Lecture Notes in Computer Science   16395

Founding Editors

Gerhard Goos
Juris Hartmanis

Editorial Board Members

Elisa Bertino, *Purdue University, West Lafayette, IN, USA*
Wen Gao, *Peking University, Beijing, China*
Bernhard Steffen, *TU Dortmund University, Dortmund, Germany*
Moti Yung, *Columbia University, New York, NY, USA*

Viviana Mascardi · Andrea Omicini
Editors

The Agents Journey

Twenty-Five Years of Multi-agent Systems

 Springer

Editors
Viviana Mascardi [iD]
Università di Genova
Genoa, Italy

Andrea Omicini [iD]
Università di Bologna
Bologna, Italy

ISSN 0302-9743   ISSN 1611-3349 (electronic)
Lecture Notes in Computer Science
ISBN 978-3-032-22939-7   ISBN 978-3-032-22940-3 (eBook)
https://doi.org/10.1007/978-3-032-22940-3

Preface

Silver Jubilee. What does it mean to you? To us, the Silver Jubilee is the definitive certification that something – a couple in love, an organisation, an event – has stood the test of time.

Let us consider, as an example, a scientific workshop. It may consolidate after ten years; it may be mature after fifteen. But only after twenty-five years one can assert that the workshop created a stable community around it, and that such a community in turn created scientific value. After twenty-five years, a workshop – and the community behind it – demonstrates that it had good ideas to share, and that they were shared in an effective way.

WOA is the Workshop on Objects and Agents. It is the most relevant event organised by the Working Group on Autonomous Agents and Multi-Agent Systems (MAS-AIIA) of the Italian Association for Artificial Intelligence, AIxIA—initially, with the cooperation of TABOO, the Italian Association for Advanced Technologies based on Object-Oriented concepts. Its first edition dates back to 2000 and took place in Parma, co-organised by Antonio Corradi, Andrea Omicini, and Agostino Poggi. Since then, WOA has been run without interruptions up to now, with editions in Modena (2001), Milano (2002), Villasimius (2003), Torino (2004), Camerino (2005), Catania (2006), Genova (2007), Palermo (2008), Parma (2009), Rimini (2010), Rende (2011), Milano (2012), Torino (2013), Catania (2014), Napoli (2015), Catania (2016), Scilla (2017), Palermo (2018), Parma (2019), Bologna (2020, online), Bologna (2021), Genova (2022), and Roma (2023). The twenty-fifth edition took place in 2024, in the fairy fortress of Bard (Aosta): a great place for celebrating such an important achievement.

WOA welcomes seminal ideas that are worthy to be shared albeit not being necessarily ready for publication in more established venues, and its steering committee has always refrained – and will always refrain – from charging any participation fee: participation in WOA is for free. Being inclusive is indeed the workshop's distinguishing feature.

Scientists attend WOA because it is the place where new ideas flow, and because it is welcoming. Despite the almost 100% acceptance rate, coherent with its inclusive nature, WOA has contributed to writing the history of agents and multi-agent systems, inside and outside Italy. At the time of writing, the 447 WOA papers indexed by Scopus, going from 2005 to 2024, received 1682 citations leading to an h-index of 17 for the workshop, comparable to the h-index of MAS-related events with similar size at European and international level. While we do not believe that bibliometric indicators are a complete and faithful representation of scientific impact, figures suggest that the ideas presented at WOA have often turned into significant results and shaped the research panorama.

This book tells the history of agents and multi-agent systems (MASs) through the lens of twenty-five WOA editions.

All the authors who published in a significant and continuous way at WOA were invited to prepare a chapter focussed on one specific subject, in order to ensure full coverage of the WOA topics of interest and minimise overlaps. Most of them accepted enthusiastically, and collaborated to create the book that you are reading.

The book is divided into four parts for a total of 14 chapters. The first part covers *Languages and Models for Computational Agents* and contains three chapters. The second part also contains three chapters and covers *Designing Agent Interaction: Putting MAS Together*. The third part deals with *Software and System Engineering with Agents and MAS* and includes four chapters, while the fourth and last part discusses *Agents and MAS for Artificial Intelligence*, with four chapters as well.

Part I of the book is about agent languages and models, and starts with a chapter by Alina Vozna, Andrea Monaldini, Stefania Costantini, Giovanni De Gasperis, Pierangelo dell'Acqua, Andrea Formisano, and Andrea Rafanelli who discuss the *Evolution of Programming Languages in Agent Systems and the Role of Computational Logic*. The chapter illustrates the evolution over time of the programming languages adopted for implementing agents and MASs and presents the authors' DALI framework, some of its applications, and how Epistemic Logic may be exploited for modelling group dynamics.

In the second chapter, Domenico Rosaci and Giuseppe M. L. Sarnè aim at *Looking for the Best Partners* for interaction and cooperation. They illustrate different strategies, including trust, reliability, reputation, cyphering, and commitment, that provide means for assessing credibility, trustworthiness, and identity, for reducing information asymmetry between agents, and for preventing malicious activities.

The third chapter complements the second by analysing *Trust Evolution in Agent and Multi-Agent Systems: A Computational Modeling Perspective*. In this chapter, Alessandro Sapienza, Filippo Cantucci, Cristiano Castelfranchi, and Rino Falcone discuss the usage and evolution of the trust concept within MASs, with the objectives of understanding how and why the choice to utilise trust was made, and of outlining the future directions to be pursued and the challenges to be taken into account.

Part II of the book moves from the single-agent dimension to the multi-agent one. The first chapter in this part is by Matteo Baldoni, Cristina Baroglio, and Roberto Micalizio who overview *Interaction Protocols: from AUML to Social Commitments, from Artifacts to BSPL*. The chapter reviews the diverse approaches in the literature ranging from message passing (FIPA ACL, KQML, and AUML) to coordination via the environment (CArtAgO, JaCaMo), from normative multi-agent organisations (MOISE) to information-based interaction protocols (BSPL).

A close focus on *Coordination of Software Agents: Models and Languages* is provided in the second chapter of Part II, written by Giacomo Cabri, Letizia Leonardi, Stefano Mariani, and Franco Zambonelli. Besides presenting agent coordination models and languages defined in the last 25 years, the authors discuss how agent coordination mechanisms have been applied in autonomic computing, self-organising systems, energy management, and autonomous vehicles.

Gianluca Aguzzi, Roberto Casadei, Danilo Pianini, and Mirko Viroli address *Self-Organisation with Aggregate Computing: A Reflection Under the Lenses of Multi-Agent Systems Engineering*. In this chapter, the authors overview results in the aggregate computing field and elaborate on how they can contribute to the design of distributed digital signs for environment-mediated agent coordination, collective plans for agents and swarms, and reinforcement learning frameworks for many-agent systems.

Part III is devoted to approaches for engineering agents and multi-agent systems, and starts with a chapter by Federico Bergenti and Stefania Monica who propose *Rethinking Software Agents as Building Blocks of Software Systems*. The chapter examines the implications of adopting cognitive agents within mainstream software development practice and presents a cognitive-agent level as a theoretical foundation for such an adoption.

The chapter *Designing Agent-Oriented Systems* by Massimo Cossentino, Luca Sabatucci, and Valeria Seidita explores the rich trajectory of Agent-Oriented Software Engineering (AOSE), delineates its path from conceptual foundations to contemporary applications, and presents a forward-looking perspective on AOSE, outlining innovative directions and potential research areas.

Alfredo Garro elaborates on *Agent-Based Computing for Science and Engineering: Back to the Future and Beyond...* The chapter explores the historical roots of agent-based approaches, tracing their evolution and renaissance in contemporary research, and highlights recent developments that extend the boundaries of agent-based approaches, pushing the paradigm "beyond" traditional confines.

The last chapter of Part III covers *Simulation and Agent-Based Simulation at WOA: 25 of Years of Simulation-Related Contributions, and an Outlook of What Awaits Us*. Therein, Giuseppe Vizzari and Daniela Briola discuss, through examples presented at WOA, how simulations may be carried out to demonstrate the working of an agent-based model or software system, to calibrate or evaluate it. They also show how agent-based approaches are particularly in tune with some of the characteristics of complex systems.

Part IV addresses agents and MASs for artificial intelligence (AI). The first chapter in this part presents *25 Years of Declarative Agent Technologies in Italy*. The authors – Davide Ancona, Daniela Briola, Angelo Ferrando, Maurizio Martelli, and Viviana Mascardi – illustrate declarative technologies for agents and MASs and how they can be exploited in the specification of the agents and MAS architecture, in the specification of their conversational flow, in their implementation, and in the representation of the agents' knowledge.

With the rise, consolidation, and success of machine learning approaches and neural networks, a discussion on *Intelligent Agents from Symbolic to Neurosymbolic Systems: The Quest for Integration* inside the WOA community is needed. Andrea Agiollo, Roberta Calegari, Giovanni Ciatto, Matteo Magnini, Andrea Omicini, and Federico Sabbatini explore the development of rational agents and integration with machine learning techniques, discussing their transition from pure symbolic to subsymbolic and neurosymbolic systems.

Daniel-Costel Bouleanu, Marco Loaiza, Claudio Savaglio, Costin Bădică, Raffaele Gravina, and Giancarlo Fortino delve into the Internet of Things (IoT) and Agent-Based Computing (ABC) duo, in their chapter *From Objects to Agents, and Back to Smart Objects: Software Agents for Intelligent Internet of Things (IoT) Systems*. There, they discuss how ABC enables the development of advanced IoT systems from the design to the implementation and simulation phases, and present application examples, technologies and IoT platforms that make use of agents.

The book ends with the vision of Andrea Omicini, Alessandro Ricci, and Viviana Mascardi on the *AI Infrastructure: From Gigastructure to Edge Intelligence with Multi-Agent Systems*. In this chapter, the authors observe how the rise of generative AI and large language models is reshaping the global landscape of computational infrastructures, and argue for a different long-term perspective on AI development, one where agents and MASs serve as the conceptual and technical foundation of scalable, sustainable, and open AI frameworks.

As this book shows, the WOA community has worked with continuity and coherence, and has a very clear vision of the road ahead. What the book cannot show is what the WOA community is for real, and which values it promotes. WOA has lovingly acted as a 'nursery' for many PhD students who gave their first talk there, and are now renowned scientists; we respect each other and are happy to meet, making the atmosphere at the workshop warm and relaxed; we look forward to moments of conviviality that are always cheerful and rewarding.

Actually, WOA's long-lasting success is rooted in long-lasting friendship among community members that goes far beyond common scientific interests. Thanks to our tight-knit community many bright years are waiting for us, full of ideas, engaging discussions, and joy to share.

September 2025

Viviana Mascardi
Andrea Omicini

Acknowledgements

The scientific and technical activity that has led to this book has seen the invaluable participation of the whole WOA community along a time span of twenty-five years, and has involved many friends and colleagues, several of whom appear as authors of this book's chapters.

In turn, the specific work devoted to the design and construction of this book as a collection of survey contributions spanning the whole MAS research area has developed over the past couple of years, during which the editors of the volume have been supported by the project "ENGINES – ENGineering INtElligent Systems around intelligent agent technologies" project, funded by the European Union – Next Generation EU within the framework of the National Recovery and Resilience Plan NRRP – Mission 4 "Education and Research" – Component 2 – Investment 1.1 "National Research Program and Projects of Significant National Interest Fund (PRIN)" – Call PRIN 2022 – D.D. n. 104 of 02/02/2022, under grant number 20229ZXBZM.

Organization

WOA Program and Editorial Chairs

WOA 2000 (Parma, Italy)

Antonio Corradi	Università di Bologna, Italy
Andrea Omicini	Università di Bologna, Italy
Agostino Poggi	Università di Parma, Italy

WOA 2001 (Modena, Italy)

Marco Cadoli	Università "La Sapienza", Roma, Italy
Flavio De Paoli	Università di Milano-Bicocca, Italy
Letizia Leonardi	Università di Modena e Reggio Emilia, Italy
Agostino Poggi	Università di Parma, Italy
Andrea Omicini	Università di Bologna, Italy
Mirko Viroli	Università di Bologna, Italy

WOA 2002 (Milano, Italy)

Flavio De Paoli	Università di Milano-Bicocca, Italy
Sara Manzoni	Università di Milano-Bicocca, Italy
Agostino Poggi	Università di Parma, Italy

WOA 2003 (Villasimius, Italy)

Giuliano Armano	Università di Cagliari, Italy
Flavio De Paoli	Università di Milano-Bicocca, Italy
Andrea Omicini	Università di Bologna, Italy
Eloisa Vargiu	Università di Cagliari, Italy

WOA 2004 (Torino, Italy)

Matteo Baldoni	Università di Torino, Italy
Flavio De Paoli	Università di Milano-Bicocca, Italy
Alberto Martelli	Università di Torino, Italy
Andrea Omicini	Università di Bologna, Italy

WOA 2005 (Camerino, Italy)

Flavio Corradini	Università di Camerino, Italy
Flavio De Paoli	Università di Milano-Bicocca, Italy
Emanuela Merelli	Università di Camerino, Italy
Andrea Omicini	Università di Bologna, Italy

WOA 2006 (Catania, Italy)

Flavio De Paoli	Università di Milano-Bicocca, Italy
Andrea Omicini	Università di Bologna, Italy
Corrado Santoro	Università di Catania, Italy

WOA 2007 (Genova, Italy)

Matteo Baldoni	Università di Torino, Italy
Antonio Boccalatte	Università di Genova, Italy
Flavio De Paoli	Università di Milano-Bicocca, Italy
Maurizio Martelli	Università di Genova, Italy
Viviana Mascardi	Università di Genova, Italy

WOA 2008 (Palermo, Italy)

Matteo Baldoni	Università di Torino, Italy
Massimo Cossentino	CNR Palermo, Italy
Flavio De Paoli	Università di Milano-Bicocca, Italy
Valeria Seidita	Università di Palermo, Italy

WOA 2009 (Parma, Italy)

Federico Bergenti — Università di Parma, Italy

WOA 2010 (Rimini, Italy)

Andrea Omicini — Università di Bologna, Italy
Mirko Viroli — Università di Bologna, Italy

WOA 2011 (Rende, Italy)

Giancarlo Fortino — Università della Calabria, Italy
Alfredo Garro — Università della Calabria, Italy
Luigi Palopoli — Università della Calabria, Italy
Wilma Russo — Università della Calabria, Italy
Giandomenico Spezzano — Università di Parma, Italy

WOA 2012 (Milano, Italy)

Flavio De Paoli — Università di Milano-Bicocca, Italy
Giuseppe Vizzari — Università di Milano-Bicocca, Italy

WOA 2013 (Torino, Italy)

Matteo Baldoni — Università di Torino, Italy
Cristina Baroglio — Università di Torino, Italy
Federico Bergenti — Università di Parma, Italy
Alfredo Garro — Università della Calabria, Italy

WOA 2014 (Catania, Italy)

Corrado Santoro — Università di Catania, Italy
Federico Bergenti — Università di Parma, Italy

WOA 2015 (Napoli, Italy)

Claudia Di Napoli   CNR Napoli, Italy
Silvia Rossi   Università di Napoli "Federico II", Italy
Mariacarla Staffa   Università di Napoli "Federico II", Italy

WOA 2016 (Catania, Italy)

Corrado Santoro   Università di Catania, Italy
Fabrizio Messina   Università di Catania, Italy
Massimiliano De Benedetti Università di Catania, Italy

WOA 2017 (Scilla, Italy)

Pasquale De Meo   Università di Messina, Italy
Maria Nadia Postorino   Università Mediterranea di Reggio Calabria, Italy
Domenico Rosaci   Università Mediterranea di Reggio Calabria, Italy
Giuseppe M. L. Sarnè   Università Mediterranea di Reggio Calabria, Italy
Massimo Cossentino   CNR Palermo, Italy
Luca Sabatucci   CNR Palermo, Italy
Valeria Seidita   Università di Palermo, Italy

WOA 2019 (Parma, Italy)

Federico Bergenti   Università di Parma, Italy
Stefania Monica   Università di Parma, Italy

WOA 2020 (Bologna, Italy/Online)

Roberta Calegari   Università di Bologna, Italy
Giovanni Ciatto   Università di Bologna, Italy
Enrico Denti   Università di Bologna, Italy
Andrea Omicini   Università di Bologna, Italy
Giovanni Sartor   Università di Bologna, Italy

WOA 2021 (Bologna, Italy)

Roberta Calegari	Università di Bologna, Italy
Giovanni Ciatto	Università di Bologna, Italy
Enrico Denti	Università di Bologna, Italy
Andrea Omicini	Università di Bologna, Italy
Giovanni Sartor	Università di Bologna, Italy

WOA 2022 (Genova, Italy)

Angelo Ferrando	Università di Genova, Italy
Viviana Mascardi	Università di Genova, Italy

WOA 2023 (Roma, Italy)

Rino Falcone	CNR Roma, Italy
Cristiano Castelfranchi	CNR Roma, Italy
Alessandro Sapienza	CNR Roma, Italy
Filippo Cantucci	CNR Roma, Italy

WOA 2024 (Bard, Italy)

Marco Alderighi	Università della Valle d'Aosta, Italy
Matteo Baldoni	Università di Torino, Italy
Cristina Baroglio	Università di Torino, Italy
Roberto Micalizio	Università di Torino, Italy
Stefano Tedeschi	Università della Valle d'Aosta, Italy

Sponsors and Contributors

MUR
Ministero dell'Università e della Ricerca

Funded by
the European Union
NextGenerationEU

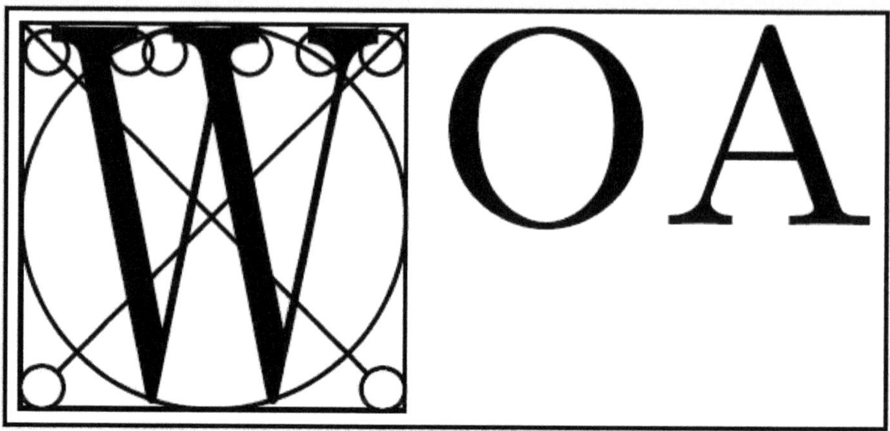

Contents

Agents and MAS for Artificial Intelligence

Languages and Models
for Computational Agents

Evolution of Programming Languages in Agent Systems and the Role of Computational Logic

Alina Vozna[1,2], Andrea Monaldini[1,2], Stefania Costantini[2,4],
Giovanni De Gasperis[2], Pierangelo dell'Acqua[5(✉)], Andrea Formisano[3,4],
and Andrea Rafanelli[1,2]

[1] Università di Pisa, Pisa, Italy
{alina.vozna,andrea.monaldini,andrea.rafanelli}@phd.unipi.it,
{stefania.costantini,giovanni.degasperis}@univaq.it
[2] Department of Information Engineering, Computer Science and Mathematics,
Università degli Studi dell'Aquila, L'Aquila, Italy
[3] Department of Mathematics, Informatics and Physics, Università degli Studi di
Udine, Udine, Italy
andrea.formisano@uniud.it
[4] Gruppo Nazionale per il Calcolo Scientifico – INdAM, Rome, Italy
[5] Department of Science and Technology, Linköping University, Linköping, Sweden
pierangelo.dellacqua@liu.se

Abstract. In this chapter we first report the evolution over time of the programming languages adopted for implementing agents and Multi-Agent Systems (MAS). Then, we briefly illustrate our own contribution to the field of agents and MAS, which concerns a programming language and framework called DALI, some significant applications of DALI, and a study relating to Epistemic Logic to model group dynamics in agent systems. All of the above is based on papers published in the Proceedings of the WOA series of workshops.

Keywords: Agent-Oriented Programming Languages · Computational Logic · Epistemic Logic

1 Introduction

Over the last decades, the field of agent-based systems has expanded and diversified dramatically, resulting in a boom in research targeted at maximizing intelligent agent application and performance across multiple domains. The selection and evolution of programming languages used in constructing intelligent agents and Multi-Agent Systems (MAS) has been critical to their advancement. Accordingly, the first part of this chapter consists of a study that presents a complete systematic evaluation of programming languages used in agent systems from 2000

A. Vozna and A. Monaldini—First author.

V. Mascardi and A. Omicini (Eds.): *The Agents Journey*, LNCS 16395, pp. 3–51, 2026.
https://doi.org/10.1007/978-3-032-22940-3_1

to 2024. We aim to analyze the evolution of these languages in this time window, highlighting their growth and adaptation to the shifting demands of agent-based research and applications. Our investigation, which involved a comprehensive review of a corpus of 395 papers published at WOA, was rigorously chosen to cover the full range of agent-centric research initiatives in Italy. Our main goal was to identify the most common programming languages used in agent creation and to determine trends, shifts, and adaptations over time. Whereas the trends were extracted from WOA contributions, the value of our work extends far beyond a survey limited to Italian research, as it also incorporates studies and contributions from non-Italian contexts, offering a more comprehensive perspective.

The resulting study reveals the importance of using specific languages and analyzes their trajectory over time, providing essential insights into their evolution within the agent systems area. Our analysis of the various programming languages used in agent systems has resulted in identifying five major languages: C++, JADE, Java, Prolog, and Python. These languages, with their unique characteristics and functionalities, have significantly impacted the landscape of agent-based systems. By tracing their use across nearly two decades, we hope to provide not only a broad overview of programming language trends but also more profound insights into the mechanisms driving their adoption and evolution within the dynamic environment of agent-based systems.

In the second part, we concentrate on languages based upon computational logic—some originate from the contribution of (some of) the authors to the field of agents and MAS. Concerning the DALI language, defined and developed by some of the authors of this paper, we will illustrate some of its significant applications. We will then present an Epistemic Logic, L-DINF, that we have originally developed as a foundation to formalize and understand DALI MAS. It is, however, of general importance, as it is capable of formalizing and reasoning upon group dynamics in agent systems.

The chapter is therefore structured as follows: Sect. 2 presents the methodology adopted for the systematic review of WOA papers, detailing the process of data collection and analysis. Section 3 provides a comprehensive overview of the programming paradigms and languages used in agent-oriented programming, highlighting the evolution of key languages such as Java, Prolog, and Python. Section 4 explores other relevant programming languages and their applications in the development of agents and MAS. Finally, Sect. 5 focuses on the DALI framework and on the epistemic logic L-DINF. Section 6 concludes by outlining the broader implications of this study and potential directions for future research.

2   Methodology of the WOA Papers Review

A systematic review was conducted in March 2024 using the DBLP computer science bibliography to examine and analyze previous existing research on agents and MAS as appeared in the Proceedings of the WOA series of workshops.

The research initially involved gathering papers from 2000 onwards, subdivided by the names, titles, and abstracts of articles with open access. After that, an attempt was made to determine which programming language was utilized to build the agents across each study. Some of these works do not mention the language used, as they primarily focus on the architecture rather than implementation details.

Out of 395 articles initially collected, 216 were selected for further analysis. To conduct a more comprehensive investigation, the next step involved identifying languages that appeared more than twice in the collection. The five most frequently utilized languages that emerged from this process are listed in alphabetic order: *(i)* C++, *(ii)* JADE, *(iii)* Java, *(iv)* Prolog, and *(v)* Python.

2.1 General Overview on Programming Languages

Before analyzing the history of programming languages in the field of agent programming, a broader and more general overview of the usage and popularity of some well-known programming languages will be briefly presented.[1] This provides us with a foundation when investigating the specific context of agent (or 'agent-oriented') programming.

In 2020, a team from the University of Edinburgh published a paper aiming to find out which programming languages are most frequently used in open-source projects on GitHub[2] and which programming languages are most frequently discussed on StackOverflow, a social coding community [203]; the first set of data is used as a measure to evaluate the most widely used languages, and the second set is used as a measure of their popularity.

According to the review, as seen in Fig. 1, JavaScript is the most frequently used language in GitHub projects between 2008 and 2020. The plot shows that other frequently used languages are: HTML, Shell, CSS, Ruby, Python, makefile, C, Java, and C++. In Fig. 2, however, you can see a graph showing the programming languages most discussed on StackOverflow: the first one is JavaScript, followed by Python, Java, C++, C#, HTML, CSS, Swift, TypeScript, and C (Table 1).

The degree of linear correlation between the two data samples is summed up using the Pearson correlation coefficient:[3] a positive correlation between the data is shown by a positive r-value. In contrast, a negative value suggests a negative correlation.[4]

Regarding practical usage and discussion, Python exhibits the highest correlation (0.65), while C++ exhibits the lowest correlation (-0.46). Given the breadth of Pearson coefficients discovered across programming languages, no universal relationship between language usage and its discussion rate that applies to all languages can be elicited.

---

[1] A list of programming languages introduced and used either at present or in the past can be found at https://en.wikipedia.org/wiki/List_of_programming_languages#D.

[2] https://github.com/.

[3] https://en.wikipedia.org/wiki/Pearson_correlation_coefficient.

[4] https://realpython.com/numpy-scipy-pandas-correlation-python/.

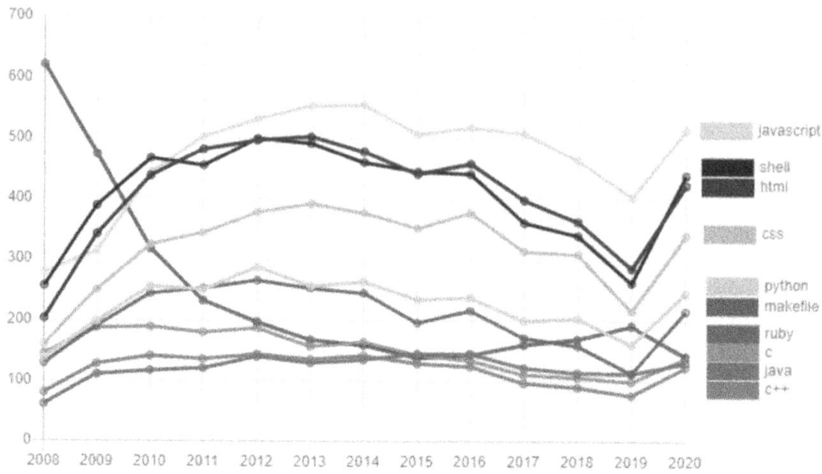

Fig. 1. Most used languages

3   Programming Paradigms and Languages for Agents and Multi-Agent Systems: A Comprehensive Overview

From 2005, a varied range of agent-oriented programming languages and frameworks have been proposed. Prolog, Java, and JADE emerged as the most popular choices, dominating the agent-oriented programming environment, as seen in Fig. 3.

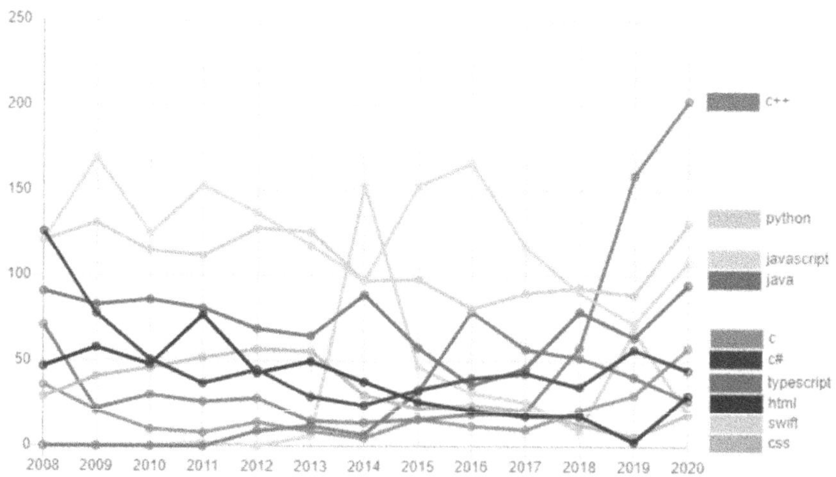

Fig. 2. Most popular languages

Table 1. Temporal analysis of metrics for architecture, toolkits and applications.

Year	THEORY	ARCHITECTURE	TOOLKIT	APPLICATIONS
2000	[180]	[14, 30, 38, 72]	[43, 55, 155]	[13, 14, 43]
2001	[202]	[31, 66, 86, 135, 199]	[31, 156, 218]	[31, 135, 156, 199, 218]
2002	[62, 221]	[27, 32, 34, 54, 198, 220, 221]	[45, 62, 175]	[32, 34, 54, 198]
2003	[26, 33, 178, 238]	[26, 33, 37, 39, 88, 96, 140, 174, 235, 240]	[37, 140]	[33, 77, 88, 174]
2004	[65]	[176]	[141, 232]	
2005	[126]	[142]	[17, 126, 142, 189, 219, 223]	[17, 35, 223]
2006	[18, 36, 58, 191]	[36, 154, 158]	[18, 36, 58, 154, 158, 191]	
2007	[22, 25, 181]	[82, 240]	[22, 82, 240]	[15, 25, 240]
2008	[152]	[64]	[64, 152]	
2009	[1, 239]	[1, 239]		
2010	[226]	[226]		
2011	[91]	[8, 47, 57, 131, 151]	[8, 47, 57, 131, 151]	
2012	[76, 173, 187, 211]	[76, 173, 187, 211]		
2013	[230]	[2, 23, 137, 178, 197, 209, 230]	[2, 23, 137]	
2014	[24, 121, 177, 182]	[46, 89]	[139]	
2015	[48]	[7, 11, 67, 128, 185, 210]	[75, 210]	[67, 83, 129]
2016	[10, 163, 179, 222]	[163]	[10]	
2017	[146]	[96, 128, 146, 150, 185]		
2018	[12, 91]	[84, 91, 143, 170, 231]	[143, 149]	[231]
2019	[68, 69, 229]	[6, 9, 92]	[167]	[16, 136, 148]
2020	[168]	[81, 85, 93, 213]	[162, 188, 189]	
2021	[5, 169]	[73, 80, 169, 201, 206]	[204, 225]	[5, 50, 73, 80]
2022	[51]	[215]		
2023	[119, 195]	[183, 196, 224]	[237, 241]	[200, 201]
2024	[109]	[78]	[74, 131, 204, 213]	

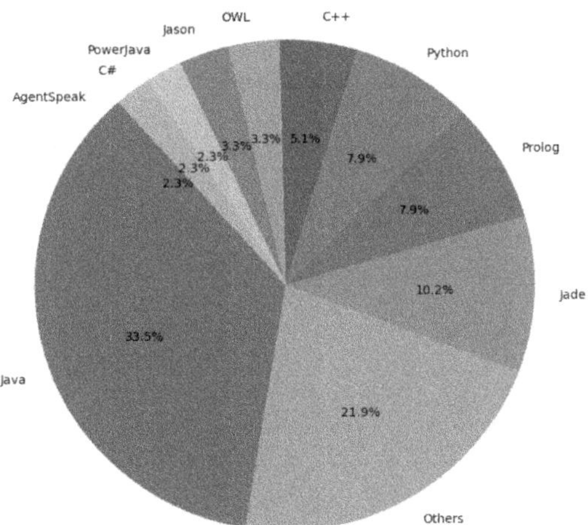

Fig. 3. Languages frequency

Prolog, with its symbolic representation and logic-based reasoning capabilities, offers a powerful tool to implement intelligent agents with complex decision-making abilities. Meanwhile, Java, which is well known for its versatility and widespread support, serves as the foundational language for many agent-oriented applications, providing stability and scalability for agent systems. JADE[5] [45–47,197] provides a robust framework for agent development in Java, leveraging its features for efficient agent creation and management.

Figure 4 shows the most used programming languages for each year based on an analysis of the WOA workshop papers. This analysis highlights trends in programming language adoption over time, offering valuable insights into the evolution of agent-oriented programming.

In general, this period marked a significant era of innovation and experimentation in agent-oriented programming, with languages and frameworks like JADE, Prolog, and Java leading the way in shaping the landscape of intelligent software agents.

3.1   Java's Evolution

Java's object-oriented design, platform neutrality, and strong networking capabilities have made it a key programming language for creating MAS. The following body of work demonstrates the versatility and effectiveness of Java in the implementation of agent-based frameworks, distributed systems, and adaptive simulations across diverse application domains.

In [78], NPI-mas is introduced, which is a multi-agent simulator implemented in Java using the JATLite framework. It supports TCP/IP messaging, scalable agent interactions, and real-time network state updates.

In [42], the SOMA framework is introduced, leveraging Java's platform independence for secure agent mobility and CORBA integration. Extending SOMA, the PUPA system enables resource monitoring and accounting in pervasive environments using Java-based mobile agents.

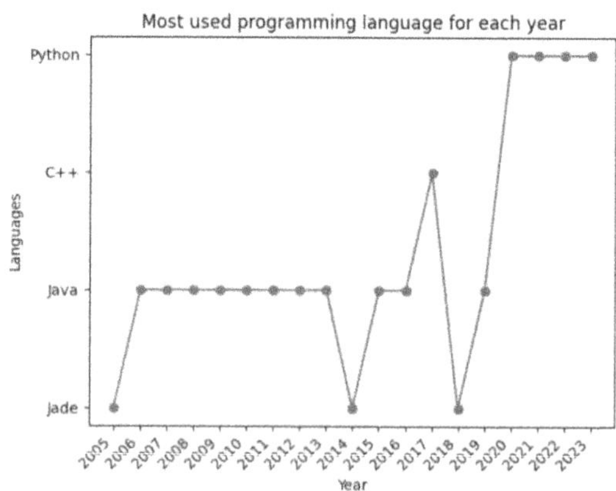

Fig. 4. Most used programming language for each year (based on WOA workshop papers)

---

[5] https://jade.tilab.com/.

In [34], the authors introduce a multi-agent simulation model, by using Java, based on the Reaction-Diffusion Machine (RDM) to study complex phenomena such as pesticide percolation through the soil. The RDM approach integrates reaction and diffusion processes with external field effects, modeled using autonomous agents.

In [58], the feasibility of real-time programming using Java is explored, by introducing a custom package that extends Java's capabilities. This package provides mechanisms for thread scheduling, synchronization primitives, and inter-process communication through semaphores, events, and messages.

For healthcare systems, in [15], the authors develop an experimental electronic patient record (EPR) system using Java InfoBus, XML, and JavaBeans to enable secure and collaborative access to patient data through web browsers.

In [16], the authors implement an agent-based framework in Java for enhancing web search tools, focusing on local search using the VSEARCH tool as a case study. The framework integrates agents with properties such as autonomy, reactivity, and proactivity to manage local search tasks, reducing the need for continuous user interaction.

Java-based technologies like programmable tuple spaces (e.g., MARS) were employed in [71] to enable localized coordination among agents. This approach separates intra-agent computations from inter-agent interactions, simplifying the development of mobile agent applications.

In [92], a policy-based approach to manage mobile agent mobility in distributed systems is proposed. By decoupling mobility logic from application code, their method enables dynamic migration strategies without altering agent functionality. A layered architecture integrates the Ponder policy language within the Java-based SOMA framework to govern agent behavior and migration dynamically.

The feasibility of integrating web services with object-oriented paradigms was explored in [164], where Java facilitated seamless HTML-to-class mapping for data extraction and organization. Similarly, the Tropos methodology introduced in [210] aligned agent-oriented platforms, such as the Java-based JACK Intelligent Agents, with goal and actor diagrams to analyze stakeholder interactions and system requirements.

A language and framework for creating situated MAS based on the Reaction Diffusion Machine (RDM) model is presented in [35]. Java is used to create the framework, taking advantage of its object-oriented capabilities for distributed execution and modularity. Agents are defined by their type, state, and interaction rules, which govern their perception and actions within a decentralized spatial environment.

In [38], Java is used for implementing the multi-agent system within the MadKit framework, enabling the creation and management of agents that observe, analyze, and enhance user interactions in interactive systems. The paper introduces an agent-based architecture to support knowledge management across the life cycle of interactive systems, emphasizing the co-evolution of users and systems.

Further innovations include the Zeus toolkit, employed in [36], where the authors develop Java-based MAS integrated with web interfaces and databases. In [66], the authors introduce WIPPONG, a Java language for expressing transitions in discrete systems, and abstracting semantics for seamless integration with visual languages.

In [182], Java is used to develop the TOTA (Tuples On The Air), a middleware designed to support context-aware and adaptive interactions in MAS operating in dynamic and distributed environments.

Paper [41] demonstrates how Java is used to implement a middleware to support service continuity in Mobile Ad-hoc Networks (MANET); the language offers a transparent interface with system-level services and functions.

In [71], Java is used to develop a role-based agent interaction system to manage mobile agents. Java enables the system to implement agent mobility and interaction logic through roles, ensuring high portability, flexibility, and compatibility across different platforms.

In [181], Java is used for the implementation of self-organizing algorithms and simulations in spray computing systems. Java enables the modeling and testing of emergent behaviors in distributed networks, particularly for applications involving mobile robots and sensor networks.

In [242], authors are concerned with the use of Java to create the architecture of a dynamic name property-based system able to manage agents and places without a network-dependent architecture.

Paper [37] uses Java as the programming language for the development of the simulation framework to create a model of the immune system.

The aim of [43] is to propose a comprehensive resource management solution for highly dynamic and heterogeneous smart environments using a Java-based middleware.

Paper [141] uses Java to realize a distributed mechanism to support selective diffusion based on contextual information in the Multilayered Multi-Agent Situated System (MMASS) model.

The aim of [101] is to address the challenges associated with transitioning from the design phase to the implementation phase in MAS modeling using Java.

In [83] the Multichannel Object REnderer (MORE) is described, a framework that can create user interfaces using Java code used to define the application model and a reflective analysis of data.

Regarding evaluating trust among agents, in [70], the authors implemented a set of Java classes that agents can exploit to present their approach.

The work by Mari *et al.* [183] presents RAP (Remote Assistant for Programmers), a web-based, multi-agent system designed to assist remote students and programmers with common projects or activities based on Java.

From 2006 to 2016, Java established itself as the dominant language in the field of agent-oriented programming. Java, known for its versatility, resilience, and widespread acceptance, has become the preferred language for constructing intelligent software agents in a wide range of domains and applications. Its extensive ecosystem of libraries, frameworks, and tools provided developers with the resources needed to create complex agent systems capable of addressing a wide range of challenges and requirements. During this period, Java's prominence highlighted its long-term significance and adaptability in determining the evolution of agent-oriented programming, establishing its position as a key technology in the area.

For example, in [40], the Hermes framework is used, employing Java to design proactive, activity-based agents. The Java platform is extended with simpA-WS in [227], enabling service-oriented architectures through the Agents and Artifacts (A&A) meta-model [200].

Java is often used to develop frameworks for multi-agent systems. Specifically, it is used to implement agents within a system [61], which are software components that can perform actions, interact with other agents, and adapt to changes in the Web application environment. In [100], Java is utilized as a part of the JaCaMo framework [59] (seen below). The use of Java allows for creating flexible and dynamic MAS capable of supporting adaptive web applications. In fact, it provides the necessary features for building complex software systems, including object-oriented programming capabilities, for modeling agents and their interactions within the MAS. For instance, Java contributes to the development of BDI (Belief, Desires, Intention) agents within the PRACTIONIST suite [88]. Specifically, it is used in conjunction with the PRACTIONIST runtime and framework (PRF) to support execution logic and provide built-in components for creating these agents. In addition, it is paired with a Prolog belief base to facilitate the development process. The PRACTIONIST Development Tool (PDT), which is part of the suite, assists developers in designing and generating code for multi-agent systems, leveraging Java as the programming language for the generated source code.

Paper [158] highlights the agent-oriented programming paradigm's suitability for Wireless Sensor Networks (WSNs), given their shared traits of distribution, decentralized control, and adaptiveness. They propose the MAPS framework, which facilitates efficient WSN application development using Java-based mobile agents.

The lack of universal, integrated platforms for creating negotiation protocols across domains is highlighted in the study [69]. The authors suggest establishing a uniform platform for the creation of negotiation protocols by starting with their FYPA system, which is implemented in Java.

Paper [217] presents ASiDE, an actor-based framework designed to simplify the development and execution of large-scale, distributed, and concurrent systems. The framework focuses on: supporting both active and passive threading solutions for efficient execution and facilitating the development of agent-based modeling and simulation (ABMS) tools. ASiDE is implemented entirely in Java, leveraging Java's multi-threading capabilities and libraries for concurrency and distribution.

In [218], the authors introduce an actor-based software framework called CoDE (Concurrent Development Environment). CoDE is a software environment that is implemented in Java and makes use of pre-existing Java software frameworks and solutions to facilitate distribution and concurrency. This framework aims to guarantee scalable and effective applications while streamlining the creation of large and distributed complex systems.

Another actor-based program is described in [169], where ActoDeS, which facilitates the construction of concurrent and distributed complex systems and guarantees effective application execution, is implemented using the Java programming language.

In [226], the authors demonstrate that replaceable implementations provide actor systems with much-needed flexibility and scalability for modern distributed applications. By supporting multiple execution strategies and enabling runtime replacement, the architecture ensures that actor systems, implemented in Java, can adapt dynamically to varying workloads and performance requirements.

A conceptual and computational methodology for creating and deploying knowledge-based agents is presented in [238]. These agents can use their internal knowledge structures to carry out activities like learning, reasoning, and making decisions. Java's implementation of the ANDROID framework makes it possible to create scalable and modular agents.

In [184], the authors formally define uniform coordination primitives. These primitives are a simplified version of standard LINDA coordination primitives[6], but instead of using uncertain non-determinism, they utilize probabilistic non-determinism. They contend that implementing uniform primitives provides a straightforward yet powerful mechanism that improves tuple-based coordination by allowing for the expression and prediction of stochastic behaviors. This, in turn, enables the design of intricate coordinated systems that possess adaptiveness and self-organization.

Java was also utilized to develop GIMT (Goal Identification and Modeling Tool), a CASE tool specifically designed to aid in the design and development of BDI MAS [100]. The tool aims to enhance the level of abstraction in the initial phases of system development by integrating goal-oriented analysis techniques within design and implementation.

In order to enable automated integration of web services in dispersed and dynamic environments, the paper [2] proposes a framework for trust negotiation that is implemented in Java. The main concept is to allow agents to dynamically build trust while integrating services by exchanging credentials incrementally. During the negotiating process, efficiency, security, and privacy are guaranteed by this trust-based strategy.

Mariani and Omicini [185] propose a contribution in the field of multi-agent systems based on the TuCSoN coordination model and technology. They highlight how crucial it is to use coordination artifacts to manage dependencies within a MAS, both social and situated. The article describes an agent-oriented approach, showing how TuCSoN helps MAS programmers at various phases of software development, starting with the TuCSoN meta-model and ending with its programming environment.

---

[6] https://en.wikipedia.org/wiki/Linda_(coordination_language).

The study [89] used Java to construct the server layer of the architecture, which contrasts a social robot with a smartphone application, in terms of movie recommendations. Java plays a crucial role in the server-side implementation of the recommendation system, which serves both the social robot and the mobile application clients.

In [73], the control module of an artificial neural network (ANN) to be used in a robot is implemented in Java. The authors emulated a three-layer feed-forward net with distinct input, hidden, and output units for the ANN using the Neuroph Java framework.[7] This architecture made building the neural network easier, which is essential to the robot agent's ability to avoid obstacles and accomplish its goals. The job of the ANN is to interpret the sensor data and adjust the robot motor actuators as necessary.

Poggi [219] introduce ActoMoS, an actor-based library for developing scalable agent-based models and simulations. Built on the Concurrent Development Environment (CoDE), ActoMoS simplifies the creation of complex simulations by leveraging the actor model. The library's architecture and functionality are detailed through successful applications across various domains, showcasing its flexibility and performance over traditional tools.

In a later work, a larger research team produced the software library Actomata [156], which was created to make the modeling and simulation of cellular automata easier. Actomata, which was built on top of the ActoDeS framework, makes it easier to create large, distributed complex systems while guaranteeing effective application execution.

In [186], the authors discuss the integration of heterogeneous coordination approaches within MAS technologies. They emphasize the need for MAS featuring autonomous components to have efficient coordination mechanisms that handle both functional and non-functional properties despite the heterogeneity of components and interaction paradigms.

In [230], the Delta Infrastructure for Cognition and Emotion (DICE) framework uses Java. DICE is a system designed to provide real-time control over non-player characters (NPCs) in virtual reality environments. It is compatible with AOS's JACK, an agent-oriented development environment constructed using Java. The basic programming language support for DICE is provided by Java, which makes it possible to create autonomous agents capable of controlling cognitive NPCs.

In [239], the authors propose the ACOSO-Meth methodology, intended to facilitate the systematic development of Internet of Things (IoT) systems, including their interoperability, distributed intelligence, and self-management. ACOSO-Meth also makes it easier to re-engineer existing IoT systems to increase their extensibility, re-usability, and maintainability. The goal is to improve the capabilities of IoT systems while resolving the difficulties brought about by their inherent heterogeneity and complexity.

In the field of E-health, Java was used in [143] for the UPA4SAR project, which aims to develop an Ambient Assisted Living (AAL) system using a social

---

[7] https://neuroph.sourceforge.net/.

robot to support home care for patients with Alzheimer's disease. The goal is to improve the acceptability of social robotics by adapting the robot's behavior to the patient's personality profile, preferences, and cognitive status. This adaptation seeks to provide personalized and adaptive interaction, improving the quality of life of patients by monitoring their activities and offering cognitive support.

In [174], the authors use the ActoDeS framework to create concurrent and distributed applications. In particular, the ActoDeS framework uses Java to implement actors,[8] which are concurrent objects that communicate with one another asynchronously. In addition to delivering messages, generating new actors, and altering their states or behaviors, these actors can also process incoming messages. The framework facilitates distributed deployment on numerous computing nodes by supporting the execution of applications across multiple actor spaces, each of which corresponds to a Java virtual machine.

Java's ability to manage distribution and concurrency is crucial to the design and operation of the ActoDeS framework.

In the field of affective computing, the authors of [155] advance the understanding of emotions by comparing a single multi-class classifier to a set of binary classifiers, each focused on recognizing a specific dimension of the Lovheim cube of emotions [180]. They utilize the ActoDeS framework to enable distributed emotion classification via asynchronous messaging and dynamic reconfiguration, enhancing accuracy in analyzing tweets for applications in business, physiology, and neuroscience.

During the pandemic, ActoDeS was further explored for building scalable epidemic forecasting simulations. It supported defining COVID-19 diffusion models and simulating large populations. In [209], the authors extend this with Acto-Demic, a Java-based framework for large-scale, agent-based epidemic simulations. Using asynchronous messaging and multi-threading, ActoDemic simulated millions of agents, demonstrated through a COVID-19 case study in Lombardy, Italy.

In general, these studies demonstrate how Java's adaptability and strong concurrency characteristics may be used to create concurrent, distributed, and scalable applications in various fields, such as virtual reality, robotics, and complex systems.

The **JaCaMo** framework [59], built on Java-based technologies, enables the creation of multi-agent systems by integrating various dimensions of intelligent agent programming, such as agent behavior, organizational structure, and shared environments. This integration supports the development of sophisticated simulation environments where the cognitive abilities of robots can be assessed and tested for dependability and cooperation with human users.

---

[8] The *actor model* was introduced by Carl Hewitt *et al.* [3,168] as a formalism to describe concurrent systems for history, description and semantics; see https://en.wikipedia.org/wiki/Actor_model.

For instance, in [79], the authors employed JaCaMo to implement an experimental setup designed to evaluate a cognitive architecture aimed at enhancing reliable human-robot collaboration.

In [247] a multi-level explainability framework for BDI agent systems is discussed. Here, JaCaMo is used to develop a tool to explore the multi-level explainability framework in practice.

Akka[9] is a Java-based framework whose basic construct is an "Actor". It features a strong hierarchical structure created by actors connected using the parent-son tactic. It is an open-source platform made available using Scala programming language libraries, and Akka actors communicate with one another asynchronously [97]. A multi-paradigm approach to developing Smart Cyber-Physical Systems (CPS) is covered in the paper [98], particularly regarding reconfiguring a ship's power system. Because of its strong actor model and hierarchical structure, Akka is used to create reactive, scalable, and effective systems. In summary, Java plays a crucial role in the above-mentioned papers for implementing agent-oriented systems, coordinating agents, supporting adaptive web applications, and facilitating the development of activity-based applications and SOA/WS applications.

Nonetheless, alongside Java, a myriad of other languages emerged and gained prominence in the landscape of agent-oriented programming, each contributing unique features and capabilities to the field.

3.2   C++'s Evolution

Up to the year 2009, C++ was widely used for various applications, ranging from advanced simulations to software development. Specifically, it was adopted as a foundation for integrating complex systems and algorithms, particularly in the domains of optimization, agent-based modeling, and 3D visualization. The following examples illustrate its multifaceted role across different tasks:

- **Integration with 3D Engine.** In [246], C++ was used to seamlessly integrate the Multilayered Multi-Agent Situated System (MMASS) model with the Irrlicht 3D engine. This integration enabled advanced 3D visualization capabilities by leveraging the features of Irrlicht, an open-source C++ 3D engine, to visualize the dynamic outputs generated by the model.
- **MMASS Framework.** According to [246], a custom C++ library was developed to represent the MMASS model. This library provided specialized classes for defining environmental conditions and agent behaviors within a virtual space.
- **Execution and Visualization.** In [245], the C++ framework facilitated the execution of agent behaviors and enabled real-time visualization of these interactions within an immersive 3D environment.
- **Algorithm Implementation.** As detailed in [17], C++ was employed to implement the Discrete Particle Swarm Optimization (DPSO) algorithm, providing efficient and optimized code execution for computational tasks.

---

[9] http://doc.akka.io/libraries/akka-core/.

In [163], the authors implemented the GOBLIN framework in C++. This framework has an object-oriented design and an XMLSchema to define communication protocols and templates. It uses a combination of TCP/IP streams, UNIX pipes, and shared memory for message transfer. Multiple mailboxes and protocol-specific methods streamline message processing, while XMLBinary encoding enhances inter-agent communication efficiency.

The Agent Developer Studio (ADS), a tool designed for the development of rule-based agents with a focus on workflow management systems (WFMS), is presented in [225]. ADS uses C++ for its implementation, integrating libraries such as ADO (Active Data Objects) and MAPI (Mail Application Program Interface) to support database and communication functionality. It uses CLIPS, a C-based language for expert systems, as the execution environment for the generated agents.

In [133] an algorithm for coordinating a flock of multirotor UAVs (Unmanned Aerial Vehicles) to perform wide-area monitoring missions is proposed. The system can identify faults in the UAVs and re-scout areas to avoid data loss. Its coordination is decentralized, which means that there is no single point of failure. In 2017, the same authors expanded their work [134] by adding a 3D simulator designed to simulate UAVs, helping developers design multi-agent applications for UAV missions. This work emphasizes the importance of simulating real physics and dynamics of UAVs, including reactions to forces and torques, and 3D visualization.

Postorino and Sarnè [221] provide an agent-based simulator implemented in C++ that takes into account vehicle interactions in both ground and aerial modes, transition processes, security concerns, and air traffic control challenges.

Capizzi *et al.* [81] propose a distributed system for Acoustic Echo Cancellation (AEC) implemented in C++. The system is composed of mobile agents equipped with Recurrent Neural Networks (RNNs) or Pipelined Recurrent Neural Networks (PRNNs). The authors highlight the advantages of these agents, such as task adaptivity and energy efficiency, and present results showing significant echo reduction.

In the field of robotics, the work presented in [7] proposes the integration of a real-time BDI model into ROS 2.[10] Here, the authors propose a MAS approach that considers the agents' internal status and environmental stimuli, along with time restrictions, to implement agents capable of practical reasoning with real-time performance.

Pagliuca and Vitanza [204] aim to present a new method called n-mates evaluation to enhance the performance of genetic algorithms in heterogeneous multi-agent systems. This work addresses the challenge of evolving collective abilities in diverse agent groups, where randomness can affect performance evaluation.

In [191], the authors present the C++ multi-agent platform DEMOCLE. Utilizing language features like lambdas, object orientation, and macros, makes

---

[10] The Robot Operating System (ROS) is a set of software libraries and tools for building robot applications that make use of C++—see https://docs.ros.org/en/foxy/index.html.

logic/declarative agent programming possible. The platform is low overhead, lightweight, and appropriate for micro-controllers with constrained capabilities.

The aim of [84] is to provide a unified API for developers to utilize various wireless communication protocols in a black-box manner. In their work, they cite the *DEMOCLE* [191]platform, a multi-agent system for embedded systems written in C++.

In [221] the authors propose an agent-based framework to simulate Mobility as a Service (MaaS) programs using diachronic representations of transport services; the simulator used is written in C++.

De Gasperis *et al.* [136] introduce SkRobot, a software platform that makes robot development easier, particularly for people with cognitive abilities; it used C++ as its foundation.

3.3   JADE's Evolution

The Java Agent DEvelopment (JADE) framework is a software framework designed to support the development of multi-agent systems and offers a run-time environment and a collection of tools for developing agent systems that meet the FIPA (Foundation for Intelligent Physical Agents) [44] requirements for intelligent multi-agent systems that are interoperable. Developed in Java, JADE provides a robust platform to build, deploy, and manage distributed agent-based applications [1,39].

Paper [47] presents an object-oriented framework for developing multi-agent systems using JADE. Scalability, interoperability, and ease of integration are guaranteed by the framework's adherence to FIPA standards and utilization of Java's modular design.

The MIKS (Mediator agent for Integration of Knowledge Sources) system, which supports information integration and querying across heterogeneous data sources, is enhanced with an agent-based framework presented in [48]. By adding intelligent and mobile agents, MIKS improves the MOMIS (Mediator environment for Multiple Information Sources) infrastructure. JADE is utilized to manage agent mobility, autonomy, and communication, ensuring robust and efficient agent interactions.

In [57] a multi-agent system for knowledge management is presented, based on the Implicit Culture Framework to enable the transfer of tacit knowledge through shared experiences. The system uses JADE to implement agents and their interactions, ensuring compliance with FIPA standards for communication protocols and behaviors.

The aim of [244] is to propose a robust authentication system for agent ownership using user fingerprints in addition to the standard username/password pair and it's full implementd in JADE.

The authors of [95] propose a programming environment for large-scale distributed systems modeled as workflows of activities sharing resources, knowledge, know-how, and services and they used JADE as a core layer.

In [19], JADE is utilized as an agent development framework to implement the ANEMONE network, which provides services to the academic community, e.g. academic support services, student-focused services, document sharing and collaboration, and software development assistance.

In [161], the authors create a hierarchical structure of agents in JADE that could efficiently manage and enact distributed workflow.

Instead, in [166] JADE is used to test the framework's support activities by simulating single and continuous sequences of Consumer Buying Behavior (CBB) processes in a small Business-to-Consumer (B2C) scenario. The prototype developed in JADE allowed the performance and effectiveness of the system in supporting e-commerce activities to be evaluated.

The role of JADE is also crucial to creating a dynamic and responsive system that takes advantage of the capabilities of BDI in pervasive environments. Indeed, in [8] it is used to support the implementation of intelligent agents capable of utilizing pervasive sensors as their perceptors. This allows the agents to provide context-aware services, making mobile services more useful and profitable.

In [26], the authors present 2COMM, an interaction-oriented architecture that integrates commitment-based protocols into the JADE platform using the CArtAgO framework. The goal is to address the lack of a social layer in JADE by reifying interaction protocols into artifacts.

In the paper [144], a framework is introduced to evaluate the negotiation cost associated with the composition of the QoS-aware service. This framework employs multi-agent negotiation protocols to facilitate service selection while balancing the cost-efficiency and QoS guarantees for composed services. The negotiation process is implemented using JADE, that facilitates agent communication and service discovery.

In [27], the authors present 2COMM4JADE, a unique framework that integrates the JADE and CArtAgO[11] platforms to create social interactions among agents through social commitments. Through this integration, agents in MAS can communicate according to pre-established social relationships, improving autonomy and decoupling. With a particular focus on enhancing the JADE platform's agent interaction design, the study highlights the importance of integrating social ties to enable agents in MAS to behave more autonomously and in a decoupled way.

In [137] it is presented the PROCE system that demonstrates how multi-agent systems can facilitate the composition and execution of software engineering processes. By leveraging JADE and web services technologies, PROCE automates method fragment management, process definition, and service orchestration in SOA environments.

Paper [50] explores the suitability of agent-based systems for Business Process Management (BPM) and highlights Wade, a platform that leverages agents to execute and manage workflows. Wade builds on JADE and extends it to support workflows by incorporating additional components, tools, and features.

Paper [82] introduces a multi-agent system for a peer-to-peer energy market, where residential users equipped with renewable energy devices (e.g., solar

---

[11] http://cartago.apice.unibo.it.

panels) can act as both energy producers and consumers (prosumers). JADE manages agent creation, communication, and discovery of other agents using a Directory Facilitator (DF) for dynamic registration and lookup of peers.

In [220] an innovative agent-based sensor grid designed to monitor urban traffic is presented. The purpose of this system is to manage transport networks more effectively using the acoustic signatures of road vehicles to estimate traffic flows. The grid employs a trust system among neighboring sensor agents to enhance performance.

Still, in the field of agent design, the authors of [49] deploy JADE agents on Android, which is a significant step in mobile agent technology. The authors detail the architecture and API of the platform module, emphasizing its modularity and ability to adapt to different device capabilities and network conditions.

The paper presented in [146] describes a prototype in JADE of a smart parking application designed for Smart Cities, aimed at alleviating the common urban challenge of finding parking spaces. This application uses software agent negotiation to dynamically allocate parking spaces based on user preferences and to consider the city's needs, such as avoiding congestion in certain areas. This negotiation mechanism offers a solution that finds a compromise between the needs of the individual and social welfare by taking into account real-time dynamic information regarding city conditions and user requests.

To manage power in smart grids, [9] suggests a learning-based strategy that places a strong emphasis on the requirement for intelligent agents with the ability to learn, negotiate, and make decisions, using JADE platfmorm to run the experiments.

After more than 15 years of practical use of JADE, [51] emphasizes the need for formal semantics, with the intent to improve the understanding and development of complex software systems managed by JADE. The authors' purpose is to provide a structured semantic framework to support reasoning in JADE-based software systems. This paper outlines the main entities involved in JADE systems, such as MAS, agents, behaviors, and their respective classes.

In [193] an optimization-based localization algorithm is described, which uses WiFi networks to position JADE agents in indoor environments. The goal is to make it possible for JADE agents to locate themselves within a familiar environment on smart devices without requiring specialized infrastructure. The algorithm solves an optimization problem derived from estimates of the distances between WiFi access points and the device using particle swarm optimization (PSO).

The 2020 pandemic has highlighted the importance of sophisticated strategies and tools to monitor and prevent the transmission of novel and unpredictable diseases. Considering these factors when trying to address such events can significantly impact the effectiveness and efficiency of virus responses. In [198], the authors introduce a MAS that enhances existing multi-agent-based approaches by incorporating additional features to manage the outbreak during simulation. The aim is to assess how government strategies can influence the dynamic spread of the disease.

Last, the paper in [212] introduces Jadescript, an agent-oriented programming language specifically designed to seamlessly integrate with the Java Agent DEvelopment (JADE) framework. The paper's main objective is to examine the advancement of productivity tools that enhance the suitability of Jadescript for professional applications: integrating Jadescript with mainstream development environments is crucial to promote its adoption by the JADE user community.

3.4 Prolog's Evolution

Prolog [67,173] is a high-level programming language associated with artificial intelligence and computational linguistics. It is rooted in formal logic and precisely predicate logic and is known for its use in symbolic reasoning, problem-solving, and expert systems. Prolog programs consist of facts, rules, and queries, allowing developers to express complex relationships and, in general, a program underlying logic straightforwardly. Thus, Prolog is a *declarative* language in the sense that to write a program, one expresses *what* results must be obtained, rather than *how* to obtain them.

An agent-based architecture for enabling linguistic communication between software agents is presented in paper [207]. The system addresses communication and knowledge-sharing problems between agents with different ontologies and conceptualizations. In this case, Prolog is used for agent reasoning and query processing, namely for concept alignment and ontology mediation.

Paper [206] introduces ALINAs (Architecture for LINguistic Agents), a multi-layer agent-based framework designed to support linguistic communication. SWI-Prolog is used to implement reasoning capabilities, linguistic translation, and ontology mediation. Its features for handling XML, RDF, and other semantic web formats make it suitable for managing linguistic and ontological data.

In [231] tuProlog[12] is utilized to implement agents within the DCaseLP environment based on the JADE platform. The agents created were part of a library designed to simulate auction mechanisms, allowing for quick prototyping of realistic auctions.

In [21,162,199,229], the authors discuss the use of Prolog in the context of the TuCSoN infrastructure for agent coordination, which is implemented using the tuProlog technology for Java-Prolog integration. Here, Prolog facilitates logic-based coordination among agents and to program tuple centers—which are coordination artefacts in the MAS environment, where agents interact by exchanging logic tuples. This is part of implementing the ReSpecT language, which specifies the reactive behavior of tuple centers in response to observable events.

Coordination is an essential aspect of multi-agent systems to regulate interactions among agents and environments. Flexible and adaptable models, such as those leveraging Linda-like tuple spaces, have been extensively explored to facilitate asynchronous and loosely coupled interactions. Cabri et al. [72] highlight how these models provide active and reactive coordination, enabling agents to

---

[12] http://tuprolog.unibo.it/.

adapt to dynamic environments while supporting a wide range of applications, from grid computing to autonomous vehicles.

The idea of Agent Coordination Contexts (ACCs) in the context of the TuC-SoN coordination infrastructure is examined in [228]. In order to control and model agent interactions in distributed contexts, ACCs are presented. They capture the responsibilities, regulations, and limitations that control how agents engage with and participate in a coordination space. The study shows how ACCs may enforce organizational policies, facilitate dynamic role-based interactions, and adjust to changing conditions.

Additionally, in [159], the authors discuss the use of Prolog in the context of dispute resolution, specifically for the design and implementation of a system that supports argumentation. Prolog is utilized for its ability to handle logical representations and reasoning, which are essential for modeling the argumentation process.

In another study [69], the authors use Prolog for developing a MAS prototype for the monitoring of railway signals.

In [13], the authors employ Prolog to present a framework for designing, formalizing, and implementing monitoring agents called sentinels and controllers in MAS and ambient intelligence (AmI) systems. In their second work [12], they discussed an algorithm for decentralized monitoring of MAS. By dividing a MAS into independently monitorable sub-MASs and guaranteeing that the interactions are independent and separate from one another, this algorithm allows for decentralized runtime verification. Finally, in a third paper [14], the authors present an algorithm that uses mappings that consider agent and message syntax differences to establish the conformance between local agent interaction protocols (LAIPs) in multi-agent systems.

Since 2019, two papers have used Prolog in the field of XAI (eXplainable Artificial Intelligence). To improve the interpretability and explainability of machine learning (ML) predictors, the first one [74] proposes a framework for combining symbolic and sub-symbolic techniques. The proposed technique allows tree predictors[13] to be converted into logical programs, which can then be utilized to produce narrative explanations for machine learning predictions. The second one [216] presents a unified model for neural-symbolic computation in the context of XAI: it proposes guidelines for integrating symbolic and sub-symbolic approaches to create intelligent systems (IS) that are both effective and understandable.

The same authors of the above-mentioned paper (i.e. [216]) used Prolog to develop a cooperative argumentation model for multi-agent systems [214]. Here, they address the challenges of conflict resolution in distributed MAS environments and propose a computational model that facilitates argument evaluation through message passing. The model leverages the Arg2P framework [215] for logic-based agreement and focuses on the distribution issues of cooperative argumentation.

---

[13] A survey on tree predictors can be found at https://www.nature.com/articles/nmeth.4370.

3.5 Python's Evolution

Python[14] is a versatile and widely-used programming language renowned for its simplicity, readability, and flexibility. Created by Guido van Rossum, it was initially made available in 1991. Python has grown to become an essential tool in several fields, including web development, data science, artificial intelligence, and scientific computing.

Python has found an extensive application in the realm of mobility and autonomous agents, offering a powerful platform to develop software solutions in these domains. It is used for various purposes, ranging from data analysis and visualization in transportation planning to building simulation models for traffic flow optimization. Moreover, Python serves as the foundation for developing autonomous agents, including autonomous vehicles, drones, and robotic systems.

In [150], a software architecture designed to accurately and realistically simulate a group of unmanned aerial vehicles (UAVs) engaged in a particular task is discussed. A series of tools are deployed, each one to mimic a specific part of the entire UAV hardware and software structure: a 3D visualization engine, a physical simulator, the flying stack, and a network simulator to handle interactions among UAVs.

To evaluate how well a state-of-the-art model supports modelers in the field of complex systems simulation, specifically pedestrian and crowd simulation, in [167], the authors introduce an examination of the model's preparedness to address challenges related to orientation and exploration within a randomly generated environment.

Cavallaro and Tramontanta [86] focus on the bike-sharing system and, in particular, on a possible method of estimating the number of bikes in bike stations to promote the use of such a mode of transportation. When users know in advance that bikes are available, they can select this form of transportation with more ease. The paper shows that it is possible to predict with precision where bikes will be in the near future using a quick algorithm to analyze data that record every bike movement. This can be achieved by mapping out the common bike routes based on their origins and most likely destinations.

In the field of micro-mobility, in [178] the authors introduce ESB-DQN, a multi-agent system built on Deep Reinforcement Learning (DRL) that can communicate with a simulator to discover different drop-off and pick-up locations for e-scooter sharing services. The primary goal is to address the imbalance issue by offering user incentives to maximize vehicle availability and facilitate battery replacement and relocation activities.

Finally, concerning the use of Python in mobility, the study of [5] aims to test the suitability of using Reinforcement Learning (RL) approaches for pedestrian simulation, particularly regarding the requirement for general models that can be applied to a variety of scenarios without requiring training for every case examined.

---

[14] https://www.python.org/.

In the field of assistant agents, Longo and Santoro [177] present a software architecture and the working scheme of an assistant agent capable of interacting with the user through natural language. The key elements of the work presented are the organization of a flexible software architecture to leverage cloud computing for speech-to-text and text-to-speech services and the use of the Python-based framework PROFETA BDI, which is presented in this paper as the execution platform. Afterward, the same group of authors presented the CASPAR architecture [175], able to implement agents capable of both reactive and cognitive reasoning. This work aims to find a comprehensive strategy for making deductions in Knowledge Bases (KBs) whose content is parsed directly from natural language. This architecture functions by utilizing a KB that is split into two separate sections (Clauses KB and Beliefs KB), which can also communicate with one another during decision-making. The final work [176] of this research group proposes an open-world assumption transposition of the cognitive architecture CASPAR, whose heuristic takes into account meta-reasoning in the closed-world assumption, namely SW-CASPAR. In this cognitive architecture, the domain is represented by an instance of a novel fundamental ontology called Linguistic Oriented Davidsonian Ontology (LODO), which is included in a module for semi-automatic ontology learning from sentences in natural language.

In [232] an extension of the PSyKE framework [233] is introduced to support explainable clustering, aiming to improve cognitive agent capabilities, and discusses the application and purpose of explainable clustering algorithms for cognitive agents, which include both human users and AI systems.

In [9] the transformation of objects into smart objects with intelligence is discussed, which is crucial for the IoT. The authors emphasize the addition of communication, negotiation, learning, and distributed reasoning to applications and propose an agent-oriented modeling approach for power management in smart grids, balancing consumption profile resolution with system performance and real-time requirements.

In [10], the authors propose a peer-to-peer system provided with a spanning tree to distribute online notifications within a group of interested peers. These notifications may regard discussion messages for a chat system or any update messages for spreading social activities performed by users of a Distributed Online Social Network. In particular, they describe and compare different mechanisms for creating and managing the spanning tree.

The study [87] presents a distributed system for social media scraping that uses an actor-based solution that can effectively orchestrate many cloud services to obtain an arbitrarily huge amount of data from social networks. Using a master node built on the ActoDeS architecture, which handles managing communications, interfaces, and messages shared by client nodes, the objective is to ensure that the correct operations are performed among the actors. As a use case, the authors use Twitter.

In the field of market simulations, the study by Bertolotti and Roman [53] offers a potential explanation for seasonal patterns observed in the time series of the number of films released and the total box-office earnings of the top 10 films (arranged according to box-office performance) in the US movie market data. The authors reproduce this market by creating and fine-tuning an agent-based model of the US movie theater industry. The same authors in [54] propose an agent-based model of a basic sustainability game where agents make decisions based on an evolutionary meta-model and risk-preference factors. The purpose of the study is to demonstrate how environmental factors, such as the amount of natural stock present at the beginning of the simulated game (such as brown blocks), the survival rate per generation, and the weight assigned to each type of victory (lone victory or shared victory), influence the evolution of risk sensitivities.

In [205] a novel approach to Federated Learning (FL) is discussed, called Peer-Reviewed Federated Learning (PRFL). The purpose of the paper is to propose a solution to improve the performance of FL systems and to provide a flexible tool to implement review-based FL algorithms.

In the field of E-Health, Python is used in [208] for a pilot study on an IoT-based tracking system for patients in the operating room (OR). This work aims to improve the management of operating blocks by using machine learning algorithms to develop a new organizational model. Here, the authors introduce a system that tracks patients in real-time through wearable tags, enhancing data accuracy for the patient management process. The collected data are used to predict surgery times for patients, allowing for better planning and resource optimization.

Python is used also in the work of [194] to develope an integrated hybrid agent architecture for personal medical digital assistant agents.

In [60], the authors introduce MAKKSim, an agent-based simulation platform for pedestrian dynamics developed in Python. MAKKSim models crowd behaviors, including pedestrian groups and cultural elements. Blender,[15] a free 3D modeling software, is used for visualization and creating realistic 3D environments via its Python API. While Blender enhances visualization, the focus of the paper is on MAKKSim's architecture, behavioral models, and simulation capabilities.

In [243], the authors discuss the integration of Runtime Verification (RV) with RL to address the challenges of specifying precise behaviors in RL agents. The goal here is to simplify problem-solving, improve efficiency through off-policy learning, and enable the specification of intricate behaviors within RL environments.

4   Other Programming Languages and Their Application

DyLOG [29,30] is a logic programming language extending Prolog with constructs for handling dynamic knowledge bases. It is used in agent systems to reason about actions, policies, and interactions within evolving environments. DyLOG has been applied to model and analyze communicative behaviors,

---

[15] http://www.blender.org/.

enabling agents to customize web service interactions through speech acts and protocols [28] and in the field of MAS [240].

In [25], the authors investigate the use of **Promela**[16] and **UML**[17] modeling languages for curriculum verification. Promela is a tool to simulate and validate curricula represented through UML activity diagrams. Its role extends to identifying competency gaps, ensuring the achievement of learning objectives, and validating compliance with curriculum models.

AgentSpeak, introduced in [65, 224], is a popular language in the logic programming community where an agent's behavior is defined through a set of executable plans, contributing significantly to the MAS framework. In a broader context, AgentSpeak is highlighted as an abstract agent language rooted in the BDI architecture. It embodies an agent's beliefs, desires, and intentions, forming the basis for cognitive agent development within MAS. Jason [64] is an open-source interpreter written in Java for an extended version of AgentSpeak. Distributed under the GNU LGPL, Jason[18] implements the operational semantics of AgentSpeak and serves as a robust platform for developing multi-agent systems. It offers a wide range of user-customizable features, enabling flexibility and adaptability for diverse applications in multi-agent system development. Jason is so popular, that the name is often used as a synonym of AgentSpeak. AgentSpeak is frequently used in WOA papers, such as in [96, 192, 234]. The first two papers explore the use of AgentSpeak within the JaCa platform but focus on distinct application domains. In [234] the discussion revolves around the creation of web client applications employing the JaCa-Web framework. This framework leverages AgentSpeak for agent implementation within the web environment, focusing on scenarios and interactions specific to web-based systems. Instead, in [192], the authors explore the use of AgentSpeak to design Android applications. Here, AgentSpeak serves as the programming language within the JaCa platform, specifically tailored for the development of Android apps.

The **DALI** language[19] [103, 104, 106–109, 114, 128–132] is an Active Logic Programming language designed to empower developers to specify logical agents. Offering seamless support for both reactive and proactive behaviors, event handling, knowledge manipulation, and planning, DALI facilitates the creation of sophisticated agent systems with unprecedented ease and flexibility. An Answer Set Solver (cf. [68, 151, 171] and references therein for Answer Set Programming (ASP)) has been integrated into the DALI implementation. The DALI communication architecture [130] is designed to facilitate agent-based communication by filtering incoming and out-coming messages. DALI is compatible with Docker, allowing agents to be deployed within containers.

DALI and AgentSpeak belong to several computational-logic-based agent-oriented languages and frameworks that have been introduced over time to specify agents and MAS (for a survey of these languages and architectures, the

---

[16] http://en.wikipedia.org/wiki/Promela.
[17] https://it.wikipedia.org/wiki/Unified_Modeling_Language.
[18] https://jason-lang.github.io/.
[19] https://github.com/AAAI-DISIM-UnivAQ/DALI.

reader may refer, among many, to [62,77,165]). Their added value concerning non-logical approaches is to provide clean semantics, readability, verifiability, transparency, and explainability 'by design' (or almost), as logical rules can easily be transposed into natural-language explanations.

A comparison between DALI and AgentSpeak, which shows that, despite some differences, the two languages have many affinities and share the same declarative semantics, is reported in [63].

C/Erlang, also known as Concurrent Erlang, is a variant of the **Erlang**[20] programming language designed to support concurrent programming paradigms. Erlang, a functional programming language, is primarily used for building distributed, fault-tolerant, and highly scalable systems, especially in telecommunications and large-scale distributed environments. It has been applied to agent platforms [149], robot behavior modeling [190], and MAS [147,148].

NetLogo[21] is a multi-agent programmable modeling environment that uses its own programming language based on the **Logo** programming language. This language is designed explicitly for creating multi-agent simulations and defining the behaviors of agents within those simulations. Its effectiveness in the fields of complex systems science, agent-based modeling, and computational social science has made it a good choice in research on agent trust modeling [153,213, 237].

Scala[22] is a high-level programming language that combines functional and object-oriented paradigms. In [157], Scala is employed for its support of the Actor model, which enables efficient, scalable concurrent systems.[23] Scala achieves scalability by unifying thread-based and event-based programming while maintaining simplicity.

In multi-agent systems [99], Scala is used to automatically generate MOISE organizational specifications.[24] An algorithm processes XML templates interleaved with rules to produce MOISE specification code.

RDF & SPARQL are used to represent and manipulate services within the SAPERE framework in [195]. RDF triples are used to model services as Live Semantic Annotations (LSAs), allowing for scalable and flexible descriptions. Service composition, contextualization, and feedback integration are made possible by SPARQL's definition of eco-laws, which are chemical-like reaction rules that match and modify RDF data. A rule might, for instance, dynamically modify a gradient service according to the audience levels in real time. In pervasive ecosystems, this integration offers a versatile and effective method for the spontaneous self-composition of services. While, in [179] RDF is employed

---

[20] https://www.erlang.org/.

[21] https://ccl.northwestern.edu/netlogo/.

[22] https://www.scala-lang.org/.

[23] The Actor model, introduced by Hewitt et al. in 1973 [3,168], describes concurrent systems. For history, description, and semantics, see https://en.wikipedia.org/wiki/Actor_model.

[24] MOISE is an organizational model for MAS based on roles, groups, and missions, integrated into the JaCaMo platform [59].

to create machine-understandable metadata that characterizes the home environment, appliances, and user preferences. This allows for a more flexible and dynamic interaction within the home automation system.

Kotlin[25] is a contemporary programming language that gained popularity due to its compatibility with Java. In the context of object-oriented programming (OOP), Kotlin is used to create a domain-specific language (DSL) for Prolog. The goal of the work [91] is to help general-purpose programming environments better integrate logic programming (LP) by examining how LP can be enhanced by OOP and functional programming (FP), two of Kotlin's multi-paradigm capabilities. Paper [233] highlights Kotlin's use in the design and development of PSyKE due to its support for the JVM (Java Virtual Machine), which allows for easy integration with Smile's API,[26] a machine learning engine.

HEMASL [187] is a meta-language for specifying heterogeneous agent architectures in MAS. It supports modularity and abstraction, enabling the modeling of reactive and deliberative agents within a unified framework. HEMASL's operational semantics facilitate rigorous verification and integration with CaseLP, a logic programming environment. The language also allows translating specifications into Java, bridging high-level design and practical implementation..

KIF[27] (Knowledge Interchange Format) is a computer-oriented language designed to facilitate the exchange of knowledge between diverse programs. The language features a declarative semantics. It is logically comprehensive, allowing for the representation of arbitrary sentences within first-order predicate calculus. Additionally, it supports the representation of meta-knowledge, accommodates nonmonotonic reasoning rules, and enables the definition of objects, functions, and relationships, making it a versatile tool for advanced knowledge representation and reasoning.

KIF [188], was essential in developing the DOLCE ontology (Descriptive Ontology for Linguistic and Cognitive Engineering).[28] DOLCE is a foundational ontology developed as part of the WONDERWEB Foundational Ontologies Library[29] (WFOL).

Complementing KIF in this endeavor is OWL (Web Ontology Language)[30] [241], which also played a significant role. OWL is a powerful tool for defining ontologies specifically tailored for the Web. OWL offers robust capabilities for defining and reasoning within ontologies, providing expressive tools for delineating classes, properties, individuals, and relationships within the ontology structure.

JSON[31] (JavaScript Object Notation) is a lightweight format for storing and transmitting data. The JSON format, which includes data on text, graph-

---

ics, sender user data, message date and time, and any geolocation information, is used to standardize the representations of different messages. A web-based system designed to function as an ad hoc Customer Relationship Management (CRM) system using the JSON format to manage reports in an organized way [18]. The development and application of a voice assistant for ER patient triage is examined in [196]. This open-source, extensible voice assistant, Mycroft, is a key component of this human-centered intelligent system. Patients can report their symptoms to the agent, who acknowledges the urgency and takes appropriate action. During triage, the voice assistant gathers data, which is subsequently exported as a JSON file and saved to a Python dictionary. The voice assistant may be easily integrated with current healthcare systems without requiring any changes thanks to the standard JSON format.

In [90] knowledge representation in collaborative human-agent systems using Jason, CArtAgO, and OWL is explored. A controlled semantic system, built with Jason and CArtAgO, governs the agents' beliefs during runtime. OWL Ontology, integrated via Jena, manages and updates the knowledge base dynamically as the system operates.

In [85] the improvement of human-robot interactions is explored by integrating trust theory with robot self-modeling capabilities. It uses the BDI agent paradigm with Jason and CArtAgO, as they fully support BDI theory and enable the development of a reference model for the robot's environment without significant modifications.

Jason is also used to implement the robot's decision-making system in [80], which follows a BDI model. It enables the robot to reason dynamically about user goals, adapt its behavior, and select appropriate strategies for task adoption, such as "literal help" or "critical help".

4.1 Applications of DALI

The DALI framework consists of a comprehensive environment built on Sicstus Prolog with additional scripting support and web-based integration, offering multiplatform capabilities and the ability to connect with external applications. The framework has been extended to "DALI 2.0" [109] to support cloud-based applications, enabling MAS to be integrated into various environments, including robotic systems. Furthermore, DALI agents can interact with other MASs programmed in different languages and integrate with object-oriented applications (see, for example, [222]).

The DALI framework has been experimented with, e.g., in applications for unattended hardware testing of hardware-software platforms in the telecommunication industry [56]; user monitoring and training [115]; emergency management (such as first aid triage assignment), patient monitoring [172], flood monitoring [223], and healthcare [55]; tourist routing [211]; security or automation contexts; home automation and processes control. More generally, DALI has proved to be useful in every situation characterized by asynchronous event sources that require reasoning over a dynamic data collection: simple events and/or events that are correlated to other ones, even in complex patterns. To be able to perform *Complex Event Processing*, i.e., to actively monitor event data to make automated decisions and take time-critical actions, DALI has been empowered with CEP capabilities [105], of which the implementation at this day is partial, but is being actively developed: since the 2018 release, DALI supports the double concurring events occurrence in a predefined time window, so that reaction rules can be defined where two events from different asynchronous sources happen to fall in the same time interval. An architecture encompassing DALI agents called F&K (Friendly-and-Kind) system [4] has been proposed for (though not restricted to) applications in the e-Health domain.

We are currently conducting experiments in the field of emotion recognition in the context of cognitive robotics, where real-time analysis of the non-verbal communication interaction between a human and the anthropomorphic NAO robot is performed by an extended DALI, consisting of an ASP_DALI and QuLog/Teleor multi-agent system. DALI has been integrated with various machine-learning techniques, giving rise to neural-symbolic approaches for applications. One concerns improving Reinforcement Learning performance [135]. Another one integrates a neural agent in a DALI MAS for flood detection [222,223].

A recent application presented at WOA, where DALI and Prolog have been used as implementation languages, concerns Behavior trees (BTs) [110], where a BT is a mathematical model of plan execution. In [170], the authors extend the core definition of BTs to incorporate the notion of emotions. They called the resulting model *emotional behavior trees*. This model is further extended in [110] to include the notion of empathy. This ability allowed the design of agents that were emotional and empathic. This is strongly related to the Theory of Mind (ToM) and allows the design of agents with social-cognitive skills, which involves the ability to attribute mental states, including emotions, desires, beliefs, and knowledge of both one's own and those of others, and to reason about the practical consequences of such mental states. To enable the integration of deep learning models for emotion recognition and symbolic models for planning and decision-making in [111–113] the authors extend the BT model with neural-symbolic capabilities.

5 Conceptual Basis of Modeling Group Dynamics in Agents: the Epistemic Logic Framework *L-DINF*

Besides developing practical agent-oriented programming languages and applications, formal tools are, in our opinion, needed at a design level to specify and study agents and modality of interaction. Our attention has been, in particular, focused on studying group dynamics in MAS and, to this aim, (some of) the authors of this chapter have been developing and experimenting with a suitable epistemic logic.

Declarative methodologies have long been recognized as essential for ensuring transparency, explainability, and formal verification in multi-agent systems. Ancona et al. [11] discuss how declarative technologies provide structured and rule-based approaches to system design, enabling the specification and verification of agent behaviors with clarity and reliability. Their survey underscores the enduring relevance of logic-based tools in addressing the growing complexity of MAS, particularly in domains requiring trustworthy AI solutions

The epistemic logic of "*Inferable*", L-DINF, first introduced in [127] is born as an extension of a pre-existing logic described in [22,23,116], is an agent-oriented logical framework that allows a designer to formalize and formally verify multi-agent systems. It has been devised for general use, but especially to provide a principled way to model DALI MAS.

The core framework of the logic allows the modeling of the reasoning activity of agents that are endowed with a *long-term memory* and a *short-term memory* (or *working memory*). The former constitutes the agent's background knowledge whereas the agent's working memory includes, instead, the "beliefs" acquired by the agent during its "life". Each agent's working memory evolves as a consequence of its actions, its reasoning activity, and its interaction with other agents and with the common environment (e.g., through perceptions). The working memory can be enlarged by combining contents from long- and short-term memories, employing the agent's inner *inferential* actions.

Formally, L-DINF is a multi-modal logic where two modalities, namely $\mathbf{K}_i$ and $\mathbf{B}_i$, express the knowledge and beliefs of the agent i, respectively (refer, for instance, to [122,126] for a detailed formal treatment). The semantics of L-DINF is a standard possible-world semantics, where $\mathbf{K}_i$ turns out to be the well-known S5 modal operator whereas semantics of $\mathbf{B}_i$ is determined by the collection of the inference actions agents can perform to modify their short-term memory. Typical inferential actions are (i) the introduction of a new belief, in the working memory, by applying *modus ponens* to knowledge and/or given beliefs; (ii) the removal of a belief as consequence of new beliefs and the contents of the long-term memory (i.e., a restricted form of *belief revision*); (iii) the closure of given beliefs under conjunction.

L-DINF allows the modeling of executability conditions of physical and inferential actions, the former being triggered by the completion of some inferential activity of agents (i.e., a sequence of inferential actions).

The basic framework has been extended over time along various directions, enriching it with many functionalities and making it sufficiently expressive to model significant aspects of MAS. Group dynamics for L-DINF has been formalized in [117,120,126], The capability of agents to form groups share beliefs, cooperate [121], and model other agents' beliefs, allows them not only to construct and execute joint plans but also to represent the mental states of other agents. This opens to the formalization, within L-DINF, of aspects of the *Theory of Mind*, namely, the social-cognitive skill involving the ability to attribute mental states, including emotions, desires, beliefs, and knowledge to oneself and to others. Consequently, an agent can reason by impersonating other agents and drawing consequences of such mental states [122], even developing *false-beliefs* about the mental state of other agents.

Resources, budget, and costs have been introduced in [118, 119]. This enables modeling reasoning in context where action execution involves resource consumption, and agents activity can be affected by their preferences [125] and by the roles [123] that agents play in their groups.

The temporal dimension has been introduced in [116, 124]. In this case, a (modal) temporal operator embodies a notion of explicit time and allows to reason on *timed beliefs*, the intervals in which such beliefs hold, and the "timed" effects of agents' actions.

5.1   An Example of Use

In this subsection, we propose an example to explain the usefulness of this kind of logic underlying the cognitive aspects of agents and agent systems. To the best of our knowledge, no one in literature uses logic in this way. For simplicity of illustration and brevity, the example is in "skeletal" form. Consider a group of four agents which are the crew of an ambulance, including a driver, two nurses, and a medical doctor. The driver is the only one allowed to drive the ambulance. Nurses can perform several tasks, such as administering a pain reliever, cleaning, disinfecting, and bandaging a wound, and measuring vital signs. It is however the task of a doctor to make a diagnosis, to prescribe medications, to order, perform, and interpret diagnostic tests, and to perform complex medical procedures. Let us identify the four agents by integer numbers and, accordingly, let $G = \{1, 2, 3, 4\}$ be their group.

Imagine that the hospital received notice of a car accident with an injured person. Then, it will inform the group of the fact that a patient needs help (how exactly is not treated here, because this depends on how the multi-agent system is implemented, but a message exchange will presumably suffice). The group will reason and devise the intention/goal:

$$\mathbf{K}_i(intend_G(rescue\_patient))$$

shared by all group agents, i.e., $i \leq 4$.

Among the physical actions that agents in G can perform, there are the following:

diagnose_patient	*administer_urgent_treatment*
measure_vital_signs	*pneumothorax_aspiration*
local_anesthesia	*bandage_wounds*
drive_to_patient	*drive_to_hospital.*

The group will now be required to perform a planning activity. Assume that, as a result of the planning phase, the knowledge base of each agent i contains the following rule that specifies how to reach the intended goal in terms of actions to perform and sub-goals to achieve:

$$\mathbf{K}_i\big(intend_G(rescue\_patient) \rightarrow$$
$$intend_G(drive\_to\_patient) \wedge$$
$$intend_G(diagnose\_patient) \wedge$$
$$intend_G(stabilize\_patient) \wedge$$
$$intend_G(drive\_to\_hospital)$$

Thanks to the axiomatization for *L-DINF*, each agent has the specialized rule (for $i \leq 4$):

$$\mathbf{K}_i\big(intend_G(rescue\_patient) \rightarrow$$
$$intend_i(drive\_to\_patient) \wedge$$
$$intend_i(diagnose\_patient) \wedge$$
$$intend_i(stabilize\_patient) \wedge$$
$$intend_i(drive\_to\_hospital))$$

While driving to the patient and returning to the hospital are actions, $intend_G(stabilize\_patient)$ is a goal.

Assume that each agent's knowledge base also contains the following general rules, stating that the group is available to perform each action included in the plan, i.e., drive to reach the patient, diagnose the patient's health status, and drive the patient to the hospital. Which agent will, in particular, perform each action ϕ_A According to the definition of L-DINF, this agent will be chosen as the one that best prefers to perform this action among those that can do it. Formally, $pref\_do_G(i, \phi_A)$ identifies an agent i in the group with a maximum degree of preference on performing ϕ_A (any rule can be applied to select i in case more agents qualify), and $can\_do_G(\phi_A)$ is true if there is some agent i in the group which is able and allowed to perform ϕ_A.

So, for each action ϕ_A required by the plan, there will be some agent (let us assume for simplicity only one), for which $do_i(\phi_A)$ will be concluded. In our case, the agent driver j will conclude $do_j(drive\_to\_patient)$ and $do_j(drive\_to\_hospital)$; the agent doctor ℓ will conclude $do_\ell(stabilize\_patient)$. Whenever an agent derives $do_i(\phi_A)$ for any physical action ϕ_A, the action is supposed to be executed via some *semantic attachment*, i.e., via some specifically implemented procedure which *actuates* an action and thus links the agent to the external environment.

Since $intend_G(stabilize\_patient)$ is not an action but a sub-goal, the group will have to devise a plan to achieve it. This will imply sensing actions and forms of reasoning not shown here. Assume that the diagnosis has been pneumothorax and that the patient has also some wounds that are bleeding. Upon completion of the planning phase, the knowledge base of each agent i contains the following rule, that specifies how to reach the intended goal in terms of actions to be performed:

$$\mathbf{K}_i\big(intend_G(stabilize\_patient) \rightarrow$$
$$intend_G(measure\_vital\_signs) \wedge intend_G(local\_anesthesia) \wedge$$
$$intend_G(bandage\_wounds) \wedge intend_G(pneumothorax\_aspiration))$$

As before, these rules will be instantiated and elaborated by the single agents, and there will be some agents who will finally perform each action. Specifically, the doctor will be the one to perform pneumothorax aspiration, and the nurses (according to their competencies and preferences) will measure vital signs, administer local anesthesia, and bandage the wounds. The semantics guarantees, in this case, that each procedure is administered by some agent which capable of and also enabled by the group to take responsibility for the action.

An interesting point concerns derogation, i.e. life-or-death situations where, unfortunately, no one who is enabled to perform some urgently needed action is available; in such situations, perhaps anyone capable of performing this action might perform it. For instance, a nurse, in the absence of a doctor, might attempt urgent pneumothorax aspiration. In its last version, L-DINF semantics allow derogation, thus enhancing the approach's ductility and relevance to modeling agents' cognitive aspects.

6   Conclusion

In this chapter, we presented the results of our exploration into the programming languages most commonly used for modeling agents and MAS. Following a comprehensive introduction, we focused on languages rooted in Computational Logic, examining their applications and theoretical underpinnings.

Our survey, covering the period from 2000 to 2024, revealed several key trends in the evolution of agent and MAS programming. In particular, languages such as Java, Prolog, and Python have maintained a dominant presence due to their versatility, logical reasoning capabilities, and adaptability to modern frameworks. The rise of Python, in particular, highlights a shift toward accessible and powerful languages that cater to both academic and practical applications, making it a preferred choice for contemporary MAS development.

Another crucial observation is the growing importance of computational logic-based languages such as DALI and AgentSpeak. These languages excel in offering transparent semantics and robust frameworks for programming agents capable of symbolic reasoning. They have proven not only effective in practical implementations but also instrumental in advancing theoretical insights into MAS. By providing formal tools to model agent behaviors, group dynamics, and complex interactions, these languages have become pivotal in the field.

Looking to the future, the field of agents and MAS is flexible enough to accommodate transformative advancements. The integration of MAS with emerging technologies, such as neural-symbolic systems and Large Language Models (LLMs), presents a unique opportunity to revolutionize the domain. This fusion could enable agents to seamlessly combine the strengths of symbolic reasoning—offering clarity, structure, and logical rigor—with the adaptability, pattern recognition, and learning capabilities of neural networks. Such convergence has the potential to create highly dynamic systems that can reason, learn, and adapt in increasingly sophisticated and unpredictable environments.

In conclusion, the findings of this chapter underscore the importance of both practical and theoretical advancements in the field of MAS. As the technology landscape continues to evolve, the ability of MAS to incorporate and leverage cutting-edge innovations will drive the development of smarter, more resilient, and highly collaborative systems. The continued exploration and integration of programming languages and paradigms will undoubtedly shape the future of MAS, enabling them to tackle complex real-world challenges and contribute to the broader progress of artificial intelligence.

Acknowledgements. This work has been partially supported by Projects PRIN 2022 TRUSTPACTX (CUP E53D23007850001), PRIN 2022 ADVISOR (CUP: E53D23016270001), PNNR ENABLE-FAIR (CUP E13C24000430006), INdAM-GNCS (CUP E53C 22001930001), and by the Interdepartmental Project on AI (Strategic Plan Uni UD—22-25).

References

1. Addis, A., Armano, G., Vargiu, E.: Monitoring boats in marine reserves: a MAS solution. In: Bergenti, F., (ed.) WOA 2009 – 10th Workshop "From Objects to Agents", pp. 52–57. Seneca Edizioni Torino, Parma (2009). http://www.ailab.unipr.it/woa09/papers/Addis1.pdf
2. Agazzi, F., Tomaiuolo, M.: Trust negotiation for automated service integration. In: Baldoni, et al., (eds.) [24] , pp. 97–103. http://ceur-ws.org/Vol-1099/paper6.pdf
3. Agha, G., Hewitt, C.: Actors: a conceptual foundation for concurrent object-oriented programming. In: Shriver, B.D., Wegner, P. (eds.) Research Directions in Object-Oriented Programming, pp. 49–74. MIT Press (1987)
4. Aielli, F., et al.: FRIENDLY & KIND with your health: human-friendly knowledge-intensive dynamic systems for the e-health domain. In: Bajo, J., et al., (eds.) Highlights of Practical Applications of Scalable Multi-Agent Systems. The PAAMS Collection - International Workshops of PAAMS 2016, Proceedings. Communications in Computer and Information Science, vol. 616, pp. 15–26. Springer (2016). https://doi.org/10.1007/978-3-319-39387-2_2
5. Albericci, T., Cecconello, T., Gibertini, A., Vizzari, G.: A curriculum-based reinforcement learning approach to pedestrian simulation. In: Calegari, et al., (eds.) [76] , pp. 224–240. http://ceur-ws.org/Vol-2963/paper11.pdf
6. Alderighi, M., Baldoni, M., Baroglio, C., Micalizio, R., Tedeschi, S. (eds.) : WOA 2024 – 25th Workshop "From Objects to Agents", CEUR Workshop Proceedings, vol. 3735. Bard (2024). http://ceur-ws.org/Vol-3735/
7. Alzetta, F., Giorgini, P.: Towards a real-time BDI model for ROS 2. In: Bergenti and Monica [52] , pp. 1–7. http://ceur-ws.org/Vol-2404/paper01.pdf
8. Amato, A., Di Martino, B., Venticinque, S.: BDI intelligent agents for augmented exploitation of pervasive environments. In: Fortino, et al., (eds.) [160], pp. 81–88. http://ceur-ws.org/Vol-741/ID16_AmatoDiMartinoVenticinque.pdf
9. Amato, A., Scialdone, M., Venticinque, S.: An application of learning agents to smart energy domains. In: Napoli, D., et al., (eds.) [145], pp. 11–18. http://ceur-ws.org/Vol-1382/paper2.pdf
10. Amoretti, M., Gandolfi, L., Tomaiuolo, M.: A peer-to-peer notification system for distributed online social networks. In: Bergenti and Monica (eds.) [52], pp. 142–148. http://ceur-ws.org/Vol-2404/paper21.pdf

11. Ancona, D., Briola, D., Ferrando, A., Martelli, M., Mascardi, V.: 25 years of declarative agent technologies in Italy. In: Mascardi and Omicini [189]
12. Ancona, D., Briola, D., Ferrando, A., Mascardi, V.: MAS-DRiVe: a practical approach to decentralized runtime verification of agent interaction protocols. In: Santoro, et al., (eds.) [236], pp. 35–43. http://ceur-ws.org/Vol-1664/w7.pdf
13. Ancona, D., Briola, D., Mascardi, V.: Protocols with exceptions, timeouts, and handlers: a uniform framework for monitoring fail-uncontrolled and ambient intelligence systems. In: Napoli, D., et al., (eds.) [145], pp. 65–75. http://ceur-ws.org/Vol-1382/paper10.pdf
14. Ancona, D., Ferrando, A., Mascardi, V.: Agents interoperability via conformance modulo mapping. In: Cossentino, et al., (eds.) [102], pp. 109–115. http://ceur-ws.org/Vol-2215/paper_18.pdf
15. Anedda, P., Brelstaff, G., Moehrs, S., Tuveri, M., Zanetti, G.: Cartella clinica elettronica su piattaforma Java InfoBus. In: Corradi, et al., (eds.) [93], pp. 98–103. http://giuseppevizzari.github.io/WOA-proceedings-archive/pdfs/woa2000/WOA19.pdf
16. Angelaccio, M., Buttarazzi, B.: Agent architecture for score-based web local search. In: Corradi, et al., (eds.) [93], pp. 104–108. http://giuseppevizzari.github.io/WOA-proceedings-archive/pdfs/woa2000/WOA20.pdf
17. Anghinolfi, D., Boccalatte, A., Grosso, A., Paolucci, M., Passadore, A., Vecchiola, C.: A swarm intelligence method applied to manufacturing scheduling. In: Baldoni, et al., (eds.) [31], pp. 65–70. http://woa07.dibris.unige.it/papers/AnghinolfiSwarm.pdf
18. Angiani, G., Fornacciari, P., Lombardo, G., Mordonini, M., Poggi, A., Tomaiuolo, M.: Intelligent collection and analysis of citizens' reports. In: Bergenti and Monica [52], pp. 84–89. http://ceur-ws.org/Vol-2404/paper13.pdf
19. Armano, G., et al.: ANEMONE-a network of multi-agent platforms for academic communities. In: Corradini, et al., (eds.) [94], pp. 120–126. http://lia.deis.unibo.it/books/woa2005/papers/17.pdf
20. Armano, G., Paoli, F.D., Omicini, A., Vargiu, E., (eds.): WOA 2003 – 4th Workshop "From Objects to Agents". Pitagora Editrice Bologna, Villasimius (2003). http://giuseppevizzari.github.io/WOA-proceedings-archive/woa-2003.html
21. Augimeri, A., Folino, G., Forestiero, A., Spezzano, G.: A multidimensional flocking algorithm for clustering spatial data. In: Paoli, D., et al., (eds.) [139], pp. 16–20. http://ceur-ws.org/Vol-204/D05.pdf
22. Balbiani, P., Fernández-Duque, D., Lorini, E.: The dynamics of epistemic attitudes in resource-bounded agents. Stud. Logica. **107**(3), 457–488 (2019)
23. Balbiani, P., Duque, D.F., Lorini, E.: A logical theory of belief dynamics for resource-bounded agents. In: Proceedings of the 2016 International Conference on Autonomous Agents & Multiagent Systems, AAMAS 2016, pp. 644–652. ACM (2016)
24. Baldoni, M., Baroglio, C., Bergenti, F., Garro, A., (eds.) : WOA 2013 – 14th Workshop "From Objects to Agents", CEUR Workshop Proceedings, vol. 1099. Turin (2013). http://ceur-ws.org/Vol-1099/
25. Baldoni, M., Baroglio, C., Berio, G., Marengo, E.: Declarative representation of curricula models: an LTL-and UML-based approach. In: Baldoni, et al., (eds.) [31], pp. 34–41. http://woa07.dibris.unige.it/papers/BaldoniDeclarative.pdf
26. Baldoni, M., Baroglio, C., Capuzzimati, F.: 2COMM: a commitment-based MAS architecture. In: Baldoni, et al., (eds.) [24], pp. 38–57. http://ceur-ws.org/Vol-1099/paper11.pdf

27. Baldoni, M., Baroglio, C., Capuzzimati, F.: Social relationships for designing agent interaction in JADE. In: Santoro and Bergenti [235], pp. 36–43. http://ceur-ws.org/Vol-1260/paper6.pdf

28. Baldoni, M., Baroglio, C., Martelli, A., Patti, V.: Reasoning about interaction for personalizing web service fruition. In: Armano, et al., (eds.) [20], pp. 29–35. http://giuseppevizzari.github.io/WOA-proceedings-archive/pdfs/woa2003/06.pdf

29. Baldoni, M., Baroglio, C., Martelli, A., Patti, V., Schifanella, C.: Preserving players goals: a choreography-driven matchmaking approach. In: Baldoni, et al., (eds.) [31], pp. 132–139. http://woa07.dibris.unige.it/papers/BaldoniPlayers.pdf

30. Baldoni, M., Baroglio, C., Patti, V.: Supporting users in adaptive web-based applications: techniques from reasoning about actions. In: Paoli, D., et al., (eds.) [140], pp. 49–55. http://giuseppevizzari.github.io/WOA-proceedings-archive/pdfs/woa2002/02.pdf

31. Baldoni, M., Boccalatte, A., De Paoli, F., Martelli, M., Mascardi, V. (eds.): WOA 2007 – 8th Workshop "From Objects to Agents". Seneca Edizioni Torino, Genova (2007). http://woa07.disi.unige.it/ProceedingsWOA2007.zip

32. Baldoni, M., Cossentino, M., De Paoli, F., Seidita, V., (eds.): WOA 2008 – 9th Workshop "From Objects to Agents". Seneca Edizioni Torino, Palermo (2008). http://www.pa.icar.cnr.it/woa08/materiali/Proceedings.pdf

33. Baldoni, M., De Paoli, F., Martelli, A., Omicini, A., (eds.): WOA 2004 – 5th Workshop "From Objects to Agents". Pitagora Editrice Bologna, Torino (2004). http://lia.deis.unibo.it/books/woa2004/atti.pdf

34. Bandini, S., De Paoli, F., Manzoni, S., Simone, C.: OO reactive agents for RDM-based simulations. In: Corradi, et al., (eds.) [93], pp. 19–22. http://giuseppevizzari.github.io/WOA-proceedings-archive/pdfs/woa2000/WOA04.pdf

35. Bandini, S., De Paoli, F., Manzoni, S., Simone, C.: A OO framework for multi-agent systems. In: Omicini and Viroli [201], pp. 78–83. http://giuseppevizzari.github.io/WOA-proceedings-archive/pdfs/woa2001/pdf/02.pdf

36. Bandini, S., Manzoni, S., Vizzari, G.: RPG-Profiler: a MAS for role playing games based tests in employee assessment. In: Paoli, D., et al., (eds.) [140], pp. 72–77. http://giuseppevizzari.github.io/WOA-proceedings-archive/pdfs/woa2002/16.pdf

37. Bandini, S., Manzoni, S., Vizzari, G.: Situated cellular agents and immune system modelling. In: Armano, et al., (eds.) [20], pp. 36–41. http://giuseppevizzari.github.io/WOA-proceedings-archive/pdfs/woa2003/02.pdf

38. Baroni, P., Fogli, D., Mussio, P.: An agent-based architecture to support knowledge management in interactive system life-cycle. In: Paoli, D., et al., (eds.) [140], pp. 42–48. http://giuseppevizzari.github.io/WOA-proceedings-archive/pdfs/woa2002/01.pdf

39. Baroni, P., Gerevini, A., Toninelli, P.: MAgentA: un sistema multi agente per la gestione di agende e riunioni. In: Corradini, et al., (eds.) [94], pp. 127–135. http://lia.deis.unibo.it/books/woa2005/papers/18.pdf

40. Bartocci, E., Corradini, F., Merelli, E., Vito, L.: Model driven design and implementation of activity-based applications in Hermes. In: Paoli, D., et al., (eds.) [139], pp. 25–31. http://ceur-ws.org/Vol-204/D07.pdf

41. Bellavista, P., Corradi, A., Magistretti, E.: Proxy-based middleware for service continuity in mobile ad hoc networks. In: Armano, et al., (eds.) [20], pp. 1–8. http://giuseppevizzari.github.io/WOA-proceedings-archive/pdfs/woa2003/01.pdf

42. Bellavista, P., Corradi, A., Montanari, R., Stefanelli, C.: How a secure and open mobile agent framework suits electronic commerce applications. In: Corradi, et al., (eds.) [93], pp. 13–18. http://giuseppevizzari.github.io/WOA-proceedings-archive/pdfs/woa2000/WOA03.pdf
43. Bellavista, P., Corradi, A., Vecchi, S.: An integrated resource management architecture for wireless smart environments. In: Armano, et al., (eds.) [20], pp. 49–56. http://giuseppevizzari.github.io/WOA-proceedings-archive/pdfs/woa2003/15.pdf
44. Bellifemine, F., Poggi, A., Rimassa, G.: JADE–a FIPA-compliant agent framework. In: Proceedings of PAAM'99, pp. 97–108. London (1999)
45. Bellifemine, F., Poggi, A., Rimassa, G.: Developing multi-agent systems with JADE. In: Castelfranchi, C., Lespérance, Y. (eds.) Intelligent Agents VII. Agent Theories Architectures and Languages, 7th International Workshop, ATAL 2000, Boston, July 7-9, 2000, Proceedings. Lecture Notes in Computer Science, vol. 1986, pp. 89–103. Springer (2000). https://doi.org/10.1007/3-540-44631-1_7
46. Bellifemine, F., Poggi, A., Rimassa, G.: Developing multi-agent systems with a FIPA-compliant agent framework. Softw. Pract. Exper. **31**(2), 103–128 (2001). https://doi.org/10.1002/1097-024X(200102)31:2<103::AID-SPE358>3.0.CO;2-O
47. Bellifemine, F., Poggi, A., Rimassa, G., Turci, P.: An object-oriented framework to realize agent systems. In: Corradi, et al., (eds.) [93], pp. 52–57. http://giuseppevizzari.github.io/WOA-proceedings-archive/pdfs/woa2000/WOA11.pdf
48. Beneventano, D., Bergamaschi, S., Gelati, G., Guerra, F., Vincini, M.: An agent framework for supporting the MIKS integration process. In: Paoli, D., et al., (eds.) [140], pp. 35–41. http://giuseppevizzari.github.io/WOA-proceedings-archive/pdfs/woa2002/25.pdf
49. Bergenti, F., Caire, G., Gotta, D.: Agents on the move: JADE for android devices. In: Santoro and Bergenti [235], pp. 44–47. http://ceur-ws.org/Vol-1260/paper9.pdf
50. Bergenti, F., Caire, G., Gotta, D., Long, D., Sacchi, G.: Enacting BPM-oriented workflows with Wade. In: Fortino, et al., (eds.) [160], pp. 112–116. http://ceur-ws.org/Vol-741/ID7_BergentiCaireGottaLongSacchi.pdf
51. Bergenti, F., Iotti, E., Poggi, A.: Outline of a formalization of JADE multi-agent systems. In: Napoli, D., et al., (eds.) [145], pp. 123–128. http://ceur-ws.org/Vol-1382/paper19.pdf
52. Bergenti, F., Monica, S. (eds.): WOA 2019 – 20th Workshop "From Objects to Agents", CEUR Workshop Proceedings, vol. 2404. Parma (2019). http://ceur-ws.org/Vol-2404/
53. Bertolotti, F., Roman, S.: Risk sensitivity of production studios on the US movie market: an agent-based simulation. In: Calegari, et al., (eds.) [76], pp. 210–223. http://ceur-ws.org/Vol-2963/paper6.pdf
54. Bertolotti, F., Roman, S.: The evolution of risk sensitivity in a sustainability game: an agent-based model. In: Ferrando and Mascardi [154], pp. 101–115. http://ceur-ws.org/Vol-3261/paper8.pdf
55. Bertoncelli, C.M., Costantini, S., Persia, F., Bertoncelli, D., D'Auria, D.: Predictmed-epilepsy: a multi-agent based system for epilepsy detection and prediction in neuropediatrics. Comput. Methods Programs Biomed. **236**, 107548 (2023). https://doi.org/10.1016/J.CMPB.2023.107548

56. Bevar, V., Costantini, S., De Gasperis, G., Tocchio, A.: A multi-agent system for industrial fault detection and repair. In: Advances on Practical Applications of Agents and Multi-Agent Systems: 10th International Conference on Practical Applications of Agents and Multi-Agent Systems. Advances in Intelligent and Soft Computing, vol. 155. Springer (2012). https://doi.org/10.1007/978-3-642-28786-2_5

57. Blanzieri, E., Giorgini, P., Giunchiglia, F., Zanoni, C.: A multi-agent system for knowledge management based on the implicit culture framework. In: Paoli, D., et al., (eds.) [140], pp. 56–63. http://giuseppevizzari.github.io/WOA-proceedings-archive/pdfs/woa2002/06.pdf

58. Boccalatte, A., Coccoli, M.: Java for real-time object-oriented programming. In: Corradi, et al., (eds.) [93], pp. 41–46. http://giuseppevizzari.github.io/WOA-proceedings-archive/pdfs/woa2000/WOA09.pdf

59. Boissier, O., Bordini, R.H., Hübner, J.F., Ricci, A., Santi, A.: Multi-agent oriented programming with JaCaMo. Sci. Comput. Program. **78**(6), 747–761 (2013). https://doi.org/10.1016/j.scico.2011.10.004

60. Bonomi, A., Manenti, L., Manzoni, S., Vizzari, G.: MAKKSim: dealing with pedestrian groups in MAS-based crowd simulation. In: Fortino, et al., (eds.) [160], pp. 166–170. http://ceur-ws.org/Vol-741/DEM01_BonomiManentiManzoniVizzari.pdf

61. Bonomi, A., Vizzari, G., Sarini, M.: A heterogeneous multi-agent system for adaptive web applications. In: Paoli, D., et al., (eds.) [139], pp. 66–75. http://ceur-ws.org/Vol-204/P03.pdf

62. Bordini, R.H., et al.: A survey of programming languages and platforms for multi-agent systems. Informatica (Slovenia) **30**(1), 33–44 (2006)

63. Bordini, R.H., Costantini, S., Monaldini, A., Vozna, A.: From pure prolog to logic agent-oriented programming languages. In: Alderighi, et al., (eds.) [6], pp. 271–285. http://ceur-ws.org/Vol-3735/paper_20.pdf

64. Bordini, R.H., Hübner, J.F., Wooldridge, M.J.: Programming multi-agent systems in agentSpeak using Jason. Wiley (2007). https://www.wiley.com/Programming+Multi-Agent+Systems+in+AgentSpeak+using+Jason-p-9780470061831

65. Bordini, R.H., Hübner, J.F.: Semantics for the Jason variant of AgentSpeak (plan failure and some internal actions). In: Coelho, H., Studer, R., Wooldridge, M.J. (eds.) ECAI 2010 - 19th European Conference on Artificial Intelligence, Lisbon, August 16-20, 2010, Proceedings. Frontiers in Artificial Intelligence and Applications, vol. 215, pp. 635–640. IOS Press (2010). https://doi.org/10.3233/978-1-60750-606-5-635

66. Bottoni, P., De Marsico, M., Di Tommaso, P., Levialdi, S., Ventriglia, D.: Un linguaggio per esprimere transizioni. In: Paoli, D., et al. [140], pp. 78–85. http://giuseppevizzari.github.io/WOA-proceedings-archive/pdfs/woa2002/03.pdf

67. Bratko, I.: Prolog Programming for Artificial Intelligence, 3rd edn. Pearson Education, USA (2001)

68. Brewka, G., Eiter, T., (eds.), M.T.: Answer set programming: special issue. AI Magazine **37**(3) (2016)

69. Briola, D., Mascardi, V., Martelli, M., Arecco, G., Caccia, R., Milani, C.: A prolog-based MAS for railway signalling monitoring: implementation and experiments. In: Baldoni, et al., (eds.) [32], pp. 11–18. http://www.pa.icar.cnr.it/woa08/materiali/paper/paper_4.pdf

70. Cabri, G., Ferrari, L., Leonardi, L.: Evaluating trust among agents. In: Baldoni, et al., (eds.) [33], pp. 1–4. http://giuseppevizzari.github.io/WOA-proceedings-archive/pdfs/woa2004/1.pdf

71. Cabri, G., Leonardi, L., Mamei, M., Zambonelli, F.: Mobile agent organizations. In: Omicini and Viroli [201], pp. 30–35. http://giuseppevizzari.github.io/WOA-proceedings-archive/pdfs/woa2001/pdf/07.pdf

72. Cabri, G., Leonardi, L., Mariani, S., Zambonelli, F.: Coordination of software agents: models and languages. In: Mascardi and Omicini [189]

73. Caianiello, P., Presutti, D.: A case study on goal oriented obstacle avoidance. In: Napoli, D., et al., (eds.) [145], pp. 142–145. http://ceur-ws.org/Vol-1382/paper22.pdf

74. Calegari, R., Ciatto, G., Dellaluce, J., Omicini, A.: Interpretable narrative explanation for ML predictors with LP: a case study for XAI. In: Bergenti and Monica [52], pp. 105–112. http://ceur-ws.org/Vol-2404/paper16.pdf

75. Calegari, R., Ciatto, G., Denti, E., Omicini, A., Sartor, G. (eds.): WOA 2020 – 21st Workshop "From Objects to Agents", CEUR Workshop Proceedings, vol. 2706. Bologna (2020). http://ceur-ws.org/Vol-2706/

76. Calegari, R., Ciatto, G., Denti, E., Omicini, A., Sartor, G. (eds.): WOA 2021 – 22nd Workshop "From Objects to Agents", CEUR Workshop Proceedings, vol. 2963. Bologna (2021). http://ceur-ws.org/Vol-2963/

77. Calegari, R., Ciatto, G., Mascardi, V., Omicini, A.: Logic-based technologies for multi-agent systems: a systematic literature review. Auton. Agents Multi-Agent Syst. 35(1) (2021). https://doi.org/10.1007/s10458-020-09478-3

78. Calisti, M., Faltings, B.: An agent-based paradigm for allocating multi-provider service demands. In: Corradi, et al., (eds.) [93], pp. 7–12. http://giuseppevizzari.github.io/WOA-proceedings-archive/pdfs/woa2000/WOA02.pdf

79. Cantucci, F., Falcone, R., Castelfranchi, C.: Investigating adjustable social autonomy in human robot interaction. In: Calegari, et al., (eds.) [76], pp. 49–60. http://ceur-ws.org/Vol-2963/paper12.pdf

80. Cantucci, F., Marini, M., Falcone, R.: Effects of robot's adaptive autonomy on users experience in a museum scenario. In: Alderighi, et al., (eds.) [6], pp. 5–19. http://ceur-ws.org/Vol-3735/paper_01.pdf

81. Capizzi, G., Bonanno, F., Lo Sciuto, G.: Mobile agents with recurrent neural networks-based computing model for echo cancellation problem. In: Napoli, D., et al., (eds.) [145], pp. 109–114. http://ceur-ws.org/Vol-1382/paper17.pdf

82. Capodieci, N., Cabri, G., Pagani, G.A., Aiello, M.: Agent modeling of a pervasive application to enable deregulated energy markets. In: Paoli, D., Vizzari [142], pp. 8–16. http://ceur-ws.org/Vol-892/paper3.pdf

83. Carboni, D., Piras, A., Sanna, S., Paddeu, G.: Filling the gap between users and objects: a multichannel interactive environment. In: Armano, et al., (eds.) [20], pp. 187–190. http://giuseppevizzari.github.io/WOA-proceedings-archive/pdfs/woa2003/29.pdf

84. Carnemolla, D., Messina, F., Santoro, C., Santoro, F.F.: Hermes: a wireless communication interface for edge computing. In: Alderighi, et al., (eds.) [6], pp. 33–41. http://ceur-ws.org/Vol-3735/paper_03.pdf

85. Castelfranchi, C., Chella, A., Falcone, R., Lanza, F., Seidita, V.: Endowing robots with self-modeling abilities for trustful human-robot interactions. In: Bergenti and Monica [52], pp. 22–28. http://ceur-ws.org/Vol-2404/paper04.pdf

86. Cavallaro, C., Tramontana, E.: User assistance for predicting the availability of bikes at bike stations. In: Calegari, et al., (eds.) [76], pp. 132–143. http://ceur-ws.org/Vol-2963/paper15.pdf

87. Cavalli, S., Cagnoni, S., Lombardo, G., Poggi, A.: Actor-based architecture for cloud services orchestration: the case of social media data extraction. In: Calegari, et al., (eds.) [75], pp. 174–183. http://ceur-ws.org/Vol-2706/paper12.pdf

88. Centineo, F., Marguglio, A., Morreale, V., Puccio, M.: The PRACTIONIST development tool. In: Baldoni, et al., (eds.) [31], pp. 20–21. http://woa07.disi.unige.it/papers/D3_CenMarMorPuc-WOA07-Demo.pdf

89. Cervone, F., Sica, V., Staffa, M., Tamburro, A., Rossi, S.: Comparing a social robot and a mobile application for movie recommendation: a pilot study. In: Napoli, D., et al., (eds.) [145], pp. 32–38. http://ceur-ws.org/Vol-1382/paper5.pdf

90. Chella, A., Lanza, F., Seidita, V.: Representing and developing knowledge using Jason, Cartago and OWL. In: Cossentino, et al., (eds.) [102], pp. 147–152. http://ceur-ws.org/Vol-2215/paper_23.pdf

91. Ciatto, G., Calegari, R., Siboni, E., Denti, E., Omicini, A.: 2P-KT: logic programming with objects & functions in Kotlin. In: Calegari, et al., (eds.) [75], pp. 219–236. http://ceur-ws.org/Vol-2706/paper14.pdf

92. Corradi, A., Montanari, R., Tonti, G., Stefanelli, C.: How to support adaptive mobile applications. In: Omicini and Viroli [201], pp. 42–47. http://giuseppevizzari.github.io/WOA-proceedings-archive/pdfs/woa2001/pdf/10.pdf

93. Corradi, A., Omicini, A., Poggi, A. (eds.): WOA 2000 – 1st Workshop "From Objects to Agents", Atti di Congressi, vol. 1195. Pitagora Editrice Bologna, Parma (2000). http://giuseppevizzari.github.io/WOA-proceedings-archive/woa-2000.html

94. Corradini, F., De Paoli, F., Merelli, E., Omicini, A. (eds.): WOA 2005 – 6th Workshop "From Objects to Agents". Pitagora Editrice Bologna, Camerino (2005). http://lia.deis.unibo.it/books/woa2005/atti.pdf

95. Corradini, F., Mariani, L., Merelli, E.: A programming environment for global activity-based applications. In: Armano, et al., (eds.) [20], pp. 163–169. http://giuseppevizzari.github.io/WOA-proceedings-archive/pdfs/woa2003/27.pdf

96. Cossentino, M., Lodato, C., Lopes, S., Ribino, P., Seidita, V., Chella, A.: A UML-based notation for representing MAS organizations. In: Fortino, et al., (eds.) [160], pp. 133–139. http://ceur-ws.org/Vol-741/ID20_CossentinoLodatoLopesRibiniSeiditaChella.pdf

97. Cossentino, M., Lopes, S., Nuzzo, A., Renda, G., Sabatucci, L.: A comparison of the basic principles and behavioural aspects of Akka, JaCaMo and Jade development frameworks. In: Cossentino, et al., (eds.) [102], pp. 133–141. http://ceur-ws.org/Vol-2215/paper_21.pdf

98. Cossentino, M., Lopes, S., Renda, G., Sabatucci, L., Zaffora, F.: A metamodel of a multi-paradigm approach to smart cyber-physical systems development. In: Bergenti and Monica [52], pp. 35–41. http://ceur-ws.org/Vol-2404/paper06.pdf

99. Cossentino, M., Lopes, S., Sabatucci, L.: A tool for the automatic generation of MOISE organisations from BPMN. In: Calegari, et al., (eds.) [75], pp. 69–82. http://ceur-ws.org/Vol-2706/paper11.pdf

100. Cossentino, M., et al.: GIMT: A tool for ontology and goal modeling in BDI multi-agent design. In: Santoro and Bergenti [235], pp. 81–88. http://ceur-ws.org/Vol-1260/paper10.pdf

101. Cossentino, M., Poggi, A., Rimassa, G., Turci, P.: Implementation level issues in MAS modeling. In: Armano, et al., (eds.) [20], pp. 155–162. http://giuseppevizzari.github.io/WOA-proceedings-archive/pdfs/woa2003/25.pdf

102. Cossentino, M., Sabatucci, L., Seidita, V. (eds.): WOA 2018 – 19th Workshop "From Objects to Agents", CEUR Workshop Proceedings, vol. 2215. Palermo (2018). http://ceur-ws.org/Vol-2215/
103. Costantini, S., Tocchio, A.: DALI: an architecture for intelligent logical agents. In: Proceedings of the Int. Workshop on Architectures for Intelligent Theory-Based Agents (AITA08). AAAI Spring Symposium Series (2008)
104. Costantini, S.: Self-checking logical agents. In: Osorio, M., Zepeda, C., Olmos, I., Carballido, J.L., Ramírez, R.C.M. (eds.) LANMR 2012: Logic / Languages, Algorithms and New Methods of Reasoning 2012. Proceedings of the Eighth Latin American Workshop on Logic / Languages, Algorithms and New Methods of Reasoning 2012. CEUR Workshop Proceedings, vol. 911, pp. 3–30. CEUR-WS.org (2012). https://ceur-ws.org/Vol-911/01_LANMR12.pdf
105. Costantini, S.: ACE: a flexible environment for complex event processing in logical agents. In: Baldoni, M., Baresi, L., Dastani, M. (eds.) Engineering Multi-Agent Systems, Third International Workshop, EMAS 2015, Revised Selected Papers. Lecture Notes in Computer Science, vol. 9318, pp. 70–91. Springer (2015). https://doi.org/10.1007/978-3-319-26184-3_5
106. Costantini, S., D'Andrea, A., De Gasperis, G., Florio, N., Tocchio, A.: DALI logical agents into play. In: Proceedings of the AI*IA Workshop "Popularize Artificial Intelligence" (PAI-2012) (2012). https://ceur-ws.org/Vol-860/paper10.pdf
107. Costantini, S., De Gasperis, G.: Complex reactivity with preferences in rule-based agents. In: Bikakis, A., Giurca, A. (eds.) Rules on the Web: Research and Applications - 6th International Symposium, RuleML 2012, Montpellier, France, August 27-29, 2012. Proceedings. Lecture Notes in Computer Science, vol. 7438, pp. 167–181. Springer (2012). https://doi.org/10.1007/978-3-642-32689-9_13
108. Costantini, S., De Gasperis, G., Nazzicone, G.: Exploration of unknown territory via DALI agents and ASP modules. In: Omatu, S., et al., (eds.) Distributed Computing and Artificial Intelligence, 12th International Conference, DCAI 2015. Proceedings. Advances in Intelligent Systems and Computing, vol. 373, pp. 285–292. Springer (2015)
109. Costantini, S., De Gasperis, G., Nazzicone, G.: DALI for cognitive robotics: principles and prototype implementation. In: Lierler, Y., Taha, W. (eds.) Practical Aspects of Declarative Languages - 19th International Symposium, PADL 2017, Proceedings. Lecture Notes in Computer Science, vol. 10137, pp. 152–162. Springer (2017)
110. Costantini, S., Dell'Acqua, P.: Emotional behavior trees for empathetic human-automation interaction. In: Ferrando and Mascardi [154], pp. 1–16. http://ceur-ws.org/Vol-3261/paper1.pdf
111. Costantini, S., Dell'Acqua, P., De Gasperis, G., Gullo, F., Rafanelli, A.: NEMO - A neural, emotional architecture for human-ai teaming. In: Angelis, E.D., Proietti, M. (eds.) Proceedings of the 39th Italian Conference on Computational Logic, Rome, June 26-28, 2024. CEUR Workshop Proceedings, vol. 3733. CEUR-WS.org (2024). https://ceur-ws.org/Vol-3733/paper11.pdf
112. Costantini, S., Dell'Acqua, P., De Gasperis, G., Gullo, F., Rafanelli, A.: The NEMO co-pilot. In: Martino, S.D., Sansone, C., Masciari, E., Rossi, S., Gravina, M. (eds.) Proceedings of the Ital-IA Intelligenza Artificiale - Thematic Workshops co-located with the 4th CINI National Lab AIIS Conference on Artificial Intelligence (Ital-IA 2024), Naples, May 29-30, 2024. CEUR Workshop Proceedings, vol. 3762, pp. 124–128. CEUR-WS.org (2024). https://ceur-ws.org/Vol-3762/543.pdf

113. Costantini, S., Dell'Acqua, P., De Gasperis, G., Rafanelli, A.: Empowering emotional behavior trees with neural computation for digital forensic. In: 15th European Symposium on Computational Intelligence and Mathematics (ESCIM 2024) (2024)

114. Costantini, S., Dell'Acqua, P., Pereira, L.M.: A multi-layer framework for evolving and learning agents. In: M.T. Cox, A.R. (ed.) Proceedings of Metareasoning: Thinking About Thinking Workshop at AAAI 2008, Chicago, USA (2008)

115. Costantini, S., Dell'Acqua, P., Pereira, L.M., Toni, F.: Learning and evolving agents in user monitoring and training. In: Inverardi, P. (ed.) Proceedings of the 2010 AICA Italian Conference. L'Aquila, Italy (2010), special Event held in L'Aquila, after the earthquake of April 6th (2009)

116. Costantini, S., Formisano, A., Pitoni, V.: Timed memory in resource-bounded agents. In: Ghidini, C., Magnini, B., Passerini, A., Traverso, P. (eds.) AI*IA 2018 - Advances in Artificial Intelligence - XVIIth International Conference of the Italian Association for Artificial Intelligence, Trento, November 20-23, 2018, Proceedings. Lecture Notes in Computer Science, vol. 11298, pp. 15–29. Springer (2018). https://doi.org/10.1007/978-3-030-03840-3_2

117. Costantini, S., Formisano, A., Pitoni, V.: An epistemic logic for modular development of multi-agent systems. In: Alechina, N., Baldoni, M., Logan, B. (eds.) Engineering Multi-Agent Systems - 9th International Workshop, EMAS 2021, Virtual Event, May 3-4, 2021, Revised Selected Papers. Lecture Notes in Computer Science, vol. 13190, pp. 72–91. Springer (2021). https://doi.org/10.1007/978-3-030-97457-2_5

118. Costantini, S., Formisano, A., Pitoni, V.: An epistemic logic for multi-agent systems with budget and costs. In: Faber, W., Friedrich, G., Gebser, M., Morak, M. (eds.) Logics in Artificial Intelligence - 17th European Conference, JELIA 2021, Virtual Event, May 17-20, 2021, Proceedings. Lecture Notes in Computer Science, vol. 12678, pp. 101–115. Springer (2021). https://doi.org/10.1007/978-3-030-75775-5_8

119. Costantini, S., Formisano, A., Pitoni, V.: A logic of inferable in multi-agent systems with budget and costs. In: Dignum, F., Lomuscio, A., Endriss, U., Nowé, A. (eds.) AAMAS '21: 20th International Conference on Autonomous Agents and Multiagent Systems, Virtual Event, United Kingdom, May 3-7, 2021, pp. 1483–1485. ACM (2021).https://doi.org/10.5555/3463952.3464133

120. Costantini, S., Formisano, A., Pitoni, V.: Cognitive aspects in epistemic logic L-DINF. In: Heyninck, J., Meyer, T., Ragni, M., Thimm, M., Kern-Isberner, G. (eds.) Proceedings of the Workshop on Cognitive Aspects of Knowledge Representation co-located with the 31st International Joint Conference on Artificial Intelligence (IJCAI-ECAI 2022), Vienna, July 23, 2022. CEUR Workshop Proceedings, vol. 3251. CEUR-WS.org (2022)

121. Costantini, S., Formisano, A., Pitoni, V.: Cooperation among groups of agents in the epistemic logic L-DINF. In: Governatori, G., Turhan, A. (eds.) Rules and Reasoning - 6th International Joint Conference on Rules and Reasoning, RuleML+RR 2022, Berlin, September 26-28, 2022, Proceedings. Lecture Notes in Computer Science, vol. 13752, pp. 280–295. Springer (2022). https://doi.org/10.1007/978-3-031-21541-4_18

122. Costantini, S., Formisano, A., Pitoni, V.: An epistemic logic for formalizing group dynamics of agents. Interact. Stud. **23**(3), 391–426 (2022). https://doi.org/10.1075/is.22019.cos

123. Costantini, S., Formisano, A., Pitoni, V.: Modelling agents roles in the epistemic logic L-DINF. In: Arieli, O., Casini, G., Giordano, L. (eds.) Proceedings of the 20th International Workshop on Non-Monotonic Reasoning, NMR 2022, Part of the Federated Logic Conference (FLoC 2022), Haifa, August 7-9, 2022. CEUR Workshop Proceedings, vol. 3197, pp. 70–79. CEUR-WS.org (2022)

124. Costantini, S., Formisano, A., Pitoni, V.: Temporalizing epistemic logic L-DINF. In: Calegari, R., Ciatto, G., Omicini, A. (eds.) Proceedings of the 37th Italian Conference on Computational Logic, Bologna, June 29 - July 1, 2022. CEUR Workshop Proceedings, vol. 3204, pp. 119–133. CEUR-WS.org (2022)

125. Costantini, S., Formisano, A., Pitoni, V.: Preference management in epistemic logic L-DINF. In: Dovier, A., Formisano, A. (eds.) Proceedings of the 38th Italian Conference on Computational Logic, Udine, June 21-23, 2023. CEUR Workshop Proceedings, vol. 3428. CEUR-WS.org (2023)

126. Costantini, S., Formisano, A., Pitoni, V.: A timed epistemic logic for formalizing cooperation among groups of agents. In: Falcone, et al., (eds.) [152], pp. 151–166. http://ceur-ws.org/Vol-3579/paper11.pdf

127. Costantini, S., Pitoni, V.: Towards a logic of "Inferable" for self-aware transparent logical agents. In: Musto, C., Magazzeni, D., Ruggieri, S., Semeraro, G. (eds.) Proceedings of the Italian Workshop on Explainable Artificial Intelligence co-located with 19th International Conference of the Italian Association for Artificial Intelligence, XAI.it@AIxIA 2020, Online Event, November 25-26, 2020. CEUR Workshop Proceedings, vol. 2742, pp. 68–79. CEUR-WS.org (2020)

128. Costantini, S., Tocchio, A.: A logic programming language for multi-agent systems. In: Flesca, S., Greco, S., Leone, N., Ianni, G. (eds.) Logics in Artificial Intelligence: European Conference, JELIA 2002, Cosenza, Italy, September, 23-26, Proceedings, Lecture Notes in Artificial Intelligence, vol. 2424, pp. 1–13. Springer-Verlag, Berlin (2002). https://doi.org/10.1007/3-540-45757-7_1

129. Costantini, S., Tocchio, A.: Strips-like planning in the DALI logic programmming language. In: Armano, et al., (eds.) [20], pp. 115–120. http://giuseppevizzari.github.io/WOA-proceedings-archive/pdfs/woa2003/05.pdf

130. Costantini, S., Tocchio, A.: The DALI logic programming agent-oriented language. In: Alferes, J.J., Leite, J.A. (eds.) Logics in Artificial Intelligence, 9th European Conference, JELIA 2004, Lisbon, September 27-30, 2004, Proceedings. Lecture Notes in Computer Science, vol. 3229, pp. 685–688. Springer (2004). https://doi.org/10.1007/978-3-540-30227-8_57

131. Costantini, S., Tocchio, A.: About declarative semantics of logic-based agent languages. In: Baldoni, M., Endriss, U., Omicini, A., Torroni, P. (eds.) Declarative Agent Languages and Technologies III, Third International Workshop, DALT 2005, Selected and Revised Papers, Lecture Notes in Computer Science, vol. 3904, pp. 106–123. Springer (2005).https://doi.org/10.1007/11691792_7

132. Costantini, S., Tocchio, A., Verticchio, A.: Communication and trust in the DALI logic programming agent-oriented language. Intelligenza Artificiale 2(1), 39–46 (2005), journal of the Italian Association AI*IA

133. De Benedetti, M., D'Urso, F., Messina, F., Pappalardo, G., Santoro, C.: Self-organising UAVs for wide area fault-tolerant aerial monitoring. In: Napoli, D., et al., (eds.) [145], pp. 135–141. http://ceur-ws.org/Vol-1382/paper21.pdf

134. De Benedetti, M., D'Urso, F., Messina, F., Pappalardo, G., Santoro, C.: 3D simulation of unmanned aerial vehicles. In: Meo, D., et al., (eds.) [138], pp. 7–12. http://ceur-ws.org/Vol-1867/w2.pdf

135. De Gasperis, G., Costantini, S., Rafanelli, A., Migliarini, P., Letteri, I., Dyoub, A.: Extension of constraint-procedural logic-generated environments for deep q-learning agent training and benchmarking. J. Log. Comput. **33**(8), 1712–1733 (2023). https://doi.org/10.1093/LOGCOM/EXAD032

136. De Gasperis, G., Di Ottavio, D., Migliarini, P., Costantini, S.: SkRobot: a pseudo-realtime multiplatform framework for robotics agents development. In: Alderighi, et al., (eds.) [6], pp. 286–301. http://ceur-ws.org/Vol-3735/paper_21.pdf

137. De Luca, F., Tundis, A., Garro, A.: PROCE: an agent-based PROcess composition and execution environment. In: Fortino, et al., (eds.) [160], pp. 171–174. http://ceur-ws.org/Vol-741/DEM02_DeLucaTundisGarro.pdf

138. De Meo, P., Postorino, M.N., Rosaci, D., Sarnè, G.M.L. (eds.): WOA 2017 – 18th Workshop "From Objects to Agents", CEUR Workshop Proceedings, vol. 1867. Scilla (2017). http://ceur-ws.org/Vol-1867/

139. De Paoli, F., Di Stefano, A., Omicini, A., Santoro, C. (eds.): WOA 2006 – 7th Workshop "From Objects to Agents", CEUR Workshop Proceedings, vol. 204. Catania (2006). http://ceur-ws.org/Vol-204/

140. De Paoli, F., Manzoni, S., Poggi, A. (eds.): WOA 2002 – 3rd Workshop "From Objects to Agents". Pitagora Editrice Bologna, Milano (2002). http://giuseppevizzari.github.io/WOA-proceedings-archive/woa-2002.html

141. De Paoli, F., Vizzari, G.: Context dependent management of field diffusion: an experimental framework. In: Armano, et al., (eds.) [20], pp. 78–84. http://giuseppevizzari.github.io/WOA-proceedings-archive/pdfs/woa2003/19.pdf

142. De Paoli, F., Vizzari, G. (eds.): WOA 2012 – 13th Workshop "From Objects to Agents", CEUR Workshop Proceedings, vol. 892. Milano (2012). http://ceur-ws.org/Vol-892/

143. Di Napoli, C., et al.: Assessing usability of a robotic-based AAL system: a pilot study with dementia patients. In: Bergenti and Monica [52], pp. 59–64. http://ceur-ws.org/Vol-2404/paper09.pdf

144. Di Napoli, C., Di Nocera, D., Rossi, S.: Evaluating negotiation cost for QoS-aware service composition. In: Baldoni, et al., (eds.) [24], pp. 54–59. http://ceur-ws.org/Vol-1099/paper2.pdf

145. Di Napoli, C., Rossi, S., Staffa, M. (eds.): WOA 2015 – 16th Workshop "From Objects to Agents", CEUR Workshop Proceedings, vol. 1382. Naples (2015) http://ceur-ws.org/Vol-1382/

146. Di Nocera, D., Di Napoli, C., Rossi, S.: A social-aware smart parking application. In: Santoro and Bergenti [235], pp. 24–29. http://ceur-ws.org/Vol-1260/paper4.pdf

147. Di Stefano, A., Santoro, C.: eXAT: an experimental tool for programming multi-agent systems in Erlang. In: Armano, et al., (eds.) [20], pp. 121–127. http://giuseppevizzari.github.io/WOA-proceedings-archive/pdfs/woa2003/09.pdf

148. Di Stefano, A., Santoro, C.: On the use of Erlang as a promising language to develop agent systems. In: Baldoni, et al., (eds.) [33], pp. 22–29. http://giuseppevizzari.github.io/WOA-proceedings-archive/pdfs/woa2004/4.pdf

149. Di Stefano, A., Santoro, C.: Building semantic agents in eXAT. In: Corradini, et al. [94], pp. 28–36. http://lia.deis.unibo.it/books/woa2005/papers/5.pdf

150. D'Urso, F., Santoro, C., Santoro, F.F.: Integrating heterogeneous tools for physical simulation of multi-unmanned aerial vehicles. In: Cossentino, et al., (eds.) [102], pp. 10–15. http://ceur-ws.org/Vol-2215/paper_2.pdf

151. Dyoub, A., Costantini, S., De Gasperis, G.: Answer set programming and agents. Knowl. Eng. Rev. **33**, e19 (2018). https://doi.org/10.1017/S0269888918000164

152. Falcone, R., Castelfranchi, C., Sapienza, A., Cantucci, F. (eds.): WOA 2023 – 24th Workshop "From Objects to Agents", CEUR Workshop Proceedings, vol. 3579. Roma (2023). http://ceur-ws.org/Vol-3579/

153. Falcone, R., Sapienza, A.: How can subjective impulsivity play a role among information sources in weather scenarios? In: Meo, D., et al., (eds.) [138], pp. 19–24. http://ceur-ws.org/Vol-1867/w4.pdf

154. Ferrando, A., Mascardi, V. (eds.): WOA 2022 – 23rd Workshop "From Objects to Agents", CEUR Workshop Proceedings, vol. 3261. Genova (2022). http://ceur-ws.org/Vol-3261/

155. Fornacciari, P., Cagnoni, S., Mordonini, M., Tarollo, L., Tomaiuolo, M.: Application of Lovheim model for emotion detection in English tweets. In: Bergenti and Monica [52], pp. 149–155. http://ceur-ws.org/Vol-2404/paper22.pdf

156. Fornacciari, P., Lombardo, G., Mordonini, M., Poggi, A., Tomaiuolo, M.: Agent based cellular automata simulation. In: Cossentino, et al., (eds.) [102], pp. 16–20. http://ceur-ws.org/Vol-2215/paper_3.pdf

157. Fornacciari, P., Mordonini, M., Poggi, A., Tomaiuolo, M.: Software actors for continuous social media analysis. In: Meo, D., et al., (eds.) [138], pp. 84–89. http://ceur-ws.org/Vol-1867/w15.pdf

158. Fortino, G., Galzarano, S., Gravina, R., Guerrieri, A.: Agent-based development of wireless sensor network applications. In: Fortino, et al., (eds.) [138], pp. 123–132. http://ceur-ws.org/Vol-741/ID19_FortinoGalzaranoGravinaGuerrieri.pdf

159. Fortino, G., Garro, A., Mascillaro, S., Russo, W.: Using multi-coordination for the design of mobile agent interactions. In: Baldoni, et al., (eds.) [32], pp. 122–128. http://www.pa.icar.cnr.it/woa08/materiali/paper/paper_11.pdf

160. Fortino, G., Garro, A., Palopoli, L., Russo, W., Spezzano, G. (eds.): WOA 2011 – 12th Workshop "From Objects to Agents", CEUR Workshop Proceedings, vol. 741. Rende (2011). http://ceur-ws.org/Vol-741/

161. Fortino, G., Garro, A., Russo, W.: Distributed workflow enactment: an agent-based framework. In: Paoli, D., et al., (eds.) [139], pp. 110–117. http://ceur-ws.org/Vol-204/P08.pdf

162. Fredriksson, M., Ricci, A., Omicini, A., Gustavsson, R.: A framework for systemic coordination in open computational systems. In: Paoli, D., et al., (eds.) [140], pp. 86–93. http://giuseppevizzari.github.io/WOA-proceedings-archive/pdfs/woa2002/11.pdf

163. Garelli, F., Ferrari, C.: GOBLINS: un modello computazionale per la progettazione e lo sviluppo di sistemi multiagenti. In: Corradi, et al., (eds.) [93], pp. 58–63. http://giuseppevizzari.github.io/WOA-proceedings-archive/pdfs/woa2000/WOA12.pdf

164. Garelli, F., Ferrari, C.: Object oriented mapping for HTML documents. In: Omicini and Viroli [201], pp. 66–71. http://giuseppevizzari.github.io/WOA-proceedings-archive/pdfs/woa2001/pdf/13.pdf

165. Garro, A., et al.: Intelligent agents: multi-agent systems. In: Ranganathan, S., Gribskov, M., Nakai, K., Schönbach, C. (eds.) Encyclopedia of Bioinformatics and Computational Biology - vol. 1, pp. 315–320. Elsevier (2019). https://doi.org/10.1016/b978-0-12-809633-8.20328-2

166. Garruzzo, S., Rosaci, D., Sarnè, G.M.L.: MAST: an agent framework to support B2C e-commerce. In: Paoli, D., et al., (eds.) [139], pp. 76–82. http://ceur-ws.org/Vol-204/P04.pdf

167. Habbash, N., Bottoni, F., Vizzari, G.: Reinforcement learning for autonomous agents exploring environments: an experimental framework and preliminary results. In: Calegari, et al., (eds.) [75], pp. 84–100. http://ceur-ws.org/Vol-2706/paper5.pdf
168. Hewitt, C., Bishop, P., Steiger, R.: A universal modular actor formalism for artificial intelligence. In: 3rd International Joint Conference on Artificial Intelligence (IJCAI 1973). Stanford (1973). https://www.ijcai.org/Proceedings/73/Papers/027B.pdf
169. Iotti, E., Poggi, A., Tomaiuolo, M.: Agent based P2P social neworks modeling. In: Santoro, et al., (eds.) [236], pp. 74–78. http://ceur-ws.org/Vol-1664/w13.pdf
170. Johansson, A., Dell'Acqua, P.: Emotional behavior trees. In: 2012 IEEE Conference on Computational Intelligence and Games, CIG 2012, pp. 355–362. IEEE, Granada (2012). https://doi.org/10.1109/CIG.2012.6374177
171. Kaufmann, B., Leone, N., Perri, S., Schaub, T.: Grounding and solving in answer set programming. AI Mag. **37**(3), 25–32 (2016). https://doi.org/10.1609/AIMAG.V37I3.2672
172. Lauretis, L.D., Persia, F., Costantini, S., D'Auria, D.: How to leverage intelligent agents and complex event processing to improve patient monitoring. J. Log. Comput. **33**(4), 900–935 (2023). https://doi.org/10.1093/LOGCOM/EXAD016
173. Lloyd, J.W.: Foundations of Logic Programming. Springer, Berlin Heidelberg (2012). https://doi.org/10.1007/978-3-642-83189-8
174. Lombardo, G., Poggi, A.: A scalable and distributed actor-based version of the Node2Vec algorithm. In: Bergenti and Monica [52], pp. 134–141. http://ceur-ws.org/Vol-2404/paper20.pdf
175. Longo, C.F., Longo, F., Santoro, C.: A reactive cognitive architecture based on natural language processing for the task of decision-making using a rich semantic. In: Calegari, et al., (eds.) [75], pp. 201–218. http://ceur-ws.org/Vol-2706/paper2.pdf
176. Longo, C.F., Santoro, C., Nicolosi Asmundo, M., Santamaria, D.F., Cantone, D.: SW-CASPAR: reactive-cognitive architecture based on natural language processing for the task of decision-making in the open-world assumption. In: Calegari, et al., (eds.) [76], pp. 178–193. http://ceur-ws.org/Vol-2963/paper10.pdf
177. Longo, F., Santoro, C.: A python-based assistant agent able to interact with natural language. In: Cossentino, et al., (eds.) [102], pp. 142–146. http://ceur-ws.org/Vol-2215/paper_22.pdf
178. Losapio, G., Minutoli, F., Mascardi, V., Ferrando, A.: Smart balancing of e-scooter sharing systems via deep reinforcement learning. In: Calegari, et al., (eds.) [76], pp. 83–97. http://ceur-ws.org/Vol-2963/paper16.pdf
179. Loseto, G., Scioscia, F., Ruta, M., Di Sciascio, E.: Semantic-based smart homes: a multi-agent approach. In: Paoli, D., Vizzari, (eds.) [142]. http://ceur-ws.org/Vol-892/paper7.pdf
180. Lövheim, H.: A new three-dimensional model for emotions and monoamine neurotransmitters. Med. Hypotheses **78**(2), 341–348 (2012). https://doi.org/10.1016/j.mehy.2011.11.016
181. Mamei, M., Zambonelli, F.: Spray computers: frontiers of self-organization for pervasive computing. In: Armano, et al. [20], pp. 16–24. http://giuseppevizzari.github.io/WOA-proceedings-archive/pdfs/woa2003/22.pdf
182. Mamei, M., Zambonelli, F., Leonardi, L.: *Tuples On The Air*: a middleware for context-aware multiagent systems. In: Paoli, D., et al. [140], pp. 108–116. http://giuseppevizzari.github.io/WOA-proceedings-archive/pdfs/woa2002/26.pdf

183. Mari, M., Lazzari, L., Poggi, A., Turci, P.: A multi-agent system to support remote software development. In: Baldoni, et al., (eds.) [33], pp. 30–36. http://giuseppevizzari.github.io/WOA-proceedings-archive/pdfs/woa2004/5.pdf

184. Mariani, S., Omicini, A.: Tuple-based coordination of stochastic systems with uniform primitives. In: Baldoni, et al., (eds.) [24], pp. 8–15. http://ceur-ws.org/Vol-1099/paper4.pdf

185. Mariani, S., Omicini, A.: TuCSoN coordination for MAS situatedness: towards a methodology. In: Santoro and Bergenti, (eds.) [235], pp. 48–57. http://ceur-ws.org/Vol-1260/paper11.pdf

186. Mariani, S., Omicini, A.: Multi-paradigm coordination for MAS: integrating heterogeneous coordination approaches in MAS technologies. In: Santoro, et al., [236], pp. 91–99. http://ceur-ws.org/Vol-1664/w16.pdf

187. Marini, S., Martelli, M., Mascardi, V., Zini, F.: HEMASL: a flexible language to specify heterogeneous agents. In: Corradi, et al., [93], pp. 76–81. http://giuseppevizzari.github.io/WOA-proceedings-archive/pdfs/woa2000/WOA15.pdf

188. Mascardi, V., Cordì, V., Rosso, P.: A comparison of upper ontologies. In: Baldoni, et al., (eds.) [31], pp. 55–64. http://woa07.dibris.unige.it/papers/mascardi.pdf

189. Mascardi, V., Omicini, A. (eds.): The Agents Journey: Twenty-five Years of Multi-agent Systems at WOA. Lecture Notes in Computer Science – State-of-the-Art Surveys, Springer (2026)

190. Messina, F., Pappalardo, G., Santoro, C.: Designing autonomous robots using GOLEM. In: Santoro and Bergenti [235], pp. 89–95. http://ceur-ws.org/Vol-1260/paper15.pdf

191. Messina, F., Santoro, C., Santoro, F.F.: A declarative C++ agent platform for agent-based edge computing. In: Falcone, et al., (eds.) [152], pp. 206–215. http://ceur-ws.org/Vol-3579/paper16.pdf

192. Minotti, M., Santi, A., Ricci, A.: Developing web client applications with JaCa-Web. In: Omicini and Viroli [202], pp. 72–79. http://ceur-ws.org/Vol-621/paper11.pdf

193. Monica, S., Bergenti, F.: An optimization-based algorithm for indoor localization of JADE agents. In: Meo, D., et al. [138], pp. 65–70. http://ceur-ws.org/Vol-1867/w12.pdf

194. Montagna, S., Sirocchi, C.: Hybrid personal medical digital assistant agents. In: Alderighi, et al., (eds.) [6], pp. 58–72. http://ceur-ws.org/Vol-3735/paper_05.pdf

195. Montagna, S., Viroli, M., Pianini, D., Fernandez-Marquez, J.L.: Towards a comprehensive approach to spontaneous self-composition in pervasive ecosystems. In: Paoli, D., Vizzari [142], pp. 89–97. http://ceur-ws.org/Vol-892/paper1.pdf

196. Montali, S., Lombardo, G., Mordonini, M., Tomaiuolo, M.: Voice assistants in hospital triage operations. In: Calegari, et al., (eds.) [75], pp. 147–159. http://ceur-ws.org/Vol-2706/paper13.pdf

197. Morreale, V., Bonura, S., Centineo, F., Rossi, A., Cossentino, M., Gaglio, S.: PRACTIONIST: implementing PRACTIcal reasONIng sySTems. In: Corradini, et al., (eds.) [94], pp. 66–74. http://lia.deis.unibo.it/books/woa2005/papers/10.pdf

198. Nanna, G.A., Quatraro, N.F., De Carolis, B.: A multi-agent system for simulating the spread of a contagious disease. In: Calegari, et al., (eds.) [75], pp. 119–134. http://ceur-ws.org/Vol-2706/paper7.pdf

199. Oliva, E., Viroli, M., Omicini, A.: Minority game: a logic-based approach in TuCSoN. In: Paoli, d., et al. [139], pp. 181–186. http://ceur-ws.org/Vol-204/P02.pdf

200. Omicini, A., Ricci, A., Viroli, M.: *Agens Faber*: toward a theory of artefacts for MAS. Electron. Notes Theoretic. Comput. Sci. **150**(3), 21–36 (2006). https://doi.org/10.1016/j.entcs.2006.03.003, 1st International Workshop "Coordination and Organization" (CoOrg 2005), COORDINATION 2005, Namur, Belgium, 22 Apr. 2005. Proceedings

201. Omicini, A., Viroli, M. (eds.): WOA 2001 – 2nd Workshop "From Objects to Agents". Pitagora Editrice Bologna, Modena (2001). http://giuseppevizzari.github.io/WOA-proceedings-archive/woa-2001.html

202. Omicini, A., Viroli, M. (eds.): WOA 2010 – 11th Workshop "From Objects to Agents", CEUR Workshop Proceedings, vol. 621. Rimini (2010). http://ceur-ws.org/Vol-621/

203. Orlowska, A., Chrysoulas, C., Jaroucheh, Z., Liu, X.: Programming languages: a usage-based statistical analysis and visualization. In: Proceedings of the 4th International Conference on Information Science and Systems, pp. 143–148. ICISS'21, Association for Computing Machinery, New York (2021). https://doi.org/10.1145/3459955.3460614

204. Pagliuca, P., Vitanza, A.: N-Mates evaluation: a new method to improve the performance of genetic algorithms in heterogeneous multi-agent systems. In: Falcone, et al., (eds.) [152], pp. 123–137. http://ceur-ws.org/Vol-3579/paper9.pdf

205. Passeri, M., Agiollo, A., Omicini, A.: Peer-reviewed federated learning. In: Falcone, et al., (eds.) [152], pp. 49–65. http://ceur-ws.org/Vol-3579/paper4.pdf

206. Pazienza, M.T., Stellato, A., Vindigni, M.: Alinas: un'architettura multi-layer ad agenti per il supporto alla comunicazione linguistica. In: Paoli, D., et al., (eds.) [140], pp. 100–107. http://giuseppevizzari.github.io/WOA-proceedings-archive/pdfs/woa2002/20.pdf

207. Pazienza, M.T., Vindigni, M.: Un pool di agenti a supporto della comunicazione linguistica. In: Omicini and Viroli [201], pp. 95–100. http://giuseppevizzari.github.io/WOA-proceedings-archive/pdfs/woa2001/pdf/18.pdf

208. Pellegrino, M., et al.: A system for tracking patients in the operating room – a pilot study. In: Falcone, et al., (eds.) [152], pp. 181–190. http://ceur-ws.org/Vol-3579/paper14.pdf

209. Pellegrino, M., Lombardo, G., Mordonini, M., Tomaiuolo, M., Cagnoni, S., Poggi, A.: ActoDemic: a distributed framework for fine-grained spreading modeling and simulation in large scale scenarios. In: Calegari, et al., (eds.) [76], pp. 194–209. http://ceur-ws.org/Vol-2963/paper7.pdf

210. Perini, A., Bresciani, P., Giorgini, P., Giunchiglia, F., Mylopoulos, J.: Towards an agent oriented approach to software engineering. In: Omicini and Viroli [201], pp. 72–77. http://giuseppevizzari.github.io/WOA-proceedings-archive/pdfs/woa2001/pdf/19.pdf

211. Persia, F., et al.: Leveraging DALI to refine route planning by dynamically avoiding risky pois. In: 18th IEEE International Conference on Semantic Computing, ICSC 2024, Laguna Hills, February 5-7, 2024, pp. 351–354. IEEE (2024). https://doi.org/10.1109/ICSC59802.2024.00061

212. Petrosino, G., Iotti, E., Monica, S., Bergenti, F.: Prototypes of productivity tools for the Jadescript programming language. In: Calegari, et al., [76], pp. 14–28. http://ceur-ws.org/Vol-2963/paper4.pdf

213. Piras, A., Bertolotti, F.: How risk preferences shape city-state success: an agent-based model of resource management. In: Alderighi, et al., (eds.) [6], pp. 302–316. http://ceur-ws.org/Vol-3735/paper_22.pdf

214. Pisano, G., Calegari, R., Omicini, A.: Towards cooperative argumentation for MAS: an actor-based approach. In: Calegari, et al., (eds.) [76], pp. 162–177. http://ceur-ws.org/Vol-2963/paper17.pdf

215. Pisano, G., et al.: Arg-tuProlog: a tuProlog-based argumentation framework. In: Calimeri, F., Perri, S., Zumpano, E. (eds.) CILC 2020 – Italian Conference on Computational Logic. Proceedings of the 35th Italian Conference on Computational Logic. CEUR Workshop Proceedings, vol. 2710, pp. 51–66. Rende (2020). http://ceur-ws.org/Vol-2710/paper4.pdf

216. Pisano, G., Ciatto, G., Calegari, R., Omicini, A.: Neuro-symbolic computation for XAI: towards a unified model. In: Calegari, et al., (eds.) [75], pp. 101–117. http://ceur-ws.org/Vol-2706/paper18.pdf

217. Poggi, A.: An actor-based software framework for developing and simulating complex systems. In: Paoli, D., Vizzari [142], pp. 49–54. http://ceur-ws.org/Vol-892/paper9.pdf

218. Poggi, A.: Replaceable implementations for actor systems. In: Baldoni, et al., (eds.) [24], pp. 91–96. http://ceur-ws.org/Vol-1099/paper13.pdf

219. Poggi, A.: Agent based modeling and simulation with ActoMoS. In: Napoli, D., et al., (eds.) [145], pp. 91–96. http://ceur-ws.org/Vol-1382/paper14.pdf

220. Postorino, M.N., Sarnè, G.M.L.: An agent-based sensor grid to monitor urban traffic. In: Santoro and Bergenti [235], pp. 18–23. http://ceur-ws.org/Vol-1260/paper2.pdf

221. Postorino, M.N., Sarnè, G.M.L.: An agent-based framework including diachronic MaaS represention. In: Alderighi, et al., (eds.) [6], pp. 98–112. http://ceur-ws.org/Vol-3735/paper_08.pdf

222. Rafanelli, A., Costantini, S., De Gasperis, G.: A multi-agent-system framework for flooding events. In: Ferrando and Mascardi [154], pp. 142–151. http://ceur-ws.org/Vol-3261/paper11.pdf

223. Rafanelli, A., Costantini, S., De Gasperis, G.: Neural-logic multi-agent system for flood event detection. Intell. Artifi. **17**(1), 19–35 (2023). https://doi.org/10.3233/IA-230004

224. Rao, A.S., Georgeff, M.: Modeling rational agents within a BDI-architecture. In: Proc. of the Second Int. Conf. on Principles of Knowledge Representation and Reasoning (KR'91), pp. 473–484. Morgan Kaufmann (1991)

225. Repetto, M., Vecchiola, C., Boccalatte, A.: A knowledge modeling tool for rule-based agents. In: Omicini and Viroli [201], pp. 24–29. http://giuseppevizzari.github.io/WOA-proceedings-archive/pdfs/woa2001/pdf/05.pdf

226. Ribino, P., Cossentino, M., Lodato, C., Lopes, S., Sabatucci, L., Seidita, V.: Ontology and goal model in designing BDI multi-agent systems. In: Baldoni, et al., (eds.) [24], pp. 66–72. http://ceur-ws.org/Vol-1099/paper12.pdf

227. Ricci, A., Buda, C., Zaghini, N., Natali, A., Viroli, M., Omicini, A.: simpA-WS: an agent-oriented computing technology for WS-based SOA applications. In: Paoli, D., et al. [139], pp. 1–3. http://ceur-ws.org/Vol-204/D01.pdf

228. Ricci, A., Omicini, A.: Ricci, A., Omicini, A.: Agent coordination contexts: experiments in TuCSoN. In: Paoli, D., et al., (eds.) [140], pp. 14 21. http://giuseppevizzari.github.io/WOA-proceedings-archive/pdfs/woa2002/17.pdf

229. Ricci, A., Omicini, A., Denti, E.: Enlightened agents in TuCSoN. In: Omicini and Viroli [201], pp. 101–106. http://giuseppevizzari.github.io/WOA-proceedings-archive/pdfs/woa2001/pdf/21.pdf

230. Robol, M., Giorgini, P., Busetta, P.: Applying social norms to implicit negotiation among non-player characters in serious games. In: Santoro, et al. [236], pp. 23–28. http://ceur-ws.org/Vol-1664/w5.pdf

231. Roggero, D., Patrone, F., Mascardi, V.: Designing and implementing electronic auctions in a multiagent system environment. In: Corradini, et al., [94], pp. 157–163. http://lia.deis.unibo.it/books/woa2005/papers/22.pdf
232. Sabbatini, F., Calegari, R.: Unlocking insights and trust: the value of explainable clustering algorithms for cognitive agents. In: Falcone, et al., [152], pp. 232–245. http://ceur-ws.org/Vol-3579/paper18.pdf
233. Sabbatini, F., Ciatto, G., Calegari, R., Omicini, A.: On the design of PSyKE: a platform for symbolic knowledge extraction. In: Calegari, et al., (eds.) [76], pp. 29–48. http://ceur-ws.org/Vol-2963/paper14.pdf
234. Santi, A., Guidi, M., Ricci, A.: Exploiting agent-oriented programming for developing Android applications. In: Omicini and Viroli [202], pp. 48–54. http://ceur-ws.org/Vol-621/paper07.pdf
235. Santoro, C., Bergenti, F. (eds.): WOA 2014 – 15th Workshop "From Objects to Agents", CEUR Workshop Proceedings, vol. 1260. Catania (2014). http://ceur-ws.org/Vol-1260/
236. Santoro, C., Messina, F., De Benedetti, M. (eds.): WOA 2016 – 17th Workshop "From Objects to Agents", CEUR Workshop Proceedings, vol. 1664. Catania (2016). http://ceur-ws.org/Vol-1664/
237. Sapienza, A., Falcone, R.: A theoretical model for the human-iot systems interaction. In: Bergenti and Monica [52], pp. 90–97. http://ceur-ws.org/Vol-2404/paper14.pdf
238. Sartori, F., Manenti, L., Grazioli, L.: A conceptual and computational model for knowledge-based agents in ANDROID. In: Baldoni, et al., (eds.) [24], pp. 41–46. http://ceur-ws.org/Vol-1099/paper8.pdf
239. Savaglio, C., Leppänen, T., Russo, W., Riekki, J., Fortino, G.: Re-engineering IoT systems through ACOSO-Meth: the IETF CoRE based agent framework case study. In: Cossentino, et al., (eds.) [24], pp. 81–89. http://ceur-ws.org/Vol-2215/paper_14.pdf
240. Schifanella, C., Lusso, L., Baldoni, M., Baroglio, C.: Design and development of a visual environment for writing DyLOG programs. In: Baldoni, et al., (eds.) [33], pp. 43–50. http://giuseppevizzari.github.io/WOA-proceedings-archive/pdfs/woa2004/7.pdf
241. Szeredi, P., Lukácsy, G., Benkő, T.: The Web Ontology Language, chap. 8, pp. 407–450. Cambridge University Press (2014). https://doi.org/10.1017/CBO9781139194129.009
242. Tarantino, F., Ravani, A., Zambrini, M.: Using a properties based naming system in mobile agents environments for pervasive computing. In: Armano, et al., (eds.) [20], pp. 25–28. http://giuseppevizzari.github.io/WOA-proceedings-archive/pdfs/woa2003/28.pdf
243. Unniyankal, H., Belardinelli, F., Ferrando, A., Malvone, V.: RMLGym: a formal reward machine framework for reinforcement learning. In: Falcone, et al., (eds.) [152], pp. 1–16. http://ceur-ws.org/Vol-3579/paper1.pdf
244. Vitabile, S., Pilato, G., Conti, V., Ferrara, C., Sorbello, F.: Agents ownership setting by user fingerprints. In: Armano, et al., (eds.) [20], pp. 135–139. http://giuseppevizzari.github.io/WOA-proceedings-archive/pdfs/woa2003/26.pdf
245. Vizzari, G., Olivieri, F.: A hybrid agent architecture for situated agents based virtual environments. In: Proc. of the 2009 IEEE/WIC/ACM International Joint Conference on Web Intelligence and Intelligent Agent Technology (WI-IAT'09). vol. 3 (2009)

246. Vizzari, G., Pizzi, G., Corrêa da Silva, F.S.: A framework for interacting situated agents in virtual environments. In: Baldoni, et al., (eds.) [31], pp. 96–103. http://woa07.dibris.unige.it/papers/D4_VizPizSoa-WOA07-Demo.pdf
247. Yan, E., Burattini, S., Hübner, J.F., Ricci, A.: Towards a multi-level explainability framework for engineering and understanding BDI agent systems. In: Falcone, et al., (eds.) [152], pp. 216–231. http://ceur-ws.org/Vol-3579/paper17.pdf

Looking for the Best Partners

Domenico Rosaci[1] and Giuseppe M. L. Sarnè[2(✉)]

[1] Department DIIES, University Mediterranea of Reggio Calabria,
via Graziella, loc. Feo di Vito, 98123 Reggio Calabria, Italy
`domenico.rosaci@unirc.it`
[2] Department of Psychology, University of Milan Bicocca, Piazza dell'Ateneo Nuovo,
1, 20126 Milan, Italy
`giuseppe.sarne@unimib.it`

Abstract. Interaction and cooperation among agents are two fundamental activities having place in multi-agent systems. In this regard, in a generally large universe of agents, the main difficulty lies in determining which agents are the most promising candidates for achieving fruitful interaction (i.e., cooperation). In a holistic view, several strategies like trust, reliability, reputation, cyphering or commitment can play, for example, a crucial role in various online environments. They provide a multitude of mechanisms for assessing credibility, trustworthiness, identity and so on, not only with respect to agents but also considering entities such as users, products or services. Agent-based scenarios can take advantage from these techniques, which are also able to reduce information asymmetry between agents, enhancing their mutual confidence and, in this way, encouraging their participation by limiting the probability of deception. Moreover, such systems form the basis for a potentially large number of countermeasures to prevent, depotentiate or nullify malicious activities intended at altering a correct perception about the counterpart by means of misrepresentation or manipulation activities carried out by bad agents. In this context, the goal of this chapter is to provide an overview of the several specific proposals, made at Workshop on Objects and Agents (WOA) over more than two decades, aimed at identifying the best partners for interaction and cooperation based on the above-cited approaches.

Keywords: Multiagent System · Partnership · Trust · Reputation · Cyphering · Commitment

1 Introduction

In the digital age, virtual communities are essential in the execution of several activities, and all without the need of physical interactions [53]. This relational paradigm requires a strategic approach for choosing one or more partners to be engaged in interaction and collaboration tasks, regardless of their real or virtual nature [46]. In fact, in online contexts, such tasks are characterized by

V. Mascardi and A. Omicini (Eds.): *The Agents Journey*, LNCS 16395, pp. 52–78, 2026.
https://doi.org/10.1007/978-3-032-22940-3_2

a complex web of relationships and connections [76], and in the decision to establish collaborations, participate in transactions, or share resources, aspects such as comfort and trustworthiness play a key role in shaping the experience of participants in these activities [77].

In detail, in virtual communities the multi-agent systems (MASs) represent a cornerstone of distributed computing, in which individual agents can collaborate with each other to achieve common or individual goals [132]. This approach is inspired by the concept of distributed intelligence observed in biological and social systems, where interactions between independent entities lead to emergent and adaptive behaviors [79].

Specifically, an agent is an autonomous computational entity with the ability to perceive the environment where it is living [135], process information [128], and act autonomously [136] to achieve assigned or independently identified goals. In the particular context of MASs, social relationships between agents can occur directly, through communication between agents, or indirectly, through observation of the results of other actors' actions in the shared environment [134]. Such social interaction mechanisms often underlie learning, also known as social learning [91], that provides agents with a dynamic adaptivity to the environment and improve their strategies and skills over time [16]. For such reasons, MASs find application in a wide range of fields, from robotics [81] to finance [9], from logistics [56] to health care [73], and have significantly contributed to the way we conceive and implement computing solutions.

In this scenario, as in human activities, successful interactions and cooperative tasks are essential for achieving complex goals in MASs [133]. So that the choice of the partners with whom to carry out such activities is crucial to obtain goals that could not be achievable individually [45]. This decision can significantly influence the outcome of the agents, bringing with it a number of challenges and considerations that must be carefully evaluated for achieving effective results, reaching common goals and promoting individual and collective success [45]. However, agent activities in MASs can also include situations of conflict, competition, or maliciousness [44] in which agents compete for limited resources, for the achievement of conflicting goals, or simply to gain undue advantages to the detriment of other actors [60].

One of the main challenges in selecting the best agent partners for interaction (i.e., cooperation) is the wide range of parameters that must be considered to build meaningful relationships within the community, thereby strengthening social capital and creating a connective tissue that extends beyond individual activities [96]. This because each potential partner brings with it a (unique) set of skills and experience [78]. Furthermore, another crucial aspect is to assess the alignment between the expectations, goals, and operating modes of the actors involved as well as their reliability and credibility, aspects that can undermine confidence between the parties [60].

Therefore, choosing the best partners is not only an individual decision, but has broader implications for the virtual community on the whole [92]. Indeed, well-considered decisions based on reliable information contribute to building a strong, resilient and sustainable community over time [60]; conversely, poor choices can undermine overall confidence and community cohesion.

In conclusion, the choice of the best partners is based on sophisticated relational dynamics, and the continuous evolution of virtual communities accentuates the awareness in the importance of building positive relationships. All this in the perspective that virtual communities become even more resilient, connected and capable of facing the emerging challenges of the digital society. The careful choice of the best partners thus becomes a foundation for the future of relationships having place both in real and virtual worlds.

The background described above is fully supported by scientific literature, spanning multiple research fields. In fact, finding the best partner for interaction and cooperation is a problem that cuts across various application domains. Solving this problem has always been a challenge for researchers, maintaining its appeal over time, as evidenced by the overwhelming number of scientific contributions that annually enrich the body of knowledge. Over the past thirty years, these proposals have become more and more sophisticated, and complex, keeping pace with the evolution of society and technology, as well as advancements in languages and tools. From this perspective, the scientific research presented over the first twenty-five years of WOA meetings of the Italian community of agents aligns closely with the above context. Indeed, the numerous studies presented at WOA over the years have factually enriched the scientific literature, contributing to the anticipation and expansion of trends that later became well-established in both academic and industrial fields. In particular, the theme of partner search has been addressed in a significant number of WOA's papers.

In this celebratory book, this chapter focuses on highlighting WOA's contributions to the topic of identifying the best candidates for interaction or cooperation. As previously mentioned, a significant number of WOA papers have addressed this issue, and these contributions can be categorized into several strategies encompassing all research proposals. In particular, we have identified key strategies that rely on mechanisms of trust and reputation, ciphering, and commitment. This selection is based on the ability of these approaches to reduce information asymmetry among agents by assessing credibility, trustworthiness, and identity. These strategies encourage participation, limit the probability of deception, and, complementarily, identify malicious agents through their past actions, their identification, or their accountability. This overview, although focused on a specific theme, provides an interesting snapshot of the activity carried out by WOA in the field of agents, thanks to the significant number of papers described.

Moreover, this chapter is linked to that of Sapienza and colleagues in [119]. Here, trust is considered a key social construct that significantly influences decision-making and relationships in human, artificial, and hybrid societies. Specifically, Sapienza et colleagues investigate the evolution of the concept of trust in multi-agent systems through a systematic analysis of studies presented at the WOA workshop. In particular, the aim of [119] is to explore how the literature on trust in MAS has evolved over time. The chapter emphasizes that as interactions become more complex, so does the importance of trust, requiring a deeper investigation of its various forms and dimensions. Furthermore, building on both the issues that have been addressed and those that remain open, they aim to outline future research directions and the challenges that still need tobeaddressed.

The remaining of the chapter is organized as follows. Section 2 describes the adopted methodology to select the most interesting papers presented at the WOA workshops and in detail the contribution of this chapter. Section 3 deals with trust, reputation and reliability issues, while Sect. 4 focuses on cipher-based systems, and Sect. 5 describe some commitment based solutions. Finally, some conclusions are drawn in Sect. 6.

2   Methodology and Contribution

From the first edition of WOA, which took place in the year 2000, to the 25th in 2024, 515 regular papers have been presented. The selection process for identifying the most relevant papers on looking for the best partners for interaction and cooperation tasks involved two consecutive steps. The first step involved searching for a range of relevant keywords (e.g., trust, reliability, reputation, cryptography, commitment, partner, cooperation, etc.) across all the 515 regular WOA papers. In the second step, each of these pre-selected papers was evaluated not only based on the frequency of the keywords used but also on their consistency and relevance to the focus of this chapter. After this selection process 53 scientific contributions resulted.

Building on this foundation, the contribution of this chapter aims to provide a systematic overview of the theme of identifying the best partners for interaction and cooperation. To achieve this, the 53 selected papers have been organized into three main sections: *(i)* Trust and Reputation Systems; *(ii)* Ciphering Systems; and *(iii)* Commitment Systems. Particular emphasis has been placed by WOA's authors on Trust and Reputation Systems, which cover a broad range of fields. Consequently, this section has been further subdivided into additional

Table 1. Contributions for theme

Trust and Reputation Systems	WOA contributions
Models	$[22, 51, 52, 62, 86, 105]$
	$[108, 113, 124, 130]$
Social Networks	$[34, 57, 63\text{–}65, 80]$
	$[38, 40, 82, 83, 87, 112]$
Information, Knowledge and Resources	$[10, 20, 32, 49, 50, 110]$
	$[120, 122, 123, 125]$
Embodied Agents	$[25\text{–}27, 30, 58]$
e-Business	$[14, 90, 121]$
Transportation Systems	$[97, 100, 101]$
Ciphering systems	$[3, 8, 13, 66, 99, 107]$
	$[1, 131]$
Commitment Systems	$[4, 6]$

Table 2. Contribution for year

Year	WOA contributions	Year	WOA contributions
2000	[8]	2013	[1]
2001	[20]	2014	[13, 100, 112, 123]
2002		2015	[30, 124]
2003		2016	[32, 40, 120]
2004	[22, 90, 105, 130]	2017	[6, 34, 49, 63, 65, 87, 97]
2005	[10, 107]	2018	[50, 64, 80, 125]
2006		2019	[3, 25, 57, 101, 121]
2008		2020	[86]
2007	[99]	2021	[27, 58]
2009	[14]	2022	[51, 52, 82, 108]
2010	[131]	2023	[26, 83]
2011	[110, 113]	2024	[62, 122]
2012	[4, 38, 66]		

subsections. Table 1 and Table 2 present the selected papers, organized by theme and by year, respectively.

In addition, the temporal distribution of the selected papers is illustrated in Fig. 1 and Fig. 2. Specifically, Fig. 1 shows the temporal distribution across the three main themes, while Fig. 2 highlights the temporal distribution within the various fields related to trust and reputation systems. Interesting is to observe that Trust and Reputation Systems have encountered significant interest mainly in the last decade, while the remaining topics have encountered a low, but regular, interest over the 25 years of WOA meetings.

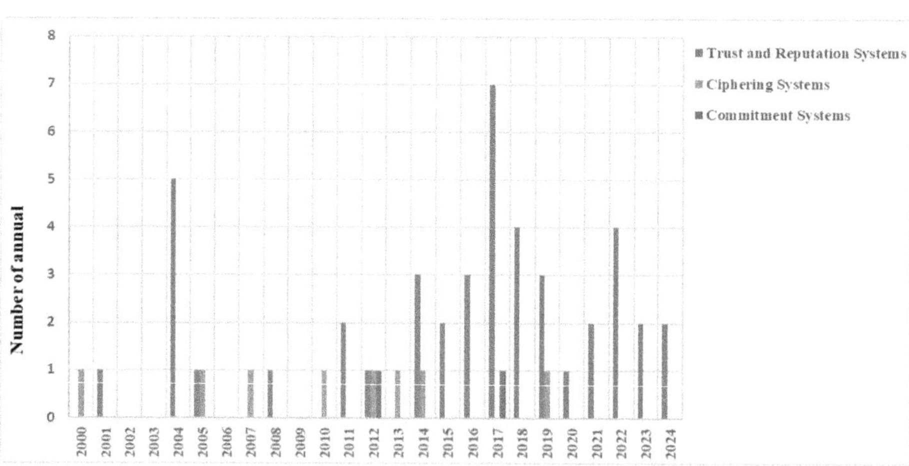

Fig. 1. Contributions in the main themes over the years.

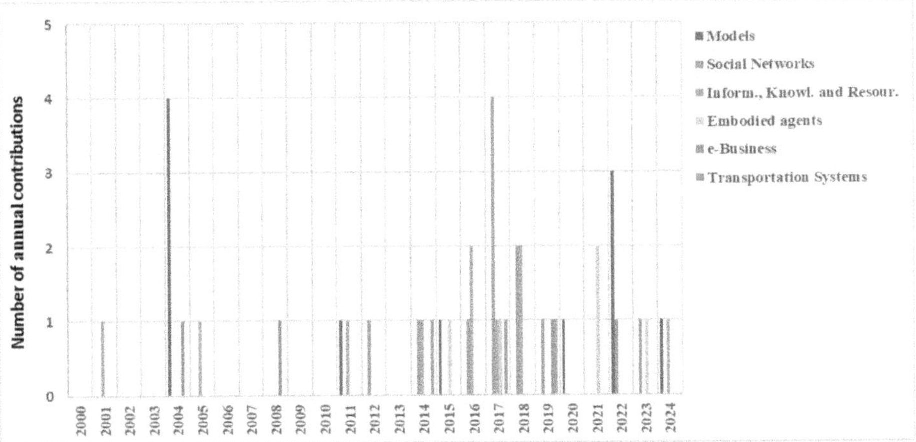

Fig. 2. Trust and Reputation Systems contributions for fields over the years.

3   Trust and Reputation Systems

In choosing an agent as a partner its perceived trustworthiness is essential to make such social interactions as comfortable and fruitful as possible. Consequently, in MAS the concepts of trust, reputation and reliability have long been adopted to optimize the process of partners choice [19]. It is a fact that in the MAS field today, such systems are increasingly used in the context of different application domains in which software agents, also distributed on a large scale, interact and cooperate with other agents.

In particular, to the best of our interest, we can consider trustworthiness as: "the quantified belief by a trustor with respect to the competence, honesty, security and dependability of a trustee within a specified context" [70]. However, it is important to note that relationships founded on trust, reputation, and reliability are typically multidimensional, as they involve varying perspectives that can shift in their practical use depending on the purpose and context of the interaction. For example, in this sense some common dimensions are competence, honesty, safety, trustworthiness, and many others [72].

More specifically, whereas reliability is a subjective measure of trust directly perceived by a trustor with respect to a trustee, reputation represents the measure of trust that an entire community perceives with respect to a specific trustee [74]. As an aggregator of others' opinions, reputation plays an essential role when a trustor has no knowledge at all, or it is partial and insufficient, with respect to a specific trustee to decide whether to interact with it or not [114]. However, frequently measures of reliability and reputation are combined together into a single measure of trust and a crucial point, in the practical use of these two measures is the choice of the most appropriate way in which to combine them together. In the context of MAS, trust, reliability and reputation (TRR) systems are widely used and there exist a rich literature and surveys on this matter to which the interested reader may refer to [18, 69, 72, 98, 103, 116]. In this scenario, numerous contributions at WOA emphasized trust and reputation as key criteria for selecting suitable partners.

3.1 Models

Proposals that appear applicable in different application contexts and thus emerge to be of more general use will be presented below.

Starting both from the potential overwhelming number of relationships existing among agents over the Internet and considering that authentication-based approaches may be inadequate (and in any case they do not provide information about agents' skills), Cabri et al. describe in [22] a preliminary approach for evaluating trust in agent interactions, taking into account the specific role played by agents in a generic mobile scenario. Furthermore, since agents do not evaluate trust in the same way as humans, a computational approach based on an analytical formulation that composes several appropriately weighted components was adopted. A set of Java classes was developed to implement the proposed approach.

In several reliability-reputation models, the measures of reliability and reputation are combined together into a synthetic trust measure to support agents' decisions. In [113] the authors present a trust model that considers, from a mathematical point of view, the interdependence between reliability and reputation measures. In other words, a parameter is dynamically computed to determine the relevance of reliability versus reputation based on the agent's direct knowledge about its current counterpart. In addition, the same authors introduce in [113] a new mechanism for calculating reputation, in which the reputation perceived by a trustor agent on a trusteee agent is based on the overall trust that every other agent in the MAS has in that trustee agent. This approach requires each agent to solve a linear system. Note that this model is applicable only in MASs where agents are cooperative and share their trust measures with each other. Other researches to assess trust in selecting partners in large agent communities for collaborative processes exploiting different information sources are presented in [86, 124]. Both these studies override the problem of assessing the huge number of possible partners by exploiting agent categories (i.e. reputation classes) by assuming that members of a category that possess similar characteristics then will have similar performances about the same task (with a certain degree of uncertainty). The larger the population and ignorance about the trustworthiness of each individual, the more valuable the role of categories to trust a partner. Both these studies highlight the advantage of assessing trust based on class reputation versus reliability or reputation information to determine the possibility of anticipating a trust score of unknown agents.

The study presented in [108] investigates on group polarization/ depolarization, two critical processes underlying relevant behaviors. In other words, polarization processes occur when agents within a community or system interact with each other and gradually move away from their initial views or positions, tending to cluster around opposite poles or, conversely, opposing positions tend to converge toward a common one (i.e., depolarization). This phenomenon can emerge in a wide range of contexts. In that study, an attempt provides to clarify the role played by similarity and trust, as well as their combination (i.e., the measure of compactness [39]) in various percentages, in different behaviors for modeling the processes of dynamic polarization and proximity depolarization. To this end, a multi-agent community has been simulated, where the software agents replicated salient features of human behaviors and the relationships among the agents were assumed to be qualitatively similar to those occurring in human societies. In addition, the agents also considered the presence of other competing or cooperating agents in planning and implementing possible strategies to achieve their goals.

An operational semantics for communication is described in [130] for the DALI language in which each locution is likened to a move in a game, to which other agents can respond with other moves, following a given protocol. Each locution returns information by influencing the state of the receiving agent, while other agents must reason about both this expression and their degree of belief, trust, and confidence to assign to the counterpart. In practice, this type of formalization provides a communication architecture that realizes a filter layer in which an agent can describe its mental attitudes and its assumptions about other agents. Note that this paper does not explicitly proposes a trust model, although the protocol explicitly considers it.

In an Internet of Things (IoT) context, the paper [51] introduces a theoretical framework for developing and regulating the autonomy of IoT devices with respect to the user they interface with. Indeed, it is critical to understand how the device should behave to stimulate user trust and make the user gradually willing to grant more autonomy to IoT devices to provide better performance for him/her. Specifically, the devices represent the actors of this autonomy, while the delegators are the users. In this scenario, two different forms of autonomy (i.e., execution and decision, the latter modeled on multiple levels) were considered to represent human-IoT devices interactions. On the other hand, the reliability of a device is modeled as a vector of 5 elements, precisely to assess its ability at each level of autonomy. The results of this investigation have clarified the various relationships existing between trust, execution, and decision autonomy by suggesting what approach is suitable to be used to improve the levels of autonomy at which IoT devices can operate.

When the tasks assigned to agents go beyond their original purpose or agent abilities are limited, collaboration between virtual and human agents can be crucial to reach the desired goals. In this context, Falcone and Sapienza in [52] consider cognitive agents able to construct a representation of their own capabilities and those of others (so that they can predict reactions and/or responses), and this plays a key role in social interactions. In addition, identifying possible dependencies to achieve a goal allows agents to discover potential weaknesses or risks. To study the dynamics of dependency networks, a simulation of a block world (in which blocks have different characteristics in terms of shape, color and weight) was conducted. The simulation results confirm that the effect of dependency is very significant in agent interactions and that, with unreliable partners, better performances are achieved in situations where resources are not available, while in contexts where dependency use is limited, trust assumes a more prominent role.

Maintaining a high level of consistency in a Blockchain Distributed Ledger depends on two key factors: limiting the number of neighbor agents per node and ensuring low delivery times between nodes. Additionally, the absence of unreliable or malicious agents is often crucial, depending on the specific blockchain system. In the past, the authors propose in [61] an algorithm called Trust-based Optimum Neighbor Selection (TONS), designed to: i) enable nodes to communicate with a globally optimized selection of reliable and trustworthy neighbors, and, based on trust measures, ii) identify misbehaving nodes while optimizing neighbor selection based on delivery times and reputation scores. At the latest WOA workshop, in [62] the same authors present an improved version of TONS, named TONS2. This version introduces a heuristic strategy that reduces the computational overhead by avoiding the need to recalculate a new set of neighbors for each block validation. Simulation results demonstrated that TONS2 is more resource-efficient than its predecessor while maintaining a high quality of neighbor selection. This improvement is particularly beneficial for IoT devices, which often operate with constrained computational and energy resources.

Finally, Ricci and Omicini in [105] discuss on agent coordination artifacts and contexts and how they can play an effective role in shaping trust with regard to social trust, trust in societies, constructive trust, and organizational issues. In more detail, coordination artifacts model the role of abstractions given by the infrastructure with adequate expressiveness and effectiveness to build trust-based strategies, for example, to support the observation and tracking of agents' actions and interactions. In this structured environment, the notion of coordination context can be exploited to model both the interactions and the related events of an agent in its lifetime.

3.2 Social Networks

Online Social Networks (OSNs) enable members to connect and interact with each other over the Internet. These networks play a significant role in modern society, facilitating communication, sharing of information, and the formation of social connections among individuals or groups [67,115,126].

In the OSN context, the formation and evolution of groups is a fascinating topic because of its implications at different conceptual levels. Inspired by [39], several works study this topic on the basis of appropriately combined measures of trust and similarity to suggest a social group to an agent and, conversely, to recommend an agent to a group. In this scenario, group homogeneity is critical in determining the satisfaction of group members, and the stability of homogeneity over time is studied in [38] and [87], respectively. Another relevant aspect of OSN is the group cohesion, Fotia et al. investigate in [65] the effects of using local rather than global measures of trust were also considered. The latter topic was also taken up in [80], to measure the overall effectiveness of the groups thus formed. A practical applications of these studies can be found in [57] and [34]. The former deals with the choice of partners to cooperate in a cloud of things environment. Specifically, groups are formed by using a voting mechanism, in which each vote combines measures of trustworthiness and local reputation, while to form groups with a high level of mutual trust among its members, a distributed algorithm for group formation was designed, optimizing efficiency and effectiveness. In [34] Comi and Rosaci describe SMARTSAN, a recommender system for smart city applications, structured as a multilayer architecture that includes both a P2P platform and a network of social agents, and built on an IoT environment. In SMARTSAN, each social agent is associated with an IoT user or object, and agents can be linked together by trust relationships. Groups of social agents are dynamically formed in SMARTSAN based on measures of both trust and similarity, where trust measures in turn take into account measures of reliability and reputation. Agent groups change over time following changes in users' desires and needs.

Student interactions in OSNs are supported in [40] by means of a MAS exploiting behavioral and trust measures to improve the composition of e-learning student classes. Firstly, behavioral measures refer to a student's proficiency with respect to a set of topics of interest to give educational homogeneity to the class for balancing "offers" and "requests" of support. Trust measures are calculated by combining reliability and reputation measures. Specifically, reputation is based on students' feedback, each of which refers to past interactions, quality of interactions, and historical attitude toward interactions with peers. In turn, these two measures are combined into a single measure called "convenience" and this measure is used to evaluate how convenient it is for a student to join with a class.

In the presence of OSNs organized into thematic groups, trust can play a key role in helping consumers to overcome risk perception. In [63, 64] the author assumes that users can be helped by personal software agents in supporting product purchases. Specific trust-based models integrating reliability and reputation have been developed to identify trustworthy recommendations in virtual communities in the presence of groups. The results show that considering only reputation measures underperformed agents who had a direct interaction with another agent (i.e., reliability measures), while the combination of these two measures was found to be the most profitable approach in an online e-Commerce community.

In communities of social agents, nontrivial forms of interaction and cooperation among agents can be realized, and the choice of qualified partners is crucial to avoid being exposed to malicious behaviors. A well known mechanism to identify malicious partners is provided by the EigenTrust algorithm [75], which is a reputation management system designed to compute trust values in peer-to-peer networks. It assigns each peer a global trust score based on the aggregation of local trust values, which are derived from direct interactions. By leveraging transitive trust and iterative calculations, EigenTrust reduces malicious behavior and ensures reliable partner selection in decentralized environments. Unfortunately, this algorithm has as a side effect that in identifying malicious peers it lowers the reputation of even honest agents. To solve this problem Marcinó et al. propose in [82] a method to preliminary identify the most promising candidates to be considered as malicious and a reputation model that can accurately identify, one at time, malicious agents without introducing the side effects on reputation scores of honest ones typical of the EigenTrust algorithm. This proposal was extended by Marcianò et al. in [83] to identify multiple groups of colluding agents operating independently and simultaneously.

3.3   Information, Knowledge and Resources

In [20], the authors exploit a specific knowledge representation, semantic properties and adaptive algorithms to identify which agents are the most promising candidates to be suggested for a fruitful cooperation. Moreover, each user choice induces changes in the associated knowledge representation, so that the new computed suggestions will be always closer to the user's expectations. Note that the weight associated with each agent can be considered like reputation measures. An extended version of [20] can be found in [21].

ELSA (E-Learning Student Assistant) [112] is an agent-based recommender system assisting a community of students with suggestions about multimedia contents. In this MAS, each student's device hosts a local agent that monitors his/her behavior to build a local profile storing information on the accessed multimedia resources. This profile is then used by an assistant agent to build a student global profile. Based on their global profiles, students are affiliated with one or more partitions where each associated partition agent pre-compiles customized collaborative filtering recommendations taking into account for each student those most similar and those considered more trusted in providing high quality resources. In computing trusted students ELSA, exploits a trust system, derived from that in [114], that dynamically merges reliability and reputation into a global trust measure on the basis of the number of interactions that have occurred in the past.

In [10] Bergenti proposes a MAS where agents' interactions ensure a desired level of security, trust, and the minimum possible number of trusted parties involved. The proposal introduces *Validation-Oriented Ontologies* and *Guarantors* abstractions. To handle the trust aspects, a probabilistic model is adopted, which takes into account a number of parameters, namely: the probability of correctness of information; the probability of the agent fulfilling contractual obligations; the level of confidence placed in the trustee agent; the lower and upper bounds of the probability distribution function of trust. In addition, reward, investment, and penalty are considered in a subjective perspective.

A benefit of using agents is that they can autonomously improve both knowledge and performance through learning. An evolutionary strategy is described in [110], here the concept of cloning, to generate more effective recommendations, is exploited. Specifically, users are served by a set of agents and can replace unsatisfactory ones with others reputed more performing and associated with those users having similar interests. This reputation-driven approach supports an evolutionary behavior in the agent community, allowing to the better agents to predominate over less productive ones. In this way, individual improvements are reflected in the entire agent community. In addition, to increase the rate of change in the agent population, a proactive mechanism, in which the system independently identifies and suggests to a user, who can accept or reject the suggestion, is proposed. Extensions of [110] can be found in [109,111].

In the paper [123], the nature of trust in information sources is studied. In particular, the components that influence trust are identified and analyzed, as well as the dependence between the degree of trust in an information and that in the sources that generated it. Based on this analysis, a fuzzy-based computational approach has been designed. The study in [120] describe a tool founded on a theoretical and computational model that analyzes all possible cognitive variables that may influence the level of trust placed on an information source is described. Trust is used to assign different weights to a source in order to assess its credibility, while information is represented by using the Bayesian theory. This tool can be used in different contexts and within different applications. The same authors analyze in [49] the effects of subjective impulsivity by simulating a population of citizens (modeled through cognitive agents) handling weather information. In this situation, agents can act rationally or impulsively (by emulating their neighbors). The effects of impulsivity were shown to be non-homogeneous across the population, i.e., effects at various levels of positivity and negativity. The authors have shown that the social trust tends to have a positive impact on agents with less information and vice versa increases the correctness of the information the agents possess. In that paper, the adopted trust model is an adaptation of a cognitive confidence model [28] and, similarly to the above cited [49], information is represented as a Bayesian probability density function. The same trust model was also applied in [50], to provide a quantitative estimation of the effects of alarmism on the population in the case of hydrogeologic risks. The results show that the overestimation of risks by public authorities decreases trust in them and, as a consequence, citizens tend not to trust a reliable source. Another effect concerns the quantification of damage, so the more citizens are wrong, the more the population will not respond effectively in the case of real events. Recently, in the context of partner selection, in [122] Sapienza and Falcone explore the role of knowledge within dependence networks. Specifically, agents with limited awareness of their environment and potential partners must acquire an adequate level of knowledge about them. This learning process entails cognitive and computational costs due to the continuous updating of agents' beliefs and strategies, which form the basis of their commitments. The experiments conducted highlight the critical role of knowledge, showing that agents with limited knowledge encounter significant challenges, such as reduced collaboration opportunities, inefficient resource utilization, and limited success in achieving their goals. It is important to note, however, that acquiring knowledge comes with costs, particularly when it involves evaluating trustworthiness, which plays a pivotal role in optimizing agent interactions.

A distributed reputation model, operating within an agent-based framework, to ensure the trustworthiness of information sources in vehicle-to-vehicle interactions is presented in [125]. In detail, a reputation model detects malicious and fraudulent sources of information in order to identify the most reliable actors as sources of useful information.

Finally, to maximize the perceived global utility (i.e., QoS) in large-scale federated computing infrastructures (FCI) a trust-based MAS is proposed in [32]. Here, each FCI node (e.g., a grid computing element, a grid site, or a part of a cloud center) is associated with an agent, which manages a set of infrastructural and resource information related to its node. To satisfy complex requirements, the formation of coalitions among FCI, which are chosen on the basis of trust measures combining reliability and reputation measures, is promoted, quantifying the trustworthiness of their peers and used by an algorithm to form groups and friendships among agents (FGF) [33] and able to maximize the overall utility of the entire federation.

3.4 Embodied Agents

Activities including humans and embodied agents, such as robots or physical devices, can benefit from the adoption of TRR systems in partner selection processes in order to optimize the effectiveness and efficiency of their activities.

To this purpose, some aspects related to the trust and delegation tasks in human-robot interactions have been explored in recent editions of WOA in [25–27]. In trust theory, the principle of delegation [29] is considered one of its founding principles. In particular, cooperation and the mental attitude of delegation has been explored by Cantucci et al. in their research [25], where a declarative, knowledge-oriented, plan-based computational model, implemented on a JaCaMo Framework [17] is designed. This computational model integrates the concept of adjustable social autonomy as a basis for an effective human-robot interaction. However, each request of collaboration also poses an inherent risk of collaborative conflict between the human (the trustor) and the robot (the trustee). To investigate this problem, in [27] a cognitive architecture for profitable human-robot collaboration based on some theoretical principles (i.e., adoption and delegation, mind, adjustable social autonomy, and trust theories) is presented. Based on a Belief-Desire-Intention (BDI) model [104], this architecture enables robots with their own mental states to exhibit a wide range of cognitive abilities able to maximize user performance evaluation. Furthermore, in the proposal presented in [26] a cognitive approach to model human-robot interactions pays attention to four attributes, namely: usefulness, effectiveness, acceptability and trustworthiness. Specifically, the mental attitude of trust is related to the type of cooperation provided by the designed robot and is the mental counterpart of delegation. This means that the robot must be able to achieve the user's goals or needs, but it must also be able to delegate tasks, based on an evaluation of other agents (artificial or human) potentially involved in the interaction.

A proposal about users' acceptance of IoT systems is discussed in [121] adopting a model, also considering security and privacy issues on the user side, by adopting both the concepts of trust and control, suitably ruled by feedback about behaviors and performed actions. Fortino et al. present in [58], a trust-based model simulating an industrial scenario which optimizing the efficiency and effectiveness of groups of workers and autonomous guided vehicles (AGVs). The simulation shows how the adoption of trust in group formation processes can optimize processing time and production quality.

Robots are embodied agents and, in order to have fruitful interactions with humans, it is essential that they be perceived as potential partners with an appropriate level of trustworthiness. The study presented in [30], a study investigates this in relation to a virtual agent using three different interaction conditions (e.g., a mobile application, a humanoid robot using speech only, and a humanoid robot using both speech and gestures) to provide movie recommendations.

3.5   e-Business

The term e-Business refers to all those economic activities carried out by exploiting ITC tools. Just like traditional business activities, which require reliable counterparts to perform economically valuable tasks, it is even more intuitive that this holds true when such activities are conducted over the Internet. In this case, TRR systems can help to create a positive atmosphere in the execution of business activities by providing information about agents based on their past behaviors.

Applications of TRR systems to e-business were explored at WOA in [14, 90]. More in detail, in [14] Bergenti et al. describe a framework for exchanging customer information among e-commerce applications. A Trust Management System, leveraging stated trust relationships, supports personalized information sharing in order to select the best service providers based on their characteristics. More generally, service providers are supported in the sharing of information from a trusted third party (i.e., the User Modeling Agent) without the need to modify their individual representation models or, alternatively if they do not have their own representation model, requesting the support of the User Modeling Agent. On the other hand, an external reputation system is considered in [90] as a key element for an auction bidding process to enable an agent as a bidder, but without deepening this issue.

3.6   Transportation Systems

In the field of transportation systems, few applications of trust and reputation to qualify a counterpart were presented at the WOA events. For example, reputation is exploited in [100] to estimate the accuracy of measurements made by nodes of a sensor grid that monitor traffic parameters, and in this way, errors made by the sensors can be mitigated.

Car-sharing and car-pooling mobility, which can complement transit systems, can also benefit from the adoption of TRR systems. For instance, a trust-based MAS is adopted in a peer-to-peer car-sharing scenario [97] to encourage and support private owners to share their cars. In this study, the agents monitor the driving habits of car-sharing clients and assist them in improving their driving. Over time, the agents also build driver's reputation measures that will be used by car-owners for avoiding to rent their car to unqualified drivers and to customized rant rates awarding the best drivers. Car-pooling is another form of shared mobility that can optimize the load factor of the car, although the origin and destination of the trip must be the same for all the passengers. In this respect, in [101] the authors design an on-demand service that adopts variable rates based on the length of the trip and the number of participants. Multi-agent, reputation (to select good travel mates) and blockchain technologies are used together, and a suitable dynamic routing algorithm has been developed.

4   Ciphering Systems

In choosing the agent to interact with, the use of encryption offers a number of advantages and limitations that affect its usefulness and applicability in different contexts [54, 68]. Advantages include: privacy, confidentiality and data integrity; authentication of the parties involved; protection from security breaches; and regulatory compliance in the presence of regulations requiring protection of sensitive data. In contrast, the main limitations in adopting cryptography lie in: increased implementation complexity (with likely costs in terms of hardware, software and personnel training); possible vulnerabilities present in the cryptographic protocols themselves or in the systems that implement them; complexity in key management; and risks of security compromise in the case of key loss.

By comparing trust and reputation systems with cryptographic systems, both tools are used to assess the reliability and security of an environment, but they are based on different concepts and approaches [137]. Trust and Reputation systems are characterized by assessing trustworthiness by leveraging on users' past experience. This realizes a social evaluation mechanism based on users' shared experiences and the reputation is accumulated by an individual or entity over time [129]. Therefore, the trustworthiness of potential partners is determined by the aggregate evaluation of many users, also in order to mitigate the effects of subjectivity, that is the influence that users' subjective opinions give that may vary based on their personal experiences [15]. In addition, trust and reputation systems are adaptable over time based on changing circumstances, user interactions, and manipulation attacks such as false feedback or fraudulent ratings [89].

Encryption systems are completely different because they are based on mathematical algorithms and protocols whose robustness and adequacy realize the effect "trust". Therefore, evaluations do not involve any social aspects, but only require the proper management of every cryptographic component. However, the "aseptic objectivity" provided by cryptographic systems is not synonymous of a superiority over TRR systems.

In summary, while trust and reputation systems are based on past users' experience and social evaluation to foresee expected future behaviors, cryptographic systems offer reliability, confidentiality, resilience, and security based on mathematical and management principles. Each of the two approaches has advantages and limitations, and both can be used to improve security and trust in an online environment. However, the combination of these two technologies is able to provide a greater effectiveness with respect to the single approaches, although at the cost of significantly increasing the complexity of the system.

Among the paper presented at the WOA that in [107], presented by Roggero et al., propose an automated trust negotiation mechanism for MASs, where the term trusted refers only to a certified and verified identity of the agent acting in the Internet. Specifically, this paper describes a protocol for the creation of trusted and untamperable credentials, issued by a third-party entity, in order to evaluate an access request, verifying both the possession of attributes and pre-requisites. Conceptually similar to that in [107], Tomaiolo and Agazzi describe in [1] a trust negotiation framework for Web services based on peer-to-peer trust relationships. This framework allows users to build trust automatically by incrementally revealing credentials. It includes several components to handle a range of format conversions for messages, policies, and credentials, ensuring interoperability among services. Always, in a Web Service context, the authors of [131] discuss a cross-domain security approach, using cryptography but without leveraging centralized or hierarchical certificate authorities or public lists of names. This work adopts a peer-to-peer delegation mechanism. The results are a library for issuing and verifying delegation chains, a security service with a SOAP [71] interface, a security service with a RESTFUL [106] interface, and other components suitable for an open environment.

On the same mechanisms [13,66] present decentralized MASs for OSN, called Blogracy, deals with social information retrieval issues. It introduces a key-based identity system and a model of social relations for distributing resources. At a lower level, Blogracy uses widespread and stable peer-to-peer technologies, such as distributed hash tables [85] and BitTorrent [102]. The most salient features of Blogracy are: *i*) anonymity and resilience to censorship; *ii*) authenticated content; *iii*) semantic interoperability; and *iv*) data availability. The same Blogracy platform is also used in [3], combined with a spanning tree, to spread online notifications on a distributed OSN to solve privacy, censorship and personal data control issues. The spanning tree robustness is ensured by connection randomness to join with a group, while in the case of node failures a recursive election procedure is implemented for the tree reconstruction.

The adoption of security assertions to improve existing security systems in federated contexts poses new problems that are addressed in [99]. This paper leverages conventional Public-Key Infrastructure (PKI) [95] to witness a web of trusted relationships in open, decentralized agent-based environments. It enables direct interoperability between parties by controlling the flow of authorizations in a XML-based chain of multiple certificates within a trusted delegation chain.

That in [8] describes a mobile agent framework called Secure and Open Mobile Agent (SOMA). SOMA provides several solutions for security and interoperability, two key aspects in mobile environments to avoid of interacting with malicious agents. In this context, authentication and authorization processes (based on credentials) are essential. In particular, SOMA complies with the

OMG/CORBA [47] and MASIF [88] standards to which the management of privacy and security instances using cryptographic techniques is delegated.

5   Commitment Systems

In MASs, commitment-based partner selection is an area of research that focuses on the selection of partners or allies by agents based on the principle that potential agent partners will keep its commitments [31]. This is a key consideration in many situations where agents must collaborate or interact with each other in a distributed context.

Commitment approaches that can be implemented in partners selection include the history of interactions and reputation of partners (peculiar elements also shared with trust and reputation systems), the risks associated within a possible collaboration with a given partner (considering the probability that they will not keep their commitments and the negative consequences of this), and their stated commitment, provide a basis for assessing their trustworthiness.

However, even in systems based on commitment, it must be taken into account that the relationships between agents and their trustworthiness may vary over time [127]. Agents must balance the risk of working with untrustworthy partners against the potential benefits of the collaboration itself, and it is important that information on reputation and stated commitments be transparent and easily accessible to the agents to enable them to make informed decisions on partners selection.

The main feature of commitment protocols is their declarative nature, which allows one to specify a "commitment to do something" and whether what is promised is accomplished. In the position paper [4], agent coordination, infrastructure, event observability, and composition of coordination patterns are analyzed in light of a commitment process. Thus, commitment protocols enable each agent to know its potential counterparts and make informed choices in terms of making and fulfilling commitments.

In terms of commitment, complex activities may involve multiple parties that require each actor to fulfill commitments from a coordination and interaction perspective. To address the lack of business artifacts, a MAS approach is proposed in [6] to support the ideas both that the services for which business artifacts can be operated should be encapsulated and organized into goal-oriented containers, and that a normative layer should be introduced to capture the expected behaviors of the parties. This work could involve three main aspects, namely: an explicit normative layer, understanding how agents could plan the use of business artifacts to achieve their goals, and finally, standardizing the commitment life-cycle.

6   Conclusion

Choosing the best partners is a major strategic issue in a MAS scenario (where each agent has its own set of skills, experience and behaviors), and collaboration is an essential element in ensuring that each agent achieves its own objectives by solving from the simplest to the most complex tasks. Carrying out correct partners selection processes has a deep impact on the entire agent community, since suitable partners improve confidence between parties and lead to increasing the social capital of MAS. A number of challenges need to be addressed to solve this problem, and several techniques have been proposed in the literature for this purpose. Each of them aims to build fruitful relationships among agents and to create an atmosphere of confidence that can reduce information asymmetry among agents and marginalize malicious agents.

In the above context, this chapter provided a comprehensive overview about the scientific contributions presented at the annual WOA workshops from 2000 to 2024, focusing on the problem of selecting one or more counterparts for interaction and cooperation. This selection process is based on key criteria such as trust, reliability, reputation, encryption, and commitment across multiple domains. Over the span of 25 years, this critical issue has been consistently addressed by WOA authors in 53 papers included in this analysis, out of a total of 515 regular papers presented at WOA. This represents a significant part of the workshop's scientific production, underscoring the centrality of this theme in the WOA community. The prominence of this topic within WOA is further evidenced by the variety of strategies proposed in the papers, reflecting the diverse and innovative approaches taken to tackle the challenges of partner selection. These contributions highlight the dynamic interplay between theoretical advancements and practical applications, spanning fields such as, for instance, agent-based systems, distributed computing, and autonomous decision-making. Moreover, the relevance of these researches extend beyond WOA, as demonstrated by the broader scientific community's recognition of the value of these contributions. In many cases, these papers have been further refined and expanded, resulting in extended versions published in leading journals in the field. Such outcomes highlight the quality and originality of the work presented at WOA and its ability to anticipate and address emerging trends in agent-based research impacting on both wider academic and industrial landscapes. In conclusion, the focus on trust, reliability, reputation, encryption, and commitment within the WOA framework has not only enriched the workshop's bibliography but also contributed meaningfully to the advancement of knowledge in the field of agents. The enduring interest in this topic, as reflected in both the volume of research and its influence on the broader scientific literature, attests to its significance and the pivotal role played by WOA in fostering innovation and collaboration within this domain.

Acknowledgments. We would like to express our gratitude to the entire WOA community, which over the years has supported us in our scientific activities, but whose human aspects we have appreciated even more. Furthermore, our gratitude also goes to the editors of this book for the time and commitment they have dedicated to this editorial work.

References

1. Agazzi, F., Tomaiuolo, M.: Trust negotiation for automated service integration. In: Baldoni et al. [5], pp. 97–103 (2013). http://ceur-ws.org/Vol-1099/paper6.pdf
2. Alderighi, M., Baldoni, M., Baroglio, C., Micalizio, R., Tedeschi, S. (eds.): WOA 2024 – 25th Workshop "From Objects to Agents", CEUR Workshop Proceedings, Bard, AO, Italy, vol. 3735 (2024). http://ceur-ws.org/Vol-3735/
3. Amoretti, M., Gandolfi, L., Tomaiuolo, M.: A peer-to-peer notification system for distributed online social networks. In: Bergenti and Monica [12] pp. 142–148 (2019). http://ceur-ws.org/Vol-2404/paper21.pdf
4. Baldoni, M., Baroglio, C.: Some thoughts about commitment protocols (position paper). In: De Paoli and Vizzari [42], pp. 68–71 (2012). http://ceur-ws.org/Vol-892/paper11.pdf
5. Baldoni, M., Baroglio, C., Bergenti, F., Garro, A. (eds.): WOA 2013 – 14th Workshop "From Objects to Agents", CEUR Workshop Proceedings, Turin, Italy, vol. 1099 (2013). http://ceur-ws.org/Vol-1099/
6. Baldoni, M., Baroglio, C., Capuzzimati, F., Micalizio, R.: Endowing business artifacts with a normative coordination layer. In: De Meo et al. [41], pp. 71–77 (2017). http://ceur-ws.org/Vol-1867/w13.pdf
7. Baldoni, M., De Paoli, F., Martelli, A., Omicini, A. (eds.): WOA 2004 – 5th Workshop "From Objects to Agents". Pitagora Editrice Bologna, Torino (2004). http://lia.deis.unibo.it/books/woa2004/atti.pdf
8. Bellavista, P., Corradi, A., Montanari, R., Stefanelli, C.: How a secure and open mobile agent framework suits electronic commerce applications. In: Corradi et al. [35], pp. 13–18 (2000). http://giuseppevizzari.github.io/WOA-proceedings-archive/pdfs/woa2000/WOA03.pdf
9. Ben Abdelaziz, F., Mrad, F.: Multiagent systems for modeling the information game in a financial market. Int. Trans. Oper. Res. **30**(5), 2210–2223 (2023)
10. Bergenti, F.: Secure, trusted and privacy-aware interactions in large-scale multi-agent systems. In: Corradini et al. [36], pp. 144–150 (2005). http://lia.deis.unibo.it/books/woa2005/papers/20.pdf
11. Bergenti, F. (ed.): WOA 2009 – 10th Workshop "From Objects to Agents". Seneca Edizioni Torino, Parma (2009). http://www.ailab.unipr.it/woa09/papers/
12. Bergenti, F., Monica, S. (eds.): WOA 2019 – 20th Workshop "From Objects to Agents", CEUR Workshop Proceedings, Parma, Italy, vol. 2404 (2019). http://ceur-ws.org/Vol-2404/
13. Bergenti, F., Poggi, A., Tomaiuolo, M.: Social information retrieval with agents. In: Santoro and Bergenti [117], pp. 30–35 (2014). http://ceur-ws.org/Vol-1260/paper3.pdf
14. Bergenti, F., Rossi, L., Tomaiuolo, M.: Towards automated trust negotiation in MAS. In: Bergenti [11], pp. 76–81 (2014). http://www.ailab.unipr.it/woa09/papers/Bergenti1.pdf
15. Bhuiyan, T., Josang, A., Xu, Y.: Trust and reputation management in web-based social network. In: Web Intelligence and Intelligent Agents, pp. 207–232 (2010)
16. Bloembergen, D., Tuyls, K., Hennes, D., Kaisers, M.: Evolutionary dynamics of multi-agent learning: a survey. J. Artif. Intell. Res. **53**, 659–697 (2015)
17. Boissier, O., Bordini, R.H., Hübner, J.F., Ricci, A., Santi, A.: Multi-agent oriented programming with JaCaMo. Sci. Comput. Program. **78**(6), 747–761 (2013). https://doi.org/10.1016/j.scico.2011.10.004

18. Braga, D.D.S., Niemann, M., Hellingrath, B., Neto, F.B.D.L.: Survey on computational trust and reputation models. ACM Comput. Surv. (CSUR) **51**(5), 1–40 (2018)
19. Bravo, G., Squazzoni, F., Boero, R.: Trust and partner selection in social networks: an experimentally grounded model. Social Netw. **34**(4), 481–492 (2012)
20. Buccafurri, F., Palopoli, L., Rosaci, D., Sarnè, G.M.L.: A system implementing cooperation in multi-agent networks. In: Omicini and Viroli [93], pp. 20–23 (2001). http://giuseppevizzari.github.io/WOA-proceedings-archive/pdfs/woa2001/pdf/06.pdf
21. Buccafurri, F., Rosaci, D., Sarné, G.M.L., Palopoli, L.: Modeling cooperation in multi-agent communities. Cogn. Syst. Res. **5**(3), 171–190 (2004). https://doi.org/10.1016/j.cogsys.2004.03.001
22. Cabri, G., Ferrari, L., Leonardi, L.: Evaluating trust among agents. In: Baldoni et al. [7], pp. 1–4 (2004). http://giuseppevizzari.github.io/WOA-proceedings-archive/pdfs/woa2004/1.pdf
23. Calegari, R., Ciatto, G., Denti, E., Omicini, A., Sartor, G. (eds.): WOA 2020 – 21st Workshop "From Objects to Agents", CEUR Workshop Proceedings, Bologna, Italy, vol. 2706 (2020). http://ceur-ws.org/Vol-2706/
24. Calegari, R., Ciatto, G., Denti, E., Omicini, A., Sartor, G. (eds.): WOA 2021 – 22nd Workshop "From Objects to Agents", CEUR Workshop Proceedings, Bologna, Italy, vol. 2963 (2021). http://ceur-ws.org/Vol-2963/
25. Cantucci, F., Falcone, R.: A computational model for cognitive human-robot interaction: an approach based on theory of delegation. In: Bergenti and Monica [12], pp. 127–133 (2019). http://ceur-ws.org/Vol-2404/paper19.pdf
26. Cantucci, F., Falcone, R.: A cognitive approach to model intelligent collaboration in human-robot interaction. In: Falcone et al. [48], pp. 138–150 (2023). http://ceur-ws.org/Vol-3579/paper10.pdf
27. Cantucci, F., Falcone, R., Castelfranchi, C.: Investigating adjustable social autonomy in human robot interaction. In: Calegari et al. [24], pp. 49–60 (2021). http://ceur-ws.org/Vol-2963/paper12.pdf
28. Castelfranchi, C., Falcone, R.: Trust Theory: A Socio-Cognitive and Computational Model. John Wiley & Sons, Hoboken (2010)
29. Castelfranchi, C., Falcone, R.: Towards a theory of delegation for agent-based systems. Robot. Auton. Syst. **24**(3–4), 141–157 (1998)
30. Cervone, F., Sica, V., Staffa, M., Tamburro, A., Rossi, S.: Comparing a social robot and a mobile application for movie recommendation: a pilot study. In: Di Napoli et al. [43], pp. 32–38 (2015). http://ceur-ws.org/Vol-1382/paper5.pdf
31. Cohen, P.R., Levesque, H.J.: Intention is choice with commitment. Artif. Intell. **42**(2–3), 213–261 (1990). https://doi.org/10.1016/0004-3702(90)90055-5
32. Comi, A., Fotia, L.: Combining reliability, reputation and honesty to enhance qos on federated computing infrastructures. In: Cossentino et al. [37], pp. 45–50 (2018). http://ceur-ws.org/Vol-2215/paper_8.pdf
33. Comi, A., Fotia, L., Messina, F., Rosaci, D., Sarné, G.M.L.: A partnership-based approach to improve qos on federated computing infrastructures. Inf. Sci. **367**, 246–258 (2016)
34. Comi, A., Rosaci, D.: SMARTSAN: a P2P social agent network for generating recommendations in a smart city environment. In: De Meo et al. [41], pp. 108–112 (2017). http://ceur-ws.org/Vol-1867/w19.pdf
35. Corradi, A., Omicini, A., Poggi, A. (eds.): WOA 2000 – 1st Workshop "From Objects to Agents", Atti di Congressi, vol. 1195. Pitagora Editrice Bologna,

Parma (2000). http://giuseppevizzari.github.io/WOA-proceedings-archive/woa-2000.html

36. Corradini, F., De Paoli, F., Merelli, E., Omicini, A. (eds.): WOA 2005 – 6th Workshop "From Objects to Agents". Pitagora Editrice Bologna, Camerino (2005). http://lia.deis.unibo.it/books/woa2005/atti.pdf

37. Cossentino, M., Sabatucci, L., Seidita, V. (eds.): WOA 2018 – 19th Workshop "From Objects to Agents", CEUR Workshop Proceedings, Palermo, Italy, vol. 2215 (2018). http://ceur-ws.org/Vol-2215/

38. De Meo, P., Ferrara, E., Rosaci, D., Sarnè, G.M.L.: How to improve group homogeneity in online social networks. In: Baldoni et al. [5], pp. 73–77 (2013). http://ceur-ws.org/Vol-1099/paper1.pdf

39. De Meo, P., Ferrara, E., Rosaci, D., Sarné, G.M.L.: Trust and compactness in social network groups. IEEE Trans. Cybern. **45**(2), 205–216 (2014). https://doi.org/10.1109/TCYB.2014.2323892

40. De Meo, P., Messina, F., Rosaci, D., Sarné, G.M.L.: Supporting learner-to-learner interactions using online social network information. In: Santoro et al. [118], pp. 56–61 (2016). http://ceur-ws.org/Vol-1664/w10.pdf

41. De Meo, P., Postorino, M.N., Rosaci, D., Sarnè, G.M.L. (eds.): WOA 2017 – 18th Workshop "From Objects to Agents", CEUR Workshop Proceedings, Scilla, RC, Italy, vol. 1867 (2017). http://ceur-ws.org/Vol-1867/

42. De Paoli, F., Vizzari, G. (eds.): WOA 2012 – 13th Workshop "From Objects to Agents", CEUR Workshop Proceedings, Milano, Italy, vol. 892 (2012). http://ceur-ws.org/Vol-892/

43. Di Napoli, C., Rossi, S., Staffa, M. (eds.): WOA 2015 – 16th Workshop "From Objects to Agents", CEUR Workshop Proceedings, Naples, Italy, vol. 1382 (2015). http://ceur-ws.org/Vol-1382/

44. Dorri, A., Kanhere, S.S., Jurdak, R.: Multi-agent systems: a survey. IEEE Access **6**, 28573–28593 (2018)

45. Dunin-Keplicz, B., Verbrugge, R.: Teamwork in Multi-agent Systems: A Formal Approach. John Wiley & Sons, Hoboken (2011)

46. Ellis, D., Oldridge, R., Vasconcelos, A.: Community and virtual community. Ann. Rev. Inf. Sci. Technol. **38**(1), 145–186 (2004)

47. Emmerich, W.: An overview of OMG/CORBA. In: IEE Colloquium on Distributed Objects – Technology and Application. IET (1997). https://doi.org/10.1049/ic:19971122

48. Falcone, R., Castelfranchi, C., Sapienza, A., Cantucci, F. (eds.): WOA 2023 – 24th Workshop "From Objects to Agents", CEUR Workshop Proceedings, Roma, Italy, vol. 3579 (2023). http://ceur-ws.org/Vol-3579/

49. Falcone, R., Sapienza, A.: How can subjective impulsivity play a role among information sources in weather scenarios? In: De Meo et al. [41], pp. 19–24 (2017). http://ceur-ws.org/Vol-1867/w4.pdf

50. Falcone, R., Sapienza, A.: Institutional alarmism and the damage it provokes in case of hydrogeological disasters: a simulative estimation. In: Cossentino et al. [37], pp. 21–26 (2018). http://ceur-ws.org/Vol-2215/paper_4.pdf

51. Falcone, R., Sapienza, A.: The role of decisional autonomy in user-IoT systems interaction. In: Ferrando and Mascardi [55], pp. 77–87 (2022). http://ceur-ws.org/Vol-3261/paper6.pdf

52. Falcone, R., Sapienza, A.: Dependence networks and trust in agents societies: insights and practical implications. In: Falcone et al. [48], pp. 106–122 (2023). http://ceur-ws.org/Vol-3579/paper8.pdf

53. Faraj, S., Jarvenpaa, S.L., Majchrzak, A.: Knowledge collaboration in online communities. Organ. Sci. **22**(5), 1224–1239 (2011)
54. Ferguson, N., Schneier, B., Kohno, T.: Cryptography Engineering: Design Principles and Practical Applications. John Wiley & Sons, Hoboken (2011)
55. Ferrando, A., Mascardi, V. (eds.): WOA 2022 – 23rd Workshop "From Objects to Agents", CEUR Workshop Proceedings, Genova, Italy, vol. 3261 (2022). http://ceur-ws.org/Vol-3261/
56. Fischer, J., Lieberoth-Leden, C., Fottner, J., Vogel-Heuser, B.: Design, application, and evaluation of a multiagent system in the logistics domain. IEEE Trans. Autom. Sci. Eng. **17**(3), 1283–1296 (2020)
57. Fortino, G., Fotia, L., Messina, F., Rosaci, D., Sarné, G.M.L.: Supporting agent CoT groups formation by trust. In: Bergenti and Monica [12], pp. 71–76 (2019). http://ceur-ws.org/Vol-2404/paper11.pdf
58. Fortino, G., Fotia, L., Messina, F., Rosaci, D., Sarné, G.M.L., Savaglio, C.: A trust model to form teams of agentified AGVs in workshop areas. In: Calegari et al. [24], pp. 61–71 (2021). http://ceur-ws.org/Vol-2963/paper2.pdf
59. Fortino, G., Garro, A., Palopoli, L., Russo, W., Spezzano, G. (eds.): WOA 2011 – 12th Workshop "From Objects to Agents", CEUR Workshop Proceedings, Rende, Italy, vol. 741 (2011). http://ceur-ws.org/Vol-741/
60. Fortino, G., Messina, F., Rosaci, D., Sarné, G.M.L.: Using blockchain in a reputation-based model for grouping agents in the internet of things. IEEE Trans. Eng. Manag. **67**(4), 1231–1243 (2019)
61. Fortino, G., Messina, F., Rosaci, D., Sarnè, G.M.L.: Using trust measures to optimize neighbor selection for smart blockchain networks in IoT. IEEE Internet Things J. **10**(24), 21168–21175 (2023). https://doi.org/10.1109/JIOT.2023.3263582
62. Fortino, G., Rosaci, D., Sarné, G.M.L.: Improving computational efficiency of the TONS algorithm in selecting neighbor agents in blockchain trust-based iot environments. In: Alderighi et al. [2], pp. 84–97 (2024). http://ceur-ws.org/Vol-3735/paper_07.pdf
63. Fotia, L.: Generating trust-based recommendations for social networks organized by groups. In: De Meo et al. [41], pp. 49–54 (2017). http://ceur-ws.org/Vol-1867/w9.pdf
64. Fotia, L.: Recommending items in social networks using cliques-based trust. In: Cossentino et al. [37], pp. 51–56 (2018). http://ceur-ws.org/Vol-2215/paper_9.pdf
65. Fotia, L., Messina, F., Rosaci, D., Sarné, G.M.L.: On the impact of trust relationships on social network group formation. In: De Meo et al. [41], pp. 25–30 (2017). http://ceur-ws.org/Vol-1867/w5.pdf
66. Franchi, E., Tomaiuolo, M.: Software agents for distributed social networking. In: De Paoli and Vizzari [42], pp. 63–67 (2012). http://ceur-ws.org/Vol-892/paper4.pdf
67. Garton, L., Haythornthwaite, C., Wellman, B.: Studying online social networks. J. Comput.-Mediat. Commun. **3**(1), JCMC313 (1997)
68. Goldreich, O.: Foundations of Cryptography: Basic Applications, vol. 2. Cambridge university press, Cambridge (2001)
69. Granatyr, J., Botelho, V., Lessing, O.R., Scalabrin, E.E., Barthès, J.P., Enembreck, F.: Trust and reputation models for multiagent systems. ACM Comput. Surv. (CSUR) **48**(2), 1–42 (2015)

70. Grandison, T., Sloman, M.: Trust management tools for internet applications. In: Trust Management: First International Conference, iTrust 2003 Heraklion, Crete, Greece, 28–30 May 2003 Proceedings 1, pp. 91–107. Springer, Heidelberg (2003)
71. Gudgin, M., et al.: Soap version 1.2. W3C Recommend. **24**, 12 (2003)
72. Huynh, T.D.: Trust and reputation in open multi-agent systems. Ph.D. thesis, University of Southampton (2006)
73. Iqbal, S., Altaf, W., Aslam, M., Mahmood, W., Khan, M.U.G.: Application of intelligent agents in health-care. Artif. Intell. Rev. **46**, 83–112 (2016)
74. Jøsang, A.: Trust and reputation systems. In: International School on Foundations of Security Analysis and Design, pp. 209–245. Springer, Heidelberg (2006)
75. Kamvar, S., Schlosser, M., Garcia-Molina, H.: The eigentrust algorithm for reputation management in P2P networks. In: Proceedings of World Wide Web, 12th International Conference on, pp. 640–651. ACM (2003)
76. Kim, A.J.: Community Building on the Web: Secret Strategies for Successful Online Communities. Peachpit press (2006)
77. Lee, S.K., Kavya, P., Lasser, S.C.: Social interactions and relationships with an intelligent virtual agent. Int. J. Hum. Comput. Stud. **150**, 102608 (2021)
78. Li, L., Xie, J., Wang, R., Su, J., Sindakis, S.: The partner selection modes for knowledge-based innovation networks: a multiagent simulation. IEEE Access **7**, 140969–140979 (2019)
79. Li, Z., Sim, C.H., Low, M.Y.H.: A survey of emergent behavior and its impacts in agent-based systems. In: 2006 4th IEEE International Conference on Industrial Informatics, pp. 1295–1300. IEEE (2006)
80. Liotta, A., Messina, F., Rosaci, D., Sarné, G.M.L.: Effective group formation in agent societies. In: Cossentino et al. [37], pp. 39–4 (2018). http://ceur-ws.org/Vol-2215/paper_7.pdf
81. Liu, J., Wu, J.: Multiagent Robotic Systems. CRC press, Boca Raton (2018)
82. Marcianò, A.: Accurate colluding agents detection by reputation measures. In: Ferrando and Mascardi [55], pp. 219–231 (2022). http://ceur-ws.org/Vol-3261/paper17.pdf
83. Marcianò, A., Rosaci, D., Sarnè, G.M.L.: A strategy to detect colluding groups by reputation measures. In: Falcone et al. [48], pp. 92–105 (2023). http://ceur-ws.org/Vol-3579/paper7.pdf
84. Mascardi, V., Omicini, A. (eds.): The Agents Journey: Twenty-five Years of Multi-agent Systems at WOA. Lecture Notes in Computer Science – State-of-the-Art Surveys. Springer, Heidelberg (2026)
85. Maurer, W.D., Lewis, T.G.: Hash table methods. ACM Comput. Surv. (CSUR) **7**(1), 5–19 (1975)
86. Meo, P.D., Falcone, R., Sapienza, A.: Applying inferential processes to partner selection in large agents communities. In: Calegari et al. [23], pp. 15–27 (2020). http://ceur-ws.org/Vol-2706/paper6.pdf
87. De Meo, P., Messina, F., Rosaci, D., Sarné, G.M.L.: Improving agent group homogeneity over time. In: De Meo et al. [41], pp. 37–42 (2017). http://ceur-ws.org/Vol-1867/w7.pdf
88. Milojicic, D., et al.: MASIF: the OMG mobile agent system interoperability facility. Pers. Technol. **2**, 117–129 (1998). https://doi.org/10.1007/BF01324942
89. Momani, M., Challa, S.: Survey of trust models in different network domains. arXiv preprint arXiv:1010.0168 (2010)
90. Negro, B., et al.: Customer information sharing between e-commerce applications. In: Baldoni et al. [7], pp. 5–12 (2004). http://giuseppevizzari.github.io/WOA-proceedings-archive/pdfs/woa2004/2.pdf

91. Noble, J., Franks, D.W.: Social learning in a multi-agent system. Comput. Inf. **22**(6), 561–574 (2003)

92. Nyongesa, H.O., Musumba, G.W., Chileshe, N.: Partner selection and performance evaluation framework for a construction-related virtual enterprise: a multi-agent systems approach. Arch. Eng. Des. Manag. **13**(5), 344–364 (2017)

93. Omicini, A., Viroli, M. (eds.): WOA 2001 – 2nd Workshop "From Objects to Agents". Pitagora Editrice Bologna, Modena (2001). http://giuseppevizzari. github.io/WOA-proceedings-archive/woa-2001.html

94. Omicini, A., Viroli, M. (eds.): WOA 2010 – 11th Workshop "From Objects to Agents", CEUR Workshop Proceedings, Rimini, Italy, vol. 621 (2010). http:// ceur-ws.org/Vol-621/

95. Perlman, R.: An overview of PKI trust models. IEEE Netw. **13**(6), 38–43 (1999). https://doi.org/10.1109/65.806987

96. Petruzzi, P.E., Busquets, D., Pitt, J.: Experiments with social capital in multi-agent systems. In: PRIMA 2014: Principles and Practice of Multi-Agent Systems: 17th International Conference, Gold Coast, QLD Australia, 1–5 December 2014. Proceedings 17, pp. 18–33. Springer, Heidelberg (2014)

97. Picasso, E., Postorino, M.N., Sarné, G.M.L.: A study to promote car-sharing by adopting a reputation system in a multi-agent context. In: De Meo et al. [41], pp. 13–18 (2017). http://ceur-ws.org/Vol-1867/w3.pdf

98. Pinyol, I., Sabater-Mir, J.: Computational trust and reputation models for open multi-agent systems: a review. Artif. Intell. Rev. **40**(1), 1–25 (2013)

99. Poggi, A., Tomaiuolo, M.: XML-based trust management in MAS. In: Baldoni, M., Boccalatte, A., De Paoli, F., Martelli, M., Mascardi, V. (eds.) WOA 2007 – 8th Workshop "From Objects to Agents", pp. 126–131. Seneca Edizioni Torino, Genova (2007). http://woa07.disi.unige.it/papers/PoggiTrust.pdf

100. Postorino, M.N., Sarnè, G.M.L.: An agent-based sensor grid to monitor urban traffic. In: Santoro and Bergenti [117], pp. 18–23 (2014). http://ceur-ws.org/Vol-1260/paper2.pdf

101. Postorino, M.N., Sarné, G.M.L.: A preliminary study for an agent blockchain-based framework supporting dynamic car-pooling. In: Bergenti and Monica [12], pp. 65–70 (2019). http://ceur-ws.org/Vol-2404/paper10.pdf

102. Pouwelse, J., Garbacki, P., Epema, D., Sips, H.: The bittorrent p2p file-sharing system: measurements and analysis. In: Peer-to-Peer Systems IV: 4th International Workshop, IPTPS 2005, Ithaca, NY, USA, 24–25 February 2005. Revised Selected Papers 4, pp. 205–216. Springer, Heidelberg (2005)

103. Ramchurn, S.D., Huynh, D., Jennings, N.R.: Trust in multi-agent systems. Knowl. Eng. Rev. **19**(1), 1–25 (2004)

104. Rao, A.S., Georgeff, M.P.: BDI agents: from theory to practice. In: 1st International Conference on Multiagent Systems (ICMAS '95), vol. 95, pp. 312–319 (1995). https://cdn.aaai.org/ICMAS/1995/ICMAS95-042.pdf

105. Ricci, A., Omicini, A.: Engineering trust in complex system through mediating infrastructures. In: Baldoni et al. [7], pp. 110–115 (2004). http://giuseppevizzari. github.io/WOA-proceedings-archive/pdfs/woa2004/16.pdf

106. Richardson, L., Ruby, S.: RESTful Web Services. O'Reilly Media, Inc., Newton(2008)

107. Roggero, D., Patrone, F., Mascardi, V.: Designing and implementing electronic auctions in a multiagent system environment. In: Corradini et al. [36], pp. 157–163 (2005). http://lia.deis.unibo.it/books/woa2005/papers/22.pdf

108. Rosaci, D., Sacchi, S., Sarné, G.M.L.: Modeling dynamic web polarization and proximity depolarization processes by compactness measures. In: Ferrando and Mascardi [55], pp. 88–100 (2022). http://ceur-ws.org/Vol-3261/paper7.pdf

109. Rosaci, D., Sarné, G.M.L.: EVA: an evolutionary approach to mutual monitoring of learning information agents. Appl. Artif. Intell. **25**(5), 341–361 (2011). https://doi.org/10.1080/08839514.2011.559907

110. Rosaci, D., Sarnè, G.M.L.: Supporting evolution in learning information agents. In: Fortino et al. [59], pp. 89–94 (2011). http://ceur-ws.org/Vol-741/ID5_RosaciSarne.pdf

111. Rosaci, D., Sarné, G.M.L.: Cloning mechanisms to improve agent performances. J. Netw. Comput. Appl. **36**(1), 402–408 (2013)

112. Rosaci, D., Sarnè, G.M.L.: An agent-based architecture to recommend educational video. In: Santoro and Bergenti [117], pp. 1–6 (2014). http://ceur-ws.org/Vol-1260/paper1.pdf

113. Rosaci, D., Sarnè, G.M.L., Garruzzo, S.: TRR· an integrated reliability-reputation model for agent societies. In: Fortino et al. [59], pp. 28–33 (2011). http://ceur-ws.org/Vol-741/ID6_RosaciSarneGarruzzo.pdf

114. Rosaci, D., Sarné, G.M.L., Garruzzo, S.: Integrating trust measures in multiagent systems. Int. J. Intell. Syst. **27**(1), 1–15 (2012)

115. Sabater, J., Sierra, C.: Reputation and social network analysis in multi-agent systems. In: Proceedings of the 1st International Joint conference on Autonomous Agents and Multiagent Systems: Part 1, pp. 475–482 (2002). https://doi.org/10.1145/544741.544854

116. Sabater, J., Sierra, C.: Review on computational trust and reputation models. Artif. Intell. Rev. **24**, 33–60 (2005)

117. Santoro, C., Bergenti, F. (eds.): WOA 2014 – 15th Workshop "From Objects to Agents", CEUR Workshop Proceedings, Catania, Italy, vol. 1260 (2014). http://ceur-ws.org/Vol-1260/

118. Santoro, C., Messina, F., De Benedetti, M. (eds.): WOA 2016 – 17th Workshop "From Objects to Agents", CEUR Workshop Proceedings, Catania, Italy, vol. 1664 (2016). http://ceur-ws.org/Vol-1664/

119. Sapienza, A., Cantucci, F., Castelfranchi, C., Falcone, R.: Trust evolution in agent and multi-agent systems: a computational modeling perspective. In: Mascardi and Omicini [84] (2022)

120. Sapienza, A., Falcone, R.: A bayesian computational model for trust on information sources. In: Santoro et al. [118], pp. 50–55 (2016). http://ceur-ws.org/Vol-1664/w9.pdf

121. Sapienza, A., Falcone, R.: A theoretical model for the human-iot systems interaction. In: Bergenti and Monica [12], pp. 90–97 (2019). http://ceur-ws.org/Vol-2404/paper14.pdf

122. Sapienza, A., Falcone, R.: Exploring the dynamics of learned, pre-existing, and partial knowledge in dependence networks within multi-agent systems. In: Alderighi et al. [2], pp. 129–141 (2024). http://ceur-ws.org/Vol-3735/paper_10.pdf

123. Sapienza, A., Falcone, R., Castelfranchi, C.: Trust on information sources: a theoretical and computational approach. In: Santoro and Bergenti [117], pp. 7–11 (2014). http://ceur-ws.org/Vol-1260/paper12.pdf

124. Sapienza, A., Falcone, R., Castelfranchi, C.: The positive power of prejudice: a computational model for MAS. In: Di Napoli et al. [43], pp. 39–45 (2015). http://ceur-ws.org/Vol-1382/paper6.pdf

125. Sarnè, G.M.L.: A reputation agent model for reliable vehicle-to-vehicle information. In: Cossentino et al. [37], pp. 33–38 (2018). http://ceur-ws.org/Vol-2215/paper_6.pdf
126. Sherchan, W., Nepal, S., Paris, C.: A survey of trust in social networks. ACM Comput. Surv. (CSUR) **45**(4), 1–33 (2013)
127. Smith, M.J., Desjardins, M.: Learning to trust in the competence and commitment of agents. Auton. Agent. Multi-Agent Syst. **18**, 36–82 (2009)
128. Smithers, T.: Are autonomous agents information processing systems? In: The Artificial Life Route to Artificial Intelligence, pp. 123–162. Routledge, Abingdon (2018)
129. Such, J.M., Espinosa, A., Garcia-Fornes, A., Botti, V.: Partial identities as a foundation for trust and reputation. Eng. Appl. Artif. Intell. **24**(7), 1128–1136 (2011)
130. Tocchio, A., Costantini, S., Verticchio, A.: A game-theoretic operational semantics. In: Baldoni et al. [7], pp. 13–21 (2004). http://giuseppevizzari.github.io/WOA-proceedings-archive/pdfs/woa2004/3.pdf
131. Tomaiuolo, M., Turci, P.: Peer-to-peer delegation for accessing web services. In: Omicini and Viroli [94], pp. 65–71 (2010). http://ceur-ws.org/Vol-621/paper10.pdf
132. Torreno, A., Onaindia, E., Komenda, A., Štolba, M.: Cooperative multi-agent planning: a survey. ACM Comput. Surv. (CSUR) **50**(6), 1–32 (2017)
133. Wang, J., et al.: Cooperative and competitive multi-agent systems: from optimization to games. IEEE/CAA J. Automatica Sinica **9**(5), 763–783 (2022)
134. de Weerdt, M.M., Zhang, Y., Klos, T.: Multiagent task allocation in social networks. Auton. Agent. Multi-Agent Syst. **25**, 46–86 (2012)
135. Weyns, D., Omicini, A., Odell, J.J.: Environment as a first class abstraction in multi-agent systems. Auton. Agent. Multi-Agent Syst. **14**(1), 5–30 (2007). https://doi.org/10.1007/s10458-006-0012-0, special issue on Environments for Multi-agent Systems
136. Wooldridge, M.: Intelligent agents. In: Weiss, G. (ed.) Multiagent Systems, 2nd edn., chap. 1, pp. 3–50. The MIT Press (2013). https://mitpress.mit.edu/9780262018890/multiagent-systems/
137. Wu, B., Chen, J., Wu, J., Cardei, M.: A survey of attacks and countermeasures in mobile ad hoc networks. In: Wireless Network Security, pp. 103–135 (2007)

Trust Evolution in Agent and Multi-agent Systems: A Computational Modeling Perspective

Alessandro Sapienza[(✉)], Filippo Cantucci, Cristiano Castelfranchi, and Rino Falcone

Institute of Cognitive Sciences and Technologies, National Research Council of Italy (ISTC-CNR), 00185 Rome, Italy
{alessandro.sapienza,filippo.cantucci,cristiano.castelfranchi,
rino.falcone}@istc.cnr.it

Abstract. The concept of trust is of fundamental importance in the field of multi-agent systems. Indeed, in this context, due to the intrinsic characteristics of the agent concept (autonomy within an environment with limited knowledge and control), trust has been introduced from the beginning as a basic theoretical requirement. In recent years, the application of this concept has exponentially increased, also thanks to the relatively recent emergence of trustworthy AI. Although, at this specific historical moment, this topic is capturing the attention of the scientific community with particular interest, trust has always been a key concept for social and non-social, human or artificial interaction. An extensive body of literature has developed around the concept of trust. Focusing on the world of multi-agent systems, we can observe that as the complexity of interaction grows, so does the importance of trust and the need to investigate its different types and faces. In this contribution, we aim to trace, through the analysis of some exemplary contributions presented in different editions of the Workshop WOA, the usage and evolution of the trust concept within multi-agent systems. The purpose of this analysis is twofold: on one hand, to understand how and why the choice to utilize trust was made, and on the other hand, to comprehend the future directions to be pursued and the challenges that lie ahead.

Keywords: Trust · MAS · Social Simulation · Human-Agent Interaction

1 Introduction

Devices and technological systems are becoming increasingly sophisticated and complex. Consider, for instance, the case of autonomous vehicles [82], which are supposed to make split-second decisions to ensure the safety of passengers and pedestrians, while intelligent virtual and robotic assistants [53] need to understand and respond to user requests contextually and in the most appropriate

V. Mascardi and A. Omicini (Eds.): *The Agents Journey*, LNCS 16395, pp. 79–102, 2026.
https://doi.org/10.1007/978-3-032-22940-3_3

way. If it was once difficult to accept the idea that an object could possess intelligence and decision-making autonomy, now this idea has become widespread in the public imagination. However, as the actions these agents can perform in the world become increasingly complex, the need to incorporate social capabilities into these systems becomes increasingly important [94]. Among the many, trust plays a fundamental role.

Trust significantly influences decision-making and relationships in human societies [49,84,104] and its crucial role has been clearly recognized even in artificial societies, such as multi-agent systems (MAS) [38,68,116]. Since the introduction of MAS, trust has represented a critical theoretical requirement to ensure cooperation and coordination among autonomous agents. Indeed, the very notion of agent implies the notions of delegation, task, and the idea of acting on behalf of someone else [37,88]. Besides cooperation, it is also necessary to ensure an acceptable level of competition or conflicts [34,98]. Agents must not only collaborate with each other and with users, but they must also be capable of managing conflicts that may arise both in user interactions (such as in cases of critical help or imposition) and with other artificial agents. For instance, this is crucial to position themselves optimally within the trust market and be selected as preferred partners over others (trust reputation capital [39,91]).

Nevertheless, the inclusion of trust in MAS is neither immediate nor trivial, but requires particular attention. Among the challenges addressed, there is certainly the issue of how it should be theoretically grounded. In this regard, it is worth noting that there is still no consensus in the scientific literature on how trust should be defined, neither in human societies nor in multi-agent systems [33,110]. Additionally, since the intention is to implement the concept of trust in artificial entities, so that they can use it in their interactions with others, it is crucial to evaluate, starting from its theoretical basis, how computational models of trust should be designed, how trust should be represented and managed, and on what basis it should be calculated, starting from interaction history, reputation, and inferential processes.

Trust is undoubtedly a complex concept that requires thorough study combined with a solid theoretical approach. However, it is not just a theoretical concept. In MAS, where numerous autonomous agents interact and collaborate to achieve their goals, managing interactions and relationships between agents becomes crucial. Remarkably, trust is a practical and indispensable tool for managing the interactional complexity that emerges.

First of all, trust is an important cognitive instrument for reducing uncertainty [18,81,141]. In complex environments, agents often have to make decisions based on partial, incomplete, or uncertain information regarding the state of the world, available resources, contextual conditions, or the intentions and capabilities of other agents. Trust allows agents to make reasonable assumptions about the reliability of others, thereby reducing the need to constantly monitor every interaction. This decision-making simplification tool undoubtedly improves cooperation among agents or it helps avoid risky and unsuccessful interactions.

Furthermore, trust facilitates coordination and coalition formation [54,105]. Agents in an MAS often need to coordinate their actions to achieve individual or shared goals. Trust enables agents to better predict the behavior of others, thus facilitating the selection and planning of actions.

Trust is also intrinsically linked to the concept of reputation [48,75]. Agents who prove to be trustworthy earn a positive reputation, which in turn increases their opportunities for future collaborations. This creates a virtuous cycle where trust generates trust, enhancing overall interaction within the system. At the same time, agents who betray trust can be penalized through mechanisms of exclusion or sanction, promoting cooperative behavior and reducing opportunistic behaviors.

Additionally, trust between humans and complex systems represents another significant challenge. As the capabilities and responsibilities of autonomous agents increase, managing interactions effectively becomes more complex. Thus, trust becomes pivotal to ensure that these interactions are safe, effective, and reliable. In summary, trust is a central concept for the development and management of MAS. Understanding how to model and calculate trust, and integrating it into complex systems, is fundamental for the development of robust and reliable MAS capable of operating in dynamic and uncertain environments.

As we will see in this chapter, the WOA community has clearly acknowledged the value of trust and the importance of this concept in MAS, applying and investigating it in different contexts and with various perspectives. Complementing this chapter, Rosaci and Sarnè's contribution in Chapter [122] of this book explores the adaptive behaviors within multi-agent communities that facilitate the selection of optimal agent partners for interaction (i.e., cooperation). This process, driven by complex relational dynamics, engages the entire virtual community in fostering positive relationships and enhancing its social capital. Specifically, the authors highlight key strategies such as trust and reputation mechanisms, encryption techniques, and commitment protocols. These approaches help mitigate information asymmetry among agents by evaluating credibility, trustworthiness, and identity, ultimately reducing the likelihood of deception and identifying malicious agents. Moreover, this chapter offers a compelling overview of WOA's contributions to the field of agent-based systems, as reflected in the substantial body of research discussed.

Chapter [17] also explores how the complex concept of trust represents a powerful tool for the development of advanced IoT systems, covering design, implementation, and simulation phases.

The theme of explainability as a fundamental dimension in designing trustworthy intelligent systems is also addressed in Chapter [4] and Chapter [3]. These chapters present explainability as a crucial aspect for enhancing interpretability and trustworthiness, especially in the case of sub-symbolics systems.

Finally, Chapter [7] highlights the potential of declarative approaches in AI for building trustworthy systems, providing strong support for integrating many of the trustworthiness dimensions analyzed in this chapter.

It clearly emerges that researchers within the WOA community have explored trust from multiple angles, including its theoretical underpinnings, computational modeling, and practical applications. This multifaceted approach has allowed for a deeper understanding of how trust can enhance cooperation, coordination, and overall system efficiency in multi-agent environments. In this regard, the phenomena identified in this study extend well beyond a survey focused solely on Italian research and demonstrate that WOA, as a reference workshop for the Italian community, is also anticipatory of international research trends and perspectives.

By analyzing the historical evolution of contributions presented in the context of WOA, this chapter aims to explore the evolution of these concepts and outline future directions for managing trust in multi-agent systems.

The rest of the chapter is organized as follows: Sect. 2 will explain how the selection of the contributions has been conducted. Section 3 provides initial considerations on the works selected for the review, starting from the WOA dataset. Then, Sect. 4 illustrates the main effects and the most remarkable results of the analysis, while Sect. 5 will discuss the impact of these results.

2 Methods

The realization of this review has been inspired by the following research questions:

1. For which issues was the use of trust relevant, and how have these issues changed over time?
2. How has the use of trust in computational simulation models evolved over time?

The research of the contributions has been conducted in May 2024, by making use of the following dataset https://dblp.org/search/publ?q=stream%3Aconf %2Fwoa%3A, which contains references to all articles published at the WOA conference from 2000 to 2023. The contributions were initially selected based on their title and abstract, considering all works that contained keywords related to trust in the title or abstract. More in detail, the following keywords were considered: "trust", "confidence", "recommend", and "reputation". As a result of this process, 59 articles were identified. Additionally, 1 article [131] was included since, based on our direct knowledge, it addressed trust. Therefore, the contributions were further selected based on their content. In this way, some contributions were excluded because, although containing keywords of interest, they did not address the topic we identified. In total, 3 articles were excluded, leaving a total of 57 articles for the review.

3 WOA Coverage

Figure 1 and Fig. 2 provide a comprehensive view of the growing importance of the concept of trust within the WOA conference. The two figures presented include linear regression analyses that illustrate the trend of contributions addressing trust over time. The data is presented in terms of both the absolute number and the percentage of contributions related to trust. In fact, the interest of the international scientific community in trust has significantly increased over time. These graphs illustrate how this phenomenon has been promptly recognized within the WOA community as well, highlighting its increasing relevance at the conference.

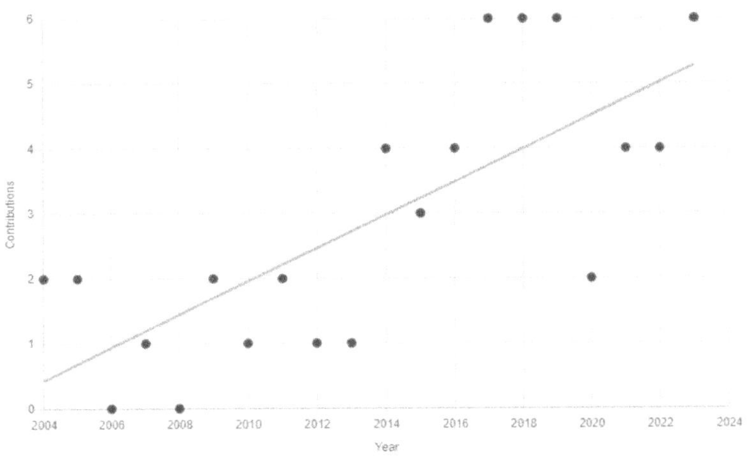

Fig. 1. Number of contributions per year presented at the WOA conference that deal with trust.

Thus, we have examined the various types of works proposed, with the aim of formulating a rationale and providing a general overview of the different methodological approaches. This allows us to focus on the structure of the studies. Table 1 reports the results of such preliminary analysis.

The types of articles can be divided into several main categories, including theoretical studies (14% of the contributions), which focus on the formulation of new theories or the critical reinterpretation of existing theories. These articles contribute to the conceptual foundation and theoretical understanding of the subject matter, offering insights for further research and practical applications.

The second category is that of computational models (10.5%), which propose implementations of theoretical trust models, thereby focusing on computational aspects. These approaches are crucial for the empirical validation of theories and for analyzing agents' behaviors in controlled or simulated contexts.

We also identified another pool of works focusing on trust in information sources and knowledge revision (8.8%). This category encompasses studies that investigate how trust in the reliability and credibility of information sources affects the process of knowledge acquisition and revision. Research in this area explores the mechanisms by which individuals and systems evaluate the trustworthiness of various information sources and the role of trust in the acceptance or rejection of new information. Furthermore, this category includes works that

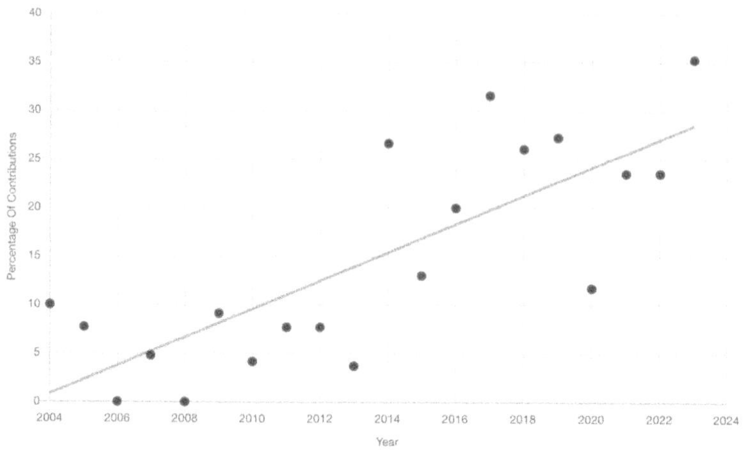

Fig. 2. Percentage of contributions per year presented at the WOA conference that deal with trust.

examine how trust dynamics influence the revision of existing knowledge. When new information is acquired, the level of trust in its source can significantly determine whether individuals or systems incorporate it into their knowledge base or discard it. Studies in this field are vital for understanding how trust shapes the evolution of knowledge and the integration of new insights in various domains, from scientific research to everyday decision-making.

Another interesting branch of work is that of recommender systems (10.5%). This category includes studies dedicated to providing personalized recommendations to users. Recommender systems are widely used across multiple domains, such as e-commerce, social media, entertainment, and online content platforms.

Furthermore, We have identified a series of works, labeled as "agent's property" (14%), that do not directly address trust but focus on various dimensions and characteristics of agents that impact their relationship with the user and, in general, with other agents. These works determine both how reliable agents are in performing a task, as in the case of autonomy, and how they are perceived in terms of reliability in delegation and execution, such as with explainability and transparency.

Besides these main categories, we also find a significant number of applied studies (35.1%), that are mainly interested in solving practical problems and on this basis they use already consolidated computational models of trust, possibly, adapting and modifying them for this purpose. These studies provide more concrete evidence and contribute to the empirical basis upon which many of the theoretical and computational models are founded. The fact that there is such a high percentage of these contributions also gives us a clear idea of how relevant the concept of trust is in practical terms.

This initial overview not only helps to understand the methodological diversity present in the literature but also serves as a foundation for critically evaluating the methodologies used and the implications of the results obtained.

Table 1. Classification of the contributions

Classification	Contributions
Computational model or solution intended to manage trust	[12, 15, 20, 112, 123, 135]
Theoretical/interaction model	[41, 45, 60, 66, 67, 100, 117, 131]
Trust on information/knowledge source	[52, 65, 96, 130, 134]
Recommender system	[1, 11, 42–44, 47, 102, 109, 113, 125]
Agents properties	[21, 24, 26, 28, 29, 32, 36, 126, 139, 152]
Practical application	[2, 46, 55, 62, 72, 78, 80, 92, 101, 114, 120, 136] [63, 73, 74, 79, 95, 115, 119, 121]

4 Results

The analysis of the contributions was aimed at identifying the main characteristics of the works and the issues addressed concerning trust. Furthermore, we examined how perspectives and approaches related to trust have evolved over time, comparing early studies with more recent ones.

Indeed, from this comprehensive analysis, several factors of particular interest emerge.

4.1 Computational Models of Trust

First of all, it should be emphasized that, even in the initial phases, particularly comprehensive models were proposed. For example, this is the case of [20], where the authors propose a rather articulated and theoretically grounded trust model. They:

1. Underline the insufficiency of security within multi-agent networks.
2. Are aware of the intrinsically dynamic nature of trust and the fact that it emerges as a result of multiple components.
3. Propose the use of the concept of trust to address the presence of malicious agents within the network.
4. Underline the link between trust, task, and context.
5. Evaluate trust in roles.
6. Support the positive vision of trust, stating that "it is more important to understand which could be the positive consequences of granting trust to a partner, rather than the negative ones (or risks) due to a bad evaluation.

Another noteworthy contribution is TRR [123], which combines reliability and reputation measures to construct a global trust evaluation for each agent. The authors define trustworthiness as an individual measure that an agent attributes to another agent in relation to a specific category of services. Therefore, the definition takes into account the task. The proposed model has been designed to adapt to changes in the system - thus the dynamic nature of trust is recognized - and to be robust to the presence of malicious agents, by relying on collective trust measures. The proposed approach takes into account both direct experiences (reliability) and the aggregated opinions of other agents (reputation). The overall trust in an agent is calculated as a weighted average of reliability and reputation, where the weight of each component varies dynamically. The peculiar characteristic of TRR is precisely the ability to dynamically calculate the weight associated with the two components, based on the number of interactions between the agents and the experience of the evaluating agent.

Furthermore, in [135], the authors propose a computational instantiation of the socio-cognitive model of trust [33]. The article specifically focuses on the importance and cognitive advantage of generalized knowledge. More specifically, the article experimentally investigates the role played by categories' reputation in comparison to the reputation and opinion of individual agents, aiming to understand if and when it is better to rely on the former type of trust source rather than the latter.

4.2 Centralized Approaches to Trust

In general, during the early years, several contributions proposed centralized or system-based solutions to the trust problem.

For example, in [12], trust is facilitated through an entity called the "Guarantor," which ensures the correctness of the information and tools used by the agents. Similarly, in [52], the figure of the "Yellow Rules Agent" is introduced, aimed at managing trust across the entire agent network by collecting feedback from the agents and subsequently providing recommendations on the best agents for each specialization.

Additionally, in [117], the authors propose the use of coordination artifacts, which act as mediation tools between agents, automating coordination activities and implementing coordination policies. The authors suggest that these artifacts can be used to track and observe the actions of agents, thereby improving the transparency and predictability of interactions.

4.3 Security Solutions for Trust

Another emerging trend during the early years of the conference is the tendency to use security solutions to manage trust. For example, this is the case of [2, 15, 112], which discuss the use of XML-based certificates for managing trust. The primary purpose of these articles is to propose frameworks and mechanisms for managing trust in decentralized systems. They aim to address the challenges posed by the lack of central authority and the need for secure inter-actions among unknown entities. In this sense, delegation chains have a central role. A delegation chain is a sequence of certificates or credentials where each certificate delegates some rights or privileges to another certificate. This chain represents a flow of trust that is transferred from one entity to another through various levels of delegation. Therefore, the main role of delegation chains is to establish a path of trust in environments where there is no central trusted authority. These chains allow agents or services to demonstrate that they have received permissions or rights from trusted entities, even if there is no direct relationship of trust between the initiator and the final recipient. XML certifi-cates are used to digitally represent credentials and attributes, facilitating the secure exchange of trust information. More recent works employ tools such as blockchain to trust anonymous and unknown actors and ensure data integrity without relying on other centralized third parties. Specifically, [115] proposed a dynamic car-pooling system using multi-agent, reputation, and blockchain tech-nologies to optimize car usage. The system included a central agency, personal agents on users' smartphones, and a permissioned blockchain for secure trans-actions. The approach aimed to provide a flexible, real-time car-pooling service with variable fares based on trip length and number of participants. It must be said that this kind of approaches to some extent force the concept of trust out-side its real canons. In fact, defining mechanisms that guarantee the certainty of correct behaviour contradicts at its basic ground the concept of trust which applies to worlds where failure remains to some extent possible.

4.4 Recommender Systems

Among the works, a topic closely related to trust also emerges: that of recom-mender systems. In fact, recommender systems, although not directly addressing the concept of trust, are inherently connected to it. Trust is crucial for users to accept and act upon the recommendations provided by the system. If the system consistently delivers relevant and useful recommendations, it enhances user trust and engagement. Moreover, transparency and explainability are vital aspects of recommender systems: when users understand the underlying mechanisms and rationale behind the recommendations, their trust in the system increases sig-nificantly [142,144,148,149]. These aspects are essential for fostering a reliable user-system relationship, ensuring that recommendations are perceived as cred-ible and trustworthy.

Let us now examine how this topic has been addressed within the WOA community. In [1], the authors propose a user profiling system based on their interests, which can be utilized, for example, in advertisement. Similarly, in [102], recommender systems are used to support patients in the daily management of chronic diseases. These systems leverage data collected through mobile devices and sensors to provide personalized feedback to patients, guiding them towards healthier lifestyle choices and optimizing their therapies. Another interesting aspect is group recommendations [11,125], where the interests, preferences, and needs of multiple users are mediated to provide a common recommendation.

In [109] authors proposed to promote car-sharing through a multi-agent system that monitored users' driving habits and builds their reputation scores. The system aimed to reduce operational costs, offer personalized fares, and make car-sharing more attractive to users and investors. In [113] authors proposed a framework to provide personalized recommendations to passengers based on their interests, location, and available commercial opportunities within the terminal. Recommendations were tailored by collecting preliminary information about passengers, tracking their movements, and considering their slack time. The paper [43] proposed a framework that exploits agents to provide personalized recommendations to passengers based on their interests, location, and available commercial opportunities within the terminal. Information about passengers were gathered through various means, including direct input and tracking via Wi-Fi/Bluetooth connections, while respecting privacy rules. Other works [42–44] exploit recommender systems based on MAS in order to recommend respectively POI (Point Of Interests), useful routes and destinations and bike availability at bike stations.

It is worth underlining that, although not present in the aforementioned works, recommender systems can also be used to recommend agents for specific tasks [90,132]. Furthermore, this tool can be combined with the inferential concept of categories, making it possible to recommend entire categories of agents [19,69,93]. This aspect is captured in some of the works produced within the WOA community, although these did not have a specific focus on recommendations [12,52].

4.5   Human-Agent Interaction and Dimensions of Trustworthiness

The increasing impact of intelligent systems in society and their integration into everyday life domains [59,108] have necessitated the design of these systems to trigger reliable dynamics with users. In this regard, intelligent systems, such as robots, to be perceived as trustworthy, must not only be able to correctly complete tasks delegated by humans but also show a strong intentionality to meet user needs and demonstrate their real motivations when interacting with humans [31,111,151]. For this reason, the trend in recent years, including within the WOA workshop, has been to investigate various dimensions and properties that artificial agents must have in their ability to interact with human agents, so that this interaction can be effective, useful, and above all, reliable. Transparency and consequently explainability are two concepts that have been explored in recent years at the WOA workshop. Specifically, the paper [21] discussed the importance of making AI systems interpretable and explainable to build trust and accountability, especially in critical fields like healthcare and finance. The authors present a framework that translates machine learning predictors into logical programs to provide narrative explanations for AI decisions. In another work [126], the authors explored the role of explainable clustering algorithms in the context of cognitive agents, which include both human users and AI systems. These algorithms offer numerous benefits, such as improved interpretability, increased trust, and more effective decision-making processes.

The paper [36] explored how robots can interact with humans to achieve common goals, emphasizing the importance of trust and self-modeling abilities in robots. By exploiting the trust model by Castelfranchi and Falcone [33], which includes self-modeling skills to enhance trust in HRI. Authors implemented a BDI robot able to justify its actions and improve trust. Seidita et al. [139] Focused the capability of robots to communicate their capabilities, intentions, and limitations clearly. Authors proposed a methodological approach for creating explainable agents, detailing phases like system requirements, team design, implementation, and testing. In the paper [152] a multi-level explainability framework for BDI agent systems were proposed, targeting developers, designers, and end-users. Authors identified three levels of abstraction: Implementation Level (technical details for developers), Knowledge Level (cognitive aspects for designers), and Domain Level (high-level behavior for end-users).

Cantucci and Falcone [26, 28, 29] investigated the impact of autonomy adaptation and behavior explaination as two fundamental capabilities in order to build trustworthy robots. They proposed experiments and computational cognitive models that try to demonstrate how autonomy and explainability play a fundamental role for fostering trustworthy HRI.

5   Discussion

The increasing impact of intelligent systems in society and their integration into everyday life domains raised up the need to design these systems in ways that foster trustworthy and effective interactions with users.

This analysis has confirmed the role of trust as a pivotal concept in managing the interactional complexity within multi-agent systems, highlighting its various components or facets, sometimes identified with different terms. Its function extends from reducing uncertainty to facilitating coordination and coalition formation among agents [129]. Trust allows agents to make reasonable assumptions about the reliability of others [70], thereby reducing the need for constant monitoring and improving overall cooperation. Regarding the theoretical aspects, although there is no explicit agreement, the complex nature of this concept has certainly been captured in the analyzed contributions. In trust modeling, important factors emerge such as its strong connection with the task being considered, its dependence on context, and its facets related to both competence and intentionality aspects. Contributions facing this topic emerged almost exclusively in the first half of the historical period we considered.

In recent years, however, there has been a tendency to focus on specific aspects related to trust. A big challenge in human-agent interaction is the design of autonomous systems that collaborate effectively with humans. For example, intelligent agents like robots becoming part of the daily life and are present in multiple environments (i.e. hospitals [83], schools [150], touristic scenarios [25]). In these contexts, robots have to coexist and interact with a wide spectrum of non expert users, that require to deal with artificial systems whose behaviors must be understandable and trustworthy. In these contexts, trustworthiness is not only a matter of safety or predictability, but above all has to be considered in terms of adaptive autonomy and behavior transparency. Numerous studies have explored the integration of cognitive capabilities into intelligent robotic systems [154], enabling them to interact with humans in ways that closely resemble human-to-human dynamics. Concepts such as Theory of Mind [137], explainability [8], and Adjustable Social Autonomy [30,33] have emerged as fundamental criteria in the design of such systems. These topics have been examined from both theoretical [27,147] perspectives and through empirical experimentation in various real-life scenarios [21,26,124]. Overall, the integration of trust-related aspects in autonomous systems, such as adaptive autonomy, behavior transparency, and cognitive capabilities, highlights a broader trend towards developing robots that are more than just tools: they are partners in daily life, capable of understanding, learning from, and adapting to human needs and preferences. As this field continues to advance, the collaboration between humans and robots will likely become more seamless, fostering environments where both can coexist and thrive harmoniously.

Equally relevant to other points is the issue of trust in information sources [6]. This is a problem that concerns both humans and artificial agents, and for the latter, the challenge is even more complex. It is necessary to identify proper mechanisms for detecting and managing incorrect information and to implement them within these agents. Generally, agents possess partial and limited knowledge of the world. When confronted with new information reported by external sources, it is not always possible to directly verify whether the information is true or not. Therefore, it is necessary to identify a mechanism that allows verifying whether this information is reliable (and thus can be internalized as their own, integrated with the rest of the knowledge, and used as a basis for reasoning and decision-making) or should be discarded. From the analyzed studies, trust has emerged as a crucial element in this process. Trust acts as a filter that helps us discern between valid information and potentially harmful or false information. For instance, an agent might want to attack another agent or a network of agents by spreading false information and beliefs. Moreover, due to the fact that the world of agents is characterized by limited beliefs and partial views of the world, an agent might report incorrect information simply because that is how it perceives it. Additionally, the reported information might simply be outdated [99]. Concerning the production of unreliable information, the phenomenon of hallucinations in Large Language Models is also of particular interest [89,153]. Undoubtedly, the trustworthiness of a source is closely related to the perceived quality of the information itself [86,146]. If it is true that it is necessary to equip artificial agents with a mechanism to discern correct information, this applies not only to the knowledge learned from the external world but also to the knowledge initially provided during training [106,118,140,155]. A discussion and reflection on the reliability of the information provided as the knowledge base to artificial agents is relevant. It is crucial to understand how reliable the a-priori knowledge given to these systems is, as the correctness of the reasoning they produce and the decision support they can provide depend on this.

A special mention must be made of what could be defined as *pseudo-trust*, which actually concerns two different trends. Firstly, it involves the attempt to use security solutions to manage trust. Security, as understood in computer science, and trust are two distinct and separate concepts, each with different goals [40, 64, 87]. Security focuses on protecting assets through three fundamental principles: confidentiality, integrity, and availability. Trust is a broader and more complex concept, especially when dealing with cognitive agents with social skills. Trust involves predicting the future behavior of an entity based on current information and past experiences, aimed at making the decision (and consequent action) to cooperate with potential partners. Trust aims to facilitate secure and cooperative interactions, reducing uncertainty and risk. Security solutions such as XML certificates and blockchain are important tools for ensuring communication security and the authenticity of digital identities. However, they do not fully address the problem of trust, which is a much broader and more complex concept. For example, these solutions are certainly excellent for confirming the identity of a person or entity. They can guarantee that the interlocutor is indeed who they claim to be. However, these tools cannot guarantee that the interlocutor will act correctly or that it is competent in a specific field. Trust requires predicting future behavior, which goes beyond simply confirming identity. Furthermore, these tools can secure digital transactions, reducing the risk of fraud and cyberattacks. But trust also involves assessing the intentions and reasons behind others' actions. For instance, a person can be authenticated and communicate securely but may have malicious intentions that are not detectable through certificates or blockchain. Therefore, while security solutions such as blockchain and XML certificates are essential for protecting communications and verifying identities, they cannot cover the entire range of aspects necessary to establish trust.

A second aspect of *pseudo-trust* concerns recommender systems. These systems are designed to help individuals make more informed decisions and find products, content, or services of interest, thereby facilitating decision-making processes. Additionally, recommender systems can be used in commercial contexts to increase sales by suggesting additional or alternative products that may interest the user. Another use is aimed at identifying reliable partners for executing specific tasks. In this sense, the recommendation is based on an evaluation of the trustworthiness of the partner in question. Thus, in general, these systems focus on optimizing the accuracy of the provided recommendations. Indeed, some systems use trust between users but always with this perspective: since user A trusts/distrusts user B - often without specifying reasons for this trust - they will trust/distrust the evaluations given by agent B. See, for instance, trust-enhanced recommender systems [145]. However, although often not considered or very limited, trust plays a fundamental role in this context. It is clear that if the recommender system is not trusted, the effectiveness of the provided recommendations will be lower, or even null. Note, for example, that individuals tend to trust recommendations more when provided by people they know rather than those given anonymously [143]. From this perspective, it is certainly necessary for the system to provide recommendations that meet the needs and desires of the user to increase the perception of the system's competence and reliability. At the same time, transparency in how the recommendations are generated can increase users' trust. Transparency is also necessary to understand the true interest motivating the recommendation [35]: within a market, is the recommendation provided in my interest or that of the seller? The recommendation is perceived as useful to the user because the recommender system knows the users better than they know themselves and is capable of producing highly "personalized" recommendations. However, this does not prove that the primary goal is not, as in marketing, to induce the user to believe, adhere, or buy. If users understand the system's decision-making process, they are more likely to trust the recommendations. Concerning all these aspects, there is ample room for improvement in the state of the art.

We would like to underline that this analysis took into consideration the articles published in the editions of WOA from 2000 to 2023. As for the 2024 edition, both the taxonomy and the trends identified in recent years are confirmed. More in detail: Agents properties [32, 85, 103, 138], Practical applications [16, 77], Theoretical/interaction model [133].

6   Conclusion

In summary, we could say that, in the early stages, research and the use of trust focused more on the fundamental aspects of trust, on the possibility of defining its fundamental characteristics and transferring them into a model capable of operating in the world of relations among artificial agents, of developing adequate computational models and of evaluating their limits and potential. The growing complexity of artificial systems, their pervasiveness in the individual e social life of all of us, the development of generative AI systems with the enormous potential to reproduce behaviours completely indistinguishable from those of humans in some areas, is putting the ways of relating to these systems at the center of scientific reflection and more generally intellectual evaluation. Trustworthiness and trust are therefore key factors on which it will be increasingly necessary to focus study and in-depth analysis in the future of scientific research on AI.

Acknowledgments. This chapter has been partially supported by the following projects: FAIR - Future Artificial Intelligence Research (MIUR-PNRR); TrustPACTX - Design of the Hybrid Society Humans-Autonomous Systems: Architecture, Trustworthiness, Trust, EthiCs, and EXplainability (the case of Patient Care) (MIUR-PRIN); ICRAS - Behavioral Interventions for Resilience to Environmental and Health Risks (MIUR-PNRR).

References

1. Addis, A., Armano, G., Vargiu, E.: Profiling users to perform contextual advertising. In: Bergenti [13], pp. 58–61. http://www.ailab.unipr.it/woa09/papers/Addis2.pdf
2. Agazzi, F., Tomaiuolo, M.: Trust negotiation for automated service integration. In: Baldoni, M., Baroglio, C., Bergenti, F., Garro, A. (eds.) WOA 2013 – 14th Workshop "From Objects to Agents". CEUR Workshop Proceedings, vol. 1099, pp. 97–103. Turin, Italy (2013). http://ceur-ws.org/Vol-1099/paper6.pdf
3. Agiollo, A., Calegari, R., Ciatto, G., Magnini, M., Omicini, A., Sabbatini, F.: Intelligent agents from symbolic to neurosymbolic systems: the quest for integration. In: Mascardi and Omicini [97]
4. Aguzzi, G., Casadei, R., Pianini, D., Viroli, M.: Self-organisation with aggregate computing: a reflection under the lenses of multi-agent systems engineering. In: Mascardi and Omicini [97]
5. Alderighi, M., Baldoni, M., Baroglio, C., Micalizio, R., Tedeschi, S.: WOA 2024 – 25th Workshop "From Objects to Agents", CEUR Workshop Proceedings, vol. 3735. Bard, AO, Italy (2024). http://ceur-ws.org/Vol-3735/
6. Amgoud, L., Demolombe, R.: An argumentation-based approach for reasoning about trust in information sources. Argument Comput. 5(2–3), 191–215 (2014)
7. Ancona, D., Briola, D., Ferrando, A., Martelli, M., Mascardi, V.: 25 years of declarative agent technologies in Italy. In: Mascardi and Omicini [97]
8. Anjomshoae, S., Najjar, A., Calvaresi, D., Främling, K.: Explainable agents and robots: results from a systematic literature review. In: 18th International Conference on Autonomous Agents and Multiagent Systems (AAMAS 2019), Montreal, Canada, May 13–17, 2019, pp. 1078–1088. International Foundation for Autonomous Agents and Multiagent Systems (2019)
9. Baldoni, M., Boccalatte, A., De Paoli, F., Martelli, M., Mascardi, V.: WOA 2007 – 8th Workshop "From Objects to Agents". Seneca Edizioni Torino, Genova, Italy (2007). http://woa07.disi.unige.it/ProceedingsWOA2007.zip
10. Baldoni, M., De Paoli, F., Martelli, A., Omicini, A.: WOA 2004 – 5th Workshop "From Objects to Agents". Pitagora Editrice Bologna, Torino, Italy (2004). http://lia.deis.unibo.it/books/woa2004/atti.pdf
11. Barile, F., Caso, A., Rossi, S.: Group recommendation for smart applications: a multi-agent view of the problem. In: Santoro and Bergenti [27], pp. 12–17. http://ceur-ws.org/Vol-1260/paper7.pdf
12. Bergenti, F.: Secure, trusted and privacy-aware interactions in large-scale multiagent systems. In: Corradini et al. [50], pp. 144–150. http://lia.deis.unibo.it/books/woa2005/papers/20.pdf
13. Bergenti, F.: WOA 2009 – 10th Workshop "From Objects to Agents". Seneca Edizioni Torino, Parma, Italy (2009). http://www.ailab.unipr.it/woa09/papers/
14. Bergenti, F., Monica, S.: WOA 2019 – 20th Workshop "From Objects to Agents", CEUR Workshop Proceedings, vol. 2404. Parma, Italy (2019). http://ceur-ws.org/Vol-2404/
15. Bergenti, F., Rossi, L., Tomaiuolo, M.: Towards automated trust negotiation in MAS. In: Bergenti [13], pp. 76–81. http://www.ailab.unipr.it/woa09/papers/Bergenti1.pdf
16. Bordini, R.H., Costantini, S., Monaldini, A., Vozna, A.: From pure Prolog to logic agent-oriented programming languages. In: Alderighi et al. [5], pp. 271–285. http://ceur-ws.org/Vol-3735/paper_20.pdf

17. Bouleanu, D.C., Loaiza Carrillo, M.A., Savaglio, C., Bădică, C., Gravina, R., Fortino, G.: From objects to agents, and back to smart objects: software agents for intelligent Internet of Things (IoT) systems. In: Mascardi and Omicini [97]
18. Burnett, C., Norman, T.J., Sycara, K.: Trust decision-making in multi-agent systems. In: Twenty-Second International Joint Conference on Artificial Intelligence (2011)
19. Burnett, C., Norman, T.J., Sycara, K.: Stereotypical trust and bias in dynamic multiagent systems. ACM Trans. Intell. Syst. Technol. (TIST) 4(2), 1–22 (2013)
20. Cabri, G., Ferrari, L., Leonardi, L.: Evaluating trust among agents. In: Baldoni et al. [10], pp. 1–4. http://giuseppevizzari.github.io/WOA-proceedings-archive/pdfs/woa2004/1.pdf
21. Calegari, R., Ciatto, G., Dellaluce, J., Omicini, A.: Interpretable narrative explanation for ML predictors with LP: a case study for XAI. In: Bergenti and Monica [14], pp. 105–112. http://ceur-ws.org/Vol-2404/paper16.pdf
22. Calegari, R., Ciatto, G., Denti, E., Omicini, A., Sartor, G.: WOA 2020 – 21st Workshop "From Objects to Agents", CEUR Workshop Proceedings, vol. 2706. Bologna, Italy (2020). http://ceur-ws.org/Vol-2706/
23. Calegari, R., Ciatto, G., Denti, E., Omicini, A., Sartor, G.: WOA 2021 – 22nd Workshop "From Objects to Agents", CEUR Workshop Proceedings, vol. 2963. Bologna, Italy (2021). http://ceur-ws.org/Vol-2963/
24. Cantucci, F., Falcone, R.: A computational model for cognitive human-robot interaction: an approach based on theory of delegation. In: Bergenti and Monica [14], pp. 127–133. http://ceur-ws.org/Vol-2404/paper19.pdf
25. Cantucci, F., Falcone, R.: Autonomous critical help by a robotic assistant in the field of cultural heritage: a new challenge for evolving human-robot interaction. Multimodal Technol. Interact. 6(8), 69 (2022a)
26. Cantucci, F., Falcone, R.: Autonomous critical help provided by an artificial agent in the field of cultural heritage. In: Ferrando and Mascardi [71], pp. 152–163. http://ceur-ws.org/Vol-3261/paper12.pdf
27. Cantucci, F., Falcone, R.: Collaborative autonomy: human-robot interaction to the test of intelligent help. Electronics 11(19), 3065 (2022b)
28. Cantucci, F., Falcone, R.: A cognitive approach to model intelligent collaboration in human-robot interaction. In: Falcone et al. [61], pp. 138–150. http://ceur-ws.org/Vol-3579/paper10.pdf
29. Cantucci, F., Falcone, R., Castelfranchi, C.: Investigating adjustable social autonomy in human robot interaction. In: Calegari et al. [23], pp. 49–60. http://ceur-ws.org/Vol-2963/paper12.pdf
30. Cantucci, F., Falcone, R., Castelfranchi, C.: Human-robot interaction through adjustable social autonomy. Intelligenza Artificiale 16(1), 69–79 (2022)
31. Cantucci, F., Falcone, R., Marini, M.: Redefining user expectations: the impact of adjustable social autonomy in human-robot interaction. Electronics 13(1), 127 (2023)
32. Cantucci, F., Marini, M., Falcone, R.: Effects of robot's adaptive autonomy on users experience in a museum scenario. In: Alderighi et al. [5], pp. 5–19. http://ceur-ws.org/Vol-3735/paper_01.pdf
33. Castelfranchi, C., Falcone, R.: Trust Theory: A Socio-Cognitive and Computational Model. Wiley, Hoboken (2010)
34. Castelfranchi, C.: The cognition of conflict: ontology, dynamics, and ideology. Conflict and Multimodal Communication: Social Research and Machine Intelligence, pp. 3–32 (2015)

35. Castelfranchi, C.: For a science-oriented, socially responsible, and self-aware AI: beyond ethical issues. In: 2020 IEEE International Conference on Human-Machine Systems (ICHMS), pp. 1–4. IEEE (2020)

36. Castelfranchi, C., Chella, A., Falcone, R., Lanza, F., Seidita, V.: Endowing robots with self-modeling abilities for trustful human-robot interactions. In: Bergenti and Monica [14], pp. 22–28. http://ceur-ws.org/Vol-2404/paper04.pdf

37. Castelfranchi, C., Falcone, R.: Delegation conflicts. In: Multi-Agent Rationality: 8th European Workshop on Modelling Autonomous Agents in a Multi-Agent World, MAAMAW'97 Ronneby, Sweden, May 13–16, 1997 Proceedings 8, pp. 234–254. Springer, Cham (1997)

38. Castelfranchi, C., Falcone, R.: Principles of trust for mas: cognitive anatomy, social importance, and quantification. In: Proceedings International Conference on Multi Agent Systems (Cat. No. 98EX160), pp. 72–79. IEEE (1998)

39. Castelfranchi, C., Falcone, R., Marzo, F.: Being trusted in a social network: trust as relational capital. In: International Conference on Trust Management, pp. 19–32. Springer, Cham (2006)

40. Castelfranchi, C., Tan, Y.H.: Trust and Deception in Virtual Societies. Springer, Cham (2001)

41. Castelli, G., Mamei, M., Rosi, A., Zambonelli, F.: Behavior predictability despite non-determinism in the SAPERE ecosystem preliminary ideas. In: De Paoli and Vizzari [57], pp. 82–88. http://ceur-ws.org/Vol-892/paper8.pdf

42. Cavallaro, C., Tramontana, E.: User assistance for predicting the availability of bikes at bike stations. In: Calegari et al. [23], pp. 132–143. http://ceur-ws.org/Vol-2963/paper15.pdf

43. Cavallaro, C., Verga, G., Tramontana, E., Muscato, O.: Multi-agent architecture for point of interest detection and recommendation. In: Bergenti and Monica [14], pp. 98–104. http://ceur-ws.org/Vol-2404/paper15.pdf

44. Cavallaro, C., Verga, G., Tramontana, E., Muscato, O.: Suggesting just enough (un)crowded routes and destinations. In: Calegari et al. [22], pp. 237–251. http://ceur-ws.org/Vol-2706/paper17.pdf

45. Cervone, F., Sica, V., Staffa, M., Tamburro, A., Rossi, S.: Comparing a social robot and a mobile application for movie recommendation: a pilot study. In: Napoli, D., (eds.) et al. [58], pp. 32–38. http://ceur-ws.org/Vol-1382/paper5.pdf

46. Comi, A., Fotia, L.: Combining reliability, reputation and honesty to enhance QoS on federated computing infrastructures. In: Cossentino et al. [51], pp. 45–50. http://ceur-ws.org/Vol-2215/paper_8.pdf

47. Comi, A., Rosaci, D.: SMARTSAN: a P2P social agent network for generating recommendations in a smart city environment. In: De Meo et al. [56], pp. 108–112. http://ceur-ws.org/Vol-1867/w19.pdf

48. Conte, R., Paolucci, M.: Reputation in Artificial Societies: Social Beliefs for Social Order, vol. 6. Springer, Cham (2002)

49. Cook, K.: Trust in Society. Russell Sage Foundation (2001)

50. Corradini, F., De Paoli, F., Merelli, E., Omicini, A.: WOA 2005 – 6th Workshop "From Objects to Agents". Pitagora Editrice Bologna, Camerino, MC, Italy (2005). http://lia.deis.unibo.it/books/woa2005/atti.pdf

51. Cossentino, M., Sabatucci, L., Seidita, V.: WOA 2018 – 19th Workshop "From Objects to Agents", CEUR Workshop Proceedings, vol. 2215. Palermo, Italy (2018). http://ceur-ws.org/Vol-2215/

52. Costantini, S., Tocchio, A.: Learning by knowledge exchange in logical agents. In: Corradini et al. [50], pp. 1–8. http://lia.deis.unibo.it/books/woa2005/papers/1.pdf

53. Cowan, B.R., et al.: "what can i help you with?" infrequent users' experiences of intelligent personal assistants. In: Proceedings of the 19th International Conference on Human-Computer Interaction with Mobile Devices and Services, pp. 1–12 (2017)

54. Das, T.K., Teng, B.S.: Between trust and control: developing confidence in partner cooperation in alliances. Acad. Manag. Rev. **23**(3), 491–512 (1998)

55. De Meo, P., Messina, F., Rosaci, D., Sarné, G.M.L.: Supporting learner-to-learner interactions using online social network information. In: Santoro et al. [128], pp. 56–61. http://ceur-ws.org/Vol-1664/w10.pdf

56. De Meo, P., Postorino, M.N., Rosaci, D., Sarné, G.M.L.: WOA 2017 – 18th Workshop "From Objects to Agents", CEUR Workshop Proceedings, vol. 1867. Scilla, RC, Italy (2017). http://ceur-ws.org/Vol-1867/

57. De Paoli, F., Vizzari, G.: WOA 2012 – 13th Workshop "From Objects to Agents", CEUR Workshop Proceedings, vol. 892. Milano, Italy (2012). http://ceur-ws.org/Vol-892/

58. Di Napoli, C., Rossi, S., Staffa, M.: WOA 2015 – 16th Workshop "From Objects to Agents", CEUR Workshop Proceedings, vol. 1382. Naples, Italy (2015). http://ceur-ws.org/Vol-1382/

59. Doncieux, S., Chatila, R., Straube, S., Kirchner, F.: Human-centered ai and robotics. AI. Perspectives **4**(1), 1 (2022)

60. Falcone, R., Castelfranchi, C.: Transitivity in trust: a discussed property. In: Omicini and Viroli [107], pp. 155–160. http://ceur-ws.org/Vol-621/paper22.pdf

61. Falcone, R., Castelfranchi, C., Sapienza, A., Cantucci, F.: WOA 2023 – 24th Workshop "From Objects to Agents", CEUR Workshop Proceedings, vol. 3579. Roma, Italy (2023). http://ceur-ws.org/Vol-3579/

62. Falcone, R., Sapienza, A.: How can subjective impulsivity play a role among information sources in weather scenarios? In: De Meo et al. [56], pp. 19–24. http://ceur-ws.org/Vol-1867/w4.pdf

63. Falcone, R., Sapienza, A.: Institutional alarmism and the damage it provokes in case of hydrogeological disasters: a simulative estimation. In: Cossentino et al. [51], pp. 21–26. http://ceur-ws.org/Vol-2215/paper_4.pdf

64. Falcone, R., Sapienza, A.: On the users' acceptance of IoT systems: a theoretical approach. Information **9**(3), 53 (2018)

65. Falcone, R., Sapienza, A.: Information seeking behavior at the time of COVID-19. In: Calegari et al. [23], pp. 241–258. http://ceur-ws.org/Vol-2963/paper8.pdf

66. Falcone, R., Sapienza, A.: The role of decisional autonomy in user-IoT systems interaction. In: Ferrando and Mascardi [71], pp. 77–87. http://ceur-ws.org/Vol-3261/paper6.pdf

67. Falcone, R., Sapienza, A.: Dependence networks and trust in agents societies: Insights and practical implications. In: Falcone et al. [61], pp. 106–122. http://ceur-ws.org/Vol-3579/paper8.pdf

68. Falcone, R., Sapienza, A., Cantucci, F., Castelfranchi, C.: To be trustworthy and to trust: the new frontier of intelligent systems. Handb. Hum.-Mach. Syst. 213–223 (2023)

69. Falcone, R., Sapienza, A., Castelfranchi, C.: Recommendation of categories in an agents world: the role of (not) local communicative environments. In: 2015 13th Annual Conference on Privacy, Security and Trust (PST), pp. 7–13. IEEE (2015)

70. Falcone, R., Sapienza, A., Castelfranchi, C.: Trusting information sources through their categories. In: Advances in Practical Applications of Agents, Multi-Agent

Systems, and Sustainability: The PAAMS Collection: 13th International Conference, PAAMS 2015, Salamanca, Spain, June 3-4, 2015, Proceedings 13, pp. 80–92. Springer, Cham (2015)

71. Ferrando, A., Mascardi, V.: WOA 2022 – 23rd Workshop "From Objects to Agents", CEUR Workshop Proceedings, vol. 3261. Genova, Italy (2022). http://ceur-ws.org/Vol-3261/

72. Fornaia, A., Napoli, C., Pappalardo, G., Tramontana, E.: Using AOP neural networks to infer user behaviours and interests. In: Di Napoli et al. [58], pp. 46–52. http://ceur-ws.org/Vol-1382/paper7.pdf

73. Fortino, G., Fotia, L., Messina, F., Rosaci, D., Sarné, G.M.L.: Supporting agent CoT groups formation by trust. In: Bergenti and Monica [58], pp. 71–76. http://ceur-ws.org/Vol-2404/paper11.pdf

74. Fortino, G., Fotia, L., Messina, F., Rosaci, D., Sarné, G.M.L., Savaglio, C.: A trust model to form teams of agentified AGVs in workshop areas. In: Calegari et al. [14], pp. 61–71. http://ceur-ws.org/Vol-2963/paper2.pdf

75. Fortino, G., Fotia, L., Messina, F., Rosaci, D., Sarnè, G.M.: Trust and reputation in the internet of things: state-of-the-art and research challenges. IEEE Access **8**, 60117–60125 (2020)

76. Fortino, G., Garro, A., Palopoli, L., Russo, W., Spezzano, G.: WOA 2011 – 12th Workshop "From Objects to Agents", CEUR Workshop Proceedings, vol. 741. Rende, Italy (2011). http://ceur-ws.org/Vol-741/

77. Fortino, G., Rosaci, D., Sarné, G.M.L.: Improving computational efficiency of the TONS algorithm in selecting neighbor agents in blockchain trust-based IoT environments. In: Alderighi et al. [5], pp. 84–97. http://ceur-ws.org/Vol-3735/paper_07.pdf

78. Fotia, L.: Generating trust-based recommendations for social networks organized by groups. In: De Meo et al. [56], pp. 49–54. http://ceur-ws.org/Vol-1867/w9.pdf

79. Fotia, L.: Recommending items in social networks using cliques-based trust. In: Cossentino et al. [51], pp. 51–56. http://ceur-ws.org/Vol-2215/paper_9.pdf

80. Fotia, L., Messina, F., Rosaci, D., Sarné, G.M.L.: On the impact of trust relationships on social network group formation. In: De Meo et al. [56], pp. 25–30. http://ceur-ws.org/Vol-1867/w5.pdf

81. Frederiksen, M.: Trust in the face of uncertainty: a qualitative study of intersubjective trust and risk. Int. Rev. Sociol. **24**(1), 130–144 (2014)

82. Gill, T.: Ethical dilemmas are really important to potential adopters of autonomous vehicles. Ethics Inf. Technol. **23**(4), 657–673 (2021)

83. González-González, C.S., Violant-Holz, V., Gil-Iranzo, R.M.: Social robots in hospitals: a systematic review. Appl. Sci. **11**(13), 5976 (2021)

84. Govier, T.: Social Trust and Human Communities. McGill-Queen's Press-MQUP (1997)

85. Grimaldi, C., Rossi, S.: Towards transparent computational models of theory of mind in collaborative environments. In: Alderighi et al. [5], pp. 73–83. http://ceur-ws.org/Vol-3735/paper_06.pdf

86. Hertzum, M., Andersen, H.H., Andersen, V., Hansen, C.B.: Trust in information sources: seeking information from people, documents, and virtual agents. Interact. Comput. **14**(5), 575–599 (2002)

87. Hoffman, L.J., Lawson-Jenkins, K., Blum, J.: Trust beyond security: an expanded trust model. Commun. ACM **49**(7), 94–101 (2006)

88. Huynh, T.D., Jennings, N.R., Shadbolt, N.R.: An integrated trust and reputation model for open multi-agent systems. Auton. Agent. Multi-Agent Syst. **13**, 119–154 (2006)

89. Ji, Z., Yu, T., Xu, Y., Lee, N., Ishii, E., Fung, P.: Towards mitigating LLM hallucination via self reflection. In: Findings of the Association for Computational Linguistics: EMNLP 2023, pp. 1827–1843 (2023)
90. Keung, S.N.L.C., Griffiths, N.: Towards improved partner selection using recommendations and trust. In: International Workshop on Trust in Agent Societies, pp. 43–64. Springer, Cham (2008)
91. Klewes, J., Wreschniok, R.: Reputation capital building and maintaining trust in the 21st century. In: Reputation Capital: Building and Maintaining Trust in the 21st Century, pp. 1–8. Springer, Cham (2009)
92. Liotta, A., Messina, F., Rosaci, D., Sarné, G.M.L.: Effective group formation in agent societies. In: Cossentino et al. [51], pp. 39–44. http://ceur-ws.org/Vol-2215/paper_7.pdf
93. Liu, X., Datta, A., Rzadca, K.: Trust beyond reputation: a computational trust model based on stereotypes. Electron. Commer. Res. Appl. **12**(1), 24–39 (2013)
94. Mahdi, H., Akgun, S.A., Saleh, S., Dautenhahn, K.: A survey on the design and evolution of social robots–past, present and future. Robot. Auton. Syst. **156**, 104193 (2022)
95. Marcianò, A.: Accurate colluding agents detection by reputation measures. In: Ferrando and Mascardi [71], pp. 219–231. http://ceur-ws.org/Vol-3261/paper17.pdf
96. Marcianò, A., Rosaci, D., Sarnè, G.M.L.: A strategy to detect colluding groups by reputation measures. In: Falcone et al. [61], pp. 92–105. http://ceur-ws.org/Vol-3579/paper7.pdf
97. Mascardi, V., Omicini, A.: The Agents Journey: Twenty-five Years of Multi-agent Systems at WOA. Lecture Notes in Computer Science – State-of-the-Art Surveys, Springer (2026)
98. Matthews, P., Greenspan, S., Matthews, P., Greenspan, S.: Robots in teams. Automation and Collaborative Robotics: A Guide to the Future of Work, pp. 109–140 (2020)
99. Melo, V.S., Panisson, A.R., Bordini, R.H.: Trust on beliefs: source, time and expertise. In: Proceedings of the 18th International Workshop on Trust in Agent Societies co-located with the 15th International Conference on Autonomous Agents and Multiagent Systems (TRUST@ AAMAS 2016), 2016, Cingapura (2016)
100. Meo, P.D., Falcone, R., Sapienza, A.: Applying inferential processes to partner selection in large agents communities. In: Calegari et al. [22], pp. 15–27. http://ceur-ws.org/Vol-2706/paper6.pdf
101. Messina, F., Rosaci, D., De Meo, P., Sarné, G.M.L.: Improving agent group homogeneity over time. In: De Meo et al. [56], pp. 37–42. http://ceur-ws.org/Vol-1867/w7.pdf
102. Montagna, S., Omicini, A., Angeli, F.D., Donati, M.: Towards the adoption of agent-based modelling and simulation in mobile health systems for the self-management of chronic diseases. In: Santoro et al. [128], pp. 100–105. http://ceur-ws.org/Vol-1664/w17.pdf
103. Montagna, S., Sirocchi, C.: Hybrid personal medical digital assistant agents. In: Alderighi et al. [5], pp. 58–72. http://ceur-ws.org/Vol-3735/paper_05.pdf
104. Morrone, A., Tontoranelli, N., Ranuzzi, G.: How good is trust?: measuring trust and its role for the progress of societies. OECD Statistics Working Papers 2009/03, OECD (2009). https://doi.org/10.1787/220633873086

105. Nhu Phu, D., Cong Vinh, P., Kim Quoc, N.: A self-organization model for mas based on trust. In: International Conference on Nature of Computation and Communication, pp. 52–69. Springer, Cham (2023)
106. Noor, P.: Can we trust AI not to further embed racial bias and prejudice? BMJ **368** (2020)
107. Omicini, A., Viroli, M.: WOA 2010 – 11th Workshop "From Objects to Agents", CEUR Workshop Proceedings, vol. 621. Rimini, Italy (2010). http://ceur-ws.org/Vol-621/
108. Perconti, P., Plebe, A.: Anthropomorphizing and trusting social robots. In: Challenges of the Technological Mind: Between Philosophy and Technology, pp. 29–42. Springer, Cham (2024)
109. Picasso, E., Postorino, M.N., Sarné, G.M.L.: A study to promote car-sharing by adopting a reputation system in a multi-agent context. In: De Meo et al. [56], pp. 13–18. http://ceur-ws.org/Vol-1867/w3.pdf
110. Pinyol, I., Sabater-Mir, J.: Computational trust and reputation models for open multi-agent systems: a review. Artif. Intell. Rev. **40**(1), 1–25 (2013)
111. Pipitone, A., Geraci, A., D'Amico, A., Seidita, V., Chella, A.: Robot's inner speech effects on human trust and anthropomorphism. Int. J. Soc. Robot. **16**(6), 1333–1345 (2024)
112. Poggi, A., Tomaiuolo, M.: XML-based trust management in MAS. In: Baldoni et al. [9], pp. 126–131. http://woa07.disi.unige.it/papers/PoggiTrust.pdf
113. Postorino, M.N., Mantecchini, L.: An agent framework to support air passengers in departure terminals. In: Cossentino et al. [51], pp. 75–80. http://ceur-ws.org/Vol-2215/paper_13.pdf
114. Postorino, M.N., Sarnè, G.M.L.: An agent-based sensor grid to monitor urban traffic. In: Santoro and Bergenti [127], pp. 18–23. http://ceur-ws.org/Vol-1260/paper2.pdf
115. Postorino, M.N., Sarné, G.M.L.: A preliminary study for an agent blockchain-based framework supporting dynamic car-pooling. In: Bergenti and Monica [14], pp. 65–70. http://ceur-ws.org/Vol-2404/paper10.pdf
116. Ramchurn, S.D., Huynh, D., Jennings, N.R.: Trust in multi-agent systems. Knowl. Eng. Rev. **19**(1), 1–25 (2004). https://doi.org/10.1017/S0269888904000116
117. Ricci, A., Omicini, A.: Engineering trust in complex system through mediating infrastructures. In: Baldoni et al. [10], pp. 110–115. http://giuseppevizzari.github.io/WOA-proceedings-archive/pdfs/woa2004/16.pdf
118. Rich, A.S., Gureckis, T.M.: Lessons for artificial intelligence from the study of natural stupidity. Nat. Mach. Intell. **1**(4), 174–180 (2019)
119. Rosaci, D., Sacchi, S., Sarné, G.M.L.: Modeling dynamic web polarization and proximity depolarization processes by compactness measures. In: Ferrando and Mascardi [71], pp. 88–100. http://ceur-ws.org/Vol-3261/paper7.pdf
120. Rosaci, D., Sarnè, G.M.L.: Supporting evolution in learning information agents. In: Fortino et al. [76], pp. 89–94. http://ceur-ws.org/Vol-741/ID5_RosaciSarne.pdf
121. Rosaci, D., Sarnè, G.M.L.: An agent-based architecture to recommend educational video. In: Santoro and Bergenti [127], pp. 1–6. http://ceur-ws.org/Vol-1260/paper1.pdf
122. Rosaci, D., Sarnè, G.M.L.: Looking for the best partners. In: Mascardi and Omicini [97]
123. Rosaci, D., Sarnè, G.M.L., Garruzzo, S.: TRR· an integrated reliability-reputation model for agent societies. In: Fortino et al. [76], pp. 28–33. http://ceur-ws.org/Vol-741/ID6_RosaciSarneGarruzzo.pdf

124. Rossi, A., Andriella, A., Rossi, S., Torras, C., Alenyà, G.: Evaluating the effect of theory of mind on people's trust in a faulty robot. In: 2022 31st IEEE International Conference on Robot and Human Interactive Communication (RO-MAN), pp. 477–482. IEEE (2022)

125. Rossi, S., Di Napoli, C., Barile, F., Liguori, L.: Conflict resolution profiles and agent negotiation for group recommendations. In: Santoro et al. [128], pp. 29–34. http://ceur-ws.org/Vol-1664/w6.pdf

126. Sabbatini, F., Calegari, R.: Unlocking insights and trust: the value of explainable clustering algorithms for cognitive agents. In: Falcone et al. [61], pp. 232–245. http://ceur-ws.org/Vol-3579/paper18.pdf

127. Santoro, C., Bergenti, F.: WOA 2014 – 15th Workshop "From Objects to Agents", CEUR Workshop Proceedings, vol. 1260. Catania, Italy (2014). http://ceur-ws.org/Vol-1260/

128. Santoro, C., Messina, F., De Benedetti, M.: WOA 2016 – 17th Workshop "From Objects to Agents", CEUR Workshop Proceedings, vol. 1664. Catania, Italy (2016). http://ceur-ws.org/Vol-1664/

129. Sapienza, A., Cantucci, F., Falcone, R.: Modeling interaction in human-machine systems: a trust and trustworthiness approach. Automation **3**(2), 242–257 (2022)

130. Sapienza, A., Falcone, R.: A Bayesian computational model for trust on information sources. In: Santoro et al. [128], pp. 50–55. http://ceur-ws.org/Vol-1664/w9.pdf

131. Sapienza, A., Falcone, R.: A theoretical model for the human-IoT systems interaction. In: Bergenti and Monica [14], pp. 90–97. http://ceur-ws.org/Vol-2404/paper14.pdf

132. Sapienza, A., Falcone, R.: Evaluating agents' trustworthiness within virtual societies in case of no direct experience. Cogn. Syst. Res. **64**, 164–173 (2020)

133. Sapienza, A., Falcone, R.: Exploring the dynamics of learned, pre-existing, and partial knowledge in dependence networks within multi-agent systems. In: Alderighi et al. [5], pp. 129–141. http://ceur-ws.org/Vol-3735/paper_10.pdf

134. Sapienza, A., Falcone, R., Castelfranchi, C.: Trust on information sources: a theoretical and computational approach. In: Santoro and Bergenti [127], pp. 7–11. http://ceur-ws.org/Vol-1260/paper12.pdf

135. Sapienza, A., Falcone, R., Castelfranchi, C.: The positive power of prejudice: a computational model for MAS. In: Di Napoli et al. [58], pp. 39–45. http://ceur-ws.org/Vol-1382/paper6.pdf

136. Sarnè, G.M.L.: A reputation agent model for reliable vehicle-to-vehicle information. In: Cossentino et al. [51], pp. 33–38. http://ceur-ws.org/Vol-2215/paper_6.pdf

137. Scassellati, B.: Theory of mind for a humanoid robot. Auton. Robot. **12**, 13–24 (2002)

138. Seidita, V., Chella, A.: Enhancing robotic systems in healthcare: a preliminary analysis of agent-based paradigms and simulation environments. In: Alderighi et al. [5], pp. 200–208. http://ceur-ws.org/Vol-3735/paper_15.pdf

139. Seidita, V., Sabella, A.M.P., Chella, A.: Agents showing self-disclosure. A preliminary methodological approach. In: Falcone et al. [61], pp. 78–91. http://ceur-ws.org/Vol-3579/paper6.pdf

140. Shah, M., Sureja, N.: A comprehensive review of bias in deep learning models: methods, impacts, and future directions. Arch. Comput. Methods Eng. 1–13 (2024)

141. Siegrist, M.: Trust and risk perception: a critical review of the literature. Risk Anal. **41**(3), 480–490 (2021)

142. Sinha, R., Swearingen, K.: The role of transparency in recommender systems. In: CHI 2002 Extended Abstracts on Human Factors in Computing Systems, pp. 830–831 (2002)
143. Sinha, R.R., Swearingen, K., et al.: Comparing recommendations made by online systems and friends. DELOS **106**(1), 1–6 (2001)
144. Sonboli, N., Smith, J.J., Cabral Berenfus, F., Burke, R., Fiesler, C.: Fairness and transparency in recommendation: the users' perspective. In: Proceedings of the 29th ACM Conference on User Modeling, Adaptation and Personalization, pp. 274–279 (2021)
145. Victor, P., De Cock, M., Cornelis, C.: Trust and Recommendations. Recommender Systems Handbook, pp. 645–675 (2011)
146. Villata, S., Boella, G., Gabbay, D.M., Van Der Torre, L.: Arguing about the trustworthiness of the information sources. In: Symbolic and Quantitative Approaches to Reasoning with Uncertainty: 11th European Conference, ECSQARU 2011, Belfast, UK, June 29–July 1, 2011. Proceedings 11, pp. 74–85. Springer, Cham (2011)
147. Vinanzi, S., Patacchiola, M., Chella, A., Cangelosi, A.: Would a robot trust you? Developmental robotics model of trust and theory of mind. Philos. Trans. R. Soc. B **374**(1771), 20180032 (2019)
148. Vorm, E., Miller, A.D.: Assessing the value of transparency in recommender systems: An end-user perspective. In: Brusilovsky, P., de Gemmis, M., Felfernig, A., Lops, P., O'Donovan, J., Semeraro, G., Willemsen, M.C. (eds.) Proceedings of the 5th Joint Workshop on Interfaces and Human Decision Making for Recommender Systems, IntRS 2018, co-located with ACM Conference on Recommender Systems (RecSys 2018), Vancouver, Canada, October 7, 2018. CEUR Workshop Proceedings, vol. 2225, pp. 61–68. CEUR-WS.org (2018). https://ceur-ws.org/Vol-2225/paper9.pdf
149. Vultureanu-Albişi, A., Bădică, C.: Recommender systems: an explainable ai perspective. In: 2021 International conference on innovations in intelligent systems and applications (INISTA), pp. 1–6. IEEE (2021)
150. Woo, H., LeTendre, G.K., Pham-Shouse, T., Xiong, Y.: The use of social robots in classrooms: a review of field-based studies. Educ. Res. Rev. **33**, 100388 (2021)
151. Xie, Y., Bodala, I.P., Ong, D.C., Hsu, D., Soh, H.: Robot capability and intention in trust-based decisions across tasks. In: 2019 14th ACM/IEEE International Conference on Human-Robot Interaction (HRI), pp. 39–47. IEEE (2019)
152. Yan, E., Burattini, S., Hübner, J.F., Ricci, A.: Towards a multi-level explainability framework for engineering and understanding BDI agent systems. In: Falcone et al. [61], pp. 216–231. http://ceur-ws.org/Vol-3579/paper17.pdf
153. Yao, J.Y., Ning, K.P., Liu, Z.H., Ning, M.N., Yuan, L.: LLM lies: hallucinations are not bugs, but features as adversarial examples. arXiv preprint arXiv:2310.01469 (2023)
154. Ye, P., Wang, T., Wang, F.Y.: A survey of cognitive architectures in the past 20 years. IEEE Trans. Cybern. **48**(12), 3280–3290 (2018)
155. Yeh, K.C., Chi, J.A., Lian, D.C., Hsieh, S.K.: Evaluating interfaced LLM bias. In: Proceedings of the 35th Conference on Computational Linguistics and Speech Processing (ROCLING 2023), pp. 292–299 (2023)

Designing Agent Interaction: Putting MAS Together

Interaction Protocols: From AUML to Social Commitments, from Artifacts to BSPL

Matteo Baldoni, Cristina Baroglio, and Roberto Micalizio^(✉)

Università degli Studi di Torino, Turin, Italy
`{matteo.baldoni,cristina.baroglio,roberto.micalizio}@unito.it`

Abstract. This chapter surveys the contributions of the WOA workshop series to the area of *interaction protocols* for communicating agents. Interaction protocols are among the main means for agent coordination, and have drawn the attention of many researchers within the WOA community, and internationally, since the effectiveness and scalability of a distributed systems may strongly depend on how interacting protocols are specified and implemented.

The chapter reviews the diverse approaches in literature starting from message passing, with protocol specifications in FIPA ACL, KQML, and AUML, and implementations in well-known platforms and systems like Jason, JADE and SARL. Then, the chapter explores the alternative approaches relying on the environment as a means of coordination, and briefly introduces proposals such as CArtAgO and JaCaMo. Environments allow the realization of agent organizations, where MOISE is particularly important since it is also representative of normative multi-agent organizations. Specifically, in organizations, agents are expected to abide by the rules encoded by the interaction protocols. Consequently, great attention was posed to *a priori* conformance verification and to monitoring the run-time behavior of the agents. Social approaches have then emerged as an alternative solution to the specification of an organization. We briefly survey social commitments and their use for defining interaction protocols, and some proposal for introducing them in agent platforms. More recently, the focus has shifted to the information that is exchanged, leading to the proposal of information-based interaction protocols.

Keywords: Interaction Protocols · Social Commitments · Artifacts · Agent Platforms · Verification and Monitoring

1 Introduction

Interaction plays a fundamental role in multi-agent systems (MAS), as it is one of the means that allow a set of individual agents to coordinate their actions and to exchange information, consequently enacting sophisticate patterns of action. The term "interaction protocol" is commonly used to denote a pattern of behavior

© The Author(s) 2026
V. Mascardi and A. Omicini (Eds.): *The Agents Journey*, LNCS 16395, pp. 105–126, 2026.
https://doi.org/10.1007/978-3-032-22940-3_4

that is followed by a MAS, whose agents may either be cooperative or self-interested.

This problem is not unique of the MAS research area, but rather it appears in all those contexts where there is the need of composing the functionalities/abilities of some independent components, such as in the case of (Web) Services [1,23], as it is also witnessed by the works on this theme that were presented at WOA [21,24,26,85,86,88,89,104].

This chapter reports about the efforts and the achievements of the Italian research community, in the context of the main research lines that gained particular importance in the last twenty-five years. We will follow the steps of development on international research on the topic, recalling the main concepts and positioning in this landscape the contributions that were presented at WOA. Thus, we start from message orientation and agent communication languages (or ACL), to continue with approaches where environments become essential means that enable and mediate the interaction, and with so called "social approaches" where the way in which agents should interact is captured with the help of social commitments and other regulations. The chapter also explains how capturing in a well-formed way an interaction protocol allows the automatization of a range of good properties of the MAS. We will, thus, talk briefly also about type checking, conformance checking, and monitoring of on-going interactions.

Table 1. WOA papers per period and main topics: speech act based languages (SPL), environment-based coordination (ENV), social approaches (SOC), and property verification (PROP).

years	papers	SPL	ENV	SOC	PROP
2000–2002	[71, 76, 84, 90, 91, 100]	X	X		
2003–2005	[20, 24, 30, 36, 68, 78, 101]	X		X	X
2006–2008	[5, 21, 22, 26, 83, 85, 88, 89, 104]	X	X		X
2009–2011	[7, 19, 29, 63, 86]		X	X	
2012–2014	[6, 9, 38, 72, 73, 93]	X	X	X	
2015–2017	[2, 11, 40, 74]	X	X	X	
2018–2020	[3]				X
2021-2024	[17, 39, 82]	X	X		X

The reader can have an organized overview of the considered papers from Table 1. Here, references are positioned along two dimensions: the years in which the proposals were made, and the main topics that are tackled by the proposal. As it can be seen at a glance, the Italian community's contribution is consistent along the years, distributing through a few main lines of research. Concerning the communication model, on one hand, we find research focusing on speech acts based languages–principally centering around the JADE agent platform–, while, on the other hand, we find research focusing on environment-based coordination, mainly centering around TuCSoN and CArtAgO. Somewhat orthogonal, we find research focusing on social approaches, mainly centering around the notion of social commitment or other kinds of norms. Spanning across all such lines of research, theoretical research on the verification of properties. The results of such research are recognized world-widely.

2   ACL and Message-Based Interaction Protocols

The earliest approach to agent interaction was agent communication, realized by means of message exchange and message protocols. An example is the well-known Contract Net Protocol (CNP) [99] that allows a group of agents to carry out a negotiation process. The agents, which interact thanks to a message-based communication protocol, need to include, in their behaviors, also the necessary communication actions. Such actions often refer to some standard ACL, or action communication language, the most famous being FIPA ACL.[1] This approach was later criticized for overly tying the agent implementations and for mixing the interaction logic with the agent control logic: all factors that have a negative impact on software decoupling and reuse. As reported in Sect. 3, a clear separation of the agents from the specification of their coordination introduces advantages both on the design and on the implementation of MAS by bringing in a greater decoupling.

2.1   KQML and FIPA

The FIPA agent interaction model, or FIPA ACL [87], might be erroneously thought of as a declarative agent communication language. Instead, it is much more than that as it involves many features, namely: Interaction Process, Communicative Acts, Content Logic, and Content Ontologies. FIPA standardizes the ways in which one can specify the structure of messages, their encoding and their message transport. The heart of the FIPA ACL model is the so called *Communicative Act protocol*, which defines communication based on a set of communicative acts of different kinds -based upon John Searle's speech act theory [96]. The protocol proposes a logical semantic definition for each kind of communicative act. The semantics is provided in terms of BDI formulas, that specify the kind of exchange occurring between the sender and the receiver agents. The *Interaction Process protocol*, or interaction protocol, captures how communicative acts can be used to specify message workflows to support complex interactions and task delegation. FIPA has standardized several interaction protocols to tackle request, recruit, subscribe, auctions, the best-known probably being the contract net protocol. The content of protocol messages is specified by using an ontology.

For the sake of completeness, it is important to remember that FIPA ACL was not the first proposal for an agent communication language. In the early '90 s, the Knowledge Query and Manipulation Language (better known as KQML)

---

[1] http://www.fipa.org/repository/aclspecs.html.

was proposed [66]. Its main characteristic is the specification of an extensible set of performatives (that amount to speech acts), that can be used as building blocks to realize complex models of agent interaction.

2.2 Agent UML

Agent UML (or AUML) is a tool that allows representing interaction protocols by a formal graphical language [70]. It is based on OMG's UML 2.0 specification. The metamodel of agent UML 2 sequence diagrams contain classes like interaction, lifeline, message, constraint, gate, protocol template. These allow drawing protocols in an intuitive way, which is particularly familiar to all those designers and software developers who use UML in their daily activities. AUML sequence diagrams closely resemble a service choreography as they describe in an abstract and global way the expected interaction without specifying how agents should be implemented.

2.3 Communication in Agent Platforms

Generally speaking, different models of communication can be thought of, backing up to message-passing and to shared memory. The former (followed by the already mentioned FIPA ACL and KQML) requires information to be shaped into messages, having a strictly specified structure. Messages are delivered to their receivers by some middleware. Primitives, like *send* and *receive* allow the message exchange. The latter is not adopted as-is by the literature on agent communication because too low level. Rather, some proposals introduce a *notification mechanism*. So, for instance, should an agent need to send a quote to another agent, in one case it would use the quote as content of a message, while in the other case, the quote would be stored in a shared environment and the receiver would be notified of this event.

The main agent platforms make different choices on how communication is realized. JADE [35] is one of the most successful and widely adopted agent frameworks, first released in the early 2000s. It is a framework for developing MAS, it is written in Java, fully complies to FIPA ACL, and adopts the message exchange paradigm for agent communication. Connected to JADE, JADEL [40] is an agent-oriented, domain-specific, programming language that was designed in order to simplify the realization of MAS in JADE, thanks to a lighter syntax and specific abstractions. JADEL also simplifies the use of ontologies and of interaction protocols.

Coming to WOA, the proposal in [85] combines JADE technology with web services technology, realizing a framework for the development of agent-based service-oriented applications, allowing the joint use of workflows, rule engines and the semantic Web. JADE is used to realize the agents, thus their communication relies on message exchange, with a particular attention to the ontology layer, which is necessary in order to support service interoperability. Another extension of JADE presented at WOA, this time to the Android world, is described in [38]. Instead, [86] tries to make the agents world and the industrial world meet.

The proposal continues previous work on the integration of JADE agents with knowledge and internet-oriented technologies, by integrating agents with workflow and rule technologies. The approach exploits rule engines as part of service implementation and the use of business process engines for service orchestration. Agents play a mediation role and their coordination properties are essential for the realization of an increasingly flexible and effective business process management.

On the other side, platforms and approaches that belong to the Agents & Artifacts (A&A) meta-model [77] (which find an ancestor in tuple spaces and the Linda project [45]) allow forms of communication which are mediated by the environment or by specific artifacts, that are part of the environment in which agents act. Along this line, the WOA paper [89] describes simpA-WS, a Java-based framework for developing web services and service-oriented applications by relying on the A&A meta-model. In simpA-WS services (and applications using services) are workspaces, in which pro-active entities (agents) work together and use passive, function-oriented entities (artifacts) as resources, in order to communicate and to perform their business activities. The next section provides more details by surveying frameworks and platforms.

Noticeably, all the main agent platforms are implemented in Java but this language was used also for realizing actor-based platforms. If interested, a comparison concerning also te interaction model, between JADE and JaCaMo, on a side, and the actor platform Akka, on the other side, can be found in [52].

We conclude this section by observing that agents are not the only abstractions practically used to realize distributed systems. Microservices are another common conceptual framework for such a purpose. The communication model is one of the aspects that main differentiate these two approaches, essentially because microservices are not agents and have not an explicit notion of goal, for more details see [41].

3   Environment as a Means of Coordination

One of the features characterizing the agent-oriented paradigm is that agents are assumed to be situated in an *environment*, that they are able to perceive and change through actions. Flipping through the WOA proceedings, we can observe an increasing interest in the environment dimension since 2006 (see Table 1), and a significant change of perspective: from a background component sometimes not even modelled, to a first-class entity that takes its own place in the architecture of MAS.

One of the early works recognizing the importance to explicitly modeling not only the agent components, but also their environment, is [30]. In this paper, the authors introduce a new view about roles in Object-Oriented Programming. This view attributes to roles three main properties: (*i*) a role is always associated not only with an object instance playing the role, but also with another object instance which constitutes the context of the role, named as *institution*. (*ii*) The definition of a role depends on the definition of the institution in which it is contextualized. (*iii*) Roles within an institution are endowed with a set of powers to modify the state of the institution itself and of the other roles of the same institution. An early implementation in Java is also discussed. Such an implementation will be the basis for further developments that led to powerJava [5] and to its variant powerJADE [28], which provides the primitive to program organizations in Java and JADE, respectively.

In the following we progress along a series of interconnected proposals, from the conceptual inception of objective coordination vs subjective coordination through the realization of many platforms and frameworks.

3.1   Objective Coordination and Organizations

In [29], the authors argue that organizations and roles are not only mental constructs, good to be used during the design phase of a MAS, but they also deserve to be considered as first class citizens in a MAS, in particular when *objective coordination* is needed. Objective coordination refers to the approach where coordination-related concerns are encapsulated within dedicated abstractions, such as coordination artifacts (the medium), offering coordination as a service to coordinables. Coordination abstractions coordinate agents towards the achievement of social goals, by managing the dependencies between their activities [74]. This perspective is opposed to subjective coordination (typical of message passing), where agents are directly in charge of addressing coordination issues, determining their best course of (inter-)action in the attempt to achieve their own goals. While in this chapter we just analyze coordination along the objective vs subjective dimension, coordination models are also explored along temporal and space dimensions in [43]. In particular, that chapter analyzes how coordination models affect coordination languages.

In order to support the realization of agent organizations, however, appropriate primitives should be made available to the programmers. To this end, [29] proposes an extension to the JADE framework, providing classes and protocols which allow agents to enact new organizational roles, to interact with their roles by invoking the execution of powers, and to receive new goals to be fulfilled. Due to software distribution, roles and organizations, on the one side, and role players, on the other side, might reside on different platforms and need to communicate. To this aim the framework foresees communication to be realized by way of protocols, that are implemented by extending the JADE agent class. The authors' objective was to give to programmers a middle tier, built on the JADE platform, useful to solve many coordination problems with a minimal implementation effort. The proposal is interesting because it offers a first, implicit management of norms and sanctions.

3.2   Tuple Spaces

Another perspective that was studied concerns the realization of a middleware for spatio-temporal distributed applications. Spatial issues emerge as essential, for instance in pervasive, situated, multi-agent, self-organising systems. In such scenarios, understanding the basic mechanisms of spatial coordination becomes a critical issue for coordination models and languages. Along this line, [72,104] propose ReSpecT: a space-aware coordination media based on tuple centres, that exploits mechanisms and constructs for tackling most of the main challenges of spatial coordination in complex software systems. In particular, the probabilistic specialisation of standard tuple-based coordination primitives, makes ReSpecT apt to capture the stochastic behaviours that must typically be tackled in order to enable adaptivity and self-organisation.

The idea of a common middleware as a way to support coordination is put forward also in [73,74], where the TuCSoN middleware is proposed as a solution to cope with open distributed MAS. The basic idea is that autonomous components must be provided with coordination mechanisms for guaranteeing both functional and non-functional properties. Moreover, heterogeneity of requirements regarding interaction, means, and paradigms, stemming from the diverse nature of components, should not affect the effectiveness of coordination. In particular, [74] shows the process of integration of objective and subjective, synchronous and asynchronous, reactive and proactive coordination approaches within JADE and Jason, by way of TuCSoN, enabling coordinating components to dynamically adapt their interaction means, based on static preference or run-time contingencies.

3.3 A&A Meta-model

We have already cited the A&A meta-model [83], where the environment is explicitly modeled via a set of artifacts, which provide agents with external facilities, services and coordination media, that are explicitly conceived for promoting their activities. The WOA workshop series hosted many works on A&A. In [83] the authors analyse A&A systems by focusing on the functional roles played by artifacts. In particular, they examine the function of artifacts once they are employed in the context of societies of cognitive agents, i.e., agents capable of reasoning about their epistemic and motivational states. In this context, two types of interaction are envisaged. Firstly, the artifact representational function allows agents to improve their epistemic states by representing and sharing strategic knowledge in the overall system. Secondly, artifacts operations allow agents to expand their repertoire of actions when needed, that is, when such actions are functional to pursuing the agent's goals.

The A&A meta-model has provided a foundation for numerous subsequent works. For instance, [88,93] rely on A&A as a backbone for the implementation of simpA-WS, and simpAL, respectively. simpA-WS [88] is a Java-based technology that makes it possible to build WS-I SOA/WS compliant applications adopting an agent-oriented style in designing and developing the systems. It provides a framework API to build user applications in terms of sets of agents that flexibly interact and use Web Services, represented as artifacts. In addition, simpA-WS provides an API framework and a middleware for building WS-I compliant Web Services in terms of set of agents as providers of the services. The

A&A meta-model is also at the basis of the approach proposed in [14], where business artifacts are put forward as means of coordination. Instead of using orchestration and choreography languages, to coordinate business processes, the work proposes to enrich business artifacts with a normative layer, based on social commitments, that defines the coordination. Business artifacts, thus, enable a form of objective coordination that promotes a clear decoupling between the coordination logic and the business logic, fostering the reuse of both processes and business artifacts.

3.4 Organizations

The metaphor of *organization* has found practical application in several distributed contexts. A very important framework, certainly one of the most successful agent platforms nowadays, is JaCaMo [42] which, interestingly, is also an heir of the A&A meta-model. JaCaMo [42] is an agent framework for realizing MAS that encompasses not only agents and artifacts, but also organizations. Agents can enter an organization by playing organizational roles. In doing so, they commit to abide by the obligations that will be directed to them along the execution. JaCaMo agents can use message exchange but, more typically, their coordination relies on the artifacts in their environment.

Agent organizations find a natural match in human organizations, which often exploit some formalization of business processes to capture, share, and regulate how internal procedures are carried out. In [53], it is shown how MAS can very easily enact business processes due to their peculiar features: on the one hand, tasks can be distributed among several agents, and possibly performed in parallel, on the other hand, agents can cooperate and coordinate to accomplish their tasks. MAS adoption in enacting processes becomes even more interesting if they exhibit adaptation capabilities. In particular, [53] proposes to generate automatically a MOISE organisation from the BPMN specification of a business process. This organisation, then, supports adaptation because of the possibility to adapt its configuration at runtime according to emerging needs. Along this line, [25] proposes a business process programming approach that provides abstractions for capturing goals and relationships between the actors. The novelty of the work stands in a paradigm shift from a procedural (activity-oriented) to a declarative (agent-based) approach, where processes are implemented as agents by way of the platform JaCaMo+ [12].

Another attempt to apply the organization metaphor in real-world scenarios is discussed in [17], facing the challenges of Industry 4.0. Specifically, the paper presents a simulation environment for MAS that is based on a real-world production cell. Its aim is to provide a realistic testbed for MAS applications, demonstrating the suitability of an agent-oriented approach for the design and implementation of modern industrial systems.

In parallel to the outlined studies, a special mention must be given to a particular family of approaches to the coordination of agents which finds inspiration in natural systems, where interaction is driven, e.g., by chemical laws, physical laws, and the instinct of survival. Thanks to such laws, the observer can perceive (complex) patters, an "ecosystem", whose parts can be as different as cells, organisms or particles. The proposal in [104] explores the realization of pervasive computing services that may exploit technologies like GPS and RFID, and that exhibit capabilities of self-organization, adaptability, self-management, and eventually also of evolvability. Such services are immersed in an ecosystem of other services, data sources, and pervasive devices, all of are governed by a limited set of spatial rules. The paper proposes both a reference architecture and a research agenda.

4   The Social Approach

In Sect. 3, we have seen how MAS have been designed taking advantage of the metaphor of an organization as a context for the specification of roles and powers. An orthogonal approach to organizations is the idea of a society of peers, where interactions are expressed through social relationships, such as commitments, that shape the society in virtue of their normative power.

Early works on agent societies originate from Software Engineering approaches, which reconsidered the traditional idea of software design in terms of a socio-tecnical problem: human agents were seen as an integral part of the system, along with hardware and software components. The design of Socio-Technical Systems requires appropriate modeling techniques and innovative infrastructures, that can be realized thanks to the abstractions of the agent-oriented paradigm. In this respect, Tropos [56] represents a first contribution. Tropos is an agent-oriented software engineering methodology, grounded on the BDI paradigm. In Tropos, a system is modeled as a set of agents, each with its own goals, that need to interact in order to achieve them. Agents are characterized by tasks, that describe how to obtain goals. Interactions amount to the exchange of resources needed to complete the tasks (see also [55]).

In agent societies, agents are substantially self-interested, and their behavior is not driven by the predefined roles they are enacting. Rather, agents act to achieve their own goal independently of others. Creating expectations on the behaviors of others, thus, requires specific solutions, and trust is a critical issue. In [63], for instance, it is pointed out that, in agent societies, there is a high probability that an agent has to interact with other agents never met before: the ability of attributing trustworthiness to the potential partners becomes a fundamental prerequisite. The authors propose to exploit transitivity as a means for analysing trust properties in highly complex scenarios.

It is worth noting that the vision of a MAS as a society of agents is not in opposition with agent organizations. Rather, some of the solutions developed for organizations, can be useful also for agent societies. This is the case of the MERCURIO proposal [7], where the **A&A** meta-model is exploited for modeling the environment objects that agents directly manipulate for interacting with each other. In this case, the attention is put on the development of formal models of interactions by explicitly representing not only the agents, but also the computational environment in terms of rules, conventions, resources, tools, and services that are functional to the coordination and cooperation of the agents. This paves the way to the formal verification of interaction properties both from a global (system-wise) and from a local (agent-wise) point of view. The innovative aspect of the proposal is the adoption of *social commitments* [46,97] as a means for modeling the social semantics of the interactions.

4.1 Social Commitments and Agent Coordination

After the seminal work on MERCURIO, social commitments have extensively been used in the realization of sophisticated social interactions by way of protocols. For instance, [19] takes into account business interactions in open MAS, it argues that these scenarios are characterized by a high degree of regulation, and hence traditional commitment-based protocols, which account only for the constitutive specification of actions, should be enriched with a regulative specification. By extending the notion of commitment machines [103] with temporal regulations in 2CL, the paper shows how business protocols can be analysed to determine possible violations.

Despite commitments being a powerful tool for establishing interaction standards, with a solid and verifiable semantics (a critical feature in open worlds), as discussed in [6], in order to capture useful coordination patterns, the language for expressing commitment conditions (both antecedents and consequents) needs to encompass temporal expressions. Furthermore, there is the need of reifying interaction protocols as first-class elements, that can be manipulated and inspected by the agents, in line with the A&A meta-model, rather than relegating them to be handled exclusively by the middleware. A more critical aspect concerns the observability of events, that in the real world are not uniformly observable by all the interacting parties, and this might have consequences on the alignment of commitment states. To overcome this issues, it is suggested that commitment protocols should be able to manipulate objects such as claims, assertions, and declarations. Finally, there is the need for an appropriate software engineering methodology, that enables the reuse and composition of interaction patterns.

These issues are tackled in [11], where business artifacts [50] and commitments are integrated within a single component taking the best of the two worlds. In particular, commitments are reified within business artifacts, which are directly manipulated by the agents via a set of operations which are disclosed by the artifacts themselves. In addition, commitments provide artifacts with a normative layer that is used to represent the data lifecycle in a form that is inspectable, and that can be reasoned upon by the agents. Agents can therefore create expectations about each other's behavior and, leveraging on norms, they can act on artifacts in order to entice, or to oblige, other agents to act.

In other words, while tools like JADE [35], TuCSoN [74], and JaCaMo [42] see coordination and communication mechanisms as services that are provided a middleware, an explicit representation of agent social relationships promotes a clear separation of the agents' logic from their coordination logic, and this yields in modularity and flexibility. In a software engineering perspective, code decoupling and reuse are increased. Several agent platforms have been extended to include social commitments as first-class elements. The 2COMM library [9, 10], for instance, was developed initially for integrating commitment-based protocols in JADE, and subsequently also in JaCaMo, where the integration goes under the name JaCaMo+ [12].

4.2   Social Commitment and Requirements Specification

Social commitments have proved to be effective not only for coordination purposes, but also for the specification of requirements that agents must satisfy to take part into an interaction. Indeed, one of the major challenges in the implementation of an open MAS is that it is composed of heterogeneous and independently developed agents, and that the agents' code cannot be inspected. So, it is not possible to carry out static type-checking and verify whether the agents satisfy the requirements. Some proposals maintain that a typing system should be expresses in terms of those abstractions that are typical of agents, and that it should be the least prescriptive in order to foster agent autonomy. In [13] an agent-based, dynamic, and declarative type checking system for agent interactions is proposed, and it is modeled via commitment-based protocols. The objective of the typing system is to ensure that, when an agent joins an interaction, it owns all the behaviors that are required in order to carry out its part of the interaction. This is done by exploiting one of the peculiar features of commitments: they can only be created by their debtor. That is, an agent can only commit itself, and cannot oblige others to commit. When an agent joins an interaction by playing a specific role, the agent can inspect the set of commitments in which it could possibly be involved, and can therefore check whether it has behaviors that will allow it to satisfy all these commitments. Thus, joining an interaction protocol implies accepting to create and satisfy the commitments associated with a specific role.

An alternative approach to typing interactions is proposed in [2] and it is based on *constrained global types*, that model expected patterns of actions along with exceptions, timeouts, and their handlers. On top of the interaction, special agents–sentinels and controllers–are in charge of monitoring the actual events occurring in the system, and intervene in case of errors and exceptions. Of course, the solution assumes that the special agents will be able to observe all the relevant events and have the power to change the system, which is not always possible in real-world cases.

5   Verification and Monitoring of Interactive Agents

As also explained in the previous sections, the problem of aggregating communicating agents into (open) societies is at the core of research on MAS. A lot of attention has been devoted to the verification of agents interoperability based on dialogical capacities, and to the verification of the conformance of given policies to some global communication protocol. See [62] for an early survey.

Two levels are identified: 1) the overall, abstract design of a system as a whole, which is independent from the specific agents that will animate it, and 2) the implementation of the such design, where specific players are identified and will interact. Following [69], the architectural design of a MAS often amounts to an interaction protocol. There is close similarity between the role played by an interaction protocol and the one played by a service choreography–like those represented in the W3C language WS-CDL.[2] When actual agents, whose behavior is specified by programs, come into the picture there is the need to understand if they fit the specification. This means, first, to verify if they have the right *capabilities* to play the desired protocol role. Supposing they have, it is also important to monitor if the actual behavior of the agents respects the *rules* that are encoded in the protocol; that is to say, the agents execute the required capabilities when it is expected. The first problem is known as *conformance checking*, while the second problem is known as *run-time compliance monitoring*.

Many works presented at the WOA workshop series tackle these problems. One of the earliest proposals for the specification and verification of systems of communicating agents suggests the use of temporal logic [68] and uses, as an application domain, a complex and real-world scenario: actual clinical guidelines, that are used in hospitals to represent the way in which certain health conditions are to be treated. Here, temporal constraints are used to specify interaction protocols (clinical guidelines), and the communicative actions are described in terms of their effects on the social state of the MAS. The paper addresses a problem that is particularly important in clinical applications, that is, the possibility of combining interactions for tackling complex situations.

Also the proposal in [47] has a potential application in medicine, although the authors foresee applications to fields as diverse as electronic commerce and e-learning. The authors claim that the formalism that is adopted for protocol description should be as intuitive as possible, but it should also be formally defined, thus allowing a formal verification of its properties, like deadlock or termination. The authors propose to exploit the SOCS - SI logic-based framework. They also present a graphical notation to express medical guidelines, which could be automatically translated into the SOCS formalism.

Other works, and in particular [24], investigate the issue of personalization. Indeed, many apparently different personalization tasks can be obtained by the applications of reasoning techniques to a declarative specification of interaction. The authors investigated the application of automated reasoning about actions and change both to the personalized selection and composition of web services, and to the construction of personalized courseware that takes into account the user's learning goals and initial competences. The proposed reasoning techniques were integrated in the DCaseLP MAS prototyping environment.

Guaranteeing the interoperability of a set of services in an open environment is the main topic of [21]. This is done by an approach to conformance verification that fits a context where the set of interacting agents (or services) are not all known in advance and interoperability must be guaranteed by verifying one

---

[2] https://www.w3.org/TR/ws-cdl-10/.

agent at a time. Verification is done against a choreography the specifies the overall design of the interaction. Before the interaction takes place, agents can verify their own conformance, each by itself and without the need of disclosing information about their behaviors to the others, and this will be enough to guarantee the interoperability of the group of agents. The achievement of the goals of the choreography as well as the achievement of the goals of the individual agents depend both on the interaction protocol and on each participant's capabilities (intuitively, their practical skills). The work described in [22] overcomes some limits of traditional approaches to matchmaking (i.e. the strategies that allows choosing among a set of agents/services to fill in a choreography) claiming that the choice of which capability to perform cannot rely totally on local criteria, as instead it is commonly implemented. Rather it should take into account also the choreography/protocol that defines the context in which the execution will take place. The authors also propose an extended "plugin match" that takes into account the choreography when performing the capability selection.

This early proposal was further developed into a more complex study of flexible matchmaking [26]. A web service specification can be quite complex, including various operations and message exchange patterns. Flexible matchmaking fosters (web) service reuse because it is generally difficult that a service perfectly matches a choreography-provided specification. However, non-exact matches have the drawback of not preserving the goals that can be proved as reachable over the specification itself. The authors explain how to enrich various kinds of match, that can be found in the literature [105], so as to produce substitutions that preserve choreography goals.

Flexibility is also a concern of [3]. The authors present an algorithm for establishing a flexible conformance relation between two local agent interaction protocols which is based on mappings involving agents and messages, respectively. Conformance is in fact computed *modulo mapping*. This means that, even though different agents may be involved, and hence use different syntax for their messages, still the algorithm can prove their conformance. To do so, a proper map is to be applied. The proposal uses trace expressions whose high expressive power allows for the design of protocols that could not be specified using classical finite state automata.

6   Conclusion and Perspectives

Interaction is the key issue in the design and development of distributed systems and of MAS. This chapter has outlined several methodologies and technologies to establish interaction protocols, enabling the agents to interact, cooperate, negotiate, and coordinate with each other. The WOA community has been very active on this topic from the start, as shown by Table 1, and all the most relevant directions of research in the field, raised internationally, have been discussed within the WOA community. Notably, these approaches still amount to active lines of research, including the early approaches on speech acts, as witnessed, for instance, by the contributions on Jadescript [39,81,82]. Speech acts are, in fact, quite intuitive and this contributes to their appeal.

The assumption, however, is that all the parties will be cooperative and trustworthy. We have seen that challenges about trust, monitoring and verification of the interactions, have moved the research to more sophisticated solutions. Cooperation and trustworthiness cannot, indeed, be granted when one considers open systems. Here agents are generally developed by independent parties, and act on behalf of possibly competing human actors. They are, therefore, opaque to each other, and no assumption can be made on whether they will comply with the desired protocol. A first turning point has been the A&A meta-model which explicitly represents the environment where agents operate: the interaction is mediated by means of computational artifacts. Then, artifacts have allowed the researchers to conceptualize and implement forms of objective coordination, that reduce the coupling between the interacting agents.

Moving one further step forward, agent organizations and agent societies have been proposed as ways to conceptualize MAS. Agent organizations take a global perspective: a MAS exists and is structured in a way that is functional to the achievement of an organizational goal. An organization, thus, represents a top-down solution where agents play roles in a global, centrally designed structure. On the other hand, agent societies capture a bottom-up view where agents are free to establish relationships dynamically, e.g., by exploiting social commitments [6,97]. In this case, agents create their own norms in order to entice the cooperation of others.

To conclude, this chapter has shown how interaction protocols are a still active research area within the WOA community, as well as in the field of MAS engineering. In [102] Winikoff observed that, despite the importance of modeling interactions, agent programming languages typically supported pretty plain message-oriented approaches by providing primitives for sending and receiving messages. Moreover, AUML notations for representing *interaction protocols*, being message-centric, over-constrained agent interaction, thus reducing their autonomy and, consequently, their flexibility when coping with unexpected situations. Sending and receiving messages is compared to the label-goto mechanism for transfering control. He advocates the introduction of higher level abstractions in order to hide the explicit use of messages, in the same way as transactional memory hides the use of locks, making certain errors impossible to make. In 2024, agent programming languages still suffer from these shortcomings. In the last years, however, a new line of research on *information protocols*, initiated by Munindar Singh, who proposed BSPL [98], started to raise attention. BSPL is declarative and information-oriented. Interestingly, the protocol does not specify any ordering of the possible messages; rather, it captures dependencies among data. A message can be sent only when the data it involves is available. It is up to the agent to choose if and when sending one or more of abilitated messages [16]. As the invited speaker at WOA 2024, Amit Chopra [48] has outlined the flexibility and the expressivity of the language, and its possible usage for developing concrete distributed systems by relying on adapters that translate a BSPL specification into agent code. BSPL deserves attention from the WOA community, that could take advantage of information protocols for coming up with novel engineering methodologies and for the development of practical applications. A first step in this direction is represented by Orpheus [31,32] and Azorus [49]. Orpheus allows information protocols, in particular BSPL, to be integrated into the BDI agent programming language Jason. By means of the Orpheus, Jason overcomes the message-centric interaction protocols that is typical of AgentUML approach. Azorus further extends Orpheus by adding commitments that capture the social meaning of a communicative act, introducing a programming model based on declarative specifications centered on commitments and aligned with information protocols.

Another direction of research concerns system models where agents can only perceive events generated by others. The SARL platform [92] is one of such systems: it relies on the two basic concepts of agent and space, which is close, but not identical, to an environment. SARL allows agent-to-agent message exchange, but it also allows an agent to observe events occurring within spaces that have been generated by others. Agents can thus react to these events by generating new ones. SARL does not support, so far, native primitives to implement interaction protocols, this is a still ongoing challenge that requires further research, apart from an attempt to introduce BSPL protocols [18]. In [15] an exception handling mechanism set up among SARL agents is presented. Although the paper is not precisely focused on interaction protocols, the handling of an exception calls for the coordinated intervention of all the involved agents, and gives some intuitions about the underlying challenges.

References

1. van der Aalst, W.M., Dumas, M., ter Hofstede, A.H.M., Russell, N., Verbeek, H.M.W., Wohed, P.: Life after BPEL? In: Bravetti, M., Kloul, L., Zavattaro, G. (eds.) Formal Techniques for Computer Systems and Business Processes, European Performance Engineering Workshop, EPEW 2005 and International Workshop on Web Services and Formal Methods, WS-FM 2005, Versailles, France, September 1-3, 2005, Proceedings. LNCS, vol. 3670, pp. 35–50. Springer, Cham (2005). https://doi.org/10.1007/11549970_4

2. Ancona, D., Briola, D., Mascardi, V.: Protocols with exceptions, timeouts, and handlers: a uniform framework for monitoring fail-uncontrolled and ambient intelligence systems. In: Di Napoli et al. [61], pp. 65–75. http://ceur-ws.org/Vol-1382/paper10.pdf

3. Ancona, D., Ferrando, A., Mascardi, V.: Agents interoperability via conformance modulo mapping. In: Cossentino et al. [54], pp. 109–115. http://ceur-ws.org/Vol-2215/paper_18.pdf

4. Armano, G., Paoli, F.D., Omicini, A., Vargiu, E. (eds.): WOA 2003 – 4th Workshop "From Objects to Agents". Pitagora Editrice Bologna, Villasimius, CA, Italy (2003). http://giuseppevizzari.github.io/WOA-proceedings-archive/woa-2003.html

5. Arnaudo, E., Baldoni, M., Boella, G., Genovese, V., Grenna, R.: An implementation of roles as affordances: powerJava. In: Baldoni et al. [27], pp. 8–13. http://woa07.disi.unige.it/papers/powerJavaWOA07-R2.pdf

6. Baldoni, M., Baroglio, C.: Some thoughts about commitment protocols (position paper). In: De Paoli and Vizzari [60], pp. 68–71. http://ceur-ws.org/Vol-892/paper11.pdf
7. Baldoni, M., et al.: MERCURIO: an interaction-oriented framework for designing, verifying and programming multi-agent systems. In: Omicini and Viroli [80], pp. 87–94. http://ceur-ws.org/Vol-621/paper13.pdf
8. Baldoni, M., Baroglio, C., Bergenti, F., Garro, A. (eds.): WOA 2013 – 14th Workshop "From Objects to Agents", CEUR Workshop Proceedings, vol. 1099. Turin, Italy (2013). http://ceur-ws.org/Vol-1099/
9. Baldoni, M., Baroglio, C., Capuzzimati, F.: 2COMM: a commitment-based MAS architecture. In: Baldoni et al. [8], pp. 38–57. http://ceur-ws.org/Vol-1099/paper11.pdf
10. Baldoni, M., Baroglio, C., Capuzzimati, F.: Social relationships for designing agent interaction in JADE. In: Santoro and Bergenti [94], pp. 36–43. http://ceur-ws.org/Vol-1260/paper6.pdf
11. Baldoni, M., Baroglio, C., Capuzzimati, F., Micalizio, R.: Endowing business artifacts with a normative coordination layer. In: De Meo et al. [57], pp. 71–77. http://ceur-ws.org/Vol-1867/w13.pdf
12. Baldoni, M., Baroglio, C., Capuzzimati, F., Micalizio, R.: Commitment-based agent interaction in JaCaMo+. Fund. Inform. **159**(1–2), 1–33 (2018). https://doi.org/10.3233/FI-2018-1656
13. Baldoni, M., Baroglio, C., Capuzzimati, F., Micalizio, R.: Type checking for protocol role enactments via commitments. Auton. Agent. Multi-Agent Syst. **32**(3), 349–386 (2018). https://doi.org/10.1007/S10458-018-9382-3
14. Baldoni, M., Baroglio, C., Capuzzimati, F., Micalizio, R.: Process coordination with business artifacts and multiagent technologies. J. Data Semant. **8**(2), 99–112 (2019). https://doi.org/10.1007/S13740-019-00100-8
15. Baldoni, M., Baroglio, C., Chiappino, G., Micalizio, R., Tedeschi, S.: Exception handling in SARL as a responsibility distribution. In: Shakshuki, E.M., Yasar, A. (eds.) The 13th International Conference on Ambient Systems, Networks and Technologies (ANT 2022)/The 5th International Conference on Emerging Data and Industry 4.0 (EDI40 2022)/Affiliated Workshops, 22–25 March 2022, Porto, Portugal. Procedia Computer Science, vol. 201, pp. 795–800. Elsevier (2022)
16. Baldoni, M., Baroglio, C., Chopra, A.K., Günay, A.: Interaction protocols. In: Chopra, A.K., van der Torre, L., Verhagen, H., Villata, S. (eds.) Handbook of Normative Multiagent Systems, chap. 7, pp. 209–230. College Publications (2018). https://www.collegepublications.co.uk/handbooks/?00004
17. Baldoni, M., Baroglio, C., Ditano, V., Micalizio, R., Tedeschi, S.: Agents for industry 4.0: the case study of a production cell. In: Falcone et al. [64], pp. 167–180. http://ceur-ws.org/Vol-3579/paper12.pdf
18. Baldoni, M., Baroglio, C., Galland, S., Micalizio, R., Outay, F., Tedeschi, S.: Interaction protocols in an imperative agent-oriented programming language: the case of BSPL and SARL. In: Proceedings of the 24th International Conference on Autonomous Agents and Multiagent Systems, AAMAS. IFAAMAS, Detroit, Michigan, USA (2025)
19. Baldoni, M., Baroglio, C., Marengo, E., Patti, V., Capuzzimati, F.: Learn the rules so you know how to break them properly. In: Fortino et al. [67], pp. 11–18. http://ceur-ws.org/Vol-741/ID1_BaldoniBaroglioMarengoPattiCapuzzimati.pdf
20. Baldoni, M., Baroglio, C., Martelli, A., Patti, V.: Reasoning about interaction for personalizing web service fruition. In: Armano et al. [4], pp. 29–35. http://giuseppevizzari.github.io/WOA-proceedings-archive/pdfs/woa2003/06.pdf

21. Baldoni, M., Baroglio, C., Martelli, A., Patti, V.: Conformance and interoperability in open environments. In: De Paoli et al. [58], pp. 151–157. http://ceur-ws.org/Vol-204/P11.pdf
22. Baldoni, M., Baroglio, C., Martelli, A., Patti, V., Schifanella, C.: Preserving players goals: a choreography-driven matchmaking approach. In: Baldoni et al. [27], pp. 132–139. http://woa07.dibris.unige.it/papers/BaldoniPlayers.pdf
23. Baldoni, M., Baroglio, C., Martelli, A., Patti, V., Schifanella, C.: Reasoning on choreographies and capability requirements. Int. J. Bus. Process. Integr. Manag. **2**(4), 247–261 (2007). https://doi.org/10.1504/IJBPIM.2007.017751
24. Baldoni, M., et al.: Personalization, verification and conformance for logic-based communicating agents. In: Corradini et al. [51], pp. 177–183. http://lia.deis.unibo.it/books/woa2005/papers/25.pdf
25. Baldoni, M., Baroglio, C., Micalizio, R., Tedeschi, S.: Implementing business processes in JaCaMo+ by exploiting accountability and responsibility. In: Elkind, E., Veloso, M., Agmon, N., Taylor, M.E. (eds.) Proceedings of the 18th International Conference on Autonomous Agents and MultiAgent Systems, AAMAS '19, Montreal, QC, Canada, 13–17 May 2019, pp. 2330–2332. International Foundation for Autonomous Agents and Multiagent Systems (2019). http://dl.acm.org/citation.cfm?id=3332102
26. Baldoni, M., Baroglio, C., Patti, V., Schifanella, C.: Conservative re-use ensuring matches for service selection. In: Baldoni et al. [33], pp. 28–36. http://www.pa.icar.cnr.it/woa08/materiali/paper/paper_8.pdf
27. Baldoni, M., Boccalatte, A., De Paoli, F., Martelli, M., Mascardi, V. (eds.): WOA 2007 – 8th Workshop "From Objects to Agents". Seneca Edizioni Torino, Genova, Italy (2007). http://woa07.disi.unige.it/ProceedingsWOA2007.zip
28. Baldoni, M., Boella, G., Dorni, M., Mugnaini, A., Grenna, R.: powerJADE: organizations and roles as primitives in the JADE framework. In: Baldoni et al. [33], pp. 84–92. http://www.pa.icar.cnr.it/woa08/materiali/paper/paper_1.pdf
29. Baldoni, M., Boella, G., Grenna, R.: Modeling organizations and roles using a middleware Jade-based. In: Bergenti [37], pp. 100–107. http://www.ailab.unipr.it/woa09/papers/Baldoni.pdf
30. Baldoni, M., Boella, G., van der Torre, L.W.N.: Social roles, from agents back to objects. In: Corradini et al. [51], pp. 164–170. http://lia.deis.unibo.it/books/woa2005/papers/23.pdf
31. Baldoni, M., Christie V, S.H., Singh, M.P., Chopra, A.K.: Orpheus: engineering multiagent systems via communication agents. In: The 39th Annual AAAI Conference on Artificial Intelligence, AAAI. Philadelphia, Pennsylvania, USA (2025)
32. Baldoni, M., Christie V, S.H., Singh, M.P., Chopra, A.K.: Orpheus: programming protocol-based BDI agents. In: Proc. of 24th International Conference on Autonomous Agents and Multiagent Systems, AAMAS, Demonstration Track. IFAAMAS, Detroit, Michigan, USA (2025)
33. Baldoni, M., Cossentino, M., De Paoli, F., Seidita, V. (eds.): WOA 2008 – 9th Workshop "From Objects to Agents". Seneca Edizioni Torino, Palermo, Italy (2008). http://www.pa.icar.cnr.it/woa08/materiali/Proceedings.pdf
34. Baldoni, M., De Paoli, F., Martelli, A., Omicini, A. (eds.): WOA 2004 – 5th Workshop "From Objects to Agents". Pitagora Editrice Bologna, Torino, Italy (2004). http://lia.deis.unibo.it/books/woa2004/atti.pdf
35. Bellifemine, F., Bergenti, F., Caire, G., Poggi, A.: JADE - a java agent development framework. In: Bordini, R.H., Dastani, M., Dix, J., El Fallah Seghrouchni, A.

(eds.) Multi-Agent Programming: Languages, Platforms and Applications, Multiagent Systems, Artificial Societies, and Simulated Organizations, vol. 15, pp. 125–147. Springer, Cham (2005). https://doi.org/10.1007/0-387-26350-0_5

36. Bergamaschi, S., Gelati, G., Guerra, F., Vincini, M.: Experiencing AUML for the WINK multi-agent system. In: Armano et al. [4], pp. 148–154. http://giuseppevizzari.github.io/WOA-proceedings-archive/pdfs/woa2003/20.pdf

37. Bergenti, F. (ed.): WOA 2009 – 10th Workshop "From Objects to Agents". Seneca Edizioni Torino, Parma, Italy (2009). http://www.ailab.unipr.it/woa09/papers/

38. Bergenti, F., Caire, G., Gotta, D.: Agents on the move: JADE for android devices. In: Santoro and Bergenti [94], pp. 44–47. http://ceur-ws.org/Vol-1260/paper9.pdf

39. Bergenti, F., Galliera, L., Giannini, P., Monica, S., Nazzari, R.: Global types for agent interaction protocols (short paper). In: de'Liguoro, U., Palazzo, M., Roversi, L. (eds.) Proceedings of the 25th Italian Conference on Theoretical Computer Science, Torino, Italy, 11–13 September 2024. CEUR Workshop Proceedings, vol. 3811, pp. 284–291. CEUR-WS.org (2024). https://ceur-ws.org/Vol-3811/paper120.pdf

40. Bergenti, F., Iotti, E., Monica, S., Poggi, A.: A case study of the JADEL programming language. In: Santoro et al. [95], pp. 85–90. http://ceur-ws.org/Vol-1664/w15.pdf

41. Bergenti, F., Monica, S.: Rethinking software agents as building blocks of software systems. In: Mascardi and Omicini [75]

42. Boissier, O., Bordini, R.H., Hübner, J.F., Ricci, A.: Multi-Agent Oriented Programming: Programming Multi-Agent Systems Using JaCaMo. The MIT Press, Cambridge (2020). https://mitpress.mit.edu/9780262044578/multi-agent-oriented-programming/

43. Cabri, G., Leonardi, L., Mariani, S., Zambonelli, F.: Coordination of software agents: models and languages. In: Mascardi and Omicini [75]

44. Calegari, R., Ciatto, G., Denti, E., Omicini, A., Sartor, G. (eds.): WOA 2020 – 21st Workshop "From Objects to Agents", CEUR Workshop Proceedings, vol. 2706. Bologna, Italy (2020). http://ceur-ws.org/Vol-2706/

45. Carriero, N., Gelernter, D.: Linda in context. Commun. ACM **32**(4), 444–458 (1989). https://doi.org/10.1145/63334.63337

46. Castelfranchi, C.: Commitments: from individual intentions to groups and organizations. In: Lesser, V.R., Gasser, L. (eds.) Proceedings of the First International Conference on Multiagent Systems, 12–14 June 1995, San Francisco, California, USA, pp. 41–48. The MIT Press (1995)

47. Chesani, F., et al.: Protocol specification and verification by using computational logic. In: Corradini et al. [51], pp. 184–192. http://lia.deis.unibo.it/books/woa2005/papers/26.pdf

48. Chopra, A.K.: Communication meaning: Why multiagent abstractions are foundational to software systems research (2024). http://www.univda.it/woa2024/program/, "Fabio Bellifemine" Keynote Speech @ WOA 2024

49. Chopra, A.K., Baldoni, M., Christie V, S.H., Singh, M.P.: Azorus: commitments over protocols for BDI agents. In: Proceedings of the 24th International Conference on Autonomous Agents and Multiagent Systems, AAMAS. IFAAMAS, Detroit, Michigan, USA (2025)

50. Cohn, D., Hull, R.: Business artifacts: a data-centric approach to modeling business operations and processes. IEEE Data Eng. Bull. **32**(3), 3–9 (2009). http://sites.computer.org/debull/A09sept/david.pdf

51. Corradini, F., De Paoli, F., Merelli, E., Omicini, A. (eds.): WOA 2005 – 6th Workshop "From Objects to Agents". Pitagora Editrice Bologna, Camerino, MC, Italy (2005). http://lia.deis.unibo.it/books/woa2005/atti.pdf

52. Cossentino, M., Lopes, S., Nuzzo, A., Renda, G., Sabatucci, L.: A comparison of the basic principles and behavioural aspects of Akka, JaCaMo and Jade development frameworks. In: Cossentino et al. [54], pp. 133–141. http://ceur-ws.org/Vol-2215/paper_21.pdf

53. Cossentino, M., Lopes, S., Sabatucci, L.: A tool for the automatic generation of MOISE organisations from BPMN. In: Calegari et al. [44], pp. 69–82. http://ceur-ws.org/Vol-2706/paper11.pdf

54. Cossentino, M., Sabatucci, L., Seidita, V. (eds.): WOA 2018 – 19th Workshop "From Objects to Agents", CEUR Workshop Proceedings, vol. 2215. Palermo, Italy (2018). http://ceur-ws.org/Vol-2215/

55. Cossentino, M., Sabatucci, L., Seidita, V.: Designing agent-oriented systems. In: Mascardi and Omicini [75]

56. Dalpiaz, F., Ali, R., Asnar, Y., Bryl, V., Giorgini, P.: Applying Tropos to sociotechnical system design and runtime configuration. In: Baldoni et al. [33], pp. 101–107. http://www.pa.icar.cnr.it/woa08/materiali/paper/paper_14.pdf

57. De Meo, P., Postorino, M.N., Rosaci, D., Sarnè, G.M.L. (eds.): WOA 2017 – 18th Workshop "From Objects to Agents", CEUR Workshop Proceedings, vol. 1867. Scilla, RC, Italy (2017). http://ceur-ws.org/Vol-1867/

58. De Paoli, F., Di Stefano, A., Omicini, A., Santoro, C. (eds.): WOA 2006 – 7th Workshop "From Objects to Agents", CEUR Workshop Proceedings, vol. 204. Catania, Italy (2006). http://ceur-ws.org/Vol-204/

59. De Paoli, F., Manzoni, S., Poggi, A. (eds.): WOA 2002 – 3rd Workshop "From Objects to Agents". Pitagora Editrice Bologna, Milano, Italy (2002). http://giuseppevizzari.github.io/WOA-proceedings-archive/woa-2002.html

60. De Paoli, F., Vizzari, G. (eds.): WOA 2012 – 13th Workshop "From Objects to Agents", CEUR Workshop Proceedings, vol. 892. Milano, Italy (2012). http://ceur-ws.org/Vol-892/

61. Di Napoli, C., Rossi, S., Staffa, M. (eds.): WOA 2015 – 16th Workshop "From Objects to Agents", CEUR Workshop Proceedings, vol. 1382. Naples, Italy (2015). http://ceur-ws.org/Vol-1382/

62. Dignum, F. (ed.): Advances in Agent Communication, International Workshop on Agent Communication Languages, ACL 2003, Melbourne, Australia, 14 July 2003, LNCS, vol. 2922. Springer, Cham (2004). https://doi.org/10.1007/B94813

63. Falcone, R., Castelfranchi, C.: Transitivity in trust: a discussed property. In: Omicini and Viroli [80], pp. 155–160. http://ceur-ws.org/Vol-621/paper22.pdf

64. Falcone, R., Castelfranchi, C., Sapienza, A., Cantucci, F. (eds.): WOA 2023 – 24th Workshop "From Objects to Agents", CEUR Workshop Proceedings, vol. 3579. Roma, Italy (2023). http://ceur-ws.org/Vol-3579/

65. Ferrando, A., Mascardi, V. (eds.): WOA 2022 – 23rd Workshop "From Objects to Agents", CEUR Workshop Proceedings, vol. 3261. Genova, Italy (2022). http://ceur-ws.org/Vol-3261/

66. Finin, T.W., Fritzson, R., McKay, D.P., McEntire, R.: KQML as an agent communication language. In: Proceedings of the Third International Conference on Information and Knowledge Management (CIKM'94), Gaithersburg, Maryland, USA, November 29– 2 December 2 1994, pp. 456–463. ACM (1994). https://doi.org/10.1145/191246.191322

67. Fortino, G., Garro, A., Palopoli, L., Russo, W., Spezzano, G. (eds.): WOA 2011 – 12th Workshop "From Objects to Agents", CEUR Workshop Proceedings, vol. 741. Rende, Italy (2011). http://ceur-ws.org/Vol-741/

68. Giordano, L., Martelli, A., Terenziani, P., Bottrighi, A., Montani, S.: A temporal approach to the specification and verification of interaction protocols. In: Corradini et al. [51], pp. 171–176. http://lia.deis.unibo.it/books/woa2005/papers/24.pdf

69. Huget, M., Koning, J.: Interaction protocol engineering. In: Huget, M. (ed.) Communication in Multiagent Systems, Agent Communication Languages and Conversation Policies. LNCS, vol. 2650, pp. 179–193. Springer, Cham (2003). https://doi.org/10.1007/978-3-540-44972-0_9

70. Huget, M., Odell, J.: Representing agent interaction protocols with agent UML. In: 3rd International Joint Conference on Autonomous Agents and Multiagent Systems (AAMAS 2004), 19-23 August 2004, New York, NY, USA, pp. 1244–1245. IEEE Computer Society (2004). https://doi.org/10.1109/AAMAS.2004.10151

71. Mamei, M., Zambonelli, F., Leonardi, L.: *Tuples On The Air*: a middleware for context-aware multiagent systems. In: De Paoli et al. [59], pp. 108–116. http://giuseppevizzari.github.io/WOA-proceedings-archive/pdfs/woa2002/26.pdf

72. Mariani, S., Omicini, A.: Space-aware coordination in ReSpecT. In: Baldoni et al. [8], pp. 1–7. http://ceur-ws.org/Vol-1099/paper3.pdf

73. Mariani, S., Omicini, A.: TuCSoN coordination for MAS situatedness: towards a methodology. In: Santoro and Bergenti [94], pp. 48–57. http://ceur-ws.org/Vol-1260/paper11.pdf

74. Mariani, S., Omicini, A.: Multi-paradigm coordination for MAS: integrating heterogeneous coordination approaches in MAS technologies. In: Santoro et al. [95], pp. 91–99. http://ceur-ws.org/Vol-1664/w16.pdf

75. Mascardi, V., Omicini, A. (eds.): The Agents Journey: Twenty-five Years of Multiagent Systems at WOA. Lecture Notes in Computer Science – State-of-the-Art Surveys, Springer (2026)

76. Menezes, R., Omicini, A., Viroli, M.: Have ReSpecT for LogOp. In: De Paoli et al. [59], pp. 94–99. http://giuseppevizzari.github.io/WOA-proceedings-archive/pdfs/woa2002/18.pdf

77. Omicini, A.: Formal ReSpecT in the A&A perspective. Electron. Notes Theor. Comput. Sci. **175**(2), 97–117 (2007). https://doi.org/10.1016/j.entcs.2007.03.006, proceedings of the Fifth International Workshop on the Foundations of Coordination Languages and Software Architectures (FOCLASA 2006)

78. Omicini, A., Ricci, A., Rimassa, G., Viroli, M.: Integrating objective & subjective coordination in FIPA: a roadmap to TuCSoN. In: Armano et al. [4], pp. 85–91. http://giuseppevizzari.github.io/WOA-proceedings-archive/pdfs/woa2003/07.pdf

79. Omicini, A., Viroli, M. (eds.): WOA 2001 – 2nd Workshop "From Objects to Agents". Pitagora Editrice Bologna, Modena, Italy (2001). http://giuseppevizzari.github.io/WOA-proceedings-archive/woa-2001.html

80. Omicini, A., Viroli, M. (eds.): WOA 2010 – 11th Workshop "From Objects to Agents", CEUR Workshop Proceedings, vol. 621. Rimini, Italy (2010). http://ceur-ws.org/Vol-621/

81. Petrosino, G., Monica, S., Bergenti, F.: Delayed and periodic execution of tasks in Jadescript programming language. In: Distributed Computing and Artificial Intelligence, 19th International Conference (DCAI 2022), pp. 50–59. Springer, Cham (2022). https://doi.org/10.1007/978-3-031-20859-1_6

82. Petrosino, G., Monica, S., Bergenti, F.: Robust software agents with the jadescript programming language. In: Ferrando and Mascardi [65], pp. 194–208. http://ceur-ws.org/Vol-3261/paper15.pdf
83. Piunti, M., Ricci, A.: From agents to artifacts back and forth: Operational and doxastic use of artifacts in MAS. In: Baldoni et al. [33], pp. 76–83. http://www.pa.icar.cnr.it/woa08/materiali/paper/paper_13.pdf
84. Poggi, A., Rimassa, G., Turci, P.: Engineering comma multiagent system with agent UML. In: De Paoli et al. [59], pp. 22–28. http://giuseppevizzari.github.io/WOA-proceedings-archive/pdfs/woa2002/19.pdf
85. Poggi, A., Tomaiuolo, M., Turci, P.: An agent-based service oriented architecture. In: Baldoni et al. [27], pp. 157–165. http://woa07.disi.unige.it/papers/PoggiSOA.pdf
86. Poggi, A., Turci, P.: An agent-based bridge between business process and business rules. In: Bergenti [37], pp. 134–139. http://www.ailab.unipr.it/woa09/papers/Poggi.pdf
87. Poslad, S.: Specifying protocols for multi-agent systems interaction. ACM Trans. Auton. Adapt. Syst. 2(4), 15 (2007). https://doi.org/10.1145/1293731.1293735
88. Ricci, A., Buda, C., Zaghini, N., Natali, A., Viroli, M., Omicini, A.: simpA-WS: an agent-oriented computing technology for WS-based SOA applications. In: De Paoli et al. [58], pp. 1–3. http://ceur-ws.org/Vol-204/D01.pdf
89. Ricci, A., Denti, E.: simpA-WS: a simple agent-oriented programming model & technology for developing SOA & web services. In: Baldoni et al. [27], pp. 140–156. http://woa07.disi.unige.it/papers/ricci_simpaws.pdf
90. Ricci, A., Omicini, A.: Agent coordination contexts: experiments in TuCSoN. In: De Paoli et al. [59], pp. 14–21. http://giuseppevizzari.github.io/WOA-proceedings-archive/pdfs/woa2002/17.pdf
91. Ricci, A., Omicini, A., Denti, E.: Enlightened agents in TuCSoN. In: Omicini and Viroli [79], pp. 101–106. http://giuseppevizzari.github.io/WOA-proceedings-archive/pdfs/woa2001/pdf/21.pdf
92. Rodriguez, S., Gaud, N., Galland, S.: SARL: a general-purpose agent-oriented programming language. In: The 2014 IEEE/WIC/ACM International Conference on Intelligent Agent Technology. IEEE Computer Society Press, Warsaw, Poland (2014). https://doi.org/10.1109/WI-IAT.2014.156
93. Santi, A., Ricci, A.: Programming distributed multi-agent systems in simpAL. In: De Paoli and Vizzari [60], pp. 39–48. http://ceur-ws.org/Vol-892/paper5.pdf
94. Santoro, C., Bergenti, F. (eds.): WOA 2014 – 15th Workshop "From Objects to Agents", CEUR Workshop Proceedings, vol. 1260. Catania, Italy (2014). http://ceur-ws.org/Vol-1260/
95. Santoro, C., Messina, F., De Benedetti, M. (eds.): WOA 2016 – 17th Workshop "From Objects to Agents", CEUR Workshop Proceedings, vol. 1664. Catania, Italy (2016). http://ceur-ws.org/Vol-1664/
96. Searle, J.R.: Speech Acts: An Essay in the Philosophy of Language. Cambridge University Press, Cambridge (1969). https://doi.org/10.1017/CBO9781139173438
97. Singh, M.P.: An ontology for commitments in multiagent systems. Artif. Intell. Law 7(1), 97–113 (1999). https://doi.org/10.1023/A:1008319631231
98. Singh, M.P.: Information-driven interaction-oriented programming: bspl, the blindingly simple protocol language. In: Sonenberg, L., Stone, P., Tumer, K., Yolum, P. (eds.) 10th International Conference on Autonomous Agents and Multiagent Systems (AAMAS 2011), Taipei, Taiwan, 2–6 May 2011, vol. 1–3, pp. 491–498. IFAAMAS (2011). https://dl.acm.org/doi/10.5555/2031678.2031687

99. Smith, R.G.: The contract net protocol: high-level communication and control in a distributed problem solver. IEEE Trans. Comput. **29**(12), 1104–1113 (1980). https://doi.org/10.1109/TC.1980.1675516
100. Stefano, A.D., Santoro, C.: Coordinating mobile agents by means of communicators. In: Omicini and Viroli [79], pp. 48–53. http://giuseppevizzari.github.io/WOA-proceedings-archive/pdfs/woa2001/pdf/12.pdf
101. Viroli, M., Ricci, A.: Timed coordination artifacts with **ReSpecT**. In: Baldoni et al. [34], pp. 77–85. http://giuseppevizzari.github.io/WOA-proceedings-archive/pdfs/woa2004/12.pdf
102. Winikoff, M.: Challenges and directions for engineering multi-agent systems. CoRR **abs/1209.1428** (2012). https://doi.org/10.48550/arXiv.1209.1428
103. Winikoff, M., Liu, W., Harland, J.: Enhancing commitment machines. In: Leite, J.A., Omicini, A., Torroni, P., Yolum, P. (eds.) Declarative Agent Languages and Technologies II, Second International Workshop, DALT 2004, New York, NY, USA, July 19, 2004, Revised Selected Papers. LNCS, vol. 3476, pp. 198–220. Springer, Cham (2004). https://doi.org/10.1007/11493402_12
104. Zambonelli, F.: Nature-inspired spatial metaphors for pervasive service ecosystems. In: Baldoni et al. [33], pp. 61–67. http://www.pa.icar.cnr.it/woa08/materiali/paper/paper_10.pdf
105. Zaremski, A.M., Wing, J.M.: Specification matching of software components. ACM Trans. Softw. Eng. Methodol. **6**(4), 333–369 (1997). https://doi.org/10.1145/261640.261641

Coordination of Software Agents: Models and Languages

Giacomo Cabri[1(✉)] [iD], Letizia Leonardi[2] [iD], Stefano Mariani[3] [iD], and Franco Zambonelli[3] [iD]

[1] Dipartimento FIM, Università di Modena e Reggio Emilia, Via Campi 213/B, 41125 Modena, Italy
giacomo.cabri@unimore.it
[2] Dipartimento DIEF, Università di Modena e Reggio Emilia, Via Vivarelli 10, 41125 Modena, Italy
letizia.leonardi@unimore.it
[3] Dipartimento DISMI, Università di Modena e Reggio Emilia, Via G. Amendola 2, 42122 Reggio Emilia, Italy
{stefano.mariani,franco.zambonelli}@unimore.it

Abstract. Software agents are autonomous components that perform tasks on the behalf of users. In many contexts, agents do not exist in isolation, but they must interact with other agents, leading to multi-agent systems (MASs). No matter whether they collaborate or compete in MASs, coordination is needed to rule their interactions and to support them in their activities. In this chapter, we present the agent coordination models defined in the last 25 years taking the contributions to the WOA workshops as fil rouge, along with the languages that have been proposed to allow agent coordination. In addition, we sketch how the research on agent coordination has paved the way to be applied in several application fields, such as autonomic computing, self-organizing systems, energy management, and autonomous vehicles.

Keywords: Coordination · multi-agent system · models · languages

1 Introduction

Software agents represent a useful paradigm in the development of complex distributed systems [28]. They exhibit some specific features that make them useful for different kinds of application areas. Let us start from the feature that could perhaps be considered the most important one, i.e. *autonomy*, which enables software agents to carry out tasks on behalf of humans with the ability to take autonomous decisions. In addition to this, there are other features that turn out to be relevant to achieving the benefits of exploiting agents. In fact, software agents are *reactive*, which means that they sense and react to environment changes; moreover, they are *proactive*, which means that they have plans to achieve goals, and last but not least, they are *social*, which means that they

V. Mascardi and A. Omicini (Eds.): *The Agents Journey*, LNCS 16395, pp. 127–146, 2026.
https://doi.org/10.1007/978-3-032-22940-3_5

interact with other agents and the environment in which they act. The *sociality* feature of the agent enables building systems composed of several agents, which allows the definition of multi-agent systems (MASs). Therefore, MASs are the natural way to design complex distributed systems that determine two different scenarios. On the one hand, a MAS can be considered from an individualistic perspective: an aggregation of agents that simply interact with each other; in this scenario, the resulting MAS is closed, meaning that participant agents must be designed only referring to the specific problem. On the other hand, a MAS can be used to determine an open scenario to provide a conceptual model for vast organizations. In the latter scenario, the agent sociality not only enables technical powers but also enables to model, in the agents, a behavior very similar to the human one. This calls for ruling out the interactions among agents in some way. In particular, agents can compete to exploit shared resources and/or can exploit each other features to achieve self-interested goals (competitive agents); nevertheless, agents can collaborate to carry out a common goal (cooperative agents); in both cases, a coordination model/language is needed. Another interesting feature of agents can be the *mobility*, which allows agents to move to different execution contexts and introduces some interesting challenges in agent coordination.

The aim of this chapter is to provide the reader with a wide illustration of the approaches present in the literature with regard to agent coordination. This survey poses a particular emphasis to the approaches that have been presented at the Workshop on Objects and Agents (WOA) over the years to underline that the Italian research is absolutely in line with the research carried out at the international level. Our analysis on agent coordination ranges from the models to the languages, to finish discussing what application fields can benefit from using MASs.

More in detail, this chapter is organized as follows. In Sect. 2, we describe the *methodology* used to gather the WOA papers, summarizing them in a table. In Sect. 3, we provide a survey of the *coordination models* that have been defined in the last 25 years to model the agents' interactions; in this Section we first consider the two possible couplings of coordination, spatially and temporally, to arrive at defining another aspect that makes the coordination more active or reactive, i.e. the adaptability. In particular, we present MARS and other models that apply this point of view. In Sect. 4, we consider some specific coordination approaches that have again been defined in the last 25 years to rule the agents' interactions, but focusing in particular on the relative *coordination languages*. In Sect. 5, we include a discussion of application areas where the use of a MAS together with a specific model/language for agent coordination can be particularly relevant. Section 6 concludes the chapter.

2   Methodology

To select the WOA papers to analyze in this chapter, we started from two sources of information tracked year after year by the WOA organization: a bibliography file tracking citation metadata about all papers presented at WOA, and a spreadsheet with abstracts of such papers. We automatically have filtered relevant contributions for the current chapter by searching for keywords "coordination model" and "coordination language", and then removing duplicates (since in some WOA editions, demo papers had the same title as main event papers). Afterwards, we manually further filtered the partial results by reading the abstracts and, when needed, the paper itself to evaluate whether the contribution is relevant to the chapter. The end result of this process is the collection of papers cited in this chapter and summarized in Table 1.

Table 1. Summary of coordination related contributions discussed at WOA. In the "Category" column, M = model, L = language, W = middleware, A = application.

Year	Refs	Brief description	Category
'98–14	[39,41,52,53]	TuCSoN, programmable tuple-based coordination	M W
2000	[11]	MARS, programmable coordination model	M L W
'02–13	[38,43,59]	ReSpecT, programmable tuples	M L
2004	[32]	TOTA, distributed, self-organising tuples	M W
2006	[45]	Coordination for autonomic computing	A
'08–12	[46,57,62,64]	SAPERE, distributed, self-organising semantic tuples	M L W
2010	[44]	Coordination for grid computing	A
'10–13	[36,47]	Bio-chemical inspired, self-organising tuples	M
2012	[14]	Coordination for energy regulation	A
'12–17	[2,4,6]	Commitment-based architecture	M W
2015	[20]	Coordination for unmanned vehicles	A
2018	[54]	Coordination for smart factories	A

3 Coordination Models

During its life, an agent is in need to coordinate its activities with other entities, let them be other agents or resources on hosting execution environments. More in particular:

- an application may be composed of several agents that cooperatively perform a task and, then, are in need of coordinating their activities;
- an agent, in case it is mobile, is usually in need to roam across remote sites to access resources, services, and even other agents there allocated.

As a case study application, let us consider a simple WWW information retrieval application. An agent is sent to a remote site to analyze the WWW pages and returns to the starting site with the URLs of the pages that contain a specific keyword. The agent clones itself for any remote link found in the pages of interest and sends the clones to the found sites, to recursively continue the searching work. Inter-agent coordination is needed to avoid multiple visits of different agents on the same site (since it is common to find cross-references in HTML pages). The coordination of the agents with regard to the hosting execution environment aims to define a precise protocol to access and retrieve information on a site.

Although coordination models have been extensively studied in the past, the openness of the agent environment introduces new problems and needs. In this section, we define a simple taxonomy of the possible coordination models for agent applications [12]. Two main characteristics distinguish different coordination models: spatial and temporal coupling. In particular:

- *spatially* coupled coordination models require the involved entities to share a common name space; conversely, spatially uncoupled models enforce anonymous interactions;
- *temporally* coupled coordination models imply synchronization of the involved entities; conversely, temporally uncoupled coordination models achieve asynchronous interactions.

Therefore, four categories of coordination models can be derived (see Fig. 1): (i) direct, both spatially and temporally coupled; (ii) meeting-oriented, spatially uncoupled and temporally coupled; (iii) blackboard-based, spatially coupled and temporally uncoupled; (iv) Linda-like, both spatially and temporally uncoupled. In the following (Sects. 3.1 to 3.4), we detail these four coordination models.

| | | Temporal | |
		coupled	uncoupled
Spatial	coupled	Direct	Blackboard-based
	uncoupled	Meeting-oriented	Linda-like

Fig. 1. Coordination Models for Agents

However, from our research work we can affirm that all these models exhibit a possible limitation. In fact, they are "passive" and therefore do not provide active support for applications. So, we decided to explore "active" or "reactive" coordination models that can introduce another aspect of coordination, i.e. *adaptability* (see Sect. 3.5).

3.1   Direct Coordination

In direct coordination models, agents can initiate a communication by explicitly naming the involved partners (spatial coupling). This usually implies their synchronization (temporal coupling). In the case of inter-agent coordination, two agents must agree on a communication protocol, typically a peer-to-peer one. In the case of access to the resources of the hosting environment, coordination usually occurs in a client-server way.

The general adoption of direct coordination models in agent applications is not suitable. Repeated interactions require stable network connections, making communication highly dependent on network reliability. In addition, wide-area communications between entities require complex and highly informed routing protocols. Finally, because several agent applications are intrinsically dynamic (through dynamic agent creation), it may be difficult to adopt a spatially coupled model in which the communication partners must be identified. In the case study application, the agents cannot know how many other agents make up the application because the agents are dynamically created depending on the found links. In addition, to establish a communication session, agents must be forced to synchronize their activities, which instead are intrinsically asynchronous and autonomous. In the presence of many agents, direct coordination models can be effectively exploited only for accessing local resources: a local server has to be provided as a manager, and an agent interacts with it in a client-server way. In our case study application, local WWW servers may supply HTML pages to agents.

3.2   Meeting-Oriented Coordination

In meeting-oriented coordination, agents can interact without the need to explicitly name the partners involved. Interactions occur in the context of known meeting points that agents join, either explicitly or implicitly, to communicate and synchronize with each other. Apart from always-opened meetings - which can abstract the role of servers in an execution environment – an active entity must assume the role of initiator to open a meeting point. Often, meetings are locally constrained: to avoid the problems related to non-local communication (i.e., unpredictable delay and unreliability), a meeting takes place at a given execution environment, and only local agents can participate in it. Clearly, because agents must share common knowledge of either the meeting names or of the events that force them to join a meeting, full spatial uncoupling is not achieved.

Although the meeting model partially solves the problem of exactly identifying the involved partners, it has the drawback of enforcing strict synchronization between agents. Because in many applications, the schedule and the position of agents cannot be predicted, the risk of missing interactions is very high. In the case study application, to avoid multiple visits to the same site with a meeting-oriented model, an additional agent must be introduced for each site visited. When an agent has explored a site, it creates a "meeting" agent before returning to the user site. The meeting agent is forced to reside on the creation site: as any other agent arrives at this site, it tries to enter a meeting with the meeting agent to detect whether the site has been already visited or not. In our opinion, this solution is not generally suitable for the case study application because there is no possibility that the meeting agent will know when to die. In addition, to let an agent remain on one visited site is not safe: a malicious agent can exploit the time it is on a site to furnish private information to the external.

3.3   Blackboard-Based Coordination

In blackboard-based coordination, interactions occur through shared data spaces, local to each hosting environment, used by agents as common repositories to store and retrieve messages. Insofar as agents must agree on a common message identifier to communicate and exchange data via a blackboard, they are not spatially uncoupled.

The most significant advantage of this coordination model derives from fully temporal uncoupling: messages can be left on blackboards without needing to know neither where the corresponding receivers are nor when they will read the messages. This clearly suits a scenario in which the position and the schedules of the agents can be neither monitored nor granted easily. In addition, being any inter-agent interaction forced to be performed via a blackboard, hosting environments can easily control all interactions, thus leading to an execution environment model more secure than that of the coordination approaches described above. Our case study application can effectively exploit the blackboard model for inter-agent coordination. When an agent arrives at a site, it first checks on the local blackboard for a "marker" message, coming from another agent of the same application. If the agent reads the "marker" message, it knows that the site has already been visited; otherwise, it is in charge of placing the "marker" message on the blackboard. With regard to agent-to-hosting execution environment interactions, a blackboard can be exploited to let agents retrieve the needed information without requiring the presence of a specialized resource manager and to let the local environment provide in the blackboard all the data it wants to publish while protecting private data. In the case study application, the execution environment could provide, in the form of messages, the pathnames of all its publicly accessible files. However, there is no way for an agent to retrieve the pathnames of the HTML files only, but all messages have to be retrieved and successively selected to search those corresponding to HTML files.

3.4   Linda-like Coordination

In Linda-like coordination, the accesses to a local blackboard are based on associative mechanisms [15]: Information is organized into tuples and retrieved associatively through a pattern matching mechanism. Associative blackboards (called tuple spaces) enforce full uncoupling, requiring neither temporal agreement nor mutual knowledge to let agents coordinate.

Linda-like coordination suits agent applications well. In a wide and dynamic environment, such as the Internet, having complete and updated knowledge of hosting execution environments and other application agents may be difficult or even impossible. Then, because agents would somehow require pattern matching mechanisms to adaptively deal with uncertainty, dynamicity, and heterogeneity, it is worthwhile to integrate these mechanisms directly into the coordination model, to simplify agent programming, and to reduce application complexity. In the testbed application, associative mechanisms may be not necessary for inter-agent interactions, because agents know which message to retrieve from the blackboard to avoid multiple visits, as shown in the previous subsection. However, let our application be composed of several types of agent, each devoted to the search for a different keyword. In this case, an associative mechanism would be necessary: an agent must check the presence of marker messages in the tuple space with the keyword field that matches the agent's own keyword; instead, it must ignore the messages left by agents searching for different keywords. With regard to agent-to-hosting execution environment interactions, if the pathnames of all public readable files are available in the tuple space, agents can simply look for tuples corresponding to pathnames matching the "html" extension.

3.5   Adaptable Coordination

As mentioned above, we further study the possibility of making the coordination medium *active* or *reactive*, to provide *adaptable* coordination and better support to the development of agent applications. In this way, the environment can become an actor in the coordination, taking an active part in the coordination process. This allows the coordination to be adaptable to the context in which it occurs, leading to *context-aware* coordination [13]. With "context" we mean a broad range of aspects, from the environment where the coordination takes place to the specific agents that need to coordinate with each other, from external information to the history of the involved agents.

In the following, we present an example of a coordination architecture that implements the idea of adaptable coordination (MARS), and then briefly present other approaches. As the readers will see, the most suitable model for facing adaptability is the Linda-like one.

MARS (Mobile Agent Reactive Spaces). MARS [11] has been proposed by the researchers of the University of Modena and Reggio Emilia. MARS is a programmable coordination architecture for Java-based mobile agents. Nevertheless, it can be associated to different agent systems with little modifications.

MARS adopts the Linda-like model and makes many independent *tuple spaces* available to the agents. It was originally conceived for *mobile* agents, but can be used with any kind of agent. Each tuple space is associated with a node and is accessed by locally executing agents. For each space, MARS provides a *metalevel tuple space*, which contains tuples that represent actions that can be executed in reaction of agents' access to the "normal" space. In this way, each MARS tuple space can "react" to accesses performed by agents that exhibit a behavior programmed by the space administrator or by the agents themselves (see Fig. 2).

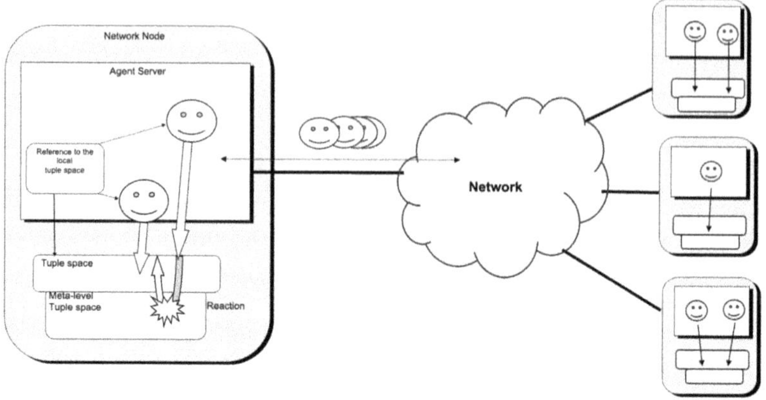

Fig. 2. The MARS coordination architecture (image adapted from [11]).

The MARS tuple space enables inter-agent coordination and allows agents to access primitive data items and references to execution environment resources. The local tuple space is the only node resource that agents can directly access, reducing the problem of dynamically binding local references to mobile entities.

Other Approaches. PageSpace [17], an architecture for interactive Web applications, uses Linda-like coordination. Both mobile and fixed agents can use its tuple spaces to store and associatively retrieve object references. In addition, agents can create tuple spaces to interact privately without affecting host execution environments. To influence the coordination activities of application agents, PageSpace is not reactive in itself but instead defines special-purpose agents to access the space and change its contents. These special-purpose agents can be limited both in monitoring interaction events and in tuning their effects.

The IBM T Spaces [61] project uses Linda-like interaction spaces as general-purpose information repositories for mobile and network applications. Rather than defining agent-oriented coordination media, the T Spaces architecture aims to provide a powerful and standard interface for accessing large amounts of information organized as a database. Therefore, the designers of T Spaces integrated a special programmability to add new behaviors to a tuple space. This occurs through new admissible operations on a tuple space rather than by programming the effects on the basic Linda operations; of course, this requires application agents to either be aware of operations available in a given tuple space or somehow dynamically acquire this knowledge.

The MOLE system [10] defines a meeting-oriented coordination model rather than a tuple-based one. MOLE meetings use shared, non-mobile objects that agents must access to send or receive messages. MOLE meetings enforce temporal uncoupling by permitting asynchronous message notification to agents and can be programmed to integrate specific policies for managing the exchanged messages. These characteristics provide an uncoupled and programmable coordination model that enforces a control-oriented coordination style, in contrast to a data-oriented one, and requires the definition of meeting points at the application level.

TuCSoN [40] extends the Linda coordination model that defines *tuple centers* whose behavior can be programmed by a specific language. TuCSoN is detailed in Sect. 4.3.

4   Coordination Languages

Coordination *models* abstractly define the concepts necessary to give shape to a desired interaction paradigm, i.e., one with desired properties. For instance, the blackboard or Linda models mentioned in previous section, respectively, offer temporal, and both temporal and spatial uncoupling properties. Coordination *languages*, instead, concretely define the vocabulary and grammar of programming languages specifically meant to deal with the *interaction* space of computing, not the more common algorithmic space [60]. Of course, several of the coordination models proposed throughout the years also brought along their own coordination language to give the model an operational incarnation suitable for practical experiments, implementations, and real-world deployments.

The WOA workshop series has seen some of such languages:

- the "Tuples Over The Air" (*TOTA*) model, language, and middleware [32];
- the "Self-Aware PERvasive Ecosystems" (*SAPERE*) model, language, and middleware [46,57,62,64], originated in the context of the homonym EU FP7 project;
- the "TUple Centres Spread Over the Network" (TuCSoN) model, language, and middleware [39,41,52,53];
- the *commitment-based* languages proposed by Baldoni et al. [2,4,6];
- the "Reaction SPECification Tuples" (ReSpecT) adopted in TuCSoN and proposed by Omicini et al. [38,43,59];
- the *biochemistry-inspired* languages [36,47] that were either precursors of or inspired by the SAPERE approach already mentioned.

4.1   TOTA

TOTA is a framework that utilizes *distributed tuples* to represent contextual information and allows uncoupled interaction between the components of a distributed application. Unlike other shared data-space models, TOTA tuples are not node specific or tied to a particular data space within the network. Instead, they are put into the network and *autonomously propagate* according to the specific *propagation rules*. Consequently, TOTA tuples form a *spatially distributed data structure* that conveys both information exchange among the application components and contextual information about the distributed environment itself. In TOTA, such an environment features a peer-to-peer network of possibly mobile nodes, each running a local instance of the TOTA middleware—as depicted in Fig. 3. The middleware maintains references to a limited set of *neighboring nodes*, and *automatically adapts* to dynamic changes caused by node mobility or failures. In scenarios like Mobile Ad Hoc Networks (MANETs), TOTA nodes identify neighbors within their wireless communication range. The propagation rules for tuples diffusion are automatically triggered by the TOTA middleware when the appropriate conditions occur (e.g., a new node enters the neighborhood, a certain tuple is added/removed to the current tuple space, and other conditions). Such rules may not only modify the location of the tuple, but also its content, allowing the creation of an *overlay* of distributed tuples meant to transmit information across the network and represent *contextual information* about the application environment in a distributed way. TOTA has been used to program coordinated motion patterns [35], implement location and content-based information access [31], implement mobile particle systems [30], in order to enable stigmergic coordination [33], and to program modular robots [34].

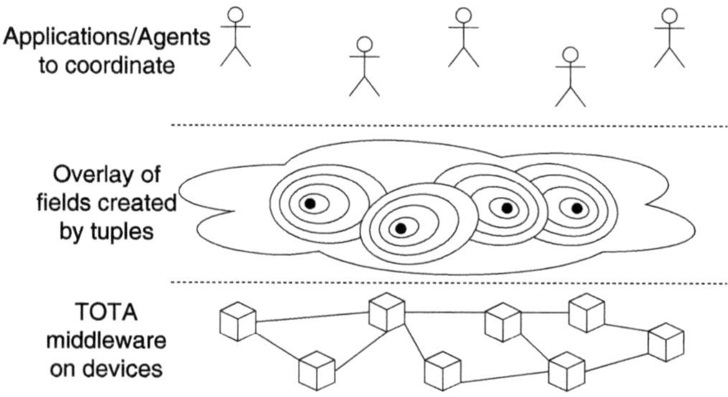

Fig. 3. The TOTA coordination model and language.

4.2 SAPERE

SAPERE [16,63] is a coordination model for multi-agent pervasive systems inspired by natural *chemical reactions*, featuring its own coordination language ("eco-laws"). The SAPERE architecture is depicted in Fig. 4. SAPERE is based on four main concepts: Live Semantic Annotations (LSAs), LSA Tuple Space, Agents, and Eco-laws. LSAs are tuples of types (name, value) that are used to store application data. LSAs belonging to a computing node are stored in a shared container named LSA Tuple Space. Each LSA is associated with an agent, such as sensors, services, or general applications, that wants to interact with the LSA space, e.g., injecting or retrieving LSAs from the LSA space. Inside the shared container, tuples react in a virtual chemical solution by using a predefined set of *coordination rules* named eco-laws, which can (i) instantiate relationships among LSAs (Bonding eco-law), (ii) aggregate them (Aggregate eco-law), (iii) delete them (Decay eco-law), and (iv) spread them across remote LSA Tuples Spaces (Spreading eco-law). When a tuple is modified by an eco-law, its relative agent is notified. The implementation of the SAPERE middleware allowed several kinds of real distributed self-adaptive and self-organizing applications to be developed [63]. More discussion about these sort of self-organising coordination models, languages, and middleware is provided by Chapter [1].

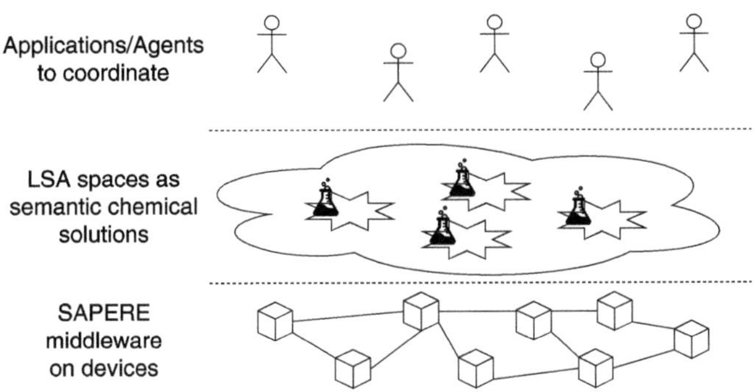

Fig. 4. The SAPERE coordination model and language.

4.3   TuCSoN

TuCSoN is a coordination model that adopts *Linda* as its core but extends it in several ways, such as by adopting nested tuples (expressed as first-order logic terms), adding primitives (i.e., bulk [55] and uniform [40]), and replacing tuple spaces with *tuple centres* [50]—that is, tuple spaces whose behavior can be programmed with a dedicated language: ReSpecT [48]. As such, the main driving concepts behind the TuCSoN model and technology are (i) *first-order logic tuples* and ReSpecT reactions to enable the declarative expression of coordination policies, (ii) asynchronous communication and coordination primitives by default (although synchronous versions are also available) to enable *full decoupling*, and (iii) programmable tuple spaces to enable full control over the *coordination policies* to be followed by the system at hand, there included security policies [19]. TuCSoN comes with a Java-based implementation that provides coordination as a service [58] in the form of a Java library (defining an API) and a middleware runtime, especially targeting distributed Java processes, but open to rational agents implemented in tuProlog [25]—see Fig. 5.

4.4   Commitments

Commitment-based communication artifacts [5] (i.e., computational tools providing functions) in multi-agent systems implement interaction protocols and monitoring functionalities—as thoroughly described in Chapter [7]. These artifacts

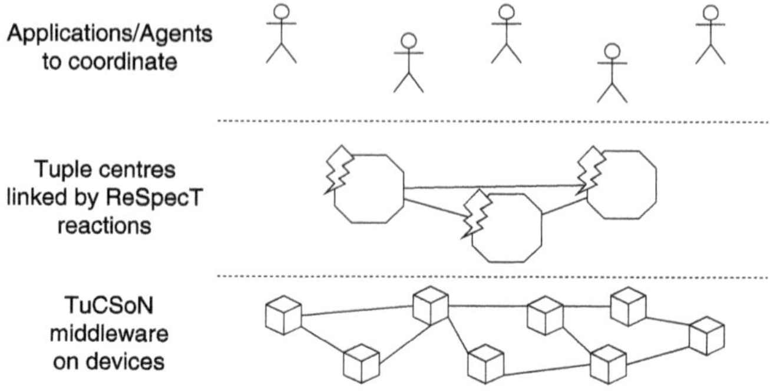

Fig. 5. The TuCSoN coordination model and language.

verify ongoing interactions for protocol adherence, detect violations, and identify violators. As *programmable* communication channels, artifacts encapsulate what commitment protocols refer to as "the social state", which captures the interaction session between parties and provides the necessary social actions for agents to enter and comply with commitments. Consequently, the artifacts encode the *coordination rules* of the protocol. A commitment, denoted as $C(x, y, r, p)$, represents a contractual relationship between a debtor (x) and a creditor (y). Specifically, the debtor commits to the realization of the consequent condition (p) when the antecedent condition (r) is satisfied. Commitments thus function as directed obligations from the debtor to the creditor. Unlike traditional obligations, commitments are subject to manipulation, for example, delegation, assignment, or release. Importantly, commitments serve a regulative purpose: social expectations dictate that agents respect the commitments that involve them, e.g. to preserve reputation. In particular, the debtor bears the responsibility for fulfilling the consequent condition. Thus, agents' behavior is influenced by the commitments present in the social state. Commitment protocols typically consist of a set of shared actions agreed upon by all interacting agents. These social actions modify the social state, for example, by adding new commitments, releasing agents from existing commitments, or satisfying commitments.

4.5   ReSpecT

The ReSpecT language [48] is rooted in first-order logic and serves to define *tuple centres'* behavior within TuCSoN. A tuple centre is a tuple space that introduces *programmability* into the coordination environment. Unlike a traditional tuple space, where the response to communication events (adding, reading, and removing tuples) is predetermined and unchangeable, a tuple centre's behavior can be changed. This flexibility is achieved by programming a collection of *specification tuples*, also known as *reactions*. ReSpecT, as a language for behavior specification, facilitates the creation of internal computations in a tuple centre, and their linkage to specific communication events. It enables the declarative pairing of events with reactions through unique logic constructs termed specification tuples, formatted as $reaction(E, G, C)$. For an event Ev, a specification tuple $reaction(E, G, C)$ will execute a computation C upon the happening of the event Ev, provided that E and Ev "match"—in ReSpecT, the matching is defined on top of Prolog unification mechanisms [49]. Moreover, computation C is executed only if the guard predicates defined in G, which express conditions on the event or the state of the tuple centre, evaluate to `true`. ReSpecT thus allows for the procedural programming of reactions as sequences of computations (in terms of logical goals), with each computation potentially achieving success or encountering failure. Every reaction elicited by a communication event is processed prior to addressing any subsequent events. Consequently, agents experience the outcome of the communication event (e.g., invocation of a Linda primitive) and the simultaneous execution of all related responses as one unified shift in the state of the tuple center. Therefore, the impact of a communication operation on a tuple centre can be tailored to be as intricate as necessary, depending on the coordination demands of the application at hand.

4.6   Biochemical Tuple Spaces

Biochemical tuple spaces [56] are the basis of a coordination model inspired by biochemical solutions where tuples always have an associated activity or pertinency value. This value represents the concept of *chemical concentration* to determine how much a tuple can influence the coordination state. For example, a low concentration tuple would participate in the execution of coordination rules infrequently. In fact, this model incorporates coordination laws that resemble *chemical reactions*. These laws are integrated into the space of the tuples, and they cause the concentration of tuples to change over time, mirroring the behavior of chemical substances in a solution. This allows for the use of chemical patterns to bring about interesting self-organizing properties. Note that if t is a tuple specified by *in* (extract) or *rd* (read) operations, a tuple existing in the space that matches t as in Linda is looked up. However, unlike Linda, the matching function here is application dependent and returns a degree of matching (e.g. $\in [0, 1]$) instead of a yes/no: stronger matching (e.g. higher semantic matching) implies a higher *probability* of finding a certain tuple. This probabilistic aspect is the crucial mechanism that ultimately enables self-organization and adaptiveness. Furthermore, these laws include a mechanism for the diffusion of tuples, which simulates the movement of chemical substances across the boundaries of biological compartments. This adds another layer of realism to the model, making it a powerful tool for studying biochemical systems, and promotes its usage in networked systems.

Common to all these heterogeneous languages is their inspiration for other fields of research, such as physics, sociology, chemistry, made not just to appear "fancy", but to inherit some desirable properties and to attack the peculiar challenges of some application domains [29]. For example, biochemical coordination approaches directly enable and support self-organization and the resulting self-* properties [26]. Chapter [1] provides ample discussion about these kinds of self-organising coordination models, languages, and middleware.

5   Application Fields

In this section, we sketch some application fields in which the coordination of software agents can be exploited in an effective way.

Autonomic computing is a context in which agent coordination has been exploited to achieve flexible and adaptable systems [45]. In fact, the autonomic computing and multi-agent systems share different aspects that enable synergies between them. Autonomic computing requires a general purpose component model, in order to enforce autonomic behavior in both the forms of self-adaptation and self-organization, to handle "situatedness" in complex knowledge environments, and to tolerate scalable forms of dynamic aggregation. Multi-agent systems research can play a major role in the definition of such component model and, more generally, in the advance of the autonomic communication research area.

Coordination has been exploited in the field of energy regulation [14]. Since private houses can produce renewable energy, for example, by means of solar panels, owners could sell the unused energy to neighbors. A peer-to-peer model seems the most suitable for energy negotiation (i.e., between single producers and single consumers), even in a deregulated way. On the one hand, this situation could lead to advantages for both producers and consumers, but on the other hand it is very complex and dynamic. An agent-based approach can help to tackle complexity, thanks to the autonomy of agents. Their coordination can grant that the system meets defined policies, both at the producers/consumers level and at the community level. In addition, a suitable coordination enables the optimization of energy production and supply costs by means of negotiation and learning.

Another interesting field in which coordination models and languages can be exploited is the management of autonomous vehicles [37]. An autonomous vehicle can be modeled as an agent that has some goals, for example, to reach the destination as soon as possible or to park near the office. To achieve the goals, the vehicle must compete with other vehicles to exploit common resources, such as roads, intersections, and parking slots. Sometimes, they must collaborate to exploit the resources, for instance, aggregating in platoons. To complete the scenario, the local administration can have some goals, for instance reducing the pollution caused by the vehicles. In any case, their coordination is needed to regulate the movements and to apply local or global polices.

In general, self-organizing approaches take advantage of the experience in the agent world, in particular reusing the coordination models and languages in other different areas, such as computational grids [44], unmanned vehicles [20], smart factories [54].

6   Conclusion

In this chapter, we have addressed the topic of the coordination of software agents, starting from the point that the agents are *social*, and this implies their interaction and then their coordination. We have focused on *coordination models* and *coordination languages*, about which we have reported an overview. We have reported in particular the research works presented at WOA in it 25 years. We have also sketched some application fields that can take advantage of the coordination of software agents.

After this overview work, we can provide some considerations.

First, only 23 WOA papers over almost 400 tackled the coordination issue in a sharp way. Of course, WOA addressed and addresses a broad range of topics, from agent modeling to Agent-Oriented Software Engineering, from intelligent agents to agents applications, so it is reasonable that the coordination issue concerns only a slice of the total number of papers.

The second consideration is about the fact that WOA papers on coordination models and languages are not recent. Most of them have been published before 2010. This can mean that the agent coordination is quite settled and no further specific research is needed. In any case, we believe that this requires some reflection from the WOA community.

Acknowledgments. The authors would like to thank all students and researchers who have contributed to the implementation of the models and the languages, and also the applications presented in this chapter.

Disclosure of Interests. The authors have no competing interests.

References

1. Aguzzi, G., Casadei, R., Pianini, D., Viroli, M.: Self-organisation with aggregate computing: a reflection under the lenses of multi-agent systems engineering. In: Mascardi and Omicini [42] (2026)
2. Baldoni, M., Baroglio, C.: Some thoughts about commitment protocols (position paper). In: De Paoli and Vizzari [24], pp. 68–71 (2012). http://ceur-ws.org/Vol-892/paper11.pdf
3. Baldoni, M., Baroglio, C., Bergenti, F., Garro, A. (eds.): WOA 2013 – 14th Workshop "From Objects to Agents". CEUR Workshop Proceedings, vol. 1099. Turin, Italy (2013). http://ceur-ws.org/Vol-1099/
4. Baldoni, M., Baroglio, C., Capuzzimati, F.: 2COMM: a commitment-based MAS architecture. In: Baldoni et al. [3], pp. 38–57 (2013). http://ceur-ws.org/Vol-1099/paper11.pdf
5. Baldoni, M., Baroglio, C., Capuzzimati, F., Micalizio, R.: Exploiting social commitments in programming agent interaction. In: Chen, Q., Torroni, P., Villata, S., Hsu, J.Y., Omicini, A. (eds.) PRIMA 2015: Principles and Practice of Multi-Agent Systems - 18th International Conference, Bertinoro, Italy, 26–30 October 2015. Proceedings. Lecture Notes in Computer Science, vol. 9387, pp. 566–574. Springer (2015). https://doi.org/10.1007/978-3-319-25524-8_39
6. Baldoni, M., Baroglio, C., Capuzzimati, F., Micalizio, R.: Endowing business artifacts with a normative coordination layer. In: De Meo et al. [21], pp. 71–77 (2017). http://ceur-ws.org/Vol-1867/w13.pdf
7. Baldoni, M., Baroglio, C., Micalizio, R.: Interaction protocols: from AUML to social commitments, from artifacts to BSPL. In: Mascardi and Omicini [42] (2026)

8. Baldoni, M., Cossentino, M., De Paoli, F., Seidita, V. (eds.): WOA 2008 – 9th Workshop "From Objects to Agents". Seneca Edizioni Torino, Palermo, Italy (2008). http://www.pa.icar.cnr.it/woa08/materiali/Proceedings.pdf

9. Baldoni, M., De Paoli, F., Martelli, A., Omicini, A. (eds.): WOA 2004 – 5th Workshop "From Objects to Agents". Pitagora Editrice Bologna, Torino, Italy (2004). http://lia.deis.unibo.it/books/woa2004/atti.pdf

10. Baumann, J., Hohl, F., Rothermel, K., Straßer, M.: Mole-concepts of a mobile agent system. World Wide Web **1**, 123–137 (1998)

11. Cabri, G., Leonardi, L., Zambonelli, F.: MARS: a programmable coordination architecture for mobile agents. IEEE Internet Comput. **4**(4), 26–35 (2000). https://doi.org/10.1109/4236.865084

12. Cabri, G., Leonardi, L., Zambonelli, F.: Mobile-agent coordination models for internet applications. Computer **33**(2), 82–89 (2000). https://doi.org/10.1109/2.820044

13. Cabri, G., Leonardi, L., Zambonelli, F.: Engineering mobile agent applications via context-dependent coordination. IEEE Trans. Software Eng. **28**(11), 1039–1055 (2002). https://doi.org/10.1109/TSE.2002.1049403

14. Capodieci, N., Cabri, G., Pagani, G.A., Aiello, M.: Agent modeling of a pervasive application to enable deregulated energy markets. In: De Paoli and Vizzari [24], pp. 8–16 (2012). http://ceur-ws.org/Vol-892/paper3.pdf

15. Carriero, N., Gelernter, D.: Linda in context. Commun. ACM **32**(4), 444–458 (1989)

16. Castelli, G., Mamei, M., Rosi, A., Zambonelli, F.: Pervasive middleware goes social: the SAPERE approach. In: Fifth IEEE Conference on Self-Adaptive and Self-Organizing Systems, SASOW 2011, Ann Arbor, MI, USA, 3–7 October 2011, Workshops Proceedings, pp. 9–14. IEEE Computer Society (2011). https://doi.org/10.1109/SASOW.2011.6

17. Ciancarini, P., Tolksdorf, R., Vitali, F., Rossi, D., Knoche, A.: Coordinating multiagent applications on the WWW: a reference architecture. IEEE Trans. Software Eng. **24**(5), 362–375 (1998)

18. Cossentino, M., Sabatucci, L., Seidita, V. (eds.): WOA 2018 – 19th Workshop "From Objects to Agents". CEUR Workshop Proceedings, vol. 2215. Palermo, Italy (2018). http://ceur-ws.org/Vol-2215/

19. Cremonini, M., Omicini, A., Zambonelli, F.: Coordination and access control in open distributed agent systems: the TuCSoN approach. In: Porto, A., Roman, G.C. (eds.) Coordination Languages and Models. Lecture Notes in Computer Science, vol. 1906, pp. 99–114. Springer, Cham (2000). https://doi.org/10.1007/3-540-45263-X_7. 4th International Conference (COORDINATION 2000), Limassol, Cyprus, 11–13 September 2000. Proceedings

20. De Benedetti, M., D'Urso, F., Messina, F., Pappalardo, G., Santoro, C.: Self-organising uavs for wide area fault-tolerant aerial monitoring. In: Di Napoli, C., Rossi, S., Staffa, M. (eds.) WOA 2015 – 16th Workshop "From Objects to Agents". CEUR Workshop Proceedings, vol. 1382, pp. 135–141. Naples, Italy (2015). http://ceur-ws.org/Vol-1382/paper21.pdf

21. De Meo, P., Postorino, M.N., Rosaci, D., Sarnè, G.M.L. (eds.): WOA 2017 – 18th Workshop "From Objects to Agents". CEUR Workshop Proceedings, vol. 1867. Scilla, RC, Italy (2017). http://ceur-ws.org/Vol-1867/

22. De Paoli, F., Di Stefano, A., Omicini, A., Santoro, C. (eds.): WOA 2006 – 7th Workshop "From Objects to Agents". CEUR Workshop Proceedings, vol. 204. Catania, Italy (2006). http://ceur-ws.org/Vol-204/

23. De Paoli, F., Manzoni, S., Poggi, A. (eds.): WOA 2002 – 3rd Workshop "From Objects to Agents". Pitagora Editrice Bologna, Milano, Italy (2002). http://giuseppevizzari.github.io/WOA-proceedings-archive/woa-2002.html

24. De Paoli, F., Vizzari, G. (eds.): WOA 2012 – 13th Workshop "From Objects to Agents". CEUR Workshop Proceedings, vol. 892. Milano, Italy (2012). http://ceur-ws.org/Vol-892/

25. Denti, E., Omicini, A., Ricci, A.: tuProlog: a light-weight prolog for internet applications and infrastructures. In: Ramakrishnan, I. (ed.) Practical Aspects of Declarative Languages, Lecture Notes in Computer Science, vol. 1990, pp. 184–198. Springer, Heidelberg (2001). https://doi.org/10.1007/3-540-45241-9_13. 3rd International Symposium (PADL 2001), Las Vegas, NV, USA, 11–12 March 2001. Proceedings

26. Fernandez-Marquez, J.L., Serugendo, G.D.M.: From self-organizing mechanisms to design patterns to engineering self-organizing applications. In: 7th IEEE International Conference on Self-Adaptive and Self-Organizing Systems, SASO 2013, Philadelphia, PA, USA, 9–13 September 2013, pp. 267–268. IEEE Computer Society (2013). https://doi.org/10.1109/SASO.2013.21

27. Fortino, G., Garro, A., Palopoli, L., Russo, W., Spezzano, G. (eds.): WOA 2011 – 12th Workshop "From Objects to Agents". CEUR Workshop Proceedings, vol. 741. Rende, Italy (2011). http://ceur-ws.org/Vol-741/

28. Jennings, N.R.: An agent-based approach for building complex software systems. Commun. ACM **44**(4), 35–41 (2001)

29. Mamei, M., Menezes, R., Tolksdorf, R., Zambonelli, F.: Case studies for self-organization in computer science. J. Syst. Archit. **52**(8–9), 443–460 (2006). https://doi.org/10.1016/J.SYSARC.2006.02.002

30. Mamei, M., Vasirani, M., Zambonelli, F.: Self-organizing spatial shapes in mobile particles: the TOTA approach. In: Brueckner, S., Serugendo, G.D.M., Karageorgos, A., Nagpal, R. (eds.) Engineering Self-Organising Systems, Methodologies and Applications [revised versions of papers presented at the Engineering Selforganising Applications (ESOA 2004) Workshop, held During the Autonomous Agents and Multi-agent Systems conference (AAMAS 2004) in New York in July 2004, and selected invited papers]. Lecture Notes in Computer Science, vol. 3464, pp. 138–153. Springer (2004). https://doi.org/10.1007/11494676_9

31. Mamei, M., Zambonelli, F.: Location-based and content-based information access in mobile peer-to-peer computing: the TOTA approach. In: Moro, G., Sartori, C., Singh, M.P. (eds.) Agents and Peer-to-Peer Computing, Second International Workshop, AP2PC 2003, Melbourne, Australia, 14 July 2003, Revised and Invited Papers. Lecture Notes in Computer Science, vol. 2872, pp. 162–173. Springer (2003). https://doi.org/10.1007/978-3-540-25840-7_17

32. Mamei, M., Zambonelli, F.: Spatial computing: the TOTA approach. In: Baldoni et al. [9], pp. 126–142 (2004). http://giuseppevizzari.github.io/WOA-proceedings-archive/pdfs/woa2004/18.pdf

33. Mamei, M., Zambonelli, F.: Programming stigmergic coordination with the TOTA middleware. In: Dignum, F., Dignum, V., Koenig, S., Kraus, S., Singh, M.P., Wooldridge, M.J. (eds.) 4th International Joint Conference on Autonomous Agents and Multiagent Systems (AAMAS 2005), 25–29 July 2005, Utrecht, The Netherlands, pp. 415–422. ACM (2005). https://doi.org/10.1145/1082473.1082537

34. Mamei, M., Zambonelli, F.: Programming modular robots with the TOTA middleware. In: Nakashima, H., Wellman, M.P., Weiss, G., Stone, P. (eds.) 5th International Joint Conference on Autonomous Agents and Multiagent Systems (AAMAS

2006), Hakodate, Japan, 8–12 May 2006, pp. 485–487. ACM (2006). https://doi.org/10.1145/1160633.1160722

35. Mamei, M., Zambonelli, F., Leonardi, L.: Programming coordinated motion patterns with the TOTA middleware. In: Kosch, H., Böszörményi, L., Hellwagner, H. (eds.) Euro-Par 2003. Parallel Processing, 9th International Euro-Par Conference, Klagenfurt, Austria, 26–29 August 2003. Proceedings. Lecture Notes in Computer Science, vol. 2790, pp. 1027–1037. Springer (2003). https://doi.org/10.1007/978-3-540-45209-6_140

36. Mariani, S.: Parameter engineering vs. parameter tuning: the case of biochemical coordination in MoK. In: Baldoni et al. [3], pp. 16–23 (2013). http://ceur-ws.org/Vol-1099/paper5.pdf

37. Mariani, S., Cabri, G., Zambonelli, F.: Coordination of autonomous vehicles: taxonomy and survey. ACM Comput. Surv. (CSUR) **54**(1), 1–33 (2021)

38. Mariani, S., Omicini, A.: Space-aware coordination in ReSpecT. In: Baldoni et al. [3], pp. 1–7 (2013). http://ceur-ws.org/Vol-1099/paper3.pdf

39. Mariani, S., Omicini, A.: Tuple-based coordination of stochastic systems with uniform primitives. In: Baldoni et al. [3], pp. 8–15 (2013). http://ceur-ws.org/Vol-1099/paper4.pdf

40. Mariani, S., Omicini, A.: Coordination mechanisms for the modelling and simulation of stochastic systems: The case of uniform primitives. SCS M&S Mag. IV **4**(3), 6–25 (2014). https://hdl.handle.net/11585/480572

41. Mariani, S., Omicini, A.: TuCSoN coordination for MAS situatedness: towards a methodology. In: Santoro, C., Bergenti, F. (eds.) WOA 2014 – 15th Workshop "From Objects to Agents". CEUR Workshop Proceedings, vol. 1260, pp. 48–57. Catania, Italy (2014). http://ceur-ws.org/Vol-1260/paper11.pdf

42. Mascardi, V., Omicini, A. (eds.): The Agents Journey: Twenty-five Years of Multi-agent Systems at WOA. Lecture Notes in Computer Science – State-of-the-Art Surveys. Springer (2026)

43. Menezes, R., Omicini, A., Viroli, M.: Have ReSpecT for LogOp. In: De Paoli et al. [23], pp. 94–99 (2002). http://giuseppevizzari.github.io/WOA-proceedings-archive/pdfs/woa2002/18.pdf

44. Messina, F., Pappalardo, G., Santoro, C.: A self-organising system for resource finding in large-scale computational grids. In: Omicini and Viroli [51], pp. 110–116 (2010). http://ceur-ws.org/Vol-621/paper16.pdf

45. De Mola, F., Quitadamo, R.: An agent model for future autonomic communications. In: De Paoli et al. [22], pp. 51–59 (2006). http://ceur-ws.org/Vol-204/P07.pdf

46. Montagna, S., Viroli, M., Pianini, D., Fernandez-Marquez, J.L.: Towards a comprehensive approach to spontaneous self-composition in pervasive ecosystems. In: De Paoli and Vizzari [24], pp. 89–97 (2012). http://ceur-ws.org/Vol-892/paper1.pdf

47. Nardini, E., Viroli, M., Casadei, M., Omicini, A.: A self-organising infrastructure for chemical-semantic coordination: experiments in TuCSoN. In: Omicini and Viroli [51], pp. 117–125 (2010). http://CEUR-WS.org/Vol-621/paper17.pdf

48. Omicini, A.: Formal ReSpecT in the A&A perspective. Electron. Notes Theor. Comput. Sci. **175**(2), 97–117 (2006). https://doi.org/10.1016/J.ENTCS.2007.03.006

49. Omicini, A., Denti, E.: Formal ReSpecT. Electron. Notes Theor. Comput. Sci. **48**, 179–196 (2001). https://doi.org/10.1016/S1571-0661(04)00156-2. Declarative Programming – Selected Papers from AGP 2000, La Habana, Cuba, 4–6 December 2000

50. Omicini, A., Denti, E.: From tuple spaces to tuple centres. Sci. Comput. Program. **41**(3), 277–294 (2001). https://doi.org/10.1016/S0167-6423(01)00011-9
51. Omicini, A., Viroli, M. (eds.): WOA 2010 – 11th Workshop "From Objects to Agents". CEUR Workshop Proceedings, vol. 621. Rimini, Italy (2010). http://ceur-ws.org/Vol-621/
52. Omicini, A., Zambonelli, F.: Co-ordination of mobile information agents in TuCSoN. Internet Res. **8**(5), 400–413 (1998). https://doi.org/10.1108/10662249810241266
53. Ricci, A., Omicini, A.: Agent coordination contexts: Experiments in TuCSoN. In: De Paoli et al. [23], pp. 14–21 (2002). http://giuseppevizzari.github.io/WOA-proceedings-archive/pdfs/woa2002/17.pdf
54. Rosendahl, R., Cala, A., Kirchheim, K., Lueder, A., D'Agostino, N.: Towards smart factory: multi-agent integration on industrial standards for service-oriented communication and semantic data exchange. In: Cossentino et al. [18], pp. 124–132 (2018). http://ceur-ws.org/Vol-2215/paper_20.pdf
55. Rowstron, A.I.T.: Bulk primitives in Linda run-time systems. Ph.D. thesis, University of York, UK (1996). https://rowstron.azurewebsites.net/papers/thesis_double.pdf
56. Viroli, M., Casadei, M.: Biochemical tuple spaces for self-organising coordination. In: Field, J., Vasconcelos, V.T. (eds.) Coordination Models and Languages, 11th International Conference, COORDINATION 2009, Lisboa, Portugal, 9–12 June 2009. Proceedings. Lecture Notes in Computer Science, vol. 5521, pp. 143–162. Springer (2009). https://doi.org/10.1007/978-3-642-02053-7_8
57. Viroli, M., Nardini, E., Castelli, G., Mamei, M., Zambonelli, F.: Coordinating spatially-situated pervasive service ecosystems. In: Fortino et al. [27], pp. 19–27 (2011). http://ceur-ws.org/Vol-741/ID13_ViroliNardiniCastelliMameiZambonelli.pdf
58. Viroli, M., Omicini, A.: Coordination as a service. Fundam. Inform. **73**(4), 507–534 (2006). http://content.iospress.com/articles/fundamenta-informaticae/fi73-4-04
59. Viroli, M., Ricci, A.: Timed coordination artifacts with ReSpecT. In: Baldoni et al. [9], pp. 77–85 (2004). http://giuseppevizzari.github.io/WOA-proceedings-archive/pdfs/woa2004/12.pdf
60. Wegner, P.: Why interaction is more powerful than algorithms. Commun. ACM **40**(5), 80–91 (1997). https://doi.org/10.1145/253769.253801
61. Wyckoff, P., McLaughry, S.W., Lehman, T.J., Ford, D.A.: T spaces. IBM Syst. J. **37**(3), 454–474 (1998)
62. Zambonelli, F.: Nature-inspired spatial metaphors for pervasive service ecosystems. In: Baldoni et al. [8], pp. 61–67 (2008). http://www.pa.icar.cnr.it/woa08/materiali/paper/paper_10.pdf
63. Zambonelli, F., et al.: Developing pervasive multi-agent systems with nature-inspired coordination. Pervasive Mob. Comput. **17**, 236–252 (2015). https://doi.org/10.1016/j.pmcj.2014.12.002. Special issue "10 years of Pervasive Computing" In Honor of Chatschik Bisdikian
64. Zambonelli, F., Viroli, M.: From service-oriented architectures to nature-inspired pervasive service ecosystems. In: Omicini and Viroli [51], pp. 102–109 (2010). http://ceur-ws.org/Vol-621/paper15.pdf

Self-organisation with Aggregate Computing: A Reflection Under the Lenses of Multi-agent Systems Engineering

Gianluca Aguzzi$^{(\boxtimes)}$, Roberto Casadei , Danilo Pianini ,
and Mirko Viroli

Alma Mater Studiorum – Università di Bologna, Via dell'Università 50, Cesena, Italy
{gianluca.aguzzi,roby.casadei,danilo.pianini,mirko.viroli}@unibo.it

Abstract. In multi-agent systems research, large-scale is traditionally addressed by bio-inspired self-organisation: starting from the paradigmatic case of ant colonies, potentially miriads of agents can be designed to bring about global complex behaviour by simple individual tasks and local interactions, by emergence. With that inspiration, the research on aggregate computing developed a theoretical and programming framework to express and engineer resilient collective behaviour in a compositional and declarative fashion, completely abstracting from population size and shape. This grounds on previous work on co-fields for agent coordination, macro-languages for amorphous computing, and environment design for MASs, and culminated in the field calculus computing model, novel programming languages, and libraries for complex and distributed situation recognition, swarm behaviour, agent-assisted crowd engineering, and the like. Overall, after a decade, several results have been provided in the area of coordination, programming languages, distributed algorithms and platforms, and self-adaptive and self-organising systems. In this chapter we seek to pave the way for bringing some of such results back the agent community. We overview such results and elaborate on how can they provide contributions and research perspectives to traditional MAS research threads, and especially in the design of (i) distributed digital signs for environment-mediated agent coordination, (ii) collective plans for agents and swarms, and (iii) reinforcement learning frameworks for many-agent systems.

Keywords: Multi-agent systems · self-organisation · collective adaptive systems · aggregate computing · macro-programming · distributed artificial intelligence

1 Introduction

Multi-agent systems (MASs) involve multiple agents that coordinate to carry out joint goals. In this chapter, we focus on a particular kind of MASs, consisting of *homogeneous* populations operating at *large scale* (thousands or millions

© The Author(s) 2026
V. Mascardi and A. Omicini (Eds.): *The Agents Journey*, LNCS 16395, pp. 147–178, 2026.
https://doi.org/10.1007/978-3-032-22940-3_6

of agents, also called *many-agent* systems [99]). For these kinds of MASs, indeed, peculiar engineering techniques applied, often based on *nature-inspired self-organisation* mechanisms [42,185]. Self-organisation is the ability of a system to autonomously seek and maintain ordered structure and behaviour [42,185], promoting several applications [39,71,88,93,122,127]. Being intimately connected with *emergence* [141,180], its engineering is a challenge, as it involves expressing rules to promote a robust link between the *micro* level and the *macro* level in MASs [50,156]. Therefore, self-organisation is generally meant as something that can be *guided* or *steered* [13,140], but which is difficult to guarantee or assess in general. Indeed, common ways to test self-organising behaviour are by extensive simulation [93].

One of the most prominent approaches to self-organisation engineering is *aggregate computing* [170]. Originating from the multi-agent and coordination communities [49,172] (see [170] for a historical account and the chapter about coordination and agents in this book for a detailed overview [45]), it has been investigated around several directions including computational models, programming languages, distributed algorithms, middlewares, multi-agent learning, deployment on edge-cloud infrastructures. In this chapter, we look at these developments through the multi-agent systems lens, focusing particularly on research advancements emerged in 25 years of the Workshop on Objects and Agents (WOA), a venue that has contributed considerably to this research thread. These developments provide insights highly relevant to scientists and engineers of WOA.

The chapter is structured as follows. Section 2 describes the methodology used to identify relevant papers and provides an overview of the research landscape within the WOA community. Section 3 provides background on the connection between MASs and self-organisation. Section 4 provides the overview on aggregate computing approach, emphasising the connection with MASs. Finally, Sect. 5 delineates trends in self-organising MASs stimulating further research on the topic.

2   Methodology

To connect research in the WOA community with aggregate computing and its broader context of self-organisation and spatial computing, we employed a multi-stage process to systematically identify and analyse relevant primary studies.[1] Initially, a comprehensive bibliography of all WOA papers was downloaded using DBLP as the primary source.[2] This bibliography was then filtered using a set of *keywords* associated with the research carried out on the aggregate computing thread. The chosen keywords included `reinforcement learning`, `machine learning`, `adaptive`, `coordination`, `situated`, `self`, `programming`,

---

[1] The repository providing the infrastructure to reproduce the steps of the literature review and its outputs (data and pictures) can be found at https://github.com/cric96/experiments-2024-chapter-woa-literature-analysis.

[2] http://dblp.uni-trier.de/db/conf/woa.

`interaction`, `design`, `bdi`. This automated filtering process helped narrow down the initial set of papers to those potentially relevant to the research area. Following the automated filtering (which selected **244** papers), a *manual review* of the remaining papers was conducted to assess their relevance and ensure alignment with the specific focus on self-organisation in multi-agent systems. This manual curation process resulted in a final corpus of **64** papers deemed pertinent to the research area.

The significance of these topics within the WOA community is evident in the publication trends over the years, as illustrated in Fig. 1. Figure 1a shows that research interest in self-organisation and spatial coordination has been consistently present since 2001, with notable peaks around 2005–2006 and a recent resurgence of interest.

Figure 1b depicts the keywords extracted from the selected papers, highlighting the interconnected nature of the core research themes. The prominence of terms like "multi-agent systems", "self-organisation", and "coordination" underscores the community's focus on collective behaviours and distributed intelligence. We extracted the main topics from the selected papers using Gemini [12] (Fig. 2):

Self-* *Self-**: Research focusing on systems capable of self-management, self-adaptation, and autonomous behaviour, particularly in complex and dynamic environments.

Prog *Programming Agents*: Studies on agent-oriented programming languages, frameworks, and methodologies for developing multi-agent systems.

Coord *Coordination Protocol*: Work on coordination models and languages for managing interactions and dependencies between agents.

Apps *Multi-Agents Applications*: Research on applications of multi-agent systems in various domains, including smart cities, IoT, and social networks.

Perv *Pervasive Computing*: Research on ubiquitous and pervasive computing scenarios where agents operate in physical spaces with sensing and actuation capabilities.

Learn *Reinforcement Learning*: Recent research exploring the integration of learning capabilities in multi-agent systems, particularly through reinforcement learning approaches.

Know *Knowledge Representation*: Studies on knowledge representation and reasoning in multi-agent systems, including ontologies, logics, and reasoning mechanisms.

Space *Spatial Computing*: Research on spatial coordination and interaction models for agents operating in physical environments.

This analysis reveals important trends within our selected papers focusing on self-organisation and aggregate computing (see Table 1). Among these papers, coordination and self-* properties emerge as prominent research directions, representing a significant portion of the publications ($\sim$50%). However, there is

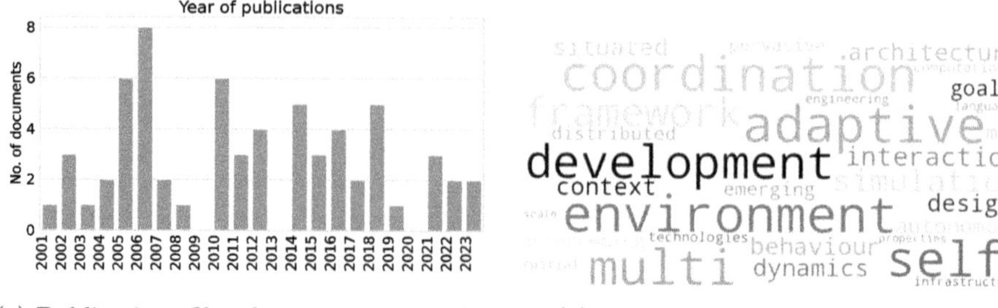

(a) Publications filter by year – 2001-2024   (b) Keywords of the selected papers

Fig. 1. Publication trends and keywords extracted from the selected papers.

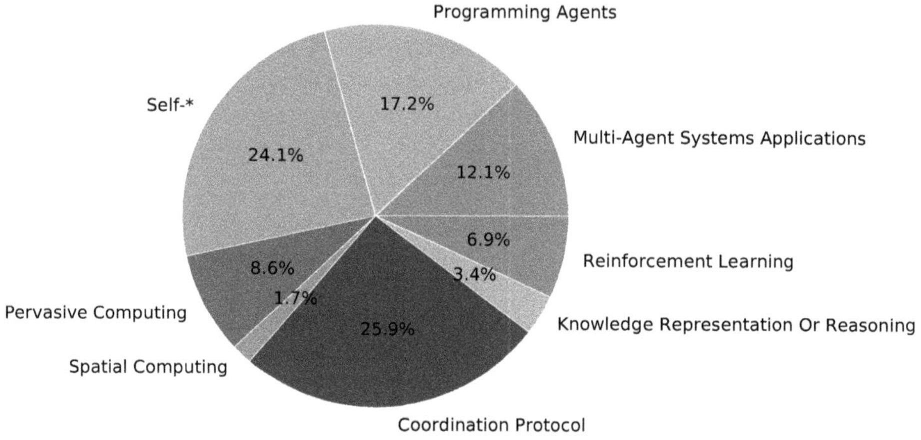

Fig. 2. Topics extracted using Gemini from the selected papers.

a notable evolution in the topics, with earlier works focusing more on foundational aspects of coordination and self-organisation, while recent years have seen increased attention to learning approaches and pervasive computing applications. The emergence of reinforcement learning and knowledge representation as a significant topic, despite being relatively new to the community, signals an important shift towards integrating modern AI techniques with traditional multi-agent systems approaches. This trend aligns well with the goals of aggregate computing, which seeks to combine rigorous foundations for collective behaviour with practical engineering approaches, including learning and adaptation mechanisms. This topical landscape demonstrates significant overlap between the WOA community's interests and aggregate computing's objectives, particularly in areas such as self-organisation, coordination, and the integration of learning capabilities. In the following sections, we explore these connections in detail, examining how aggregate computing can both benefit from and contribute to these research directions.

Table 1. Distribution of papers across topics and years

Year	Self-*	Prog	Coord	Apps	Perv	Learn	Know	Space	Total
2001			[146]						1
2002			[121, 145]		[111]				3
2003			[131]						1
2004			[175]					[108]	2
2005	[93]	[119]		[14, 31, 32]	[109]				6
2006	[124]	[158]	[48, 129, 130]	[43]	[39]			[20]	8
2007		[61]	[26]						2
2008				[138]					1
2010	[122]	[139]	[23, 127]		[89, 189]				6
2011	[60, 88]		[172]						3
2012	[58, 126]	[153]			[49]				4
2014	[123, 125]		[25, 91, 116]						5
2015	[68, 70, 71]								3
2016		[59]	[10, 117, 148]						4
2017		[37]	[118]						2
2018	[152]	[47]		[150, 151]			[62]		5
2019						[168]			1
2021						[8, 107]	[2]		3
2022		[135]	[79]						2
2023	[183]					[166]			2
Total	14	9	20	7	6	4	2	2	**64**

3 Multi-agent Systems and Self-organisation

In this section, we review the connection between multi-agent systems and self-organisation, by the WOA perspective. In particular, we will discuss the broader context of self-*/autonomic computing (Sect. 3.1), the problem of self-organisation engineering (Sect. 3.2), and then we will review tuples (Sect. 3.3) and fields (Sect. 3.4) as useful mechanisms for guided self-organisation. These concepts are also preparatory for introducing aggregate computing in Sect. 4.

3.1 Autonomic Computing and Communications

As systems get more distributed, interconnected, heterogeneous, and large-scale, their overall design and management become more challenging. In the vision of *autonomic computing* [103], computing systems should be able to *self-manage* themselves, given high-level goals from human administrators. In order words, both structure and behaviour of systems should *dynamically adapt* to new situations, to deal with change, perturbations, and disruption [14, 43, 60, 68, 70, 150, 152, 168]. From this idea, multiple adaptation goals or *self-** properties can be envisioned [103]: self-(re-)configuration [59, 152], self-optimisation [100], self-integration [36] and self-composition [126], self-healing [157], self-protection [186], etc.

Adaptation can happen at various levels. For instance, the importance of interaction and coordination promotes *autonomic communication services* [142], where networks and corresponding services are context-aware and able to self-configure, self-monitor, self-heal, and self-organise [124]. Such autonomic communication services should satisfy various requirements including autonomicity, adaptivity, situation-awareness, scalability, and the ability to support heterogeneity [124]. Various mechanism can help in satisfying such requirements. For instance, in the agent-based model for autonomic communications presented in [124], a *self-aggregation* mechanism is proposed to organise adaptation by means of dynamic coalitions, possibly formed in a *self-similar* fashion across multiple scales (cf. holonic agents [149], [68]). As also discussed in Sect. 4.2, regional coordination is indeed a recurrent pattern of self-organisation.

3.2 Self-organisation and Its Engineering

Self-organisation can be defined as the ability of a system to autonomously seek and maintain structure, order, and coherent behaviour [42, 185]. Intimately connected with *emergence* [141, 180], among self-* properties, self-organisation is one of the most fundamental and desired properties, as also witnessed in the WOA community [39, 71, 88, 93, 122, 127]. Indeed, as self-organisation implies *robustness* and *adaptability* to perturbation and change, and may promote *desired emergents*, it is often a target property in distributed systems engineering [187]. Self-organising mechanisms can also be an ingredient to promote the emergence of *collective intelligence* [42], supporting collective tasks (e.g., collective sorting of tuples into coherent clusters [48]). The connection to emergence implies that it is difficult to *design* self-organising behaviours—a problem referred to by different terms like *guided self-organisation* [140], *self-organisation steering* [13], *micro-macro link* [50, 156], *forward/inverse problem* [165], *local-global connection* [33], just to name a few. Methodologically, the problem is addressed by extensive *simulation* [93], possibly combined with theories providing some formal guarantees (cf. self-stabilisation [78, 80, 125]).

In Sect. 4, we will present the *aggregate computing* approach [170] to self-organisation engineering, discussing how it promotes the emergence of robust, ordered behaviour through macro-level abstractions [50].

3.3 Stigmergy and Tuple-Based Coordination

Communication among multiple autonomous entities can be achieved through two main paradigms: *direct* and *indirect* communication (for an in-depth discussion on these communication paradigms—see the corresponding chapter of this book [27]. The former communication introduces *coupling* in time and space: in time because, to communicate directly, agents must be active contemporaneously; and in space as agents must be able to address (thus, know) each other.[3] Indirect communication, on the other hand, *decouples* agents both in time and space: in time, as a message can exist regardless of the lifetime of the sender and potential receivers, and in space, as there is no need to explicitly address a receiver.

A convenient way to implement indirect communication is through *stigmergy* [41,82], where agents communicate by leaving marks on the environment, which, in turn, may influence the behaviour of other agents. The word origins from the Greek *stigma* (mark) and *ergon* (work), and was first introduced in biology to describe the indirect communication among social insects.

In the context of multi-agent systems, stigmergy has been a successful mean to implement coordination mechanisms [48,91,109,117,118,126,129,130,138], particularly in the form of *tuple spaces*, an abstract environment on which tuples can be written, read, and withdrawn through coordination primitives, such as those (`out`, `read`, and `in`) first introduced in Linda [95].

As a single shared tuple space can be limiting for distributed system, the notion of tuple-based coordination moved first to multiple tuple spaces [96], then to networked multiple tuple spaces (for instance, as in the case of Tuple Centres Spread on the Network (TuCSoN) [116,127,131,145,146]), and finally to *programmable* tuple spaces [115], capable of reacting to the environment events. During the years, multiple languages for programmable tuple spaces have been proposed after different metaphors and paradigms. A notable example is Reaction Specification Tuples (ReSpecT) [114,121,175], on which re-writing rules could be triggered to respond to the insertion/retrieval/read of tuples. Other languages come instead from nature-inspired computing. The most successful metaphors have been those of chemistry, for instance as in Molecules of Knowledge (MoK) [113] (indeed, chemical reactions closely resemble re-writing rules); biochemistry, as in Biochemical Tuple Spaces [171]; physical fields, notably in Tuples-On-The-Air (TOTA) [108,111]; and natural ecosystems, as exemplified by the Self-Aware Pervasive service Ecosystems (SAPERE) approach [58,172,188,189].

Since the inception of TOTA, it was increasingly evident that distributed programmable tuple-spaces could have been a mean to implement stigmergically a form of coordination that was instead meant at considering space and time as first-class abstractions. This idea lead to works that used tuple spaces to understand and verify programs based on computational fields [49], and laid the basis upon which frameworks such as Spatial Tuples [57,147] (where tuples are enriched with spatio-temporal properties); and $\sigma\tau$-Linda [173] (in which the evolution of tuple spaces is driven by spatial and temporal activities) were built.

---

[3] This is true for single- and multicast communication. Arguably, some forms of broadcast, such as sending wireless messages omnidirectionally for everyone to receive them, could be considered decoupled in space. However, this could be considered a communication *mediated* by the environment, thus, in some sense, indirect.

3.4 Potential Fields and Field-Based Coordination

An emerging pattern in multi-agent coordination leverages *fields of values* to guide systems towards desired collective goals. This area of research originated from early works based on *artificial potential fields* [177]. These fields extend electromagnetic field theory by calculating a direction vector at each point to guide an agent as if it were a particle. The fields can be *repulsive* (to avoid obstacles) or *attractive* (to reach a target), guiding agents' movement through the sum of these fields that work as the collective objective of the system. Initially, these ideas were applied to coordinated movement in swarm robotics [178], particularly in path planning [167], search and rescue [176], and exploration [137] scenarios.

The generalisation of this concept has led to *field-based coordination* [110], where fields guide agents more broadly, such as in task allocation or information distribution. This development stems from the introduction of *co-fields* [112] by Mamei et al., where agents and the environment create *abstract coordination fields* to coordinate actions and disseminate information. *Co-fields* has been utilised in various scenarios, including spatially-situated pervasive applications [49,172]. Even though the concept of fields has been widely used in multi-agent systems, a practical method to engineer applications utilising fields was lacking. This gap has been addressed by the aggregate computing (AC) [170] model and language, which provide a way to *program* these fields and the agents that interact with them.

4 The Aggregate Computing Approach to Self-organising Multi-agent Systems

Aggregate computing [170] is a macro-programming paradigm [50] that is quite different from other approaches to MAS programming (cf. [23,25,37,61,89, 119,123,135,139,153]). It is based on the computational field abstraction (cf. Sect. 3.4), distributed and dynamic data structures mapping devices to values. In some way, however, it shares the *global perspective* also promoted by organisation programming approaches like Moise [98] and e-institutions [161] (frameworks that regulate agent interactions through norms and protocols, similar to how human institutions regulate society). These topics are discussed in the WOA community, such as the integration of agents, organisations, and environments [139], the development of formal models for agent interactions and coordination [23], and the use of social commitments to shape interaction patterns [25]. E-institutions relate to these works by providing a framework for regulating agent interactions through norms and protocols.

4.1 The AC Model and Language

To understand AC, it is convenient to consider three distinct but related pieces (an overall picture can Fig. 3): the *system model*, which delineates the constraints and characteristics of an abstract system employed to execute an aggregate program; the *execution model*, which specifies the steps each agent must undertake to produce the aggregate computation; and finally, the *programming model*, which identifies the main constructs and operations necessary to achieve the defined specifications of the collective program. The following sections will elaborate on these aspects in detail.

System Model. An aggregate system is populated by *agents* that can perceive their *environment* through *sensors* and change its state using *actuators*. Each agent has a perception of its *neighbourhood*, which consists of agents it can directly *communicate* with, and a *state*, which is the memory of what occurs as time evolves. The definition of how agents perceive their neighbourhood can vary and may be based on proximity or communication channels. Additionally, each agent can execute a program at certain intervals, which potentially alter internal its state. Interactions between agents do not have a fixed frequency. However, since we are modeling self-organising systems, we assume that interactions occur *continuously* and *frequently*, as done is nature and in related works [71].

Execution Model. To execute a specific aggregate program, an agent must adhere to a particular execution cycle called *round*. A round is viewed as an atomic execution of these three main steps:

- **Context acquisition**: In this step, agents gather information from sensors, receive messages from neighbors, and read their state.
- **Program execution**: The program is executed against this context and results in i) the outcome of the program executed locally and ii) the set of messages to be sent to their neighbors.
- **Actuation**: Given the program's output, nodes can then perform actuations (e.g., movement) and finally send the collected messages to the perceived neighborhood.

This asynchronous and continuous execution performed by all nodes with dynamics similar to those observed in self-organising systems eventually leads to the collective structure defined by the aggregate program.

Programming Model. Field-based computing involves the use of *computational fields*, which are spatial-temporal structures associating each device in a network with a specific computational value. These fields can embody a variety of data types such as sensor data, actuator states, or even constant values. The manipulation of these fields is governed by field calculi, an extension of functional programming paradigms designed to incorporate spatial-temporal computational expressions as first-class entities. Over time, numerous variations of field calculi have emerged [19] with several programming languages and libraries developed to support the field-based computing model [16,56].

In the programming model of field-based computing, expressions are interpreted both locally and globally. For example, a simple arithmetic expression like

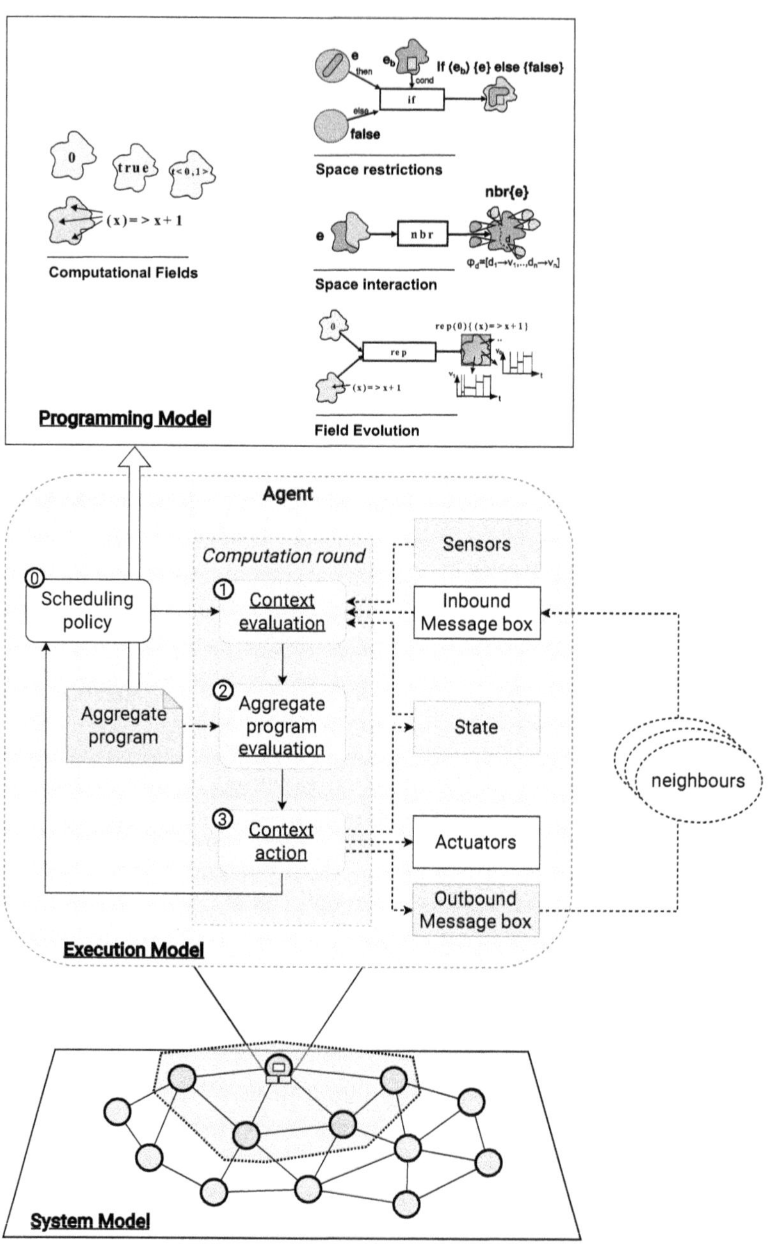

Fig. 3. The three levels of the aggregate computing model, which are the system model (i.e., the structure of the system), the execution model (i.e., the behaviour of the nodes), and the programming model (i.e., the specification of the collective stance).

$a + b$ traditionally computes the sum of two integers locally. However, within a field-based program, this expression acquires a global dimension where it represents the operation of addition applied across corresponding values in fields a and b throughout a network. This global interpretation produces a new field where each device's local value reflects the sum of a and b specific to its location.

Field calculus avoids direct interactions with global fields and instead focuses on the interactions within *neighboring fields* (i.e., the local fields of neighboring devices). By aggregating data from immediate neighbors and manipulating these interactions both spatially and temporally, devices within the network can give rise to complex global behaviours and structures, often based on gradients and other distributed algorithms. In particular, the essential constructs of field-based programming include i) temporal operators used to evolve field values over time, transforming data obtained in one computational round into the values used in the next; ii) spatial interaction: involving the exchange of data with neighboring devices, where the incoming data forms new, collective fields that represent the collective state of the neighboring area, and iii) space restrictions: allowing the computation to be segmented into distinct non-communicating domains, allowing for specialised processing within localised areas. By manipulating these constructs it is possible to create complex and global behaviours across the network, which are presented in the following sections.

4.2   Aggregate Algorithms and Patterns

Reuse across design and implementation is a major goal, generally in software engineering [104] and specifically for MASs [158] [67]. Functional composition of algorithms is arguably one of the key aspects of AC. Self-organising behaviours can be encoded into functions, collected, and reused stand-alone or as part of richer behaviours. This kind of compositionality marks a stark difference with respect to other approaches to self-organisation, in which behaviours are often hard to reuse or compose. Composed behaviours can thus be leveraged to build increasingly complex systems, hiding most of the nuances of the core AC primitives.

Self-stabilising Building Blocks. Self-stabilisation [78,80] [125] is the property of a system to reach a stable correct state in finite time, regardless of its the initial state. It is a desirable property for many systems, especially in the presence of faults or perturbations. Programming a system in AC using its primitives, however, provides no guarantee of self-stabilisation. However, some common patterns can be constructed in a self-stabilising way, and then used to build more complex algorithms. In aggregate computing research [170], four main fundamental self-stabilising building blocks are identified: *gradient-cast* (**G**), implementing information spreading; *converge-cast* (**C**), implementing information collection; *sparse-choice* (**S**), implementing symmetry breaking; and *time-evolution* (**T**), implementing change in time. Crucially, the functional composition of these self-stabilising building blocks is itself self-stabilising [169]. Additionally, each block permits multiple diverse and interchangeable implementations, enabling fine-tuning of the performance depending on the specific problem at hand [169]. More complex algorithms can then be built by composing these building blocks, and many of them have been collected in a specialised library of standard functions [92].

Self-organising Coordination Regions. A prominent example of how rich self-stabilising behaviour can be obtained by combination of the basic building blocks is a pattern named Self-Organising Coordination Regions (SCR) [136]. The pattern consists of four phases:

1. *local leader election*, where a leader is elected in each neighbourhood (the metric by which some device can be considered a "neighbor" depends on the specific context);
2. *area formation*, where every device is assigned to a leader;
3. *upstream information flow*, collecting the area information into the leader; and
4. *downstream information flow*, where the leader, after deliberation, propagates the result in the area.

From an AC point of view, this pattern can be implemented by functional composition of the following building blocks:

$$\text{SCR} \approx \mathbf{G}_{\text{downstream}} (\ \mathbf{C}_{\text{upstream}} (\ \mathbf{G}_{\text{area formation}} (\ \mathbf{S}_{\text{leader election}}\ )\ ))$$

Besides its applicability in multiple contexts, as it fundamentally provides a simple encoding of the idea of local decision-making, SCR is also a good example of how the AC approach can be used to build complex behaviours with self-sabilising guarantees by composition of simpler blocks.

Self-organising Coordination Regions. A prominent example of how rich self-stabilising behaviour can be obtained by combination of the basic building blocks is a pattern named SCR [136]. The pattern consists of four phases:

1. *local leader election*, where a leader is elected in each neighbourhood (the metric by which some device can be considered a "neighbor" depends on the specific context);
2. *area formation*, where every device is assigned to a leader;
3. *upstream information flow*, collecting the area information into the leader; and
4. *downstream information flow*, where the leader, after deliberation, propagates the result in the area.

From an AC point of view, this pattern can be implemented by functional composition of the following building blocks:

$$\text{SCR} \approx \mathbf{G}_{\text{downstream}} (\ \mathbf{C}_{\text{upstream}} (\ \mathbf{G}_{\text{area formation}} (\ \mathbf{S}_{\text{leader election}}\ )\ ))$$

Besides its applicability in multiple contexts, as it fundamentally provides a simple encoding of the idea of local decision-making, SCR is also a good example of how the AC approach can be used to build complex behaviours with self-sabilising guarantees by composition of simpler blocks.

4.3   Learning in AC

Learning is the main technique that can be utilised to enhance adaptation against dynamic systems. In multi-agent systems, learning has been a longstanding theme, dating back to the late 1990s with initial works on multi-agent reinforcement learning (MARL) [164]. The renewal recent interest in MARL, particularly following advances in deep learning [97,101,162], has seen significant practical successes across various scenarios such as video games [159], pedestrian dynamics [8], e-scooter sharing [107], and traffic management.

In systems targeting AC, learning is even more complex due to several considerations such as scale, the multi-agent assignment problem, the simulation cost for verifying multi-agent interactions, and the variety of tasks within this domain. Dispite these challenges, several works have been proposed to integrate learning into AC systems, at different levels of abstraction. Notably, this integration can be realised at the *application level*, where the aim is to create more robust collective applications; at *the middleware* level to configure certain execution strategy; and at the *deployment level* to better manage the placement of aggregate computation components.

Application Level. At the application level, AC has been combined in two distinct ways. Firstly, reinforcement learning (RL) has been to improve AC in a collective program synthesis approach. This idea was inspired by *program sketching*, where a program is partially specified and completed using a machine learning technique, such as genetic algorithms. In [6] the authors proposed using RL because it is challenging to know the correct output without executing the system as such. In particular, this work demonstrated how learning could synthesize some basic blocks more optimised than the state of the art.

Another approach to utilising machine learning (ML) is using AC to enhance the learning process itself. For example, in [7] a multi-agent version of deep Q-learning has been developed where the state of agents was computed through AC, creating a form of stigmergic communication that enhanced the agents' state and simplified the learning task. This particular combination of AC and graph neural networks (GNNs) [181] has shown benefits in the synthesis of collective programs, such as those covering a spatiotemporal phenomenon.

Middleware Level. Given a collective aggregate computing specification, it is possible to configure various aspects of the middleware, including round scheduling, communication, and neighbor messages retention, to alter the collective behaviour of the system. This can primarily be done to improve the *efficiency* of a specific collective program, such as reducing consumption to align with green computing principles, or to achieve faster convergence to stable collective states.

Among these topics, the first work to apply learning to improve middleware aspects focused on round scheduling. Indeed, it may sometimes be unnecessary to compute at a fixed frequency because i) environmental conditions are not changing, and ii) a globally stable configuration has already been reached, eliminating the need for fast reactivity to new changes. In particular, in [5] it was observed that by applying a variant of Q-learning for multi-agent systems, it was possible to learn distributed scheduling strategies capable of reducing the number of rounds performed by the systems while still maintaining certain convergence times and reactivity to changes. This demonstrated that, depending on the QoS requirements of a particular aggregate system, it is possible to configure it appropriately to maximize these requirements (e.g., high reactivity or low consumption).

Deployment Level. Aggregate programming provides a high-level logical model that can be mapped to various physical architectures. Although it is primarily designed for peer-to-peer scenarios, it can be easily extended to cloud-based computing, fog computing, or edge computing environments. This flexibility is discussed in the pulverisation approach [85], where a collective specification is broken down into a set of basic blocks that can be deployed differently depending on the architecture. However, this decomposition can affect non-functional aspects such as battery consumption in constrained devices or the energy required for message exchange. Therefore, applying modern learning approaches to select the appropriate subdivision of blocks might be an effective way to optimize their placement to meet specific requirements. Additionally, in mobility contexts, selecting the right policies for shifting computation from the edge to the cloud is crucial, especially in opportunistic environments where services must follow users.

Combining ML and AC is particularly advantageous in these scenarios. AC captures essential collective aspects of these applications, while ML creates adaptable systems capable of optimising non-functional requirements such as bandwidth and energy consumption. This synergy is essential for developing modern and versatile systems.

4.4 Agent-Oriented Aggregate Computing

In the years, research has been carried out to connect the "unconventional" programming model of aggregate computing with other paradigms, e.g., across the object–actor–agent thread [128,144]. This connection is particularly interesting for the WOA community as it enables structured agent-oriented engineering of self-organising systems. Several works explore this direction, as discussed next.

In [54], an actor-based design of an AC middleware is proposed, also supporting the integration of AC-based behaviour with more traditional applications. In the proposal, an "aggregate computing actor" deployed in each device can provide the results of a collective service to other local actors, enabling the interfacing of collective and traditional applications. In the programming language contribution of the eXchange Calculus [17], actor-based designs and pub-sub-designs of aggregate computing behaviours are used as a metric for comparing the practical expressiveness of the programming model. In [52], it is shown how actor-based designs of AC systems can be refined by applying principles of separation of concerns and reusability. Then, the work describes an Akka-based distributed middleware for AC systems, implemented as part of the ScaFi toolkit [56].

A conceptual connection with agents, through the fundamental property of *autonomy*, is provided in [51]. In particular, it is shown that the AC execution model (cf. Sect. 4.1) can be regarded as an *agent control architecture* (cf. Fig. 3). Regarding the *individual autonomy* of agents, in aggregate computing, there are three multiple degrees of freedom or autonomy acceptations: (i) the autonomy to follow the suggested execution protocol, (ii) the autonomy to follow the prescriptions resulting from the AC program, (ii) the *endogenous* or *delegated autonomy* from the program to the individual, and (iii) the *exogeneous autonomy* undergone by the AC program, due to the environment (e.g., people moving, carrying the device around). Then, it is observed that an AC system also exhibits a form of *collective autonomy* that interacts (e.g., it may limit) the autonomy of the individuals.

In [174], a bridge between AC and MAS programming is proposed. In particular, the proposal is based on a notion of *aggregate plan*: a dynamically evolving "field of actions" (an extension of co-fields [112]) which is diffused across the MAS and that can be selected and executed by each agent based on an autonomous deliberation process. However, there are further directions to be explored, such as aggregates of Belief-Desire-Intention (BDI) agents, and language-level integrations of BDI programming and aggregate programming.

5   Future Trends in Self-organising Multi-agent Systems Engineering

5.1   Multi-scale Modelling

Complex systems can be described at different levels (e.g., micro-, meso-, and macro-levels) [105]. One example is given by human crowds, whose dynamics can be captured by models ranging from the sub-micro to the super-macro scales [65]. Working at different levels of abstractions is key for proper software and MAS engineering (cf. [183]). Indeed, MAS can be engineered by exploiting artefacts at different levels, e.g., to support design and debugging [106]. For instance, *holonic* MASs have been adopted for multi-scale simulation of complex systems [94]. Though micro-level descriptions are the most common in the context of MASs, research, especially on *macro-programming* and aggregate computing (cf. Sect. 4) [50,170], shows that macro-level descriptions are both feasible and useful [106]. In particular, macro-programming implementations can promote a sort of *global-to-local* mapping [170], whereby a macro-program can be used to derive micro-level activity, with reasonable guarantees in terms of emergence steering. Also, the inherent *declarativity* of macro-level programs [55] has shown to provide benefits in terms of operational flexibility, enabling optimisation and dynamic adaptation [85].

However, research is only at the beginning of multi-scale MAS engineering. First of all, it would be key to understand the (limits of) applicability of macro-level models. This would also shed light how on micro-level and macro-level descriptions could be integrated to achieve different trade-offs—e.g., with respect to expressiveness, adaptation, and efficiency. Holonic MASs and macro-programming approaches, which aims at capturing micro-macro links, could provide ideas for such integration [50,94]. Explainability is another goal that may be promoted by macroscopic descriptions.

5.2 Foundational Models for Collective Applications

For many years, the typical approach in machine learning involved performing a training phase for each new task. However, this approach was highly costly and risky when dealing with large amounts of data. Consequently, efforts have been made to develop techniques for *transfer learning* [194], which aims to reuse knowledge acquired in certain domains in others. This has proven particularly effective in supervised contexts, particularly in the field of computer vision. However, the situation is more challenging in the context of RL [193], where transfer learning has always been an open challenge, further complicated in multi-agent [162] settings, also already discussed in recent vision papers [81].

A modern approach in this direction involves creating *foundational* models [21], which are trained on a large amount of data and capable of extrapolating various high-level tasks and subsequently adapting to new domains. This is particularly evident in the context of natural natural language processing (NLP) with the advent of large language models (LLMs) [191]. However, these models are not designed for collective work, nor are they intended for real-time tasks. In this direction, GATO [143] has attempted to create such models in the context of robotics and video games. Nevertheless, the collective or group aspect is still not captured. Therefore, we anticipate that in the coming years, these studies will be applied to self-organisation with the aim of synthesising one (or more) models capable of executing collective applications based on the dynamics of self-organisation. This would allow the reuse of the same model across a wide variety of tasks without the need for retraining, simply by specialising and instrumenting it to solve a specific collective task.

5.3 Synergistic Integration of Symbolic and Sub-symbolic Design

Currently, MAS engineering approaches are clearly divided into symbolic (i.e., programmatic) methods [22,25,35,44,62,64,135], and sub-symbolic methods (i.e., utilising black-box models) [40,134,184]—see the dedicated chapter on these learning-based approaches in this volume [1]. Symbolic methods offer the advantage of *interpretability*, allowing to understand the behaviour of agents and the rationale behind their actions. On the other hand, sub-symbolic methods, particularly those based on neural network models, pose significant challenges in terms of interpretability, making it difficult to understand why a particular model responded in a specific way. Despite these challenges, the advent of deep learning models and foundational models has made the use of sub-symbolic approaches inevitable for scaling the complexity of MAS applications [97]. We believe that in the future, these two worlds will increasingly converge, leveraging the benefits of both symbolic and sub-symbolic methods. An essential aspect of this convergence is the role of explainable AI (XAI) [182] (also extended to multi-agent systems [63,102]). XAI seeks to make the decision-making processes of AI systems more transparent and understandable to humans. By integrating explainability into sub-symbolic models, we can enhance their interpretability and *trustworthiness*, making it easier to diagnose issues, ensure compliance with regulations, and gain insights into the system's behaviour. This is particularly important in critical applications where understanding the *rationale* behind decisions is crucial. Recent research [2] has discussed how GNNs might be a promising model in this regard, as they can take inputs in the form of graphs (e.g., knowledge base expressed in Prolog). This approach could facilitate the integration of symbolic knowledge representation and sub-symbolic learning, offering a pathway to combine interpretability with the powerful learning capabilities of sub-symbolic models. The integration of these approaches aims to leverage the strengths of both methodologies. Symbolic methods provide clarity and precision in understanding and designing agent behaviours, while sub-symbolic methods, with their deep learning capabilities, allow for handling more complex and large-scale problems. Moreover, we propose that using a macro-programming approach as an *explainer* for the sub-symbolic model could be a promising direction. Specifically, aggregate computing has been effective in capturing the collective behaviour of multi-agent systems [18] and has a similar execution model to that of GNNs. This similarity could be leveraged to explain the decisions made by the sub-symbolic model, thus elucidating self-organising behaviours created with sub-symbolic models.

5.4   Other Directions

Space-Time(-Aware) Modelling. Since many MAS-based applications are *situated* in space-time, or must be *aware* of it, research has devoted efforts in coping with, modelling, and exploiting space. A wide range of scenarios are crucially dependent on the ability of agents to represent space and act in a spatially-aware manner [76], including environmental monitoring [160], teleoperation [76], and emergency management [190]. This has also led to the *spatial computing* research thread [33,76,83], which is one precursor of aggregate computing. Indeed, situated activity and spatial coordination are crucial themes both in the WOA [20,31,32,47,71,79,114,116,172] and the specific aggregate computing threads [3,4,53,57]. Space, as a prominent macro abstraction [50], can be leveraged to engineer self-organisation, or be a target, i.e., something to be coped with, by self-organising. More research would be valuable to address challenges related to spatiotemporal situation and evolution, such as dealing with the sparsity and density of devices [34], modelling and simulating complex spatiotemporal phenomena [87], and supporting dynamic or multi spatiotemporal granularity of distributed tasks [192].

Synergistic Integration of Individual and Collective Intelligence. In the MAS research panorama, the systems of interest and approaches seem implicitly split into different classes, e.g.: small-scale systems involving agents that are individually very intelligent or that follow well-defined protocols (cf. choreographies [26]); large-scale systems involving individually very simple agents, that however make collective intelligence emerge by interaction [42]; or large-scale systems involving individually very intelligent agents, whose contributions get aggregated or integrated through either ML models or proper collaborative structures (cf. wisdom of crowd and crowdsourcing [163]). It is still quite unclear how these these different perspectives could interact and be combined. This makes the case for *socially intelligent agents* [148, 151] and social structures promoting effective coordination and achievement of global goals from possibly self-interested agents. Moreover, more research on emergence steering and guided self-organisation should be carried out to understand the mechanisms that individuals may use to positively affect collective dynamics.

Verification and Runtime Monitoring. The general problem of self-organisation engineering is guaranteeing the desired emergent outcomes are reached while preventing undesired emergent outcomes. Some guarantees may be provided by verifying via model-checking (exhaustively, or statistically) or simulation, possibly for a subset of the possible environments and configurations, or may be provided by correct-by-construction techniques (cf. composition of self-stabilising fragments in field calculus [169]). Also, uncertainty stemming, e.g., from deviation from assumptions, incomplete models, low-quality data used in learning, lack of knowledge about non-local/non-linear effects, and human activity (cf. human-in-the-loop cyber-physical systems), may require dealing with change at runtime [179]. In this context, a relevant issue revolves around *distributed runtime verification and monitoring*. An interesting work in this direction is [18], where an approach to map spatial logic formulas to field calculus fragments is proposed, enabling the automatic construction of distributed monitors out of the formulas of the spatial properties to check. This is an interesting paradigm, combining self-organisation with formal specification languages, to provide a support for runtime verification in large-scale MAS.

Other approaches to runtime verification include MAS-DRiVe [10], an algorithm that partitions a multi-agent system into sub-systems which can be monitored independently, and RMLGym [166], a framework that allows users to define reward functions using RML specifications [11] and generates reward monitors that evaluate the agent's performance and provide feedback at each step.

6 Conclusion

This chapter has discussed the state-of-the-art in self-organising systems engineering, focusing on recent developments in the aggregate computing paradigm and exploring research trends from the perspective of the WOA community. Particularly, we have discussed how aggregate computing currently provides a robust method for describing collective computations in MAS. In this direction, we examined the computational model and how it simplifies the definition of self-organising systems. We connected this to the WOA perspective, describing how agent-oriented paradigms can be integrated with aggregate computing and how multi-agent learning techniques can enhance the paradigm. We also provide a future outlook on self-organising MAS engineering, focusing on multi-scale modeling, foundational models for collective applications, the integration of symbolic and sub-symbolic methods via explainable AI, as well as other emerging trends such as space-time-aware modeling, the synergistic integration of individual and collective intelligence, human-cyber-physical collectives, and runtime monitoring of self-organising systems.

This chapter can therefore serve as a guide for researchers in the ongoing development of this branch of MAS, enabling the creation of self-organising applications that are more intelligent, resilient, and adaptive.

Acknowledgments. This work has been partially supported by the Italian MUR PRIN 2020 Project "COMMON-WEARS" (2020HCWWLP).

References

1. Agiollo, A., Calegari, R., Ciatto, G., Magnini, M., Omicini, A., Sabbatini, F.: Intelligent agents from symbolic to neurosymbolic systems: the quest for integration. In: Mascardi and Omicini [120]
2. Agiollo, A., Ciatto, G., Omicini, A.: Graph neural networks as the copula mundi between logic and machine learning: a roadmap. In: Calegari et al. [46], pp. 98–115. http://ceur-ws.org/Vol-2963/paper18.pdf
3. Aguzzi, G., Audrito, G., Casadei, R., Damiani, F., Torta, G., Viroli, M.: A field-based computing approach to sensing-driven clustering in robot swarms. Swarm Intell. **17**(1–2), 27–62 (2023). https://doi.org/10.1007/S11721-022-00215-Y
4. Aguzzi, G., Casadei, R., Pianini, D., Viroli, M.: Dynamic decentralization domains for the internet of things. IEEE Internet Comput. **26**(6), 16–23 (2022). https://doi.org/10.1109/MIC.2022.3216753
5. Aguzzi, G., Casadei, R., Viroli, M.: Addressing collective computations efficiency: towards a platform-level reinforcement learning approach. In: IEEE International Conference on Autonomic Computing and Self-Organizing Systems, ACSOS 2022, pp. 11–20. IEEE (2022). https://doi.org/10.1109/ACSOS55765.2022.00019
6. Aguzzi, G., Casadei, R., Viroli, M.: Towards reinforcement learning-based aggregate computing. In: Coordination Models and Languages - 24th IFIP WG 6.1 International Conference, COORDINATION 2022, Proceedings. LNCS, vol. 13271, pp. 72–91. Springer, Cham (2022). https://doi.org/10.1007/978-3-031-08143-9_5

7. Aguzzi, G., Viroli, M., Esterle, L.: Field-informed reinforcement learning of collective tasks with graph neural networks. In: IEEE International Conference on Autonomic Computing and Self-Organizing Systems, ACSOS 2023, pp. 37–46. IEEE (2023). https://doi.org/10.1109/ACSOS58161.2023.00021

8. Albericci, T., Cecconello, T., Gibertini, A., Vizzari, G.: A curriculum-based reinforcement learning approach to pedestrian simulation. In: Calegari et al. [46], pp. 224–240. http://ceur-ws.org/Vol-2963/paper11.pdf

9. Alderighi, M., Baldoni, M., Baroglio, C., Micalizio, R., Tedeschi, S. (eds.): WOA 2024 – 25th Workshop "From Objects to Agents", CEUR Workshop Proceedings, vol. 3735. Bard, AO, Italy (2024). http://ceur-ws.org/Vol-3735/

10. Ancona, D., Briola, D., Ferrando, A., Mascardi, V.: MAS-DRiVe: a practical approach to decentralized runtime verification of agent interaction protocols. In: Santoro et al. [155], pp. 35–43. http://ceur-ws.org/Vol-1664/w7.pdf

11. Ancona, D., Franceschini, L., Ferrando, A., Mascardi, V.: RML: theory and practice of a domain specific language for runtime verification. Sci. Comput. Program. **205**, 102610 (2021). https://doi.org/10.1016/J.SCICO.2021.102610

12. Anil, R., et al.: Gemini: a family of highly capable multimodal models. CoRR abs/2312.11805 (2023). https://doi.org/10.48550/ARXIV.2312.11805

13. Araújo, N.A.M., et al.: Steering self-organisation through confinement. Soft Matter **19**(9), 1695–1704 (2023). https://doi.org/10.1039/d2sm01562e

14. Armano, G., Cherchi, G., Manconi, A., Vargiu, E.: PACMAS: a personalized, adaptive, and cooperative multiagent system architecture. In: Corradini et al. [66], pp. 54–60. http://lia.deis.unibo.it/books/woa2005/papers/8.pdf

15. Armano, G., Paoli, F.D., Omicini, A., Vargiu, E. (eds.): WOA 2003 – 4th Workshop "From Objects to Agents". Pitagora Editrice Bologna, Villasimius, CA, Italy (2003). http://giuseppevizzari.github.io/WOA-proceedings-archive/woa-2003.html

16. Audrito, G.: FCPP: an efficient and extensible field calculus framework. In: IEEE International Conference on Autonomic Computing and Self-Organizing Systems, ACSOS 2020, Washington, DC, USA, 17–21 August 2020, pp. 153–159. IEEE (2020). https://doi.org/10.1109/ACSOS49614.2020.00037

17. Audrito, G., Casadei, R., Damiani, F., Salvaneschi, G., Viroli, M.: Functional programming for distributed systems with XC. In: 36th European Conference on Object-Oriented Programming, ECOOP 2022. LIPIcs, vol. 222, pp. 20:1–20:28. Schloss Dagstuhl - LZI (2022). https://doi.org/10.4230/LIPICS.ECOOP.2022.20

18. Audrito, G., Casadei, R., Damiani, F., Stolz, V., Viroli, M.: Adaptive distributed monitors of spatial properties for cyber-physical systems. J. Syst. Softw. **175**, 110908 (2021). https://doi.org/10.1016/J.JSS.2021.110908

19. Audrito, G., Casadei, R., Damiani, F., Viroli, M.: Computation against a neighbour: addressing large-scale distribution and adaptivity with functional programming and scala. Log. Methods Comput. Sci. **19**(1) (2023). https://doi.org/10.46298/LMCS-19(1:6)2023

20. Augimeri, A., Folino, G., Forestiero, A., Spezzano, G.: A multidimensional flocking algorithm for clustering spatial data. In: De Paoli et al. [73], pp. 16–20. http://ceur-ws.org/Vol-204/D05.pdf

21. Awais, M., et al.: Foundational models defining a new era in vision: a survey and outlook. CoRR abs/2307.13721 (2023). https://doi.org/10.48550/ARXIV.2307.13721

22. Baiardi, M., Burattini, S., Ciatto, G., Pianini, D.: JaKtA: BDI agent-oriented programming in pure Kotlin. In: Multi-Agent Systems - 20th European Conference, EUMAS 2023, Naples, Italy, 14–15 September 2023, Proceedings. LNCS, vol. 14282, pp. 49–65. Springer, Cham (2023). https://doi.org/10.1007/978-3-031-43264-4_4
23. Baldoni, M., et al.: MERCURIO: an interaction-oriented framework for designing, verifying and programming multi-agent systems. In: Omicini and Viroli [133], pp. 87–94. http://ceur-ws.org/Vol-621/paper13.pdf
24. Baldoni, M., Baroglio, C., Bergenti, F., Garro, A. (eds.): WOA 2013 – 14th Workshop "From Objects to Agents", CEUR Workshop Proceedings, vol. 1099. Turin, Italy (2013). http://ceur-ws.org/Vol-1099/
25. Baldoni, M., Baroglio, C., Capuzzimati, F.: Social relationships for designing agent interaction in JADE. In: Santoro and Bergenti [154], pp. 36–43. http://ceur-ws.org/Vol-1260/paper6.pdf
26. Baldoni, M., Baroglio, C., Martelli, A., Patti, V., Schifanella, C.: Preserving players goals: a choreography-driven matchmaking approach. In: Baldoni et al. [28], pp. 132–139. http://woa07.dibris.unige.it/papers/BaldoniPlayers.pdf
27. Baldoni, M., Baroglio, C., Micalizio, R.: Interaction protocols: from AUML to social commitments, from artifacts to BSPL. In: Mascardi and Omicini [120]
28. Baldoni, M., Boccalatte, A., De Paoli, F., Martelli, M., Mascardi, V. (eds.): WOA 2007 – 8th Workshop "From Objects to Agents". Seneca Edizioni Torino, Genova, Italy (2007). http://woa07.disi.unige.it/ProceedingsWOA2007.zip
29. Baldoni, M., Cossentino, M., De Paoli, F., Seidita, V. (eds.): WOA 2008 – 9th Workshop "From Objects to Agents". Seneca Edizioni Torino, Palermo, Italy (2008). http://www.pa.icar.cnr.it/woa08/materiali/Proceedings.pdf
30. Baldoni, M., De Paoli, F., Martelli, A., Omicini, A. (eds.): WOA 2004 – 5th Workshop "From Objects to Agents". Pitagora Editrice Bologna, Torino, Italy (2004). http://lia.deis.unibo.it/books/woa2004/atti.pdf
31. Bandini, S., Federici, M.L., Vizzari, G.: A methodology for crowd modelling with situated cellular agents. In: Corradini et al. [66], pp. 91–98. http://lia.deis.unibo.it/books/woa2005/papers/13.pdf
32. Bandini, S., Manzoni, S., Redaelli, S.: Towards the interpretation of emergent spatial patterns through GO game: the case of forest population dynamics. In: Corradini et al. [66], pp. 99–103. http://lia.deis.unibo.it/books/woa2005/papers/14.pdf
33. Beal, J., Dulman, S., Usbeck, K., Viroli, M., Correll, N.: Organizing the aggregate: languages for spatial computing. In: Formal and Practical Aspects of Domain-Specific Languages: Recent Developments, chap. 16, pp. 436–501. IGI Global (2013). https://doi.org/10.4018/978-1-4666-2092-6.ch016
34. Beal, J., Viroli, M., Pianini, D., Damiani, F.: Self-adaptation to device distribution in the internet of things. ACM Trans. Auton. Adapt. Syst. 12(3), 12:1–12:29 (2017). https://doi.org/10.1145/3105758
35. Bellifemine, F., Poggi, A., Rimassa, G.: Developing multi-agent systems with JADE. In: Intelligent Agents VII. Agent Theories Architectures and Languages, 7th International Workshop, ATAL 2000, Boston, MA, USA, 7–9 July 2000, Proceedings. LNCS, vol. 1986, pp. 89–103. Springer, Cham (2000). https://doi.org/10.1007/3-540-44631-1_7
36. Bellman, K.L., et al.: Self-improving system integration: mastering continuous change. Future Gener. Comput. Syst. 117, 29–46 (2021). https://doi.org/10.1016/J.FUTURE.2020.11.019

37. Bergenti, F., Iotti, E., Monica, S., Poggi, A.: Overview of a formal semantics for the JADEL programming language. In: De Meo et al. [72], pp. 55–60. http://ceur-ws.org/Vol-1867/w10.pdf
38. Bergenti, F., Monica, S. (eds.): WOA 2019 – 20th Workshop "From Objects to Agents", CEUR Workshop Proceedings, vol. 2404. Parma, Italy (2019). http://ceur-ws.org/Vol-2404/
39. Bicocchi, N., Mamei, M., Zambonelli, F.: Mechanisms of self-organization in pervasive computing. In: De Paoli et al. [73], pp. 41–50. http://ceur-ws.org/Vol-204/P06.pdf
40. Bloembergen, D., Tuyls, K., Hennes, D., Kaisers, M.: Evolutionary dynamics of multi-agent learning: a survey. J. Artif. Intell. Res. **53**, 659–697 (2015). https://doi.org/10.1613/JAIR.4818
41. Bonabeau, E.: Editor's introduction: stigmergy. Artif. Life **5**(2), 95–96 (1999). https://doi.org/10.1162/106454699568692
42. Bonabeau, E., Dorigo, M., Theraulaz, G.: Swarm Intelligence: From Natural to Artificial Systems. Oxford University Press, Oxford (1999)
43. Bonomi, A., Vizzari, G., Sarini, M.: A heterogeneous multi-agent system for adaptive web applications. In: De Paoli et al. [73], pp. 66–75. http://ceur-ws.org/Vol-204/P03.pdf
44. Bordini, R.H., Hübner, J.F., Vieira, R.: Jason and the golden fleece of agent-oriented programming. In: Multi-Agent Programming: Languages, Platforms and Applications, Multiagent Systems, Artificial Societies, and Simulated Organizations, vol. 15, pp. 3–37. Springer, Cham (2005)
45. Cabri, G., Leonardi, L., Mariani, S., Zambonelli, F.: Coordination of software agents: models and languages. In: Mascardi and Omicini [120]
46. Calegari, R., Ciatto, G., Denti, E., Omicini, A., Sartor, G. (eds.): WOA 2021 – 22nd Workshop "From Objects to Agents", CEUR Workshop Proceedings, vol. 2963. Bologna, Italy (2021). http://ceur-ws.org/Vol-2963/
47. Calegari, R., Ciatto, G., Mariani, S., Denti, E., Omicini, A.: Logic programming in space-time: the case of situatedness in LPaaS. In: Cossentino et al. [69], pp. 63–68. http://ceur-ws.org/Vol-2215/paper_11.pdf
48. Casadei, M., Gardelli, L., Viroli, M.: Collective sorting tuple spaces. In: De Paoli et al. [73], pp. 173–180. http://ceur-ws.org/Vol-204/P01.pdf
49. Casadei, M., Viroli, M.: A framework to specify and verify computational fields for pervasive computing systems. In: De Paoli and Vizzari [75], pp. 72–81. http://ceur-ws.org/Vol-892/paper2.pdf
50. Casadei, R.: Macroprogramming: concepts, state of the art, and opportunities of macroscopic behaviour modelling. ACM Comput. Surv. **55**(13s), 275:1–275:37 (2023). https://doi.org/10.1145/3579353
51. Casadei, R., Aguzzi, G., Viroli, M.: A programming approach to collective autonomy. J. Sens. Actuator Netw. **10**(2), 27 (2021). https://doi.org/10.3390/JSAN10020027
52. Casadei, R., Damiani, F., Torta, G., Viroli, M.: Actor-based designs for distributed self-organisation programming. In: Active Object Languages: Current Research Trends. LNCS, vol. 14360, pp. 37–58. Springer, Cham (2024). https://doi.org/10.1007/978-3-031-51060-1_2
53. Casadei, R., Mariani, S., Pianini, D., Viroli, M., Zambonelli, F.: Space-fluid adaptive sampling by self-organisation. Log. Methods Comput. Sci. **19**(4) (2023). https://doi.org/10.46298/LMCS-19(4:29)2023

54. Casadei, R., Viroli, M.: Programming actor-based collective adaptive systems. In: Programming with Actors - State-of-the-Art and Research Perspectives. LNCS, vol. 10789, pp. 94–122. Springer, Cham (2018). https://doi.org/10.1007/978-3-030-00302-9_4

55. Casadei, R., Viroli, M.: Declarative macro-programming of collective systems with aggregate computing: an experience report. In: 26th International Symposium on Principles and Practice of Declarative Programming, PPDP 2024, Milano, Italy, 9–11 Sep 2024, pp. 5:1–5:5. ACM (2024). https://doi.org/10.1145/3678232.3678235

56. Casadei, R., Viroli, M., Aguzzi, G., Pianini, D.: ScaFi: a Scala DSL and toolkit for aggregate programming. SoftwareX **20**, 101248 (2022). https://doi.org/10.1016/J.SOFTX.2022.101248

57. Casadei, R., Viroli, M., Ricci, A., Audrito, G.: Tuple-based coordination in large-scale situated systems. In: Coordination Models and Languages - 23rd IFIP WG 6.1 International Conference, COORDINATION 2021, Proceedings. LNCS, vol. 12717, pp. 149–167. Springer, Cham (2021). https://doi.org/10.1007/978-3-030-78142-2_10

58. Castelli, G., Mamei, M., Rosi, A., Zambonelli, F.: Behavior predictability despite non-determinism in the SAPERE ecosystem preliminary ideas. In: De Paoli and Vizzari [75], pp. 82–88. http://ceur-ws.org/Vol-892/paper8.pdf

59. Cavaleri, A., Cossentino, M., Lodato, C., Lopes, S., Sabatucci, L.: Self-configuring mashup of cloud applications. In: Santoro et al. [155], pp. 68–73. http://ceur-ws.org/Vol-1664/w12.pdf

60. Cavone, D., Carolis, B.D., Ferilli, S., Novielli, N.: An agent-based approach for adapting the behavior of a smart home environment. In: Fortino et al. [90], pp. 105–111. http://ceur-ws.org/Vol-741/ID14_CavoneDeCarolisFerilliNovelli.pdf

61. Centineo, F., Marguglio, A., Morreale, V., Puccio, M.: The PRACTIONIST development tool. In: Baldoni et al. [28], pp. 20–21. http://woa07.disi.unige.it/papers/D3_CenMarMorPuc-WOA07-Demo.pdf

62. Chella, A., Lanza, F., Seidita, V.: Representing and developing knowledge using Jason, Cartago and OWL. In: Cossentino et al. [69], pp. 147–152. http://ceur-ws.org/Vol-2215/paper_23.pdf

63. Ciatto, G., Calegari, R., Omicini, A., Calvaresi, D.: Towards XMAS: explainability through multi-agent systems. In: 1st Workshop on Artificial Intelligence and Internet of Things, Rende, Italy. CEUR Workshop Proceedings, vol. 2502, pp. 40–53 (2019). https://ceur-ws.org/Vol-2502/paper3.pdf

64. Collier, R.W., Russell, S.E., Lillis, D.: Reflecting on agent programming with AgentSpeak(L). In: PRIMA 2015: Principles and Practice of Multi-Agent Systems - 18th International Conference, Bertinoro, Italy, 26–30 October 2015, Proceedings. LNCS, vol. 9387, pp. 351–366. Springer, Cham (2015). https://doi.org/10.1007/978-3-319-25524-8_22

65. Corbetta, A., Toschi, F.: Physics of human crowds. Ann. Rev. Condensed Matter Phys. **14**(1), 311–333 (2023). https://doi.org/10.1146/annurev-conmatphys-031620-100450

66. Corradini, F., De Paoli, F., Merelli, E., Omicini, A. (eds.): WOA 2005 – 6th Workshop "From Objects to Agents". Pitagora Editrice Bologna, Camerino, MC, Italy (2005). http://lia.deis.unibo.it/books/woa2005/atti.pdf

67. Cossentino, M., Burrafato, P., Lombardo, S., Sabatucci, L.: Introducing pattern reuse in the design of multi-agent systems. In: Agent Technologies, Infrastructures, Tools, and Applications for E-Services, NODe 2002 Agent-Related Workshops, Erfurt, Germany, 7–10 October 2002. Revised Papers. LNCS, vol. 2592, pp. 107–120. Springer, Cham (2002). https://doi.org/10.1007/3-540-36559-1_10
68. Cossentino, M., Lodato, C., Lopes, S., Sabatucci, L.: MUSA: a middleware for user-driven service adaptation. In: Di Napoli et al. [77], pp. 1–10. http://ceur-ws.org/Vol-1382/paper1.pdf
69. Cossentino, M., Sabatucci, L., Seidita, V. (eds.): WOA 2018 – 19th Workshop "From Objects to Agents", CEUR Workshop Proceedings, vol. 2215. Palermo, Italy (2018). http://ceur-ws.org/Vol-2215/
70. Crociani, L., Piazzoni, A., Vizzari, G.: Adaptive hybrid agents for tactical decisions in pedestrian environments. In: Di Napoli et al. [77], pp. 115–122. http://ceur-ws.org/Vol-1382/paper18.pdf
71. De Benedetti, M., D'Urso, F., Messina, F., Pappalardo, G., Santoro, C.: Self-organising UAVs for wide area fault-tolerant aerial monitoring. In: Di Napoli et al. [77], pp. 135–141. http://ceur-ws.org/Vol-1382/paper21.pdf
72. De Meo, P., Postorino, M.N., Rosaci, D., Sarnè, G.M.L. (eds.): WOA 2017 – 18th Workshop "From Objects to Agents", CEUR Workshop Proceedings, vol. 1867. Scilla, RC, Italy (2017). http://ceur-ws.org/Vol-1867/
73. De Paoli, F., Di Stefano, A., Omicini, A., Santoro, C. (eds.): WOA 2006 – 7th Workshop "From Objects to Agents", CEUR Workshop Proceedings, vol. 204. Catania, Italy (2006). http://ceur-ws.org/Vol-204/
74. De Paoli, F., Manzoni, S., Poggi, A. (eds.): WOA 2002 – 3rd Workshop "From Objects to Agents". Pitagora Editrice Bologna, Milano, Italy (2002). http://giuseppevizzari.github.io/WOA-proceedings-archive/woa-2002.html
75. De Paoli, F., Vizzari, G. (eds.): WOA 2012 – 13th Workshop "From Objects to Agents", CEUR Workshop Proceedings, vol. 892. Milano, Italy (2012). http://ceur-ws.org/Vol-892/
76. Delmerico, J.A., et al.: Spatial computing and intuitive interaction: bringing mixed reality and robotics together. IEEE Robotics Autom. Mag. **29**(1), 45–57 (2022). https://doi.org/10.1109/MRA.2021.3138384
77. Di Napoli, C., Rossi, S., Staffa, M. (eds.): WOA 2015 – 16th Workshop "From Objects to Agents", CEUR Workshop Proceedings, vol. 1382. Naples, Italy (2015). http://ceur-ws.org/Vol-1382/
78. Dijkstra, E.W.: Self-stabilizing systems in spite of distributed control. Commun. ACM **17**(11), 643–644 (1974). https://doi.org/10.1145/361179.361202
79. Dinaharison, J.B., Marilleau, N., Rakotonirainy, H.L., Corson, N., Bernard, L., Müller, J.: Agent-based spatial model coupling using a coordination unit. In: Ferrando and Mascardi [86], pp. 164–175. http://ceur-ws.org/Vol-3261/paper13.pdf
80. Dolev, S.: Self-stabilization. MIT Press (2000). https://mitpress.mit.edu/9780262041782/self-stabilization/
81. Domini, D., Farabegoli, N., Aguzzi, G., Viroli, M.: Towards intelligent pulverized systems: a modern approach for edge-cloud services. In: Alderighi et al. [9], pp. 252–270. http://ceur-ws.org/Vol-3735/paper_19.pdf
82. Dorigo, M., Bonabeau, E., Theraulaz, G.: Ant algorithms and stigmergy. Future Gener. Comput. Syst. **16**(8), 851–871 (2000). https://doi.org/10.1016/S0167-739X(00)00042-X
83. Duckham, M.: Decentralized Spatial Computing - Foundations of Geosensor Networks. Springer, Cham (2013). https://doi.org/10.1007/978-3-642-30853-6

84. Falcone, R., Castelfranchi, C., Sapienza, A., Cantucci, F. (eds.): WOA 2023 – 24th Workshop "From Objects to Agents", CEUR Workshop Proceedings, vol. 3579. Roma, Italy (2023). http://ceur-ws.org/Vol-3579/

85. Farabegoli, N., Pianini, D., Casadei, R., Viroli, M.: Scalability through pulverisation: declarative deployment reconfiguration at runtime. Future Gener. Comput. Syst. **161**, 545–558 (2024). https://doi.org/10.1016/J.FUTURE.2024.07.042

86. Ferrando, A., Mascardi, V. (eds.): WOA 2022 – 23rd Workshop "From Objects to Agents", CEUR Workshop Proceedings, vol. 3261. Genova, Italy (2022). http://ceur-ws.org/Vol-3261/

87. Filatova, T., Verburg, P.H., Parker, D.C., Stannard, C.A.: Spatial agent-based models for socio-ecological systems: challenges and prospects. Environ. Model. Softw. **45**, 1–7 (2013). https://doi.org/10.1016/J.ENVSOFT.2013.03.017

88. Forestiero, A., Mastroianni, C.: Description of the self-chord P2P application. In: Fortino et al. [90], pp. 175–177. http://ceur-ws.org/Vol-741/DEM03_ForestieroMastroianni.pdf

89. Fortino, G., Galzarano, S.: Programming wireless body sensor network applications through agents. In: Omicini and Viroli [133], pp. 137–144. http://ceur-ws.org/Vol-621/paper20.pdf

90. Fortino, G., Garro, A., Palopoli, L., Russo, W., Spezzano, G. (eds.): WOA 2011 – 12th Workshop "From Objects to Agents", CEUR Workshop Proceedings, vol. 741. Rende, Italy (2011). http://ceur-ws.org/Vol-741/

91. Fortino, G., Zedadra, O., Jouandeau, N., Seridi, H.: A decentralized ant colony foraging model using only stigmergic communication. In: Santoro and Bergenti [154], pp. 63–67. http://ceur-ws.org/Vol-1260/paper13.pdf

92. Francia, M., Pianini, D., Beal, J., Viroli, M.: Towards a foundational API for resilient distributed systems design. In: 2nd IEEE International Workshops on Foundations and Applications of Self* Systems, FAS*W@SASO/ICCAC'17, Tucson, USA, pp. 27–32. IEEE Computer Society (2017). https://doi.org/10.1109/FAS-W.2017.116

93. Gardelli, L., Viroli, M., Omicini, A.: On the role of simulation in the engineering of self-organising systems: Detecting abnormal behaviour in MAS. In: Corradini et al. [66], pp. 85–90. http://lia.deis.unibo.it/books/woa2005/papers/12.pdf

94. Gaud, N., Galland, S., Gechter, F., Hilaire, V., Koukam, A.: Holonic multilevel simulation of complex systems: application to real-time pedestrians simulation in virtual urban environment. Simul. Model. Pract. Theory **16**(10), 1659–1676 (2008). https://doi.org/10.1016/j.simpat.2008.08.015

95. Gelernter, D.: Generative communication in Linda. ACM Trans. Program. Lang. Syst. **7**(1), 80–112 (1985). https://doi.org/10.1145/2363.2433

96. Gelernter, D.: Multiple tuple spaces in Linda. In: PARLE 1989: Parallel Architectures and Languages Europe, Volume II: Parallel Languages, Proceedings. LNCS, vol. 366, pp. 20–27. Springer, Cham (1989). https://doi.org/10.1007/3-540-51285-3_30

97. Gronauer, S., Diepold, K.: Multi-agent deep reinforcement learning: a survey. Artif. Intell. Rev. **55**(2), 895–943 (2022). https://doi.org/10.1007/S10462-021-09996-W

98. Hannoun, M., Boissier, O., Sichman, J.S., Sayettat, C.: MOISE: an organizational model for multi-agent systems. In: Advances in Artificial Intelligence, International Joint Conference, 7th Ibero-American Conference on AI, 15th Brazilian Symposium on AI, IBERAMIA-SBIA 2000, Proceedings. LNCS, vol. 1952, pp. 156–165. Springer, Cham (2000). https://doi.org/10.1007/3-540-44399-1_17

99. He, K., Doshi, P., Banerjee, B.: Modeling and reinforcement learning in partially observable many-agent systems. Auton. Agents Multi-Agent Syst. **38**(1) (2024). https://doi.org/10.1007/s10458-024-09640-1

100. Henrichs, E., Lesch, V., Straesser, M., Kounev, S., Krupitzer, C.: A literature review on optimization techniques for adaptation planning in adaptive systems: state of the art and research directions. Inf. Softw. Technol. **149**, 106940 (2022). https://doi.org/10.1016/J.INFSOF.2022.106940

101. Hernandez-Leal, P., Kartal, B., Taylor, M.E.: A survey and critique of multiagent deep reinforcement learning. Auton. Agents Multi Agent Syst. **33**(6), 750–797 (2019). https://doi.org/10.1007/S10458-019-09421-1

102. Heuillet, A., Couthouis, F., Rodríguez, N.D.: Collective explainable AI: explaining cooperative strategies and agent contribution in multiagent reinforcement learning with Shapley values. IEEE Comput. Intell. Mag. **17**(1), 59–71 (2022). https://doi.org/10.1109/MCI.2021.3129959

103. Kephart, J.O., Chess, D.M.: The vision of autonomic computing. Computer **36**(1), 41–50 (2003). https://doi.org/10.1109/MC.2003.1160055

104. Krueger, C.W.: Software reuse. ACM Comput. Surv. **24**(2), 131–183 (1992). https://doi.org/10.1145/130844.130856

105. Lachowicz, M.: Microscopic, mesoscopic and macroscopic descriptions of complex systems. Probab. Eng. Mech. **26**(1), 54–60 (2011). https://doi.org/10.1016/j.probengmech.2010.06.007

106. Lamarche-Perrin, R., Demazeau, Y., Vincent, J.: How to build the best macroscopic description of your multi-agent system? In: Advances on Practical Applications of Agents and Multi-Agent Systems, 11th International Conference, PAAMS 2013. Proceedings, vol. 7879, pp. 157–169. Springer, Cham (2013). https://doi.org/10.1007/978-3-642-38073-0_14

107. Losapio, G., Minutoli, F., Mascardi, V., Ferrando, A.: Smart balancing of e-scooter sharing systems via deep reinforcement learning. In: Calegari et al. [46], pp. 83–97. http://ceur-ws.org/Vol-2963/paper16.pdf

108. Mamei, M., Zambonelli, F.: Spatial computing: the TOTA approach. In: Baldoni et al. [30], pp. 126–142. http://giuseppevizzari.github.io/WOA-proceedings-archive/pdfs/woa2004/18.pdf

109. Mamei, M., Zambonelli, F.: Pervasive pheromone-based interaction with RFID tags. In: Corradini et al. [66], pp. 104–110. http://lia.deis.unibo.it/books/woa2005/papers/15.pdf

110. Mamei, M., Zambonelli, F.: Field-Based Coordination for Pervasive Multiagent Systems. Springer, Cham (2006). https://doi.org/10.1007/3-540-27969-5

111. Mamei, M., Zambonelli, F., Leonardi, L.: *Tuples On The Air*: a middleware for context-aware multiagent systems. In: De Paoli et al. [74], pp. 108–116. http://giuseppevizzari.github.io/WOA-proceedings-archive/pdfs/woa2002/26.pdf

112. Mamei, M., Zambonelli, F., Leonardi, L.: Co-fields: a physically inspired approach to motion coordination. IEEE Pervasive Comput. **3**(2), 52–61 (2004). https://doi.org/10.1109/MPRV.2004.1316820

113. Mariani, S.: Parameter engineering vs. parameter tuning: the case of biochemical coordination in MoK. In: Baldoni et al. [24], pp. 16–23. http://ceur-ws.org/Vol-1099/paper5.pdf

114. Mariani, S., Omicini, A.: Space-aware coordination in ReSpecT. In: Baldoni et al. [24], pp. 1–7. http://ceur-ws.org/Vol-1099/paper3.pdf

115. Mariani, S., Omicini, A.: Tuple-based coordination of stochastic systems with uniform primitives. In: Baldoni et al. [24], pp. 8–15. http://ceur-ws.org/Vol-1099/paper4.pdf

116. Mariani, S., Omicini, A.: TuCSoN coordination for MAS situatedness: towards a methodology. In: Santoro and Bergenti [154], pp. 48–57. http://ceur-ws.org/Vol-1260/paper11.pdf

117. Mariani, S., Omicini, A.: Multi-paradigm coordination for MAS: integrating heterogeneous coordination approaches in MAS technologies. In: Santoro et al. [155], pp. 91–99. http://ceur-ws.org/Vol-1664/w16.pdf

118. Mariani, S., Omicini, A., Ciatto, G.: Novel opportunities for tuple-based coordination: XPath, the Blockchain, and stream processing. In: De Meo et al. [72], pp. 61–64. http://ceur-ws.org/Vol-1867/w11.pdf

119. Mascardi, V., Demergasso, D., Ancona, D.: Languages for programming BDI-style agents: an overview. In: Corradini et al. [66], pp. 9–15. http://lia.deis.unibo.it/books/woa2005/papers/2.pdf

120. Mascardi, V., Omicini, A. (eds.): The Agents Journey: Twenty-Five Years of Multi-agent Systems at WOA. LNCS – State-of-the-Art Surveys. Springer, Cham (2026)

121. Menezes, R., Omicini, A., Viroli, M.: Have ReSpecT for LOGOP. In: De Paoli et al. [74], pp. 94–99. http://giuseppevizzari.github.io/WOA-proceedings-archive/pdfs/woa2002/18.pdf

122. Messina, F., Pappalardo, G., Santoro, C.: A self-organising system for resource finding in large-scale computational grids. In: Omicini and Viroli [133], pp. 110–116. http://ceur-ws.org/Vol-621/paper16.pdf

123. Messina, F., Pappalardo, G., Santoro, C.: Designing autonomous robots using GOLEM. In: Santoro and Bergenti [154], pp. 89–95. http://ceur-ws.org/Vol-1260/paper15.pdf

124. Mola, F.D., Quitadamo, R.: An agent model for future autonomic communications. In: De Paoli et al. [73], pp. 51–59. http://ceur-ws.org/Vol-204/P07.pdf

125. Monica, S., Bergenti, F.: A stochastic model of self-stabilizing cellular automata for consensus formation. In: Santoro and Bergenti [154], pp. 75–80. http://ceur-ws.org/Vol-1260/paper8.pdf

126. Montagna, S., Viroli, M., Pianini, D., Fernandez-Marquez, J.L.: Towards a comprehensive approach to spontaneous self-composition in pervasive ecosystems. In: De Paoli and Vizzari [75], pp. 89–97. http://ceur-ws.org/Vol-892/paper1.pdf

127. Nardini, E., Viroli, M., Casadei, M., Omicini, A.: A self-organising infrastructure for chemical-semantic coordination: Experiments in TuCSoN. In: Omicini and Viroli [133], pp. 117–125. http://CEUR-WS.org/Vol-621/paper17.pdf

128. Odell, J.: Objects and agents compared. J. Object Technol. **1**(1), 41–53 (2002). https://doi.org/10.5381/JOT.2002.1.1.C4

129. Oliva, E., Viroli, M., Omicini, A.: Minority Game: a logic-based approach in TuCSoN. In: De Paoli et al. [73], pp. 181–186. http://ceur-ws.org/Vol-204/P02.pdf

130. Oliva, E., Viroli, M., Omicini, A.: Simulation of minority game in TuCSoN. In: De Paoli et al. [73], pp. 6–9. http://ceur-ws.org/Vol-204/D03.pdf

131. Omicini, A., Ricci, A., Rimassa, G., Viroli, M.: Integrating objective & subjective coordination in FIPA: a roadmap to TuCSoN. In: Armano et al. [85], pp. 85–91. http://giuseppevizzari.github.io/WOA-proceedings-archive/pdfs/woa2003/07.pdf

132. Omicini, A., Viroli, M. (eds.): WOA 2001 – 2nd Workshop "From Objects to Agents". Pitagora Editrice Bologna, Modena, Italy (2001). http://giuseppevizzari.github.io/WOA-proceedings-archive/woa-2001.html

133. Omicini, A., Viroli, M. (eds.): WOA 2010 – 11th Workshop "From Objects to Agents", CEUR Workshop Proceedings, vol. 621. Rimini, Italy (2010). http://ceur-ws.org/Vol-621/

134. Panait, L., Luke, S.: Cooperative multi-agent learning: the state of the art. Auton. Agents Multi Agent Syst. **11**(3), 387–434 (2005). https://doi.org/10.1007/S10458-005-2631-2

135. Petrosino, G., Monica, S., Bergenti, F.: Robust software agents with the jadescript programming language. In: Ferrando and Mascardi [86], pp. 194–208. http://ceur-ws.org/Vol-3261/paper15.pdf

136. Pianini, D., Casadei, R., Viroli, M., Natali, A.: Partitioned integration and coordination via the self-organising coordination regions pattern. Future Gener. Comput. Syst. **114**, 44–68 (2021). https://doi.org/10.1016/J.FUTURE.2020.07.032

137. Pianini, D., Pettinari, F., Casadei, R., Esterle, L.: A collective adaptive approach to decentralised k-coverage in multi-robot systems. ACM Trans. Auton. Adapt. Syst. **17**, 4:1–4:39 (2022). https://doi.org/10.1145/3547145

138. Piunti, M., Ricci, A.: From agents to artifacts back and forth: operational and doxastic use of artifacts in MAS. In: Baldoni et al. [29], pp. 76–83. http://www.pa.icar.cnr.it/woa08/materiali/paper/paper_13.pdf

139. Piunti, M., Ricci, A., Boissier, O., Hübner, J.F.: Programming open systems with agents, environments and organizations. In: Omicini and Viroli [133], pp. 39–47. http://ceur-ws.org/Vol-621/paper06.pdf

140. Prokopenko, M.: Guided self-organization (2009)

141. Prokopenko, M., Boschetti, F., Ryan, A.J.: An information-theoretic primer on complexity, self-organization, and emergence. CompLex **15**(1), 11–28 (2009). https://doi.org/10.1002/CPLX.20249

142. Quitadamo, R., Zambonelli, F.: Autonomic communication services: a new challenge for software agents. Auton. Agents Multi Agent Syst. **17**(3), 457–475 (2008). https://doi.org/10.1007/S10458-008-9054-9

143. Reed, S.E., Zolna, K., Parisotto, E., Colmenarejo, S.G., Novikov, A., et al: A generalist agent. CoRR abs/2205.06175 (2022). https://doi.org/10.48550/ARXIV.2205.06175

144. Ricci, A.: Programming with event loops and control loops - from actors to agents. Comput. Lang. Syst. Struct. **45**, 80–104 (2016). https://doi.org/10.1016/J.CL.2015.12.003

145. Ricci, A., Omicini, A.: Agent coordination contexts: Experiments in TuCSoN. In: De Paoli et al. [74], pp. 14–21. http://giuseppevizzari.github.io/WOA-proceedings-archive/pdfs/woa2002/17.pdf

146. Ricci, A., Omicini, A., Denti, E.: Enlightened agents in TuCSoN. In: Omicini and Viroli [132], pp. 101–106. http://giuseppevizzari.github.io/WOA-proceedings-archive/pdfs/woa2001/pdf/21.pdf

147. Ricci, A., Viroli, M., Omicini, A., Mariani, S., Croatti, A., Pianini, D.: Spatial tuples: augmenting reality with tuples. Expert Syst. J. Knowl. Eng. **35**(5) (2018). https://doi.org/10.1111/EXSY.12273

148. Robol, M., Giorgini, P., Busetta, P.: Applying social norms to implicit negotiation among non-player characters in serious games. In: Santoro et al. [155], pp. 23–28. http://ceur-ws.org/Vol-1664/w5.pdf

149. Rodriguez, S., Hilaire, V., Gaud, N., Galland, S., Koukam, A.: Holonic multi-agent systems. In: Self-organising Software - From Natural to Artificial Adaptation. Natural Computing Series, pp. 251–279. Springer, Cham (2011). https://doi.org/10.1007/978-3-642-17348-6_11

150. Rossi, S., Ercolano, G., Raggioli, L., Valentino, M., Di Napoli, C.: A framework for personalized and adaptive socially assistive robotics. In: Cossentino et al. [69], pp. 90–95. http://ceur-ws.org/Vol-2215/paper_15.pdf

151. Ruta, M., Scioscia, F., Loseto, G., Gramegna, F., Pinto, A., Sciascio, E.D.: Semantic-based social intelligence through multi-agent systems. In: Cossentino et al. [69], pp. 96–102. http://ceur-ws.org/Vol-2215/paper_16.pdf

152. Sabatucci, L., Cossentino, M., Lopes, S.: Self-adaptive reconfigurations of shipboard power systems. In: Cossentino et al. [69], pp. 103–108. http://ceur-ws.org/Vol-2215/paper_17.pdf

153. Santi, A., Ricci, A.: Programming distributed multi-agent systems in simpAL. In: De Paoli and Vizzari [75], pp. 39–48. http://ceur-ws.org/Vol-892/paper5.pdf

154. Santoro, C., Bergenti, F. (eds.): WOA 2014 – 15th Workshop "From Objects to Agents", CEUR Workshop Proceedings, vol. 1260. Catania, Italy (2014). http://ceur-ws.org/Vol-1260/

155. Santoro, C., Messina, F., De Benedetti, M. (eds.): WOA 2016 – 17th Workshop "From Objects to Agents", CEUR Workshop Proceedings, vol. 1664. Catania, Italy (2016). http://ceur-ws.org/Vol-1664/

156. Sawyer, R.K.: Artificial societies: multiagent systems and the micro-macro link in sociological theory. Sociol. Methods Res. **31**(3), 325–363 (2003). https://doi.org/10.1177/0049124102239079

157. Schneider, C., Barker, A., Dobson, S.A.: A survey of self-healing systems frameworks. Softw. Pract. Exp. **45**(10), 1375–1398 (2015). https://doi.org/10.1002/SPE.2250

158. Seidita, V., Cossentino, M., Gaglio, S.: A repository of fragments for agent systems design. In: De Paoli et al. [73], pp. 130–137. http://ceur-ws.org/Vol-204/P18.pdf

159. Shao, K., Tang, Z., Zhu, Y., Li, N., Zhao, D.: A survey of deep reinforcement learning in video games. CoRR abs/1912.10944 (2019). http://arxiv.org/abs/1912.10944

160. Shekhar, S.: Technical perspective: progress in spatial computing for flood prediction. Commun. ACM **63**(9), 93 (2020). https://doi.org/10.1145/3410410

161. Sierra, C., Noriega, P.: Agent-mediated interaction. From auctions to negotiation and argumentation. In: Foundations and Applications of Multi-Agent Systems, UKMAS Workshop 1996-2000, Selected Papers. LNCS, vol. 2403, pp. 27–48. Springer, Cham (2002). https://doi.org/10.1007/3-540-45634-1_3

162. da Silva, F.L., Costa, A.H.R.: A survey on transfer learning for multiagent reinforcement learning systems. J. Artif. Intell. Res. **64**, 645–703 (2019). https://doi.org/10.1613/JAIR.1.11396

163. Suran, S., Pattanaik, V., Draheim, D.: Frameworks for collective intelligence: a systematic literature review. ACM Comput. Surv. **53**(1), 14:1–14:36 (2021). https://doi.org/10.1145/3368986

164. Tan, M.: Multi-agent reinforcement learning: independent versus cooperative agents. In: Machine Learning, 10th International Conference, USA, 27–29 June 1993, pp. 330–337. Morgan Kaufmann (1993). https://doi.org/10.1016/B978-1-55860-307-3.50049-6

165. Tumer, K., Wolpert, D.H.: A survey of collectives. In: Collectives and the Design of Complex Systems, chap. 1. Springer, Cham (2004)

166. Unniyankal, H., Belardinelli, F., Ferrando, A., Malvone, V.: RMLGym: a formal reward machine framework for reinforcement learning. In: Falcone et al. [84], pp. 1–16. http://ceur-ws.org/Vol-3579/paper1.pdf

167. Vadakkepat, P., Tan, K.C., Wang, M.: Evolutionary artificial potential fields and their application in real time robot path planning. In: 2000 Congress on Evolutionary Computation, CEC, USA, pp. 256–263. IEEE (2000). https://doi.org/10.1109/CEC.2000.870304

168. Vidali, A., Crociani, L., Vizzari, G., Bandini, S.: A deep reinforcement learning approach to adaptive traffic lights management. In: Bergenti and Monica [38], pp. 42–50. http://ceur-ws.org/Vol-2404/paper07.pdf

169. Viroli, M., Audrito, G., Beal, J., Damiani, F., Pianini, D.: Engineering resilient collective adaptive systems by self-stabilisation. ACM Trans. Model. Comput. Simul. **28**(2), 16:1–16:28 (2018). https://doi.org/10.1145/3177774

170. Viroli, M., Beal, J., Damiani, F., Audrito, G., Casadei, R., Pianini, D.: From distributed coordination to field calculus and aggregate computing. J. Log. Algebraic Methods Program. **109** (2019). https://doi.org/10.1016/J.JLAMP.2019.100486

171. Viroli, M., Casadei, M., Montagna, S., Zambonelli, F.: Spatial coordination of pervasive services through chemical-inspired tuple spaces. ACM Trans. Auton. Adapt. Syst. **6**(2), 14:1–14:24 (2011). https://doi.org/10.1145/1968513.1968517

172. Viroli, M., Nardini, E., Castelli, G., Mamei, M., Zambonelli, F.: Coordinating spatially-situated pervasive service ecosystems. In: Fortino et al. [90], pp. 19–27. http://ceur-ws.org/Vol-741/ID13_ViroliNardiniCastelliMameiZambonelli.pdf

173. Viroli, M., Pianini, D., Beal, J.: Linda in space-time: an adaptive coordination model for mobile ad-hoc environments. In: Coordination Models and Languages - 14th International Conference, COORDINATION 2012, Stockholm, Sweden, 14–15 June 2012. Proceedings. LNCS, vol. 7274, pp. 212–229. Springer, Cham (2012). https://doi.org/10.1007/978-3-642-30829-1_15

174. Viroli, M., Pianini, D., Ricci, A., Croatti, A.: Aggregate plans for multiagent systems. Int. J. Agent Oriented Softw. Eng. **5**(4), 336–365 (2017). https://doi.org/10.1504/IJAOSE.2017.10008554

175. Viroli, M., Ricci, A.: Timed coordination artifacts with ReSpecT. In: Baldoni et al. [30], pp. 77–85. http://giuseppevizzari.github.io/WOA-proceedings-archive/pdfs/woa2004/12.pdf

176. Waharte, S., Trigoni, N.: Supporting search and rescue operations with UAVs. In: 2010 International Conference on Emerging Security Technologies, EST 2010. pp. 142–147. IEEE Computer Society (2010). https://doi.org/10.1109/EST.2010.31

177. Warren, C.W.: Global path planning using artificial potential fields. In: IEEE International Conference on Robotics and Automation, Scottsdale, AZ, USA, 14–19 May 1989, pp. 316–321. IEEE Computer Society (1989). https://doi.org/10.1109/ROBOT.1989.100007

178. Warren, C.W.: Multiple robot path coordination using artificial potential fields. In: 1990 IEEE International Conference on Robotics and Automation, Cincinnati, Ohio, USA, 13–18 May 1990, pp. 500–505. IEEE (1990). https://doi.org/10.1109/ROBOT.1990.126028

179. Weyns, D.: An Introduction to Self-adaptive Systems: A Contemporary Software Engineering Perspective. Wiley, Hoboken (2020)

180. Wolf, T.D., Holvoet, T.: Emergence versus self-organisation: different concepts but promising when combined. In: Engineering Self-Organising Systems, Methodologies and Applications. LNCS, vol. 3464, pp. 1–15. Springer, Cham (2004). https://doi.org/10.1007/11494676_1

181. Wu, Z., Pan, S., Chen, F., Long, G., Zhang, C., Yu, P.S.: A comprehensive survey on graph neural networks. IEEE Trans. Neural Netw. Learn. Syst. **32**(1), 4–24 (2021). https://doi.org/10.1109/TNNLS.2020.2978386

182. Xu, F., Uszkoreit, H., Du, Y., Fan, W., Zhao, D., Zhu, J.: Explainable AI: a brief survey on history, research areas, approaches and challenges. In: Natural Language Processing and Chinese Computing - 8th CCF International Conference, NLPCC 2019, Proceedings, Part II. LNCS, vol. 11839, pp. 563–574. Springer, Cham (2019). https://doi.org/10.1007/978-3-030-32236-6_51
183. Yan, E., Burattini, S., Hübner, J.F., Ricci, A.: Towards a multi-level explainability framework for engineering and understanding BDI agent systems. In: Falcone et al. [84], pp. 216–231. http://ceur-ws.org/Vol-3579/paper17.pdf
184. Yang, Y., Wang, J.: An overview of multi-agent reinforcement learning from game theoretical perspective. CoRR abs/2011.00583 (2020). https://arxiv.org/abs/2011.00583
185. Ye, D., Zhang, M., Vasilakos, A.V.: A survey of self-organization mechanisms in multiagent systems. IEEE Trans. Syst. Man Cybern. Syst. **47**(3), 441–461 (2017). https://doi.org/10.1109/TSMC.2015.2504350
186. Yuan, E., Esfahani, N., Malek, S.: A systematic survey of self-protecting software systems. ACM Trans. Auton. Adapt. Syst. **8**(4), 17:1–17:41 (2014). https://doi.org/10.1145/2555611
187. Zambonelli, F., Rana, O.: Self-organization in distributed systems engineering: introduction to the special issue. IEEE Trans. Syst. Man Cybern. - Part A: Syst. Hum. **35**(3), 313–315 (2005). https://doi.org/10.1109/tsmca.2006.846372
188. Zambonelli, F., et al.: Developing pervasive multi-agent systems with nature-inspired coordination. Pervasive Mob. Comput. **17**, 236–252 (2015). https://doi.org/10.1016/j.pmcj.2014.12.002, special issue "10 years of Pervasive Computing" In Honor of Chatschik Bisdikian
189. Zambonelli, F., Viroli, M.: From service-oriented architectures to nature-inspired pervasive service ecosystems. In: Omicini and Viroli [133], pp. 102–109. http://ceur-ws.org/Vol-621/paper15.pdf
190. Zhang, H., Huang, Y., Thill, J., Guo, D., Liu, Y.: Guest editorial: special issue on spatial computing in emergency management. GeoInformatica **22**(2), 307–309 (2018). https://doi.org/10.1007/S10707-018-0321-X
191. Zhao, W.X., et al.: A survey of large language models. CoRR abs/2303.18223 (2023). https://doi.org/10.48550/ARXIV.2303.18223
192. Zhou, Z., Wang, Y., Xie, X., Chen, L., Zhu, C.: Foresee urban sparse traffic accidents: a spatiotemporal multi-granularity perspective. IEEE Trans. Knowl. Data Eng. **34**(8), 3786–3799 (2022). https://doi.org/10.1109/TKDE.2020.3034312
193. Zhu, Z., Lin, K., Jain, A.K., Zhou, J.: Transfer learning in deep reinforcement learning: a survey. IEEE Trans. Pattern Anal. Mach. Intell. **45**(11), 13344–13362 (2023). https://doi.org/10.1109/TPAMI.2023.3292075
194. Zhuang, F., et al.: A comprehensive survey on transfer learning. Proc. IEEE **109**(1), 43–76 (2021). https://doi.org/10.1109/JPROC.2020.3004555

Software and System Engineering with Agents and MAS

Rethinking Software Agents as Building Blocks of Software Systems

Federico Bergenti[1]([✉])[iD] and Stefania Monica[2][iD]

[1] Dipartimento di Scienze Matematiche, Fisiche e Informatiche, Università degli Studi di Parma, Parco Area delle Scienze 53/A, 43124 Parma, Italy
federico.bergenti@unipr.it
[2] Dipartimento di Scienze e Metodi dell'Ingegneria, Università degli Studi di Modena e Reggio Emilia, Via Amendola 2, 42122 Reggio Emilia, Italy
stefania.monica@unimore.it

Abstract. The idea of using software agents as fundamental building blocks within software systems has been a subject of relevant interest over the past three decades. This chapter seeks to contextualize the longstanding debate surrounding the role of software agents as building blocks of software systems within the framework of contemporary software development. Specifically, the focus of this chapter is on the programmatic dimension of development with the intent to emphasize the integration of cognitive agents as fine-grained modular units within software architectures. The metaphors that characterize cognitive agents are explored as promising means to enable the treatment of agents as effective building blocks of fine-grained software architectures. A relevant part of this chapter is dedicated to examine the implications of adopting cognitive agents within mainstream software development practice. Additionally, this chapter presents a preliminary proposal of a novel system level to use cognitive agents in the scope of contemporary software development.

Keywords: Agent-oriented software engineering · Agent-based software systems · Software agents · Agent-oriented programming

1 Introduction

The primary goal of *AOSE (Agent-Oriented Software Engineering)* [43] is to provide the necessary tools for the design and development of agent-based software systems. These tools encompass, but are not limited to, methodologies and software frameworks. To date, AOSE has made partial progress in this regard, with the establishment of several research-focused methodologies and software frameworks documented in the large literature on AOSE (e.g., [1]). However, these advancements may be insufficient if the AOSE community continues to overlook some fundamental questions. For example, the reason why agents should be employed in the construction of software systems is still debated. Additionally, the quantitative motivations that justify the adoption of agents over other

V. Mascardi and A. Omicini (Eds.): *The Agents Journey*, LNCS 16395, pp. 181–212, 2026.
https://doi.org/10.1007/978-3-032-22940-3_7

existing approaches are still under investigation. These questions, among others, present significant challenges for proponents of agent-based approaches. In essence, there is no conclusive answer to these inquiries. The ongoing debate surrounding the distinctions between agents and other development technologies, like objects and microservices [225], has further complicated the issue. The perceived advantages of agent-based approaches over microservices appear marginal, and the results of the proposals to match them (e.g., [93]) appear preliminary and partial.

This chapter represents a preliminary attempt to address the fundamental question of why agents constitute a viable paradigm for software development. To this end, a comparative analysis is conducted between agents and contemporary software development technologies, specifically microservices. The first significant outcome of this comparison is discussed, namely that agents exhibit superior reusability and composability relative to microservices. The second key finding is presented, which indicates that agents elevate the level of abstraction in software development beyond that of microservice architectures. This new level of abstraction is formalized in terms of a preliminary proposal of a novel system level to be used to frame cognitive agents in the scope of the contemporary software development.

This chapter is organized as follows. Section 2 discusses the role of the community of researchers and practitioners that annually gathers at Workshop on Objects and Agents (WOA). The contribution of this community to the understanding of the role of software agents in the scope of software development is particularly relevant. Section 3 briefly describes the specific notion of software agents targeted in this chapter, namely cognitive agents. Section 4 compares the studied software agents with one of the most relevant development technologies available today, namely microservices. Section 5 briefly provides a preliminary proposal of a novel system level for cognitive agents. Finally, Sect. 6 concludes the chapter with a concise overview of some planned research directions.

2   The Contribution of the WOA Community

The community of researchers and practitioners that annually gathers at WOA has been significantly contributing to AOSE and to the various aspects of the use of agents as building blocks of software systems. The relevance of this contribution is spread in most of the 518 papers of the first 25 editions of WOA, and it can be succinctly exemplified as follows.

First, an early prototype of one of the most widely adopted tools for the practical development of agent-based software systems, namely the *JADE (Java Agent DEvelopment framework)* [37,38], was initially presented [39] at the first edition of WOA. Also, the major evolutions of JADE, which were mostly developed by members of the initial team together with other researchers, were all presented at WOA. For example, JADE for Android [48], *WADE (Workflows and Agents Development Environment)* [49], and *AMUSE (Agent-based Multi-User Social Environment)* [47] were all presented at WOA. Then, one of the major proposals to retarget JADE in the current development landscape, namely Jadescript [42], was discussed several times [54,180–182] at WOA. Immediately before Jadescript, also JADEL [41], which is the direct predecessor of Jadescript, was presented [50–52] at WOA.

Second, two of the editors of the book [43] that marked a milestone in the initial development of AOSE are active members of the WOA community. One of them was a co-author of 17 papers in the first 25 editions of the workshop. The other organized WOA two times and was the co-editor of four editions of the proceedings of the workshop. Moreover, he contributed 31 papers in the first 25 editions of the workshop.

Third, one of the most significant approaches for modeling and engineering agent-based software systems, namely *A&A (Agents & Artefacts)* [173], which is also the base for relevant tools like *CArtAgO (Common Artifact Infrastructure for Agent Open Environments)* [198], was presented at WOA [186].

Fourth, several papers presented at the first 25 editions of WOA have contributed to the understanding of how agents can be used as building blocks of software systems. These contributions can be classified as:

1. AOSE methodologies: papers that discuss an AOSE methodology or methodological approach (see also another chapter of this book [106]);
2. Models of interactions: papers that discuss an approach to support effective interactions among agents (see also other chapters of this book [3,23,71]);
3. Programming languages: papers that discuss a programming language, or an extension of a programming language, for agent-based software systems (see also other chapters of this book [2,6,229]);
4. Interoperability and ontologies: papers that discuss relevant aspects related to interoperability and ontologies; and
5. Domain-agnostic infrastructures: papers that talk about domain-agnostic infrastructures for agent-based software systems (see also another chapter of this book [61]).

Table 1, Table 2, and Table 3 list 179 out of the 518 papers presented at the first 25 editions of WOA. These tables allocate the listed papers in the considered five classes. Note that some of the listed papers are allocated in more than one class because their contributions are relevant for more than one of the considered aspects. Similarly, the papers included in the proceedings of the first 25 editions of WOA that are not listed in the tables are not relevant for the considered classes.

3 A Reference Model for Cognitive Agents

Prior to addressing one of the primary focuses of this chapter, which is the comparison between agents and microservices, it is necessary to briefly outline the agent model employed in the subsequent analysis. This discussion is essential, as microservices represent a concrete and well-established approach, and a corresponding concrete agent model is required to facilitate a meaningful comparison.

Table 1. Papers in the editions of WOA from 2000 to 2006 targeting relevant aspects of agent-based software development

WOA year	Paper reference	AOSE methodologies	Models of interactions	Programming languages	Interoperability and ontologies	Domain-agnostic infrastructures
2000	[10]				•	
	[39]				•	•
	[56]			•		
	[89]		•			
	[127]		•			
	[155]				•	
	[171]	•	•			
2001	[55]		•			
	[70]		•			
	[86]	•				
	[217]		•			
	[179]	•			•	
	[193]					•
	[196]				•	
	[203]	•				•
	[233]	•				
2002	[68]		•			
	[119]	•				
	[139]		•			
	[141]	•				
	[148]					•
	[159]		•			
	[201]					•
2003	[36]					•
	[62]	•				•
	[63]			•		
	[98]				•	
	[109]			•		
	[120]			•		•
	[146]		•			
	[172]		•		•	
	[204]	•	•			•
	[223]			•		
2004	[58]	•				
	[134]	•				
	[147]	•				
	[174]	•				
	[202]	•				•
	[121]			•		•
	[213]			•		
	[220]			•		
	[222]				•	•
	[227]		•			
	[228]		•			
2005	[22]		•			
	[28]		•			
	[33]	•				
	[45]					•
	[69]					•
	[88]		•			
	[94]				•	
	[96]				•	
	[122]			•		•
	[142]					•
	[157]			•		
	[166]			•		•
2006	[20]		•			
	[29]		•			
	[34]	•				
	[57]	•	•			
	[72]					•
	[107]			•		
	[114]		•			
	[167]			•		•
	[168]			•		•
	[170]		•			
	[199]					•
	[214]	•				
	[224]					•

Table 2. Papers in the editions of WOA from 2007 to 2014 targeting relevant aspects of agent-based software development

WOA year	Paper reference	AOSE methodologies	Models of interactions	Programming languages	Interoperability and ontologies	Domain-agnostic infrastructures
2007	[12]			•		
	[21]		•			•
	[30]			•		
	[85]			•		•
	[136]			•		
	[156]				•	
	[194]					•
	[185]	•	•			
	[200]			•		•
2008	[24]					•
	[26]			•		
	[65]				•	
	[92]			•		
	[110]	•				
	[111]	•				
	[132]		•			
	[149]			•		•
	[162]	•				
	[165]					•
	[178]					•
	[186]	•				
2009	[27]			•		•
	[81]	•				
	[140]	•				
	[188]	•				•
	[195]	•				•
	[208]			•		
2010	[14]			•		•
	[128]	•				
	[163]	•				
	[189]					•
	[187]	•		•		•
	[206]			•		•
	[235]	•				•
2011	[19]	•		•		
	[49]			•		•
	[66]	•				
	[99]	•				
	[84]	•				
	[112]	•		•		•
	[129]		•			•
	[131]	•				
	[138]					•
	[219]					•
	[226]	•				
2012	[13]		•			
	[79]		•			
	[164]	•				
	[190]					•
	[207]			•		•
2013	[16]					•
	[150]		•			
	[151]		•			
	[191]					•
	[197]				•	
	[211]	•				
2014	[17]		•			•
	[48]					•
	[103]				•	
	[135]		•			
	[152]	•				

Table 3. Papers in the editions of WOA from 2015 to 2024 targeting relevant aspects of agent-based software development

WOA year	Paper reference	AOSE methodologies	Models of interactions	Programming languages	Interoperability and ontologies	Domain-agnostic infrastructures
2015	[8]		•			
	[52]	•				•
	[100]					•
	[130]	•		•		•
	[177]			•		•
	[192]					•
	[231]	•				•
2016	[7]					•
	[50]			•		
	[76]			•		•
	[82]					•
	[153]	•				
	[234]	•				
2017	[18]		•			
	[51]			•		
	[104]	•				
	[154]	•				•
2018	[9]		•			
	[54]			•		
	[67]				•	
	[75]			•		•
	[90]			•		•
	[87]				•	•
	[101]			•		
	[212]			•		
2019	[5]			•		•
	[77]				•	
	[180]			•		
2020	[83]					•
	[102]					•
	[91]			•		
2021	[181]			•		
	[184]		•			
	[183]	•				•
2022	[35]				•	
	[215]	•				
	[218]	•				
	[182]			•		•
2023	[108]		•			
	[145]	•				•
	[160]					•
	[232]	•		•		
2024	[60]			•		
	[78]					•
	[123]	•	•			•
	[125]					•
	[143]				•	
	[205]	•			•	

For this purpose, an abstract view on cognitive agents is presented in terms of a model inspired by the *BDI (Belief-Desire-Intention)* model [64]. The considered model is designed to emphasize the core characteristics of cognitive agents in terms of reusability, composability, and interoperability. For the sake of conciseness, an exhaustive and detailed description of the model is not provided, limiting the discussion to the aspects necessary to support the comparison with microservices.

Agent-based software refers to software systems constructed through the composition of interacting agents. In an idealized scenario, agents are sourced from a repository of agents, and the *MAS (Multi-Agent System)* is dynamically assembled and reconfigured to adapt to changing conditions. The agents within the MAS are identified by a unique agent identifier, and their internal state is represented through beliefs and intentions. The term *goals* is sometimes used interchangeably with *intentions*, as there is no substantive distinction between the two concepts within this context. To maintain generality and support various agent models, a formal definition of beliefs and intentions is omitted, and their specific properties are not delineated. In addition to the unique identifier and mental state, each agent possesses capabilities, which are described in terms of the possible outcomes of its actions and the ways in which the agent interacts with other agents within the MAS.

Agents communicate through message passing, enabling the exchange of representations of their beliefs, intentions, and capabilities. These mental states are typically represented using logical formulae, and the primary objective of communication is to facilitate the exchange of such formulae, incorporating modalities for beliefs, intentions, and capabilities. While this may appear to be an overly formal approach to agent communication, it essentially extends the existing body of work on *ACLs (Agent Communication Languages)* [137]. For example, the ACL standardized by FIPA (Foundation for Intelligent Physical Agents) [137] defines performatives, along with associated feasibility preconditions and rational effects. When an agent receives a message, it can assert that the feasibility precondition holds for the sender and that the sender is attempting to achieve the corresponding rational effect. This approach, though complex, serves to provide the receiver with a detailed understanding of the sender's mental state. The use of a structured ACL, rather than a more informal exchange of mental state representations, offers the advantage of simplifying the development of reactive agents capable of engaging in complex interactions. Performatives are sufficient to guide reactive agents even if they may not have explicit internal representations of beliefs, intentions, and capabilities.

The semantics commonly associated with most widely used ACLs often rely on strong assumptions regarding the agents' capabilities. For example, the FIPA ACL requires an agent to reason about the receiver's mental state prior to sending any message. This represents a significant and potentially impractical requirement, especially in large-scale MASs involving numerous, and often unpredictable, interactions. To address this limitation, the discussed framework for cognitive agents introduces an ACL with minimalistic semantics. This language provides an operational mechanism for agents to exchange representations of their beliefs, intentions, and capabilities, while minimizing the cognitive demands placed on agents. Table 4 presents a selection of performatives from the considered ACL, along with their associated semantics. The semantics are modeled as the intended effect that the sender seeks to achieve through the transmission of the message.

The considered ACL offers a mechanism for exchanging complex logical formulae through simple messages, enabling the receiver to assert the sender's intentions. This approach ensures semantic interoperability [44] while preserving the encapsulation of the sender's mental state by not exposing excessive details. It

Table 4. Semantics of the core performatives used by the considered cognitive agents

Message	Semantics
$\text{inform}(s, r, p)$	$I_s B_r p$
$\text{achieve}(s, r, p)$	$I_s I_r p$
$\text{request}(s, r, a)$	$\|\text{achieve}(s, r, done(a))\|$
$\text{agree}(s, r, a)$	$\|\text{inform}(s, r, I_s done(a))\|$
$\text{refuse}(s, r, a)$	$\|\text{inform}(s, r, \neg I_s done(a))\|$

is important to note that, strictly speaking, the specific form of the ACL is not an integral component of the agent model being presented. However, this ACL is introduced here to provide a foundation for the subsequent discussions in the following section.

Isolated messages are insufficient to facilitate effective communication among agents. A well-known example of this limitation arises when one agent requests another to perform an action. First, messages are typically asynchronous, meaning that there is no guarantee that the receiver will respond by performing the requested action. Second, the semantics of a single message may not fully capture the application-specific constraints that caused the interaction. For instance, the semantics of a *request* message do not require the receiver to inform the sender that the requested action has been completed. As a result, the sender could potentially remain in a state of indefinite waiting, expecting confirmation from the receiver that the action has been performed, without any assurance that such a confirmation will occur.

To facilitate effective communication, the agent model discussed here incorporates interaction rules. These rules are predefined rules that an agent chooses to adopt in order to govern its interactions with other agents. The interaction rules selected by an agent are considered part of its capabilities and are explicitly published, thereby making them accessible to other agents within the MAS. The following interaction rules, where agent s is the sender and agent r is the receiver, are sufficient to solve the mentioned problem of *request* messages regarding action a:

$$I_r done(a) \implies B_s I_r done(a) \tag{1}$$

$$\neg I_r done(a) \implies B_s \neg I_r done(a) \tag{2}$$

$$B_r done(a) \implies B_s done(a) \tag{3}$$

The first interaction rule stipulates that if agent r intends to perform action a, then agent s must be aware of this intention. The second rule addresses the inverse scenario: if agent r decides not to perform action a, then agent s must also be informed of this decision. The third rule asserts that as soon as agent r becomes aware that action a has been completed, agent s must be informed of this outcome.

An interaction rule has a precondition and a postcondition from the perspective of each interacting agent. An agent starts applying an interaction rule when the precondition is verified and stops as soon as the postcondition holds. In the example regarding *request* messages, the precondition for agent r is $I_s done(a)$, i.e., agent r received the request to perform action a. The postcondition for agent r is $B_r done(a) \vee \neg I_r done(a)$, i.e., agent r performed action a or decided not to perform it.

The introduction of preconditions and postconditions enhances the elegance and flexibility of interaction rules as a means of defining interaction protocols. The example of *request* messages illustrates an interaction rules that models the FIPA request protocol [137]. Similar approaches, which address well-known issues in traditional descriptions of interaction protocols, have been proposed [216]; however, these approaches do not fully leverage the semantics inherent to the underlying ACL. Finally, note that the interaction rules than an agent may adopt are linked to the possible roles it can play in the MAS, and they may vary over time.

Table 5. Comparison between the abstractions that characterize agents and the abstractions that characterize microservices

Abstraction	Microservices	Agents
Communication model	Task delegation	Task and goal delegation
Messages	Requests for actions	ACL messages
State representation	Properties and relations	Mental attitudes
Interactions	Interfaces	Capabilities
Interactions with the environment	Events	Updates of beliefs
Runtime support	Cloud infrastructure	Agent platform

4   Comparison with Microservices

A preliminary comparison between agents and microservices is summarized in Table 5, which presents the key abstractions related to microservices and align them with their agent-oriented counterparts. Specifically, Table 5 contrasts certain abstractions from the considered metamodel of microservices with those from the considered metamodel of agents. This comparison suggests that a comprehensive analysis would also need to address additional abstractions not included in Table 5. However, this work may be excessive, as many abstractions within these metamodels are fundamentally different, making a direct comparison challenging and potentially unproductive.

4.1   Comparing Abstractions

The following paragraphs compare the abstractions that characterize microservices with the corresponding abstractions that characterize agents, as shown in Table 5. At this stage, no specific ranking criteria is established, and thus, it is not possible to determine which of the two approaches is superior.

Communication Model. The primary distinction between agents and microservices lies in the mechanisms they employ for communication. Agents utilize ACLs, such as the one introduced in the previous section, while microservices rely on a their *APIs (Application Programming Interfaces).* In the agent-oriented paradigm, communication is achieved through messages that convey a portion of the sender's mental state to the receiver. A particular instance of this communication mechanism occurs when the sender seeks to delegate a goal to the receiver, as exemplified by the *achieve* performative. This process, known as goal delegation [80], serves as a fundamental mechanism through which agents delegate responsibilities.

The metamodel of microservices does not include an abstraction for goals, which limits microservices to task delegation [80] rather than goal delegation. In the approach that underlies microservices, microservices achieve their (implicit) goals by requesting other microservices to perform actions, whereas agents achieve their (explicit) goals by delegating them to other agents. This distinction is the basis for referring to the agent-oriented communication model as declarative message passing [40]: agents communicate to other agents what to do without specifying how to accomplish it. In contrast, the communication model of microservices can be called imperative message passing [40], as microservices are required to not only instruct other microservices on what to do but also how to perform the task.

The limitation of relying solely on task delegation represents a significant constraint for microservices, as goal delegation offers a more general and flexible mechanism. First, task delegation can be viewed as a special case of goal delegation, where the delegated goal takes the form of $done(a)$, akin to the semantics of the *request* performative. Moreover, task delegation may hinder potential optimizations. For example, consider a microservice s with a goal g that requires microservice r to perform actions a_1 and a_2 in order to achieve it. Using task delegation, s would request r to perform a_1 and then subsequently request a_2. However, since these two requests are not coupled by the underlying goal g, microservice r is unable to exploit any opportunities for cross-optimization between the actions a_1 and a_2.

If s and r were agents rather than microservices, s would delegate the goal g to r, which would then autonomously determine the course of action to achieve g. For instance, r could decide to perform actions a_1 and a_2. This approach effectively couples a_1 and a_2 through the shared goal g, thereby enabling r to perform potential cross-optimizations between the two actions.

Messages. Agents communicate via message passing, allowing them to exchange representations of their beliefs, intentions, and capabilities. This facilitates goal delegation, as when an agent receives a message, it can infer that the precondition for sending the message holds for the sender and that the sender is working toward achieving the corresponding goal. In contrast, the messages exchanged among microservices are solely meant to support task delegation. Thus, a microservice sends a message only to request that another microservice perform a specific task.

State Representation. Both agents and microservices are abstractions that encapsulate a state, yet they adopt fundamentally different approaches to representing and exposing their states. In the model of microservices, the state is represented by a set of properties that can be manipulated by other microservices; these properties are essentially the attributes of the microservice itself. In addition to these properties, the state of a microservice also encompasses its relationships with other microservices, which describe the microservice's knowledge about, and interactions with, other microservices. In contrast, the agent model introduced in the previous section represents the state of an agent through a set of beliefs, intentions, and capabilities. The main differences with the approach of microservices can be summarized as follows. First, agents have an explicit representation of their goals. Second, agents have explicit knowledge of their environment and not only of other agents. Third, except for a unique identifier, agents do not have properties because they only have relations with other agents and with the entities in the environment. Fourth, agents may use reasoning to come to know more than what other agents told them and more than what they sensed.

It is pertinent to further elaborate on the previous point. Microservices can infer the value of a property through application-specific mechanisms. However, a key distinction lies in the fact that properties and relations are not easily amenable to formalization within a logical framework, making the application of general-purpose reasoning techniques challenging. Consequently, any reasoning performed by microservices is typically hardcoded within the microservice itself, limiting the flexibility and reusability of reasoning processes across different contexts.

Interactions. The communication mechanisms employed by agents and microservices significantly affect how they interact with the external environment. Microservices expose their functionality through interfaces, which enumerate the services they provide and specify how clients can interact with them. Advanced models of microservices enhance interfaces by incorporating features to facilitate design by contract [161]. However, a critical issue remains unresolved: the provision of a formal description of the semantics of services directly within the interface.

The agent-oriented approach eliminates the need for interfaces, instead equipping agents with capabilities that define both what the agent can do and how the agent can interact with other agents, including the interaction rules it can adopt. The use of capabilities instead of interfaces has the advantage that the semantics of the actions that an agent offers can be easily described using high-level, mentalistic abstractions, i.e., beliefs and intentions in the discussed agent model, and the model of the environment, i.e., entities in the environment and their relationships.

Interactions with the Environment. The environment constitutes an integral component of the agents' metamodel. Agents operate within an environment that they can utilize to acquire knowledge. They are capable of sensing the environment and receiving events from it. Agents respond to any changes in the environment by adjusting their mental state. This interaction model significantly contrasts with the approach of microservices, where the environment communicates with microservices via reified events that are explicitly notified through dedicated APIs. Microservices respond to reified events by first establishing a relation with them.

The approach of microservices appears to more rigorously adhere to the principle of encapsulation compared to the agent-oriented approach. In microservices, the internal state of a microservices is modified only when the microservices itself determines a change in response to an event. However, a closer examination reveals that the agent-oriented approach also maintains encapsulation. Agents possess reasoning capabilities that are responsible for any changes to the mental state. The connections from sensors to the mental state are mediated through reasoning processes, thus ensuring that the mental state remains encapsulated.

Runtime Support. FIPA initiated its work with the development of a run-time environment designed to support interoperable agent-based software systems [42]. This effort remains valuable, and the idea of agent platforms can be considered today the agent-oriented counterpart of cloud infrastructures. However, cloud infrastructures are large software systems that offer enterprise-level features, such as transactional persistency and security, which are not yet fully supported by existing agent platforms. Acknowledging this limitation, FIPA has moved toward defining an abstract architecture for its agent platforms [42], which can be instantiated using either an available FIPA platform or other run-time environments, such as those based on cloud infrastructures. This approach accommodates both agent-oriented and enterprise needs, making it a reasonable and pragmatic compromise to save the agent-oriented characteristics of agent platforms while ensuring enterprise features.

Nevertheless, it is important to recognize that a straightforward approach of encapsulating an agent within a microservice to run it using a cloud infrastructure introduces relevant challenges. The most significant of these challenges is the potential incompatibility between the threading model imposed by the cloud infrastructure and the requirements of agent-based software systems. Specifically, the developer is often forced to choose between sacrificing enterprise features, e.g., fault tolerance and transparent scalability, and implementing only reactive agents.

4.2   Some Relevant Properties of Agents

The comparison outlined previously highlights both differences and similarities between microservices and agents. However, it does not assert the superiority of one approach over the other, as no specific ranking criteria is adopted. Here, the focus is on two key attributes of development technologies, namely, reusability and composability, to assess how and under what conditions agents outperform microservices in these aspects. As noted previously, agents can use goal delegation instead of task delegation only, which is a characterizing feature of microservices. Moreover, agents use ACLs that exploit the agent model to give a formal semantics to interactions, which is something that microservices cannot achieve because they cannot attach a formal semantics to their interfaces. Finally, agents have mental states and they can use their reasoning capabilities to generate knowledge from events and messages, which is a capability that microservices express only in terms of preprogrammed procedures. These properties improve the reusability and the composability of agents with respect of microservices. These three characteristics of agents are detailed as follows.

First, goal delegation partially decouples the agent delegating a goal from the delegate agent, as the two are linked not through a sequence of actions, but through a shared goal. This approach addresses the interface mismatching problem, which arises when substituting one microservice with another that provides the same services but through a different interface. While clients may accept the services of the new microservice, they often cannot utilize them because they do not know how to access those services. In the agent-oriented model, this issue is mitigated, as the client agent delegates the goal, and the delegate agent autonomously determines the actions required to achieve it. However, the interface mismatching problem is not entirely resolved, as agents may operate with different ontologies. This challenge is more manageable, particularly in the context of open software systems that employ standardized ontologies, which facilitate easier interoperability [65]. There are additional challenges related to reusability and composability that are addressed by goal delegation. While a comprehensive catalog of these issues does not exist in the literature, the enumeration and detailed analysis of all such challenges falls outside the scope of this chapter.

Second, further improvements in reusability and composability are afforded by the agent-oriented approach to communication. This approach generalizes many common tasks, such as informing and querying, by making them application-specific only to the extent that they depend on the ontology [221]. While messages also depend on the chosen content language, this is generally not a significant issue. In contrast, microservices implement informing and querying through properties and relations, which inherently couples communication with the information model, which essentially is the microservice counterpart of the ontology, and with the semantics of dedicated messages. The agent-oriented approach mitigates this dependency on dedicated messages, thereby enhancing reusability and composability, provided that the ontology does not change.

Third, the logic-based model of mental states enables the use of deduction and means-end reasoning to infer knowledge and plans, thereby allowing a broad range of messages and events to be reduced to a limited set of common situations. In this framework, the agent's concrete behavior is defined for a restricted set of scenarios, yet it remains capable of responding to a wide set of events and messages. This design promotes reusability and composability, as the agent's behavior is partially decoupled from the specific messages and events it processes, facilitating greater flexibility in diverse contexts.

The three characteristics of agents discussed previously explain their superior performance in terms of reusability and composability. Generalizing this result, it is evident that such superiority is well-founded, as agents support semantic composability [40]. Agents operate within a unified executor model, specifically the agent model, which delegates most of the semantics of composition to the semantics of the ACL. This stands in stark contrast to microservices, where the majority of the compositional semantics is embedded within the specific procedures a microservice performs in response to a message or event. This latter approach can be described as syntactic composability [40], as the semantics of communication is not supported by a shared executor model, limiting its flexibility and adaptability. If a shared and accepted ACL is adopted, e.g., the FIPA ACL, then agents become semantically interoperable [40] while microservices remain syntactically interoperable [40].

5   The Cognitive-Agent Level

The benefits of operating at a high level of abstraction were recognized early in the history of computer science. In the era when programming was limited to assembly language, there was a clear demand for higher-level abstractions, such as types and procedures. In the present day, the approach of microservices offers high-level abstractions, including interfaces and reified events. At first glance, further increases in the level of abstraction may appear unnecessary. However, the level of abstraction employed by developers has a profound impact on various quality metrics used to assess a product. It is therefore unsurprising that elevating the level of abstraction significantly enhances the quality of the final product.

To show that the agent-oriented approach operates at a higher level of abstraction than the approach of microservices, the following quote is considered: "at any given level of abstraction, we find meaningful collections of entities that collaborate to achieve some higher level view" [59]. In the agent-oriented paradigm, the meaningful collections of entities include beliefs, goals, and capabilities, which are conceptually closer to human intuition than their microservice counterparts, such as properties, events, and messages. Building on this distinction, these higher-level abstractions are presented by introducing a new system level.

A system level [169] refers to a set of concepts that facilitates the modeling of implementable systems. These system levels are organized hierarchically in a layered stack, with each level corresponding to a lower-level abstraction. System levels are designed to abstract away implementation details, with higher levels offering concepts that are more aligned with human intuition and more distanced from the implementation.

This hierarchical structure represents the reason for system levels to be commonly treated as levels of abstraction. System levels are structured in terms of the following elements:

1. Components: atomic blocks for building systems at the level;
2. Laws of compositions: laws that rule how components can be assembled into a system;
3. Medium: concepts that are processed at the level; and
4. Laws of behavior: laws that determine how the behavior of the system depends on the behavior of each component and on the designed structure of the system.

Newell's knowledge level [169] offers a more suitable framework for characterizing agents than any operational approach. However, it is important to note that Newell's work, dating back to 1982, did not account for many features that are central to modern agent-based software systems. Specifically, Newell's focus was primarily on the realization of individual agents capable of exhibiting intelligent behavior. In contrast, contemporary approaches no longer emphasize the creation of monolithic, single agents. Instead, agents are increasingly viewed as modular building blocks within MASs because "Interaction enhances dumb algorithms so they become smart agents." [230]

Jennings' proposal of the social level [144] aims to elevate the abstraction of the knowledge level, focusing on the interaction between agents within a MAS. This approach offers the advantage of minimal requirements for agent capabilities, thereby encompassing a wide variety of agent models described in the literature. However, its generality may limit its effectiveness in constructing complex systems, as the abstraction may lack sufficient specificity to address the nuanced requirements of sophisticated system architectures.

In response to the limitations of both Newell's and Jennings' approaches, a novel system level is proposed here, referred to as the *cognitive-agent level*. The justification for this terminology will be provided shortly. Note that this proposal retargets and extends a previous proposal [40]. Also, note that this proposal is still preliminary and it is not meant to be considered complete.

The proposed cognitive-agent level represents a balanced compromise between Newell's perspective, which avoids addressing interactions structurally, and Jennings' emphasis on interaction as the central element of a system. At the cognitive-agent level, individual agents exhibit rational behavior and are characterized by mental attitudes. Moreover, these agents are embedded within a social context, interacting through an ACL. Therefore, the cognitive-agent level facilitates the distribution of complexity across the MAS rather than centralizing intelligence in a monolithic agent.

In order to define the cognitive-agent level, the components that it comprises are first enumerated:

1. Agents, which interact to implement the functionality of the MAS;
2. Beliefs, which an agent has;
3. Intentions, which an agent is trying to achieve;
4. Actions, which an agent can perform on the environment where it executes;
5. Roles, which agents can play in the system; and
6. Interaction rules, which rule how agents playing different roles can interact.

The inclusion of agents and mental attitudes as fundamental components of the cognitive-agent level justifies its designation. This distinction contrasts with the knowledge level, where the agent is synonymous with the system being implemented. Similarly, it is not applicable to the social level, where agents are treated as components without specific characteristics, and the primary focus is on the structure of the society. According to the laws of composition, a MAS is constituted by a set of interacting agents, each associated with a set of beliefs, intentions, actions, and roles. Agent interactions are governed by a set of interaction laws. Importantly, this framework does not undermine agent autonomy, as agents autonomously choose to adopt specific roles in pursuit of their goals.

Exploiting the components of the cognitive-agent level, two familiar concepts, which are no longer atomic, can be defined:

1. Responsibility: an intention that an agent is constantly bringing about and that the agent does not drop even if it has already been achieved; and
2. Capability: the post-conditions of an agent's action, i.e., what the agent is capable to achieve on its own, and the interaction laws that it follows, i.e., how it can interact with other agents in the system to achieve its intentions.

The medium of the cognitive-agent level consists of the representations that each agent holds regarding its own beliefs, intentions, and capabilities, as well as those of other agents. Agents process this medium by interacting with one another to acquire knowledge about others' beliefs, intentions, and capabilities, with the aim of achieving their respective goals. In the proposed framework, communication is the primary means of interaction, and agents utilize an ACL to exchange representations of beliefs, intentions, and capabilities. Only agents produce and consume messages, and the computation of the MAS emerges from the messages that agents exchange and manipulate.

The law of behavior, as proposed here, is an adaptation of Newell's principle of rationality: an agent will select an action from its set of capabilities if it has knowledge that the chosen action will contribute to satisfying one of its intentions or fulfilling one of its responsibilities. This principle serves to link the components of the cognitive-agent level with the process of action selection, without specifying the underlying mechanisms for this selection at lower system levels. The mechanism for action selection may involve means-end reasoning, or it may be explicitly encoded within the agent's program. Table 6 provides a summary of the elements comprising the cognitive-agent level. Many of the concepts discussed by Newell in the context of the knowledge level remain applicable to the cognitive-agent level. In particular, as with the knowledge level, the cognitive-agent level is inherently incomplete, and the behavior of an agent cannot be fully determined at this level alone. A model at the cognitive-agent level is not operational without a concrete implementation at a lower level. If the cognitive-agent level is to be situated atop another system level, a clear mapping must exist between the elements of the cognitive-agent level and the components at the lower level. In this context, any development tool supporting the abstractions of the cognitive-agent level effectively implements this mapping.

Table 6. Elements of the cognitive-agent level

System-level element	Element of the cognitive-agent level
System	MAS
Components	Beliefs, intentions, actions, roles, and interaction laws
Medium	Representations of beliefs, intentions, and capabilities
Behavior	Principle of rationality

6 Conclusion

This chapter aims to provide a preliminary justification for why developers should consider the adoption of agent-based approaches in their software development processes. The section on the cognitive-agent level serves to offer a theoretical foundation for these arguments. The two primary outcomes of the discussions presented in this work are: agents offer high-level abstractions that can simplify development, and agents possess advantages over microservices in terms of reusability and composability.

The first outcome–working with high-level abstractions–presents well-established benefits, such as improved modularity and ease of maintenance. However, it also introduces a common drawback: performance overhead. To fully leverage the potential of agents, an agent model akin to the one briefly discussed in this chapter is required. This model depends significantly on reasoning processes, which can result in slower performance. Nevertheless, this performance issue is not necessarily a critical concern in contemporary development contexts, where factors such as time-to-market and flexibility often take precedence over raw execution speed.

The second point–namely, reusability and composability–merits further discussion, particularly given the widespread advocacy for microservices as the most reusable and composable technology. However, the advantages that agents offer in these areas come at a cost: performance. Specifically, the shift from task delegation to goal delegation necessitates means-end reasoning, which normally introduces additional computational overhead. As a result, the implementation of agents, particularly those employing goal delegation, may lead to performance trade-offs, with the potential for slower execution times compared to software systems based on microservices.

Fortunately, in both cases, agent performance degrades in a controlled and predictable manner. Developers have the flexibility to adjust the extent of reasoning applied to each agent, thereby controlling the trade-off between computational overhead and functionality. Specifically, complex agents that benefit from high-level abstractions can be equipped with reasoning capabilities, allowing for greater reusability and composability across different projects. In contrast, for scenarios where performance is critical, reactive agents–or even microservices–can be employed, which bypass more computationally intensive reasoning mechanisms. This approach is well-justified, as the more complex and value-added an agent is, the greater the need for its reuse and composition with other agents. Furthermore, reactive agents are functionally equivalent to microservices, meaning that adopting the agent-oriented paradigm does not incur a loss of capability compared to the approach of microservices, particularly in terms of performance.

Acknowledgments. The authors were supported by the Italian Ministry of University and Research under the PRIN 2020 grant number 2020TL3X8X for the project Typeful Language Adaptation for Dynamic, Interacting and Evolving Systems (T-LADIES).

References

1. Abdalla, R., Mishra, A.: Agent-oriented software engineering methodologies: analysis and future directions. Complexity **2021**(1), 1629419 (2021). https://doi.org/10.1155/2021/1629419
2. Agiollo, A., Calegari, R., Ciatto, G., Magnini, M., Omicini, A., Sabbatini, F.: Intelligent agents from symbolic to neurosymbolic systems: the quest for integration. In: Mascardi and Omicini [158]
3. Aguzzi, G., Casadei, R., Pianini, D., Viroli, M.: Self-organisation with aggregate computing: a reflection under the lenses of multi-agent systems engineering. In: Mascardi and Omicini [158]
4. Alderighi, M., Baldoni, M., Baroglio, C., Micalizio, R., Tedeschi, S. (eds.): WOA 2024 – 25th Workshop "From Objects to Agents", CEUR Workshop Proceedings, vol. 3735. Bard, AO, Italy (2024). http://ceur-ws.org/Vol-3735/
5. Alzetta, F., Giorgini, P.: Towards a real-time BDI model for ROS 2. In: Bergenti and Monica [53], pp. 1–7. http://ceur-ws.org/Vol-2404/paper01.pdf
6. Ancona, D., Briola, D., Ferrando, A., Martelli, M., Mascardi, V.: 25 years of declarative agent technologies in Italy. In: Mascardi and Omicini [158]
7. Ancona, D., Briola, D., Ferrando, A., Mascardi, V.: MAS-DRiVe: a practical approach to decentralized runtime verification of agent interaction protocols. In: Santoro et al. [210], pp. 35–43. http://ceur-ws.org/Vol-1664/w7.pdf
8. Ancona, D., Briola, D., Mascardi, V.: Protocols with exceptions, timeouts, and handlers: a uniform framework for monitoring fail-uncontrolled and ambient intelligence systems. In: Di Napoli et al. [118], pp. 65–75. http://ceur-ws.org/Vol-1382/paper10.pdf
9. Ancona, D., Ferrando, A., Mascardi, V.: Agents interoperability via conformance modulo mapping. In: Cossentino et al. [105], pp. 109–115. http://ceur-ws.org/Vol-2215/paper_18.pdf

10. Armando, A., Zini, D.: Towards interoperable mechanized reasoning systems: the logic broker architecture. In: Corradi et al. [95], pp. 70–75. http://lia.disi.unibo.it/books/woa00/pdf/14.pdf

11. Armano, G., Paoli, F.D., Omicini, A., Vargiu, E. (eds.): WOA 2003 – 4th Workshop "From Objects to Agents". Pitagora Editrice Bologna, Villasimius, CA, Italy (2003). http://giuseppevizzari.github.io/WOA-proceedings-archive/woa-2003.html

12. Arnaudo, E., Baldoni, M., Boella, G., Genovese, V., Grenna, R.: An implementation of roles as affordances: powerJava. In: Baldoni et al. [25], pp. 8–13. http://woa07.disi.unige.it/papers/powerJavaWOA07-R2.pdf

13. Baldoni, M., Baroglio, C.: Some thoughts about commitment protocols (position paper). In: De Paoli and Vizzari [117], pp. 68–71. http://ceur-ws.org/Vol-892/paper11.pdf

14. Baldoni, M., et al.: MERCURIO: an interaction-oriented framework for designing, verifying and programming multi-agent systems. In: Omicini and Viroli [176], pp. 87–94. http://ceur-ws.org/Vol-621/paper13.pdf

15. Baldoni, M., Baroglio, C., Bergenti, F., Garro, A. (eds.): WOA 2013 – 14th Workshop "From Objects to Agents", CEUR Workshop Proceedings, vol. 1099. Turin, Italy (2013). http://ceur-ws.org/Vol-1099/

16. Baldoni, M., Baroglio, C., Capuzzimati, F.: 2COMM: a commitment-based MAS architecture. In: Baldoni et al. [15], pp. 38–57. http://ceur-ws.org/Vol-1099/paper11.pdf

17. Baldoni, M., Baroglio, C., Capuzzimati, F.: Social relationships for designing agent interaction in JADE. In: Santoro and Bergenti [209], pp. 36–43. http://ceur-ws.org/Vol-1260/paper6.pdf

18. Baldoni, M., Baroglio, C., Capuzzimati, F., Micalizio, R.: Endowing business artifacts with a normative coordination layer. In: De Meo et al. [113], pp. 71–77. http://ceur-ws.org/Vol-1867/w13.pdf

19. Baldoni, M., Baroglio, C., Marengo, E., Patti, V., Capuzzimati, F.: Learn the rules so you know how to break them properly. In: Fortino et al. [133], pp. 11–18. http://ceur-ws.org/Vol-741/ID1_BaldoniBaroglioMarengoPattiCapuzzimati.pdf

20. Baldoni, M., Baroglio, C., Martelli, A., Patti, V.: Conformance and interoperability in open enviroments. In: De Paoli et al. [115], pp. 151–157. http://ceur-ws.org/Vol-204/P11.pdf

21. Baldoni, M., Baroglio, C., Martelli, A., Patti, V., Schifanella, C.: Preserving players goals: a choreography-driven matchmaking approach. In: Baldoni et al. [25], pp. 132–139. http://woa07.dibris.unige.it/papers/BaldoniPlayers.pdf

22. Baldoni, M., et al.: Personalization, verification and conformance for logic-based communicating agents. In: Corradini et al. [97], pp. 177–183. http://lia.deis.unibo.it/books/woa2005/papers/25.pdf

23. Baldoni, M., Baroglio, C., Micalizio, R.: Interaction protocols: from AUML to social commitments, from artifacts to BSPL. In: Mascardi and Omicini [158]

24. Baldoni, M., Baroglio, C., Patti, V., Schifanella, C.: Conservative re-use ensuring matches for service selection. In: Baldoni et al. [31], pp. 28–36, http://www.pa.icar.cnr.it/woa08/materiali/paper/paper_8.pdf

25. Baldoni, M., Boccalatte, A., De Paoli, F., Martelli, M., Mascardi, V. (eds.): WOA 2007 – 8th Workshop "From Objects to Agents". Seneca Edizioni Torino, Genova, Italy (2007). http://woa07.disi.unige.it/ProceedingsWOA2007.zip

26. Baldoni, M., Boella, G., Dorni, M., Mugnaini, A., Grenna, R.: powerJADE: organizations and roles as primitives in the JADE framework. In: Baldoni et al. [31], pp. 84–92. http://www.pa.icar.cnr.it/woa08/materiali/paper/paper_1.pdf

27. Baldoni, M., Boella, G., Grenna, R.: Modeling organizations and roles using a middleware Jade-based. In: Bergenti [46], pp. 100–107. http://www.ailab.unipr.it/woa09/papers/Baldoni.pdf

28. Baldoni, M., Boella, G., van der Torre, L.W.N.: Social roles, from agents back to objects. In: Corradini et al. [97], pp. 164–170. http://lia.deis.unibo.it/books/woa2005/papers/23.pdf

29. Baldoni, M., Boella, G., van der Torre, L.W.N.: Importing agent-like interaction in object orientation. In: De Paoli et al. [115], pp. 158–165. http://ceur-ws.org/Vol-204/P12.pdf

30. Baldoni, M., Boella, G., van der Torre, L.W.N.: Adding roles to relationship patterns. In: Baldoni et al. [25], pp. 112–125. http://woa07.dibris.unige.it/papers/BaldoniPatterns.pdf

31. Baldoni, M., Cossentino, M., De Paoli, F., Seidita, V. (eds.): WOA 2008 – 9th Workshop "From Objects to Agents". Seneca Edizioni Torino, Palermo, Italy (2008). http://www.pa.icar.cnr.it/woa08/materiali/Proceedings.pdf

32. Baldoni, M., De Paoli, F., Martelli, A., Omicini, A. (eds.): WOA 2004 – 5th Workshop "From Objects to Agents". Pitagora Editrice Bologna, Torino, Italy (2004). http://lia.deis.unibo.it/books/woa2004/atti.pdf

33. Bandini, S., Federici, M.L., Vizzari, G.: A methodology for crowd modelling with situated cellular agents. In: Corradini et al. [97], pp. 91–98. http://lia.deis.unibo.it/books/woa2005/papers/13.pdf

34. Bartocci, E., Corradini, F., Merelli, E., Vito, L.: Model driven design and implementation of activity-based applications in Hermes. In: De Paoli et al. [115], pp. 25–31. http://ceur-ws.org/Vol-204/D07.pdf

35. Bella, G., Cantone, D., Nicolosi Asmundo, M., Santamaria, D.F.: The ontology for agents, systems and integration of services: recent advancements of OASIS. In: Ferrando and Mascardi [126], pp. 176–193. http://ceur-ws.org/Vol-3261/paper14.pdf

36. Bellavista, P., Corradi, A., Magistretti, E.: Proxy-based middleware for service continuity in mobile ad hoc networks. In: Armano et al. [11], pp. 1–8. http://giuseppevizzari.github.io/WOA-proceedings-archive/pdfs/woa2003/01.pdf

37. Bellifemine, F., Poggi, A., Rimassa, G.: Developing multi-agent systems with a FIPA-compliant agent framework. Softw. Pract. Exp. **31**, 103–128 (2001)

38. Bellifemine, F., Bergenti, F., Caire, G., Poggi, A.: Jade–a Java agent development framework. In: Multi-Agent Programming. Multiagent Systems, Artificial Societies, and Simulated Organizations, vol. 15. Springer (2005)

39. Bellifemine, F., Poggi, A., Rimassa, G., Turci, P.: An object-oriented framework to realize agent systems. In: Corradi et al. [95], pp. 52–57. http://giuseppevizzari.github.io/WOA-proceedings-archive/pdfs/woa2000/WOA11.pdf

40. Bergenti, F.: A discussion of two major benefits of using agents in software development. In: Proceedings of the 3rd International Workshop on Engineering Societies in the Agents World (ESAW 2002). Lecture Notes in Computer Science, vol. 2577, pp. 1–12. Springer (2003)

41. Bergenti, F.: An introduction to the JADEL programming language. In: Proceedings of the 2014 IEEE International Conference on Tools with Artificial Intelligence (ICTAI 2014), pp. 974–978. IEEE (2014)

42. Bergenti, F., Caire, G., Monica, S., Poggi, A.: The first twenty years of agent-based software development with JADE. Auton. Agents Multi-Agent Syst. **34**(2) (2020)

43. Bergenti, F., Gleizes, M.P., Zambonelli, F. (eds.): Methodologies and Software Engineering for Agent Systems. Multiagent Systems, Artificial Societies, and Simulated Organizations 11. Springer (2004)

44. Bergenti, F., Poggi, A.: A development toolkit to realize autonomous and interoperable agents. In: Proceedings of the 5th International Conference on Autonomous Agents, pp. 632–639 (2001)

45. Bergenti, F.: Secure, trusted and privacy-aware interactions in large-scale multiagent systems. In: Corradini et al. [97], pp. 144–150. http://lia.deis.unibo.it/books/woa2005/papers/20.pdf

46. Bergenti, F. (ed.): WOA 2009 – 10th Workshop "From Objects to Agents". Seneca Edizioni Torino, Parma, Italy (2009). http://www.ailab.unipr.it/woa09/papers/

47. Bergenti, F., Caire, G., Gotta, D.: An overview of the AMUSE social gaming platform. In: Baldoni et al. [15], pp. 85–90. http://ceur-ws.org/Vol-1099/paper9.pdf

48. Bergenti, F., Caire, G., Gotta, D.: Agents on the move: JADE for android devices. In: Santoro and Bergenti [209], pp. 44–47. http://ceur-ws.org/Vol-1260/paper9.pdf

49. Bergenti, F., Caire, G., Gotta, D., Long, D., Sacchi, G.: Enacting BPM-oriented workflows with Wade. In: Fortino et al. [133], pp. 112–116. http://ceur-ws.org/Vol-741/ID7_BergentiCaireGottaLongSacchi.pdf

50. Bergenti, F., Iotti, E., Monica, S., Poggi, A.: A case study of the JADEL programming language. In: Santoro et al. [210], pp. 85–90. http://ceur-ws.org/Vol-1664/w15.pdf

51. Bergenti, F., Iotti, E., Monica, S., Poggi, A.: Overview of a formal semantics for the JADEL programming language. In: De Meo et al. [113], pp. 55–60. http://ceur-ws.org/Vol-1867/w10.pdf

52. Bergenti, F., Iotti, E., Poggi, A.: Outline of a formalization of JADE multi-agent systems. In: Di Napoli et al. [118], pp. 123–128. http://ceur-ws.org/Vol-1382/paper19.pdf

53. Bergenti, F., Monica, S. (eds.): WOA 2019 – 20th Workshop "From Objects to Agents", CEUR Workshop Proceedings, vol. 2404. Parma, Italy (2019). http://ceur-ws.org/Vol-2404/

54. Bergenti, F., Petrosino, G.: Overview of a scripting language for JADE-based multi-agent systems. In: Cossentino et al. [105], pp. 57–62. http://ceur-ws.org/Vol-2215/paper_10.pdf

55. Bergenti, F., Poggi, A., Somacher, M.: A contract decommitment protocol for automated negotiation in time variant environments. In: Omicini and Viroli [175], pp. 54–59. http://giuseppevizzari.github.io/WOA-proceedings-archive/pdfs/woa2001/pdf/03.pdf

56. Bettini, L., De Nicola, R., Ferrari, G., Pugliese, R.: Mobile applications in X-KLAIM. In: Corradi et al. [95], pp. 1–6. http://giuseppevizzari.github.io/WOA-proceedings-archive/pdfs/woa2000/WOA01.pdf

57. Bicocchi, N., Mamei, M., Zambonelli, F.: Mechanisms of self-organization in pervasive computing. In: De Paoli et al. [115], pp. 41–50. http://ceur-ws.org/Vol-204/P06.pdf

58. Boella, G., van der Torre, L.W.N.: Organizations as socially constructed agents in the agent oriented paradigm. In: Baldoni et al. [32], pp. 93–99. http://giuseppevizzari.github.io/WOA-proceedings-archive/pdfs/woa2004/14.pdf

59. Booch, G.: Object-Oriented Analysis and Design with Applications. Addison-Wesley (1994)
60. Bordini, R.H., Costantini, S., Monaldini, A., Vozna, A.: From pure Prolog to logic agent-oriented programming languages. In: Alderighi et al. [4], pp. 271–285. http://ceur-ws.org/Vol-3735/paper_20.pdf
61. Bouleanu, D.C., Loaiza Carrillo, M.A., Savaglio, C., Bădică, C., Gravina, R., Fortino, G.: From objects to agents, and back to smart objects: software agents for intelligent Internet of Things (IoT) systems. In: Mascardi and Omicini [158]
62. Bouquet, P., Busetta, P., Adami, G., Bonifacio, M., Palmieri, F.: K-Trek: a peer-to-peer infrastructure for distributing using knowledge in large environments. In: Armano et al. [11], pp. 65–70. http://giuseppevizzari.github.io/WOA-proceedings-archive/pdfs/woa2003/12.pdf
63. Bouquet, P., Serafini, L., Zanobini, S.: Semantic coordination in systems of autonomous agents: the approach and an implementation. In: Armano et al. [11], pp. 179–186. http://giuseppevizzari.github.io/WOA-proceedings-archive/pdfs/woa2003/17.pdf
64. Bratman, M.E.: Intention, Plans, and Practical Reason. CSLI Publications (1999)
65. Briola, D., Locoro, A., Mascardi, V.: Ontology agents in FIPA-compliant platforms: a survey and a new proposal. In: Baldoni et al. [31], pp. 68–75. http://www.pa.icar.cnr.it/woa08/materiali/paper/paper_7.pdf
66. Briola, D., Mascardi, V.: Multi agent resource allocation: a comparison of five negotiation protocols. In: Fortino et al. [133], pp. 95–104. http://ceur-ws.org/Vol-741/ID9_Briola_Mascardi.pdf
67. Briola, D., Mascardi, V., Gioseffi, M.: OntologyBeanGenerator 5.0: extending ontology concepts with methods and exceptions. In: Cossentino et al. [105], pp. 116–123. http://ceur-ws.org/Vol-2215/paper_19.pdf
68. Cabri, G., Ferrari, L., Leonardi, L.: How to dynamically add roles to agents. In: De Paoli et al. [116], pp. 117–123. http://giuseppevizzari.github.io/WOA-proceedings-archive/pdfs/woa2002/07.pdf
69. Cabri, G., Ferrari, L., Leonardi, L., Quitadamo, R.: Improving Aglets with strong agent mobility through the IBM JikesRVM. In: Corradini et al. [97], pp. 136–143. http://lia.deis.unibo.it/books/woa2005/papers/19.pdf
70. Cabri, G., Leonardi, L., Mamei, M., Zambonelli, F.: Mobile agent organizations. In: Omicini and Viroli [175], pp. 30–35. http://giuseppevizzari.github.io/WOA-proceedings-archive/pdfs/woa2001/pdf/07.pdf
71. Cabri, G., Leonardi, L., Mariani, S., Zambonelli, F.: Coordination of software agents: models and languages. In: Mascardi and Omicini [158]
72. Caico, R., Cossentino, M., Sabatucci, L., Seidita, V., Gaglio, S.: MetaMeth: a tool for process definition and execution. In: De Paoli et al. [115], pp. 21–24. http://ceur-ws.org/Vol-204/D06.pdf
73. Calegari, R., Ciatto, G., Denti, E., Omicini, A., Sartor, G. (eds.): WOA 2020 – 21st Workshop "From Objects to Agents", CEUR Workshop Proceedings, vol. 2706. Bologna, Italy (2020). http://ceur-ws.org/Vol-2706/
74. Calegari, R., Ciatto, G., Denti, E., Omicini, A., Sartor, G. (eds.): WOA 2021 – 22nd Workshop "From Objects to Agents", CEUR Workshop Proceedings, vol. 2963. Bologna, Italy (2021). http://ceur-ws.org/Vol-2963/
75. Calegari, R., Ciatto, G., Mariani, S., Denti, E., Omicini, A.: Logic programming in space-time: the case of situatedness in LPaaS. In: Cossentino et al. [105], pp. 63–68. http://ceur-ws.org/Vol-2215/paper_11.pdf

76. Calegari, R., Denti, E., Mariani, S., Omicini, A.: Towards logic programming as a service: experiments in tuProlog. In: Santoro et al. [210], pp. 79–84. http://ceur-ws.org/Vol-1664/w14.pdf

77. Cantone, D., Longo, C.F., Nicolosi Asmundo, M., Santamaria, D.F., Santoro, C.: Towards an ontology-based framework for a behavior-oriented integration of the IoT. In: Bergenti and Monica [53], pp. 119–126. http://ceur-ws.org/Vol-2404/paper18.pdf

78. Carnemolla, D., Messina, F., Santoro, C., Santoro, F.F.: Hermes: a wireless communication interface for edge computing. In: Alderighi et al. [4], pp. 33–41. http://ceur-ws.org/Vol-3735/paper_03.pdf

79. Casadei, M., Viroli, M.: A framework to specify and verify computational fields for pervasive computing systems. In: De Paoli and Vizzari [117], pp. 72–81. http://ceur-ws.org/Vol-892/paper2.pdf

80. Castelfranchi, C.: Modelling social action for AI agents. Artif. Intell. **103**(1) (1998)

81. Castelli, G., Zambonelli, F.: A self-organized multiagent approach for distributed management of contextual data. In: Bergenti [46], pp. 82–91. http://www.ailab.unipr.it/woa09/papers/Castelli.pdf

82. Cavaleri, A., Cossentino, M., Lodato, C., Lopes, S., Sabatucci, L.: Self-configuring mashup of cloud applications. In: Santoro et al. [210], pp. 68–73. http://ceur-ws.org/Vol-1664/w12.pdf

83. Cavalli, S., Cagnoni, S., Lombardo, G., Poggi, A.: Actor-based architecture for cloud services orchestration: the case of social media data extraction. In: Calegari et al. [73], pp. 174–183. http://ceur-ws.org/Vol-2706/paper12.pdf

84. Cavone, D., Bergenti, F., Gotta, D.: Semantic web services and agents: a reality check. In: Fortino et al. [133], pp. 68–73. http://ceur-ws.org/Vol-741/ID3_CavoneBergentiGotta.pdf

85. Centineo, F., Marguglio, A., Morreale, V., Puccio, M.: The PRACTIONIST development tool. In: Baldoni et al. [25], pp. 20–21. http://woa07.disi.unige.it/papers/D3_CenMarMorPuc-WOA07-Demo.pdf

86. Chella, A., Cossentino, M., Infantino, I., Pirrone, R.: An agent based design process for cognitive architectures in robotics. In: Omicini and Viroli [175], pp. 84–89. http://giuseppevizzari.github.io/WOA-proceedings-archive/pdfs/woa2001/pdf/08.pdf

87. Chella, A., Lanza, F., Seidita, V.: Representing and developing knowledge using Jason, Cartago and OWL. In: Cossentino et al. [105], pp. 147–152. http://ceur-ws.org/Vol-2215/paper_23.pdf

88. Chesani, F., et al.: Protocol specification and verification by using computational logic. In: Corradini et al. [97], pp. 184–192. http://lia.deis.unibo.it/books/woa2005/papers/26.pdf

89. Ciampolini, A., Lamma, E., Mello, P., Torroni, P.: Expressing collaboration and competition among abductive logic agents. In: Corradi et al. [95], pp. 64–69. http://giuseppevizzari.github.io/WOA-proceedings-archive/pdfs/woa2000/WOA13.pdf

90. Ciatto, G., Calegari, R., Mariani, S., Denti, E., Omicini, A.: From the blockchain to logic programming and back: research perspectives. In: Cossentino et al. [105], pp. 69–74. http://ceur-ws.org/Vol-2215/paper_12.pdf

91. Ciatto, G., Calegari, R., Siboni, E., Denti, E., Omicini, A.: 2P-KT: logic programming with objects & functions in Kotlin. In: Calegari et al. [73], pp. 219–236. http://ceur-ws.org/Vol-2706/paper14.pdf

92. Ciuro, A., Cossentino, M., Fontana, G., Gaglio, S., Rizzo, R., Vitali, M.: Towards a new inheritance definition in multi-agent systems. In: Baldoni et al. [31], pp. 54–60. http://www.pa.icar.cnr.it/woa08/materiali/paper/paper_9.pdf

93. Collier, R., O'Neill, E., Lillis, D., O'Hare, G.M.P.: Multi-agent microservices. In: Proceedings of the 2019 World Wide Web Conference (WWW 2019). ACM (2019)

94. Cordì, V., Lombardi, P., Martelli, M., Mascardi, V.: An ontology-based similarity between sets of concepts. In: Corradini et al. [97], pp. 16–21. http://lia.deis.unibo.it/books/woa2005/papers/3.pdf

95. Corradi, A., Omicini, A., Poggi, A. (eds.): WOA 2000 – 1st Workshop "From Objects to Agents", Atti di Congressi, vol. 1195. Pitagora Editrice Bologna, Parma, Italy (2000). http://giuseppevizzari.github.io/WOA-proceedings-archive/woa-2000.html

96. Corradini, F., Culmone, R., Di Berardini, M.R., Merelli, E.: Integrating ontologies in mobile agents. In: Corradini et al. [97], pp. 37–45. http://lia.deis.unibo.it/books/woa2005/papers/6.pdf

97. Corradini, F., De Paoli, F., Merelli, E., Omicini, A. (eds.): WOA 2005 – 6th Workshop "From Objects to Agents". Pitagora Editrice Bologna, Camerino, MC, Italy (2005). http://lia.deis.unibo.it/books/woa2005/atti.pdf

98. Cossentino, M., Hopmans, G., Odell, J.: FIPA standardization activities in the software engineering area. In: Armano et al. [11], pp. 71–77. http://giuseppevizzari.github.io/WOA-proceedings-archive/pdfs/woa2003/23.pdf

99. Cossentino, M., Lodato, C., Lopes, S., Ribino, P., Seidita, V., Chella, A.: A UML-based notation for representing MAS organizations. In: Fortino et al. [133], pp. 133–139. http://ceur-ws.org/Vol-741/ID20_CossentinoLodatoLopesRibiniSeiditaChella.pdf

100. Cossentino, M., Lodato, C., Lopes, S., Sabatucci, L.: MUSA: a middleware for user-driven service adaptation. In: Di Napoli et al. [118], pp. 1–10. http://ceur-ws.org/Vol-1382/paper1.pdf

101. Cossentino, M., Lopes, S., Nuzzo, A., Renda, G., Sabatucci, L.: A comparison of the basic principles and behavioural aspects of Akka, JaCaMo and Jade development frameworks. In: Cossentino et al. [105], pp. 133–141. http://ceur-ws.org/Vol-2215/paper_21.pdf

102. Cossentino, M., Lopes, S., Sabatucci, L.: A tool for the automatic generation of MOISE organisations from BPMN. In: Calegari et al. [73], pp. 69–82. http://ceur-ws.org/Vol-2706/paper11.pdf

103. Cossentino, M., et al.: GIMT: a tool for ontology and goal modeling in BDI multi-agent design. In: Santoro and Bergenti [209], pp. 81–88. http://ceur-ws.org/Vol-1260/paper10.pdf

104. Cossentino, M., Sabatucci, L., Seidita, V.: Towards an approach for engineering complex systems: agents and agility. In: De Meo et al. [113], pp. 1–6. http://ceur-ws.org/Vol-1867/w1.pdf

105. Cossentino, M., Sabatucci, L., Seidita, V. (eds.): WOA 2018 – 19th Workshop "From Objects to Agents", CEUR Workshop Proceedings, vol. 2215, Palermo, Italy (2018). http://ceur-ws.org/Vol-2215/

106. Cossentino, M., Sabatucci, L., Seidita, V.: Designing agent-oriented systems. In: Mascardi and Omicini [158]

107. Costantini, S., Dell'Acqua, P., Tocchio, A.: Expressing preferences declaratively in logic-based agent languages. In: De Paoli et al. [115], pp. 138–143. http://ceur-ws.org/Vol-204/P05.pdf

108. Costantini, S., Formisano, A., Pitoni, V.: A timed epistemic logic for formalizing cooperation among groups of agents. In: Falcone et al. [124], pp. 151–166. http://ceur-ws.org/Vol-3579/paper11.pdf
109. Costantini, S., Tocchio, A.: Strips-like planning in the DALI logic programmming language. In: Armano et al. [11], pp. 115–120. http://giuseppevizzari.github.io/WOA-proceedings-archive/pdfs/woa2003/05.pdf
110. Dalpiaz, F., Ali, R., Asnar, Y., Bryl, V., Giorgini, P.: Applying Tropos to socio-technical system design and runtime configuration. In: Baldoni et al. [31], pp. 101–107. http://www.pa.icar.cnr.it/woa08/materiali/paper/paper_14.pdf
111. Dalpiaz, F., Molesini, A., Puviani, M., Seidita, V.: Towards filling the gap between AOSE methodologies and infrastructures: requirements and meta-model. In: Baldoni et al. [31], pp. 115–121. http://www.pa.icar.cnr.it/woa08/materiali/paper/paper_3.pdf
112. De Luca, F., Tundis, A., Garro, A.: PROCE: an agent-based PROcess Composition and execution Environment. In: Fortino et al. [133], pp. 171–174. http://ceur-ws.org/Vol-741/DEM02_DeLucaTundisGarro.pdf
113. De Meo, P., Postorino, M.N., Rosaci, D., Sarnè, G.M.L. (eds.): WOA 2017 – 18th Workshop "From Objects to Agents", CEUR Workshop Proceedings, vol. 1867. Scilla, RC, Italy (2017). http://ceur-ws.org/Vol-1867/
114. De Mola, F., Quitadamo, R.: Towards an agent model for future autonomic communications. In: De Paoli et al. [115], pp. 51–59. http://ceur-ws.org/Vol-204/P07.pdf
115. De Paoli, F., Di Stefano, A., Omicini, A., Santoro, C. (eds.): WOA 2006 – 7th Workshop "From Objects to Agents", CEUR Workshop Proceedings, vol. 204. Catania, Italy (2006). http://ceur-ws.org/Vol-204/
116. De Paoli, F., Manzoni, S., Poggi, A. (eds.): WOA 2002 – 3rd Workshop "From Objects to Agents". Pitagora Editrice Bologna, Milano, Italy (2002). http://giuseppevizzari.github.io/WOA-proceedings-archive/woa-2002.html
117. De Paoli, F., Vizzari, G. (eds.): WOA 2012 – 13th Workshop "From Objects to Agents", CEUR Workshop Proceedings, vol. 892. Milano, Italy (2012). http://ceur-ws.org/Vol-892/
118. Di Napoli, C., Rossi, S., Staffa, M. (eds.): WOA 2015 – 16th Workshop "From Objects to Agents", CEUR Workshop Proceedings, vol. 1382. Naples, Italy (2015). http://ceur-ws.org/Vol-1382/
119. Di Nitto, E., Pianciamore, M., Selvini, P.: The role of agents in knowledge management. In: De Paoli et al. [116], pp. 29–34. http://giuseppevizzari.github.io/WOA-proceedings-archive/pdfs/woa2002/22.pdf
120. Di Stefano, A., Santoro, C.: eXAT: an experimental tool for programming multi-agent systems in Erlang. In: Armano et al. [11], pp. 121–127. http://giuseppevizzari.github.io/WOA-proceedings-archive/pdfs/woa2003/09.pdf
121. Di Stefano, A., Santoro, C.: On the use of Erlang as a promising language to develop agent systems. In: Baldoni et al. [32], pp. 22–29. http://giuseppevizzari.github.io/WOA-proceedings-archive/pdfs/woa2004/4.pdf
122. Di Stefano, A., Santoro, C.: Building semantic agents in eXAT. In: Corradini et al. [97], pp. 28–36. http://lia.deis.unibo.it/books/woa2005/papers/5.pdf
123. Domini, D., Farabegoli, N., Aguzzi, G., Viroli, M.: Towards intelligent pulverized systems: a modern approach for edge-cloud services. In: Alderighi et al. [4], pp. 252–270. http://ceur-ws.org/Vol-3735/paper_19.pdf
124. Falcone, R., Castelfranchi, C., Sapienza, A., Cantucci, F. (eds.): WOA 2023 – 24th Workshop "From Objects to Agents", CEUR Workshop Proceedings, vol. 3579. Roma, Italy (2023). http://ceur-ws.org/Vol-3579/

125. Ferrando, A., Malvone, V.: Hands-on VITAMIN: a compositional tool for model checking of multi-agent systems. In: Alderighi et al. [4], pp. 157–169. http://ceur-ws.org/Vol-3735/paper_12.pdf

126. Ferrando, A., Mascardi, V. (eds.): WOA 2022 – 23rd Workshop "From Objects to Agents", CEUR Workshop Proceedings, vol. 3261. Genova, Italy (2022). http://ceur-ws.org/Vol-3261/

127. Ferrari, G., Pugliese, R., Tuosto, E.: Calculi for network aware programming. In: Corradi et al. [95], pp. 23–28. http://giuseppevizzari.github.io/WOA-proceedings-archive/pdfs/woa2000/WOA05.pdf

128. Fichera, L., Marletta, D., Nicosia, V., Santoro, C.: A methodology to extend imperative languages with AgentSpeak declarative constructs. In: Omicini and Viroli [176], pp. 30–38. http://ceur-ws.org/Vol-621/paper05.pdf

129. Forestiero, A., Mastroianni, C.: Description of the self-chord P2P application. In: Fortino et al. [133], pp. 175–177. http://ceur-ws.org/Vol-741/DEM03_ForestieroMastroianni.pdf

130. Fornaia, A., Napoli, C., Pappalardo, G., Tramontana, E.: An AO system for OO-GPU programming. In: Di Napoli et al. [118], pp. 24–31. http://ceur-ws.org/Vol-1382/paper4.pdf

131. Fortino, G., Galzarano, S., Gravina, R., Guerrieri, A.: Agent-based development of wireless sensor network applications. In: Fortino et al. [133], pp. 123–132. http://ceur-ws.org/Vol-741/ID19_FortinoGalzaranoGravinaGuerrieri.pdf

132. Fortino, G., Garro, A., Mascillaro, S., Russo, W.: Using multi-coordination for the design of mobile agent interactions. In: Baldoni et al. [31], pp. 122–128. http://www.pa.icar.cnr.it/woa08/materiali/paper/paper_11.pdf

133. Fortino, G., Garro, A., Palopoli, L., Russo, W., Spezzano, G. (eds.): WOA 2011 – 12th Workshop "From Objects to Agents", CEUR Workshop Proceedings, vol. 741. Rende, Italy (2011). http://ceur-ws.org/Vol-741/

134. Fortino, G., Garro, A., Russo, W.: Using method engineering for the construction of agent-oriented methodologies. In: Baldoni et al. [32], pp. 51–54. http://giuseppevizzari.github.io/WOA-proceedings-archive/pdfs/woa2004/8.pdf

135. Fortino, G., Zedadra, O., Jouandeau, N., Seridi, H.: A decentralized ant colony foraging model using only stigmergic communication. In: Santoro and Bergenti [209], pp. 63–67. http://ceur-ws.org/Vol-1260/paper13.pdf

136. Fortino, G., Garro, A., Mascillaro, S., Russo, W.: ELDATool: a statecharts-based tool for prototyping multi-agent systems. In: Baldoni et al. [25], pp. 14–19. http://woa07.dibris.unige.it/papers/D2_ForGarMasRus-WOA07-Demo.pdf

137. Foundation for Intelligent Physical Agents: Specifications. Foundation for Intelligent Physical Agents (2001). www.fipa.org

138. Franchi, E., Poggi, A., Tomaiuolo, M.: Developing applications with HDS. In: Fortino et al. [133], pp. 117–122. http://ceur-ws.org/Vol-741/ID8_FranchiPoggiTomaiuolo.pdf

139. Fredriksson, M., Ricci, A., Omicini, A., Gustavsson, R.: A framework for systemic coordination in open computational systems. In: De Paoli et al. [116], pp. 86–93. http://giuseppevizzari.github.io/WOA-proceedings-archive/pdfs/woa2002/11.pdf

140. Garro, A., Russo, W.: Exploiting the easyABMS methodology in social and economic domains. In: Bergenti [46], pp. 8–15. http://www.ailab.unipr.it/woa09/papers/Garro.pdf

141. Garzetti, M., Giorgini, P., Mylopoulos, J., Sannicolò, F.: Applying Tropos methodology to a real case study: complexity and criticality analysis. In: De Paoli et al. [116], pp. 7–13. http://giuseppevizzari.github.io/WOA-proceedings-archive/pdfs/woa2002/12.pdf

142. Grosso, A., Boccalatte, A., Vecchiola, C.: Un'infrastruttura per la mobilità in AgentService. In: Corradini et al. [97], pp. 46–53. http://lia.deis.unibo.it/books/woa2005/papers/7.pdf

143. Ivan, D., Ferrando, A., Gatti, A., Guerrini, G., Mascardi, V.: Integrating procedural ontologies in VEsNA: study, requirements, and preliminary design. In: Alderighi et al. [4], pp. 186–199. http://ceur-ws.org/Vol-3735/paper_14.pdf

144. Jennings, N.R.: On agent-based software engineering. Artif. Intell. **117**, 277–296 (2000)

145. Loaiza, M., Savaglio, C., Arijo, N.H., Aloi, G., Fortino, G., Gravina, R.: Agents in software development architectures. In: Falcone et al. [124], pp. 66–77. http://ceur-ws.org/Vol-3579/paper5.pdf

146. Mamei, M., Zambonelli, F.: Spray computers: frontiers of self-organization for pervasive computing. In: Armano et al. [11], pp. 16–24. http://giuseppevizzari.github.io/WOA-proceedings-archive/pdfs/woa2003/22.pdf

147. Mamei, M., Zambonelli, F.: Spatial computing: the TOTA approach. In: Baldoni et al. [32], pp. 126–142. http://giuseppevizzari.github.io/WOA-proceedings-archive/pdfs/woa2004/18.pdf

148. Mamei, M., Zambonelli, F., Leonardi, L.: *Tuples On The Air*: a middleware for context-aware multiagent systems. In: De Paoli et al. [116], pp. 108–116. http://giuseppevizzari.github.io/WOA-proceedings-archive/pdfs/woa2002/26.pdf

149. Marguglio, A., Cammarata, G., Bonura, S., Francaviglia, G., Puccio, M., Morreale, V.: Design and development of intentional systems with PRACTIONIST Studio. In: Baldoni et al. [31], pp. 37–45. http://www.pa.icar.cnr.it/woa08/materiali/paper/paper_16.pdf

150. Mariani, S., Omicini, A.: Space-aware coordination in ReSpecT. In: Baldoni et al. [15], pp. 1–7. http://ceur-ws.org/Vol-1099/paper3.pdf

151. Mariani, S., Omicini, A.: Tuple-based coordination of stochastic systems with uniform primitives. In: Baldoni et al. [15], pp. 8–15. http://ceur-ws.org/Vol-1099/paper4.pdf

152. Mariani, S., Omicini, A.: TuCSoN coordination for MAS situatedness: towards a methodology. In: Santoro and Bergenti [209], pp. 48–57. http://ceur-ws.org/Vol-1260/paper11.pdf

153. Mariani, S., Omicini, A.: Multi-paradigm coordination for MAS: integrating heterogeneous coordination approaches in MAS technologies. In: Santoro et al. [210], pp. 91–99. http://ceur-ws.org/Vol-1664/w16.pdf

154. Mariani, S., Omicini, A., Ciatto, G.: Novel opportunities for tuple-based coordination: XPath, the Blockchain, and stream processing. In: De Meo et al. [113], pp. 61–64. http://ceur-ws.org/Vol-1867/w11.pdf

155. Marini, S., Martelli, M., Mascardi, V., Zini, F.: HEMASL: a flexible language to specify heterogeneous agents. In: Corradi et al. [95], pp. 76–81. http://giuseppevizzari.github.io/WOA-proceedings-archive/pdfs/woa2000/WOA15.pdf

156. Mascardi, V., Cordì, V., Rosso, P.: A comparison of upper ontologies. In: Baldoni et al. [25], pp. 55–64. http://woa07.dibris.unige.it/papers/mascardi.pdf

157. Mascardi, V., Demergasso, D., Ancona, D.: Languages for programming BDI-style agents: an overview. In: Corradini et al. [97], pp. 9–15. http://lia.deis.unibo.it/books/woa2005/papers/2.pdf

158. Mascardi, V., Omicini, A. (eds.): The Agents Journey: Twenty-five Years of Multi-agent Systems at WOA. Lecture Notes in Computer Science – State-of-the-Art Surveys. Springer (2026)

159. Menezes, R., Omicini, A., Viroli, M.: Have ReSpecT for LoGOp. In: De Paoli et al. [116], pp. 94–99. http://giuseppevizzari.github.io/WOA-proceedings-archive/pdfs/woa2002/18.pdf

160. Messina, F., Santoro, C., Santoro, F.F.: A declarative C++ agent platform for agent-based edge computing. In: Falcone et al. [124], pp. 206–215. http://ceur-ws.org/Vol-3579/paper16.pdf

161. Meyer, B.: Object-Oriented Software Construction. Prentice-Hall (1997)

162. Molesini, A., Nardini, E., Denti, E., Omicini, A.: Advancing object-oriented standards toward agent-oriented methodologies: SPEM 2.0 on SODA. In: Baldoni et al. [31], pp. 108–114. http://www.pa.icar.cnr.it/woa08/materiali/paper/paper_2.pdf

163. Molesini, A., Omicini, A.: Documenting SODA: an evaluation of the process documentation template. In: Omicini and Viroli [176], pp. 95–101. http://ceur-ws.org/Vol-621/paper14.pdf

164. Montagna, S., Viroli, M., Pianini, D., Fernandez-Marquez, J.L.: Towards a comprehensive approach to spontaneous self-composition in pervasive ecosystems. In: De Paoli and Vizzari [117], pp. 89–97. http://ceur-ws.org/Vol-892/paper1.pdf

165. Mordacci, P., Poggi, A., Tiso, C.G., Turci, P.: Using agent technology as a support for an enterprise service bus. In: Baldoni et al. [31], pp. 5–10. http://www.pa.icar.cnr.it/woa08/materiali/paper/paper_15.pdf

166. Morreale, V., Bonura, S., Centineo, F., Rossi, A., Cossentino, M., Gaglio, S.: PRACTIONIST: implementing PRACTIcal reasONIng sySTems. In: Corradini et al. [97], pp. 66–74. http://lia.deis.unibo.it/books/woa2005/papers/10.pdf

167. Morreale, V., Bonura, S., Francaviglia, G., Centineo, F., Cossentino, M., Gaglio, S.: Reasoning about goals in BDI agents: the PRACTIONIST framework. In: De Paoli et al. [115], pp. 187–194. http://ceur-ws.org/Vol-204/P20.pdf

168. Morreale, V., et al.: PRACTIONIST: a framework for developing BDI agent systems. In: De Paoli et al. [115], pp. 4–5. http://ceur-ws.org/Vol-204/D02.pdf

169. Newell, A.: The knowledge level. Artif. Intell. **18**, 87–127 (1982)

170. Oliva, E., Viroli, M., Omicini, A.: Minority Game: A logic-based approach in TuCSoN. In: De Paoli et al. [115], pp. 181–186. http://ceur-ws.org/Vol-204/P02.pdf

171. Omicini, A.: From objects to agent societies: abstractions and methodologies for the engineering of open distributed systems. In: Corradi et al. [95], pp. 29–34. http://giuseppevizzari.github.io/WOA-proceedings-archive/pdfs/woa2000/WOA07.pdf

172. Omicini, A., Ricci, A., Rimassa, G., Viroli, M.: Integrating objective & subjective coordination in FIPA: a roadmap to TuCSoN. In: Armano et al. [11], pp. 85–91. http://giuseppevizzari.github.io/WOA-proceedings-archive/pdfs/woa2003/07.pdf

173. Omicini, A., Ricci, A., Viroli, M.: Artifacts in the A&A meta-model for multi-agent systems. Auton. Agents Multi-Agent Syst. **17**(3), 432–456 (2008). https://doi.org/10.1007/s10458-008-9053-x, special issue on Foundations, Advanced Topics and Industrial Perspectives of Multi-Agent Systems

174. Omicini, A., Ricci, A., Viroli, M., Castelfranchi, C., Tummolini, L.: A conceptual framework for self-organising MAS. In: Baldoni et al. [32], pp. 100–109. http://giuseppevizzari.github.io/WOA-proceedings-archive/pdfs/woa2004/15.pdf

175. Omicini, A., Viroli, M. (eds.): WOA 2001 – 2nd Workshop "From Objects to Agents". Pitagora Editrice Bologna, Modena, Italy (2001). http://giuseppevizzari.github.io/WOA-proceedings-archive/woa-2001.html

176. Omicini, A., Viroli, M. (eds.): WOA 2010 – 11th Workshop "From Objects to Agents", CEUR Workshop Proceedings, vol. 621. Rimini, Italy (2010). http://ceur-ws.org/Vol-621/

177. Omicini, A., Zambonelli, F.: Coordination of large-scale socio-technical systems: challenges and research directions. In: Di Napoli et al. [118], pp. 76–79. http://ceur-ws.org/Vol-1382/paper11.pdf

178. Passadore, A., Grosso, A., Coccoli, M., Boccalatte, A.: AgentService in a hand. In: Baldoni et al. [31], pp. 19–27. http://www.pa.icar.cnr.it/woa08/materiali/paper/paper_5.pdf

179. Perini, A., Bresciani, P., Giorgini, P., Giunchiglia, F., Mylopoulos, J.: Towards an agent oriented approach to software engineering. In: Omicini and Viroli [175], pp. 72–77. http://giuseppevizzari.github.io/WOA-proceedings-archive/pdfs/woa2001/pdf/19.pdf

180. Petrosino, G., Bergenti, F.: Extending message handlers with pattern matching in the Jadescript programming language. In: Bergenti and Monica [53], pp. 113–118. http://ceur-ws.org/Vol-2404/paper17.pdf

181. Petrosino, G., Iotti, E., Monica, S., Bergenti, F.: Prototypes of productivity tools for the Jadescript programming language. In: Calegari et al. [74], pp. 14–28. http://ceur-ws.org/Vol-2963/paper4.pdf

182. Petrosino, G., Monica, S., Bergenti, F.: Robust software agents with the jadescript programming language. In: Ferrando and Mascardi [126], pp. 194–208. http://ceur-ws.org/Vol-3261/paper15.pdf

183. Pigazzini, I., Briola, D., Arcelli Fontana, F.: Architectural technical debt of multiagent systems development platforms. In: Calegari et al. [74], pp. 1–13. http://ceur-ws.org/Vol-2963/paper13.pdf

184. Pisano, G., Calegari, R., Omicini, A.: Towards cooperative argumentation for MAS: an actor-based approach. In: Calegari et al. [74], pp. 162–177. http://ceur-ws.org/Vol-2963/paper17.pdf

185. Piunti, M., Castelfranchi, C., Falcone, R.: Expectations driven approach for situated, goal-directed agents. In: Baldoni et al. [25], pp. 104–111. http://woa07.dibris.unige.it/papers/PiuntiExpectations.pdf

186. Piunti, M., Ricci, A.: From agents to artifacts back and forth: operational and doxastic use of artifacts in MAS. In: Baldoni et al. [31], pp. 76–83. http://www.pa.icar.cnr.it/woa08/materiali/paper/paper_13.pdf

187. Piunti, M., Ricci, A., Boissier, O., Hübner, J.F.: Programming open systems with agents, environments and organizations. In: Omicini and Viroli [176], pp. 39–47. http://ceur-ws.org/Vol-621/paper06.pdf

188. Piunti, M., Ricci, A., Santi, A.: SOA/WS applications using cognitive agents working in CArtAgO environments. In: Bergenti [46], pp. 116–124. http://www.ailab.unipr.it/woa09/papers/Piunti.pdf

189. Poggi, A.: Towards a flexible development framework for multi-agent systems. In: Omicini and Viroli [176], pp. 55–58. http://ceur-ws.org/Vol-621/paper08.pdf

190. Poggi, A.: An actor-based software framework for developing and simulating complex systems. In: De Paoli and Vizzari [117], pp. 49–54. http://ceur-ws.org/Vol-892/paper9.pdf

191. Poggi, A.: Replaceable implementations for actor systems. In: Baldoni et al. [15], pp. 91–96. http://ceur-ws.org/Vol-1099/paper13.pdf

192. Poggi, A.: Agent based modeling and simulation with ActoMoS. In: Di Napoli et al. [118], pp. 91–96. http://ceur-ws.org/Vol-1382/paper14.pdf
193. Poggi, A., Rimassa, G., Tomaiuolo, M.: Multi-user and security support for multi-agent systems. In: Omicini and Viroli [175], pp. 8–13. http://giuseppevizzari.github.io/WOA-proceedings-archive/pdfs/woa2001/pdf/20.pdf
194. Poggi, A., Tomaiuolo, M., Turci, P.: An agent-based service oriented architecture. In: Baldoni et al. [25], pp. 157–165. http://woa07.disi.unige.it/papers/PoggiSOA.pdf
195. Puviani, M., Cabri, G., Leonardi, L.: The future of AOSE: exploiting SME for a new conception of methodologies. In: Bergenti [46], pp. 16–22. http://www.ailab.unipr.it/woa09/papers/Puviani.pdf
196. Repetto, M., Vecchiola, C., Boccalatte, A.: A knowledge modeling tool for rule-based agents. In: Omicini and Viroli [175], pp. 24–29. http://giuseppevizzari.github.io/WOA-proceedings-archive/pdfs/woa2001/pdf/05.pdf
197. Ribino, P., Cossentino, M., Lodato, C., Lopes, S., Sabatucci, L., Seidita, V.: Ontology and goal model in designing BDI multi-agent systems. In: Baldoni et al. [15], pp. 66–72. http://ceur-ws.org/Vol-1099/paper12.pdf
198. Ricci, A., Viroli, M., Omicini, A.: CArtAgO: a framework for prototyping artifact-based environments in MAS. In: Proceedings of the 3rd International Workshop on Environments for Multi-Agent Systems (E4MAS 2006). Lecture Notes in Computer Science, vol. 4389, pp. 67–86. Springer (2006)
199. Ricci, A., Buda, C., Zaghini, N., Natali, A., Viroli, M., Omicini, A.: simpA-WS: an agent-oriented computing technology for WS-based SOA applications. In: De Paoli et al. [115], pp. 1–3. http://ceur-ws.org/Vol-204/D01.pdf
200. Ricci, A., Denti, E.: simpA-WS: a simple agent-oriented programming model & technology for developing SOA & web services. In: Baldoni et al. [25], pp. 140–156. http://woa07.disi.unige.it/papers/ricci_simpaws.pdf
201. Ricci, A., Omicini, A.: Agent coordination contexts: Experiments in TuCSoN. In: De Paoli et al. [116], pp. 14–21. http://giuseppevizzari.github.io/WOA-proceedings-archive/pdfs/woa2002/17.pdf
202. Ricci, A., Omicini, A.: Engineering trust in complex system through mediating infrastructures. In: Baldoni et al. [32], pp. 110–115. http://giuseppevizzari.github.io/WOA-proceedings-archive/pdfs/woa2004/16.pdf
203. Ricci, A., Omicini, A., Denti, E.: Enlightened agents in TuCSoN. In: Omicini and Viroli [175], pp. 101–106. http://giuseppevizzari.github.io/WOA-proceedings-archive/pdfs/woa2001/pdf/21.pdf
204. Sabatucci, L., Cossentino, M.: A multi-platform architecture for agent patterns representation and reuse. In: Armano et al. [11], pp. 170–174. http://giuseppevizzari.github.io/WOA-proceedings-archive/pdfs/woa2003/14.pdf
205. Sabbatini, F., Sirocchi, C., Calegari, R.: Symbolic knowledge comparison: metrics and methodologies for multi-agent systems. In: Alderighi et al. [4], pp. 221–235. http://ceur-ws.org/Vol-3735/paper_17.pdf
206. Santi, A., Guidi, M., Ricci, A.: Exploiting agent-oriented programming for developing Android applications. In: Omicini and Viroli [176], pp. 48–54. http://ceur-ws.org/Vol-621/paper07.pdf
207. Santi, A., Ricci, A.: Programming distributed multi-agent systems in simpAL. In: De Paoli and Vizzari [117], pp. 39–48. http://ceur-ws.org/Vol-892/paper5.pdf
208. Santoro, C.: Towards an agent programming language. In: Bergenti [46], pp. 23–30. http://www.ailab.unipr.it/woa09/papers/Santoro.pdf

209. Santoro, C., Bergenti, F. (eds.): WOA 2014 – 15th Workshop "From Objects to Agents", CEUR Workshop Proceedings, vol. 1260. Catania, Italy (2014). http://ceur-ws.org/Vol-1260/

210. Santoro, C., Messina, F., De Benedetti, M. (eds.): WOA 2016 – 17th Workshop "From Objects to Agents", CEUR Workshop Proceedings, vol. 1664. Catania, Italy (2016). http://ceur-ws.org/Vol-1664/

211. Sartori, F., Manenti, L., Grazioli, L.: A conceptual and computational model for knowledge-based agents in ANDROID. In: Baldoni et al. [15], pp. 41–46. http://ceur-ws.org/Vol-1099/paper8.pdf

212. Savaglio, C., Leppänen, T., Russo, W., Riekki, J., Fortino, G.: Re-engineering IoT systems through ACOSO-Meth: the IETF CoRE based agent framework case study. In: Cossentino et al. [105], pp. 81–89. http://ceur-ws.org/Vol-2215/paper_14.pdf

213. Schifanella, C., Lusso, L., Baldoni, M., Baroglio, C.: Design and development of a visual environment for writing DyLOG programs. In: Baldoni et al. [32], pp. 43–50. http://giuseppevizzari.github.io/WOA-proceedings-archive/pdfs/woa2004/7.pdf

214. Seidita, V., Cossentino, M., Gaglio, S.: A repository of fragments for agent systems design. In: De Paoli et al. [115], pp. 130–137. http://ceur-ws.org/Vol-204/P18.pdf

215. Seidita, V., Lanza, F., Sabella, A.M.P., Chella, A.: Can agents talk about what they are doing? A proposal with Jason and speech acts. In: Ferrando and Mascardi [126], pp. 17–29. http://ceur-ws.org/Vol-3261/paper2.pdf

216. Singh, M.P., Yolum, P.: Commitment machines. In: Proceedings of the 8th International Workshop on Agent Theories, Architectures, and Languages, 2001 (2001)

217. Stefano, A.D., Santoro, C.: Coordinating mobile agents by means of communicators. In: Omicini and Viroli [175], pp. 48–53. http://giuseppevizzari.github.io/WOA-proceedings-archive/pdfs/woa2001/pdf/12.pdf

218. Sterling, L.S., Marshall, J.: Humans are not rational; artificial agents are not emotional. In: Ferrando and Mascardi [126], pp. 127–141. http://ceur-ws.org/Vol-3261/paper10.pdf

219. Talia, D.: Cloud computing and software agents: towards cloud intelligent services. In: Fortino et al. [133], pp. 2–6. http://ceur-ws.org/Vol-741/INV02_Talia.pdf

220. Tocchio, A., Costantini, S., Verticchio, A.: A game-theoretic operational semantics. In: Baldoni et al. [32], pp. 13–21. http://giuseppevizzari.github.io/WOA-proceedings-archive/pdfs/woa2004/3.pdf

221. Tomaiuolo, M., Turci, P., Bergenti, F., Poggi, A.: An ontology support for semantic aware agents. In: Agent-Oriented Information Systems III: 7th International Bi-Conference Workshop, AOIS 2005, Utrecht, The Netherlands, 26 July 2005, and Klagenfurt, Austria, 27 October 2005, Revised Selected Papers. Lecture Notes in Computer Science, vol. 3529, pp. 140–153 (2006)

222. Tomaiuolo, M., Bergenti, F., Poggi, A., Turci, P.: OWLBeans–from ontologies to Java classes. In: Baldoni et al. [32], pp. 116–125. http://giuseppevizzari.github.io/WOA-proceedings-archive/pdfs/woa2004/17.pdf

223. Vecchiola, C., Coccoli, M., Boccalatte, A.: Agent#: Un linguaggio di programmazione per lo sviluppo di agenti su piattaforma. In: Armano et al. [11], pp. 128–134. http://giuseppevizzari.github.io/WOA-proceedings-archive/pdfs/woa2003/13.pdf

224. Vecchiola, C., Grosso, A., Boccalatte, A.: Integrating ontology support within AgentService. In: De Paoli et al. [115], pp. 166–172. http://ceur-ws.org/Vol-204/P22.pdf

225. Velepucha, V., Flores, P.: A survey on microservices architecture: principles, patterns and migration challenges. IEEE Access **11**, 88339–88358 (2023)
226. Viroli, M., Nardini, E., Castelli, G., Mamei, M., Zambonelli, F.: Coordinating spatially-situated pervasive service ecosystems. In: Fortino et al. [133], pp. 19–27. http://ceur-ws.org/Vol-741/ID13_ViroliNardiniCastelliMameiZambonelli.pdf
227. Viroli, M., Ricci, A.: Timed coordination artifacts with ReSpecT. In: Baldoni et al. [32], pp. 77–85. http://giuseppevizzari.github.io/WOA-proceedings-archive/pdfs/woa2004/12.pdf
228. Vizzari, G., Bandini, S.: Coordinated change of state for situated agents. In: Baldoni et al. [32], pp. 69–76. http://giuseppevizzari.github.io/WOA-proceedings-archive/pdfs/woa2004/11.pdf
229. Vozna, A., et al.: Evolution of programming languages in agent systems and the role of computational logic. In: Mascardi and Omicini [158]
230. Wegner, P.: Why interaction is more powerful than algorithms. Commun. ACM **40**(5), 80–91 (1997)
231. Woźniak, M.: Recent possibilities of intelligent agents in distributed systems. In: Di Napoli et al. [118], pp. 19–23. http://ceur-ws.org/Vol-1382/paper3.pdf
232. Yan, E., Burattini, S., Hübner, J.F., Ricci, A.: Towards a multi-level explainability framework for engineering and understanding BDI agent systems. In: Falcone et al. [124], pp. 216–231. http://ceur-ws.org/Vol-3579/paper17.pdf
233. Zambonelli, F.: From design to intention: Signs of a revolution. In: Omicini and Viroli [175], pp. 1–7. http://giuseppevizzari.github.io/WOA-proceedings-archive/pdfs/woa2001/pdf/23.pdf
234. Zambonelli, F.: Towards a discipline of IoT-oriented software engineering. In: Santoro et al. [210], pp. 1–7. http://ceur-ws.org/Vol-1664/w1.pdf
235. Zambonelli, F., Viroli, M.: From service-oriented architectures to nature-inspired pervasive service ecosystems. In: Omicini and Viroli [176], pp. 102–109. http://ceur-ws.org/Vol-621/paper15.pdf

Designing Agent-Oriented Systems

Massimo Cossentino[1] , Luca Sabatucci[1] , and Valeria Seidita[2]($\boxtimes$)

[1] ICAR, National Research Council (CNR), Palermo, Italy
{massimo.cossentino,luca.sabatucci}@icar.cnr.it
[2] Department of Engineering, University of Palermo, Palermo, Italy
valeria.seidita@unipa.it

Abstract. In the era of computational complexity, autonomous agent-based systems stand as an established paradigm that simplifies various stages of project conception and design compared to classical approaches. This chapter explores the rich trajectory of Agent-Oriented Software Engineering (AOSE), delineating its path from conceptual foundations to contemporary applications with a specific focus on the contributions presented during Workshop on Objects and Agents (WOA). Our study begins with a retrospective analysis of how AOSE methodologies have evolved to implement increasingly advanced agents. We trace this progression from methodologies designed for simple state machine-based reactive systems through those supporting cognitive agents to sophisticated approaches enabling the development of Belief-Desire-Intention (BDI) models. This evolution culminates in contemporary methodologies that facilitate the creation of complex agents capable of real-time introspection, reflection, and self-adaptation.

The second part of this chapter analyzes the core principles and practices of AOSE methodologies and their development and how they evolved during WOA events. When creating an agent methodology, we emphasise that a good principle is to follow clearly defined rules that consider appropriate abstractions for each context, making it possible to move from requirements to code when applying the methodology. Also, we underline and explore that essential tools for this are the metamodel and a notation language suitable for developing models for each phase of the methodology, as well as the selected framework or implementation platform to be used.

We conclude with a forward-looking perspective on AOSE, outlining innovative directions and potential research areas.

Keywords: Agent-Oriented Software Engineering · Agent Design · Methodologies

1 Introduction

The proliferation of complex autonomous agent-based systems has become increasingly important in addressing problems characterized by intricate interactions, dynamic environments, and decentralized resource distribution, which

V. Mascardi and A. Omicini (Eds.): *The Agents Journey*, LNCS 16395, pp. 213–240, 2026.
https://doi.org/10.1007/978-3-032-22940-3_8

cannot be effectively tackled using classical methodologies. Over the years, Multi-Agent Systems (MASs) have been successfully applied across various domains, including: Smart Cities [9,30], where MASs are used to optimize energy consumption, traffic management, waste disposal, and public services, thereby contributing to sustainable and efficient city operations. Disaster Response [38,51], in which MASs play a vital role in disaster management by coordinating emergency services, allocating resources, and optimizing response strategies. Robotics, where MASs enable collaborative tasks, such as search and rescue missions, by facilitating coordination among multiple robots to achieve complex objectives [10,52]. Within Transportation systems [81], MASs manage traffic flow, route optimization, and vehicle coordination, enhancing efficiency and safety in dynamic environments. In economic contexts [16,60], MASs model complex market interactions, resource allocation, and economic phenomena. These systems help analyze market dynamics and optimize decision-making processes. Researchers also apply MASs in social structure modelling [80,87], studying collective behaviour and analyzing social networks. These systems help the designer understand emergent patterns and interactions.

Throughout all these years, it has become increasingly evident that design methodologies for agent-based systems are crucial for developing Multi-Agent Systems in such complex and mission-critical contexts. This claim is supported by the definition of many different agent-oriented methodologies over the years, answering the need for concrete support when working with high-level abstractions. As a result, there has been an evolution in modelling techniques from those treating agents as state machines to those focusing on social interactions and rational decision-making. This development has also given rise to analyzing the principles of the design process and its constituent components. The method engineering research area [22], understanding recurring patterns in methodology's rules, metamodel, and notation, has enabled the organization of a repository of fragments and provided composition guidelines for building ad-hoc methodologies.

This chapter provides an overview of agent-oriented design methodologies. The first part (Sect. 3) explores how the evolution of these methodologies followed the advancements in agent-oriented programming frameworks, from state charts to intentional systems. The section discusses design principles by emphasizing features such as autonomy, proactiveness, situatedness, and sociality. The second part of this chapter (Sect. 4) examines the fundamental principles that underlie agent-oriented methodologies, including their theoretical foundations, metamodels, guidelines and notations. Finally, this chapter concludes with some insights into future challenges and opportunities in the agent-oriented software engineering (AOSE) research area (Sect. 5).

2   AOSE: The WOA Perspective

This chapter 's statistical trends and patterns have been extracted from WOA publications. However, their significance extends far beyond merely surveying

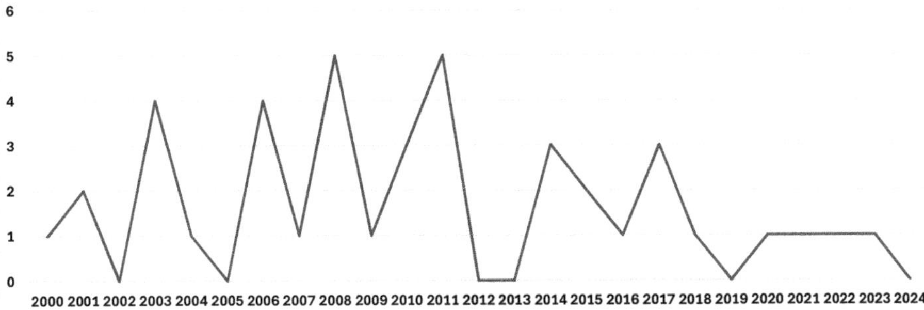

Fig. 1. Number of Agent-Oriented Software Engineering related papers at WOA per year

Italian research activities. The chapter presents a comprehensive and up-to-date perspective on international research in agent-oriented software engineering, incorporating and analyzing numerous non-Italian works that constitute the broader context of this survey. The alignment between WOA trends and international developments is particularly noteworthy, as it demonstrates not only the integration of Italian research within the global scientific community but often its anticipatory nature in relation to international trends and visions. We want to emphasize how the trends observed in WOA mirror (in many cases anticipate) international developments.

Figure 1 shows a year-by-year evolution of AOSE Publications in 25 years. The analysis of AOSE publications reveals notable fluctuations in research productivity (with peaks in 2008 and 2011). These spikes likely reflect significant developments in the field. The alternating high and low publication periods suggest a dynamic research environment that cycles between theoretical advancement and practical implementation. A recent trend of decreasing publications, especially from 2018, may indicate the field's maturation and shifting focus from foundational theory to application and refinement.

Figure 2 reveals significant patterns in research intensity over five-year periods. The data demonstrates a notable concentration of research activity during the decade spanning 2005–2014, which accounts for approximately half of all publications. This period could represent the apex of AOSE research activity at WOA, suggesting a mature phase in the field's development where key methodological approaches were being actively developed and refined. The subsequent gradual decline in publication volume, particularly evident in the 2020–2024 period, which represents only 10% of total publications, may indicate a shift in research focus or the consolidation of established methodologies rather than necessarily suggesting diminished importance of the field.

Figure 3 proposes a thematic distribution of AOSE Research. The categorization of AOSE papers provides valuable insights into the field's primary research concerns and theoretical foundations. The predominance of Autonomy and Proactivity research, comprising 24% publications, reflects the field's funda-

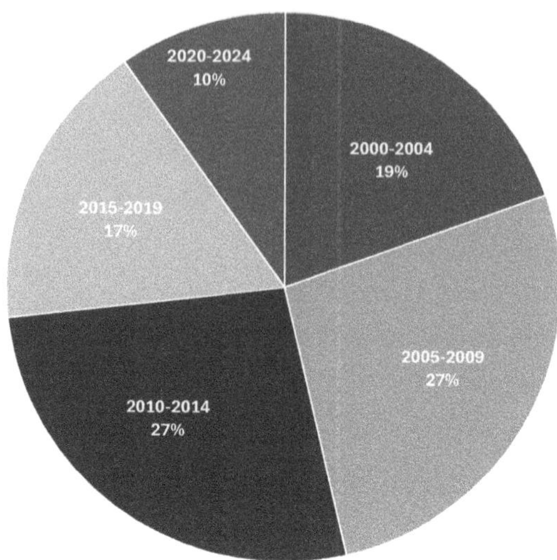

Fig. 2. Number of Agent-Oriented Software Engineering papers at WOA per lustrum

mental focus on developing systems capable of independent decision-making and goal-directed behaviour. This emphasis is complemented by substantial attention to Sociality (21%), underscoring the importance of inter-agent interactions and collaborative behaviours in Multi-Agent Systems. The significant representation

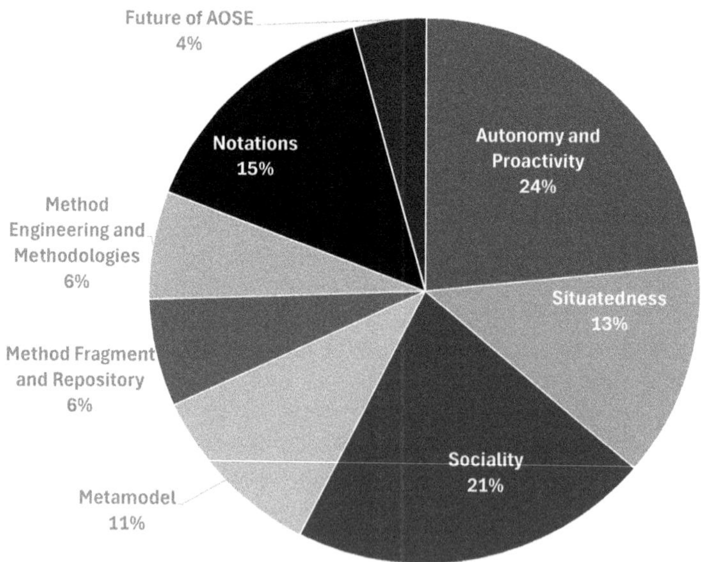

Fig. 3. Agent-Oriented Software Engineering papers at WOA by category

Table 1. WOA AOSE related papers organized according to year of publication and research category (papers may belong to more than one category).

	2000–2004	2005–2009	2010–2014	2015–2019	2020–2024	Total
Autonomy and Proactivity	[34,78]	[45,57,65,70,84]	[82]	[14,36,41]		11
Situatedness	[73]	[93]	[66,71,82,95]			6
Sociality	[34,40,73]	[44,93]	[82,95]	[30,80]	[37]	10
Metamodel	[28,61,78]	[45]			[16]	5
Method Fragment and Repository		[68,89]	[69]			3
Method Engineering and Methodologies	[46,56]	[25]				3
Notation	[12,40]		[35,39,82]	[29]	[38]	7
Future of AOSE				[94]	[90]	2

of Notations (15%) in the research corpus highlights the ongoing effort to develop and refine formal representations for agent-based systems. The equal distribution between Method Engineering and Method Fragment and Repository (6% each) indicates a balanced approach to methodology development, combining theoretical frameworks with practical implementation concerns. The presence of research on Situatedness (13%) demonstrates recognition of the importance of context-awareness in agent systems.

Table 1 details the distribution of AOSE papers over five-year periods. The data confirms the field's peak activity during 2005–2014, with each lustrum accounting for 25% of total publications. This refined analysis suggests a more gradual decline in research output than initially indicated, pointing to a measured evolution rather than a sharp decrease in scholarly attention. The sustained level of publications during these peak periods suggests a robust research community actively engaging with fundamental questions in agent-oriented software engineering.

The remaining part of this chapter examines how local developments in agent-oriented software engineering in Italy relate to global research advances. It highlights the contributions of Italian researchers and the bidirectional exchange of ideas between local and international venues.

3   Designing Agents: From State-Charts to Intentional Systems

From the beginning of Multi-Agent Systems, the objective has been to devise a decentralised computational model capable of acting proactively and adapting autonomously to changing circumstances. During the mid-1990s, Jennings and Wooldridge envisioned the grounding principles that became a research agenda of the (multi-)agent systems community [63]. Among these principles, some (autonomy, proactivity, situations, and sociality) directly involve the ability to dynamically alter agents' behaviour in response to changes in conditions, uncertainties, and objectives.

This section explores agent-oriented methodologies, aiming to show how the evolution of this research area progresses through significant milestones closely related to the characteristics of agent-based (or agent-oriented) systems.

This analysis focuses on the perspectives relevant to implementing properties like autonomy, proactivity, and situatedness. The following subsections will explore how well-known agent-oriented design methodologies propose dealing with properties.

3.1   Autonomy and Proactivity

Autonomy and proactivity are crucial features of Multi-Agent Systems. Initially, AOSE methods [59] focused more on autonomy, allowing the design of complex agent structures and internal functionalities that adhere to the agent's perceive-decide-act (PDA) cycle [83]. At the end of the 90 s, the most diffused frameworks for agent development (such as FIPA-OS and JADE) conceived them as classes. The common approach to designing an autonomous behaviour was to model agents as state charts, with GAIA [92], INGENIAS [77], and PASSI [43] falling into this category.

The GAIA methodology [92] was introduced in 1999 to develop a generic architecture for information availability. This architecture aims to make it easier to locate, deliver, and manage information, content, and digital services. GAIA's functional architecture is built on Functional Units that act as building blocks for a scalable brokerage model. A few years later, two other methodologies were presented for modelling generic Multi-Agent Systems: INGENIAS [77] and PASSI [43]. Both of them adopted Unified Modeling Language (UML) [18] and Model-Driven Engineering (MDE) [88] within their process to design a Multi-Agent System as a complex software system that will exhibit high-level properties (like autonomy and proactivity).

In these years, FIPA [34,72] (Foundation for Intelligent Physical Agents) was pushing the definition of standards for developing distributed MAS. Many FIPA-compliant development platforms, including JADE, largely supported a state-based agent model. Many contributions have been presented at WOA on this topic, and this research stream arrived at a formalization of JADE presented in [14]. Such formalization includes the identification of five main entities: Multi-Agent System, agents and their classes, behaviours and their classes. The paper also provides an example of the transition system that can be obtained from a very simple JADE agent.

The great advantage of adopting a deterministic state-chart model for modelling the agent is to inherit decades of experiences from object orientation. The use of UML (as in INGENIAS and PASSI) is an example. Moreover, using model-driven engineering facilitates the development of supporting IDEs and tools. An interesting tool (ELDATool [57]) has been presented in WOA 2007.

It has been conceived for fast prototyping of agents starting from GAIA/PASSI state-charts models (for the ELDA agent framework). Another example is [84], where a repository of design patterns is presented to solve typical problems of agent design and development.

The following step in AOSE research focused on proactive agents, i.e. agents requiring a clear understanding of their own design objectives. To this purpose, goals became first-class abstractions of agent-oriented design. The TROPOS [21] methodology introduced this concept, allowing designers to reason about intentions rather than tasks, especially when analysing user requirements. In WOA 2001, TROPOS was presented as a methodology for modelling socio-technical systems, highlighting how humans and agents are integral parts of the system along with hardware and software components [45, 78].

In the same direction, at WOA 2006, the PRACTIONIST framework was presented [70]. It recognises that goals are useful and stable abstractions in the analysis and design of software applications. According to the Belief-Desire-Intention (BDI) model, it supports a goal-oriented approach to developing agent systems. At WOA 2008, [65] introduces the PRACTIONIST Studio, an integrated design and development tool tailored explicitly for designing BDI agent systems. This environment provides tools and facilities to represent the fundamental concepts and intentional elements underlying the BDI models.

Over the years, the community has realised that the agent's conception as a class needs to be revised (at that time, most of the BDI frameworks were built on top of JADE). In 2005, [19] introduced Jason, an implementation of the AgentSpeak language, an elegant agent-oriented programming language based on logic programming and inspired by the work on BDI architectures [20]. Although attempts to define methodologies for BDI systems started in the mid-90 s [64], introducing this new language has raised the need to define specific methodological approaches in the AOSE community. Indeed, the opportunity to focus on new techniques like the plan and belief models seems evident. For example, in WOA 2013, a semantic approach and a set of guidelines have been presented to identify goals to implement BDI agents [82].

Shifting from goals as requirements towards run-time models (see the model@ run-time manifest [17]) was a fundamental step in designing and creating requirement-aware agents able to reason about their actions and change their behaviour at run-time. This may drive their adaptation to optimise performance, ensure reliability, and maintain security. In WOA 2015, a Proactive Means-end Reasoning (PMR) agent has been presented [36]. The main intuition was to decouple goals and tasks, allowing the agents to establish a link at run-time. The strength of this approach has been discussed in a methodology [41] presented at WOA 2017. It fosters collaborations between analysts and agents whereas the role played by the agents consists in addressing the goals provided/changed at run-time. Conversely, the analyst's role is to collect data during the system execution, creating a better understanding of the conditions and thus continuously designing new goals/capabilities for the agent.

3.2   Situatedness

Agents perceive and act in an environment that may include a communication channel. The environment may also be a virtual or physical place where the effects of agents' actions are observed and evaluated. Therefore Situatdness was one of the first principles of agent conceptualisation. Indeed, agent-oriented methodologies have always emphasised the need to model the environment as a specific abstraction. A common implementation of situatedness in Multi-Agent Systems (MAS) involves agents sensitive to environmental change.

In the earlier phases, the design of the agents' environment suffered because frameworks like JADE and FIPA-OS did not include specific entities for implementing it. Indeed, methodologies like MAS-Common KADS [1] focussed on the domain of interest from the agent's point of view, i.e., providing instruments to model the knowledge the agents need to act in the environment and achieve their goals. PASSI [43] uses a similar approach but emphasises the need to conceptualise the elements of the domain by using an ontology. In particular, the Ontology Description (O.D.) is a diagram that adopts a UML profile and a graphical notation for describing a semantic formalisation of the domain. Inspired by the FIPA specification of ontology, it provides three main elements: Concepts are the elements of interest in a domain; Predicates are their properties, whereas Actions represent how the agent can manipulate these domain elements. In WOA 2013, [82] extended the use of O.D. diagrams, suggesting some guidelines for using an ontology to represent the domain of interests to address possible ambiguities and incompleteness. In addition, that work proposes a process to identify agents' goals directly from the ontology.

As we anticipated, agents must be programmed to respond to environmental events. In WOA 2010, the TuCSoN coordination model [71] has been presented to support the development of information-oriented applications. It provides two abstractions: a programmable coordination model based on tuples and a computational activity called reaction. TuCSoN addresses situated, open and distributed MASs by relying on mediating abstractions (such as ACC, transducers, and tuple centres) to decouple interactions between individual components (agents and probes). Additionally, an asynchronous event-driven communication model handles common system distribution issues. In WOA 2014, the latest research results added abstractions for requirement analysis, modelling architectural components, and programming situatedness-related aspects via a coordination API [66].

In WOA 2000, the SODA methodology [73] explicitly included an environment model where logical and physical resources are mapped onto infrastructure classes and associated with topological abstractions. The main idea behind this approach is that the structure of an environment may be shifted into a run-time model that the agent can use to reason on and to make decisions.

Later on, situatedness was approached by adopting a nature-inspired perspective [2]. In WOA 2008 and 2010, Zambonelli et al. in [93,95] list situatedness and adaptivity as fundamental requirements for pervasive systems and argue that the best architecture to implement a pervasive system with such features should be a nature-inspired ecosystem where a set of spatially situated entities interact following some natural laws enforced by their living environment, and adaptively self-organize their interactions in synergy with the environment itself.

3.3 Sociality

When adopting the multi-agent perspective, agents are regarded as social entities; although each agent may have its own agenda, they are supposed to work together to achieve their goals. Cooperation is a fundamental concept that sets the MAS paradigm apart from other related disciplines, such as distributed computing and object-oriented systems. Additionally, the idea that agent organisations can produce emergent behaviour has been evident in developing Multi-Agent Systems from the beginning.

To effectively organise autonomous entities into cooperating groups, the AOSE community recognised the need for modelling techniques to manage these systems' complexity and guide the design process. This ensures that the resulting systems are reliable, maintainable, and extensible. In [81], the authors have investigated the use of Multi-Agent Systems for traffic simulation, control, and management and provide a structured overview of the most relevant research, classifying the studies according to three key criteria: The purpose of the agents, the applied artificial intelligence techniques, and the behaviours of the agents. They thus support the idea that centralized and static approaches are insufficient to manage complex and dynamic environments such as urban transportation networks, reinforcing the notion that cooperative interactions between agents exchanging information enable self-organizing mechanisms that allow agents to adapt to changing conditions, a key principle of agent societies.

A remarkable contribution to conceptualising agents' social structures comes from Moise+ [62], which introduces three dimensions: structural, functional, and deontic. The structural dimension determines the system's organisational structure regarding groups, roles, and the functional relationships between those roles. Often, the relationship between agents and the group's roles is established at run-time, as in [30]. The functional dimension focuses on how various groups of agents are expected to work together to achieve shared goals. Finally, the deontic dimension relates agents/roles to rules and constraints. It sets the standards for acceptable behaviour within the system and outlines consequences for violations.

This approach fits the need for an AOSE perspective on the social aspects of agency. In the following, we will discuss contributions presented at WOA events about sociality, clustering them according to the three dimensions introduced above.

Structural Dimension. Focussing on the contributions presented at WOA on the structural dimension of a Multi-Agent System, a significant contribution comes from SODA [73] (Societies in Open and Distributed Agent Spaces), which mainly focuses on inter-agent issues, such as engineering societies and infrastructures for Multi-Agent Systems [24]. It uses a social model to depict groups regarding social roles, tasks, permissions, and interaction rules. Societies in **SODA** are designed around coordination media, which are abstractions provided by coordination models for coordinating multi-component systems.

Some years later, ASPECS (Agent-oriented Software Process for Engineering Complex Systems) [32] proposed a holistic view instead of the classical agent organisation. This methodology deals with how to design agent societies under a holonic perspective (HMAS). The idea is that holons are agents that may be (recursively) composed of agents for developing complex software systems, looking at the problem domain with different levels of granularity. The advantage is that it provides instruments for the design of open, dynamic, and complex systems. During WOA 2013, in [82], the authors presented a methodology for designing norm-governed holonic MAS. Its metamodel was created by combining elements of ASPECS with all those concepts from Moise+, which are useful for modelling a MAS from a normative point of view. Another contribution was presented at WOA 2020; it proposed an approach for automatically defining MOISE+ organisations starting from the Business Process Modeling Notation (BPMN) specification of a business process [37].

Functional Dimension. Earlier attempts were made to adapt existing modelling techniques and notations from the Object-Oriented side, which achieved considerable maturity and widespread acceptance. A great effort, in particular, has been focused on defining interaction protocols [5] and coordination models [24]. The FIPA organisation and the OMG Agent Work Group followed and suggested this trend, supporting the exploration of UML use and the development of several extension proposals for the agent domain.

FIPA's activity comprises several Technical Committees (TCs), each responsible for producing specifications that become part of the FIPA standards. The activities of three active TCs have been presented at WOA 2003 in [34]. The first was the "Interaction Protocols TC", which aimed to develop flexible conversation policies between agents and agent-based systems. The second one was the "Methodology TC" which focussed on identifying a standard design methodology for Multi-Agent Systems (MASs) that could address various needs. The adopted approach involved creating a meta-methodology that could be instantiated in specific methodologies for different problems. This trend has been adopted in several subsequent research projects involving the international community. Finally, the "Modeling TC" worked on defining specifications for a future FIPA agent-based unified modelling language starting from the experiences done with UML and AUML.

The most notable example of accommodating UML for the distinctive requirements of agents was Agent UML or AUML [23]. AUML is primarily known for the layered approach to representing agent interaction protocols, i.e. the protocol diagram (derived from the UML sequence diagram). AUML was also adopted in a paper presented at WOA 2003 [40] for depicting the deployment details of an agent system; the paper also deals with other implementation challenges of developing agents like agents-interactions and pattern-reuse that have been deepened in many other papers in the following years.

Tropos made another significant contribution to the functional dimension of modelling agents. This design methodology focuses on collaborations between humans and agents and between different agents. This approach makes it possible to model "delegation" relationships that reveal the dependencies among the entities involved in the contest. This type of analysis allows for creating intentional, collaborative contexts in which agents interact with a specific purpose in mind. In fact, at WOA 2008, the authors of [44] explore several fundamental features of the Tropos methodology that play a crucial role in supporting the development and runtime reconfiguration of socio-technical systems (STSs). Specifically, they address two critical design challenges, risk analysis and location variability, and discuss how they are integrated and used to support the designer in choosing the best design alternative. The paper also presents a generic framework to develop self-reconfigurable STSs.

Deontic Dimension. Historically, ADELFE [79] was one of the first and most known methodologies for self-organising agents with a specific focus on deontic aspects of the MAS. It includes a cooperation view where the designer can design local rules to make the agent locally cooperative. However, in ADELFE, agents' cooperation is not directly modelled. Being cooperative means that an agent can recognise Non-Cooperative Situations (NCS), i.e. states that it judges opposing to an ideal cooperation.

Many papers have been presented at WOA events dealing with related aspects of sociality, such as delegation, collaboration, cooperation, etc. We leave the discussion of these contributions to other chapters of this book. We note that few agent-oriented methodologies in the literature deal explicitly with deontic abstraction. This open point may trigger future work in the AOSE research area.

Surely, an original point of view about agent's organisations has been presented at WOA 2008 and 2010 [93,95]. In the papers, the authors identify the need for innovative paradigms and frameworks that could allow the effective deployment and execution of pervasive computing services. They propose to model the normative part of the system by considering that the components interact and evolve based on a limited set of spatial 'laws of nature', and they introduce a reference architecture to frame these concepts consistently.

4 Agent Methodologies: Metamodel, Fragments and Notation

From the beginning of the WOA's history, we have found interesting contributions in the design of agents and agent-based robotic systems. During WOA 2001, the authors of [28] presented an initial study of a methodological approach towards designing a multi-agent robot architecture, which is an initial step towards defining the PASSI methodology.

In the same year, the TROPOS methodology was introduced in [78], and the next year, an application of this methodology was presented in [61]. This paper illustrates the TROPOS early requirements analysis phase applied to the Ice Co case study; it required the design of an agent system to enable Trentino's industries to easily access some online logistic services. As introduced in this paper, the Tropos methodology encompasses five stages of software development. Initially, early requirements analysis focuses on understanding organizational issues by creating a model that outlines the actors and their interdependencies. These actors have goals that are more effectively achieved through shared knowledge and mutual dependencies. Specifically, dependencies involve a depender, a dependee, and a dependum (which could be goals, soft goals, plans, or resources), with the depender entrusting the dependee to fulfill a particular dependum. Subsequently, late requirements analysis characterizes the intended system within its operational context, detailing its functions and attributes. The system is depicted as a set of actors with various social dependencies within their environment. In the architectural design phase, subsystems (as actors) and their interconnections (as actor dependencies) define the system's overarching structure. The detailed design then elaborates on each subsystem using a selection of AUML diagrams, specifying inputs, outputs, controls, and other pertinent details. Lastly, the implementation phase actualizes the system following the detailed design specifications.

A different research stream presented at various WOA editions regarded the adoption of metamodels in system design and the composition of design methodologies. This research finds its motivation in considerations that arose from the beginning of software engineering research and practice.

In fact, since the late 1960s, the field of software production has recognized that a disciplined approach is necessary to handle complex systems. This involves specific design activities to analyze the problem domain, identify potential goals and requirements, and convert them into software. Tying a design methodology to the programming language is a good practice.

One possible way to achieve that is through the concept of a metamodel. A metamodel is a high-abstraction model that describes a system's structure and behaviour. It provides a framework for understanding the system and its components and guides the design process.

In the initial stages of a project, it is important to conduct a theoretical analysis to identify the application domain in detail, decide which technologies to use, and then apply the appropriate design methodology. This can be done by creating a metamodel that outlines the basic principles of the design process and abstracts the agent domain. MOF (Meta-Object Facility)[1] is a metamodeling language used to define the structure and behaviour of other modelling languages, such as UML (Unified Modeling Language). UML is a modelling language commonly used in software engineering to represent the design of a system. It is based on a metamodel that includes elements such as classes, attributes,

---

[1] https://www.omg.org/spec/MOF/2.5.1/About-MOF.

and instances. Both MOF and UML are used in many engineering approaches to software development.

MOF and UML are metamodeling languages used to represent and study the world in a specific syntax. The elements in MOF and UML, such as classes, attributes, and instances, are also linked to the problem domain being studied. For instance, in the context of robotic systems, MOF and UML can be used to model the system-to-be as it happens in classical software engineering approaches. Moreover, these languages also allow the drawing of agent-related models representing the knowledge, the decision-making processes of the robot, and its actions.

At the end of 2004, a great European initiative started and actively involved the WOA community: the AgentLink Network of Excellence. Much effort has been spent during the Agentlink meetings on the AOSE topics. A specific working group has been created, giving place to a vibrant and productive exchange of experiences and several scientific collaborations. Several members of the WOA community actively participated in this initiative and brought back into the WOA events the results of that work, enriching them with new contributions. A proposal of a unifying MAS metamodel was one of the main results of the numerous meetings held around Europe during the AgentLink events [15].

In the following subsections, we will discuss details of the research presented at WOA dealing with metamodels, method fragments, the composition of ad-hoc design methodologies and modelling notations.

4.1 Metamodel

A metamodel is a model that describes the structure of all the elements that should be designed when following a specific methodology. In [45], the authors propose an integrated agent-oriented metamodel that merges the best aspects of four relevant AOSE methodologies. This metamodel is useful because it helps fill the gap between the methodology's conceptual level and the system's implementation level, resulting in more consistent and well-designed agent systems. Filling the gap refers to the process of bridging the differences and integrating the concepts and methodologies of AOSE methodologies and MAS infrastructures. This complex task involves comparing and relating the concepts, providing methodological guidelines, and introducing new concepts to make the integration successful. The ultimate goal is to create a seamless transition between the design and implementation phases, allowing for a more efficient and effective development process for agent-based software.

The core fragments of the metamodel were identified by first defining the requirements for the metamodel and then selecting fragments that fulfilled those requirements. The fragments were then analyzed and refined to provide better integration. A glossary of relevant terms was also created to aid in identifying synonyms and conflicts. Based on this work, a first version of the metamodel was then defined.

An interesting approach to using meta-model is adopted in [16] where the elements and parameters of an evolutionary Multi-Agent System are modelled at the meta-level and instantiated at runtime. The authors adopt this approach to observe how the behavioural parameters of agents adapt under evolutionary pressure at runtime.

4.2 The Method Fragment and the Repository

After the AgentLink initiative, in 2010–2014, the community of researchers working on AOSE continued to hold meetings often co-located with scientific events in Europe. The work also involved the FIPA association, which, at the time, was looking for a methodological reference specifically conceived to develop FIPA-based MASs. The result of this work was the conception of a new methodological approach where existing AOSE methodologies contributed to constructing a repository of pieces of process (called method fragments) that could be assembled to build ad-hoc design processes. The standardization perspective pursued by the FIPA association helped achieve the result of a standard approach for the documentation of the existing methodologies that enabled the identification of method fragments, the construction of a repository and the assembly of new, ad hoc processes. The WOA community has delivered several papers on these topics. The final result of this long effort was a book collecting most of the well-known agent-oriented design processes and describing them according to the FIPA standard description approach [33], again the WOA community largely contributed to that and fruitfully linked that effort to the WOA events.

A method fragment is a portion of a design process composed of two main parts: the process and the product. It is stored in a repository and can be used to construct new design processes or retrieve specific fragments for reuse. A method fragment provides a reusable piece of a design process that method engineers can use to create new methodologies. Method engineers select and assemble method fragments to construct a new process tailored to an organization's specific needs and capabilities. In [89], the authors utilized method fragments by extracting, defining, and standardizing portions of existing design processes and storing them in a repository. This database repository categorizes fragments based on process metamodel elements central to agent-systems design: process role, phase/activity, work product, and MAS Metamodel element. The fragments are described using SPEM diagrams and text documents, illustrating their use in various activities and phases of the design process. This approach allows for easy retrieval and assembly of fragments to construct new, situation-specific design processes, facilitating the reuse and adaptation of well-defined process components in Multi-Agent Systems development.

Based on this and again in [89], the authors propose to use method engineering to design, construct, and adapt methods for information systems development. This involves extracting, defining, standardizing, and storing method fragments from existing processes in a repository. The method engineer selects and assembles the appropriate fragments to create a new process. This approach allows for reuse and customization of existing methods.

The repository includes metadata such as Fragment ID, Fragment Name, File Name, and Phase ID. These are managed using a relational data structure, with relationships such as Fragment (ID, FragName, FileName, ID Phase) and Phase (ID, PAName, PADescription). Other elements in the repository may also have metadata associated with them. Creating a repository of fragments is important because it allows for easy access and retrieval of standardized method fragments, which can then be used to compose new design processes. This saves time and effort in the design process and ensures consistency and efficiency in using method fragments.

A method fragment consists of composition guidelines, aspects of the fragment, and dependency relationships. It is also important to consider the context and problem behind the fragment and the specific issues it addresses. Moreover, it comprises several elements that describe a portion of a design process. These elements include activities, process roles, and work products. Activities refer to a portion of work performed by a process role and can be further broken down into smaller parts called steps. Process roles are responsible for performing the activities and can be assigned to one or more individuals. Work products are the outputs of an activity and can include diagrams or text documents.

In addition to these core elements, a method fragment includes composition guidelines, aspects of the fragment, and dependency relationships. Composition guidelines describe the context or problem the fragment intends to address, which helps with its reuse in similar situations. Aspects of the fragment provide additional information about the fragment, such as the preferred implementation platform or application area. Dependency relationships can be used to identify other fragments strongly related to the one being considered.

A method fragment is a comprehensive representation of a portion of a design process, including the necessary elements and additional information to facilitate its use and retrieval from a repository.

A link with the previously cited FIPA activity on design methodology can be found at WOA 2010, where [69] presents an experimental evaluation of the methodology documentation template proposed by the IEEE FIPA Design Process Documentation and Fragmentation working group. This template documents the three fundamental elements of the methodology (metamodel, notation, and process) and adopts OMG's standard Software Process Engineering Metamodel (SPEM). The experiment is performed by documenting the SODA process.

Interestingly, the authors propose evaluating and comparing SPEM 2.0 (Software Process Engineering Metamodel) with SPEM 1.0 in the same case study [68]. In the paper, the authors examined the applicability of SPEM 2.0 to the SODA methodology. Their goal was to determine whether SPEM 2.0 addressed the limitations and expressiveness issues that had arisen in SPEM 1.0, particularly related to the readability of UML diagrams in the context of complex Agent-Oriented methodologies and the absence of suitable ad-hoc entities. The findings indicate that SPEM 2.0 effectively addresses some of these limitations by clearly separating Method Content and Processes. Additionally, it incorporates capability patterns and enables the expression of relationships between Work Product states and the Activities responsible for changes in those states.

4.3   Method Engineering and Creating a Methodology

In [56], method engineering is employed to construct tailored development processes by integrating various method fragments. Two principal approaches are utilized: metamodel-driven and development process-driven approaches. The metamodel-driven approach emphasizes using a MAS metamodel to guide the methodology construction. This approach requires selecting or defining a MAS metamodel that is appropriate for the specific problem and application domain. Subsequently, the elements that comprise the metamodel of the MAS under development are identified. Method fragments, which are capable of producing the identified metamodel elements, are then selected. The development process is characterized by the execution order of these method fragments, based on the relationships among the metamodel elements. This ensures that the resulting methodology comprehensively covers the MAS metamodel for the given problem and application domain, providing a flexible framework for defining methodologies and metamodels for MAS development. Conversely, the development process-driven approach focuses on instantiating a complete software development process encompassing all MAS development phases. In this approach, a suitable software development process is either chosen or defined, tailored to the specific problem and application domain. Each phase of the development process is instantiated by selecting appropriate method fragments from existing agent-oriented methodologies or by defining new fragments as needed. Fragments are integrated by identifying and defining dependencies among the work products produced in each phase. This ensures that the work products from one phase serve as the inputs for the subsequent phase, creating a coherent and seamless development process.

A tool to support development activities is crucial, whether the designer is using a methodology to develop a software product or is creating a new one.

In [25], the authors present MetaMeth, a tool for process definition and execution in software engineering. It is a Computer Aided Method Engineering (CAME) and Computer Aided Process Engineering (CAPE) tool at the same time, meaning it supports the construction of new methods through reuse and also allows for the management and execution of processes through a workflow engine, agents, and an expert system. It also has a code generator for implementation and supports design patterns for reuse. The main innovation of MetaMeth is combining CAME and CAPE functionalities, allowing method engineers to not only store and retrieve reusable method fragments but also to orchestrate all Computer Aided Software Engineering (CASE) services and design a system. It also integrates a reuse technique based on design patterns and has a code generator that uses an MDA approach to transform the design view into an implementation view and, finally, a code view. Additionally, it supports distributed design and automatic composition of work products. In MetaMeth, process definition and execution are separated using a multi-agent system. Process definition is done through a graphical workflow editor called JaWE, while process execution is done through a separate module that uses a Multi-Agent System. This allows for a clear separation of concerns and more efficient process management.

The objective of automatic composition is to automatically modify, create, or update work products related to a specific activity in the design process. This is done using auto-composition, notation interpretation, and semantic validation services offered by activity agents.

Another contribution to the stream of the composition of ad-hoc methodologies and related tools comes from [46]; in this paper presented at WOA 2011, the authors introduce PROCE (PROcess Composition and execution Environment), an agent-based CAME and CASE tool which supports the design of Multi-Agent Systems as prescribed by the Organization-based Multi-Agent System Engineering (O-MASE) methodology [58]. The tool also comprises a fragment repository inspired by the FIPA fragment specification [33]. The tool allows the development of agent systems that are compatible with the JADE platform [11].

4.4 Agent-Based Notations for Designing MAS

Notation, in general, in the metamodeling process has a very important role because it helps to define the structure and syntax of the methodology being developed. In [12], authors evidentiated a gap between agent technology and widely accepted industrial technologies. They proposed integrating Multi-Agent Systems (MAS) into real-world applications. Indeed, despite significant advancements in agent technology, its industrial and commercial applications remain limited. The authors aim to leverage the Unified Modeling Language (UML) by extending it to accommodate the concepts of software agents and MAS through Agent UML (AUML). This integration proposes MAS as an incremental extension to existing, proven industrial practices. The practical application of AUML in the WINK project, which focuses on data management and system updates, evaluated the suitability and effectiveness of AUML in a real-world scenario and identified areas for refinement and improvement in the modelling language. The authors conclude that there is a lack of development tools to support the graphical representation and code translation of AUML, and further work is needed to clarify the semantics of dependencies and cooperation between agents.

In [40], the authors argue that existing agent-oriented modelling languages, like Agent UML (AUML), need enhancements to fully capture aspects related to representing interactions between agents and their internal architecture, deployment of MAS, and pattern reuse. They propose an extended AUML that includes detailed deployment diagrams and interaction representations, aiming to provide developers with precise tools to map design models to implementation artefacts. They revealed the inadequacy of current modelling languages in addressing the implementation-level details of MAS. While significant efforts have been made to define metaphors and diagrammatic notations for MAS, these often fall short in practical implementation scenarios. Specifically, the transition from design to implementation lacks sufficient support, making it difficult to manage the complexity and heterogeneity of MAS.

The notation is also used during process execution to ensure the methodology is followed correctly and to identify any errors or inconsistencies. The MetaMeth tool allows for introducing syntactic and semantic rules to ensure that the notation is used correctly. Additionally, the tool has a graphical notation feature that allows for creating complex documents using diagrams, text, tables, and more. The work done during the realization of the Metameth tool also concerned researching in the notation field. The question was: *What are the most efficient and representative elements that can be used for a notation suitable for an agent-based design methodology?*

The main objective of this research is to propose notations and models for representing social structures and relationships in the context of organizational and agent-based systems. The UML-based notation in [35] is designed to represent organizational elements in MASs, whereas other methods may not have been specifically tailored for this purpose. Additionally, the proposed notation allows for representing all the elements of the Moise+ organizational model, whereas other methods may only represent certain aspects of the organization.

Indeed, at the time, Moise was not adequately supported by a well-defined methodological approach. Creating a specific notation for Moise makes it easier to represent and explain the organizational model to stakeholders involved in the design process, making it more readable and understandable. This also allows for the involvement of stakeholders in the development process, improving the flexibility of conventional development approaches. The proposed graphical notation allows the representation of organizations in the Moise+ organizational model. It includes three types of diagrams: structural, functional, and normative. It is designed to be easily understandable by stakeholders and can be used to support different approaches. However, it is not as comprehensive as other notations, such as the one presented in [76], including behavioural diagrams.

A complementary effort is made in [82] where the authors propose using ontology to describe the problem domain to better understand the problem and identify goals. This can lead to improvement in the goal identification process and potentially address any inconsistencies or deficiencies. Here, the authors propose a formalization for the Problem Ontology Description activity, which aims to describe the intentional behaviours of problems addressed with agent-oriented technologies. The innovation consists of introducing new elements inspired by the FIPA agent ontology to explicitly model intentional behaviours and identify the goals the solution of the problem has to satisfy. The paper presents a formalization for the Problem Ontology Description activity, which aims to describe the intentional behaviours of problems addressed with agent-oriented technologies. The innovation proposed is the introduction of new elements inspired by the FIPA agent ontology to explicitly model intentional behaviours and identify the goals the problem's solution has to satisfy.

The problem ontology can be used to improve the analyst's understanding of the problem by providing a deeper knowledge of the problem domain and identifying goals. This can be achieved through reasoning on the elements and relationships within the ontology and by identifying patterns that can provide useful information about the goals of the problem. The ontology can also help to address any inconsistencies or deficiencies in the problem specification. The ontology can also help eliminate redundancies and ambiguities in the problem specification, making it easier for stakeholders to understand and communicate their knowledge. Additionally, the ontology can assist in identifying the artefacts that will compose the environment, providing a clear framework for the design process.

One of the difficulties in defining the system ontology is correctly catching the key elements of the problem description and mapping them to corresponding elements of the ontology. At WOA 2014, [39] proposed GIMT (Goal Identification and Modeling Tool), a CASE tool for supporting ontology building and goal modelling. GIMT allows users to write the problem statement and extract significant elements to build the system's ontology. The ontology is then analysed to identify the system's goals. This is a first step in the construction of the problem ontology. By adding concepts from the solution domain, such an ontology can be evolved to support agents' communications, thus obtaining a rigorous foundation for both agents' reasoning and semantic communications.

Over the years, the need to represent and manage knowledge in Multi-Agent Systems operating in dynamic and unpredictable environments was addressed, also in mission-critical and sensitive applications like emergency management [38]. First, modern software systems must consist of increasingly autonomous and self-adaptive entities capable of performing tasks that were not always predictable in the design phase. These systems must interact and collaborate with humans as if they were a team. They must exchange knowledge, decide whether to perform actions independently or delegate them to others and adapt to changes in the environment in real time. The representation of knowledge is crucial for decision-making. Agents must be able to update and manage their knowledge while the system runs, especially in operational areas that change during runtime. In [29], the Belief-Desire-Intention (BDI) model has been used, and programming languages such as Jason enable the mapping of intentions and events at runtime, the selection of plans from a library of plans to achieve a goal even in situations that are not fully known at the design stage, and the exploration of knowledge representation and management in Multi-Agent Systems using the Jason programming language, the CArtAgO framework and the OWL ontology. The focus is on creating an agent memory system that is adaptive and autonomous in dynamic environments. The authors propose a centralized agent called Jino that manages episodic and semantic memory and improves the efficiency of agents' decision-making. The methodology enables agents to adapt to changes in real time, ensuring effective knowledge management through a centralized approach.

The development of agent-based methodologies in recent years has shown the importance of using modular and flexible methods, as supported by fragmented methods and CAME/CASE tools, which provide a solid foundation for developing increasingly complex and adaptive systems. Looking to the future, the continued integration of methods, methodologies and tools promises to further advance the application of agents in industrial contexts and improve adaptability and collaboration in dynamic environments.

5 The Future of AOSE

The future of Multi-Agent Systems still holds immense potential for revolutionizing industries and transforming how we interact with technology. In healthcare, agent-based systems can optimize patient care, manage clinical trials, and facilitate personalized medicine. In smart cities, agents can enable intelligent infrastructure management, public safety, and resource allocation in urban environments. Self-driving vehicles will become more prevalent, while agents can optimize routes, traffic flow, and logistics in transportation. Manufacturing will see improved production processes, managed supply chains, and enhanced product quality through the application of software engineering methods.

As researchers and developers, it's crucial to address the challenges and opportunities that lie ahead. There are significant challenges to overcome. One such hurdle is the need to design and manage complex systems comprising multiple autonomous and interacting agents that can adapt to changing environments, learn from experiences, and make decisions without human intervention. This requires a deep understanding of how agents establish trust with each other and maintain reputations in distributed systems.

Another crucial area of focus is the IoT and edge computing. As the number of connected devices grows, edge computing will play a vital role in processing data closer to the source, reducing latency, and improving real-time interactions between agents. Researchers must study how agents can establish trust with each other and maintain reputations in distributed systems, ensuring reliable interactions and cooperation. The WOA community has always been relevant to the research about AOSE and, consequently, has considered the future of this area of research. A relevant contribution to the discussion comes from [94], where the author states that AOSE addresses the challenge of engineering large-scale systems involving goal-oriented entities. These entities often have conflicting goals and involve multiple stakeholders. This problem relates to the challenges faced by the IoT, where accommodating services and managing many goals are crucial. While the concept of goal-oriented groups draws inspiration from AOSE, IoT necessitates specific concepts and abstractions that AOSE, in its general terms, does not directly cover.

Another contact point between IoT and AOSE is in the research for adaptivity that AOSE has pursued as a branch of the general area of software engineering. This addresses the challenges posed by dynamic and unpredictable operational environments. These dynamics also impact IoT systems, where ensuring continuous functionality involves embedding close control loops (similar to those in self-adaptive systems research). These loops continuously monitor system activities and the environment, allowing for eventual corrective actions. The author in [94] introduces and outlines some key conceptual abstractions related to the IoT domain and suggests an initial step toward establishing a broader discipline for engineering IoT systems and applications starting from the AOSE background.

The convergence of physical and computational systems will lead to more complex, adaptive, and resilient systems that require AOSE's capabilities. Complex systems will require multiple agents to interact with each other to achieve common goals, making Multi-Agent Systems a crucial aspect of AOSE's future. Researchers are currently investigating how multiple agents can learn from each other and their environment to achieve common goals or optimize individual performance. The role of AOSE is to provide models and methodologies for developing and simulating complex systems using autonomous agents, enabling a better understanding of dynamics, behaviour, and decision-making processes. The big challenge here is protecting autonomous agents from cyber threats and ensuring data integrity and system stability.

Developing seamless interfaces between humans and autonomous agents for effective collaboration is another key trend worth exploring. In this context, integrating artificial intelligence (AI) and machine learning (ML) into agents will enable more sophisticated decision-making, planning, and problem-solving capabilities. Now, the recent hype around Large Language Models (LLMs) warrants a dedicated discussion, suggesting a fascinating relationship between AOSE and LLMs. Conversational interfaces powered by LLMs can enable humans to interact with autonomous agents through natural language processing (NLP) and text-to-speech synthesis. This integration can facilitate more sophisticated coordination and negotiation among autonomous agents, leading to improved decision-making and system performance. The role of AOSE is to leverage LLMs to enable agents to better understand natural language, which is essential for effective communication and decision-making in complex systems. However, this also raises concerns about robustness against adversarial attacks and biases.

Cognitive architectures can couple symbolic reasoning to amplify agents' power in analyzing complex situations, learning from experience, reasoning about complex situations, and adapting to changing environments. For instance, LLMs can create knowledge graphs representing complex relationships between entities, concepts, and actions. This enables agents to reason about the world more effectively and make informed decisions. Interpretability and explainability become essential in this context: methods are required to interpret the output of LLM-based decision-making systems and explain decisions made by autonomous agents using LLMs.

Explainability and interpretability are also fundamental in human-agent interaction, especially when humans have to interact and collaborate with machines (such as computers, robots, or other devices) in environments that are not fully known a priori. In these cases, the challenge is to use agents not only as a design paradigm but also as a suitable technological approach. In human-robot interaction, for example, agents can solve complex problems related to ethical issues. The ability of an agent to reason and deliberate based on its own knowledge can be a crucial factor in building the right agent architecture. Indeed, an appropriate ontological description is normally needed to give an agent the means to link actions to the elements in the environment and to the goal. For instance, in a soccer scenario, the goal may be to pass the ball to a team member, and in this case, it may be possible for an agent to commit the action "to throw a ball at someone". If, on the other hand, the scenario is a small child's entertainment, throwing the ball could even be dangerous. This makes sense, and it is necessary to adequately describe the knowledge base, especially regarding ethical norms. In this context, it might be interesting to investigate using knowledge graph technologies.

In this context, the possibility of endowing an agent with self-analysis and self-disclosure abilities that lead to a clear and reasoned explanation of how and why an action is performed can be explored. Two preliminary papers have already been presented at WOA in the last two years [90,91]. Additionally, LLMs, text-to-speech techniques, and cognitive architectures could prove to be fundamental and enriching research elements in the agent world.

Another potential use of agents, particularly in robotics, is their application in designing and implementing complex robotic systems that rely on ROS and Gazebo. ROS and Gazebo have become almost a de facto standard in robot programming. The potential of agents to handle the complexity of systems, combined with the strengths of ROS and Gazebo from an implementation perspective, could lead to significant advancements in AOSE in the future.

References

1. Aguilar, J., Cerrada, M., Mousalli, G., Rivas, F., Hidrobo, F.: A multiagent model for intelligent distributed control systems. In: Knowledge-Based Intelligent Information and Engineering Systems: 9th International Conference, KES 2005, Melbourne, Australia, 14–16 September 2005, Proceedings, Part I. Lecture Notes in Artificial Intelligence, vol. 3681, pp. 191–197. Springer (2005). https://doi.org/10.1007/11552413_28
2. Aguzzi, G., Casadei, R., Pianini, D., Viroli, M.: Self-organisation with aggregate computing: a reflection under the lenses of multi-agent systems engineering. In: Mascardi and Omicini [67]
3. Armano, G., Paoli, F.D., Omicini, A., Vargiu, E. (eds.): WOA 2003 – 4th Workshop "From Objects to Agents". Pitagora Editrice Bologna, Villasimius, CA, Italy (2003). http://giuseppevizzari.github.io/WOA-proceedings-archive/woa-2003.html
4. Baldoni, M., Baroglio, C., Bergenti, F., Garro, A. (eds.): WOA 2013 – 14th Workshop "From Objects to Agents", CEUR Workshop Proceedings, vol. 1099. Turin, Italy (2013). http://ceur-ws.org/Vol-1099/
5. Baldoni, M., Baroglio, C., Micalizio, R.: Interaction protocols: from AUML to social commitments, from artifacts to BSPL. In: Mascardi and Omicini [67]
6. Baldoni, M., Boccalatte, A., De Paoli, F., Martelli, M., Mascardi, V. (eds.): WOA 2007 – 8th Workshop "From Objects to Agents". Seneca Edizioni Torino, Genova, Italy (2007). http://woa07.disi.unige.it/ProceedingsWOA2007.zip
7. Baldoni, M., Cossentino, M., De Paoli, F., Seidita, V. (eds.): WOA 2008 – 9th Workshop "From Objects to Agents". Seneca Edizioni Torino, Palermo, Italy (2008). http://www.pa.icar.cnr.it/woa08/materiali/Proceedings.pdf
8. Baldoni, M., De Paoli, F., Martelli, A., Omicini, A. (eds.): WOA 2004 – 5th Workshop "From Objects to Agents". Pitagora Editrice Bologna, Torino, Italy (2004). http://lia.deis.unibo.it/books/woa2004/atti.pdf
9. Barile, F., Caso, A., Rossi, S.: Group recommendation for smart applications: a multi-agent view of the problem. In: Santoro and Bergenti [85], pp. 12–17. http://ceur-ws.org/Vol-1260/paper7.pdf

10. Baxter, J.L., Burke, E.K., Garibaldi, J.M., Norman, M.: Multi-robot search and rescue: a potential field based approach. In: Autonomous Robots and Agents, 9–16 (2007). https://doi.org/10.1007/978-3-540-73424-6_2

11. Bellifemine, F., Poggi, A., Rimassa, G.: Developing multi-agent systems with JADE. In: Intelligent Agents VII: Agent Theories Architectures and Languages, 7th International Workshop, ATAL 2000 Boston, MA, USA, 7–9 July 2000, Proceedings, pp. 89–103. Springer (2001). https://doi.org/10.1007/3-540-44631-1_7

12. Bergamaschi, S., Gelati, G., Guerra, F., Vincini, M.: Experiencing AUML for the WINK multi-agent system. In: Armano et al. [3], pp. 148–154. http://giuseppevizzari.github.io/WOA-proceedings-archive/pdfs/woa2003/20.pdf

13. Bergenti, F. (ed.): WOA 2009 – 10th Workshop "From Objects to Agents". Seneca Edizioni Torino, Parma, Italy (2009). http://www.ailab.unipr.it/woa09/papers/

14. Bergenti, F., Iotti, E., Poggi, A.: Outline of a formalization of JADE multi-agent systems. In: Di Napoli et al. [50], pp. 123–128. http://ceur-ws.org/Vol-1382/paper19.pdf

15. Bernon, C., Cossentino, M., Pavón, J.: Agent-oriented software engineering. Knowl. Eng. Rev. **20**(2), 99–116 (2005). https://doi.org/10.1017/S0269888905000421

16. Bertolotti, F., Roman, S.: The evolution of risk sensitivity in a sustainability game: an agent-based model. In: Ferrando and Mascardi [54], pp. 101–115. http://ceur-ws.org/Vol-3261/paper8.pdf

17. Blair, G., Bencomo, N., France, R.B.: Models@run.time. Computer **42**(10), 22–27 (2009). https://doi.org/10.1109/MC.2009.326

18. Booch, G., Jacobson, I., Rumbaugh, J., et al.: The unified modeling language. Unix Rev. **14**(13), 5 (1996)

19. Bordini, R.H., Hübner, J.F.: BDI agent programming in AgentSpeak using *jason*. In: Computational Logic in Multi-Agent Systems: 6th International Workshop, CLIMA VI, London, UK, June 2005, Revised Selected and Invited Papers, pp. 143–164. Springer (2005). https://doi.org/10.1007/11750734_9

20. Bratman, M.E., Israel, D.J., Pollack, M.E.: Plans and resource-bounded practical reasoning. Comput. Intell. **4**(3), 349–355 (1988). https://doi.org/10.1111/j.1467-8640.1988.tb00284.x

21. Bresciani, P., Giorgini, P., Giunchiglia, F., Mylopoulos, J., Perini, A.: Tropos: an agent-oriented software development methodology. Auton. Agent. Multi-Agent Syst. **3**(8), 203–236 (2004). https://doi.org/10.1023/B:AGNT.0000018806.20944.ef

22. Brinkkemper, S.: Method engineering: engineering of information systems development methods and tools. Inf. Softw. Technol. **38**(4), 275–280 (1996). https://doi.org/10.1016/0950-5849(95)01059-9

23. Cabac, L., Moldt, D.: Formal semantics for AUML agent interaction protocol diagrams. In: Agent-Oriented Software Engineering V: 5th International Workshop, AOSE 2004, New York, NY, USA, July 2004, Revised Selected Papers 5, pp. 47–61. Springer (2005). https://doi.org/10.1007/978-3-540-30578-1_4

24. Cabri, G., Leonardi, L., Mariani, S., Zambonelli, F.: Coordination of software agents: models and languages. In: Mascardi and Omicini [67]

25. Caico, R., Cossentino, M., Sabatucci, L., Seidita, V., Gaglio, S.: MetaMeth: a tool for process definition and execution. In: De Paoli et al. [48], pp. 21–24. http://ceur-ws.org/Vol-204/D06.pdf

26. Calegari, R., Ciatto, G., Denti, E., Omicini, A., Sartor, G. (eds.): WOA 2020 – 21st Workshop "From Objects to Agents", CEUR Workshop Proceedings, vol. 2706. Bologna, Italy (2020). http://ceur-ws.org/Vol-2706/

27. Calegari, R., Ciatto, G., Denti, E., Omicini, A., Sartor, G. (eds.): WOA 2021 – 22nd Workshop "From Objects to Agents", CEUR Workshop Proceedings, vol. 2963. Bologna, Italy (2021). http://ceur-ws.org/Vol-2963/

28. Chella, A., Cossentino, M., Infantino, I., Pirrone, R.: An agent based design process for cognitive architectures in robotics. In: Omicini and Viroli [74], pp. 84–89. http://giuseppevizzari.github.io/WOA-proceedings-archive/pdfs/woa2001/pdf/08.pdf

29. Chella, A., Lanza, F., Seidita, V.: Representing and developing knowledge using Jason, Cartago and OWL. In: Cossentino et al. [42], pp. 147–152. http://ceur-ws.org/Vol-2215/paper_23.pdf

30. Comi, A., Rosaci, D.: SMARTSAN: a P2P social agent network for generating recommendations in a smart city environment. In: De Meo et al. [47], pp. 108–112. http://ceur-ws.org/Vol-1867/w19.pdf

31. Corradi, A., Omicini, A., Poggi, A. (eds.): WOA 2000 – 1st Workshop "From Objects to Agents", Atti di Congressi, vol. 1195. Pitagora Editrice Bologna, Parma, Italy (2000). http://giuseppevizzari.github.io/WOA-proceedings-archive/woa-2000.html

32. Cossentino, M., Gaud, N., Hilaire, V., Galland, S., Koukam, A.: ASPECS: an agent-oriented software process for engineering complex systems. Auton. Agent. Multi-Agent Syst. **20**(2), 260–300 (2010). https://doi.org/10.1007/s10458-009-9099-4

33. Cossentino, M., Hilaire, V., Molesini, A., Seidita, V. (eds.): Handbook on Agent-Oriented Design Processes. Springer (2014). https://doi.org/10.1007/978-3-642-39975-6

34. Cossentino, M., Hopmans, G., Odell, J.: FIPA standardization activities in the software engineering area. In: Armano et al. [3], pp. 71–77. http://giuseppevizzari.github.io/WOA-proceedings-archive/pdfs/woa2003/23.pdf

35. Cossentino, M., Lodato, C., Lopes, S., Ribino, P., Seidita, V., Chella, A.: A UML-based notation for representing MAS organizations. In: Fortino et al. [55], pp. 133–139. http://ceur-ws.org/Vol-741/ID20_CossentinoLodatoLopesRibiniSeiditaChella.pdf

36. Cossentino, M., Lodato, C., Lopes, S., Sabatucci, L.: MUSA: a middleware for user-driven service adaptation. In: Di Napoli et al. [50], pp. 1–10. http://ceur-ws.org/Vol-1382/paper1.pdf

37. Cossentino, M., Lopes, S., Sabatucci, L.: A tool for the automatic generation of MOISE organisations from BPMN. In: Calegari et al. [26], pp. 69–82. http://ceur-ws.org/Vol-2706/paper11.pdf

38. Cossentino, M., Lopes, S., Sabatucci, L., Tripiciano, M.: Towards a semantic layer for Italian emergency plans. In: Calegari et al. [27], pp. 144–161. http://ceur-ws.org/Vol-2963/paper9.pdf

39. Cossentino, M., et al.: GIMT: a tool for ontology and goal modeling in BDI multi-agent design. In: Santoro and Bergenti [85], pp. 81–88. http://ceur-ws.org/Vol-1260/paper10.pdf

40. Cossentino, M., Poggi, A., Rimassa, G., Turci, P.: Implementation level issues in MAS modeling. In: Armano et al. [3], pp. 155–162. http://giuseppevizzari.github.io/WOA-proceedings-archive/pdfs/woa2003/25.pdf

41. Cossentino, M., Sabatucci, L., Seidita, V.: Towards an approach for engineering complex systems: agents and agility. In: De Meo et al. [47], pp. 1–6. http://ceur-ws.org/Vol-1867/w1.pdf

42. Cossentino, M., Sabatucci, L., Seidita, V. (eds.): WOA 2018 – 19th Workshop "From Objects to Agents", CEUR Workshop Proceedings, vol. 2215. Palermo, Italy (2018). http://ceur-ws.org/Vol-2215/

43. Cossentino, M., Seidita, V.: PASSI - process for agents society specification and implementation. In: Cossentino et al. [33], pp. 287–329. https://doi.org/10.1007/978-3-642-39975-6_10

44. Dalpiaz, F., Ali, R., Asnar, Y., Bryl, V., Giorgini, P.: Applying Tropos to socio-technical system design and runtime configuration. In: Baldoni et al. [7], pp. 101–107. http://www.pa.icar.cnr.it/woa08/materiali/paper/paper_14.pdf

45. Dalpiaz, F., Molesini, A., Puviani, M., Seidita, V.: Towards filling the gap between AOSE methodologies and infrastructures: requirements and meta-model. In: Baldoni et al. [7], pp. 115–121. http://www.pa.icar.cnr.it/woa08/materiali/paper/paper_3.pdf

46. De Luca, F., Tundis, A., Garro, A.: PROCE: an agent-based PROcess Composition and execution Environment. In: Fortino et al. [55], pp. 171–174. http://ceur-ws.org/Vol-741/DEM02_DeLucaTundisGarro.pdf

47. De Meo, P., Postorino, M.N., Rosaci, D., Sarnè, G.M.L. (eds.): WOA 2017 – 18th Workshop "From Objects to Agents", CEUR Workshop Proceedings, vol. 1867. Scilla, RC, Italy (2017). http://ceur-ws.org/Vol-1867/

48. De Paoli, F., Di Stefano, A., Omicini, A., Santoro, C. (eds.): WOA 2006 – 7th Workshop "From Objects to Agents", CEUR Workshop Proceedings, vol. 204. Catania, Italy (2006). http://ceur-ws.org/Vol-204/

49. De Paoli, F., Manzoni, S., Poggi, A. (eds.): WOA 2002 – 3rd Workshop "From Objects to Agents". Pitagora Editrice Bologna, Milano, Italy (2002). http://giuseppevizzari.github.io/WOA-proceedings-archive/woa-2002.html

50. Di Napoli, C., Rossi, S., Staffa, M. (eds.): WOA 2015 – 16th Workshop "From Objects to Agents", CEUR Workshop Proceedings, vol. 1382. Naples, Italy (2015). http://ceur-ws.org/Vol-1382/

51. Domnori, E., Cabri, G., Leonardi, L.: A multi-agent approach for territorial emergency management. In: Fortino et al. [55], pp. 74–80. http://ceur-ws.org/Vol-741/ID4_DomnoriCabriLeonardi.pdf

52. Drew, D.S.: Multi-agent systems for search and rescue applications. Curr. Robot. Rep. **2**, 189–200 (2021). https://doi.org/10.1007/s43154-021-00048-3

53. Falcone, R., Castelfranchi, C., Sapienza, A., Cantucci, F. (eds.): WOA 2023 – 24th Workshop "From Objects to Agents", CEUR Workshop Proceedings, vol. 3579. Roma, Italy (2023). http://ceur-ws.org/Vol-3579/

54. Ferrando, A., Mascardi, V. (eds.): WOA 2022 – 23rd Workshop "From Objects to Agents", CEUR Workshop Proceedings, vol. 3261. Genova, Italy (2022). http://ceur-ws.org/Vol-3261/

55. Fortino, G., Garro, A., Palopoli, L., Russo, W., Spezzano, G. (eds.): WOA 2011 – 12th Workshop "From Objects to Agents", CEUR Workshop Proceedings, vol. 741. Rende, Italy (2011). http://ceur-ws.org/Vol-741/

56. Fortino, G., Garro, A., Russo, W.: Using method engineering for the construction of agent-oriented methodologies. In: Baldoni et al. [8], pp. 51–54. http://giuseppevizzari.github.io/WOA-proceedings-archive/pdfs/woa2004/8.pdf

57. Fortino, G., Garro, A., Mascillaro, S., Russo, W.: ELDATool: a statecharts-based tool for prototyping multi-agent systems. In: Baldoni et al. [6], pp. 14–19. http://woa07.dibris.unige.it/papers/D2_ForGarMasRus-WOA07-Demo.pdf

58. Garcia-Ojeda, J.C., DeLoach, S.A., Robby, Oyenan, W.H., Valenzuela, J.: O-MaSE: a customizable approach to developing multiagent development processes. In: Agent-Oriented Software Engineering VIII: 8th International Workshop, AOSE 2007, Honolulu, HI, USA, May 2007, Revised Selected Papers 8, pp. 1–15. Springer (2008). https://doi.org/10.1007/978-3-540-79488-2_1

59. Garro, A.: Agent-based computing for science and engineering: back to the future and beyond.... In: Mascardi and Omicini [67]

60. Garro, A., Russo, W.: Exploiting the easyABMS methodology in social and economic domains. In: Bergenti [13], pp. 8–15. http://www.ailab.unipr.it/woa09/papers/Garro.pdf

61. Garzetti, M., Giorgini, P., Mylopoulos, J., Sannicolò, F.: Applying Tropos methodology to a real case study: complexity and criticality analysis. In: De Paoli et al. [49], pp. 7–13. http://giuseppevizzari.github.io/WOA-proceedings-archive/pdfs/woa2002/12.pdf

62. Hübner, J.F., Sichman, J.S., Boissier, O.: Developing organised multiagent systems using the MOISE$^+$ model: programming issues at the system and agent levels. Int. J. Agent Oriented Softw. Eng. **1**(3/4), 370–395 (2007). https://doi.org/10.1504/IJAOSE.2007.016266

63. Jennings, N.R., Wooldridge, M.J.: Agent Technology: Foundations, Applications, and Markets. Springer (1998). https://doi.org/10.1007/978-3-662-03678-5

64. Kinny, D., Georgeff, M., Rao, A.: A methodology and modelling technique for systems of BDI agents. In: Agents Breaking Away: 7th European Workshop on Modelling Autonomous Agents in a Multi-Agent World, MAAMAW '96, Eindhoven, The Netherlands, January 1996. Proceedings, pp. 56–71. Springer (1996). https://doi.org/10.1007/BFb0031846

65. Marguglio, A., Cammarata, G., Bonura, S., Francaviglia, G., Puccio, M., Morreale, V.: Design and development of intentional systems with PRACTIONIST Studio. In: Baldoni et al. [7], pp. 37–45. http://www.pa.icar.cnr.it/woa08/materiali/paper/paper_16.pdf

66. Mariani, S., Omicini, A.: TuCSoN coordination for MAS situatedness: towards a methodology. In: Santoro and Bergenti [85], pp. 48–57. http://ceur-ws.org/Vol-1260/paper11.pdf

67. Mascardi, V., Omicini, A. (eds.): The Agents Journey: Twenty-Five Years of Multiagent Systems at WOA. Lecture Notes in Computer Science – State-of-the-Art Surveys. Springer (2026)

68. Molesini, A., Nardini, E., Denti, E., Omicini, A.: Advancing object-oriented standards toward agent-oriented methodologies: SPEM 2.0 on SODA. In: Baldoni et al. [7], pp. 108–114. http://www.pa.icar.cnr.it/woa08/materiali/paper/paper_2.pdf

69. Molesini, A., Omicini, A.: Documenting SODA: an evaluation of the process documentation template. In: Omicini and Viroli [75], pp. 95–101. http://ceur-ws.org/Vol-621/paper14.pdf

70. Morreale, V., Bonura, S., Francaviglia, G., Centineo, F., Cossentino, M., Gaglio, S.: Reasoning about goals in BDI agents: the PRACTIONIST framework. In: De Paoli et al. [48], pp. 187–194. http://ceur-ws.org/Vol-204/P20.pdf

71. Nardini, E., Viroli, M., Casadei, M., Omicini, A.: A self-organising infrastructure for chemical-semantic coordination: experiments in TuCSoN. In: Omicini and Viroli [75], pp. 117–125. http://CEUR-WS.org/Vol-621/paper17.pdf

72. O'Brien, P.D., Nicol, R.C.: FIPA – towards a standard for software agents. BT Technol. J. **16**, 51–59 (1998). https://doi.org/10.1023/A:1009621729979

73. Omicini, A.: From objects to agent societies: abstractions and methodologies for the engineering of open distributed systems. In: Corradi et al. [31], pp. 29–34. http://giuseppevizzari.github.io/WOA-proceedings-archive/pdfs/woa2000/WOA07.pdf

74. Omicini, A., Viroli, M. (eds.): WOA 2001 – 2nd Workshop "From Objects to Agents". Pitagora Editrice Bologna, Modena, Italy (2001). http://giuseppevizzari.github.io/WOA-proceedings-archive/woa-2001.html

75. Omicini, A., Viroli, M. (eds.): WOA 2010 – 11th Workshop "From Objects to Agents", CEUR Workshop Proceedings, vol. 621. Rimini, Italy (2010). http://ceur-ws.org/Vol-621/

76. Padgham, L., Winikoff, M., DeLoach, S., Cossentino, M.: A unified graphical notation for AOSE. In: Agent-Oriented Software Engineering IX: 9th International Workshop, AOSE 2008, Estoril, Portugal, May 2008, Revised Selected Papers, pp. 116–130. Springer (2008). https://doi.org/10.1007/978-3-642-01338-6_9

77. Pavón, J., Gómez-Sanz, J.J., Fuentes, R.: The INGENIAS methodology and tools. In: Agent-Oriented Methodologies, pp. 236–276. IGI Global (2005). https://doi.org/10.4018/978-1-59140-581-8.ch009

78. Perini, A., Bresciani, P., Giorgini, P., Giunchiglia, F., Mylopoulos, J.: Towards an agent oriented approach to software engineering. In: Omicini and Viroli [74], pp. 72–77. http://giuseppevizzari.github.io/WOA-proceedings-archive/pdfs/woa2001/pdf/19.pdf

79. Picard, G., Gleizes, M.P.: The ADELFE methodology. In: Methodologies and Software Engineering for Agent Systems: The Agent-oriented Software Engineering Handbook, pp. 157–175. Springer (2004). https://doi.org/10.1007/1-4020-8058-1_11

80. Picasso, E., Postorino, M.N., Sarné, G.M.L.: A study to promote car-sharing by adopting a reputation system in a multi-agent context. In: De Meo et al. [47], pp. 13–18. http://ceur-ws.org/Vol-1867/w3.pdf

81. Postorino, M.N., Sarnè, G.M.: Agents meet traffic simulation, control and management: a review of selected recent contributions. In: Santoro et al. [86], pp. 112–117. http://ceur-ws.org/Vol-1664/w19.pdf

82. Ribino, P., Cossentino, M., Lodato, C., Lopes, S., Sabatucci, L., Seidita, V.: Ontology and goal model in designing BDI multi-agent systems. In: Baldoni et al. [4], pp. 66–72. http://ceur-ws.org/Vol-1099/paper12.pdf

83. Russell, S.J., Norvig, P.: Artificial Intelligence: A Modern Approach, Global Edition, 4th Edition. Pearson (2021). https://elibrary.pearson.de/book/99.150005/9781292401171

84. Sabatucci, L., Cossentino, M., Gaglio, S.: Building agents with agents and patterns. In: De Paoli et al. [48], pp. 124–129. http://ceur-ws.org/Vol-204/P19.pdf

85. Santoro, C., Bergenti, F. (eds.): WOA 2014 – 15th Workshop "From Objects to Agents", CEUR Workshop Proceedings, vol. 1260. Catania, Italy (2014). http://ceur-ws.org/Vol-1260/

86. Santoro, C., Messina, F., De Benedetti, M. (eds.): WOA 2016 – 17th Workshop "From Objects to Agents", CEUR Workshop Proceedings, vol. 1664. Catania, Italy (2016). http://ceur-ws.org/Vol-1664/

87. Schaerf, A.: A survey of multi-agent systems for optimization problems. In: Fortino et al. [55], p. 1. http://ceur-ws.org/Vol-741/INV01_Schaerf.pdf

88. Schmidt, D.C.: Model-driven engineering. Computer **39**(2), 25–31 (2006). https://doi.org/10.1109/MC.2006.58

89. Seidita, V., Cossentino, M., Gaglio, S.: A repository of fragments for agent systems design. In: De Paoli et al. [48], pp. 130–137. http://ceur-ws.org/Vol-204/P18.pdf

90. Seidita, V., Sabella, A.M.P., Chella, A.: Agents showing self-disclosure. A preliminary methodological approach. In: Falcone et al. [53], pp. 78–91. http://ceur-ws.org/Vol-3579/paper6.pdf

91. Seidita, V., Sabella, A.M.P., Lanza, F., Chella, A.: Agent talks about itself: an implementation using Jason, CArtAgO and Speech Acts. Intelligenza Artificiale **17**(1), 7–18 (2023). https://doi.org/10.3233/IA-230005

92. Wooldridge, M., Jennings, N.R., Kinny, D.: The Gaia methodology for agent-oriented analysis and design. Auton. Agent. Multi-Agent Syst. **3**(3), 285–312 (2000). https://doi.org/10.1023/A:1010071910869
93. Zambonelli, F.: Nature-inspired spatial metaphors for pervasive service ecosystems. In: Baldoni et al. [7], pp. 61–67. http://www.pa.icar.cnr.it/woa08/materiali/paper/paper_10.pdf
94. Zambonelli, F.: Towards a discipline of IoT-oriented software engineering. In: Santoro et al. [86], pp. 1–7. http://ceur-ws.org/Vol-1664/w1.pdf
95. Zambonelli, F., Viroli, M.: From service-oriented architectures to nature-inspired pervasive service ecosystems. In: Omicini and Viroli [75], pp. 102–109. http://ceur-ws.org/Vol-621/paper15.pdf

Agent-Based Computing for Science and Engineering: Back to the Future and Beyond...

Alfredo Garro[(✉)] [iD]

University of Calabria, 87036 Rende, CS, Italy
`alfredo.garro@unical.it`
`http://si.deis.unical.it/garro/`

Abstract. Agent-based computing has emerged as a powerful paradigm for modeling and simulating complex natural and artificial systems as well as for software engineering. Following the path traced by several contributions presented at Workshop on Objects and Agents (WOA) during the last decades, the chapter explores the historical roots of agent-based approaches, tracing their evolution and renaissance in contemporary research. Through a synthesis of selected studies, the efficacy of agent-based computing in capturing the intricacies of dynamic systems and facing their complexity is illustrated. Moreover, recent developments that extend the boundaries of agent-based approaches, pushing the paradigm "beyond" traditional confines, are highlighted. The chapter aims at underscoring the enduring relevance of agent-based computing in scientific and engineering research, emphasizing its adaptability to contemporary challenges and its potential to shape the future of computational modeling.

Keywords: Agent-Based Computing · Complex Natural and Artificial Systems · Agent Based Modeling and Simulation (ABMS) · Agent-Oriented Software Engineering (AOSE) · Agent-based applications

1 Introduction

In recent decades, the increasing complexity of scientific and engineering problems has necessitated the development of computational approaches that can capture, simulate, and predict the behaviors of intricate systems. These systems, characterized by non-linear interactions, emergent phenomena, and dynamic adaptability, have become central to fields as diverse as climate modeling, epidemiology, urban planning, and supply chain optimization. One computational approach that has proven particularly well-suited to such challenges is Agent-Based Computing (ABC). Rooted in the principles of decentralized decision-making and local interaction, the agent-based paradigm offers a powerful method for modeling complex systems in which individual entities—referred

V. Mascardi and A. Omicini (Eds.): *The Agents Journey*, LNCS 16395, pp. 241–259, 2026.
https://doi.org/10.1007/978-3-032-22940-3_9

to as agents—interact with one another and their environment to produce emergent, often unpredictable outcomes [41].

Historically, agent-based modeling arose from early attempts to simulate social behavior and biological systems, growing out of disciplines such as artificial life, evolutionary computation, and complexity science [3, 9, 45]. Over time, ABC has matured into a versatile tool for addressing problems in fields as diverse as engineering, economics, sociology, and environmental science. The paradigm's ability to represent heterogeneous, autonomous agents and to simulate their interactions at various scales has made it invaluable for studying both micro-level processes and macro-level patterns. As computational resources and technological innovations have expanded, ABC has grown in scope and sophistication, adapting to the evolving needs of contemporary science and engineering. Indeed, the applicability of ABC extends beyond modeling and simulating complex systems as the agent-based paradigm offers significant advantages in the field of software engineering providing a robust framework for designing, developing, and managing complex software systems [14, 39].

With these premises, and following the path traced by several contributions presented at Workshop on Objects and Agents (WOA) by the author during the last decades, the chapter seeks to explore the past, present, and future of agent-based computing, contextualizing its development within the broader trajectory of computational science. The decision to base the chapter on the author's contributions was made to minimize overlaps with other Chapters in the Book, which aims to celebrate the 25th anniversary of WOA by drawing from the papers in its proceedings.

The objectives of the chapter are threefold: *(i)* To provide an overview of the historical foundations of agent-based computing with specif reference to WOA contributions, tracing its origins and early applications in various domains (Historical Perspective); *(ii)* To demonstrate the adaptability of the agent-based paradigm to current scientific and engineering challenges, particularly in light of recent technological advancements such as artificial intelligence (AI), big data, and cloud computing (Contemporary Relevance); *(iii)* To offer insights into the potential future developments of ABC, including its integration with emerging technologies and its growing role in interdisciplinary research (Future Trajectories).

The chapter is structured as follows. Section 2 presents the application of the agent-based paradigm for studying and understanding complex physical and socio-economic systems. In particular, the Agent Based Modeling and Simulation (ABMS) approach and its application to several problems in different scientific domains are discussed with specific reference to contributions presented at WOA. Following the same approach, Sect. 3 presents the application of the agent-based paradigm for the design, development and management of software systems discussing on Agent-Oriented Software Engineering (AOSE), Mobile Agents programming and Distributed software solutions. Section 4 discusses the adaptability of agent-based computing to contemporary challenges and its potential to shape the future of computational modeling. By bridging historical foundations with cutting-edge advancements in AI, virtual and augmented reality (VR/AR), (big)data analytics, pervasive, parallel and distributed computing, the section presents a holistic perspective on the current state of agent-based computing and provides insights into its promising trajectory in the years to come. Finally, Sect. 5 closes the chapter by summarizing its content, the main outcomes and by proposing future research directions.

2   Agent-Based Computing for Systems Modeling and Simulation

The agent-based paradigm is fundamentally distinguished by its decentralized, bottom-up approach to modeling. Unlike traditional equation-based models, which often rely on top-down, aggregate representations of systems, ABC models individual agents, each with its own set of behaviors, goals, and decision-making processes [3,9]. These agents interact within an environment, responding to stimuli, exchanging information, and adapting to changing conditions. The cumulative interactions of many agents can lead to complex, emergent behaviors at the system level, which may not be predictable from the behavior of individual agents alone. This capability makes ABC particularly well-suited to modeling complex adaptive systems, where global dynamics emerge from local interactions [45].

In this context, the section presents the application of the agent-based paradigm for studying and understanding complex physical and socio-economic systems. In particular, the ABMS approach and its application to several problems in different scientific domains are discussed with specific reference to some contributions presented by the author at WOA [35,36] and that paved the way for further research achievements [18,31–33] A more comprehensive view and analysis of the contributions presented at WOA in the last 25 years on Agent-Based Simulation can be found in [55].

Agent Based Modeling and Simulation (ABMS) is a multidisciplinary approach for analyzing and modeling complex system: an approach which is becoming acknowledged for its efficacy in several application domains (financial, economic, social, logistics, physical, chemical, engineering, etc.) [9,20,37,44,45]. ABMS allows for the definition of a system model based on autonomous, goal-driven and interacting entities (agents) organized into societies which is then simulated so to obtain significant information on not only the properties of the system under consideration but also its evolution. Despite the availability of several ABMS tools, few methodologies, involving well-defined processes, are able to cover all the phases from the analysis of the system under consideration to its modeling and subsequent analysis of simulation results [45]. As a result, simulation models are often obtained using the two following approaches: (i) a direct implementation based on a chosen ABMS tool of the simulation model whose abstraction level is then too low and platform dependent as a conceptual modeling phase is not available; (ii) an adaptation a given conceptual system model to a specific ABMS tool which, however, requires additional adaptation,

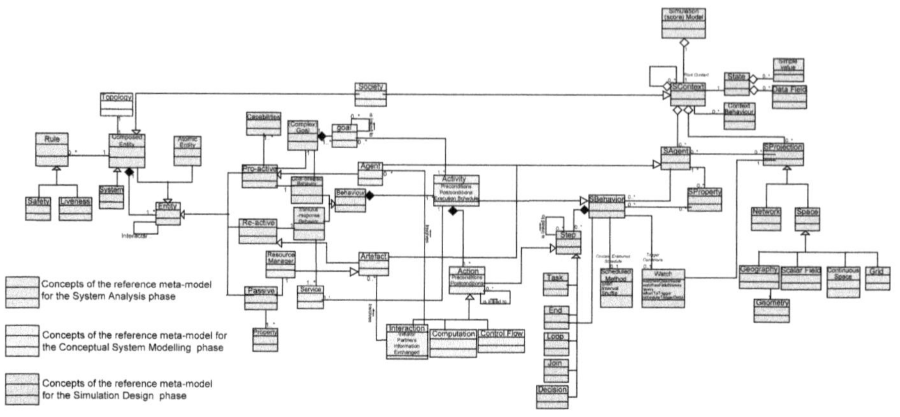

Fig. 1. The reference meta-model of easyABMS [36].

calling for extra work, the amount of which increases depending on the gap between the conceptual and the implementation model of the system. Thus, both approaches lead to simulation models which are difficult to verify, modify and update. To address these issues, in the 10th edition of WOA, the easyABMS methodology has been proposed to seamlessly covering all the phases from the analysis of the system under consideration to its modeling and analysis of simulation results [36] (see Fig. 1). easyABMS fruitfully exploits both AOSE modeling techniques (see Sect. 3) and simulation tools specifically conceived for ABMS and defines an iterative process which is integrated, model-driven and visual. In particular, each phase of the process refines the model of the system which has been produced in the preceding phase and its work-products are mainly constituted by visual diagrams based on the UML notation [50]. In addition, according to the model-driven paradigm [52] the simulation code is automatically generated from the derived system Simulation Model. On the basis of the simulation results, a new/modified and/or refined model of the system can be obtained through a new process iteration which can involve all or some process phases. easyABMS exploits the advanced features of visual modeling and of (semi)automatic code generation provided by the Repast Simphony Toolkit [46], a very popular and open source ABMS platform. easyABMS has been successfully applied in different application domains, from logistics (managing Straddle Carriers in a Container Transshipment Terminal) to social, financial, and economic domains [31,32].

Another interesting field of application of ABMS is related to Game Theory [43]. The complexity of NASH, the problem consisting in computing Nash equilibria in non-cooperative games, has been characterized in the early 2000s [16], but even in the two players case, the best algorithm known (without any constrain on the game structure) has an exponential worst-case running time [51]. Starting from these considerations SALENE, a Multi-Agent System(MAS) for learning Nash Equilibria in non cooperative games, was developed and presented durign the 7th edition of WOA [35]. In particular, considering a static non cooperative game described in its normal form, SALENE is based on the assumptions that if agents representing the players act as rational players, i.e. if each player acts to maximize his expected utility in each match of a game G, and if such agents play k matches of G they will converge in playing one of the Nash Equilibria of the game. In particular, after each match each agent decides the strategy to play in the next match on the basis of his beliefs about the strategies that the other agents are adopting. More specifically, each agent assumes that his beliefs about the other players' strategies are correct and plays a strategy that is a best response to his beliefs. Analyzing the behaviour of each agent in all the k matches of G, SALENE presents to the user an estimate of a Nash Equilibrium of the game. A set of experiments was carried out on different games that differ from each other both in the number and in the kind of Nash Equilibria. The experiments demonstrated that:

- if the game has one Pure Nash Equilibrium the agents converge in playing this equilibrium;
- if the game has one Mixed Nash Equilibrium, the frequency distributions of the pure strategies played by each player asymptotically converge to the mixed Nash Equilibrium of the game;
- if the game has $p > 1$ Pure Nash Equilibria and $s > 1$ Mixed Nash Equilibria the agents converge in playing one of the p Pure Nash Equilibria.

SALENE can be conceived as a heuristic and efficient method for computing at least one Nash Equilibria in a non-cooperative game represented in its normal form; actually, the learning algorithm adopted by the Player Agents has a polynomial running time for both average and worst case [34].

The discussed WOA contributions paved the way for the applications of the ABMS approach in other interesting application domains as reported in [18,33]. In particular, [18] presents X-Learn, an XML-based, multi-agent system for supporting "user-device" adaptive e-learning, i.e. e-learning activities which take into account the profile, past behaviour, preferences and needs of users, as well as the characteristics of the devices they use for these activities. Whereas in [33] is proposed X-MACoP, an XML multi-agent system for supporting a user in the prediction of protein of the three-dimensional structures of proteins. In particular, X-MACoP carries out the following tasks, in a way completely transparent for the user: (i) choice of the most promising predictor team to apply for the prediction problem of interest for the user; (ii) integration of the results produced by the predictors of the team for constructing a unique global prediction for the user; (iii) possible translation of predictor inputs and outputs in such a way that a user handles a unique data format.

The heterogeneity of these applications and the quality of the achieved results clearly demonstrated the potential of ABMS to represent a main scientific tool to face with the complexity of natural and artificial systems.

3 Agent-Based Computing for Software Engineering

As discussed in Sect. 2, while Agent-Based Computing is widely recognized for its effectiveness in modeling and simulating complex systems, its applicability extends beyond these domains and offers significant advantages in the field of software engineering [14,39]. Indeed, agents, as autonomous, modular entities capable of local decision-making and interaction, provide a robust framework for designing, developing, and managing complex software systems, especially as systems become more distributed, heterogeneous, and adaptive; in particular:

- The agent-based paradigm naturally supports the principles of modularity and autonomy, as each agent represents a distinct, self-contained unit of functionality. This modularity enables to create loosely coupled systems where each agent can be developed, tested, and deployed independently, reducing the risk of system-wide failures and simplifying maintenance. Moreover, the autonomous nature of agents is particularly beneficial in environments where systems must adapt dynamically to changing requirements or conditions.
- The agent paradigm is inherently well-suited to distributed and parallel computing environments due to its decentralized architecture. In distributed systems, agents can be deployed across multiple machines or nodes, each performing local computations and interacting with other agents in a networked environment. Moreover, each agent operates independently, meaning tasks can be processed concurrently, leveraging multi-core processors or parallel computing platforms. This parallelism improves the efficiency and scalability of software solutions, particularly in domains like real-time data processing, distributed simulations, or multi-agent collaborative systems.
- Agents can be designed to perceive changes in their environment, make decisions based on these perceptions, and adapt their behavior accordingly. This is particularly useful in applications where conditions evolve over time, such as autonomous robotics, adaptive user interfaces, or smart grids.
- Agents can engage in proactive behaviors, pursuing goals and reacting to unforeseen events. This level of adaptability enables software systems to handle complex interactions, anticipate user needs, or recover gracefully from unexpected failures. In dynamic environments, like real-time traffic management or automated trading systems, the ability of agents to operate autonomously and adjust to external conditions makes them a valuable paradigm for building adaptive, real-time systems.
- The agent paradigm also supports application domains requiring collaborative software systems, where different components must work together to achieve shared objectives. In MASs, agents can cooperate, negotiate, and coordinate their actions to solve problems that are too complex for a single agent or module to handle. This is particularly relevant in distributed applications, collaborative and swarm intelligence systems, where multiple agents must communicate and collaborate to complete tasks.
- Agent-based systems can facilitate and promote interoperability between heterogeneous components. Since agents are designed to be autonomous and

modular, they can be integrated into larger systems with minimal dependencies. This makes the agent paradigm well-suited for building software that must interface with diverse technologies or legacy systems, as is often the case in enterprise architectures, smart cities, or healthcare systems.
- The agent paradigm inherently supports fault-tolerance by distributing functionality across multiple agents that can operate independently. This means that the failure of a single agent does not necessarily lead to system-wide failure, allowing for greater fault tolerance.
- Agents can be deployed across multiple nodes and communicate via decentralized protocols, thus agent-based systems are inherently scalable. New agents can be added to handle additional tasks, manage higher loads, or replace failed agents without requiring major system overhauls. This makes the agent paradigm ideal for applications that need to scale dynamically, such as web services, financial trading platforms, or cloud-based applications.

Starting from such premises, this section presents the exploitation of the agent-based paradigm in the field of software engineering with specific reference to the contributions presented by the author at WOA and related to:

- methodologies for Agent-Oriented Software Engineering (AOSE) [17,25,26, 29] (see Sect. 3.1);
- frameworks for Mobile Agents Programming [22] (see Sect. 3.2);
- applications of AOSE to heterogeneous domains ranging from Content Distribution Networks (CDN) to Workflow Management Systems (WfMS) [27,28] (see Sect. 3.3).

An in depth analysis on the application of Software Agents for intelligent Internet of Things (IoT) systems can instead be found in another chapter of this book [10].

3.1 Agent-Oriented Software Engineering (AOSE)

Several methodologies supporting analysis, design and implementation of MAS have been proposed in the context of Agent Oriented Software Engineering (AOSE) [15]. Although such methodologies have different advantages when applied to specific problems it seems to be widely accepted that a unique methodology cannot be general enough to be useful to everyone without some level of customization. In fact, agent designers, for solving specific problems in a specific application context, often prefer to define their own methodology specifically tailored for their needs instead of reusing an existing one. Thus, an approach that combines the designer's need of defining his own methodology with the advantages and the experiences coming from the existing and documented methodologies is highly required. A possible solution to this problem is to adopt the method engineering paradigm so enabling designers of MAS to use phases or models or elements coming from different methodologies in order to build up a customized approach for their own problems [38]. In this direction, durign the 5th edition of WOA, two approaches for the construction of agent-oriented

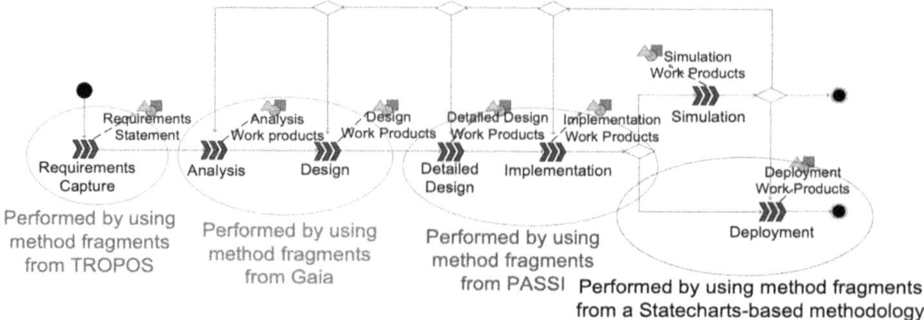

Fig. 2. The Development process-driven methods integration [25].

methodologies by using methods integration were proposed [25]: (i) meta-model-driven, which is based on the MAS meta-model adopted by the designer for the development of a MAS for a specific problem in a specific application domain; (ii) development process-driven, which is based on the instantiation of a software development process in which each phase is carried out using appropriate method fragments (see Fig. 2). These approaches were intensively experimented and have been adopted by the FIPA Methodology Technical Committee (TC) [30].

Routed on the above presented results, in [17] the authors presents PROCE (PROcess Composition and execution Environment), an agent-based CAME (Computer Aided Method-Engineering) and CASE (Computer Aided Software Engineering) tool which supports the composition of software development processes, based on the Method Engineering paradigm, and their execution. PROCE is a Multi Agent System, in which both method fragments and the processes derived from their composition are represented by agents. This approach provides an effective solution to the issue of fragment composition that can be based on the cooperation among agents. Moreover, the agent-based representation of the development process allows a more effective process execution. In fact, the agentified method fragments, in the CAME phase, cooperate to build up the development process, whereas, in the CASE stage, cooperate to support its execution (each agent is in charge of a portion of the process and interacts with the others by exchanging fragment work products). In order to verify the effectiveness and the efficacy of PROCE in method fragments composition and processes execution, an experimentation was carried out in the Service Oriented Architecture (SOA) domain showing how it represents an effective solution able to combine the definition of ad-hoc methodology with the reuse of existing ones (see Fig. 3).

Simulation of agent-based systems is another important requirement of an agent-oriented software development process. Indeed, Simulation provides developers with a powerful means to validate both agents' dynamic behavior and the agent system as a whole and investigate the implications of alternative architec-

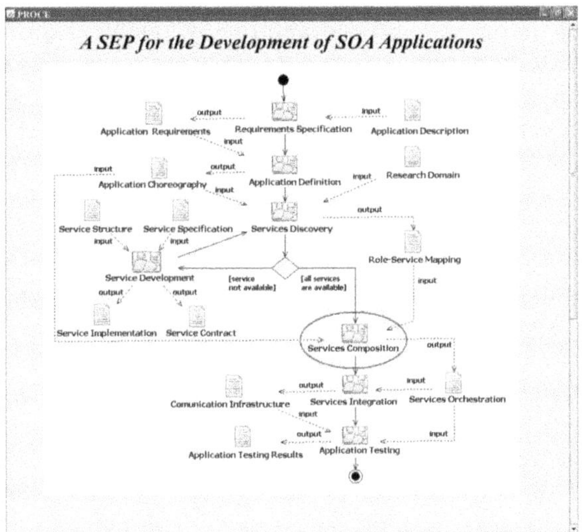

Fig. 3. The Software Engineering Process for the development of SOA Applications implemented in PROCE [17].

tures and coordination strategies. In this context, [26], presented at WOA 2005, proposes a discrete-event simulation framework which supports the validation activity of agent-based and multi-agent systems which are modeled and programmed as a set of event-driven agents by means of the Distilled StateCharts formalism and related programming tools. The simulation framework is equipped with a discrete-event simulation engine which provides support for the execution of agents by interleaving their events processing, the exchange of events among agents, the migration of agents, and the clustering of agents into agent servers interconnected by a logical network. Using this framework, an agent-based complex system can be easily validated and evaluated by defining a simulator program along with suitable test cases and performance measurements. The simulation framework is organized in four layers: (i) low-level simulation framework, which provides the basic mechanisms and classes to simulate general purpose systems; (ii) agent platform, which is built atop the low-level simulation framework and provides a distributed infrastructure formed by a network of interconnected agent servers; (iii) ELA (Event-driven Lightweight Agent) adapter, which allows to map event-driven DSC (Distilled State Charts)-based lightweight agents onto the agent platform layer; (iv) user, which provides abstractions representing interacting users and users' behaviors. Using this framework, an agent-based complex system can be easily validated and evaluated by defining a simulator program along with suitable test cases and performance measurements.

As an evolution of the previous solution, [29] describes ELDATool, a Statecharts-based visual tool for the rapid prototyping of Multi-Agent Systems based on the Event-driven Lightweight Distilled Statecharts-based Agents (ELDA) model. In particular, the ELDATool, which is implemented in Java as an Eclipse plug-in, supports an iterative process involving the following phases: detailed design, automatic code generation and simulation. The high-level design, which is the input to this iterative process, can be obtained through currently available agent-oriented methodologies (such as PASSI and GAIA) [15]. In order to show the main characteristics of the ELDATool, a simple case study concerning with the modelling of a contractor mobile agent within an agent-based e-Marketplace is presented. According to the ELDA model [21] a multi-agent system is modelled at high-level as a set of different types of agents and a set of interaction events among the agents. An ELDA agent consists of a unique identifier, a data space, a dynamic behaviour, a single thread of control, and a queue of the received events. In particular, the dynamic behaviour of an agent is specified through the Distilled Statecharts formalism, derived from the well-known Statecharts. Modelling an agent is basically carried out by specifying its behaviour as a hierarchical state machine compliant with the state-based template of the FIPA agent [30] and by defining the events which can be received and generated. While events are implicitly received through the event queue, they are explicitly emitted through the generate primitive. The received events are called IN-events, whereas the generated events are called OUT-events. In particular, events formalize three kinds of interactions: (i) internal, which are sent by the agent to itself to proactively drive its activity; (ii) management, which are used to interact with the agent management system for requesting services and resources; (iii) coordination, which are exploited to interact with local or remote agents/entities through a given coordination space.

3.2   Mobile Agents

In the application of the agent paradigm to the engineering of software systems, one of the key property of agents, which leads to several contributions in the WOA community, was mobility [40]. In particular, an interesting issue concerning with the design of mobile agent interactions regards how to clearly identify which agents will be interacting and how their interactions can be modeled. To deal with mobile agent interactions, communication paradigms and mechanisms as well as coordination models and architectures for non mobile software components, have been enhanced to be mobility-aware (message-passing, tuple space, publish/subscribe, etc.) and new ones have been purposely defined for logical and physical mobility (meeting, blackboard, shared transiently tuple spaces, reactive tuples) [12]. Moreover, several design patterns have been proposed for driving the design of mobile agent interactions [4] and programmable coordination models and related frameworks (e.g. TuCSoN [48]) are available. Although different mobile agent frameworks already offer several mechanisms based on the aforementioned communication/coordination paradigms and architectures, mobile agent interactions are typically designed on the basis of a single paradigm which is mainly based on message passing or, in some application domains, on tuple spaces. However, single model based communication/coordination might not be effective for satisfying all the needs of mobile agent interactions in all possible application scenarios. As a consequence, the exploitation of multiple communication/coordination paradigms, namely Multi-Coordination, represents an effective solution to enhance design effectiveness, improve efficiency, and enable adaptability in dynamic and heterogeneous computing environments. In particular, Multi-Coordination allows agents to choose among a variety of different communication/coordination paradigms which best fit mobile agent interaction needs. One of the first multi-coordination approach for the design and evaluation of mobile agent interactions was proposed in the 9th edition of WOA [22]. In the paper, the design is based on a procedure which uses suitable agent interaction patterns to fulfill agent coordination requirements. In particular, interaction patterns are first characterized by appositely defined parameters and associated to specific coordination models according to such parameters; then, the most appropriate coordination model is selected for implementing a given interaction pattern so providing a design solution for the related coordination requirement. The evaluation is based on a discrete-event simulation framework which allows to evaluate the designed solutions in terms of performance indices with reference to given application scenarios. In particular, the simulation framework provides effective abstractions for easily programming mobile agent interaction scenarios and flexibly supporting configuration, execution and evaluation of such scenarios. The proposed multi-coordination approach makes it possible the definition of alternative design solutions and their evaluation and comparison from qualitative (i.e. according to design effectiveness criteria) and quantitative (i.e. according to performance indices) points of view. To show a concrete application of the proposed approach, a significant case study related to mobile agent-based distributed information retrieval is also reported in the paper.

3.3   Agent-Based Applications

The methodologies and frameworks presented in the previous sections allowed to design and develop several agent-based applications in heterogeneous domains ranging from Content Distribution Networks to Workflow Systems.

In [27], presented at WOA 2006, the authors propose an agent-based approach for the distributed enactment of workflows. The workflow enactment is enabled by an Agent-based Workflow Enactment Framework (AWEF) which is instantiated on the basis of the schemas of the workflows to be enacted so obtaining specific workflow engines. A workflow schema can be defined by using the Workflow Patterns identified and proposed by van der Aalst [1] and can be represented using YAWL (Yet Another Workflow Language) [2]. A workflow engine therefore consists of a MAS capable of managing instances of the workflow schema used for the instantiation of the workflow engine. Each MAS adopts a hierarchical organizational structure composed by an EnacterAgent, which is responsible of the activation and monitoring of the workflow, one or more ManagerAgents, which are responsible of the execution and control of the workflow/subworkflows according to a parent/child model, and one or more TaskAgents, which are responsible of the execution of internal tasks and/or of the wrapping of external tasks or services (see Fig. 4). The hierarchical distribution

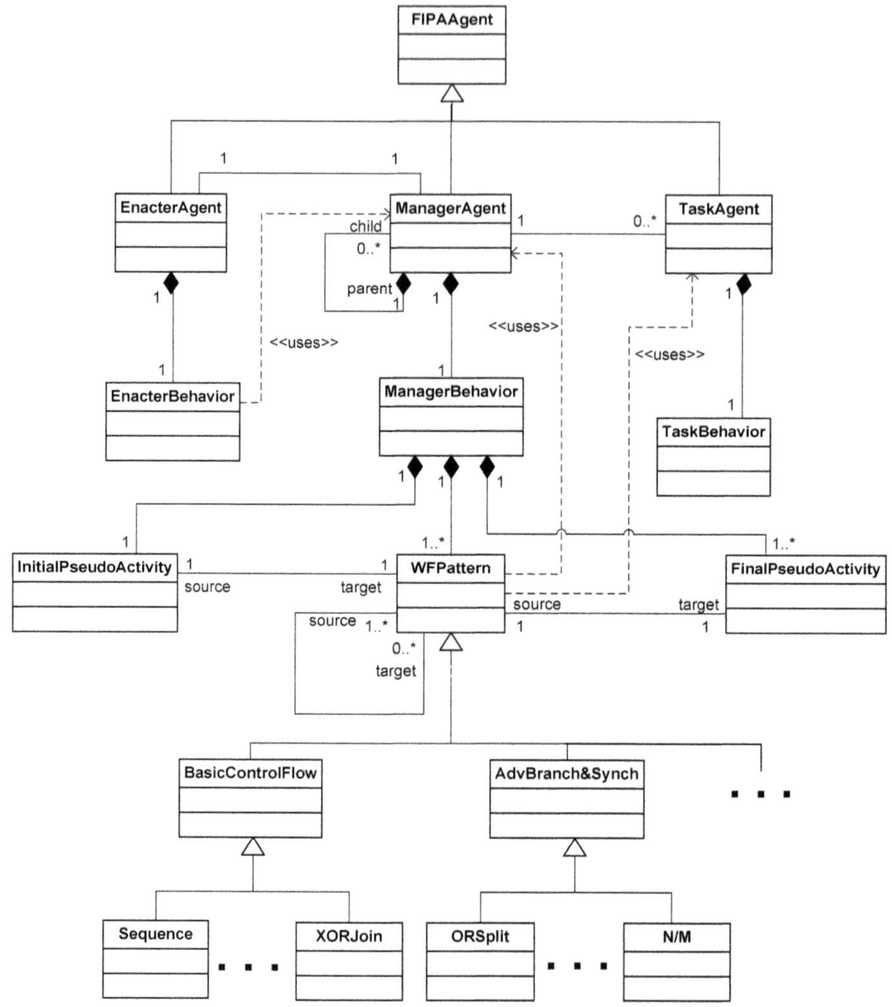

Fig. 4. The Class diagram of the AWEF Framework [27].

of the workflow execution control between the ManagerAgents and the distribution of the computation among the TaskAgents allow for more flexible, efficient, and robust enactment services. The framework is implemented by using JADE,[1] a FIPA-compliant [30] Java-based agent development environment which basically offers a distributed agent platform and an API for agent programming. The JADE-based implementation of AWEF has been applied to the development of a workflow system for the monitoring of distributed agro-industrial productive processes. The developed workflow system is a component of a larger system which

---

[1] https://jade.tilab.com.

was built in the context of the M.ENTE (Management of integrated ENTErprise) project which aims at developing a pervasive system for the control and management of productive, organizational, and business processes of companies working in the agro-alimentary industry of Calabria. The experimentation of the system provides support to a consortium of agro-industrial greenhouses.

In [28], presented at WOA 2011, the agent-based approach is exploited for modeling and evaluating through simulation different Content Distribution Networks (or, Content Delivery Networks, CDNs) architectures that represent effective solution for improving the performance of content delivery by means of coordinated content replication [11]. In particular, five distributed architectures (Conventional, Cooperative, Master/Slave, Multicast-based, Peer-to-Peer) have been modeled and extensively evaluated. Clustered and Cooperative architectures differ from Conventional architectures as surrogate servers can loosely (in the Cooperative architectures) or tightly (in the Clustered architectures) cooperate to provide the requested contents to users. To analyze the performances of the five considered architectures with respect to the most important CDN performance indices (average perceived user latency, cache hit ratio, and CDN utility) [53], for each architecture, an agent-based model has been defined and simulated by using the ELDAMeth methodology [23]. In particular, the modeling phase is driven by a Statecharts-based modeling language and supported by a CASE tool (ELDATool) which automatically translates visual specifications into platform-independent code; the simulation phase is based on an agent-oriented and event-driven simulation framework (ELDASim) which executes the code produced in the modeling phase in the context of purposely set distributed scenarios (see Sect. 3.1). The results obtained from the performance evaluation phase show that the Clustered architectures can provide higher performances, in terms of the considered performance indices, than those of Conventional and Cooperative architectures.

4   Back to the Future and Beyond

As stated by the WOA contributions illustrated in the previous sections, Agent-based computing (ABC) has demonstrated remarkable adaptability in addressing contemporary scientific and engineering challenges, emerging as a pivotal computational paradigm in a rapidly evolving technological landscape. Rooted in historical foundations that trace back to complex system modeling and distributed programming, ABC's core strength lies in its decentralized, autonomous agents that can interact, learn, and adapt dynamically. These properties make ABC especially suited to tackle the intricate, non-linear, and heterogeneous problems that increasingly define today's scientific, engineering, and societal challenges. One of the most compelling aspects of agent-based computing is its ability to bridge the past and future of computational modeling by integrating with cutting-edge technologies such as AI, VR/AR, big data analytics, and parallel and distributed computing. This confluence of technologies has significantly enhanced the potential of ABC, enabling it to respond flexibly to complex scenarios while pushing the boundaries of simulation, prediction, and optimization in various domains. In the following, the intersections between ABC and the above-mentioned technologies is shortly discussed along with their potential benefits and applications.

4.1 Synergy with AI and Machine Learning

The incorporation of AI and machine learning (ML) into ABC represents a transformative shift in the field [54]. Historically, agent-based models (ABMs) relied on rules to simulate agent behaviors. However, with advancements in AI, agents can now exhibit more sophisticated decision-making processes, learning from their environment and interactions in real time. This adaptability is crucial in fields such as robotics, autonomous systems, and smart infrastructures, where agents must operate in unpredictable or dynamic environments. By integrating ML algorithms, agents are capable of continuously evolving their strategies, leading to more realistic and scalable models in domains such as traffic management, supply chain optimization, and disaster response.

4.2 Enhanced Visualization Through VR/AR

Virtual and augmented reality technologies have also enhanced the way agent-based models are visualized and understood. Traditionally, Agent-Based Models (ABMs) provided two-dimensional or simplified three-dimensional representations of agent interactions. VR/AR, however, offers immersive environments where stakeholders, researchers, and engineers can interact with agents and their behaviors in real-time, facilitating deeper insights into complex systems [47]. In fields such as urban planning, environmental management, and healthcare, VR/AR-enhanced ABMs can simulate real-world scenarios at a granular level, allowing for more informed decision-making and experimental interventions in simulated environments before deployment in the real world.

4.3 Integration with Big Data Analytics

The rise of big data analytics has further catalyzed the relevance of agent-based computing in addressing large-scale, data-driven problems. By leveraging vast datasets generated by IoT devices, social networks, and other pervasive systems, agent-based models can be designed to simulate large populations of agents with unique characteristics and behaviors based on real-world data [44]. This approach is especially valuable in fields such as epidemiology, where agent-based models can predict the spread of diseases by analyzing real-time health and mobility data, or in economics, where consumer behavior and market dynamics can be simulated on a massive scale. The ability of ABC to integrate and analyze big data ensures that models remain relevant, accurate, and capable of generating actionable insights in an era of data-driven decision-making.

4.4 Scalability Through Pervasive, Parallel, and Distributed Computing

Scalability has traditionally been a challenge for agent-based models, particularly when simulating large systems with millions of agents. However, the advent of pervasive, parallel, and distributed computing has addressed this limitation. Cloud computing platforms, distributed networks, and multi-core processors now provide the computational resources needed to execute complex agent-based simulations at scale [49]. This has broad applications in fields like climate modeling, where the interactions between thousands of environmental agents must be computed in real-time, or in social science simulations that track the behavior of entire populations under varying policy interventions. With the computational bottlenecks alleviated, ABC is well-positioned to tackle increasingly complex and large-scale systems that demand high-performance computing.

5 Conclusion

Looking ahead, agent-based computing is set to become even more integral to the future of computational modeling, particularly as interdisciplinary collaboration between fields continues to grow. With AI continuing to evolve, future ABMs will likely feature agents with even more advanced cognitive abilities, capable of reasoning, foresight, and long-term planning. The convergence of ABC with quantum computing could unlock unprecedented computational power, allowing for simulations of complex systems that are currently infeasible due to computational constraints.

Moreover, the increasing ubiquity of edge computing and the IoT will drive the evolution of ABC into more decentralized models, where agents operate across distributed networks, processing data and making decisions locally in real-time (see [10]). This paradigm is particularly relevant in applications such as smart cities, autonomous transportation, and environmental monitoring, where the ability to process information and adapt quickly to changing conditions is critical.

In summary, agent-based computing has not only adapted to contemporary challenges but is also poised to shape the future of computational modeling in profound ways. By bridging its historical foundations with cutting-edge advancements in AI, VR/AR, big data analytics, and distributed computing, ABC is transforming from a niche modeling, simulating and programming tool into a versatile, scalable, and essential framework for addressing the complexity of modern scientific and engineering problems. As technological advancements continue, the future of ABC looks bright, promising new opportunities for innovation and discovery across a wide range of disciplines.

Acknowledgments. This chapter aimed to exploring the past, present, and future of agent-based computing following the path traced by several contributions presented at WOA during the last decades. Such contributions have been mainly written by the author of this chapter together with several colleagues: the author has just tried to provide a short but effective summary of these works! Many thanks to Wilma Russo for leading most of the contributions presented in the Chapter, Giancarlo Fortino and all the other co-authors for their invaluable contribution to the presented research results.

References

1. van der Aalst, W.M.P., ter Hofstede, A.H.M.: YAWL: yet another workflow language. Inf. Syst. **30**(4), 245–275 (2005). https://doi.org/10.1016/j.is.2004.02.002
2. van der Aalst, W.M.P., ter Hofstede, A.H.M., Kiepuszewski, B., Barros, A.P.: Workflow patterns. Distrib. Parallel Databases **14**(3), 5–51 (2003). https://doi.org/10.1023/A:1022883727209
3. Aguzzi, G., Casadei, R., Pianini, D., Viroli, M.: Self-organisation with aggregate computing: a reflection under the lenses of multi-agent systems engineering. In: Mascardi and Omicini [42]
4. Aridor, Y., Lange, D.B.: Agent design patterns: elements of agent application design. In: Sycara, K.P., Wooldridge, M. (eds.) AGENTS 1998: Proceedings of the 2nd International Conference on Autonomous Agents, pp. 108–115. ACM, Minneapolis, Minnesota, US (1998). https://doi.org/10.1145/280765.280784
5. Baldoni, M., Boccalatte, A., De Paoli, F., Martelli, M., Mascardi, V. (eds.): WOA 2007 – 8th Workshop "From Objects to Agents". Seneca Edizioni Torino, Genova, Italy (2007). http://woa07.disi.unige.it/ProceedingsWOA2007.zip
6. Baldoni, M., Cossentino, M., De Paoli, F., Seidita, V. (eds.): WOA 2008 – 9th Workshop "From Objects to Agents". Seneca Edizioni Torino, Palermo, Italy (2008). http://www.pa.icar.cnr.it/woa08/materiali/Proceedings.pdf
7. Baldoni, M., De Paoli, F., Martelli, A., Omicini, A. (eds.): WOA 2004 – 5th Workshop "From Objects to Agents". Pitagora Editrice Bologna, Torino, Italy (2004). http://lia.deis.unibo.it/books/woa2004/atti.pdf
8. Bergenti, F. (ed.): WOA 2009 – 10th Workshop "From Objects to Agents". Seneca Edizioni Torino, Parma, Italy (2009). http://www.ailab.unipr.it/woa09/papers/
9. Bonabeau, E.: Agent-based modeling: methods and techniques for simulating human systems. Proc. Natl. Acad. Sci. **99 Suppl 3**, 7280–7287 (2002). https://doi.org/10.1073/pnas.082080899
10. Bouleanu, D.C., Loaiza Carrillo, M.A., Savaglio, C., Bădică, C., Gravina, R., Fortino, G.: From objects to agents, and back to smart objects: software agents for intelligent Internet of Things (IoT) systems. In: Mascardi and Omicini [42]
11. Buyya, R., Pathan, M., Vakali, A. (eds.): Content Delivery Networks. Lecture Notes in Electrical Engineering, vol. 9. Springer (2008). https://doi.org/10.1007/978-3-540-77887-5
12. Cabri, G., Leonardi, L., Zambonelli, F.: Mobile-agent coordination models for internet applications. IEEE Comput. **33**(2), 82–89 (2000). https://doi.org/10.1109/2.820044
13. Corradini, F., De Paoli, F., Merelli, E., Omicini, A. (eds.): WOA 2005 – 6th Workshop "From Objects to Agents". Pitagora Editrice Bologna, Camerino, MC, Italy (2005). http://lia.deis.unibo.it/books/woa2005/atti.pdf
14. Cossentino, M., Sabatucci, L., Seidita, V.: Designing agent-oriented systems. In: Mascardi and Omicini [42]
15. Dam, K.H., Winikoff, M.: Comparing agent-oriented methodologies. In: Giorgini, P., Henderson-Sellers, B., Winikoff, M. (eds.) Agent-Oriented Information Systems. AOIS 2003. Lecture Notes in Computer Science, vol. 3030, pp. 78–93. Springer (2003). https://doi.org/10.1007/978-3-540-25943-5_6

16. Daskalakis, C., Goldberg, P.W., Papadimitriou, C.H.: The complexity of computing a Nash equilibrium. Technical Report TR05-115, Electronic Colloquium on Computational Complexity (ECCC) (2005). https://eccc.weizmann.ac.il/report/2005/115/
17. De Luca, F., Tundis, A., Garro, A.: PROCE: an agent-based PROcess Composition and execution Environment. In: Fortino et al. [24], pp. 171–174. http://ceur-ws.org/Vol-741/DEM02_DeLucaTundisGarro.pdf
18. De Meo, P., Garro, A., Terracina, G., Ursino, D.: Personalizing learning programs with X-Learn, an XML-based, "user-device" adaptive multi-agent system. Inf. Sci. **177**(8), 1729–1770 (2007). https://doi.org/10.1016/j.ins.2006.10.005
19. De Paoli, F., Di Stefano, A., Omicini, A., Santoro, C. (eds.): WOA 2006 – 7th Workshop "From Objects to Agents", CEUR Workshop Proceedings, vol. 204. Catania, Italy (2006). http://ceur-ws.org/Vol-204/
20. Epstein, J.M.: Generative Social Science: Studies in Agent-Based Computational Modeling. Princeton University Press, Princeton, NJ (2006)
21. Fortino, G., Russo, W., Zimeo, E.: A statecharts-based software development process for mobile agents. Inf. Softw. Technol. **46**(13), 907–921 (2004)
22. Fortino, G., Garro, A., Mascillaro, S., Russo, W.: Using multi-coordination for the design of mobile agent interactions. In: Baldoni et al. [6], pp. 122–128. http://www.pa.icar.cnr.it/woa08/materiali/paper/paper_11.pdf
23. Fortino, G., Garro, A., Mascillaro, S., Russo, W.: Using event-driven lightweight DSC-based agents for MAS modelling. Int. J. Agent-Oriented Softw. Eng. **4**(2), 113–119 (2010). https://doi.org/10.1504/IJAOSE.2010.032798, Special Issue: "From Agent Theory to Agent Implementation 6" – – a Selection of Contributions
24. Fortino, G., Garro, A., Palopoli, L., Russo, W., Spezzano, G. (eds.): WOA 2011 – 12th Workshop "From Objects to Agents", CEUR Workshop Proceedings, vol. 741. Rende, Italy (2011). http://ceur-ws.org/Vol-741/
25. Fortino, G., Garro, A., Russo, W.: Using method engineering for the construction of agent-oriented methodologies. In: Baldoni et al. [7], pp. 51–54. http://giuseppevizzari.github.io/WOA-proceedings-archive/pdfs/woa2004/8.pdf
26. Fortino, G., Garro, A., Russo, W.: A discrete-event simulation framework for the validation of agent-based and multi-agent systems. In: Corradini et al. [13], pp. 75–84. http://lia.deis.unibo.it/books/woa2005/papers/11.pdf
27. Fortino, G., Garro, A., Russo, W.: Distributed workflow enactment: an agent-based framework. In: De Paoli et al. [19], pp. 110–117. http://ceur-ws.org/Vol-204/P08.pdf
28. Fortino, G., Garro, A., Russo, W., Vaccaro, M.: Performance evaluation of content distribution network architectures through agent-based modeling and simulation. In: Fortino et al. [24], pp. 158–165. http://ceur-ws.org/Vol-741/ID18_FortinoGarroRussoVaccaro.pdf
29. Fortino, G., Garro, A., Mascillaro, S., Russo, W.: ELDATool: a statecharts-based tool for prototyping multi-agent systems. In: Baldoni et al. [5], pp. 14–19. http://woa07.dibris.unige.it/papers/D2_ForGarMasRus-WOA07-Demo.pdf
30. Foundation for Intelligent Physical Agents (FIPA): FIPA specifications. http://www.fipa.org/specifications/. Accessed 21 June 2025
31. Garro, A., Russo, W.: An integrated agent-based process for the simulation of complex systems. In: Proceedings of the International Conference on Economic Science with Heterogeneous Interacting Agents (ESHIA), Warsaw, Poland (2008)
32. Garro, A., Russo, W.: An integrated and iterative process for agent-based modeling and simulation. In: Proceedings of the 5th International Conference of the European Social Simulation Association (ESSA), Brescia, Italy (2008)

33. Garro, A., Terracina, G., Ursino, D.: A multi-agent system for supporting the prediction of protein structures. Integr. Comput.-Aided Eng. **11**(3), 259–280 (2004)
34. Garro, A.: Learning Nash equilibria in non-cooperative games. In: Encyclopedia of Artificial Intelligence, pp. 1018–1023. Information Science Reference, Hershey, PA, USA (2008)
35. Garro, A., Iusi, M.: Software agents for learning Nash equilibria in non-cooperative games. In: De Paoli et al. [19], pp. 10–15. http://ceur-ws.org/Vol-204/D04.pdf
36. Garro, A., Russo, W.: Exploiting the easyABMS methodology in social and economic domains. In: Bergenti [8], pp. 8–15. http://www.ailab.unipr.it/woa09/papers/Garro.pdf
37. Helbing, D.: Social Self-Organization: Agent-Based Simulations and Experiments to Study Emergent Social Behavior. Springer (2012)
38. Henderson-Sellers, B.: Method engineering for OO systems development. Commun. ACM **46**(10) (2003). https://doi.org/10.1145/944217.944242
39. Jennings, N.R.: On agent-based software engineering. Artif. Intell. **117**(2), 277–296 (2000). https://doi.org/10.1016/S0004-3702(99)00107-1
40. Kendall, E.A., Krishna, P.V.M., Pathak, C.V., Suresh, C.B.: Patterns of intelligent and mobile agents. In: Proceedings of the Second International Conference on Autonomous Agents (AGENTS 1998), pp. 92–99. Association for Computing Machinery, New York, NY, USA (1998)
41. Luck, M., McBurney, P., Preist, C.: Agent Technology: Enabling Next Generation Computing: A Roadmap for Agent-Based Computing. AgentLink/University of Southampton (2003). https://eprints.soton.ac.uk/257309/1/al2roadmap.pdf
42. Mascardi, V., Omicini, A. (eds.): The Agents Journey: Twenty-Five Years of Multi-agent Systems at WOA. Lecture Notes in Computer Science – State-of-the-Art Surveys. Springer (2026)
43. Maschler, M., Solan, E., Zamir, S.: Game Theory. Cambridge University Press (2020). https://doi.org/10.1017/9781108636049
44. Murić, G., et al.: Large-scale agent-based simulations of online social networks. Auton. Agents Multi-Agent Syst. **36**(38) (2022). https://doi.org/10.1007/s10458-022-09565-7
45. North, M.J., Macal, C.M.: Managing Business Complexity: Discovering Strategic Solutions with Agent-Based Modeling and Simulation. Oxford University Press (2007)
46. North, M.J., Tatara, E., Collier, N.T., Ozik, J.: Visual agent-based model development with Repast Simphony. In: Proceedings of the Agent 2007 Conference on Complex Interaction and Social Emergence. Northwestern University, Evanston, IL (2007)
47. Olshannikova, E., Ometov, A., Koucheryavy, Y., Olsson, T.: Visualizing big data with augmented and virtual reality: challenges and research agenda. J. Big Data **2**(22) (2015). https://doi.org/10.1186/s40537-015-0031-2
48. Omicini, A., Zambonelli, F.: Coordination of mobile agents for information systems: the TuCSoN model. In: Badaloni, S., Minnaja, C. (eds.) 6th Convention of the Italian Association for Artificial Intelligence (AI*IA 1998), pp. 94–98. Edizioni Progetto Padova, Padova, Italy (1998)
49. Parry, H.R., Bithell, M.: Large scale agent-based modelling: a review and guidelines for model scaling. In: Agent-Based Models of Geographical Systems, pp. 271–308. Springer (2012). https://doi.org/10.1007/978-90-481-8927-4_14
50. Rumbaugh, J., Jacobson, I., Booch, G.: The Unified Modeling Language Reference Manual, 2nd edn. Pearson Higher Education (2004)

51. Savani, R., von Stengel, B.: Exponentially many steps for finding a Nash equilibrium in a bimatrix game. In: Proceedings of the 45th Symposium on Foundations of Computer Science (FOCS), pp. 258–267 (2004)
52. Schmidt, D.C.: Model-driven engineering. IEEE Comput. **39**(2), 41–47 (2006)
53. Stamos, K., Pallis, G., Vakali, A., Dikaiakos, M.D.: Evaluating the utility of content delivery networks. In: Proceedings of the 4th edition of the UPGRADE-CN Workshop on Use of P2P, GRID and Agents for the Development of Content Networks (UPGRADE-CN 2009), pp. 11–20. ACM, New York, NY, USA (2009)
54. Tesfatsion, L.: Agent-based computational economics: growing economies from the bottom up. Artif. Life **8**(1), 55–82 (2002). https://doi.org/10.1162/106454602753694765
55. Vizzari, G., Briola, D.: Simulation and agent-based simulation at WOA: 25 of years of simulation-related contributions, and an outlook of what awaits us. In: Mascardi and Omicini [42]

Simulation and Agent-Based Simulation at WOA: 25 of Years of Simulation-Related Contributions, and an Outlook of What Awaits Us

Giuseppe Vizzari[(✉)] and Daniela Briola

Department of Informatics, Systems and Communication,
University of Milano–Bicocca, Milano, Italy
{giuseppe.vizzari,daniela.briola}@unimib.it

Abstract. The expression *computer simulation* implies the definition and adoption of a computational model to improve the understanding of some system's behavior and/or to evaluate strategies for its operation, in explanatory or predictive schemes. Computer simulation is quite diffused, since in many situations practical and/or ethical reasons make it impossible to directly observe a system that we want to study or manage. In these cases, the possibility of performing 'in-machina' experiments is often the only, hazardous way to study, analyze and evaluate models of those realities. The Workshop on Objects and Agents (WOA) venue is no exception: in several cases papers presented at WOA discussed simulations carried out to demonstrate the working of an agent-based model or software system, to calibrate or evaluate it. On the other hand, agent-based approaches also represented a set of conceptual, modeling and computational tools that are particularly suited to represent situations characterized by the presence of autonomous entities whose local behaviors (actions and interactions) determine the evolution of the overall system, often in non-trivial ways: agent-based approaches are, in other words, particularly in tune with some of the characteristics of complex systems. This chapter provides a bird's eye view of the relevant contributions presented at WOA in the last 25 years, highlighting the scientific impact of agent-based approaches in the more general area of simulation, and giving a perspective on what we can expect to witness in the near future for this area.

Keywords: Simulation · agent-based modeling · agent-based simulation

1 Introduction

"Computer simulation" belongs to a set of expressions used by a wide range of persons, belonging to very different groups, that are often employed without considering that the communication partners might not share the adopted conception and (typically informal) definition: it is a rather large set, and it also

V. Mascardi and A. Omicini (Eds.): *The Agents Journey*, LNCS 16395, pp. 260–283, 2026.
https://doi.org/10.1007/978-3-032-22940-3_10

includes terms such as "model" and "system" that are even more present in everyday discussions without being rooted on proper definitions. Although we do not have the ambition of joining the philosophical debate on definitions of simulation (or simulation models [51]), we feel the urge to provide a working definition before we start exploring the set of relevant contributions presented at WOA in the last 25 years. To do this, we will borrow elements from the literature and from our prior works (mainly [15] and [12]), clarifying some fuzzy points thanks to the occasion of being invited to contribute this chapter, and trying to consider the evolution of the field.

Let us therefore define the term **computer simulation** as the usage of a computational model to gain additional insights into some system's behavior by envisioning the implications of the modeling choices, but also to evaluate designs and plans without actually bringing them into existence in the real world (e.g. architectural designs, road networks and traffic lights). For sake of simplicity, let us assume that a model is a representation of a system that is object of study (i.e. **target system**), and that the adjective computational adds sufficient precision, formality, and in general constraints enabling the model to be coded in an executable software system. In turn, we will consider a system as "a part of the world that a person (or group of persons) chooses to regard as a whole consisting of components, each component characterized by properties that are selected as being relevant and by actions related to these properties and those of other components" [108].[1]

The usage of simulators, that are thus a sort of "synthetic environments" reproducing essential features and mechanisms that are relevant to the goals of the analyst, is often necessary because the simulated system cannot actually be observed ever in principle (since it does not exist yet, it is currently being designed), or also for ethical (e.g. the safety of humans would be involved) or practical reasons (e.g. costs of experiments or data acquisition, observation of systems characterized by a very slow evolution). As a consequence, simulation can fit both very scientific and extremely practical, application-oriented workflows, kept together by the need of a proxy of a reality (either existing or desired) to be manipulated to support analysis, study, even decision making.

In the vein of what was already proposed by [54] or [78], we can introduce a schema depicted in Fig. 1, that proposes additional concepts of the overall simulation life-cycle:

- we surely have a *synthesis* part of a simulation project, bringing the analyst to define and implement a model and a simulator representing the target system; this artifact can be configured and used to carry out a set of simulations generally in different situations that are relevant to the overall goals of the study, a *simulation campaign*, producing a (potentially very large) set of data describing the dynamics of the system in those conditions according to the defined model;

---

[1] It interesting and significant that Krysten Nygaard was one of the creators of a language called Simula 67.

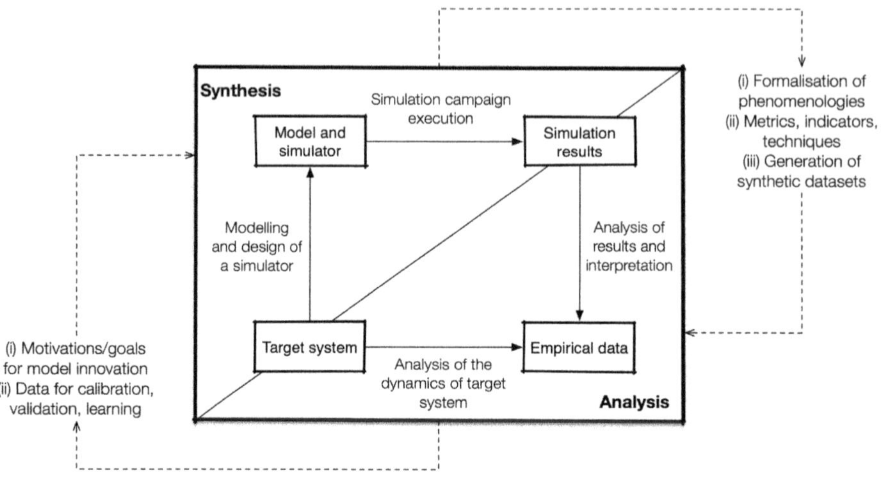

Fig. 1. Simulation as a predictive or explanatory instrument.

- there is necessarily an *analysis* part of the project, that is twofold: on the one hand, the raw data produced by the simulators need to be processed, analyzed, interpreted to produce insights. On the other hand, using a simulator in an "open loop" situation does not assure that the modeling phase led to the definition of a model and corresponding simulator producing results that are in tune with what would be observed in the simulated conditions. The loop must be closed, at least in a representative set of situations, by achieving data about the *actual target system dynamics*, that needs to be analysed to produce empirical data that can be compared with what is produced by the simulator.

For sake of simplicity, we can say that when the empirical evidences produced by simulation system are compatible with those observed in reality within a reasonably representative set of situations we can say that we have performed a *validation* of the model and simulator (the topic is of course more complicated than what we were able to say a few lines, more information can be found, for instance in [85]).

While simulation is typically more closely associated to the synthesis phase, the overall process calls for an integration among the phases, for activities of calibration and validation. Analogously, there are areas of research much more focused on the analysis of real world dynamics (e.g. time series analysis, pattern recognition in images and videos), but in some cases formalization of phenomena studies by means of simulation can provide useful information to research focusing on the analysis side (see, e.g., [139] where pedestrian group detection in videos considered mechanisms earlier adopted by pedestrian simulation models). Moreover, the exploitation of simulators for the production of synthetic datasets is a well-known, although always challenging, approach enabling machine learning (ML) based workflows for automated analysis [113].

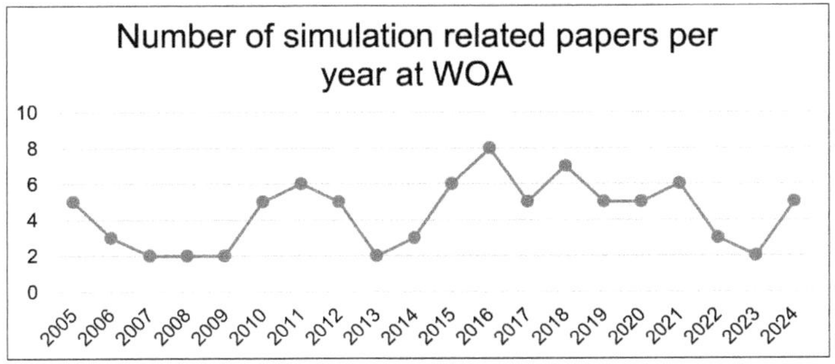

Fig. 2. Number of simulation related contributions per year at WOA.

2   Agents and Simulation: the WOA Perspective

Considering the above introduction of the scenario and especially the proposed definition of computer simulation, we considered the contributions presented at WOA and discussed at the workshop, trying to provide a bird's eye view of the types of work that have been produced by the community through time.

First of all, we started from two artifacts: (i) a large `bib` file including reference information about all papers presented at WOA since 2005, (ii) a spreadsheet including the above information plus abstracts. We selected relevant contributions for the present chapter by (i) filtering out papers not including any match to the pattern `simula*`, (ii) removing duplicates from the results (in some occasions WOA included a demo session in which poster papers could have the same title as the main workshop contribution), (iii) reading title and abstracts and evaluating if the contribution was actually relevant to the chapter.

Unfortunately, we were not able to process with analogous rigor proceedings from year 2000 to 2004: not all manuscripts were available to the authors, and having just the title was not sufficient to properly perform the following analyses[2]. Works such as [10,14,62] could be directly included in our analysis, but for many others simulation might be mentioned in the abstract as a way to evaluate a model or implemented system that is the central topic of the paper, and those works would have been impossible to consider and classify without having at least also the abstract.

As a consequence of the above process, we achieved 87 records of simulation related contributions.[3] The number of simulation related papers per year is

---

[2] This was not a light-hearted decision, but – on the contrary – we want to express our appreciation to excellent services that supported our work and the WOA community such as DBLP – https://dblp.uni-trier.de/ – and CEUR workshop proceedings – https://ceur-ws.org/ – and especially the AIxIA series, managed by Prof. Matteo Baldoni, that is also a pillar of the WOA community.

[3] In 2024 some contributions, denoted as "dissemination papers", were presented but not included in the proceedings, due to prior publication or since authors opted out of the publication process, for instance since the work was undergoing revision in another venue or was in press. These papers were not considered in our analysis, due to the fact that abstracts and manuscripts were not always available.

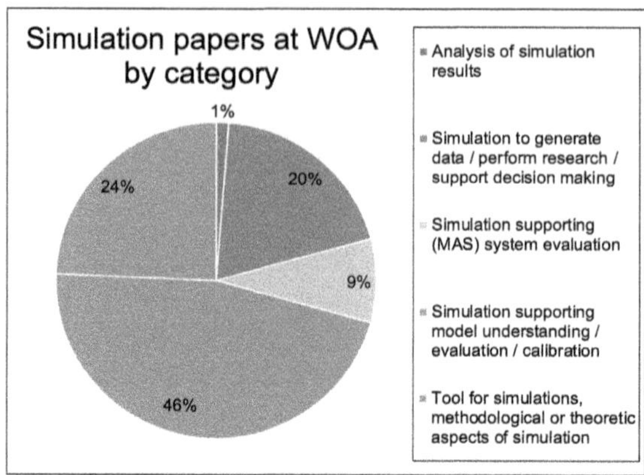

(a) Papers by category

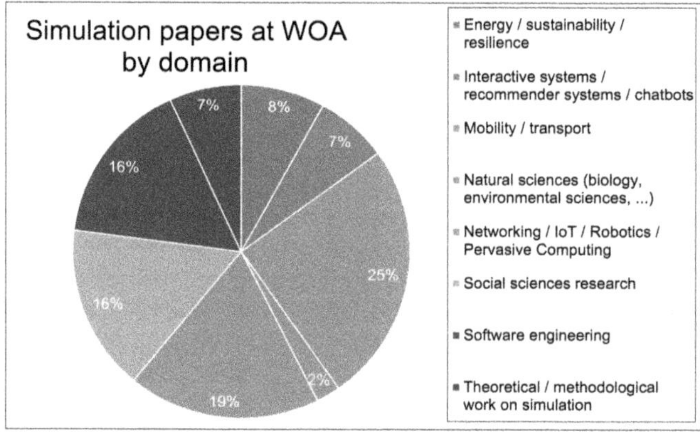

(b) Papers by domain

Fig. 3. Breakdown of simulation related papers at WOA respectively by category (left) and domain (right).

depicted in Fig. 2; the most prolific authors of WOA papers in this subset are Giuseppe Vizzari (16), Giuseppe M. L. Sarnè (14), and Giancarlo Fortino (9), with a number of authors with 7 contributions.

We also defined two controlled vocabularies to add metadata to perform a few analyses of the achieved results, in addition to the obvious ones (such as the authors and the year of publication). In particular, we defined a *category* of contribution, meaning with this vague term the nature of the contribution, the main value of the paper. In particular, we defined the following categories:

- *simulation as main topic*: to support research in some specific domain, to support decision making activities about the target system, or to generate synthetic data: papers in this category are simulation systems that are relatively close to practical applicability, they are on the border of technological transfer;

- *tools supporting simulation, methodological or theoretical aspects of simulation projects*: papers in this category deal with simulation as a central objective of the research, but they are of quite general value and applicability;
- *analysis of simulation results*: papers in this category are mostly focused on what happens after the simulation, and they deal with complex forms of analyses on data generated by simulations;
- *simulation supporting model understanding, evaluation, calibration*: papers in this category are not necessarily focused on simulation activities, but they essentially perform simulations to gain insights on the functioning of the models themselves, in controlled experiments, to support acquiring evidence of system dynamics in given conditions, or to perform evaluation, validation, or calibration activities; as such, these papers are not close to technological transfer, yet;
- *simulation supporting (MAS) system evaluation*: papers in this category are not about simulation, but they rather employ simulation as a form of evaluation of a software system, typically based on autonomous agents or a multi-agent system, or employing agent models or technologies for the simulation activity. Papers in this category are generally close to practical applicability and technological transfer.

The breakdown of papers in the above categories is shown in Fig. 3(a). As we can see, simulation is widely used to gain insights and empirical evidences on how an agent-based or multi-agent model works, or (moving closer to practical application) how a software system employing agent technologies performs in scenarios that mimic some real world deployment by means of a simulation scheme. This is particularly reasonable, since in many cases the agent-based and multi-agent paradigm is a natural choice for distributed systems (recently within cloud/edge/IoT areas), for which it is often hard to perform real-world experiments.

We therefore also defined a *domain of application* for the contribution, meaning with this vague term the areas in which the described model, approach, or software system is intended to be applied. In particular, we defined the following domains:

- *social science research*: synthetic agents have naturally been adopted as representatives of humans or aggregated forms of decision makers (e.g. households, companies) in forms of simulation trying to study socio-economical systems, in the vein of [78]; within the present volume, one chapter presents a discussion of *trust* [134], a very relevant and well studied aspect of social sciences through the lenses of computational modeling, with potential outcomes and applications also to interactive systems, discussed below;
- *natural sciences (biology, environmental sciences, etc.)*: agents have also been employed for the modeling of biological and natural systems, at difference scales and levels of analysis;

Table 1. WOA simulation related papers organized according to year of publication and category of research.

	Analysis of simulation results	Simulation as main topic	Simulation supporting (MAS) system evaluation	Simulation supporting model understanding	Tools, methodological aspects	Total
2005	[13]			[68, 74, 126]	[11]	5
2006				[33]	[60, 109]	3
2007			[72, 142]			2
2008				[9, 66]		2
2009					[76, 88]	2
2010		[92, 105]	[79, 99]		[89]	5
2011		[16, 24, 90, 100]	[69]	[115]		6
2012		[32, 148]		[73]	[91, 119]	5
2013				[45]	[40]	2
2014			[128]	[71, 101]		3
2015				[43, 102]	[27, 39, 41, 120]	6
2016		[104, 124, 130]	[70]	[46]	[30, 93, 125]	8
2017		[18]		[56, 103, 116]	[44]	5
2018		[42]		[21, 57, 131, 136]	[53, 63]	7
2019				[64, 96, 122, 135, 143]		5
2020		[107]		[87, 97, 121]	[80]	5
2021		[114]		[1, 23, 31, 58, 65]		6
2022		[86]		[59, 127]		3
2023				[5, 144]		2
2024		[38]		[112, 118, 123, 137]		5
Total	1	17	7	42	20	87

- *interactive systems, recommender systems, chatbots*: when developing interactive systems the notion of agent has turned out to be very useful, both to simulate actual users (something particularly in tune with the fact that these systems often defined and exploit some form of user model), and sometimes to design the interactive system as an agent, not necessarily but in some cases even with an embodied form; within this application domain, it is worth reminding that, within this volume, a chapter discusses models, approaches, challenges, and results on the topic of identifying (and potentially recommending) partners for interaction [129];
- *software engineering*: a long lasting line of research has seen the crossing of agent technology research and software engineering; simulation has played a role in many of these cases, mostly because the proposed system (designed or evaluated by means of software engineering principles and approaches) was a simulator or to support the evaluation or understanding of a proposed model;
- *networking, IoT, robotics, pervasive computing*: analogously as for the software engineering domain, agents are a natural approach for physically distributed systems, and simulation has been often employed to support the evaluation or understanding of a proposed model or a more mature software system, and sometimes specific simulators have been proposed to model and study very specific robotics systems (i.e. drones); with reference to this domain of application, we remind that a chapter in this volume discusses specifically how software agents can represent a viable solution for intelligent IoT systems [25], while another chapter discusses the Aggregate Computing approach [25] to the programming of collective adaptive systems;
- *mobility, transport*: the traffic and transportation application domain is a particular kind of socio-technical system that, due to the intrinsically distributed nature of the studied phenomena, has often witnessed the application of agent-based models [19];
- *energy, sustainability, resilience*: recent attention to sustainability issues and resilience (we included simulations and researches focusing on measures limiting epidemic outbreaks in this domain) has also influenced the contributions discussed at WOA;
- *theoretical or methodological works on simulation*: finally, also from the point of view of this controlled vocabulary there are works of very general nature, whose applicability spans across the above domains.

The breakdown of papers focusing on the above domains of application is shown in Fig. 3(b): on the one hand, this distribution reflects the research interests of members of the WOA community. On the other hand, it is surely influenced by exogenous tendencies (that have manifested themselves in a dramatic way during the COVID-19 outbreak) and that however see a growing push to achieve *societal impact*, that has become one of the established factors for the evaluation of scientific research, and it is basically the common element shared by the *Sustainable Development Goals* defined by the United Nations[4].

---

[4] https://sdgs.un.org/.

The results of the presented analysis are also shown in a compact way in Table 1 that lists simulation related papers organized according to year of publication and category of research.

3   Agents in Simulation Research

The above analysis of simulation related papers at WOA confirms that, besides supporting research in computer science and engineering already working with agents, research on agent related concepts, models, and technologies has also been instrumental to support scientific research in an impressive range of additional disciplines. A non exhaustive list of areas, that can be useful to have a glimpse of the pervasiveness of the approach, would include social sciences in general [78], in particular an approach called Agent-Based Computational Economics [140], biology [117], urban planning (and sustainability) [106], energy systems (and markets) of different kinds [52], traffic and transportation [19] (in particular we want to highlight the Agents in Traffic and Transportation, a long lasting workshop series that has orbited around the main international conferences in Agent technologies and AI in general for over 20 years[5]).

Various approaches developed in the different areas show, of course, significant differences from a formal, technical, and sometimes also epistemic point of view, but the common standpoint of all the above mentioned researches (and of many other ones that legitimately describe themselves as agent-based) is the fact that the analytical unit of the system is represented by the individual agent, acting and interacting with other entities in a shared environment. This represents a significant difference from models in which the observables are typically the *quantities* of agents, and what is being modeled is their variation over time. For instance, the venerable Lotka-Volterra population dynamics model [149], defined to model the complex interaction among two species, one of which feeds upon the other, is essentially defined as:

$$\frac{dx}{dt} = \alpha x - \beta xy,$$

$$\frac{dy}{dt} = -\gamma y + \delta xy,$$

where x is the number of preys, y is the number of predators, α and γ (constants) account for the efficacy of respectively the prey and predator reproduction processes, β (constant) defines the link between the prey mortality and the number of preys and predators, and δ defines the link between the increase in predators to the number of prey and predators. Despite the age of this model, the overall approach has shown its adequacy to represent nonlinear dynamics and support reasoning and scenario building in the recent COVID outbreak (through Susceptible, Infected, Removed – SIR – or Susceptible, Exposed, Infected, Removed – SEIR – models [82]), and using proper model extensions to account for spatial

---

[5] http://www.ia.urjc.es/ATT/.

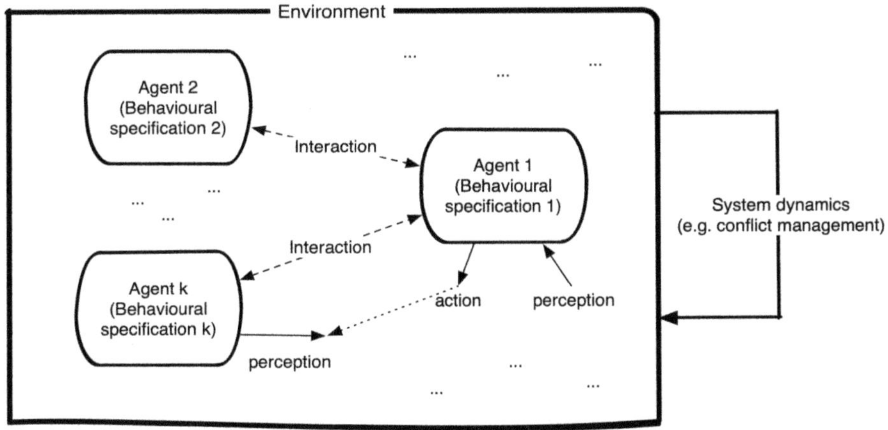

Fig. 4. A reference model for agent-based approaches to simulation.

aspects researchers were able to evaluate the impact of containment measures in terms of reduction of casualties, by exploring counterfactual scenarios [77].

Agent-based models, on the other hand, do not prescript an overall global trend of observables, whereas the overall system dynamic is rather the result of individuals' actions and interactions within the environment. Agents, within this approach, are not governed by outside global rules, but they rather perceive, choose the action to be carried out, by decision making mechanisms that can range from simple reaction rules to knowledge–level processes. It must be stressed that, in some areas of application, agents can represent entities that do act in an environment, but these actions are basically due to the application of physical laws, rather than autonomous decisions. When agents do take decisions, and especially when they represent humans, again research on the synthesis side of the research calls, and in generally interacts with, research on the analysis side, as discussed in the introduction. Whatever the action selection process, the agent attempts to carry it out in the environment, as schematized in Fig. 4. Agent naturally interact indirectly simply because they (and their actions, and the effects of their actions) can be perceived by other agents, but also direct interaction mechanisms could be employed when necessary, convenient, or simply plausible according to the specific modeled reality.

Agents and interaction are therefore central concepts in this kind of models, analogously as in any other scenario of application of agent technologies, but agents' environment [150] within simulation project plays (if possible) an even more prominent role, since:

- it deeply influences the behaviors of the simulated entities, in terms of perceptions;
- it manages dynamic process that unfold independently of agents [83], and it performs an overall regulation function on the overall system [17];

- the aim of the simulation is to observe microscopic or aggregate level behaviors (e.g. the density of a certain type of agent in an area of the environment, the average length of a given path for movements, the generation of clusters of agents), that can actually only be observed in the environment.

Compared to the macroscopic approach taken by population dynamics models, agent-based models require additional information, knowledge, insights about the structure and functioning of a system: getting back to predators and preys, we need to know substantial additional information about these organisms; we cannot simply observe real world situations and fit the constants in order to achieve a plausible overall dynamics. On the other hand, if we are able to some-how express this additional knowledge, we can perform analyses that would have been otherwise impossible, due to the fact that the concepts of interest would have been hidden in constants within equations. For instance, a particular kind of environmental structure and vegetation might make it easier for predators to catch their preys: this can be explicitly considered in an agent-based model, whereas it would be represented as changes in the values of constants β and δ in a Lotka-Volterra model. Agent-based modeling has also been suggested as a poten-tially useful tool within "learning-by-modeling" approaches that can improve our knowledge of complex phenomena [141]: basically, by requiring the modeler to specify additional knowledge about the simulated system and, in parallel, by calling for more granular experimentation, evaluation, and finally validation of the proposed model, this approach represents a potentially useful workflow to support rigorous scientific investigation leading to further discoveries.

While we discussed in pretty abstract terms the role and the specifics of agent-based models in simulation, other chapters of the present book suggest concrete ways to put together specific agent-based approaches and specific domains of application [75], by describing meta–models of agent-based systems [37] and showing how they can be applied to cases of study.

4   Concluding Remarks and a Glimpse at the Future

This chapter has discussed how simulation was an important topic within the set of researches carried out, and discussed at the WOA workshop. First of all we proposed a definition of the term simulation, and a basic workflow of simulation projects. We then analyzed the contribution of relevant research related to simu-lation carried out at WOA. Not all of these researches have taken an agent-based approach to simulation, and quite often simulation represented a way to support the understanding and evaluation of the workings of some agent-based system whose goal was not simulation. We finally therefore took a closer look at the spe-cific nature of agent-based approaches to the definition of a simulation model, comparing the approach to macroscopic modeling approaches, and proposing a reference model that can help comparing the inevitably extremely heterogeneous approaches that have been defined in extremely different disciplines and areas of research.

Although we paid particular attention to the research that was discussed at WOA, we want to stress that this local observatory mainly reflected, elaborated, and presented an original perspective on the progress of scientific research that extends its reach far beyond the Italian community.

We want to emphasize three messages that are rooted in what has been discussed in the chapter, but that we want to further elaborate here.

First of all, **agent-based models are inherently more expressive** than alternative approaches to the modeling and simulation: although agents in simulation are often simpler than those employed for the design and implementation of distributed systems, agents can be heterogeneous, they require precise and potentially complicated perceptive capabilities, behavioral specifications, mechanisms of interaction among themselves and with the environment. An agent-based model is richer, more "colorful" than most alternatives. However, **"with great powers comes great responsibility"**:[6] the risk, for the modeler, is to create extremely rich and extremely ambitious instruments, characterized by the usage of numerous parameters, including a high number of internal mechanisms leading to diverse pathways of overall system evolution. However, simulation models are tools that support rigorous forms of investigation and need to face systematic forms of evaluation and validation. The agent community has created powerful conceptual and computational tools supporting the design of intelligent distributed systems, but simulation is a quite peculiar task and one should be careful in adding elements that can hinder the possibility to perform sensitivity analyses [145], validation of the developed models and simulators, and more generally to faithfully replicate observed patterns or analyze achieved results to understand reasons for some observed effect.

Second, and sometimes related to the above point, scientific researches on complex systems have been carried out for a very long time **without agent-based models**, even without computational tools at all. While in some areas microscopic, agent-based simulation is completely accepted and used on an everyday basis supporting decision makers and designers,[7] for COVID-19 scenarios the most credible studies were carried out employing spatial extensions of SEIR based analytical models, such as the already mentioned [77]. This can certainly reflect the different level of maturity in models and tools developed in different areas, but it often reflects a deeper problem with *credibility* of a model and related simulators [111]. The role of research is, however, not quite the same as the one of professional software developers or software houses, and controversies related to the present scenario, and in particular the fact that sometimes frontier research is carried out using and sometimes producing software, were

---

[6] The proverb has been popularized by Spider-Man, but it has been used even by the Supreme Court of the United States of America (https://en.wikipedia.org/wiki/With_great_power_comes_great_responsibility), so why shouldn't we?.

[7] For instance, for pedestrian and crowd simulation, despite research is still very active, commercial tools such as PTV-Viswalk (https://www.ptvgroup.com/en-us/products/pedestrian-simulation-software-ptv-viswalk) are widely used and well reputed; analogous considerations can be done for multimodal traffic simulation (see, e.g., PTV-Vissim – https://www.ptvgroup.com/en-us/products/ptv-vissim).

already discussed in [98]: the quality of research prototypes and scientific software is often questionable, to the point of casting shade and doubts on the results achieved through their usage. We can surely say that the problem, if possible, has grown since then. Will the open science movement bring some direly needed improvements? Only time will tell, but we want to stress that even in the agents community releasing code as open source is still not that frequent [26].

The third point we want to discuss more deeply is related to the **growing adoption of ML approaches for simulation**. Gartner's Innovation Insights more broadly talks about "AI Simulation"[8] saying that the topic is about "AI and simulation increasingly work together to enable more versatile and adaptive systems". Some of the works discussed recently at the WOA workshop, and in external venues (see, e.g., [146]), do represent attempts to investigate the possibility to achieve a simulation model, more specifically an agent model to be used within a larger model for the simulation of some complex system, by means of some machine learning technique (Reinforcement Learning – RL – in particular seems a quite straightforward approach, due to the inherent presence of a learning agent in a RL setting). On the other hand, the Sim2Real [84] line of research represents an attempt to combine learning and simulation by proposing to transfer predictive models and control programs trained through simulations directly to the real world. We mainly talk about the line of work that employs ML for simulation, and we can say for sure that these attempts will increase in number and quality: it is actually already happening, also in research areas outside computer science and engineering, further increasing the fragmentation of research on or around ML. We have two warnings to researchers spending time and energies in this direction: first of all, we need to consider that **the success criterion for a simulation project is not optimality of the efficiency of the simulated system,** or some agents within the system, but rather **the capacity to plausibly reproduce some phenomena observed in the real world** [147]. Moreover, and connecting this point to the first one, let us remember that **the journey we follow within a simulation project is often a quest for the improvement of our knowledge** on a specific object of investigation, and - again - agent-based approaches can be more difficult to adopt because they might require more knowledge than what the state-of-the-art makes available. The above mentioned work describing a "learning-by-modeling" approach [141] is again very appropriate and worth mentioning again. Non ML based approaches are demanding, they often call for interdisciplinary works, sometimes with slow advancement and results of limited applicability, works with lots of *caveats*. Simulation projects are hard, people talk about "art and science" [138] for simulation, and sometimes even "dark arts" [94], but it has represented and it still represents a sound approach for conducting scientific research and increase our knowledge. ML represents a completely legitimate instrument to solve problems, and even a very practical tool not just to be employed somewhere around simulation projects, but as **a substitute of a whole simulation model.** We are, however, **not so sure that ML will be**

---

[8] https://www.gartner.com/en/documents/4037399.

as useful as manually defined models to acquire new knowledge about the object of investigation of the simulation project, due to the fact that ML models are much less transparent and interpretable.

Simulation for agent research, as well as agents within simulation research, are however both here to stay. Every new technology needs to be studied in synthetic environments to evaluate it, its effectiveness, efficiency, potentially unintended implications before being deployed in the real world. Agent technologies are no exception to this need. Microscopic level analyses of complex systems, considering the fact that overall dynamics depend on local decisions and actions taken by (to a certain extent) autonomous but interacting entities, are simply necessary to face the challenges raised by the need to regulate (or at least influence) these systems, and steer them away from global undesired destinations. Simulation models might not be able to grasp all the complexity of scenarios like global warming, global pandemics, geopolitical crises, but they do represent a useful tool to study them and possibly advance our knowledge. The interplay and synergy among research on the synthesis of agents' behaviors, potentially also by means of ML approaches, and analysis of complex systems is even more urgent and central within this kind of developments: research fragmentation, disciplinary barriers, reproducibility crisis [3], as well as the huge inflation of the number of published research papers [81] represent threats to a virtuous growth of this research area, as well as to the overall scientific research process. The whole research community should be thinking about these issues: maybe we should contribute to this discussion. Why not considering employing agent-based simulation for performing what-if scenarios? Well, let's talk about it in 25 years, at WOA 2049!

Acknowledgments. This work was partly developed within the Spoke 8—MaaS and Innovative services of the National Center for Sustainable Mobility (MOST) set up by the "Piano nazionale di ripresa e resilienza (PNRR)—M4C2, investimento 1.4, "Potenziamento strutture di ricerca e creazione di "campioni nazionali di R&S" su alcune Key Enabling Technologies" funded by the European Union. Project code CN00000023, CUP: D93C22000410001. This work was also partially supported by the MUR under the grant "Dipartimenti di Eccellenza 2023–2027" of the Department of Informatics, Systems and Communication of the University of Milano-Bicocca, Italy.

References

1. Albericci, T., Cecconello, T., Gibertini, A., Vizzari, G.: A curriculum-based reinforcement learning approach to pedestrian simulation. In: Calegari et al. [29], pp. 224–240. http://ceur-ws.org/Vol-2963/paper11.pdf
2. Alderighi, M., Baldoni, M., Baroglio, C., Micalizio, R., Tedeschi, S. (eds.): WOA 2024 – 25th Workshop "From Objects to Agents", CEUR Workshop Proceedings, vol. 3735. Bard, AO, Italy (2024). http://ceur-ws.org/Vol-3735/
3. Baker, M.: 1,500 scientists lift the lid on reproducibility. Nature **533**(7604), 452–454 (2016). https://doi.org/10.1038/533452a

4. Baldoni, M., Baroglio, C., Bergenti, F., Garro, A. (eds.): WOA 2013 – 14th Workshop "From Objects to Agents", CEUR Workshop Proceedings, vol. 1099. Turin, Italy (2013). http://ceur-ws.org/Vol-1099/
5. Baldoni, M., Baroglio, C., Ditano, V., Micalizio, R., Tedeschi, S.: Agents for industry 4.0: the case study of a production cell. In: Falcone et al. [55], pp. 167–180. http://ceur-ws.org/Vol-3579/paper12.pdf
6. Baldoni, M., Boccalatte, A., De Paoli, F., Martelli, M., Mascardi, V. (eds.): WOA 2007 – 8th Workshop "From Objects to Agents". Seneca Edizioni Torino, Genova, Italy (2007). http://woa07.disi.unige.it/ProceedingsWOA2007.zip
7. Baldoni, M., Cossentino, M., De Paoli, F., Seidita, V. (eds.): WOA 2008 – 9th Workshop "From Objects to Agents". Seneca Edizioni Torino, Palermo, Italy (2008). http://www.pa.icar.cnr.it/woa08/materiali/Proceedings.pdf
8. Baldoni, M., De Paoli, F., Martelli, A., Omicini, A. (eds.): WOA 2004 – 5th Workshop "From Objects to Agents". Pitagora Editrice Bologna, Torino, Italy (2004). http://lia.deis.unibo.it/books/woa2004/atti.pdf
9. Bandini, S., Bonomi, A., Vizzari, G.: Supporting the design of self-organizing ambient intelligent systems through agent-based simulation. In: Baldoni et al. [7], pp. 93–100. http://www.pa.icar.cnr.it/woa08/materiali/paper/paper_6.pdf
10. Bandini, S., De Paoli, F., Manzoni, S., Simone, C.: OO reactive agents for RDM-based simulations. In: Corradi et al. [34], pp. 19–22. http://giuseppevizzari.github.io/WOA-proceedings-archive/pdfs/woa2000/WOA04.pdf
11. Bandini, S., Federici, M.L., Vizzari, G.: A methodology for crowd modelling with situated cellular agents. In: Corradini et al. [35], pp. 91–98. http://lia.deis.unibo.it/books/woa2005/papers/13.pdf
12. Bandini, S., Gorrini, A., Vizzari, G.: Towards an integrated approach to crowd analysis and crowd synthesis: a case study and first results. Pattern Recogn. Lett. **44**, 16–29 (2014)
13. Bandini, S., Manzoni, S., Redaelli, S.: Towards the interpretation of emergent spatial patterns through GO game: the case of forest population dynamics. In: Corradini et al. [35], pp. 99–103. http://lia.deis.unibo.it/books/woa2005/papers/14.pdf
14. Bandini, S., Manzoni, S., Vizzari, G.: Situated cellular agents and immune system modelling. In: Armano, G., Paoli, F.D., Omicini, A., Vargiu, E. (eds.) WOA 2003 – 4th Workshop "From Objects to Agents", pp. 36–41. Pitagora Editrice Bologna, Villasimius, CA, Italy (2003). http://giuseppevizzari.github.io/WOA-proceedings-archive/pdfs/woa2003/02.pdf
15. Bandini, S., Manzoni, S., Vizzari, G.: Agent based modeling and simulation: an informatics perspective. J. Artif. Soc. Soc. Simul. **12**(4), 4 (2009)
16. Bandini, S., Rubagotti, F., Vizzari, G., Shimura, K.: A cellular automata model for pedestrian and group dynamics. In: Fortino et al. [67], pp. 34–40. http://ceur-ws.org/Vol-741/ID2_BandiniRubagottiVizzariShimura.pdf
17. Bandini, S., Vizzari, G.: Regulation function of the environment in agent-based simulation. In: Weyns, D., Parunak, H.V.D., Michel, F. (eds.) Environments for Multi-Agent Systems III, Third International Workshop, E4MAS 2006, Hakodate, Japan, May 8, 2006, Selected Revised and Invited Papers. LNCS, vol. 4389, pp. 157–169. Springer, Cham (2006). https://doi.org/10.1007/978-3-540-71103-2_9
18. Barbaro, G., Gangemi, M.D., Foti, G.: An agent-based tsunami alert system. In: De Meo et al. [47], pp. 102–107. http://ceur-ws.org/Vol-1867/w18.pdf
19. Bazzan, A.L.C., Klügl, F.: A review on agent-based technology for traffic and transportation. Knowl. Eng. Rev. **29**(3), 375–403 (2014). https://doi.org/10.1017/S0269888913000118

20. Bergenti, F. (ed.): WOA 2009 – 10th Workshop "From Objects to Agents". Seneca Edizioni Torino, Parma, Italy (2009). http://www.ailab.unipr.it/woa09/papers/
21. Bergenti, F., Monica, S.: A kinetic model of the dynamics of compromise in large multi-agent system. In: Cossentino et al. [36], pp. 27–32. http://ceur-ws.org/Vol-2215/paper_5.pdf
22. Bergenti, F., Monica, S. (eds.): WOA 2019 – 20th Workshop "From Objects to Agents", CEUR Workshop Proceedings, vol. 2404. Parma, Italy (2019). http://ceur-ws.org/Vol-2404/
23. Bertolotti, F., Roman, S.: Risk sensitivity of production studios on the US movie market: an agent-based simulation. In: Calegari et al. [29], pp. 210–223. http://ceur-ws.org/Vol-2963/paper6.pdf
24. Bonomi, A., Manenti, L., Manzoni, S., Vizzari, G.: MAKKSim: dealing with pedestrian groups in MAS-based crowd simulation. In: Fortino et al. [67], pp. 166–170. http://ceur-ws.org/Vol-741/DEM01_BonomiManentiManzoniVizzari.pdf
25. Bouleanu, D.C., Loaiza Carrillo, M.A., Savaglio, C., Bădică, C., Gravina, R., Fortino, G.: From objects to agents, and back to smart objects: Software agents for intelligent Internet of Things (IoT) systems. In: Mascardi and Omicini [95]
26. Briola, D., Ferrando, A., Mascardi, V.: Fantastic mass and where to find them: first results and lesson learned. In: Ciortea, A., Dastani, M., Luo, J. (eds.) Engineering Multi-Agent Systems - 11th International Workshop, EMAS 2023, London, UK, May 29-30, 2023, Revised Selected Papers. LNCS, vol. 14378, pp. 233–252. Springer, Cham (2023). https://doi.org/10.1007/978-3-031-48539-8_16
27. Busetta, P., Dragoni, M.: Composing cognitive agents from behavioural models in PRESTO. In: Di Napoli et al. [50], pp. 85–90. http://ceur-ws.org/Vol-1382/paper13.pdf
28. Calegari, R., Ciatto, G., Denti, E., Omicini, A., Sartor, G. (eds.): WOA 2020 – 21st Workshop "From Objects to Agents", CEUR Workshop Proceedings, vol. 2706. Bologna, Italy (2020). http://ceur-ws.org/Vol-2706/
29. Calegari, R., Ciatto, G., Denti, E., Omicini, A., Sartor, G. (eds.): WOA 2021 – 22nd Workshop "From Objects to Agents", CEUR Workshop Proceedings, vol. 2963. Bologna, Italy (2021). http://ceur-ws.org/Vol-2963/
30. Calenda, T., De Benedetti, M., Messina, F., Pappalardo, G., Santoro, C.: AgentSimJS: a web-based multi-agent simulator with 3D capabilities. In: Santoro et al. [133], pp. 118–123. http://ceur-ws.org/Vol-1664/w20.pdf
31. Cantucci, F., Falcone, R., Castelfranchi, C.: Investigating adjustable social autonomy in human robot interaction. In: Calegari et al. [29], pp. 49–60. http://ceur-ws.org/Vol-2963/paper12.pdf
32. Capodieci, N., Cabri, G., Pagani, G.A., Aiello, M.: Agent modeling of a pervasive application to enable deregulated energy markets. In: De Paoli and Vizzari [49], pp. 8–16. http://ceur-ws.org/Vol-892/paper3.pdf
33. Casadei, M., Gardelli, L., Viroli, M.: Collective sorting tuple spaces. In: De Paoli et al. [48], pp. 173–180. http://ceur-ws.org/Vol-204/P01.pdf
34. Corradi, A., Omicini, A., Poggi, A. (eds.): WOA 2000 – 1st Workshop "From Objects to Agents", Atti di Congressi, vol. 1195. Pitagora Editrice Bologna, Parma, Italy (2000). http://giuseppevizzari.github.io/WOA-proceedings-archive/woa-2000.html
35. Corradini, F., De Paoli, F., Merelli, E., Omicini, A. (eds.): WOA 2005 – 6th Workshop "From Objects to Agents". Pitagora Editrice Bologna, Camerino, MC, Italy (2005). http://lia.deis.unibo.it/books/woa2005/atti.pdf

36. Cossentino, M., Sabatucci, L., Seidita, V. (eds.): WOA 2018 – 19th Workshop "From Objects to Agents", CEUR Workshop Proceedings, vol. 2215. Palermo, Italy (2018). http://ceur-ws.org/Vol-2215/

37. Cossentino, M., Sabatucci, L., Seidita, V.: Designing agent-oriented systems. In: Mascardi and Omicini [95]

38. Cristani, M., Olivieri, F., Governatori, G., Buriola, G.: Simulating the law in a multi-agent system. In: Alderighi et al. [2], pp. 236–251. http://ceur-ws.org/Vol-3735/paper_18.pdf

39. Crociani, L., Invernizzi, A., Vizzari, G.: A hybrid agent architecture for endowing floor field pedestrian models with tactical level decisions. In: Di Napoli et al. [50], pp. 80–84. http://ceur-ws.org/Vol-1382/paper12.pdf

40. Crociani, L., Khan, S.D., Vizzari, G.: Integrated analysis and synthesis of pedestrian dynamics: First results in a real world case study. In: Baldoni et al. [4], pp. 30–40. http://ceur-ws.org/Vol-1099/paper16.pdf

41. Crociani, L., Piazzoni, A., Vizzari, G.: Adaptive hybrid agents for tactical decisions in pedestrian environments. In: Di Napoli et al. [50], pp. 115–122. http://ceur-ws.org/Vol-1382/paper18.pdf

42. Crociani, L., Vizzari, G., Bandini, S.: Between avoidance and imitation: plausible wayfinding in pedestrian agent-based models. In: Cossentino et al. [36], pp. 1–9. http://ceur-ws.org/Vol-2215/paper_1.pdf

43. De Benedetti, M., D'Urso, F., Messina, F., Pappalardo, G., Santoro, C.: Self-organising uavs for wide area fault-tolerant aerial monitoring. In: Di Napoli et al. [50], pp. 135–141. http://ceur-ws.org/Vol-1382/paper21.pdf

44. De Benedetti, M., D'Urso, F., Messina, F., Pappalardo, G., Santoro, C.: 3D simulation of unmanned aerial vehicles. In: De Meo et al. [47], pp. 7–12. http://ceur-ws.org/Vol-1867/w2.pdf

45. De Meo, P., Ferrara, E., Rosaci, D., Sarnè, G.M.L.: How to improve group homogeneity in online social networks. In: Baldoni et al. [4], pp. 73–77. http://ceur-ws.org/Vol-1099/paper1.pdf

46. De Meo, P., Messina, F., Rosaci, D., Sarné, G.M.L.: Supporting learner-to-learner interactions using online social network information. In: Santoro et al. [133], pp. 56–61. http://ceur-ws.org/Vol-1664/w10.pdf

47. De Meo, P., Postorino, M.N., Rosaci, D., Sarnè, G.M.L. (eds.): WOA 2017 – 18th Workshop "From Objects to Agents", CEUR Workshop Proceedings, vol. 1867. Scilla, RC, Italy (2017). http://ceur-ws.org/Vol-1867/

48. De Paoli, F., Di Stefano, A., Omicini, A., Santoro, C. (eds.): WOA 2006 – 7th Workshop "From Objects to Agents", CEUR Workshop Proceedings, vol. 204. Catania, Italy (2006). http://ceur-ws.org/Vol-204/

49. De Paoli, F., Vizzari, G. (eds.): WOA 2012 – 13th Workshop "From Objects to Agents", CEUR Workshop Proceedings, vol. 892. Milano, Italy (2012). http://ceur-ws.org/Vol-892/

50. Di Napoli, C., Rossi, S., Staffa, M. (eds.): WOA 2015 – 16th Workshop "From Objects to Agents", CEUR Workshop Proceedings, vol. 1382. Naples, Italy (2015). http://ceur-ws.org/Vol-1382/

51. Durán, J.M.: What is a simulation model? Mind. Mach. **30**(3), 301–323 (2020)

52. Durana, J.M.G.d., Barambones, O., Kremers, E., Varga, L.: Agent based modeling of energy networks. Energy Convers. Manag. **82**, 308–319 (2014). https://doi.org/10.1016/j.enconman.2014.03.018

53. D'Urso, F., Santoro, C., Santoro, F.F.: Integrating heterogeneous tools for physical simulation of multi-unmanned aerial vehicles. In: Cossentino et al. [36], pp. 10–15. http://ceur-ws.org/Vol-2215/paper_2.pdf

54. Edmonds, B.: The use of models - making MABS more informative. In: Moss, S., Davidsson, P. (eds.) Multi-Agent-Based Simulation. MABS 2000. LNCS, vol. 1979, pp. 15–32. Springer, Berlin, Heidelberg (2001). https://doi.org/10.1007/3-540-44561-7_2

55. Falcone, R., Castelfranchi, C., Sapienza, A., Cantucci, F. (eds.): WOA 2023 – 24th Workshop "From Objects to Agents", CEUR Workshop Proceedings, vol. 3579. Roma, Italy (2023). http://ceur-ws.org/Vol-3579/

56. Falcone, R., Sapienza, A.: How can subjective impulsivity play a role among information sources in weather scenarios? In: De Meo et al. [47], pp. 19–24. http://ceur-ws.org/Vol-1867/w4.pdf

57. Falcone, R., Sapienza, A.: Institutional alarmism and the damage it provokes in case of hydrogeological disasters: a simulative estimation. In: Cossentino et al. [36], pp. 21–26. http://ceur-ws.org/Vol-2215/paper_4.pdf

58. Falcone, R., Sapienza, A.: Information seeking behavior at the time of COVID-19. In: Calegari et al. [29], pp. 241–258. http://ceur-ws.org/Vol-2963/paper8.pdf

59. Falcone, R., Sapienza, A.: The role of decisional autonomy in user-IoT systems interaction. In: Ferrando and Mascardi [61], pp. 77–87. http://ceur-ws.org/Vol-3261/paper6.pdf

60. Federici, M.L., Redaelli, S., Vizzari, G.: Models, abstractions and phases in multi-agent based simulation. In: De Paoli et al. [48], pp. 144–150. http://ceur-ws.org/Vol-204/P15.pdf

61. Ferrando, A., Mascardi, V. (eds.): WOA 2022 – 23rd Workshop "From Objects to Agents", CEUR Workshop Proceedings, vol. 3261. Genova, Italy (2022). http://ceur-ws.org/Vol-3261/

62. Ferraris, G., Morini, M.: Simulation in the textile industry: production planning optimization. In: Baldoni et al. [8], pp. 143–149. http://giuseppevizzari.github.io/WOA-proceedings-archive/pdfs/woa2004/19.pdf

63. Fornacciari, P., Lombardo, G., Mordonini, M., Poggi, A., Tomaiuolo, M.: Agent based cellular automata simulation. In: Cossentino et al. [36], pp. 16–20. http://ceur-ws.org/Vol-2215/paper_3.pdf

64. Fortino, G., Fotia, L., Messina, F., Rosaci, D., Sarné, G.M.L.: Supporting agent CoT groups formation by trust. In: Bergenti and Monica [22], pp. 71–76. http://ceur-ws.org/Vol-2404/paper11.pdf

65. Fortino, G., Fotia, L., Messina, F., Rosaci, D., Sarné, G.M.L., Savaglio, C.: A trust model to form teams of agentified AGVs in workshop areas. In: Calegari et al. [29], pp. 61–71. http://ceur-ws.org/Vol-2963/paper2.pdf

66. Fortino, G., Garro, A., Mascillaro, S., Russo, W.: Using multi-coordination for the design of mobile agent interactions. In: Baldoni et al. [7], pp. 122–128. http://www.pa.icar.cnr.it/woa08/materiali/paper/paper_11.pdf

67. Fortino, G., Garro, A., Palopoli, L., Russo, W., Spezzano, G. (eds.): WOA 2011 – 12th Workshop "From Objects to Agents", CEUR Workshop Proceedings, vol. 741. Rende, Italy (2011). http://ceur-ws.org/Vol-741/

68. Fortino, G., Garro, A., Russo, W.: A discrete-event simulation framework for the validation of agent-based and multi-agent systems. In: Corradini et al. [35], pp. 75–84. http://lia.deis.unibo.it/books/woa2005/papers/11.pdf

69. Fortino, G., Garro, A., Russo, W., Vaccaro, M.: Performance evaluation of content distribution network architectures through agent-based modeling and simulation. In: Fortino et al. [67], pp. 158–165. http://ceur-ws.org/Vol-741/ID18_FortinoGarroRussoVaccaro.pdf

70. Fortino, G., Russo, W., Savaglio, C.: Simulation of agent-oriented Internet of Things systems. In: Santoro et al. [133], pp. 8–13. http://ceur-ws.org/Vol-1664/w2.pdf

71. Fortino, G., Zedadra, O., Jouandeau, N., Seridi, H.: A decentralized ant colony foraging model using only stigmergic communication. In: Santoro and Bergenti [132], pp. 63–67. http://ceur-ws.org/Vol-1260/paper13.pdf

72. Fortino, G., Garro, A., Mascillaro, S., Russo, W.: ELDATool: a statecharts-based tool for prototyping multi-agent systems. In: Baldoni et al. [6], pp. 14–19. http://woa07.dibris.unige.it/papers/D2_ForGarMasRus-WOA07-Demo.pdf

73. Franchi, E., Tomaiuolo, M.: Software agents for distributed social networking. In: De Paoli and Vizzari [49], pp. 63–67. http://ceur-ws.org/Vol-892/paper4.pdf

74. Gardelli, L., Viroli, M., Omicini, A.: On the role of simulation in the engineering of self-organising systems: Detecting abnormal behaviour in MAS. In: Corradini et al. [35], pp. 85–90. http://lia.deis.unibo.it/books/woa2005/papers/12.pdf

75. Garro, A.: Agent-based computing for science and engineering: back to the future and beyond.... In: Mascardi and Omicini [95]

76. Garro, A., Russo, W.: Exploiting the easyABMS methodology in social and economic domains. In: Bergenti [20], pp. 8–15. http://www.ailab.unipr.it/woa09/papers/Garro.pdf

77. Gatto, M., et al.: Spread and dynamics of the covid-19 epidemic in Italy: effects of emergency containment measures. Proc. Natl. Acad. Sci. **117**(19), 10484–10491 (2020). https://doi.org/10.1073/pnas.2004978117

78. Gilbert, N., Troitzsch, K.G.: Simulation for the Social Scientist (second edition). Open University Press (2005)

79. Grosso, A., Anghinolfi, D., Boccalatte, A., Cannata, G.: A context aware multi-robot coordination system based on agent technology. In: Omicini and Viroli [110], pp. 169–173. http://ceur-ws.org/Vol-621/paper24.pdf

80. Habbash, N., Bottoni, F., Vizzari, G.: Reinforcement learning for autonomous agents exploring environments: an experimental framework and preliminary results. In: Calegari et al. [28], pp. 84–100. http://ceur-ws.org/Vol-2706/paper5.pdf

81. Hanson, M.A., Barreiro, P.G., Crosetto, P., Brockington, D.: The strain on scientific publishing. Quant. Sci. Stud. 1–21 (2024). https://doi.org/10.1162/qss_a_00327

82. He, S., Peng, Y., Sun, K.: SEIR modeling of the COVID-19 and its dynamics. Nonlinear Dyn. **101**(3), 1667–1680 (2020). https://doi.org/10.1007/s11071-020-05743-y

83. Helleboogh, A., Vizzari, G., Uhrmacher, A.M., Michel, F.: Modeling dynamic environments in multi-agent simulation. Auton. Agents Multi Agent Syst. **14**(1), 87–116 (2007). https://doi.org/10.1007/S10458-006-0014-Y

84. Höfer, S., et al.: Sim2real in robotics and automation: applications and challenges. IEEE Trans. Autom. Sci. Eng. **18**(2), 398–400 (2021). https://doi.org/10.1109/TASE.2021.3064065

85. Klügl, F.: A validation methodology for agent-based simulations. In: Menezes, R., Viroli, M. (eds.) Symposium on Applied Computing, pp. 39–43. ACM Press (2008). https://doi.org/10.1145/1363686.1363696

86. Lombardo, G., Pellegrino, M., Poggi, A.: Unsupervised continual learning from synthetic data generated with agent-based modeling and simulation: a preliminary experimentation. In: Ferrando and Mascardi [61], pp. 116–126. http://ceur-ws.org/Vol-3261/paper9.pdf

87. Lombardo, G., Poggi, A.: A preliminary experimentation for large scale epidemic forecasting simulations. In: Calegari et al. [28], pp. 28–36. http://ceur-ws.org/Vol-2706/paper15.pdf

88. Magnolo, E., Manenti, L., Manzoni, S., Sartori, F.: Towards a MAS model for crowd simulation at pop-rock concerts exploiting ontologies and fuzzy logic. In: Bergenti [20], pp. 92–99. http://www.ailab.unipr.it/woa09/papers/Magnolo.pdf

89. Manenti, L., Manzoni, L., Manzoni, S.: Towards an application of graph structure analysis to a mas-based model of proxemic distances in pedestrian systems. In: Omicini and Viroli [110], pp. 16–22. http://ceur-ws.org/Vol-621/paper03.pdf

90. Manenti, L., Manzoni, S.: Crystals of crowd: modelling pedestrian groups using mas-based approach. In: Fortino et al. [67], pp. 51–57. http://ceur-ws.org/Vol-741/ID12_ManentiManzoni.pdf

91. Manenti, L., Manzoni, S., Vizzari, G., Dijkstra, J.: Towards modeling activity scheduling in an agent-based model for pedestrian dynamics simulation. In: De Paoli and Vizzari [49], pp. 31–38. http://ceur-ws.org/Vol-892/paper12.pdf

92. Manenti, L., Manzoni, S., Vizzari, G., Ohtsuka, K., Shimura, K.: Towards an agent-based proxemic model for pedestrian and group dynamic. In: Omicini and Viroli [110], pp. 7–15. http://ceur-ws.org/Vol-621/paper02.pdf

93. Mariani, S., Omicini, A.: Game engines to model MAS: a research roadmap. In: De Meo et al. [47], pp. 106–111. http://ceur-ws.org/Vol-1664/w18.pdf

94. Marney, J.P., Tarbert, H.F.E.: Why do simulation? Towards a working epistemology for practitioners of the dark arts. J. Artif. Soc. Soc. Simul. **3**(4) (2000). http://jasss.soc.surrey.ac.uk/3/4/4.html

95. Mascardi, V., Omicini, A. (eds.): The Agents Journey: Twenty-five Years of Multiagent Systems at WOA. LNCS – State-of-the-Art Surveys. Springer, Cham (2026)

96. Mastroeni, L., Naldi, M., Vellucci, P.: An agent-based model on scale-free networks for personal finance decisions. In: Bergenti and Monica [22], pp. 77–83. http://ceur-ws.org/Vol-2404/paper12.pdf

97. Meo, P.D., Falcone, R., Sapienza, A.: Applying inferential processes to partner selection in large agents communities. In: Calegari et al. [28], pp. 15–27. http://ceur-ws.org/Vol-2706/paper6.pdf

98. Merali, Z.: Computational science: ...error. Nature **467**(7317), 775–777 (2010). https://doi.org/10.1038/467775a, publisher: Nature Publishing Group

99. Messina, F., Pappalardo, G., Santoro, C.: A self-organising system for resource finding in large-scale computational grids. In: Omicini and Viroli [110], pp. 110–116. http://ceur-ws.org/Vol-621/paper16.pdf

100. Molesini, A., Denti, E., Omicini, A.: BaSi: multi-agent based simulation for medieval battles. In: Fortino et al. [67], pp. 140–149. http://ceur-ws.org/Vol-741/ID11_MolesiniDentiOmicini.pdf

101. Monica, S., Bergenti, F.: A stochastic model of self-stabilizing cellular automata for consensus formation. In: Santoro and Bergenti [132], pp. 75–80. http://ceur-ws.org/Vol-1260/paper8.pdf

102. Monica, S., Bergenti, F.: Simulations of opinion formation in multi-agent systems using kinetic theory. In: Di Napoli et al. [50], pp. 97–102. http://ceur-ws.org/Vol-1382/paper15.pdf

103. Monica, S., Bergenti, F.: An analytic model of the impact of skeptical agents on the dynamics of compromise. In: De Meo et al. [47], pp. 43–48. http://ceur-ws.org/Vol-1867/w8.pdf

104. Montagna, S., Omicini, A., Angeli, F.D., Donati, M.: Towards the adoption of agent-based modelling and simulation in mobile health systems for the self-management of chronic diseases. In: Santoro et al. [133], pp. 100–105. http://ceur-ws.org/Vol-1664/w17.pdf

105. Montagna, S., Omicini, A., Ricci, A.: A multiscale agent-based model of morphogenesis in biological systems. In: Omicini and Viroli [110], pp. 23–29. http://ceur-ws.org/Vol-621/paper04.pdf

106. Motieyan, H., Mesgari, M.S.: An agent-based modeling approach for sustainable urban planning from land use and public transit perspectives. Cities **81**, 91–100 (2018). https://doi.org/10.1016/j.cities.2018.03.018

107. Nanna, G.A., Quatraro, N.F., De Carolis, B.: A multi-agent system for simulating the spread of a contagious disease. In: Calegari et al. [28], pp. 119–134. http://ceur-ws.org/Vol-2706/paper7.pdf

108. Nygaard, K.: Basic concepts in object oriented programming. In: Proceedings of the 1986 SIGPLAN Workshop on Object-oriented Programming, pp. 128–132 (1986)

109. Oliva, E., Viroli, M., Omicini, A.: Minority game: a logic-based approach in TuCSoN. In: De Paoli et al. [48], pp. 181–186. http://ceur-ws.org/Vol-204/P02.pdf

110. Omicini, A., Viroli, M. (eds.): WOA 2010 – 11th Workshop "From Objects to Agents", CEUR Workshop Proceedings, vol. 621. Rimini, Italy (2010). http://ceur-ws.org/Vol-621/

111. Onggo, B.S., Yilmaz, L., Klügl, F., Terano, T., Macal, C.M.: Credible agent-based simulation – an illusion or only a step awayf. In: 2019 Winter Simulation Conference (WSC), pp. 273–284 (2019). https://doi.org/10.1109/WSC40007.2019.9004716

112. Pagliuca, P., Vitanza, A.: Enhancing aggregation in locomotor multi-agent systems: a theoretical framework. In: Alderighi et al. [2], pp. 42–57. http://ceur-ws.org/Vol-3735/paper_04.pdf

113. Paulin, G., Ivasic-Kos, M.: Review and analysis of synthetic dataset generation methods and techniques for application in computer vision. Artif. Intell. Rev. **56**(9), 9221–9265 (2023). https://doi.org/10.1007/S10462-022-10358-3

114. Pellegrino, M., Lombardo, G., Mordonini, M., Tomaiuolo, M., Cagnoni, S., Poggi, A.: ActoDemic: a distributed framework for fine-grained spreading modeling and simulation in large scale scenarios. In: Calegari et al. [29], pp. 194–209. http://ceur-ws.org/Vol-2963/paper7.pdf

115. Pianini, D., Viroli, M., Montagna, S.: A simulation framework for pervasive services ecosystems. In: Fortino et al. [67], pp. 150–157. http://ceur-ws.org/Vol-741/ID15_PianiniViroliMontagna.pdf

116. Picasso, E., Postorino, M.N., Sarné, G.M.L.: A study to promote car-sharing by adopting a reputation system in a multi-agent context. In: De Meo et al. [47], pp. 13–18. http://ceur-ws.org/Vol-1867/w3.pdf

117. Pinheiro, V.B., Gorochowski, T.E.: Agent-based modelling in synthetic biology. Essays Biochemistry **60**(4), 325–336 (2016). https://doi.org/10.1042/EBC20160037

118. Piras, A., Bertolotti, F.: How risk preferences shape city-state success: an agent-based model of resource management. In: Alderighi et al. [2], pp. 302–316. http://ceur-ws.org/Vol-3735/paper_22.pdf

119. Poggi, A.: An actor-based software framework for developing and simulating complex systems. In: De Paoli and Vizzari [49], pp. 49–54. http://ceur-ws.org/Vol-892/paper9.pdf

120. Poggi, A.: Agent based modeling and simulation with ActoMoS. In: Di Napoli et al. [50], pp. 91–96. http://ceur-ws.org/Vol-1382/paper14.pdf

121. Postorino, M.N., Sarnè, F.A., Sarnè, G.M.L.: An agent-based simulator for urban air mobility scenarios. In: Calegari et al. [28], pp. 2–14. http://ceur-ws.org/Vol-2706/paper3.pdf

122. Postorino, M.N., Sarné, G.M.L.: A preliminary study for an agent blockchain-based framework supporting dynamic car-pooling. In: Bergenti and Monica [22], pp. 65–70. http://ceur-ws.org/Vol-2404/paper10.pdf

123. Postorino, M.N., Sarnè, G.M.L.: An agent-based framework including diachronic MaaS represention. In: Alderighi et al. [2], pp. 98–112. http://ceur-ws.org/Vol-3735/paper_08.pdf

124. Postorino, M.N., Sarnè, G.M.: Agents meet traffic simulation, control and management: a review of selected recent contributions. In: Santoro et al. [133], pp. 112–117. http://ceur-ws.org/Vol-1664/w19.pdf

125. Robol, M., Giorgini, P., Busetta, P.: Applying social norms to implicit negotiation among non-player characters in serious games. In: Santoro et al. [133], pp. 23–28. http://ceur-ws.org/Vol-1664/w5.pdf

126. Roggero, D., Patrone, F., Mascardi, V.: Designing and implementing electronic auctions in a multiagent system environment. In: Corradini et al. [35], pp. 157–163. http://lia.deis.unibo.it/books/woa2005/papers/22.pdf

127. Rosaci, D., Sacchi, S., Sarné, G.M.L.: Modeling dynamic web polarization and proximity depolarization processes by compactness measures. In: Ferrando and Mascardi [61], pp. 88–100. http://ceur-ws.org/Vol-3261/paper7.pdf

128. Rosaci, D., Sarnè, G.M.L.: An agent-based architecture to recommend educational video. In: Santoro and Bergenti [132], pp. 1–6. http://ceur-ws.org/Vol-1260/paper1.pdf

129. Rosaci, D., Sarnè, G.M.L.: Looking for the best partners. In: Mascardi and Omicini [95]

130. Rossi, S., Di Napoli, C., Barile, F., Liguori, L.: Conflict resolution profiles and agent negotiation for group recommendations. In: Santoro et al. [133], pp. 29–34. http://ceur-ws.org/Vol-1664/w6.pdf

131. Sabatucci, L., Cossentino, M., Lopes, S.: Self-adaptive reconfigurations of shipboard power systems. In: Cossentino et al. [36], pp. 103–108. http://ceur-ws.org/Vol-2215/paper_17.pdf

132. Santoro, C., Bergenti, F. (eds.): WOA 2014 – 15th Workshop "From Objects to Agents", CEUR Workshop Proceedings, vol. 1260. Catania, Italy (2014). http://ceur-ws.org/Vol-1260/

133. Santoro, C., Messina, F., De Benedetti, M. (eds.): WOA 2016 – 17th Workshop "From Objects to Agents", CEUR Workshop Proceedings, vol. 1664. Catania, Italy (2016). http://ceur-ws.org/Vol-1664/

134. Sapienza, A., Cantucci, F., Castelfranchi, C., Falcone, R.: Trust evolution in agent and multi-agent systems: a computational modeling perspective. In: Mascardi and Omicini [95]

135. Sapienza, A., Falcone, R.: A theoretical model for the human-iot systems interaction. In: Bergenti and Monica [22], pp. 90–97. http://ceur-ws.org/Vol-2404/paper14.pdf

136. Sarnè, G.M.L.: A reputation agent model for reliable vehicle-to-vehicle information. In: Cossentino et al. [36], pp. 33–38. http://ceur-ws.org/Vol-2215/paper_6.pdf

137. Seidita, V., Chella, A.: Enhancing robotic systems in healthcare: a preliminary analysis of agent-based paradigms and simulation environments. In: Alderighi et al. [2], pp. 200–208. http://ceur-ws.org/Vol-3735/paper_15.pdf

138. Shannon, R.: Introduction to the art and science of simulation. In: 1998 Winter Simulation Conference. Proceedings (Cat. No.98CH36274), vol. 1, pp. 7–14 (1998). https://doi.org/10.1109/WSC.1998.744892

139. Solera, F., Calderara, S., Cucchiara, R.: Socially constrained structural learning for groups detection in crowd. IEEE Trans. Pattern Anal. Mach. Intell. **38**(5), 995–1008 (2016). https://doi.org/10.1109/TPAMI.2015.2470658

140. Tesfatsion, L.: Chapter 16 Agent-based computational economics: a constructive approach to economic theory. In: Tesfatsion, L., Judd, K.L. (eds.) Handbook of Computational Economics, Handbook of Computational Economics, vol. 2, pp. 831–880. Elsevier (2006). https://doi.org/10.1016/S1574-0021(05)02016-2, iSSN: 1574-0021

141. Triulzi, G., Pyka, A.: Learning-by-modeling: insights from an agent-based model of university–industry relationships. Cybern. Syst. **42**(7), 484–501 (2011). https://doi.org/10.1080/01969722.2011.610266

142. Vecchiola, C., Grosso, A., Passadore, A., Anghinolfi, D., Boccalatte, A., Paolucci, M.: An agent based solution for dispatching items in a distributed environment. In: Baldoni et al. [6], pp. 71–77. http://woa07.disi.unige.it/papers/VecchiolaItems.pdf

143. Vidali, A., Crociani, L., Vizzari, G., Bandini, S.: A deep reinforcement learning approach to adaptive traffic lights management. In: Bergenti and Monica [22], pp. 42–50. http://ceur-ws.org/Vol-2404/paper07.pdf

144. Vizzari, G., Briola, D., Cecconello, T.: Curriculum-based reinforcement learning for pedestrian simulation: Towards an explainable training process? In: Falcone et al. [55], pp. 32–48. http://ceur-ws.org/Vol-3579/paper3.pdf

145. Vizzari, G., Briola, D., Pisapia, F.: Curriculum-based RL for pedestrian simulation: Sensitivity analysis and hyperparameter exploration. In: Bazzan, A.L.C., Dusparic, I., Lujak, M., Vizzari, G. (eds.) Thirteenth International Workshop on Agents in Traffic and Transportation co-located with the the 27th European Conference on Artificial Intelligence (ECAI 2024), Santiago de Compostela, Spain, October 19, 2024. CEUR Workshop Proceedings, vol. 3813, pp. 136–149. CEUR-WS.org (2024). https://ceur-ws.org/Vol-3813/11.pdf

146. Vizzari, G., Cecconello, T.: Pedestrian simulation with reinforcement learning: a curriculum-based approach. Future Internet **15**(1), 12 (2023). https://doi.org/10.3390/FI15010012

147. Vizzari, G., Crociani, L., Bandini, S.: An agent-based model for plausible wayfinding in pedestrian simulation. Eng. Appl. Artif. Intell. **87** (2020). https://doi.org/10.1016/J.ENGAPPAI.2019.103241

148. Vizzari, G., Manenti, L., Ohtsuka, K., Shimura, K.: Experimental and real world applications of agent-based pedestrian group modeling. In: De Paoli and Vizzari [49], pp. 22–30. http://ceur-ws.org/Vol-892/paper13.pdf

149. Wangersky, P.J.: Lotka-volterra population models. Annu. Rev. Ecol. Syst. **9**, 189–218 (1978)

150. Weyns, D., Omicini, A., Odell, J.J.: Environment as a first class abstraction in multi-agent systems. Auton. Agents Multi-Agent Syst. **14**(1), 5–30 (2007). https://doi.org/10.1007/s10458-006-0012-0, special issue on Environments for Multi-agent Systems

Agents and MAS for Artificial Intelligence

25 Years of Declarative Agent Technologies in Italy

Davide Ancona[1] , Daniela Briola[2] , Angelo Ferrando[3] ,
Maurizio Martelli[1] , and Viviana Mascardi[1(✉)]

[1] Università degli Studi di Genova, Genova, Italy
`{davide.ancona,maurizio.martelli,viviana.mascardi}@unige.it`
[2] Università di Milano Bicocca, Milan, Italy
`daniela.briola@unimib.it`
[3] Università di Modena e Reggio Emilia, Modena, Italy
`angelo.ferrando@unimore.it`

Abstract. Since the first appearance of agents and multiagent systems (MAS), their close connection with declarative technologies was clearly devised and drove – and still drives – a large share of the research in the field. Declarative technologies play many roles in the MAS context: they can be exploited in the specification of the agents and MAS architecture, in the specification of their conversational flow, in their implementation, and in the representation of the agents' knowledge. In all of these roles, one main advantage of declarative technologies is the support to transparency and explainability thanks to a (more, w.r.t. other paradigms) readable, understandable, and interoperable description of the system, and to reliability, by means of formal verification of its properties. This chapter, guided by works presented at Workshop on Objects and Agents (WOA) starting from 2000, discusses the crucial role that declarative technologies play in a MAS context.

Keywords: Declarative approaches · Logic-based approaches · Cognitive and BDI Agents · Verification · Ontologies · Argumentation

1 Introduction

According to the widely accepted definition by Jennings, Sycara, and Wooldridge [113], an intelligent agent is a computer system situated within an environment, capable of exhibiting autonomous, social, reactive, and proactive behaviours. The strong definition of agents further incorporates the requirement of being modelled in terms of beliefs, desires, goals, and intentions, usually ascribed to humans. The Belief-Desire-Intention (BDI) model [158] is the most known architecture for cognitive agents.

AgentSpeak(L) [157] is one of the first agent oriented programming (AOP) languages for designing and implementing BDI agents and Jason [38] is one of the most well known interpreters for AgentSpeak(L). Jason has been integrated

V. Mascardi and A. Omicini (Eds.): *The Agents Journey*, LNCS 16395, pp. 287–319, 2026.
https://doi.org/10.1007/978-3-032-22940-3_11

with CArtAgO [162,163] for modelling and implementing the MAS environment as a set of artifacts, and with MOISE [111] to model the MAS organisational constraints, resulting into the JaCaMo framework [34].

Notably, the idea of integrating Jason, CArtAgO and MOISE appears for the first time in a WOA paper dating back 2010 [153], three years before the first paper on JaCaMo [35].

The study of intelligent agents, especially those built using the BDI model, provides a foundation for understanding how autonomous systems can reason and act within complex environments. These agent-based systems, particularly within the JaCaMo framework, emphasise transparency and modularity in their design, enabling explicit modelling of beliefs and intentions. However, as AI advances, especially with the rise of black-box models like deep neural networks, the focus has shifted towards balancing these foundational principles with the need for explainability in more opaque systems. This shift has sparked growing interest in combining traditional agent-based approaches with newer AI models to address challenges related to transparency and trust. These concerns become critical in high-stakes fields like healthcare, justice, and finance, where explainability is essential [106].

Declarative approaches in AI and MAS offer an advantage by focussing on *what* needs to be done rather than *how* to do it. This makes decisions more interpretable and rule-based. Unlike black-box models, declarative systems allow for explicit inspection and modification of decision-making processes, fostering greater transparency and trust. This approach aligns with the growing demand for Trustworthy AI (TAI), as outlined by the European Commission's Guidelines for Trustworthy AI[1]. These guidelines emphasise the importance of transparency, robustness, and fairness in AI systems.

Declarative models also promote fairness by making biases easier to identify and correct through explicit rule inspection, addressing a major shortcoming of black-box methods. Additionally, their modularity allows for simpler updates, enhancing reliability and robustness.

The Trustworthy AI framework emerged from both academic and industry efforts to address ethical concerns and establish principles for AI use across various domains [94,184]. Various approaches have been proposed to achieve TAI. For example, Vianello et al. [182] present a design framework based on user explainability and normative ethics, while Thiebes et al. [177] outline five foundational principles for TAI: beneficence, non-maleficence, autonomy, justice, and explicability. Similarly, Yeung [187] emphasises responsible stewardship by highlighting respect for human rights and democratic values.

Rawal et al. [159] introduced an eXplainable AI (XAI) framework that enhances trustworthiness by integrating principles such as transparency, accountability, and privacy. This framework bridges technical solutions with ethical concerns and incorporates legal standards, aligning AI systems with societal values.

Additionally, IBM's open-source toolkit for evaluating fairness and mitigating bias in machine learning models [25] exemplifies practical solutions. This effort

---

[1] https://digital-strategy.ec.europa.eu/en/library/ethics-guidelines-trustworthy-ai.

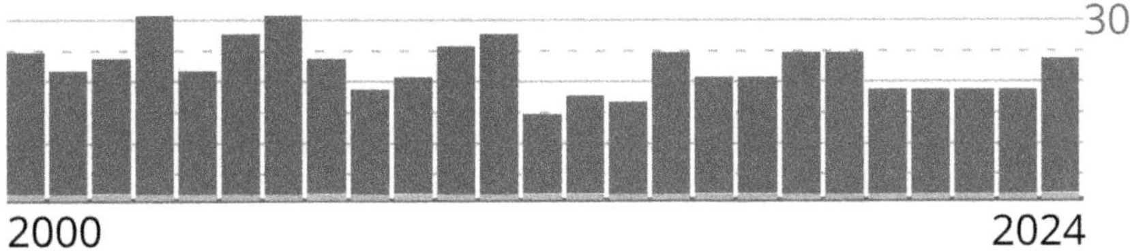

Fig. 1. Distribution of the 453 WOA papers in the range 2000–2024, from DBLP.

complements the European Commission's Guidelines for Trustworthy AI [96], which define seven key requirements for AI systems to be deemed trustworthy.

The chapter is organised as follows. Section 2 presents the WOA papers we took under consideration in this chapter and analyses them from a quantitative point of view, whereas Sect. 3 provides a qualitative evaluation of these works. Section 4 discusses our own research, always using WOA publications as fil rouge. Finally, Sect. 5 outlines the future directions of the research on declarative technologies and MAS.

2   A Look into Raw Data

We start our journey with a look into raw data. We analysed the titles and abstracts of all the papers published at WOA from 2000 to 2024, looking for relevant keywords and their syntactic variants. The results of our search are more precise for papers from 2005 onwards, as these papers' data were automatically collected into a single spreadsheet from Scopus, and this made the analysis easier. For papers published in the first five editions, data collection was manual and hence more error prone. The extensive results are shown in Table 1, Table 2, Table 3 in the Appendix: a summary is provided in the sequel.

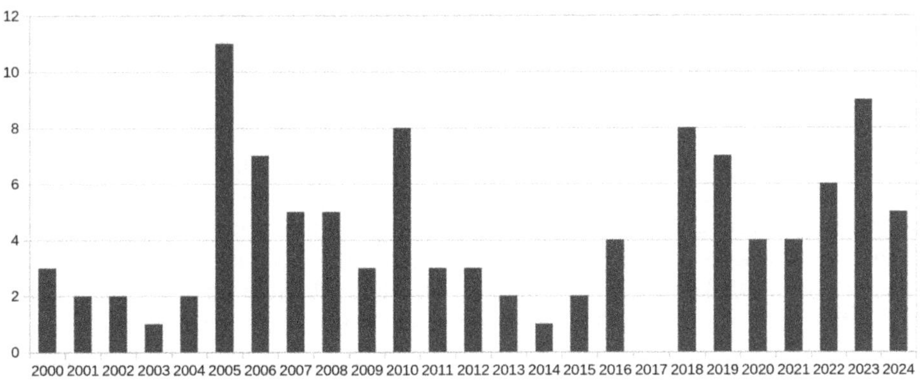

Fig. 2. Distribution of the 107 WOA papers dealing with declarative agent technologies in the range 2000–2024.

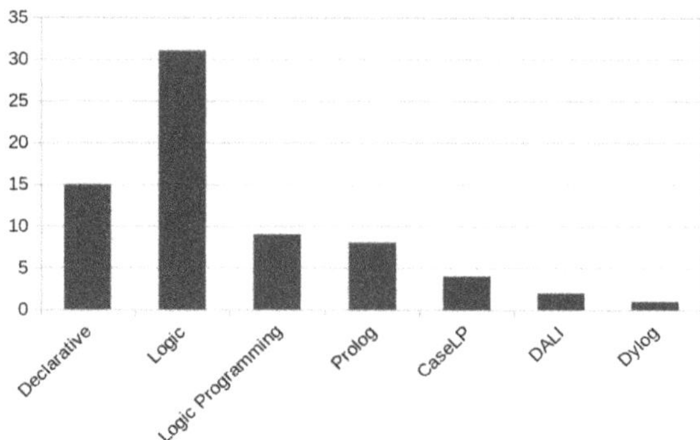

Fig. 3. WOA papers dealing with declarative and logic-based approaches. The distinct papers belonging to this category are 54.

Out of 453 WOA papers indexed in DBLP,[2] whose distribution over years is shown in Fig. 1, 107 included at least one of the keywords matching our search in their title or abstract. Their distribution over years is shown in Fig. 2.

The five areas we considered to look for papers and to group them into coherent categories, are **declarative and logic-based agents**, **cognitive and BDI agents**, **verification**, **ontologies**, and **argumentation**. These areas are not disjoint, and many papers belong to more than one.

Figure 3 shows the number of papers that include 'declarative', 'logic', or 'logic programming' in their title or abstract. Papers that deal with logic in general, but not with logic programming, are counted only in the 'logic' sub-category, and vice-versa. Papers that deal with both, contribute to increasing both counters. Sub-categories are not disjoint, and they show that the 'logic' (meant in a general, broad sense) keyword is the most popular one, appearing in 31 papers, followed by 'declarative' (15 papers) and 'logic programming' (9). 'Prolog' appears in 8 papers, while – notably – no paper mentions 'answer set' or 'stable model' at least in its title or abstract. We read the abstracts and titles of these papers, and a few programming languages and tools designed and implemented by members of the WOA community appeared almost often: DCaseLP [3, 18, 44, 129], DALI [36, 83], DyLOG [172]. They are included in Fig. 3 for reference.

Figure 4 presents figures related with papers that include 'BDI' (or the extended version of the acronym) or 'cognitive' in their title or abstract. By reading these abstracts, we realised that many papers mentioning AgentSpeak(L), Jason, or JaCaMo, did not result from our search because they did not also include the 'BDI' keyword. We searched for these three languages/technologies explicitly and we increased the BDI count any time one paper mentioned them: indeed, one paper where AgentSpeak(L) is used, is one paper on BDI agents. In Fig. 4, PRACTIONIST also appears because it was mentioned in 4 regular papers [127, 140–142].

---

[2] https://dblp.org/db/conf/woa/index.html.

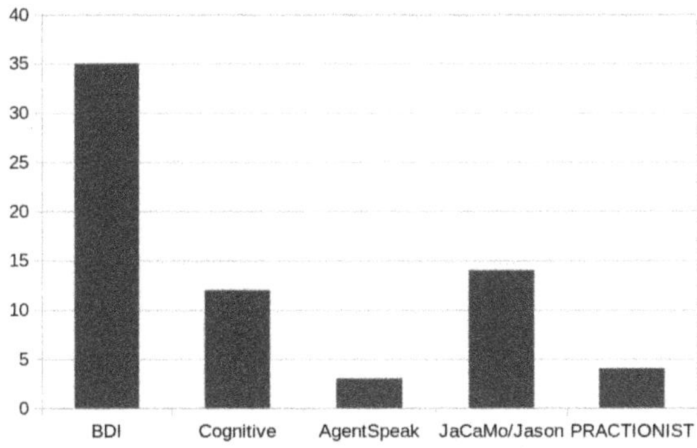

Fig. 4. WOA papers dealing with cognitive and BDI agents. The distinct papers belonging to this category are 42.

Only 13 distinct papers out of 107 deal with formal verification. The keyword recurring most often is 'verification' in general (11 papers), followed by 'model checking' and 'conformance' (3 papers both). Figure 5 shows the histogram of these data.

The distinct papers dealing with semantic web and ontologies are 29: in 26 titles/abstracts the words 'ontology' or 'OWL' appear, in 8 of them the 'semantic web' keyword appears (see Figure Fig. 6). Of course, some papers mention both. To make our search as exhaustive as possible we also looked for 'description logic' but it is not mentioned, at least in titles and abstracts.

We considered the argumentation research area, given that argumentation frameworks are often, although not always, based on logic. Only 3 papers belong to this category, which we did not divide into sub-categories.

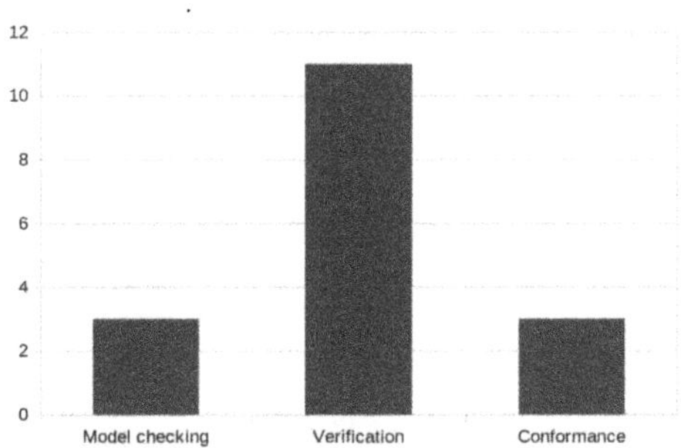

Fig. 5. WOA papers dealing with formal verification. The distinct papers belonging to this category are 13.

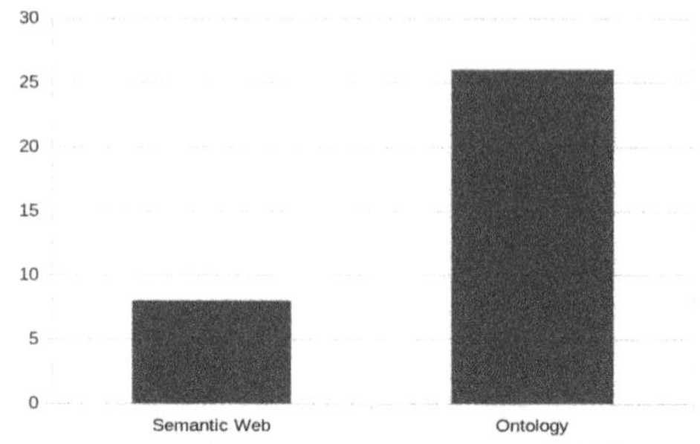

Fig. 6. WOA papers dealing with semantic web and ontologies. The distinct papers belonging to this category are 29.

Figure 7 shows that out of the 107 papers we considered in this work, 3 deal with topics in the intersection of 3 different categories, 28 cover two distinct categories, and the other 76 papers belong to one category only. Out of the 3 papers covering 3 categories, 2 deal with declarative and logic-based agents ∩ cognitive and BDI agents ∩ ontologies [112, 121], while one deals with declarative and logic-based agents ∩ cognitive and BDI agents ∩ verification [18].

The distribution of the 28 papers falling in two categories is

11 papers in declarative and logic-based agents ∩ cognitive and BDI agents;
6 papers in cognitive and BDI agents ∩ ontologies;
5 papers in declarative and logic-based agents ∩ verification;
3 papers in declarative and logic-based agents ∩ ontologies;
2 papers in declarative and logic-based agents ∩ argumentation;
1 paper in cognitive and BDI agents ∩ verification.

Finally, most papers belonging to one category only fall either in the declarative and logic-based agents one (30 papers), in the cognitive and BDI agents one (21 papers), or in the ontologies one (18 papers).

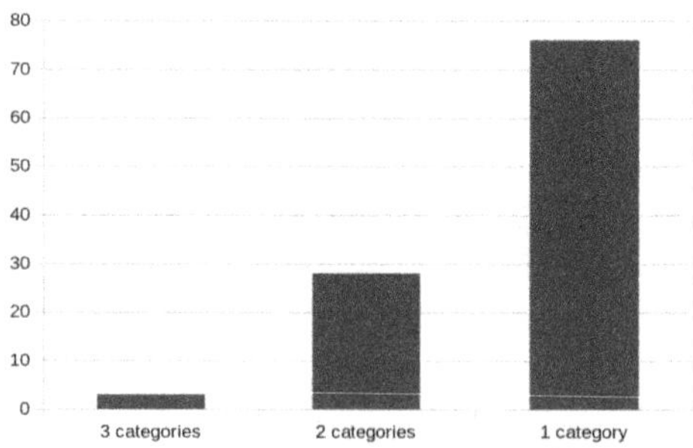

Fig. 7. Number of papers belonging to exactly one, two, or three categories among declarative and logic-based agents; cognitive and BDI agents; verification; ontologies; argumentation.

We conclude our journey by mentioning the research impact of these papers in terms of citations. Due to lack of indexing of the papers belonging to the first five editions, and to the recent publication of the 2024 proceedings, we only considered the editions from 2005 to 2023 included, for 92 papers in total. According to Scopus, at the time of writing these 92 papers obtained 5.4 citations per paper on average, with one paper obtaining more than 110 citations and 3 papers obtaining between 30 and 50 citations. The average number of citations of papers published on the International Conference on Autonomous Agents and Multiagent Systems (AAMAS) Proceedings is 11.2. With due proportions between WOA and an A* ranked conference as AAMAS, the impact of WOA publications on declarative approaches to agent technologies and languages seems extremely significant.

3   From Data to Knowledge

In this section we organise raw data in a timeline, finding semantic connections among them and positioning the WOA contribution in the wider international panorama. Papers that are not dealt with in details in this book are discussed more in depth, and cross-references to other chapters are inserted when relevant.

3.1   Declarative and Logic-Based Agents

The importance of declarative and logic-based agent languages and technologies was recognised as early as the notion of intelligent agent was conceived. It was already clear in the seminal paper by Wooldridge and Jennings [185], that – referring to agent architectures – wrote

> *The close relationship between symbolic processing systems and mathematical logic means that the semantics of such architectures can often be represented as a logical system of some kind.*

Along this line, in the same year Kowalski presented the logical foundations of MAS [116] and, one year later, he addressed the problem of how logic programming and meta-programming in particular could be adopted to reconcile reactivity and proactivity (rationality) in agents [117,118].

The Italian research community has been traditionally very active in declarative approaches and in logic programming, with the "Gruppo Ricercatori e Utenti di Logic Programming" association dating back 1986. When the notion of intelligent agent was put forward, many Italian scientists working on declarative approaches started to apply them to the specification, prototyping, implementation and verification of agents and MAS. Most of them, are still doing.

It is not a case that the first edition of the Declarative Agent Languages and Technologies (DALT) workshop was organised in 2003 by scientists with a strong background in logic programming and Prolog, and that two of them were Italian. Out of ten DALT editions, nine were co-organised by Italian scientists. Today, the Preface of the first DALT edition is still (maybe, even more) valid in its statement *the growing complexity of agent systems calls for models and technologies that promote system predictability and enable feature discovery and verification. Formal methods and declarative technologies have recently attracted a growing interest as a means to address such issues.*

The active contribution of the Italian community to the development of the research area is also witnessed by recent surveys [54].

WOA mirrors, at the local scale, the evolution of the field at the international scale.

Tools and Languages. Among the oldest WOA papers in this category, most proposed either languages for specifying and programming agents [3,83,129,172], or languages for specifying and verifying agent interaction protocols [18,67,107], or architectures [10] and applications [139,167]. Among agent programming languages, the already mentioned DALI is discussed in detail in [183], while CaseLP will be discussed later in this chapter.

Coordination. Coordination is also a relevant problem to address, and is achieved via abductive reasoning [68] or via the TuCSoN [147] infrastructure [143].

Neuro-Symbolic Integration and Other Recent Trends. In the most recent papers, besides languages [55,70], platforms and architectures [53,120,121,137], applications [87,156] that are still relevant for the community, we observe an increasing number of proposals that cross-breed neural and symbolic approaches. The importance of this topic is also witnessed by [1], which is the chapter of this book devoted to it.

This integration is often aimed at making sub-symbolic AI explainable: an example of integration of symbolic and sub-symbolic techniques in the XAI context is presented by Calegari et al. [50] while Pisano et al. [152] present a set of guidelines based on logic induction and logic constraints aimed at building explainable intelligent systems even when they exploit sub-symbolic techniques, and discuss a working prototype. PSyKE [166] supports extraction of symbolic knowledge in logic form from different sorts of black-box predictors. Finally, an analysis of problems from the field of computational logic that may benefit from graph-related problems where Graph Neural Networks (GNN) has been proved effective, along with the application of GNN to logic theories via an end-to-end toy example, are presented by Agiollo et al. [2]. Fewer works target Reinforcement Learning, either for capturing a recursive pattern in neural-symbolic RL [27] or for integrating a runtime verification tool with OpenAI Gym, a popular framework for developing and comparing RL algorithms [180].

Works addressing games [65], the law application domain [56,86], the exploitation of Theory of Mind to boost collaboration [108], are also worth mentioning among the most recent contributions to WOA, belonging to the 'declarative and logic based agents' category.

3.2 Cognitive and BDI Agents

Due to the intersection among categories that we discussed in Section Sect. 2, some papers dealing with cognitive and BDI agents also deal with verification and with knowledge representation, and will be discussed later. In this section we overview those works with no overlaps with the categories discussed in Sections Sect. 3.3 and Sect. 3.4.

The history of BDI agents and languages is covered by many surveys. Besides an old one presented at WOA in 2005 [134], recent works involving Italian scientists [37,62] represent good readings for addressing the topic.

Tools and Languages. Among the works presented at early WOA editions we mention PRACTIONIST [127,140–142]. PRACTIONIST stands for PRACTIcal reasONIng sySTem; it is an old system supporting the development of BDI agents in Java (using JADE [26]) with a Prolog belief base. A goal-oriented approach drives the PRACTIONIST reasoning cycle, that clearly separates the deliberation and the means-ends reasoning, as well as the states of affairs to pursue and the way to do it. Works involving the Jason and CArtAgO (JaCa) environments, and their integration with web services, are also relevant examples of papers in this category [138,154]. A security mechanism for SOAP-style and REST-style web services that allows the distribution of the delegation of access rights among different rational agents is presented by Tomaiuolo and Turci [179].

BDI Agents and Robots. A more recent strand of research involves the theoretical and practical relations between BDI agents and robots. On the practical side, Alzetta and Giorgini propose an integraton of the BDI model into one of the most popular robotics frameworks, ROS 2 [5], while works by Falcone and colleagues [59,64] illustrate how to include self-modelling skills involved in trustworthy interactions, and how to exploit principles underlying theory of delegation, theory of mind and BDI agent modelling, to better shape the interactions with the humanoid robot Nao. The theoretical work by Cantucci and Falcone [61], on the other hand, outlines the development of computational cognitive models aimed at supporting a useful, effective, acceptable and trustworthy interaction between humans and robots.

Applications. Applications are always in the agenda, and range from cultural heritage domain [6,60] to interaction in natural language [122,173].

3.3 Formal Verification

Formal verification is the branch of formal methods focussed on verifying whether a system – or a model of the system – meets its specifications. Verification can be exhaustive, as in model checking or theorem proving, where the entire model is explored to ensure the property holds as specified. This means that all possible execution paths or states are considered, though the property itself may require verification on some paths (existential) or all paths (universal), depending on the formula. In contrast, non-exhaustive approaches, such as runtime verification or software testing, examine only a subset of possible executions – often limited to specific test cases or the current execution in runtime verification.

The importance of formal verification of agents and MAS has been discussed in many works [115], also in connection with the pressing need of certifying autonomous software systems [103]. As expected, many papers presented at WOA address this topic.

Model Checking. One of the oldest works published at WOA in this category deals with the application of model checking to the cryptographic mechanisms designed for the protection of mobile agents from their environment, with a particular emphasis on agent data integrity [125]. In details, the authors check the properties of a protocol model proposed by Corradi et al. [72] using a model checker developed at Polytechnic of Torino.

Probabilistic model checking is exploited by Casadei and Viroli [63]. The specification language used to model computational fields in pervasive and spatial systems is a variant of the PRISM language [110]; a generation process translates the model into a PRISM module and then builds a complete PRISM specification representing the whole network, ready to be model checked.

VITAMIN (VerIficaTion of A MultI-ageNt system [100]) is a formal verification framework integrating model checking algorithms for many different logics and model formalisms while providing a user-friendly experience. In that paper, VITAMIN is exploited in the robotics domain, focussing on an extension of Alternating-time Temporal Logic with resource bounds (RB-ATL).

Protocol Conformance. A bunch of papers addressed the problem of verifying a priori conformance of *atomic services* offered by individual agents and represented as finite state automata against a global interaction protocol (a choreography), also represented as a finite state automaton [17,18]. Given such a representation, a priori conformance test amounts to answering in a positive way to the following questions:

- Is it possible to verify that a service, playing a role in a given global protocol, produces at least those conversations which guarantee interoperability with other conformant service?
- Will such a service always follow one of these conversations when interacting with the other parties in the context of the protocol?
- Will it always be able to conclude the legal conversations it is involved in?

An extension of a priori protocol conformance that takes into account the possibility for agent names and messages to have different syntax, but equivalent (hence the 'modulo mapping') semantics, is presented in [8]. Conformance check is fully implemented in SWI-Prolog.

Linear Time Logic is used in [15], where – in the domain of declarative presentation of curricula – model checking techniques are used to verify that the user's learning goal is supplied by a curriculum, that a curriculum is compliant to a curricula model, and that competence gaps are avoided.

Protocol Combination. In [107] interaction protocols are defined by a set of temporal constraints, which specify the effects and preconditions of the communicative actions on the social state. The problem of combining protocols to define new more specialised protocols is addressed and the approach is applied to the specification and verification of clinical guidelines. The work by Chesani et al. [67] is similar in the adoption of a logic-based framework and also in the medical guidelines application domain.

Runtime Verification. Papers on runtime verification appeared only recently at WOA, coherently with the recent take-up of this approach w.r.t. more consolidated techniques. In [7], we address the problem of decentralised runtime verification of agent interaction protocols by means of MAS-DRiVe, an algorithm implemented in SWI-Prolog that partitions a MAS into sub-MASs which can be monitored independently. The already cited RMLGym [180] allows users to define reward functions using RML specifications [9] and then generates reward monitors that evaluate the agent's performance and provide feedback at each step.

Testing and Validation via Explanations. Although not based on formal methods, we mention the conceptual framework, supported by a working prototype, proposed by Yan et al. [186]. The tool creates narratives explaining the behaviour of a Jason agent at multiple levels of abstractions, meant to be useful at different levels – developers, designers, users. During the testing and validation phases, developers can use the explanation of the agents, take the narrative, and check the requirements to see if they meet them, or compare the narrative with the user stories of the system to ensure alignment. While this must be made manually, so far, there is room for taking advantage of past experience of conformance check and formal verification, to make the above tasks more automatic and well grounded.

3.4   Semantic Web and Ontologies

The close relation between agents and semantic web technologies, especially ontologies, is as old as the semantic web itself [109], and is witnessed by many publications since then [85,135].

FIPA and Ontology Services. In 2000, the first FIPA Ontology Service Specification was released[3]. In the early WOA editions, many papers proposed FIPA-compliant architectures integrating ontology service providers [40,148,181] or frameworks that – albeit not being FIPA-compliant – aimed at offering services for retrieving, managing, mapping ontologies in MAS with mobile agents [74] or in service-oriented architectures [155,178]. More recently, Ruta et al. [164] follow the service-oriented architecture research line by proposing a framework where device agents self-organise in social relationships, interact autonomously and

---

[3] http://www.fipa.org/specs/fipa00086/XC00086C.pdf.

share information, cooperating and orchestrating ambient resources. A a service-oriented architecture allows collaborative dissemination, discovery and composition of service/resource descriptions by device agents. Decision and choreography capabilities of software agents leverage Semantic Web languages at the knowledge representation layer.

Ontologies and Agent Languages. JADEL [30] is the ancestor of the Jadescript language also presented at WOA [33,149], and not only [29,32]. JADEL and JadeScript provide ontologies not only to enable fruitful communication among agents, following the FIPA specifcations, but also to define structured data that can be used in the construction of the agents and their behaviours. In order to support this extended approach to the use of ontologies, Jadescript treats ontologies as organised packages of concepts, actions, predicates, and propositions.

Moving from JADE to the Jason (and its ecosystem) language, Chella et al. [66] implement a controlled semantic system to manage the belief base of a MAS at runtime. Their goal is achieved by interfacing Jason, CArtAgO and the Jena library[4] for managing OWL ontologies.

Ontology Models. In [79,161] the Problem Ontology metamodel, inspired by the FIPA standard, is used for describing the problem domain by a set of meta classes (Concept, Action and Predicate) in a BDI context. OntologyBeanGenerator 5.0 [43] is also based on the model driven approach – where the model is represented by an ontology – and injects programming components inside an ontology: OntologyBeanGenerator 5.0 extends the OntologyBeanGenerator plugin for Protégé in order to generate a Java representation of an OWL ontology for Jade, and supports the modelling of exceptions, formalised at the ontology level, and of methods associated with ontology elements, to set the interface of artifacts at design time.

Applications and Other Recent Trends. Applications where ontologies are exploited in combination with agents and MAS span very diverse domains. In [126] an ontology based on fuzzy logic is used inside a tool that analyses different crowded scenarios – in particular, concerts – according to crowd features like density and duration.

In [124], automatic interpretation and execution of laboratory protocols expressed in XPDL+OWL in the life sciences domain is carried out thanks to a MAS implemented with JADE and WADE [49].

Loseto et al. designed and implemented an agent able to perform an automated profile annotation by adopting Semantic Web languages, and tested it in a domotic environment [123].

PRESTO [47] applies agent technologies to serious gaming by creating game independent, modular Non-Player Characters behaviours based on a BDI approach. Both the environment and the internal state of the NPC are modelled via ontologies [46]. VideOWL [131] classifies video games starting from their core features, hence belonging to a domain similar to PRESTO's one.

---

[4] https://jena.apache.org/.

The Indiana MAS project [132] and the VEsNA framework [112], discussed in Section Sect. 4, also integrate ontologies and semantic web technologies.

3.5 Argumentation

The three WOA papers that – based on their title and abstract – deal with argumentation are all co-authored by Omicini and cover a range of 14 years, from 2008 to 2021.

In the oldest one [144] the authors present a system for Alternative Dispute Resolution exploiting a Co-Argumentation Artifact and a Dialogue Artifact to coordinate the agents during the argumentative process. The technological support for the artifacts is provided by the already mentioned TuCSoN infrastructure. For each argument set, the argument validity; the relations of undercut and attack between arguments; the conflict-free sets; and the preferred extensions are computed in Prolog, via metaprogramming.

Pisano et al. [150] address the problem of cooperative argumentation in the context of a MAS. The logic-based agreement framework Arg2P [151] evaluates the admissibility of a single statement without building the entire argumentation graph: starting from the Arg2P single query evaluation mode, they introduce the corresponding distributed computational model. In their WOA paper, they show how the argument evaluation algorithm of Arg2P can be parallelised, and present a complete model for decentralised reasoning based on the actor model.

Finally, the work by Calegari et al. [56] tackles argumentation from a theoretical point of view: it introduces the concept of computable law as an argumentation-based MAS and investigates the most promising approaches and technologies – among which, knowledge representation and ontologies, machine learning, argumentation models and technologies, human-computer interfaces – that may be exploited for engineering of systems and services.

4 From CaseLP to VEsNA

Nomen omen. The story of our research group starts with the design and development of CaseLP,[5] whose name has a double reading. On the one hand, the acronym expands into 'Complex Application Specification Environment based on Logic Programming', stressing our interest in developing applications that are complex enough to be challenging and exciting, and in exploiting Logic Programming for achieving our goal. On the other hand, 'Case' intentionally reminds to 'Computer Aided Software Engineering', emphasising the engineering dimension of our research, that – over years – covered the theory and practice of MAS specification, implementation, and verification, often in collaboration with industrial partners.

The first paper mentioning CaseLP was published in 1998 [130]. From a descriptive point of view, a CaseLP agent is characterised by a *kind* (logical,

---

[5] https://person.dibris.unige.it/mascardi-viviana/Software/DCaseLP.html.

interface, facilitator or manager), an *architecture* (data structures that form the agent's internal components + control flow), an *interpreter* and a *set of services*. From a computational point of view it consists of a *state*, a *behaviour* and an *engine*, that are all architecture-dependent components. Private and public *mail-boxes* are further components, needed to ensure asynchronous communication among agents. CaseLP comes with a simple engineering methodology, whose steps include: 1. identification of the set of agents and their interconnecting structure; 2. choice of the communication protocol among each pair of communicating agents; 3. specification of the behaviour of each agent in the system; 4. implementation of the prototype; 5. execution of the obtained prototype.

After 26 years, our core business is still engineering complex applications modelled and implemented as MAS, by exploiting symbolic approaches when it makes sense (and other approaches when they are more suitable). In the meantime, the world evolved, and we evolved too.

In this section, we illustrate our evolution following the most significant papers that we presented at WOA from 2000 to 2024.

Our starting point is HEMASL [129], a meta-language for specifying agent architectures in an imperative way, and translating them into a set of clauses in $\mathcal{E}_{hhf}$ [91], a language based on linear logic. $\mathcal{E}_{hhf}$ specifications can be tested and/or verified and refined in CaseLP and finally translated into Prolog, for being executed. The distributed version of CaseLP, DCaseLP, was first presented at WOA 2002 [3]. DCaseLP integrates both imperative (object-oriented) and declarative (rule-based and logic-based) languages, as well as the UML graphical notation.[6] The rationale behind DCaseLP is that MAS development requires engineering support for a diverse range of non-functional properties, such as understandability of the MAS at various conceptual levels, integrability of heterogeneous agent architectures, usability, re-usability, and testability. By providing the MAS developer with a set of languages, and allowing for the choice of the most suitable language to model, implement, or test each property, DCaseLP heads towards a modular approach to Agent-Oriented Software Engineering [114].

The development of approaches and tools to verify the agents' behaviour – whose importance had already been devised in the early papers on HEMASL and CaseLP – characterised a long and fruitful collaboration with researchers from Torino [18] and from other universities [13].

While working on the more theoretical aspects of MAS specification and verification, we also managed to design and implement real MAS, in collaboration with industries or within funded projects. Two of these projects were developed together with Ansaldo STS S.p.A., now Hitachi Rail STS S.p.A.. The first started in February 2008 and ended in September 2008, and consisted in a MAS prototype implemented in DCaseLP that monitors processes running in a railway signalling plant, detects functioning anomalies, and provides support to the early notification of problems to the Command and Control System Assistance [44]. The second was a multiagent resource allocation problem [42], solved

---

[6] https://www.uml.org/.

by means of a complex negotiation protocol named FYPA (Find Your Path, Agents!) among the involved entities. The problem is described as *"For each entity that enters the graph from a start point either confirm the validity of the plan stated in the static allocation plan, or, if some unexpected event occurred that makes the original plan no longer applicable, find a new plan for reaching an end point of the graph. The new plan should minimise the delay in which the entity exits the graph and the number of required changes with respect to the original plan, as well as the number of entities involved in the reallocation process."* [45]

Due to an NDA, we could not be explicit on what entities and graph edges represent. They can be easily guessed, given that Ansaldo STS dealt with trains that enter rail stations on pre-allocated tracks, which may no longer be available when the train is approaching, hence triggering a re-planning. A NetLogo interface for a standalone version of FYPA was also developed [41].

A project developed with SELEX Elsag S.p.A., now Leonardo S.p.A., consisted in the Jade implementation of a MAS for solving unavailability problems in a scenario inspired by the electricity power network domain [119].

The Indiana MAS project obtained a funding of 747.600 euros by the Italian Ministry of Education, University and Research "Futuro in Ricerca 2010" program.[7] It provides a framework for the digital protection and conservation of rock art natural and cultural heritage sites, by storing, organising and suitably presenting information about them. Its objectives, illustrated at WOA 2012 [132], were to develop a MAS supporting archaeologists and historians in 1. integrating heterogeneous unstructured data (multilingual textual documents, pictures, and drawings) related to rock carvings into a single repository; 2. normalising data by recognising those referring to the same object, correctly associating them with its digital representation, and removing duplicate data; 3. classifying normalised data according to the "Indiana ontology"; 4. organising classified data into a Digital Library and making the library accessible thanks to a web-based, multilingual, user-friendly interface; 5. interpreting data stored in the Digital Library, finding relations among them, and enriching them with the semantic information extracted thanks to this interpretation and relation retrieval stage. The project successfully achieved its goals: videos showing demos be found in the project's web site,[8] together with all the project's papers and deliverables.

We attended WOA on a regular basis in these 25 years: many papers published after 2012 dealt with verification and ontologies, and have been already discussed in Section Sect. 3.

Our most recent contribution, VEsNA [99,105,112], can be seen as a CaseLP 4.0: it is still conceived as an environment for engineering software prototypes of complex applications, and is still (also) rooted on logic programming but – as for Industry 4.0 – it pays more attention to human-computer interaction, to the continuum between physical and digital worlds, and to safety.

---

[7] http://indianamas.dibris.unige.it/.

[8] http://indianamas.dibris.unige.it/index.php/the-indianamas-demonstrator.

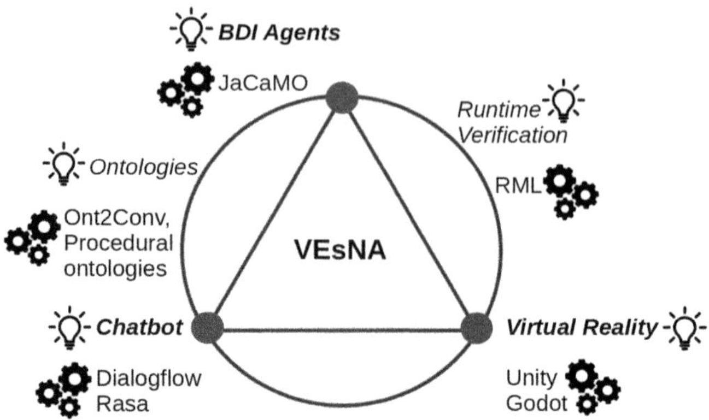

Fig. 8. VEsNA concept.

VEsNA is a general-purpose and agent-based framework for managing Virtual Environments via Natural language Agents. As shown in Fig. 8, VEsNA builds upon three pillars:

(i) a chatbot-like interface to support the sociality of agents; thanks to the chatbot supporting natural language interaction, sociality is not limited to agent-agent conversations, but it is extended to agent-human ones;

(ii) a framework for building the dynamic virtual environment; virtual reality is very suitable for supporting agents' situatendness and embodiment: therein, agents are expected to perceive the reality and to act over it;

(iii) a framework for implementing cognitive, declarative agents able to reason about knowledge (about what users say, about the environment, about themselves) and to provide human-readable explanations.

The chatbot interface can be implemented in both Dialogflow[9] and Rasa[10], and the virtual environment in both Unity[11] and Godot[12]. The framework for BDI agents is JaCaMo.

A mechanism for verifying the behaviour of the system's components, at runtime is also integrated in the VEsNA concept: runtime verification is supported by the adoption of the Runtime Monitoring Language, RML [9], compiled down into SWI-Prolog and whose monitoring engine is implemented in SWI-Prolog too.

The presence of ontologies in VEsNA was considered since the very beginning as a tool to provide a unique specification of the conversation domain, and generate skeletons for both the Jason agents in the backend and the chatbot frontend from it [95]. In our WOA 2024 paper, we illustrated the possibility to use ontologies also to describe agents' behaviours [112].

---

[9] https://cloud.google.com/dialogflow.

[10] https://rasa.com/.

[11] https://unity.com/.

[12] https://godotengine.org/.

All the VEsNA components are implemented, working, and available online under GPL 2.0 license, although they are not all fully integrated into a unique repository, yet[13].

The technological panorama changed dramatically from 2000 to nowadays, with the perceived and narrated supremacy of sub-symbolic approaches over symbolic ones, and the Large Language Models breakthrough in the last few years. We evolved and did our best to adapt to these changes, but we never retreated from our original vision of science and of agent oriented software engineering. We are confident we will continue to keep the pace: technology goes fast, but also VEsNA does!

5   Future Perspectives and Conclusions

Declarative approaches have proven to be essential in fields like MAS due to their emphasis on transparency, interpretability, and rule-based decision-making. Unlike black-box models, declarative systems allow for explicit reasoning about the system's behaviour, enabling easier identification and correction of biases and hence supporting trust and accountability. These characteristics are increasingly vital as AI systems are deployed in high-stakes domains where explainability and reliability are crucial.

In the MAS area, declarative models have been particularly successful in providing modularity and flexibility, enabling systems to adapt more easily to new rules and environments. Their ability to model complex organisational constraints, as demonstrated by frameworks like JaCaMo, highlights the practical advantages of declarative approaches in managing distributed, autonomous agents.

Looking to the future, one potential direction lies in neuro-symbolic AI, where declarative and logic approaches could complement the data-driven nature of machine learning, providing structured, rule-based reasoning alongside the adaptability of neural networks. This integration could address the opaque nature of black-box models, making AI systems more interpretable while preserving their powerful pattern recognition capabilities.

Another exciting direction is the application of declarative approaches in the development of chatbots and conversational agents. These systems, widely used today, often struggle with issues like unpredictability, lack of coherence, and ethical concerns. By combining the flexibility of machine learning-driven chatbots with the robustness, inspectability and explainability of declarative methods, we can create conversational agents that are not only more reliable but also capable of motivating their decisions and maintaining consistency with human values.

---

[13] https://github.com/VEsNA-ToolKit.

In summary, declarative approaches offer powerful tools for building trustworthy and reliable AI systems. As AI continues to evolve, their integration with other advanced techniques, particularly in areas like machine learning and conversational systems, is likely to unlock new possibilities for creating more responsible and effective intelligent systems.'

Acknowledgments. This work was partially supported by the following projects:

– *T-LADIES – Typeful Language Adaptation for Dynamic, Interacting and Evolving Systems*, funded by the Italian MUR program PRIN 2020 under grant number 2020TL3X8X

– *ENGINES – ENGineering INtElligent Systems around intelligent agent technologies*, funded by the European Union – Next Generation EU within the framework of the National Recovery and Resilience Plan NRRP – Mission 4 "Education and Research" – Component 2 – Investment 1.1 "National Research Program and Projects of Significant National Interest Fund (PRIN)" – Call PRIN 2022 – D.D. n. 104 of 02/02/2022, under grant number 20229ZXBZM

– *FAIR – Future Artificial Intelligence Research*, PNRR MUR Project PE0000013 funded by the European Union – NextGenerationEU, CUP J33C24000420007

Appendix

In this Appendix we list the 107 papers published at WOA from 2000 to 2024, dealing with declarative agent technologies. Each column stands for one feature that may or may not characterise the paper (the ✓ sign), based on our keyword-based search on the papers' titles and abstracts. Besides the reference and the publication year, tables show the family name that appears first in the list of authors as in most cases it helps identifying the research group that worked on the paper. The keywords we looked for, along with their syntactic and semantic variants, are:

Dec. Declarative;
Log. Logic (in general);
LP Logic Programming;
Prol. Prolog;
BDI;

Cog. Cognitive;
MC Model checking;
Ver. Verification;
Con. Conformance checking;
Ont. Ontology/OWL/Semantic Web;
Arg. Argumentation.

Table 1. Table 1

Ref.	1st Auth.	Yr	Dec.	Log.	LP	Prol.	BDI	Cog.	MC	Ver.	Con.	Ont.	Arg.
[10]	Armando	2000		✓									
[68]	Ciampolini	2000		✓									
[129]	Marini	2000		✓									
[139]	Montaldo	2001	✓										
[160]	Repetto	2001	✓										
[3]	Albertoni	2002				✓							
[125]	Maggi	2002								✓			
[83]	Costantini	2003			✓								
[172]	Schifanella	2004				✓						✓	
[178]	Tomaiuolo	2004										✓	
[18]	Baldoni	2005	✓	✓			✓			✓	✓		
[21]	Baldoni	2005		✓								✓	
[39]	Bouquet	2005		✓									
[48]	Cabitza	2005	✓										
[67]	Chesani	2005		✓						✓			
[71]	Cordì	2005										✓	
[74]	Corradini	2005										✓	
[84]	Costantini	2005		✓									
[107]	Giordano	2005		✓						✓			

Table 2. Table 2

Ref.	1st Auth.	Yr	Dec.	Log.	LP	Prol.	BDI	Cog.	MC	Ver.	Con.	Ont.	Arg.
[134]	Mascardi	2005		✓			✓						
[140]	Morreale	2005				✓	✓						
[17]	Baldoni	2006								✓	✓		
[81]	Costantini	2006	✓	✓									
[141]	Morreale	2006					✓						
[142]	Morreale	2006					✓						
[143]	Oliva	2006		✓			✓						
[175]	Sguera	2006										✓	
[181]	Vecchiola	2006										✓	
[15]	Baldoni	2007	✓	✓					✓	✓			
[57]	Cannata	2007		✓								✓	
[92]	Deufemia	2007		✓			✓						
[133]	Mascardi	2007										✓	
[155]	Poggi	2007										✓	
[19]	Baldoni	2008	✓										
[40]	Briola	2008										✓	
[44]	Briola	2008				✓							
[127]	Marguglio	2008					✓						
[144]	Oliva	2008				✓						✓	✓
[126]	Magnolo	2009										✓	
[148]	Passadore	2009										✓	
[154]	Piunti	2009						✓					
[13]	Baldoni	2010								✓			
[97]	Falcone	2010		✓			✓						
[102]	Fichera	2010	✓										
[124]	Maccagnan	2010										✓	
[138]	Minotti	2010					✓						
[153]	Piunti	2010					✓						
[168]	Santi	2010					✓						
[179]	Tomaiuolo	2010					✓						
[6]	Amato	2011					✓						
[16]	Baldoni	2011	✓										
[76]	Cossentino	2011					✓						
[12]	Baldoni	2012	✓										
[63]	Casadei	2012							✓	✓			
[132]	Mascardi	2012										✓	
[123]	Loseto	2013										✓	
[161]	Ribino	2013					✓					✓	
[79]	Cossentino	2014					✓					✓	
[46]	Busetta	2015					✓	✓				✓	
[171]	Sapienza	2015						✓					
[7]	Ancona	2016								✓			
[30]	Bergenti	2016										✓	
[55]	Calegari	2016			✓	✓							

Table 3. Table 3

Ref.	1st Auth.	Yr	Dec.	Log.	LP	Prol.	BDI	Cog.	MC	Ver.	Con.	Ont.	Arg.
[128]	Mariani	2016					✓						
[8]	Ancona	2018									✓		
[43]	Briola	2018					✓					✓	
[53]	Calegari	2018			✓								
[66]	Chella	2018					✓					✓	
[69]	Ciatto	2018			✓								
[77]	Cossentino	2018					✓					✓	
[122]	Longo	2018	✓				✓						
[164]	Ruta	2018										✓	
[5]	Alzetta	2019					✓						
[50]	Calegari	2019			✓								
[58]	Cantone	2019										✓	
[59]	Cantucci	2019					✓	✓					
[64]	Castelfranchi	2019					✓						
[78]	Cossentino	2019					✓						
[87]	D'Asaro	2019		✓									
[56]	Calegari	2020		✓								✓	✓
[70]	Ciatto	2020			✓	✓							
[120]	Longo	2020		✓			✓	✓					
[152]	Pisano	2020		✓									
[2]	Agiollo	2021			✓								
[121]	Longo	2021		✓				✓				✓	
[150]	Pisano	2021										✓	✓
[166]	Sabbatini	2021			✓								
[24]	Bella	2022										✓	
[60]	Cantucci	2022					✓	✓					
[65]	Catta	2022		✓									
[156]	Rafanelli	2022		✓									
[173]	Seidita	2022					✓	✓					
[176]	Sterling	2022		✓									
[27]	Beretta	2023	✓	✓									
[61]	Cantucci	2023						✓					
[82]	Costantini	2023		✓									
[131]	Martino	2023										✓	
[137]	Messina	2023	✓	✓									
[165]	Sabbatini	2023						✓					
[174]	Seidita	2023					✓						
[180]	Unniyankal	2023	✓	✓						✓			
[186]	Yan	2023					✓			✓			
[36]	Bordini	2024			✓	✓	✓						
[86]	Cristani	2024		✓			✓						
[100]	Ferrando	2024		✓						✓			
[108]	Grimaldi	2024		✓			✓						
[112]	Ivan	2024	✓					✓				✓	

References

1. Agiollo, A., Calegari, R., Ciatto, G., Magnini, M., Omicini, A., Sabbatini, F.: Intelligent agents from symbolic to neurosymbolic systems: the quest for integration. In: Mascardi and Omicini [136]
2. Agiollo, A., Ciatto, G., Omicini, A.: Graph neural networks as the copula mundi between logic and machine learning: a roadmap. In: Calegari et al. [52], pp. 98–115. http://ceur-ws.org/Vol-2963/paper18.pdf
3. Albertoni, R., Martelli, M., Mascardi, V., Miglia, S.: Specifica, implementazione ed esecuzione di un prototipo di sistema multi-agente in D-CaseLP. In: De Paoli et al. [89], pp. 149–156. http://giuseppevizzari.github.io/WOA-proceedings-archive/pdfs/woa2002/14.pdf
4. Alderighi, M., Baldoni, M., Baroglio, C., Micalizio, R., Tedeschi, S. (eds.): WOA 2024 – 25th Workshop "From Objects to Agents", CEUR Workshop Proceedings, vol. 3735. Bard, AO, Italy (2024). http://ceur-ws.org/Vol-3735/
5. Alzetta, F., Giorgini, P.: Towards a real-time BDI model for ROS 2. In: Bergenti and Monica [31], pp. 1–7. http://ceur-ws.org/Vol-2404/paper01.pdf
6. Amato, A., Di Martino, B., Venticinque, S.: BDI intelligent agents for augmented exploitation of pervasive environments. In: Fortino et al. [104], pp. 81–88. http://ceur-ws.org/Vol-741/ID16_AmatoDiMartinoVenticinque.pdf
7. Ancona, D., Briola, D., Ferrando, A., Mascardi, V.: MAS-DRiVe: a practical approach to decentralized runtime verification of agent interaction protocols. In: Santoro et al. [170], pp. 35–43. http://ceur-ws.org/Vol-1664/w7.pdf
8. Ancona, D., Ferrando, A., Mascardi, V.: Agents interoperability via conformance modulo mapping. In: Cossentino et al. [80], pp. 109–115. http://ceur-ws.org/Vol-2215/paper_18.pdf
9. Ancona, D., Franceschini, L., Ferrando, A., Mascardi, V.: RML: theory and practice of a domain specific language for runtime verification. Sci. Comput. Program. **205**, 102610 (2021)
10. Armando, A., Zini, D.: Towards interoperable mechanized reasoning systems: the logic broker architecture. In: Corradi et al. [73], pp. 70–75. http://lia.disi.unibo.it/books/woa00/pdf/14.pdf
11. Armano, G., Paoli, F.D., Omicini, A., Vargiu, E. (eds.): WOA 2003 – 4th Workshop "From Objects to Agents". Pitagora Editrice Bologna, Villasimius, CA, Italy (2003). http://giuseppevizzari.github.io/WOA-proceedings-archive/woa-2003.html
12. Baldoni, M., Baroglio, C.: Some thoughts about commitment protocols (position paper). In: De Paoli and Vizzari [90], pp. 68–71. http://ceur-ws.org/Vol-892/paper11.pdf
13. Baldoni, M., et al.: MERCURIO: an interaction-oriented framework for designing, verifying and programming multi-agent systems. In: Omicini and Viroli [146], pp. 87–94. http://ceur-ws.org/Vol-621/paper13.pdf
14. Baldoni, M., Baroglio, C., Bergenti, F., Garro, A. (eds.): WOA 2013 – 14th Workshop "From Objects to Agents", CEUR Workshop Proceedings, vol. 1099. Turin, Italy (2013). http://ceur-ws.org/Vol-1099/
15. Baldoni, M., Baroglio, C., Berio, G., Marengo, E.: Declarative representation of curricula models: an LTL-and UML-based approach. In: Baldoni et al. [20], pp. 34–41. http://woa07.dibris.unige.it/papers/BaldoniDeclarative.pdf
16. Baldoni, M., Baroglio, C., Marengo, E., Patti, V., Capuzzimati, F.: Learn the rules so you know how to break them properly. In: Fortino et al. [104], pp. 11–18. http://ceur-ws.org/Vol-741/ID1_BaldoniBaroglioMarengoPattiCapuzzimati.pdf

17. Baldoni, M., Baroglio, C., Martelli, A., Patti, V.: Conformance and interoperability in open enviroments. In: De Paoli et al. [88], pp. 151–157. http://ceur-ws.org/Vol-204/P11.pdf
18. Baldoni, M., Baroglio, C., Martelli, A., Patti, V., Schifanella, C., Torasso, L., Mascardi, V.: Personalization, verification and conformance for logic-based communicating agents. In: Corradini et al. [75], pp. 177–183. http://lia.deis.unibo.it/books/woa2005/papers/25.pdf
19. Baldoni, M., Baroglio, C., Patti, V., Schifanella, C.: Conservative re-use ensuring matches for service selection. In: Baldoni et al. [22], pp. 28–36. http://www.pa.icar.cnr.it/woa08/materiali/paper/paper_8.pdf
20. Baldoni, M., Boccalatte, A., De Paoli, F., Martelli, M., Mascardi, V. (eds.): WOA 2007 – 8th Workshop "From Objects to Agents". Seneca Edizioni Torino, Genova, Italy (2007). http://woa07.disi.unige.it/ProceedingsWOA2007.zip
21. Baldoni, M., Boella, G., van der Torre, L.W.N.: Social roles, from agents back to objects. In: Corradini et al. [75], pp. 164–170. http://lia.deis.unibo.it/books/woa2005/papers/23.pdf
22. Baldoni, M., Cossentino, M., De Paoli, F., Seidita, V. (eds.): WOA 2008 – 9th Workshop "From Objects to Agents". Seneca Edizioni Torino, Palermo, Italy (2008). http://www.pa.icar.cnr.it/woa08/materiali/Proceedings.pdf
23. Baldoni, M., De Paoli, F., Martelli, A., Omicini, A. (eds.): WOA 2004 – 5th Workshop "From Objects to Agents". Pitagora Editrice Bologna, Torino, Italy (2004). http://lia.deis.unibo.it/books/woa2004/atti.pdf
24. Bella, G., Cantone, D., Nicolosi Asmundo, M., Santamaria, D.F.: The ontology for agents, systems and integration of services: Recent advancements of OASIS. In: Ferrando and Mascardi [101], pp. 176–193. http://ceur-ws.org/Vol-3261/paper14.pdf
25. Bellamy, R.K., Dey, K., Hind, M., Hoffman, S.C., Houde, S., Kannan, K., Lohia, P., Martino, J., Mehta, S., Mojsilović, A., et al.: AI Fairness 360: An extensible toolkit for detecting and mitigating algorithmic bias. IBM J. Res. Dev. **63**(4/5), 4–1 (2019)
26. Bellifemine, F.L., Caire, G., Greenwood, D.: Developing Multi-Agent Systems with JADE. John Wiley & Sons (2007)
27. Beretta, D., Monica, S., Bergenti, F.: Capturing a recursive pattern in neural-symbolic reinforcement learning. In: Falcone et al. [98], pp. 17–31. http://ceur-ws.org/Vol-3579/paper2.pdf
28. Bergenti, F. (ed.): WOA 2009 – 10th Workshop "From Objects to Agents". Seneca Edizioni Torino, Parma, Italy (2009). http://www.ailab.unipr.it/woa09/papers/
29. Bergenti, F., Caire, G., Monica, S., Poggi, A.: The first twenty years of agent-based software development with JADE. Auton. Agents Multi-Agent Syst. **34**(36) (2020). https://doi.org/10.1007/s10458-020-09460-z
30. Bergenti, F., Iotti, E., Monica, S., Poggi, A.: A case study of the JADEL programming language. In: Santoro et al. [170], pp. 85–90. http://ceur-ws.org/Vol-1664/w15.pdf
31. Bergenti, F., Monica, S. (eds.): WOA 2019 – 20th Workshop "From Objects to Agents", CEUR Workshop Proceedings, vol. 2404. Parma, Italy (2019). http://ceur-ws.org/Vol-2404/
32. Bergenti, F., Monica, S., Petrosino, G.: A comprehensive presentation of the Jadescript agent-oriented programming language. In: EUMAS. Lecture Notes in Computer Science, vol. 14282, pp. 100–115. Springer, Cham (2023)
33. Bergenti, F., Petrosino, G.: Overview of a scripting language for JADE-based multi-agent systems. In: Cossentino et al. [80], pp. 57–62. http://ceur-ws.org/Vol-2215/paper_10.pdf

34. Boissier, O., Bordini, R.H., Hübner, J.F., Ricci, A.: Multi-Agent Oriented Programming: Programming Multi-Agent Systems Using JaCaMo. The MIT Press (2020). https://mitpress.mit.edu/9780262044578/multi-agent-oriented-programming/

35. Boissier, O., Bordini, R.H., Hübner, J.F., Ricci, A., Santi, A.: Multi-agent oriented programming with JaCaMo. Sci. Comput. Program. **78**(6), 747–761 (2013). https://doi.org/10.1016/j.scico.2011.10.004

36. Bordini, R.H., Costantini, S., Monaldini, A., Vozna, A.: From pure Prolog to logic agent-oriented programming languages. In: Alderighi et al. [4], pp. 271–285. http://ceur-ws.org/Vol-3735/paper_20.pdf

37. Bordini, R.H., El Fallah Seghrouchni, A., Hindriks, K.V., Logan, B., Ricci, A.: Agent programming in the cognitive era. Auton. Agents Multi-Agent Syst. **34**(37) (2020). https://doi.org/10.1007/s10458-020-09453-y

38. Bordini, R.H., Hübner, J.F., Wooldridge, M.J.: Programming Multi-Agent Systems in AgentSpeak using Jason. Wiley (2007). https://www.wiley.com/Programming+Multi-Agent+Systems+in+AgentSpeak+using+Jason-p-9780470061831

39. Bouquet, P., Kuper, G.M., Zanobini, S.: Asking and answering queries semantically. In: Corradini et al. [75], pp. 22–27. http://lia.deis.unibo.it/books/woa2005/papers/4.pdf

40. Briola, D., Locoro, A., Mascardi, V.: Ontology agents in FIPA-compliant platforms: a survey and a new proposal. In: Baldoni et al. [22], pp. 68–75. http://www.pa.icar.cnr.it/woa08/materiali/paper/paper_7.pdf

41. Briola, D., Mascardi, V.: Design and implementation of a NetLogo interface for the stand-alone FYPA system. In: Fortino et al. [104], pp. 41–50. http://ceur-ws.org/Vol-741/ID10_Briola_Mascardi.pdf

42. Briola, D., Mascardi, V.: Multi agent resource allocation: a comparison of five negotiation protocols. In: Fortino et al. [104], pp. 95–104. http://ceur-ws.org/Vol-741/ID9_Briola_Mascardi.pdf

43. Briola, D., Mascardi, V., Gioseffi, M.: OntologyBeanGenerator 5.0: Extending ontology concepts with methods and exceptions. In: Cossentino et al. [80], pp. 116–123. http://ceur-ws.org/Vol-2215/paper_19.pdf

44. Briola, D., Mascardi, V., Martelli, M., Arecco, G., Caccia, R., Milani, C.: A Prolog-based MAS for railway signalling monitoring: Implementation and experiments. In: Baldoni et al. [22], pp. 11–18, http://www.pa.icar.cnr.it/woa08/materiali/paper/paper_4.pdf

45. Briola, D., Mascardi, V., Martelli, M., Caccia, R., Milani, C.: Dynamic resource allocation in a MAS: A case study from the industry. In: Bergenti [28], pp. 125–133. http://www.ailab.unipr.it/woa09/papers/Briola.pdf

46. Busetta, P., Dragoni, M.: Composing cognitive agents from behavioural models in PRESTO. In: Di Napoli et al. [93], pp. 85–90. http://ceur-ws.org/Vol-1382/paper13.pdf

47. Busetta, P., Ghidini, C., Pedrotti, M., De Angeli, A., Menestrina, Z., et al.: Briefing virtual actors: a first report on the PRESTO project. In: Proceedings of the AI and Games Symposium at AISB (2014)

48. Cabitza, F., Locatelli, M.P., Sarini, M.: CASMAS: an agent-based support for modulated participation in cooperative applications. In: Corradini et al. [75], pp. 111–119. http://lia.deis.unibo.it/books/woa2005/papers/16.pdf

49. Caire, G., Gotta, D., Banzi, M.: WADE: a software platform to develop mission critical applications exploiting agents and workflows. In: AAMAS (Industry Track), pp. 29–36. IFAAMAS (2008)

50. Calegari, R., Ciatto, G., Dellaluce, J., Omicini, A.: Interpretable narrative explanation for ML predictors with LP: a case study for XAI. In: Bergenti and Monica [31], pp. 105–112. http://ceur-ws.org/Vol-2404/paper16.pdf
51. Calegari, R., Ciatto, G., Denti, E., Omicini, A., Sartor, G. (eds.): WOA 2020 – 21st Workshop "From Objects to Agents", CEUR Workshop Proceedings, vol. 2706. Bologna, Italy (2020). http://ceur-ws.org/Vol-2706/
52. Calegari, R., Ciatto, G., Denti, E., Omicini, A., Sartor, G. (eds.): WOA 2021 – 22nd Workshop "From Objects to Agents", CEUR Workshop Proceedings, vol. 2963. Bologna, Italy (2021). http://ceur-ws.org/Vol-2963/
53. Calegari, R., Ciatto, G., Mariani, S., Denti, E., Omicini, A.: Logic programming in space-time: The case of situatedness in LPaaS. In: Cossentino et al. [80], pp. 63–68. http://ceur-ws.org/Vol-2215/paper_11.pdf
54. Calegari, R., Ciatto, G., Mascardi, V., Omicini, A.: Logic-based technologies for multi-agent systems: a systematic literature review. Auton. Agents Multi-Agent Syst. **35**(1) (2021). https://doi.org/10.1007/s10458-020-09478-3
55. Calegari, R., Denti, E., Mariani, S., Omicini, A.: Towards logic programming as a service: Experiments in tuProlog. In: Santoro et al. [170], pp. 79–84. http://ceur-ws.org/Vol-1664/w14.pdf
56. Calegari, R., Omicini, A., Sartor, G.: Computable law as argumentation-based MAS. In: Calegari et al. [51], pp. 54–68. http://ceur-ws.org/Vol-2706/paper10.pdf
57. Cannata, N., Corradini, F., Piersigilli, F., Merelli, E., Vito, L.: Semantic resource management in MAS. In: Baldoni et al. [20], pp. 42–47. http://woa07.disi.unige.it/papers/CannataSemantic.pdf
58. Cantone, D., Longo, C.F., Nicolosi Asmundo, M., Santamaria, D.F., Santoro, C.: Towards an ontology-based framework for a behavior-oriented integration of the IoT. In: Bergenti and Monica [31], pp. 119–126. http://ceur-ws.org/Vol-2404/paper18.pdf
59. Cantucci, F., Falcone, R.: A computational model for cognitive human-robot interaction: An approach based on theory of delegation. In: Bergenti and Monica [31], pp. 127–133. http://ceur-ws.org/Vol-2404/paper19.pdf
60. Cantucci, F., Falcone, R.: Autonomous critical help provided by an artificial agent in the field of cultural heritage. In: Ferrando and Mascardi [101], pp. 152–163. http://ceur-ws.org/Vol-3261/paper12.pdf
61. Cantucci, F., Falcone, R.: A cognitive approach to model intelligent collaboration in human-robot interaction. In: Falcone et al. [98], pp. 138–150. http://ceur-ws.org/Vol-3579/paper10.pdf
62. Cardoso, R.C., Ferrando, A.: A review of agent-based programming for multi-agent systems. Comput. **10**(2), 16 (2021)
63. Casadei, M., Viroli, M.: A framework to specify and verify computational fields for pervasive computing systems. In: De Paoli and Vizzari [90], pp. 72–81. http://ceur-ws.org/Vol-892/paper2.pdf
64. Castelfranchi, C., Chella, A., Falcone, R., Lanza, F., Seidita, V.: Endowing robots with self-modeling abilities for trustful human-robot interactions. In: Bergenti and Monica [31], pp. 22–28. http://ceur-ws.org/Vol-2404/paper04.pdf
65. Catta, D., Leneutre, J., Malvone, V.: Subset sabotage games & attack graphs. In: Ferrando and Mascardi [101], pp. 209–218. http://ceur-ws.org/Vol-3261/paper16.pdf
66. Chella, A., Lanza, F., Seidita, V.: Representing and developing knowledge using Jason, Cartago and OWL. In: Cossentino et al. [80], pp. 147–152. http://ceur-ws.org/Vol-2215/paper_23.pdf

67. Chesani, F., et al.: Protocol specification and verification by using computational logic. In: Corradini et al. [75], pp. 184–192. http://lia.deis.unibo.it/books/woa2005/papers/26.pdf

68. Ciampolini, A., Lamma, E., Mello, P., Torroni, P.: Expressing collaboration and competition among abductive logic agents. In: Corradi et al. [73], pp. 64–69. http://giuseppevizzari.github.io/WOA-proceedings-archive/pdfs/woa2000/WOA13.pdf

69. Ciatto, G., Calegari, R., Mariani, S., Denti, E., Omicini, A.: From the blockchain to logic programming and back: research perspectives. In: Cossentino et al. [80], pp. 69–74. http://ceur-ws.org/Vol-2215/paper_12.pdf

70. Ciatto, G., Calegari, R., Siboni, E., Denti, E., Omicini, A.: 2P-KT: logic programming with objects & functions in Kotlin. In: Calegari et al. [51], pp. 219–236. http://ceur-ws.org/Vol-2706/paper14.pdf

71. Cordì, V., Lombardi, P., Martelli, M., Mascardi, V.: An ontology-based similarity between sets of concepts. In: Corradini et al. [75], pp. 16–21. http://lia.deis.unibo.it/books/woa2005/papers/3.pdf

72. Corradi, A., Montanari, R., Stefanelli, C.: Mobile agents integrity in e-commerce applications. In: Proceedings of 19th IEEE International Conference on Distributed Computing Systems. Workshops on Electronic Commerce and Web-based Applications. Middleware, pp. 59–64 (1999). https://doi.org/10.1109/ECMDD.1999.776415

73. Corradi, A., Omicini, A., Poggi, A. (eds.): WOA 2000 – 1st Workshop "From Objects to Agents", Atti di Congressi, vol. 1195. Pitagora Editrice Bologna, Parma, Italy (2000). http://giuseppevizzari.github.io/WOA-proceedings-archive/woa-2000.html

74. Corradini, F., Culmone, R., Di Berardini, M.R., Merelli, E.: Integrating ontologies in mobile agents. In: Corradini et al. [75], pp. 37–45. http://lia.deis.unibo.it/books/woa2005/papers/6.pdf

75. Corradini, F., De Paoli, F., Merelli, E., Omicini, A. (eds.): WOA 2005 – 6th Workshop "From Objects to Agents". Pitagora Editrice Bologna, Camerino, MC, Italy (2005). http://lia.deis.unibo.it/books/woa2005/atti.pdf

76. Cossentino, M., Lodato, C., Lopes, S., Ribino, P., Seidita, V., Chella, A.: A UML-based notation for representing MAS organizations. In: Fortino et al. [104], pp. 133–139. http://ceur-ws.org/Vol-741/ID20_CossentinoLodatoLopesRibiniSeiditaChella.pdf

77. Cossentino, M., Lopes, S., Nuzzo, A., Renda, G., Sabatucci, L.: A comparison of the basic principles and behavioural aspects of Akka, JaCaMo and Jade development frameworks. In: Cossentino et al. [80], pp. 133–141. http://ceur-ws.org/Vol-2215/paper_21.pdf

78. Cossentino, M., Lopes, S., Renda, G., Sabatucci, L., Zaffora, F.: A metamodel of a multi-paradigm approach to smart cyber-physical systems development. In: Bergenti, Monica (eds.) [31], pp. 35–41. http://ceur-ws.org/Vol-2404/paper06.pdf

79. Cossentino, M., et al.: GIMT: A tool for ontology and goal modeling in BDI multi-agent design. In: Santoro and Bergenti [169], pp. 81–88. http://ceur-ws.org/Vol-1260/paper10.pdf

80. Cossentino, M., Sabatucci, L., Seidita, V. (eds.): WOA 2018 – 19th Workshop "From Objects to Agents", CEUR Workshop Proceedings, vol. 2215. Palermo, Italy (2018). http://ceur-ws.org/Vol-2215/

81. Costantini, S., Dell'Acqua, P., Tocchio, A.: Expressing preferences declaratively in logic-based agent languages. In: De Paoli et al. [88], pp. 138–143. http://ceur-ws.org/Vol-204/P05.pdf

82. Costantini, S., Formisano, A., Pitoni, V.: A timed epistemic logic for formalizing cooperation among groups of agents. In: Falcone et al. [98], pp. 151–166. http://ceur-ws.org/Vol-3579/paper11.pdf

83. Costantini, S., Tocchio, A.: Strips-like planning in the DALI logic programmming language. In: Armano et al. [11], pp. 115–120. http://giuseppevizzari.github.io/WOA-proceedings-archive/pdfs/woa2003/05.pdf

84. Costantini, S., Tocchio, A.: Learning by knowledge exchange in logical agents. In: Corradini et al. [75], pp. 1–8. http://lia.deis.unibo.it/books/woa2005/papers/1.pdf

85. Cranefield, S., Finin, T.W., Tamma, V.A.M., Willmott, S. (eds.): Ontologies in Agent Systems 2003, Proceedings of the Workshop on Ontologies in Agent Systems (OAS 2003) at the 2nd International Joint Conference on Autonomous Agents and Multi-Agent Systems, Melbourne, Australia, July 15, 2003, CEUR Workshop Proceedings, vol. 73. CEUR-WS.org (2003). https://ceur-ws.org/Vol-73/

86. Cristani, M., Olivieri, F., Governatori, G., Buriola, G.: Simulating the law in a multi-agent system. In: Alderighi et al. [4], pp. 236–251. http://ceur-ws.org/Vol-3735/paper_18.pdf

87. D'Asaro, F.A., Origlia, A., Rossi, S.: Towards a logic-based approach for multi-modal fusion and decision making during motor rehabilitation sessions. In: Bergenti and Monica [31], pp. 8–13. http://ceur-ws.org/Vol-2404/paper02.pdf

88. De Paoli, F., Di Stefano, A., Omicini, A., Santoro, C. (eds.): WOA 2006 – 7th Workshop "From Objects to Agents", CEUR Workshop Proceedings, vol. 204. Catania, Italy (2006). http://ceur-ws.org/Vol-204/

89. De Paoli, F., Manzoni, S., Poggi, A. (eds.): WOA 2002 – 3rd Workshop "From Objects to Agents". Pitagora Editrice Bologna, Milano, Italy (2002). http://giuseppevizzari.github.io/WOA-proceedings-archive/woa-2002.html

90. De Paoli, F., Vizzari, G. (eds.): WOA 2012 – 13th Workshop "From Objects to Agents", CEUR Workshop Proceedings, vol. 892. Milano, Italy (2012). http://ceur-ws.org/Vol-892/

91. Delzanno, G., Martelli, M.: Proofs as computations in linear logic. In: APPIA-GULP-PRODE, pp. 155–166 (1996)

92. Deufemia, V., Polese, G., Tortora, G., Vacca, M.: Conceptual foundations of interrogative agents. In: Baldoni et al. [20], pp. 26–33. http://woa07.disi.unige.it/papers/DeufemiaConceptual.pdf

93. Di Napoli, C., Rossi, S., Staffa, M. (eds.): WOA 2015 – 16th Workshop "From Objects to Agents", CEUR Workshop Proceedings, vol. 1382. Naples, Italy (2015). http://ceur-ws.org/Vol-1382/

94. Dignum, V.: Responsible artificial intelligence: how to develop and use AI in a responsible way. Springer Nature (2019)

95. Esfahani, Z.N., Engelmann, D.C., Ferrando, A., Margarone, M., Mascardi, V.: Integrating ontologies and cognitive conversational agents in On2Conv. In: Multi-Agent Systems: 20th European Conference, EUMAS 2023, Naples, Italy, September 14–15, 2023, Proceedings, Lecture Notes in Computer Science, vol. 14282, pp. 66–82. Springer, Cham (2023). https://doi.org/10.1007/978-3-031-43264-4_5

96. European Commission: Ethics guidelines for trustworthy AI (2019). https://ec.europa.eu/digital-single-market/en/news/ethics-guidelines-trustworthy-ai

97. Falcone, R., Castelfranchi, C.: Transitivity in trust: a discussed property. In: Omicini and Viroli [146], pp. 155–160. http://ceur-ws.org/Vol-621/paper22.pdf
98. Falcone, R., Castelfranchi, C., Sapienza, A., Cantucci, F. (eds.): WOA 2023 – 24th Workshop "From Objects to Agents", CEUR Workshop Proceedings, vol. 3579. Roma, Italy (2023). http://ceur-ws.org/Vol-3579/
99. Ferrando, A., Gatti, A., Mascardi, V.: Geometric and spatial reasoning in BDI agents: a survey. In: CILC. CEUR Workshop Proceedings, vol. 3733. CEUR-WS.org (2024)
100. Ferrando, A., Malvone, V.: Hands-on VITAMIN: A compositional tool for model checking of multi-agent systems. In: Alderighi et al. [4], pp. 157–169. http://ceur-ws.org/Vol-3735/paper_12.pdf
101. Ferrando, A., Mascardi, V. (eds.): WOA 2022 – 23rd Workshop "From Objects to Agents", CEUR Workshop Proceedings, vol. 3261. Genova, Italy (2022). http://ceur-ws.org/Vol-3261/
102. Fichera, L., Marletta, D., Nicosia, V., Santoro, C.: A methodology to extend imperative languages with AgentSpeak declarative constructs. In: Omicini and Viroli [146], pp. 30–38. http://ceur-ws.org/Vol-621/paper05.pdf
103. Fisher, M., Mascardi, V., Rozier, K.Y., Schlingloff, B., Winikoff, M., Yorke-Smith, N.: Towards a framework for certification of reliable autonomous systems. Auton Agents Multi-Agent Syst. textbf35(8) (2021). https://doi.org/10.1007/s10458-020-09487-2
104. Fortino, G., Garro, A., Palopoli, L., Russo, W., Spezzano, G. (eds.): WOA 2011 – 12th Workshop "From Objects to Agents", CEUR Workshop Proceedings, vol. 741. Rende, Italy (2011). http://ceur-ws.org/Vol-741/
105. Gatti, A., Mascardi, V.: VEsNA, a framework for virtual environments via natural language agents and its application to factory automation. Robotics **12**(2), 46 (2023)
106. Giannotti, F., Naretto, F., Bodria, F.: Explainable for trustworthy AI. In: Chetouani, M., Dignum, V., Lukowicz, P., Sierra, C. (eds.) Human-Centered Artificial Intelligence: Advanced Lectures, pp. 175–195. Springer, Cham (2023). https://doi.org/10.1007/978-3-031-24349-3_10
107. Giordano, L., Martelli, A., Terenziani, P., Bottrighi, A., Montani, S.: A temporal approach to the specification and verification of interaction protocols. In: Corradini et al. [75], pp. 171–176. http://lia.deis.unibo.it/books/woa2005/papers/24.pdf
108. Grimaldi, C., Rossi, S.: Towards transparent computational models of theory of mind in collaborative environments. In: Alderighi et al. [4], pp. 73–83. http://ceur-ws.org/Vol-3735/paper_06.pdf
109. Hendler, J.A.: Agents and the semantic web. IEEE Intell. Syst. **16**(2), 30–37 (2001)
110. Hinton, A., Kwiatkowska, M.Z., Norman, G., Parker, D.: PRISM: a tool for automatic verification of probabilistic systems. In: Hermanns, H., Palsberg, J. (eds.) TACAS. Lecture Notes in Computer Science, vol. 3920, pp. 441–444. Springer, Cham (2006). https://doi.org/10.1007/11691372_29
111. Hübner, J.F., Sichman, J.S., Boissier, O.: Developing organised multiagent systems using the MOISE+ model: programming issues at the system and agent levels. Int. J. Agent Oriented Softw. Eng. **1**(3/4), 370–395 (2007). https://doi.org/10.1504/IJAOSE.2007.016266
112. Ivan, D., Ferrando, A., Gatti, A., Guerrini, G., Mascardi, V.: Integrating procedural ontologies in VEsNA: Study, requirements, and preliminary design. In: Alderighi et al. [4], pp. 186–199. http://ceur-ws.org/Vol-3735/paper_14.pdf

113. Jennings, N.R., Sycara, K.P., Wooldridge, M.J.: A roadmap of agent research and development. Auton. Agents Multi-Agent Syst. **1**, 7–38 (1998). https://doi.org/10.1023/A:1010090405266

114. Juan, T., Sterling, L., Martelli, M., Mascardi, V.: Customizing AOSE methodologies by reusing AOSE features. In: AAMAS, pp. 113–120. ACM (2003)

115. Kouvaros, P., Lomuscio, A., Pirovano, E., Punchihewa, H.: Formal verification of open multi-agent systems. In: AAMAS '19: Proceedings of the 18th International Conference on Autonomous Agents and MultiAgent System, pp. 179–187. International Foundation for Autonomous Agents and Multiagent Systems (2019). https://dl.acm.org/doi/10.5555/3306127.3331691

116. Kowalski, R.A.: Logical foundations for multi-agent systems. In: Alpuente, M., Sessa, M.I. (eds.) 1995 Joint Conference on Declarative Programming, GULP-PRODE'95, Marina di Vietri, Italy, September 11–14, 1995, pp. 39–40 (1995)

117. Kowalski, R.A.: Using meta-logic to reconcile reactive with rational agents. In: Crabtree, I.B., Jennings, N.R. (eds.) Proceedings of the First International Conference on the Practical Application of Intelligent Agents and Multi-Agent Technology, PAAM 1996, Westminster Central Hall, London, UK, April 22–24, 1996, pp. 361–374. Practical Application Company Ltd. (1996)

118. Kowalski, R.A., Sadri, F.: Towards a unified agent architecture that combines rationality with reactivity. In: Pedreschi, D., Zaniolo, C. (eds.) Logic in Databases. Lecture Notes in Computer Science, vol. 1154, pp. 137–149. Springer, Cham (1996). https://doi.org/10.1007/BFb0031739

119. Locoro, A., Mascardi, V., Mortara, F., Sanna, R.: Managing unavailabilities in a dynamic scenario following an agent-based approach. In: Fortino et al. [104], pp. 58–67. http://ceur-ws.org/Vol-741/ID17_LocoroMascardiMontaraSanna.pdf

120. Longo, C.F., Longo, F., Santoro, C.: A reactive cognitive architecture based on natural language processing for the task of decision-making using a rich semantic. In: Calegari et al. [51], pp. 201–218. http://ceur-ws.org/Vol-2706/paper2.pdf

121. Longo, C.F., Santoro, C., Nicolosi Asmundo, M., Santamaria, D.F., Cantone, D.: SW-CASPAR: Reactive-cognitive architecture based on natural language processing for the task of decision-making in the open-world assumption. In: Calegari et al. [52], pp. 178–193. http://ceur-ws.org/Vol-2963/paper10.pdf

122. Longo, F., Santoro, C.: A Python-based assistant agent able to interact with natural language. In: Cossentino et al. [80], pp. 142–146. http://ceur-ws.org/Vol-2215/paper_22.pdf

123. Loseto, G., Ruta, M., Scioscia, F., Sciascio, E.D., Mongiello, M.: Mining the user profile from a smartphone: a multimodal agent framework. In: Baldoni et al. [14], pp. 47–53. http://ceur-ws.org/Vol-1099/paper10.pdf

124. Maccagnan, A., Vardanega, T., Feltrin, E., Valle, G., Riva, M., Cannata, N.: A multi-agent system for the automated handling of experimental protocols in biological laboratories. In: Omicini and Viroli [146], pp. 126–132. http://ceur-ws.org/Vol-621/paper18.pdf

125. Maggi, P., Sisto, R.: Experiments on formal verification of mobile agent data integrity properties. In: De Paoli et al. [89], pp. 131–136. http://giuseppevizzari.github.io/WOA-proceedings-archive/pdfs/woa2002/15.pdf

126. Magnolo, E., Manenti, L., Manzoni, S., Sartori, F.: Towards a MAS model for crowd simulation at pop-rock concerts exploiting ontologies and fuzzy logic. In: Bergenti [28], pp. 92–99. http://www.ailab.unipr.it/woa09/papers/Magnolo.pdf

127. Marguglio, A., Cammarata, G., Bonura, S., Francaviglia, G., Puccio, M., Morreale, V.: Design and development of intentional systems with PRACTION-IST Studio. In: Baldoni et al. [22], pp. 37–45. http://www.pa.icar.cnr.it/woa08/materiali/paper/paper_16.pdf

128. Mariani, S., Omicini, A.: Multi-paradigm coordination for MAS: integrating heterogeneous coordination approaches in MAS technologies. In: Santoro et al. [170], pp. 91–99. http://ceur-ws.org/Vol-1664/w16.pdf
129. Marini, S., Martelli, M., Mascardi, V., Zini, F.: HEMASL: a flexible language to specify heterogeneous agents. In: Corradi et al. [73], pp. 76–81. http://giuseppevizzari.github.io/WOA-proceedings-archive/pdfs/woa2000/WOA15.pdf
130. Martelli, M., Mascardi, V., Zini, F.: Towards multi-agent software prototyping. In: PAAM, pp. 331–354. Practical Application Company Ltd. (1998)
131. Martino, S.D., Asmundo, M.N., Rizzo, S.A., Santamaria, D.F.: Modeling the video game environment: the VideOWL ontology. In: Falcone et al. [98], pp. 191–205. http://ceur-ws.org/Vol-3579/paper15.pdf
132. Mascardi, V., et al.: The Indiana MAS project: goals and preliminary results. In: De Paoli and Vizzari [90], pp. 55–62. http://ceur-ws.org/Vol-892/paper10.pdf
133. Mascardi, V., Cordì, V., Rosso, P.: A comparison of upper ontologies. In: Baldoni et al. [20], pp. 55–64. http://woa07.dibris.unige.it/papers/mascardi.pdf
134. Mascardi, V., Demergasso, D., Ancona, D.: Languages for programming BDI-style agents: an overview. In: Corradini et al. [75], pp. 9–15. http://lia.deis.unibo.it/books/woa2005/papers/2.pdf
135. Mascardi, V., Hendler, J.A., Papaleo, L.: Semantic web and declarative agent languages and technologies: current and future trends - (position paper). In: Baldoni, M., Dennis, L., Mascardi, V., Vasconcelos, W. (eds.) DALT. Lecture Notes in Computer Science, vol. 7784, pp. 197–202. Springer, Cham (2012). https://doi.org/10.1007/978-3-642-37890-4_12
136. Mascardi, V., Omicini, A. (eds.): The Agents Journey: Twenty-five Years of Multi-agent Systems at WOA. Lecture Notes in Computer Science – State-of-the-Art Surveys, Springer, Cham (2026)
137. Messina, F., Santoro, C., Santoro, F.F.: A declarative C++ agent platform for agent-based edge computing. In: Falcone et al. [98], pp. 206–215. http://ceur-ws.org/Vol-3579/paper16.pdf
138. Minotti, M., Santi, A., Ricci, A.: Developing web client applications with JaCa-Web. In: Omicini and Viroli [146], pp. 72–79. http://ceur-ws.org/Vol-621/paper11.pdf
139. Montaldo, E., Sacile, R., Boccalatte, A.: Rule-based agents for workflow applications in manifacturing information systems. In: Omicini and Viroli [145], pp. 90–94. http://giuseppevizzari.github.io/WOA-proceedings-archive/pdfs/woa2001/pdf/16.pdf
140. Morreale, V., Bonura, S., Centineo, F., Rossi, A., Cossentino, M., Gaglio, S.: PRACTIONIST: implementing PRACTIcal reasONIng sySTems. In: Corradini et al. [75], pp. 66–74. http://lia.deis.unibo.it/books/woa2005/papers/10.pdf
141. Morreale, V., Bonura, S., Francaviglia, G., Centineo, F., Cossentino, M., Gaglio, S.: Reasoning about goals in BDI agents: The PRACTIONIST framework. In: De Paoli et al. [88], pp. 187–194. http://ceur-ws.org/Vol-204/P20.pdf
142. Morreale, V., et al.: PRACTIONIST: a framework for developing BDI agent systems. In: De Paoli et al. [88], pp. 4–5. http://ceur-ws.org/Vol-204/D02.pdf
143. Oliva, E., Viroli, M., Omicini, A.: Minority game: a logic-based approach in TuCSoN. In: De Paoli et al. [88], pp. 181–186. http://ceur-ws.org/Vol-204/P02.pdf
144. Oliva, E., Viroli, M., Omicini, A.: Arguments and artifacts for dispute resolution. In: Baldoni et al. [22], pp. 46–53. http://www.pa.icar.cnr.it/woa08/materiali/paper/paper_12.pdf
145. Omicini, A., Viroli, M. (eds.): WOA 2001 – 2nd Workshop "From Objects to Agents". Pitagora Editrice Bologna, Modena, Italy (2001). http://giuseppevizzari.github.io/WOA-proceedings-archive/woa-2001.html

146. Omicini, A., Viroli, M. (eds.): WOA 2010 – 11th Workshop "From Objects to Agents", CEUR Workshop Proceedings, vol. 621. Rimini, Italy (2010). http://ceur-ws.org/Vol-621/

147. Omicini, A., Zambonelli, F.: Co-ordination of mobile information agents in TuCSoN. Internet Res. **8**(5), 400–413 (1998). https://doi.org/10.1108/10662249810241266

148. Passadore, A., Grosso, A., Boccalatte, A.: Indexing enterprise knowledge bases with AgentSeeker. In: Bergenti [28], pp. 69–75. http://www.ailab.unipr.it/woa09/papers/Passadore.pdf

149. Petrosino, G., Bergenti, F.: Extending message handlers with pattern matching in the Jadescript programming language. In: Bergenti and Monica [31], pp. 113–118. http://ceur-ws.org/Vol-2404/paper17.pdf

150. Pisano, G., Calegari, R., Omicini, A.: Towards cooperative argumentation for MAS: an actor-based approach. In: Calegari et al. [52], pp. 162–177. http://ceur-ws.org/Vol-2963/paper17.pdf

151. Pisano, G., Calegari, R., Omicini, A., Sartor, G.: Arg-tuProlog: a tuProlog-based argumentation framework. In: CILC. CEUR Workshop Proceedings, vol. 2710, pp. 51–66. CEUR-WS.org (2020)

152. Pisano, G., Ciatto, G., Calegari, R., Omicini, A.: Neuro-symbolic computation for XAI: towards a unified model. In: Calegari et al. [51], pp. 101–117. http://ceur-ws.org/Vol-2706/paper18.pdf

153. Piunti, M., Ricci, A., Boissier, O., Hübner, J.F.: Programming open systems with agents, environments and organizations. In: Omicini and Viroli [146], pp. 39–47. http://ceur-ws.org/Vol-621/paper06.pdf

154. Piunti, M., Ricci, A., Santi, A.: SOA/WS applications using cognitive agents working in CArtAgO environments. In: Bergenti [28], pp. 116–124. http://www.ailab.unipr.it/woa09/papers/Piunti.pdf

155. Poggi, A., Tomaiuolo, M., Turci, P.: An agent-based service oriented architecture. In: Baldoni et al. [20], pp. 157–165. http://woa07.disi.unige.it/papers/PoggiSOA.pdf

156. Rafanelli, A., Costantini, S., De Gasperis, G.: A multi-agent-system framework for flooding events. In: Ferrando and Mascardi [101], pp. 142–151. http://ceur-ws.org/Vol-3261/paper11.pdf

157. Rao, A.S.: AgentSpeak(L): BDI agents speak out in a logical computable language. In: Van de Velde, W., Perram, J.W. (eds.) European workshop on modelling autonomous agents in a multi-agent world, pp. 42–55. Springer, Cham (1996). https://doi.org/10.1007/BFb0031845

158. Rao, A.S., Georgeff, M.P.: BDI agents: From theory to practice. In: ICMAS, pp. 312–319. The MIT Press (1995)

159. Rawal, A., McCoy, J., Rawat, D.B., Sadler, B.M., Amant, R.S.: Recent advances in trustworthy explainable artificial intelligence: status, challenges, and perspectives. IEEE Trans. Artif. Intell. **3**(6), 852–866 (2022). https://doi.org/10.1109/TAI.2021.3133846

160. Repetto, M., Vecchiola, C., Boccalatte, A.: A knowledge modeling tool for rule-based agents. In: Omicini and Viroli [145], pp. 24–29. http://giuseppevizzari.github.io/WOA-proceedings-archive/pdfs/woa2001/pdf/05.pdf

161. Ribino, P., Cossentino, M., Lodato, C., Lopes, S., Sabatucci, L., Seidita, V.: Ontology and goal model in designing BDI multi-agent systems. In: Baldoni et al. [14], pp. 66–72. http://ceur-ws.org/Vol-1099/paper12.pdf

162. Ricci, A., Piunti, M., Viroli, M., Omicini, A.: Environment programming in CArtAgO. In: El Fallah Seghrouchni, A., Dix, J., Dastani, M., Bordini, R. (eds.) Multi-Agent Programming, Languages, Tools and Applications, pp. 259–288. Springer, Cham (2009). https://doi.org/10.1007/978-0-387-89299-3_8

163. Ricci, A., Viroli, M., Omicini, A.: CArtAgO: A framework for prototyping artifact-based environments in MAS. In: Weyns, D., Parunak, H.V.D., Michel, F. (eds.) Environments for MultiAgent Systems III, Lecture Notes in Computer Science, vol. 4389, chap. 4, pp. 67–86. Springer Berlin Heidelberg (May 2007). https://doi.org/10.1007/978-3-540-71103-2_4, 3rd International Workshop (E4MAS 2006), Hakodate, Japan, 8 May 2006. Selected Revised and Invited Papers

164. Ruta, M., Scioscia, F., Loseto, G., Gramegna, F., Pinto, A., Sciascio, E.D.: Semantic-based social intelligence through multi-agent systems. In: Cossentino et al. [80], pp. 96–102. http://ceur-ws.org/Vol-2215/paper_16.pdf

165. Sabbatini, F., Calegari, R.: Unlocking insights and trust: the value of explainable clustering algorithms for cognitive agents. In: Falcone et al. [98], pp. 232–245. http://ceur-ws.org/Vol-3579/paper18.pdf

166. Sabbatini, F., Ciatto, G., Calegari, R., Omicini, A.: On the design of PSyKE: a platform for symbolic knowledge extraction. In: Calegari et al. [52], pp. 29–48. http://ceur-ws.org/Vol-2963/paper14.pdf

167. Sacile, R., Montaldo, E., Paolucci, M., Boccalatte, A.: Intelligent agents applied to manufacturing: the MAKE-IT approach. In: Corradi et al. [73], pp. 92–97. http://giuseppevizzari.github.io/WOA-proceedings-archive/pdfs/woa2000/WOA18.pdf

168. Santi, A., Guidi, M., Ricci, A.: Exploiting agent-oriented programming for developing Android applications. In: Omicini and Viroli [146], pp. 48–54. http://ceur-ws.org/Vol-621/paper07.pdf

169. Santoro, C., Bergenti, F. (eds.): WOA 2014 – 15th Workshop "From Objects to Agents", CEUR Workshop Proceedings, vol. 1260. Catania, Italy (2014). http://ceur-ws.org/Vol-1260/

170. Santoro, C., Messina, F., De Benedetti, M. (eds.): WOA 2016 – 17th Workshop "From Objects to Agents", CEUR Workshop Proceedings, vol. 1664. Catania, Italy (2016). http://ceur-ws.org/Vol-1664/

171. Sapienza, A., Falcone, R., Castelfranchi, C.: The positive power of prejudice: A computational model for MAS. In: Di Napoli et al. [93], pp. 39–45. http://ceur-ws.org/Vol-1382/paper6.pdf

172. Schifanella, C., Lusso, L., Baldoni, M., Baroglio, C.: Design and development of a visual environment for writing DyLOG programs. In: Baldoni et al. [23], pp. 43–50. http://giuseppevizzari.github.io/WOA-proceedings-archive/pdfs/woa2004/7.pdf

173. Seidita, V., Lanza, F., Sabella, A.M.P., Chella, A.: Can agents talk about what they are doing? A proposal with Jason and speech acts. In: Ferrando and Mascardi [101], pp. 17–29. http://ceur-ws.org/Vol-3261/paper2.pdf

174. Seidita, V., Sabella, A.M.P., Chella, A.: Agents showing self-disclosure. A preliminary methodological approach. In: Falcone et al. [98], pp. 78–91. http://ceur-ws.org/Vol-3579/paper6.pdf

175. Sguera, S., Stellato, A., Griesi, D., Pazienza, M.T.: J-ALINAs: a JADE-based architecture for linguistic agents. In: De Paoli et al. [88], pp. 83–89. http://ceur-ws.org/Vol-204/P09.pdf

176. Sterling, L.S., Marshall, J.: Humans are not rational; artificial agents are not emotional. In: Ferrando and Mascardi [101], pp. 127–141. http://ceur-ws.org/Vol-3261/paper10.pdf

177. Thiebes, S., Lins, S., Sunyaev, A.: Trustworthy artificial intelligence. Electron. Mark. **31**, 447–464 (2021)
178. Tomaiuolo, M., Bergenti, F., Poggi, A., Turci, P.: OWLBeans–from ontologies to Java classes. In: Baldoni et al. [23], pp. 116–125. http://giuseppevizzari.github. io/WOA-proceedings-archive/pdfs/woa2004/17.pdf
179. Tomaiuolo, M., Turci, P.: Peer-to-peer delegation for accessing web services. In: Omicini and Viroli [146], pp. 65–71. http://ceur-ws.org/Vol-621/paper10.pdf
180. Unniyankal, H., Belardinelli, F., Ferrando, A., Malvone, V.: RMLGym: a formal reward machine framework for reinforcement learning. In: Falcone et al. [98], pp. 1–16. http://ceur-ws.org/Vol-3579/paper1.pdf
181. Vecchiola, C., Grosso, A., Boccalatte, A.: Integrating ontology support within AgentService. In: De Paoli et al. [88], pp. 166–172. http://ceur-ws.org/Vol-204/ P22.pdf
182. Vianello, A., Laine, S., Tuomi, E.: Improving trustworthiness of AI solutions: a qualitative approach to support ethically-grounded AI design. Int. J. Human-Comput. Inter. **39**(7), 1405–1422 (2023)
183. Vozna, A., Monaldini, A., Costantini, S., De Gasperis, G., Dell'Acqua, P., Formisano, A., Rafanelli, A.: Evolution of programming languages in agent systems and the role of computational logic. In: Mascardi and Omicini [136]
184. Wickramasinghe, C.S., Marino, D.L., Grandio, J., Manic, M.: Trustworthy AI development guidelines for human system interaction. In: 2020 13th International Conference on Human System Interaction (HSI). pp. 130–136 (2020). https://doi. org/10.1109/HSI49210.2020.9142644
185. Wooldridge, M.J., Jennings, N.R.: Intelligent agents: theory and practice. Knowl. Eng. Rev. **10**(2), 115–152 (1995). https://doi.org/10.1017/S0269888900008122
186. Yan, E., Burattini, S., Hübner, J.F., Ricci, A.: Towards a multi-level explainability framework for engineering and understanding BDI agent systems. In: Falcone et al. [98], pp. 216–231. http://ceur-ws.org/Vol-3579/paper17.pdf
187. Yeung, K.: Recommendation of the council on artificial intelligence (OECD). Int. Leg. Mater. **59**(1), 27–34 (2020). https://doi.org/10.1017/ilm.2020.5

Intelligent Agents from Symbolic to Neurosymbolic Systems: The Quest for Integration

Andrea Agiollo[1]([✉]) , Roberta Calegari[2] , Giovanni Ciatto[2] ,
Matteo Magnini[2] , Andrea Omicini[2] , and Federico Sabbatini[3]

[1] Faculty of Electrical Engineering, Mathematics and Computer Science (EEMCS),
Delft University of Technology, Delft, The Netherlands
`A.Agiollo-1@tudelft.nl`
[2] Department of Computer Science and Engineering (DISI), Alma Mater
Studiorum–Università di Bologna, Bologna, Italy
`{roberta.calegari,giovanni.ciatto,matteo.magnini,andrea.omicini}@unibo.it`
[3] Department of Pure and Applied Sciences (DiSPeA), Università degli Studi di
Urbino Carlo Bo, Urbino, Italy
`f.sabbatini1@campus.uniurb.it`

Abstract. In this chapter we take as our reference twenty-five years of
scientific and technical results presented at the Workshop on Objects,
and explore the development of *rational agents* and integration with
machine learning (ML) techniques, discussing their transition from pure
symbolic to *subsymbolic* and *neurosymbolic* systems. Given the growing importance of combining rational agent reasoning with ML, we first
outline the current state of technology by highlighting key milestones
and breakthroughs. Pinpointing logics and logic programming as the
main foundational tool for the design and implementation of rational
agents, we discuss successful implementations and applications of *logic-
based agents*, then we identify some of the main integration strands of
subsymbolic techniques within rational agents. In particular, we focus
on *symbolic knowledge injection (SKI)* and *symbolic knowledge extraction (SKE)* as some of the most relevant neurosymbolic techniques, and
on their impact on intelligent agents and multi-agent systems (MASs).
Current gaps and challenges in the integration of rational agents with
ML are finally discussed along with future research directions.

Keywords: Rational Agents · Logic Programming · Multi-agent
Systems · Symbolic-Subsymbolic Integration

1 Introduction

In the twenty-five years of the Workshop on Objects and Agents (WOA), agents
and multi-agent systems (MASs) have obviously been at the core of the scientific
and technical discussion: after a few years when the computational paradigm for

© The Author(s) 2026
V. Mascardi and A. Omicini (Eds.): *The Agents Journey*, LNCS 16395, pp. 320–339, 2026.
https://doi.org/10.1007/978-3-032-22940-3_12

distributed and situated systems was the main focus – as the " objects vs. agents" debate –, the general attention critically shifted towards intelligent agents and their role in the engineering of intelligent MASs. There, mainly, the notion of intelligent agent mostly referred to rational agent architectures, exploiting classical *symbolic* artificial intelligence (AI) approaches such automated reasoning, and exploiting the power of logics – e.g., in belief-desire-intention (BDI) architectures and frameworks [12] – and logic programming—for logic-based, or, *logic agents* [25].

In the last years, instead, the explosion of the general interest towards deep learning as one of the main trend in intelligent systems has led to the re-emergence of the so-called *AI agents* – a revamped term from the Nineties, see e.g. [29] –, nowadays understood as technical abstractions aimed at encapsulating machine learning (ML)-based *subsymbolic* techniques, so as to make their exploitation possible as legitimate interoperable components of intelligent systems. However, while on the one hand the strictly-cognitive properties of ML-based agents are up to some debate, their overall ability to exhibit sophisticated forms of intelligent behaviour is no longer disputable. Unlike *symbolic agents*, *subsymbolic agents* are already fast and effective, and behave well in real-world application scenarios, and capable of dealing efficiently with vast amounts of heterogeneous and possibly partially-specified or incomplete data. At the same time, any subsymbolic approach to AI inherently brings about the issues of transparency and interpretability of intelligent behaviours, mostly preventing actual human understanding of AI systems [15]—thus opening new critical problems, such as trustability and *explainability*, e.g. [2,77].

Rational agents – exploiting symbolic techniques based on first-order cognitive abstractions for their cognitive processes –, even with their well-known shortcomings in terms of computational efficiency and limited ability to deal with real-world scenarios, are instead to some extent *understandable by design*: their behaviour is typically easy to be interpreted by both intelligent agents and humans. For instance, a rational planning agent could straightforwardly justify and explain any action from its observable behaviour by just sharing its view of the world and its goals, along with its rational plan. Generally speaking, rational agents – such as logic agents, using formal logics as the foundation of their reasoning process –, offer a robust foundation for understanding and explaining decisions and behaviours by intelligent systems.

Thus, as AI systems become increasingly complex and ubiquitous, whereas the need for frameworks that are both interpretable and reliable has never been more critical [59], the integration of ML techniques within rational agents has clearly the potential of representing a transformative approach to AI, merging the strengths of symbolic reasoning with data-driven learning [25,89]. Blending symbolic reasoning with subsymbolic techniques, and integrating them in *neurosymbolic systems* – e.g., [84] – aims at addressing all of the aforementioned challenges by framing the real-world effectiveness of ML-based approaches within well-founded rational frameworks constraining and driving decision-making processes and intelligent behaviours [26].

Despite that promise of integration, however, several gaps and challenges still persist. Issues such as scalability, biases inherent in data, and the reliability of decision-making processes in high-stakes environments need to be critically examined. On the other hand, the roles that rational agents could potentially play within many different critical sectors – including healthcare, finance, autonomous systems, and smart cities – highlight the practical implications of this research line.

Accordingly, in this chapter we start by sketching the current landscape of rational agents, focussing on logic-based agents (*logic agents*, henceforth), as well as on their integration with subsymbolic techniques, typically as they emerge from the ML field. After discussing the existing challenges, we point out possible future directions for research, by exploiting the twenty-five years of WOA as our main reference.

There, rational and logic agents, along with the integration of symbolic and subsymbolic approaches in agents and MASs, have represented a recurring theme over the past twenty-five years. So, in the remainder of this chapter we first outline the key milestones and achievements in the field, then we introduce the two main integration strands that have characterised the most recent and effective developments: *symbolic knowledge extraction (SKE)* and *symbolic knowledge injection (SKI)*. We delve into these topics, by assessing their potential to enhance the interpretability and explainability of intelligent systems, and also by addressing specific relevant issues such as their ability to improve ethical alignment of AI systems to human values. Finally, we analyse current gaps, challenges, and future directions towards the effective integration of symbolic and subsymbolic techniques.

2   Logic and Rational Agents in Multi-agent Systems

The scientific and technical histories of computational logic and MASs are deeply intertwined. As remarkable examples, well-known workshop lines such as CLIMA (Computational Logic in Multi-Agent Systems)[1] and DALT (Declarative Agent Languages and Technologies)[2] have carried on and developed that specific scientific landscape for more than a decade. Overall, in the years, logic has proven to be a powerful tool for modelling, verifying, and reasoning about the behaviour of agents in complex systems [14].

Computational logic provides the foundation for many aspects of MASs— way beyond formal specification, as one may think at first glance. The history of WOA itself – which started by focussing on the power of objects and agents as abstractions for distributed systems, and nowadays is instead mostly devoted to elaborate on the role of multi-agent systems in the engineering of intelligent systems – corroborates such a connection, as demonstrated by the large number of contributions about logic that can be found in WOA proceedings. In fact, WOA has featured papers about the many different aspects of logic for several

---

[1] https://dblp.org/db/conf/clima/.
[2] https://dblp.org/db/conf/dalt/.

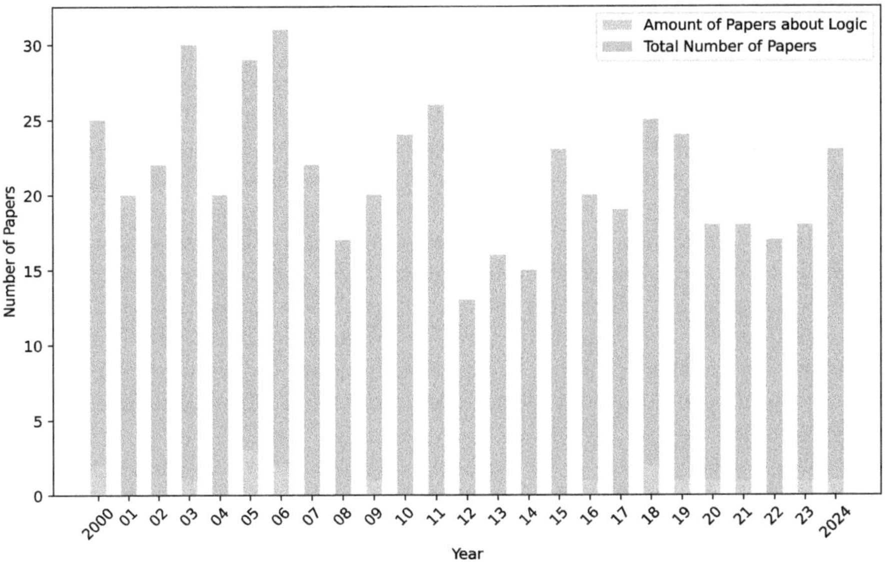

Fig. 1. Number of papers on logic-based approaches in MASs at WOA per year (2000–2024).

years since the inception of the workshop in 2000—as shown in Fig. 1. The recurring, almost continuous presence of those sorts of contributions straightforwardly emphasises the enduring relevance of logic in the area of intelligent agent and MAS research.

More in detail, logic has played a range of different roles in the MAS area, serving as a cornerstone for declarative specification, communication protocols, formal verification, agent programming, and – more recently – hybrid systems integrating ML techniques with MASs. Below, we proceed by categorising the many roles that logic has played in the MAS fields according to the papers that can be found in the twenty-five years of WOA proceedings.

2.1   Declarative Specification

Declarativeness is a warhorse of programming languages based on computational logic: by evaluating the truth value of logic formulas, logic-based programs can just specify *what* a machine should do, instead of *how* to do it [20]. In particular, logic programming languages like Prolog are amenable of both a declarative and an operational interpretation, and can exploit the fact that the two corresponding semantics match [58], so that they can be used as languages for executable specification. This makes logic-based systems particularly suitable for MASs when it comes to create high-level agent specifications or programs, as well as when agents have to reason about their environment, or interact with other agents.

Contributions focussing on declarativeness are manifold. For instance, in [13] a declarative language aimed at customising agent-based systems is discussed, focussing on interaction with web services and interoperability. There, Baldoni *et al.* highlight how personalised service selection and composition – particularly in web-based and multi-agent system – can benefit from reasoning about actions and conformance to policies—which are made simple by declarative programming.

Similarly, Costantini *et al.* [43] propose a novel method for expressing preferences within logic-based agent languages. There, agents can define preferences in the body of rules, allowing them to choose among multiple actions based on evolving preferences, via a declarative language. The paper discusses how that approach makes it possible to support dynamic decision-making in agents, enabling them to modify and adjust their actions as their goals and priorities change over time.

Declarativeness is also a key concern in [34], where Ciatto *et al.* discuss the interplay between blockchain technology and logic programming, and argue that logic programming has the potential to enhance the intrinsic capabilities of blockchain—in particular in the development of smart contracts. There, the authors argue that logic-based approaches could make smart contracts more expressive and reliable, whereas blockchain could in turn provide logic-based systems with the distributed infrastructure they typically need in real-world scenarios.

Finally, a timed epistemic logic is introduced in [44], aimed at modelling cooperation and belief changes within groups of agents. There, logic is used to formalise agents willing to either join or leave groups, and even agents temporarily "lent" to other groups. By leveraging on temporal reasoning, the system is able to express and check the validity of agents' beliefs and knowledge, making it particularly useful for dynamic, time-sensitive MASs.

2.2 Communication and Interoperability

In MASs, agents often need to communicate and collaborate across distributed systems. To this end, logic has been mostly exploited so as to ensure that agents can interact with each other effectively, while adopting specific communication protocols, as well as ensuring system interoperability. For instance, this is the case of the aforementioned work by Baldoni*et al.* [13], as well as of the work by Chesani *et al.* [32], which is discussed later in this section. Another example is [33], where Ciampolini *et al.* propose a language for coordinating abductive logic agents, focusing on how agents can interact within MASs, either they are competing or collaborating. The language allows agents to solve problems based on incomplete knowledge by formulating hypotheses via adductive reasoning. In order to showcase the ability of the proposed system to handle both collaboration and competition among agents, the paper presents a medical diagnosis example.

Furthermore, computational logic has also been exploited as the foundation for "programming the interaction space" [38] within MASs, exploiting a declarative model for the coordination [37] of both intelligent and non-intelligent agents – namely, TuCSoN [71] – aimed at enabling and governing both the explicit communication and the stigmergic interaction of agents within MASs. Along this line, WOA proceedings are disseminated with contributions, which we mention in chronological order on the following.

First of all, Ricci *et al.* [76] demonstrate how the TuCSoN coordination infrastructure helps manage autonomous agents in network-centric applications using intelligent light management as a case study. The notion of *agent coordination contexts* (ACC) in TuCSoN is introduced in [75], enabling agents to model, interact, and affect their environment while providing a flexible framework for MAS organisation. Omicini *et al.* [68] investigate the combination of *subjective* (intra-agent) and *objective* (inter-agent) *coordination* within FIPA agents using the TuCSoN framework. Oliva *et al.* [66,67] focus on how the TuCSoN coordination model and technology support multi-agent-based simulation (MABS), by showing how to simulate Minority Game with TuCSoN, with the aim of studying emergent behaviour in complex systems using logic-based agents for flexible and controllable simulations. Nardini *et al.* [65] explore a chemistry-inspired approach for the coordination of services in pervasive computing environments, where the ReSpecT logic-based coordination engine is used to enable adaptive and self-organising behaviour of TuCSoN agents. The main guidelines for a methodology specifically targeting the issue of *situatedness* in MASs are introduced in [63]; based on the TuCSoN coordination model, the methodology is meant to be centred around the notion of coordination as the key to managing dependencies between agents and their environment. Finally, Mariani *et al.* [64] try and go beyond logic towards other declarative mainstream languages for MAS coordination, by integrating XPath, blockchain, and stream processing with tuple-based coordination models so as to enhance MAS expressive power in the Internet of Things (IoT) as well as in general pervasive intelligence scenarios.

The generalised exploitation of logic programming engines at the core of distributed architectures – obviously including distributed MASs – has also been the subject of exploration in the early works by Calegari *et al.* [24], leading to the notion of logic programming as a service (LPaaS, which first appeared in the WOA proceedings in 2016. For instance, in [27] the authors introduce tuProlog as a lightweight logic programming engine suitable to provide rational agents with *as-a-service* logic programming capabilities – such as interactive goal demonstration – in distributed systems. Later on, Calegari *et al.* [23] explore the potential of computational logic in the realm of spatial and temporal reasoning by extending the LPaaS model and architecture towards *situated intelligence*, allowing agents to improve on their ability to take context-aware, location-specific decisions.

2.3 Formal Verification and Semantics

As in many other sorts of computational systems, logic has been instrumental in verifying the behaviour of agents within MASs, typically by ensuring that their interactive behaviour conforms to expected communication protocols and rules. This is especially crucial when engineers are concerned with the reliability of distributed, open, and dynamic MASs.

For instance, verification – see also [4] in this book – plays a primary role in [13] and [32], where the results of the MASSIVE projects are framed and shared. In particular, a logic-based framework for the specification and verification of agent interaction protocols in distributed MASs is discussed; examples in applications scenarios – e-commerce, medicine, and e-learning – are discussed. The framework leverages on formal logic for protocol specification, so that the compliance of agent observable behaviour with the protocols can be automatically verified, thus ensuring agent and MAS correctness.

Armando *et al.* [5] push formal verification even further by introducing the Logic Broker Architecture aimed at facilitating the integration of automated verification systems, such as theorem provers and model checkers, which commonly operate in isolation. The architecture enables different verification systems to interoperate by means of a registration/subscription mechanism and a translation process that ensure the safe and sound exchange of logical services across different systems.

2.4 Agent Programming, Reasoning and Planning

Another topic that is recurrent in the twenty-five years of WOA is obviously agent-oriented computing (AOC), and more specifically *agent programming*. Whenever rational agents are involved, agent programming mostly deals with agent *reasoning* and *planning*, where logics obviously play a crucial role. Rational agent architectures are generally designed around specific logics – e.g., BDI logic [74] –, so as to enable the declarative specification of actions, goals, beliefs, and plans, while ensuring sound agent decision making, deliberation, and planning processes.

One remarkable example of logic-based agent language is DALI, which firstly appeared in the WOA proceedings in 2003 [45]. There, Costantini *et al.* demonstrate how DALI can be used to implement STRIPS-like planning, allowing agents to plan and execute actions to achieve their goals. The DALI framework enables agents to engage in proactive behaviour by continuously checking for goals and actions, making it suitable for dynamic and adaptive environments.

Another example is the work by Magnolo *et al.* [62], which leverages fuzzy logic and ontologies so as to simulate crowd behaviour at large social events such as concerts. By analysing factors like crowd density and duration, the model aims at providing for more accurate simulations of crowd dynamics, which can be used to inform the design of safer and more efficient event management strategies.

More recently, the focus shifted towards the exploitation of the Prolog language [57] for agent programming. For instance, Ciatto *et al.* [36] introduce a

Kotlin-based domain-specific language (DSL) for Prolog, embedding logic programming directly into Kotlin – via the 2P-Kt ecosystem [35] –, thus providing a seamless way for object-oriented and functional developers to leverage logic-based reasoning within their projects—which could be expected to help promoting wider adoption of logic programming in mainstream programming environments. As expected, later on, the same approach propelled the development of [12], a BDI framework based on Kotlin.

Finally, Bordini *et al.* [19] compare agent-oriented logic programming languages in the literature, showing how those languages extend traditional logic programming (most of them leveraging on Prolog) so as to model autonomous agents and MASs. There, the practical applications of those languages in the context of complex, real-world MASs are discussed, highlighting their utility in scenarios requiring autonomous decision-making.

3   Rational Agents and Machine Learning in Multi-agent Systems

3.1   Hybrid Systems

More recent developments in MAS research try and bridge agents and ML, to let agents learn either from data or from other agents. In all cases, logic lies in the middle, enabling the definition of hybrid systems that leverage both symbolic and/or subsymbolic approaches.

For instance, the work by Costantini *et al.* [46] introduces a method for agents to learn through the exchange of rule sets, as a form of *cultural transmission* akin to human learning: in this case, learning is purely symbolic. Agents evaluate new knowledge based on its potential for the achievements of specific goals, and are equipped with mechanisms for discarding unhelpful or incorrect information. Overall, this allows agents in a MAS to adapt and improve their behaviour through cooperative knowledge sharing.

Conversely, D'Asaro *et al.* [47] introduce a system that combines subsymbolic ML and logic-based techniques to assist in motor rehabilitation. The system uses data from multiple sources (e.g., sensors) in order to model users' cognitive and motor abilities, and help therapists making decisions in the evaluation and adjustment of rehabilitation exercises. There, the intrinsic transparency of logic-based approaches allows for an easier understanding of decisions by human patients, which is critical in therapeutic settings.

Many other works that explore the integration of logic and machine learnin in multi-agent system can be found in the WOA proceedings, especially in recent years, when the field has seen a surge in hybrid systems that aim at combining the strengths of both approaches. Accordingly, here and in the next subsections, we explore the related contributions, highlighting some of the most relevant slices of literature.

3.2 Towards Neurosymbolic Agents

The integration of logic agents and ML is transforming the AI landscape by merging the strengths of symbolic reasoning with the adaptability, effectiveness, and efficiency of data-driven approaches (subsymbolic techniques). At the core of the integration is typically the ability of logic agents to represent complex knowledge using formal logic, which provides them with a structured foundation for their reasoning process. Meanwhile, ML excels in learning patterns and making predictions from large datasets, allowing systems to adapt and improve based on empirical evidence. Such a symbiotic relationship enhances the capabilities of intelligent systems across various domains.

One significant area where synergies are likely to be found is knowledge representation and learning, where logic programming can be used to define a rich structure for a problem domain, providing for a formal framework for representing rules, relationships, and constraints. A structured representation in principle enables ML to continuously refine the knowledge base through data-driven insights, thus enabling or facilitating a dynamic learning environment. As ML algorithms analyse incoming data, they can update and adjust the logic framework, thus ensuring that the system not only adheres to logic constraints, but also evolves based on new information—and its evolution fosters greater accuracy and reliability in decision-making processes.

Furthermore, the inclusion of logical constraints into ML models helps harnessing the learning processes by embedding domain-specific knowledge within the model. Techniques such as constraint-based learning allow for the specification of acceptable solution spaces, ensuring that the learned models stay consistent with respect to the established domain knowledge. This approach can improve the robustness of the decision-making process by preventing the model from exploring infeasible or irrelevant solutions. Other techniques, such as neurosymbolic approaches, further blend neural networks with symbolic reasoning, creating systems that ideally are able to leverage on the strengths of both paradigms. By combining the generalisation capabilities of neural networks with the rationality of symbolic reasoning, integrated neurosymbolic systems can achieve a more nuanced understanding of complex tasks.

Finally, and most interestingly, recent advancements have introduced promising techniques for SKI and SKE, which further enhance the integration of LP and ML. Symbolic extraction focuses on the derivation of interpretable models from complex ML systems, allowing for the extraction of meaningful patterns and rules. Conversely, symbolic injection involves incorporating logical rules into ML frameworks, thus enriching the learning process with structured knowledge. Those techniques have exhibited significant potential in improving the transparency and reliability of AI systems, and many recent works presented at WOA over the years have explored their applications in depth—so, they will be detailed further in the remainder of this section.

3.3   Symbolic Knowledge Extraction in Intelligent Agent Systems

When transposing the ML workflow into the realm of logic agents, symbolic knowledge can be seen as a common means to enable agent communication, information sharing, and cooperation. Symbolic knowledge is produced in several ways—e.g., it may be encoded by domain experts, or, distilled via dedicated SKE algorithms. More in detail, SKE focuses on extracting a symbolic representation out of the knowledge acquired by subsymbolic predictors. This approach offers a higher degree of interpretability for opaque ML predictions, making it possible to inspect the subsymbolic model. Here and in the following we stick to the definition provided in [39]: accordingly, SKE refers to

> any algorithmic procedure accepting trained subsymbolic predictors as input and producing symbolic knowledge as output, so that the extracted knowledge reflects the behaviour of the predictor with high fidelity

In the context of intelligent agents, SKE provides effective tools to inspect the agents' knowledge and behaviour.

Generally speaking, the main benefit of SKE for intelligent agents is that it makes it possible to inspect agents' knowledge—for instance, to check whether it satisfies domain requirements, fairness constraints, or other behavioural specifications. Even as a recent technique, SKE has already found practical application in a wide range of fields, including credit-risk evaluation [10,11,87], credit card screening [85], intrusion detection in computer networks [56], keyword extraction [7], space mission diagnostic [81], and in the medical field as well [18,53,55]. Overall, the apparent wide applicability of SKE techniques suggests that neurosymbolic agents based on SKE have the potential to extend MAS effective operation over a large range of diverse real-word scenarios.

The actual applicability of SKE techniques is enhanced by the availability of public software libraries implementing state-of-the-art extraction algorithms, such as PSyKE,[3] ruleex,[4] and `Rule_Extraction_From_Trees`.[5]

In particular, PSyKE [28,79] – first presented at WOA [78] – is a Python framework supporting a significant set of pedagogical SKE techniques while maintaining complete compatibility with other mainstream Python packages as Scikit-Learn [72], also supporting Semantic Web interoperability for intelligent agents [80].

3.4   Symbolic Knowledge Injection in Intelligent Agent Systems

Quite intuitively, SKI serves a dual purpose w.r.t. to SKE, since it constrains an ML predictor to take into account some symbolic knowledge when drawing predictions. According to the definition provided in [39], SKI refers to

---

[3] https://github.com/psykei/psyke-python.
[4] https://github.com/fantamat/ruleex.
[5] https://github.com/Yimeng-Zhang/Rule_Extraction_from_Trees.

> any algorithmic procedure affecting how subsymbolic predictors draw their inferences in such a way that predictions are either computed as a function of, or made consistent with, some given symbolic knowledge

Overall, SKI accounts for a wide set of techniques aimed at improving subsymbolic systems – such as neural networks (NNs) – by "injecting" them with some sort of structured and explicit symbolic knowledge, available at the rational agent level, affecting their overall behaviour.

Depending on the agent's context and task, symbolic knowledge can represent different things such as the agent's beliefs, some well-known concepts, a societal norm, or, any desirable rule to be taken into account. Therefore, the agent can solve a task by exploiting both the symbolic knowledge – deductive process – and the subsymbolic system—inductive process. The goals of SKI can be manifold, including: *(i)* improving the agent's predictive performances—e.g., accuracy, precision, recall, etc., *(ii)* making the agent's decisions more robust—e.g., against data degradation, adversarial attacks, etc., *(iii)* making the agent's decisions more compliant with some normative or ethical constraints, *(iv)* reducing the amount of data needed to train the subsymbolic system, *(v)* reducing learning time by providing straight away the very knowledge that subsymbolic predictors would otherwise struggle to learn by processing huge amounts of data, *(vi)* preventing subsymbolic predictors from working as full black boxes during their training—hence avoiding the need for explanations.

SKI can be performed in different ways, depending on the desired outcome, properties, and the nature of the symbolic knowledge to be injected. According to the taxonomy proposed in [39], SKI can be classified into three main categories:

predictor structuring – where the structure of the subsymbolic predictor is extended in order to accommodate the symbolic knowledge. This can be done by introducing new items – new layers, new neurons, new connections, new activation functions – that are specifically designed to mimic the symbolic knowledge. Relevant examples of this approach are knowledge based artificial neural networks (KBANNs) [88], fibred neural networks (FNNs) [54], logic tensor networks (LTNs) [9], and knowledge injection via network structuring (KINS) [60].

guided learning – where the training process of the subsymbolic predictor is altered so as to take into account the symbolic knowledge. This is usually done by modifying the loss function—for instance, by adding a new regularisation term that penalises the predictor when it does not comply with the symbolic knowledge. Examples of this approach are guiding backpropagation by inserting rules (GBIR) [8], and knowledge injection via lambda layer (KILL) [61].

knowledge embedding – where the subsymbolic predictor is provided with the symbolic knowledge as additional input data. This can be done by converting the symbolic knowledge into some numerical form (a.k.a. embedding) that can be fed to the subsymbolic predictor [30, 31, 86].

In the context of intelligent agents, SKI methods can be exploited to pursue different aims, such as:

agent learning enrichment – where SKI lets *sub*-symbolic methods consume *symbolic* knowledge to either improve or enrich the agent's learning capabilities. Along this line, SKI improves ordinary ML tasks inside the agent workflow, by allowing the subsymbolic predictors to process (or, to take into account) the structured symbolic knowledge available at the agent level. The fundamental idea underlying those approaches is that there exist some concepts that can be either cumbersome or troublesome to learn from examples – e.g., syntactical concepts, semantics, etc. –: those concepts can represent complex beliefs that an agent has gained about the external environment, normative, or bounding expressions regarding the agent's acceptable actions—and much more. Therefore, the symbolic knowledge expressing those high-level concepts can be injected directly into the model to be used inside the agent workflow.

agent knowledge manipulation – where SKI enables the *sub*-symbolic manipulation of an agent's *symbolic* knowledge, by enabling subsymbolic predictors to handle it similarly to symbolic engines. In doing so, SKI supports classic symbolic AI tasks while aiming at boosting their performance, either extending their capabilities or improving their raw processing latency. In this context, common tasks are:

> **logic inference** in its many forms – e.g. deductive, inductive, probabilistic, etc. –, i.e. drawing conclusions out of a symbolic (KB);
>
> **information retrieval** looking for information in a symbolic KB;
>
> **KB completion** finding (and adding) missing information in a symbolic KB;
>
> **KB fusion** merging several KBs into a single one, taking care of (possibly, syntactically different) overlaps;
>
> The key point here is supporting tasks where both inputs and outputs are symbolic in nature, but leveraging upon subsymbolic methods to gain speed, fuzziness, and robustness against noise [73].

Finally, in the context of SKI techniques, the usage of graph neural networks (GNNs) has recently gained popularity in tackling relevant tasks which are hard to formalise or solve in the logic realm, because of either their numerical nature or their algorithmic infeasibility [1].

4   Conclusion

In this chapter we explore the emergence of subsymbolic techniques in the area of multi-agent systems, and their integration with rational architectures for intelligent agents based on symbolic approaches, focussing in particular on the incorporation of machine learning techniques within logic-based agents.

By taking as our reference twenty-five years of scientific and technical results presented at the Workshop on Objects and Agents – from 2000 to 2024 –, we first overview the main reasons for combining rational agent reasoning with subsymbolic ML techniques, outlining the current state of models and technologies in the field. Special attention is given to computational logic in general, and logic programming in particular, as a foundational tool for designing rational agents: successful implementations and applications of logic-based agents are discussed, and the benefits derived from logic programming are emphasised. Some of the most prominent roles that logic has played in the MAS area in the last decades are pointed out—such as declarative specification, communication and interoperability, formal verification and semantics, agent programming, reasoning, and planning.

We then identify some of the main strands of integration of subsymbolic techniques within rational agents, mostly focussing on how logic-based agents can leverage on machine learning techniques, and showcasing some relevant cases where this sort of integration has actually been proven as effective. Some of the current gaps and challenges in the integration of rational agents with ML are discussed along with potential and promising future research directions. In particular, we finally focus on symbolic knowledge injection and symbolic knowledge extraction techniques: we summarise the key findings, and emphasise their remarkable potential in improving the transparency and reliability of intelligent MASs and, in general, of AI systems.

Acknowledgments. This chapter was partially supported by *(i)* the "ENGINES – ENGineering INtElligent Systems around intelligent agent technologies" project, funded by the European Union – Next Generation EU within the framework of the National Recovery and Resilience Plan NRRP – Mission 4 "Education and Research" – Component 2 – Investment 1.1 "National Research Program and Projects of Significant National Interest Fund (PRIN)" – Call PRIN 2022 – D.D. n. 104 of 02/02/2022, under grant number 20229ZXBZM, *(ii)* the "AEQUITAS" project funded by European Union's Horizon Europe research and innovation programme under grant number 101070363, *(iii)* PNRR – M4C2 – Investimento 1.3, Partenariato Esteso PE00000013 – "FAIR—Future Artificial Intelligence Research" – Spoke 8 "Pervasive AI' ', funded by the European Commission under the Next Generation EU programme.

Disclosure of Interests. The authors have no competing interests to declare that are relevant to the content of this article.

References

1. Agiollo, A., Ciatto, G., Omicini, A.: Graph neural networks as the copula mundi between logic and machine learning: a roadmap. In: Calegari et al. [22], pp. 98–115. http://ceur-ws.org/Vol-2963/paper18.pdf
2. Agiollo, A., Siebert, L.C., Murukannaiah, P.K., Omicini, A.: From large language models to small logic programs: building global explanations from disagreeing local post-hoc explainers. Auton. Agent. Multi-Agent Syst. **38**, 1–33 (2024). https://doi.org/10.1007/s10458-024-09663-8
3. Alderighi, M., Baldoni, M., Baroglio, C., Micalizio, R., Tedeschi, S. (eds.): WOA 2024 – 25th workshop "From Objects to Agents. In: CEUR Workshop Proceedings, vol. 3735. Bard, AO, Italy (2024). http://ceur-ws.org/Vol-3735/

4. Ancona, D., Briola, D., Ferrando, A., Martelli, M., Mascardi, V.: 25 years of declarative agent technologies in Italy. In: Mascardi, V., Omicini, A. (eds.) The Agents Journey: Twenty-five Years of Multi-agent Systems at WOA. Springer, Lecture Notes in Computer Science - State-of-the-Art Surveys (2026)

5. Armando, A., Zini, D.: Towards interoperable mechanized reasoning systems: the logic broker architecture. In: Corradi et al. [40], pp. 70–75. http://lia.disi.unibo.it/books/woa00/pdf/14.pdf

6. Armano, G., Paoli, F.D., Omicini, A., Vargiu, E. (eds.): WOA 2003 – 4th workshop "From Objects to Agents". Pitagora Editrice Bologna, Villasimius, CA, Italy (2003). http://giuseppevizzari.github.io/WOA-proceedings-archive/woa-2003.html

7. Azcarraga, A., Liu, M.D., Setiono, R.: Keyword extraction using backpropagation neural networks and rule extraction. In: The 2012 International Joint Conference on Neural Networks (IJCNN 2012), pp. 1–7. IEEE (2012). https://doi.org/10.1109/IJCNN.2012.6252618

8. Bader, S., Hölldobler, S., Marques, N.C.: Guiding backprop by inserting rules. In: Garcez, A.S.D., Hitzler, P. (eds.) 4th International Workshop on Neural-Symbolic Learning and Reasoning (NeSy'08), CEUR Workshop Proceedings, vol. 366, pp. 19–22. CEUR-WS.org, Patras, Greece (2008). http://ceur-ws.org/Vol-366/paper-5.pdf

9. Badreddine, S., d'Avila Garcez, A.S., Serafini, L., Spranger, M.: Logic tensor networks. Artif. Intell. **303**, 103649 (2022). https://doi.org/10.1016/J.ARTINT.2021.103649

10. Baesens, B., Setiono, R., De Lille, V., Viaene, S., Vanthienen, J.: Building credit-risk evaluation expert systems using neural network rule extraction and decision tables. In: Storey, V.C., Sarkar, S., DeGross, J.I. (eds.) ICIS 2001 Proceedings, pp. 159–168. Association for Information Systems (2001). http://aisel.aisnet.org/icis2001/20

11. Baesens, B., Setiono, R., Mues, C., Vanthienen, J.: Using neural network rule extraction and decision tables for credit-risk evaluation. Manage. Sci. **49**(3), 312–329 (2003). https://doi.org/10.1287/mnsc.49.3.312.12739

12. Baiardi, M., Burattini, S., Ciatto, G., Pianini, D.: JaKtA: BDI agent-oriented programming in pure Kotlin. In: Malvone, V., Murano, A. (eds.) 20th European Conference on Multi-Agent Systems (EUMAS 2023), Lecture Notes in Computer Science, pp. 49–65. Springer, Napoli, Italy (2023). https://doi.org/10.1007/978-3-031-43264-4_4

13. Baldoni, M., et al.: Personalization, verification and conformance for logic-based communicating agents. In: Corradini et al. [41], pp. 177–183. http://lia.deis.unibo.it/books/woa2005/papers/25.pdf

14. Baldoni, M., Baroglio, C., Mascardi, V., Omicini, A., Torroni, P.: Agents, multi-agent systems and declarative programming: who, what, when, where, why, how? In: Dovier, A., Pontelli, E. (eds.) A 25 Year Perspective on Logic Programming. Achievements of the Italian Association for Logic Programming, GULP, LNAI: State-of-the-Art Survey, vol. 6125, chap. 10, pp. 200–225. Springer, Heidelberg (2010). https://doi.org/10.1007/978-3-642-14309-0_10

15. Belle, V., Papantonis, I.: Principles and practice of explainable machine learning. Front. Big Data **4**(688969), 1–25 (2021). https://doi.org/10.3389/fdata.2021.688969

16. Bergenti, F. (ed.): WOA 2009 – 10th workshop "From Objects to Agents". Seneca Edizioni Torino, Parma, Italy (2009). http://www.ailab.unipr.it/woa09/papers/

17. Bergenti, F., Monica, S. (eds.): WOA 2019 – 20th workshop "From Objects to Agents", CEUR Workshop Proceedings, vol. 2404. Parma, Italy (2019). http://ceur-ws.org/Vol-2404/

18. Bologna, G., Pellegrini, C.: Three medical examples in neural network rule extraction. Physica Medica **13**, 183–187 (1997). https://archive-ouverte.unige.ch/unige:121360

19. Bordini, R.H., Costantini, S., Monaldini, A., Vozna, A.: From pure prolog to logic agent-oriented programming languages. In: Alderighi et al. [3], pp. 271–285. http://ceur-ws.org/Vol-3735/paper_20.pdf

20. Calegari, R., Ciatto, G., Denti, E., Omicini, A.: Logic-based technologies for intelligent systems: state of the art and perspectives. Information **11**(3), 1–29 (2020). https://doi.org/10.3390/info11030167

21. Calegari, R., Ciatto, G., Denti, E., Omicini, A., Sartor, G. (eds.): WOA 2020 – 21st workshop "From Objects to Agents". In: CEUR Workshop Proceedings, vol. 2706. Bologna, Italy (2020). http://ceur-ws.org/Vol-2706/

22. Calegari, R., Ciatto, G., Denti, E., Omicini, A., Sartor, G. (eds.): WOA 2021 – 22nd workshop "From Objects to Agents. In: CEUR Workshop Proceedings, vol. 2963. Bologna, Italy (2021). http://ceur-ws.org/Vol-2963/

23. Calegari, R., Ciatto, G., Mariani, S., Denti, E., Omicini, A.: Logic programming in space-time: the case of situatedness in LPaaS. In: Cossentino et al. [42], pp. 63–68. http://ceur-ws.org/Vol-2215/paper_11.pdf

24. Calegari, R., Ciatto, G., Mariani, S., Denti, E., Omicini, A.: LPaaS as micro-intelligence: enhancing IoT with symbolic reasoning. Big Data Cogn. Comput. **2**(3) (2018). https://doi.org/10.3390/bdcc2030023

25. Calegari, R., Ciatto, G., Mascardi, V., Omicini, A.: Logic-based technologies for multi-agent systems: a systematic literature review. Auton. Agents Multi-Agent Syst. **35**(1) (2021). https://doi.org/10.1007/s10458-020-09478-3

26. Calegari, R., Ciatto, G., Omicini, A.: On the integration of symbolic and sub-symbolic techniques for XAI: a survey. Intelligenza Artificiale **14**(1), 7–32 (2020). https://doi.org/10.3233/IA-190036

27. Calegari, R., Denti, E., Mariani, S., Omicini, A.: Towards logic programming as a service: Experiments in tu prolog. In: Santoro et al. [83], pp. 79–84. http://ceur-ws.org/Vol-1664/w14.pdf

28. Calegari, R., Federico, S.: The PSyKE technology for trustworthy artificial intelligence. In: Dovier, A., Montanari, A., Orlandini, A. (eds.) AIxIA 2022 – Advances in Artificial Intelligence, Lecture Notes in Computer Science, vol. 13796, pp. 3–16. Springer, Udine, Italy (2023). https://doi.org/10.1007/978-3-031-27181-6_1

29. Castelfranchi, C.: Modelling social action for AI agents. Artif. Intell. **103**(1), 157–182 (1998). https://doi.org/10.1016/S0004-3702(98)00056-3

30. Chang, K., Yih, W., Yang, B., Meek, C.: Typed tensor decomposition of knowledge bases for relation extraction. In: Moschitti, A., Pang, B., Daelemans, W. (eds.) 2014 Conference on Empirical Methods in Natural Language Processing (EMNLP), Doha, Qatar, pp. 1568–1579 (2014). https://doi.org/10.3115/v1/d14-1165

31. Chang, M., Ullman, T., Torralba, A., Tenenbaum, J.B.: A compositional object-based approach to learning physical dynamics. In: Proceedings of the 5th International Conference on Learning Representations (ICLR), Toulon, France, 24–26 April 2017. OpenReview.net (2017). https://openreview.net/forum?id=Bkab5dqxe

32. Chesani, F., et al.: Protocol specification and verification by using computational logic. In: Corradini et al. [41], pp. 184–192. http://lia.deis.unibo.it/books/woa2005/papers/26.pdf

33. Ciampolini, A., Lamma, E., Mello, P., Torroni, P.: Expressing collaboration and competition among abductive logic agents. In: Corradi et al. [40], pp. 64–69. http://giuseppevizzari.github.io/WOA-proceedings-archive/pdfs/woa2000/WOA13.pdf
34. Ciatto, G., Calegari, R., Mariani, S., Denti, E., Omicini, A.: From the blockchain to logic programming and back: research perspectives. In: Cossentino et al. [42], pp. 69–74. http://ceur-ws.org/Vol-2215/paper_12.pdf
35. Ciatto, G., Calegari, R., Omicini, A.: 2P-KT: a logic-based ecosystem for symbolic AI. SoftwareX **16**, 1–7 (2021). https://doi.org/10.1016/j.softx.2021.100817
36. Ciatto, G., Calegari, R., Siboni, E., Denti, E., Omicini, A.: 2P-KT: logic programming with objects & functions in Kotlin. In: Calegari et al. [21], pp. 219–236. http://ceur-ws.org/Vol-2706/paper14.pdf
37. Ciatto, G., Di Marzo Serugendo, G., Louvel, M., Mariani, S., Omicini, A., Zambonelli, F.: Twenty years of coordination technologies: COORDINATION contribution to the state of art. J. Logical Algebraic Methods Program. **113**(100531), 1–25 (2020). https://doi.org/10.1016/j.jlamp.2020.100531
38. Ciatto, G., Mariani, S., Omicini, A.: ReSpecTX: programming interaction made easy. Comput. Sci. Inf. Syst. **15**(3), 655–682 (2018). https://doi.org/10.2298/CSIS180111031C
39. Ciatto, G., Sabbatini, F., Agiollo, A., Magnini, M., Omicini, A.: Symbolic knowledge extraction and injection with sub-symbolic predictors: a systematic literature review. ACM Comput. Surv. **56**(6), 1–35 (2024). https://doi.org/10.1145/3645103
40. Corradi, A., Omicini, A., Poggi, A. (eds.): WOA 2000 – 1st workshop "From Objects to Agents", Atti di Congressi, vol. 1195. Pitagora Editrice Bologna, Parma, Italy (2000). http://giuseppevizzari.github.io/WOA-proceedings-archive/woa-2000.html
41. Corradini, F., De Paoli, F., Merelli, E., Omicini, A. (eds.): WOA 2005 – 6th workshop "From Objects to Agents". Pitagora Editrice Bologna, Camerino, MC, Italy (2005). http://lia.deis.unibo.it/books/woa2005/atti.pdf
42. Cossentino, M., Sabatucci, L., Seidita, V. (eds.): WOA 2018 – 19th workshop "From Objects to Agents". In: CEUR Workshop Proceedings, vol. 2215. Palermo, Italy (2018). http://ceur-ws.org/Vol-2215/
43. Costantini, S., Dell'Acqua, P., Tocchio, A.: Expressing preferences declaratively in logic-based agent languages. In: De Paoli et al. [49], pp. 138–143 .http://ceur-ws.org/Vol-204/P05.pdf
44. Costantini, S., Formisano, A., Pitoni, V.: A timed epistemic logic for formalizing cooperation among groups of agents. In: Falcone et al. [51], pp. 151–166. http://ceur-ws.org/Vol-3579/paper11.pdf
45. Costantini, S., Tocchio, A.: Strips-like planning in the DALI logic programming language. In: Armano et al. [6], pp. 115–120. http://giuseppevizzari.github.io/WOA-proceedings-archive/pdfs/woa2003/05.pdf
46. Costantini, S., Tocchio, A.: Learning by knowledge exchange in logical agents. In: Corradini et al. [41], pp. 1–8. http://lia.deis.unibo.it/books/woa2005/papers/1.pdf
47. D'Asaro, F.A., Origlia, A., Rossi, S.: Towards a logic-based approach for multimodal fusion and decision making during motor rehabilitation sessions. In: Bergenti and Monica [17], pp. 8–13. http://ceur-ws.org/Vol-2404/paper02.pdf
48. De Meo, P., Postorino, M.N., Rosaci, D., Sarnè, G.M.L. (eds.): WOA 2017 – 18th workshop "From Objects to Agents". In: CEUR Workshop Proceedings, vol. 1867. Scilla, RC, Italy (2017). http://ceur-ws.org/Vol-1867/
49. De Paoli, F., Di Stefano, A., Omicini, A., Santoro, C. (eds.): WOA 2006 – 7th workshop "From Objects to Agents". In: CEUR Workshop Proceedings, vol. 204. Catania, Italy (2006). http://ceur-ws.org/Vol-204/

50. De Paoli, F., Manzoni, S., Poggi, A. (eds.): WOA 2002 – 3rd workshop "From Objects to Agents". Pitagora Editrice Bologna, Milano, Italy (2002). http://giuseppevizzari.github.io/WOA-proceedings-archive/woa-2002.html
51. Falcone, R., Castelfranchi, C., Sapienza, A., Cantucci, F. (eds.): WOA 2023 – 24th workshop "From Objects to Agents". In: CEUR Workshop Proceedings, vol. 3579. Roma, Italy (2023). http://ceur-ws.org/Vol-3579/
52. Ferrando, A., Mascardi, V. (eds.): WOA 2022 – 23rd workshop "From Objects to Agents". In: CEUR Workshop Proceedings, vol. 3261. Genova, Italy (2022). http://ceur-ws.org/Vol-3261/
53. Franco, L., Subirats, J.L., Molina, I., Alba, E., Jerez, J.M.: Early breast cancer prognosis prediction and rule extraction using a new constructive neural network algorithm. In: Computational and Ambient Intelligence (IWANN 2007). LNCS, vol. 4507, pp. 1004–1011. Springer (2007). https://doi.org/10.1007/978-3-540-73007-1_121
54. d'Avila Garcez, A.S., Gabbay, D.M.: Fibring neural networks. In: McGuinness, D.L., Ferguson, G. (eds.) 19th National Conference on Artificial Intelligence, 16th Conference on Innovative Applications of Artificial Intelligence, pp. 342–347. AAAI Press/The MIT Press, San Jose, CA, USA (2004). https://cdn.aaai.org/AAAI/2004/AAAI04-055.pdf
55. Hayashi, Y., Setiono, R., Yoshida, K.: A comparison between two neural network rule extraction techniques for the diagnosis of hepatobiliary disorders. Artif. Intell. Med. **20**(3), 205–216 (2000). https://doi.org/10.1016/s0933-3657(00)00064-6
56. Hofmann, A., Schmitz, C., Sick, B.: Rule extraction from neural networks for intrusion detection in computer networks. In: 2003 IEEE International Conference on Systems, Man and Cybernetics, vol. 2, pp. 1259–1265. IEEE (2003). https://doi.org/10.1109/ICSMC.2003.1244584
57. Körner, P., et al.: Fifty years of Prolog and beyond. Theory Pract. Logic Program. **22**(6), 776–858 (2022). https://doi.org/10.1017/S1471068422000102
58. Kowalski, R.A.: Predicate logic as programming language. In: Information Processing 74 – Proceedings of the 1974 IFIP Congress, pp. 569–574. North-Holland Publishing Company (1974). http://dblp.uni-trier.de/rec/html/conf/ifip/Kowalski74
59. Laato, S., Tiainen, M., Najmul Islam, A., Mäntymäki, M.: How to explain AI systems to end users: a systematic literature review and research agenda. Internet Res. **32**(7), 1–31 (2022). https://doi.org/10.1108/INTR-08-2021-0600
60. Magnini, M., Ciatto, G., Omicini, A.: KINS: knowledge injection via network structuring. In: Calegari, R., Ciatto, G., Omicini, A. (eds.) CILC 2022 – Italian Conference on Computational Logic. CEUR Workshop Proceedings, vol. 3204, pp. 254–267. CEUR-WS (2022). http://ceur-ws.org/Vol-3204/paper_25.pdf
61. Magnini, M., Ciatto, G., Omicini, A.: A view to a KILL: knowledge injection via lambda layer. In: Ferrando and Mascardi [52], pp. 61–76. http://ceur-ws.org/Vol-3261/paper5.pdf
62. Magnolo, E., Manenti, L., Manzoni, S., Sartori, F.: Towards a MAS model for crowd simulation at pop-rock concerts exploiting ontologies and fuzzy logic. In: Bergenti [16], pp. 92–99. http://www.ailab.unipr.it/woa09/papers/Magnolo.pdf
63. Mariani, S., Omicini, A.: TuCSoN coordination for MAS situatedness: Towards a methodology. In: Santoro and Bergenti [82], pp. 48–57. http://ceur-ws.org/Vol-1260/paper11.pdf
64. Mariani, S., Omicini, A., Ciatto, G.: Novel opportunities for tuple-based coordination: XPath, the Blockchain, and stream processing. In: De Meo et al. [48], pp. 61–64. http://ceur-ws.org/Vol-1867/w11.pdf

65. Nardini, E., Viroli, M., Casadei, M., Omicini, A.: A self-organising infrastructure for chemical-semantic coordination: experiments in TuCSoN. In: Omicini and Viroli [70], pp. 117–125. http://CEUR-WS.org/Vol-621/paper17.pdf
66. Oliva, E., Viroli, M., Omicini, A.: Minority game: a logic-based approach in TuCSoN. In: De Paoli et al. [49], pp. 181–186. http://ceur-ws.org/Vol-204/P02.pdf
67. Oliva, E., Viroli, M., Omicini, A.: Simulation of minority game in TuCSoN. In: De Paoli et al. [49], pp. 6–9. http://ceur-ws.org/Vol-204/D03.pdf
68. Omicini, A., Ricci, A., Rimassa, G., Viroli, M.: Integrating objective & subjective coordination in FIPA: a roadmap to TuCSoN. In: Armano et al. [6], pp. 85–91. http://giuseppevizzari.github.io/WOA-proceedings-archive/pdfs/woa2003/07.pdf
69. Omicini, A., Viroli, M. (eds.): WOA 2001 – 2nd workshop "From Objects to Agents". Pitagora Editrice Bologna, Modena, Italy (2001). http://giuseppevizzari.github.io/WOA-proceedings-archive/woa-2001.html
70. Omicini, A., Viroli, M. (eds.): WOA 2010 – 11th workshop "From Objects to Agents". In: CEUR Workshop Proceedings, vol. 621. Rimini, Italy (2010). http://ceur-ws.org/Vol-621/
71. Omicini, A., Zambonelli, F.: Co-ordination of mobile information agents in TuCSoN. Internet Res. **8**(5), 400–413 (1998). https://doi.org/10.1108/10662249810241266
72. Pedregosa, F., et al.: Scikit-learn: machine learning in Python. J. Mach. Learn. Res. (JMLR) **12**, 2825–2830 (2011). https://dl.acm.org/doi/10.5555/1953048.2078195
73. Rafanelli, A., Magnini, M., Agiollo, A., Ciatto, G., Omicini, A.: An empirical study on the robustness of knowledge injection techniques against data degradation. In: Alderighi et al. [3] , pp. 20–32. http://ceur-ws.org/Vol-3735/paper_02.pdf
74. Rao, A.S.: AgentSpeak(L): BDI agents speak out in a logical computable language. In: Van de Velde, W., Perram, J.W. (eds.) Agents Breaking Away, Lecture Notes in Computer Science, vol. 1038, pp. 42–55. Springer (1996). https://doi.org/10.1007/BFb0031845
75. Ricci, A., Omicini, A.: Agent coordination contexts: experiments in TuCSoN. In: De Paoli et al. [50], pp. 14–21. http://giuseppevizzari.github.io/WOA-proceedings-archive/pdfs/woa2002/17.pdf
76. Ricci, A., Omicini, A., Denti, E.: Enlightened agents in TuCSoN. In: Omicini and Viroli [69], pp. 101–106. http://giuseppevizzari.github.io/WOA-proceedings-archive/pdfs/woa2001/pdf/21.pdf
77. Sabbatini, F., Calegari, R.: Unveiling opaque predictors via explainable clustering: the CReEPy algorithm. In: Boella, G., et al. (eds.) Proceedings of the 2nd Workshop on Bias, Ethical AI, Explainability and the role of Logic and Logic Programming co-located with the 22nd International Conference of the Italian Association for Artificial Intelligence (AI*IA 2023), Rome, Italy, 6 November 2023. CEUR Workshop Proceedings, vol. 3615, pp. 1–14. CEUR-WS.org (2023). https://ceur-ws.org/Vol-3615/paper1.pdf
78. Sabbatini, F., Ciatto, G., Calegari, R., Omicini, A.: On the design of PSyKE: a platform for symbolic knowledge extraction. In: Calegari et al. [22], pp. 29–48. http://ceur-ws.org/Vol-2963/paper14.pdf
79. Sabbatini, F., Ciatto, G., Calegari, R., Omicini, A.: Symbolic knowledge extraction from opaque ML predictors in PSyKE: platform design & experiments. Intelligenza Artificiale **16**(1), 27–48 (2022). https://doi.org/10.3233/IA-210120

80. Sabbatini, F., Ciatto, G., Omicini, A.: Semantic web-based interoperability for intelligent agents with PSyKE. In: Calvaresi, D., Najjar, A., Winikoff, M., Främling, K. (eds.) Explainable and Transparent AI and Multi-Agent Systems, Lecture Notes in Computer Science, vol. 13283, chap. 8, pp. 124–142. Springer (2022). https://doi.org/10.1007/978-3-031-15565-9_8

81. Sabbatini, F., Grimani, C., Calegari, R.: Bridging machine learning and diagnostics of the ESA LISA space mission with equation discovery via explainable artificial intelligence. Adv. Space Res. **74**(1), 505–517 (2024). https://doi.org/10.1016/j.asr.2024.04.041

82. Santoro, C., Bergenti, F. (eds.): WOA 2014 – 15th workshop "From Objects to Agents". In: CEUR Workshop Proceedings, vol. 1260. Catania, Italy (2014). http://ceur-ws.org/Vol-1260/

83. Santoro, C., Messina, F., De Benedetti, M. (eds.): WOA 2016 – 17th workshop "From Objects to Agents". In: CEUR Workshop Proceedings, vol. 1664. Catania, Italy (2016). http://ceur-ws.org/Vol-1664/

84. Sen, P., de Carvalho, B.W.S.R., Riegel, R., Gray, A.G.: Neuro-symbolic inductive logic programming with logical neural networks. In: 36th AAAI Conference on Artificial Intelligence, pp. 8212–8219. AAAI Press (2022). https://doi.org/10.1609/aaai.v36i8.20795

85. Setiono, R., Baesens, B., Mues, C.: Rule extraction from minimal neural networks for credit card screening. Int. J. Neural Syst. **21**(04), 265–276 (2011). https://doi.org/10.1142/S0129065711002821

86. Spillo, G., Musto, C., de Gemmis, M., Lops, P., Semeraro, G.: Knowledge-aware recommendations based on neuro-symbolic graph embeddings and first-order logical rules. In: Golbeck, J., et al. (eds.) RecSys '22: Sixteenth ACM Conference on Recommender Systems, Seattle, WA, USA, 18–23 September 2022, pp. 616–621. ACM (2022). https://doi.org/10.1145/3523227.3551484

87. Steiner, M.T.A., Steiner Neto, P.J., Soma, N.Y., Shimizu, T., Nievola, J.C.: Using neural network rule extraction for credit-risk evaluation. Int. J. Comput. Sci. Netw. Secur. **6**(5A), 6–16 (2006). http://paper.ijcsns.org/07_book/200605/200605A02.pdf

88. Towell, G.G., Shavlik, J.W., Noordewier, M.O.: Refinement of approximate domain theories by knowledge-based neural networks. In: Shrobe, H.E., Dietterich, T.G., Swartout, W.R. (eds.) Proceedings of the 8th National Conference on Artificial Intelligence. Boston, Massachusetts, USA, July 29–August 3 1990, vol. 2, pp. 861–866. AAAI Press/The MIT Press (1990). http://www.aaai.org/Library/AAAI/1990/aaai90-129.php

89. Zhang, W., Valencia, A., Chang, N.B.: Synergistic integration between machine learning and agent-based modeling: a multidisciplinary review. IEEE Trans. Neural Netw. Learn. Syst. **34**(5), 2170–2190 (2021). https://doi.org/10.1109/TNNLS.2021.3106777

From Objects to Agents, and Back to Smart Objects: Software Agents for Intelligent Internet of Things (IoT) Systems

Daniel-Costel Bouleanu[1,2,3], Marco Loaiza[1], Claudio Savaglio[1(✉)], Costin Bădică[3], Raffaele Gravina[1], and Giancarlo Fortino[1]

[1] DIMES, Università della Calabria, Rende, Italy
{m.loaiza,csavaglio,r.gravina}@dimes.unical.it,
giancarlo.fortino@unical.it
[2] DEI, Politecnico di Bari, Bari, Italy
d.bouleanu@phd.poliba.it
[3] CIT, University of Craiova, Craiova, Romania
costin.badica@edu.ucv.ro

Abstract. The chapter delves into the Internet of Things (IoT) and Agent-based Computing (ABC) duo. From the first sensor networks to the current IoT systems (e.g. smart cities, smart factories, smart homes), the ABC has been widely exploited to make devices truly "smart objects" by providing them with different degrees of autonomy, cognitivity, sociality and proactiveness. With particular, though not exclusive, focus on contributions from Workshop on Objects and Agents (WOA), in the following, we discuss how the ABC enables the development of advanced IoT systems, from the design to the implementation and simulation phases. Then, we present application examples, technologies and IoT platforms that make use of agents and, finally, we discuss future directions of an "agentified" IoT in the light of the emerging computing continuum.

Keywords: Multi-agent systems · IoT · Smart-Objects · Intelligent Systems

1 Introduction

The Internet of Things (IoT) [40, 45] is a rapidly evolving paradigm poised to transform our world by promising an interconnected future. In this future, technology seamlessly integrates into every aspect of our lives. Through the utilization of "Smart Objects" (SOs), IoT holds the promise of creating a more interconnected and intelligent world, aiming to address pressing social issues [60]. This shift paves the way for a smarter, more responsive world, heralding a new era of innovation and social impact. By harnessing the power of intelligence in both

© The Author(s) 2026
V. Mascardi and A. Omicini (Eds.): *The Agents Journey*, LNCS 16395, pp. 340–365, 2026.
https://doi.org/10.1007/978-3-032-22940-3_13

systems and devices, IoT is already bringing transformative changes across various sectors, including smart industries, smart homes, smart agriculture, smart cities, healthcare, and energy efficiency.

However, to fully unlock IoT's disruptive potential, it is essential to confront and resolve several well-known, multifaceted development issues and related requirements. A significant challenge is the heterogeneity among devices, which vary widely in type, resources, and capabilities. This spans a wide array of components such as NFC tags, sensors, microcomputers, wearable gadgets, industrial robots, domotic devices, and vehicles. It also involves a diverse range of IoT stakeholders, including individuals, companies, and public administrations. Managing and facilitating interaction between this vast number of different devices is not trivial, as there is no specific standard to follow [33,38,60,65]. Cyberphysicality, a cornerstone of IoT, merges the digital and physical realms through SOs, introducing unique functionalities and challenges. This intersection emphasizes the need for addressing advanced cyber-physical security and personal data privacy issues, which transcend traditional computer engineering boundaries, showcasing the intricate interplay between the virtual and real worlds facilitated by the IoT [11,54,60,61]. Beyond the characteristics previously outlined, IoT systems inherently integrate essential features crucial for their optimal operation and development. These features address the complexities and dynamic nature of IoT environments. Given the annual increase in the number of interconnected IoT devices, and with forecasts anticipating upwards of 29 billion devices by 2030[1], a shift toward their autonomous configuration and management becomes imperative. This shift is driven by the impracticality of manually overseeing the vast number of devices, highlighting the importance of self-steering, decentralization and high-performance intelligence as foundational to the system's architecture. Furthermore, integrating capabilities that support context-awareness and spatio-temporal positioning, as noted in [15], along with the necessity for pervasive intelligence [16], is crucial. These elements enhance the system's efficiency and scalability, while also strengthening a robust framework that enables autonomous adaptation to changes and challenges. Still, managing and facilitating interactions among a multitude of diverse devices presents a significant challenge, primarily due to the lack of a universal standard or protocol. Each device may operate on different platforms, utilize unique communication protocols, and adhere to various security standards, which complicates the integration process. The absence of a uniform standard not only increases the complexity of device interactions but also heightens the potential for inefficiencies and diminishes the overall reliability and scalability of the systems.

A methodological approach grounded in Agent-based Computing (ABC) is crucial for navigating the aforementioned complexities of IoT systems, enabling the creation of computational activities that are autonomous, socially reactive, and proactive [37,66]. This strategy allows IoT systems to dynamically adapt to environmental changes and user needs. ABC not only inspires the integra-

---

[1] https://www.statista.com/statistics/1183457/iot-connected-devices-worldwide/ accessed on March 9, 2026.

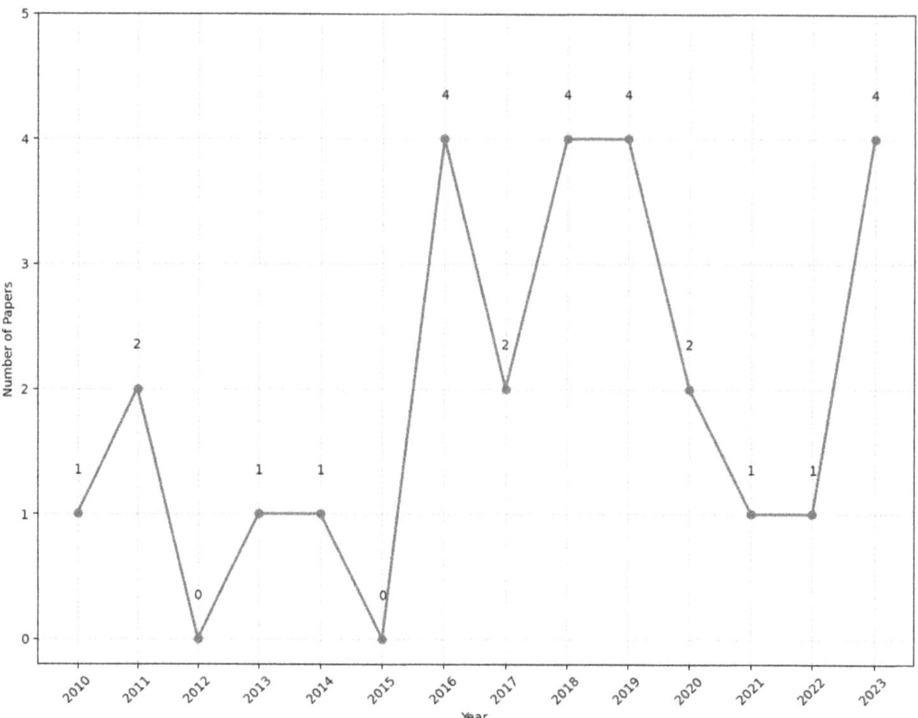

Fig. 1. Per-year distribution of WOA referenced papers on IoT and ABC.

tion of these sophisticated computational behaviors but also offers a robust programming paradigm for implementing agents with advanced features [68]. This facilitates meeting the essential requirements of modern distributed applications, thereby enhancing the IoT ecosystem's efficiency, adaptability, and user engagement. This chapter explores how ABC facilitates the development of IoT systems. As shown in Fig. 1, from 2010, a relevant number of WOA publications started exploring the potential of agents in intelligent cyberphysical domains and applications, and they are surveyed in this review, along with other relevant related works.

We have classified those studies with respect to their contribution to the modeling, programming and simulation phase of IoT systems, by specifying also their applications scenarios and their deployment setting across the computing spectrum, as reported in the comparison framework of Table 1. In particular, with respect to [39], the focus is specifically on the engineering of agentified IoT systems, whose inherent and distinctive features, cyberphysical devices and services can be successfully coupled with agent-based platforms, technologies, and applications, as depicted in Fig. 2.

The remainder of this chapter is organized as follows: Sect. 2 highlights how ABC aligns with IoT requirements, addressing complexities and showcas-

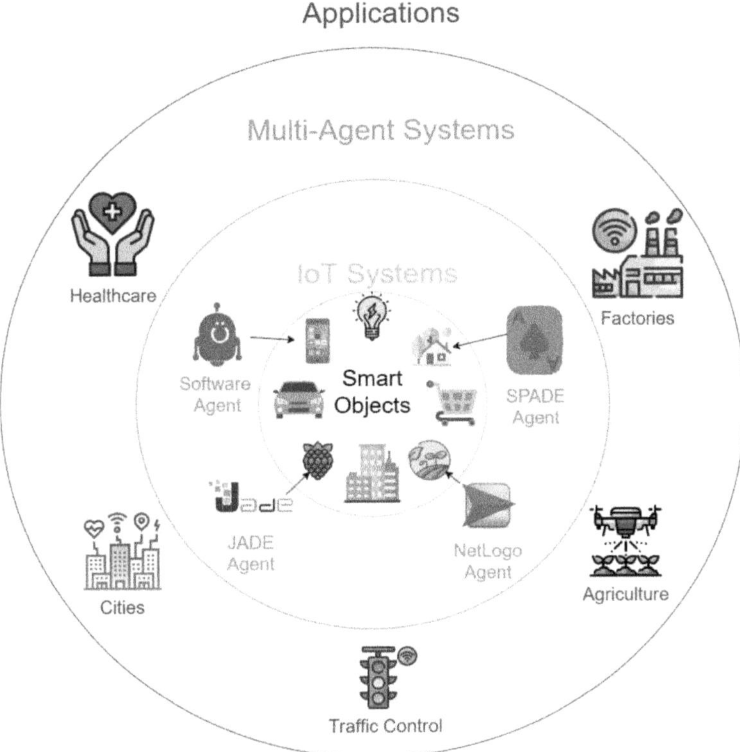

Fig. 2. Overview of the agentified IoT ecosystem.

ing the paradigm through the design, implementation, and simulation phases. Section sec:agentification presents a selection of agentified IoT applications and platforms. Section sec:continuum explores integration of agents within the computing continuum (device-edge-cloud). The chapter concludes with final remarks and summarizes key findings in Section sec:conclusion.

2   The Alignment of ABC and IoT

The ABC paradigm leverages agents—autonomous, social, reactive, and proactive software entities—to model complex systems across various domains. These agents constitute Multi-Agent Systems (MASs), which are distinguished by their nature as distributed, self-regulating societies operating within a specific environment. ABC stands out in its ability to model complex systems, interactions, and organizational frameworks, offering a refined programming paradigm. This paradigm emphasizes autonomous behavior and high-level asynchronous message passing for agent coordination. It enhances computational efficiency, reliability, and scalability, offering advantages over centralized systems. Additionally,

Table 1. Comparison Framework for the WOA ABC-IoT related papers

Year	The Alignment of ABC and IoT			Agentified IoT Applications and platforms		Agents in the continuum			
	Agent based modelling for IoT	Agent based programming for IoT	Agent based simulation for IoT	Applications	Platforms	Device	Edge Computing	Cloud computing	Continuum
2010		[32]							
2011				[25,33]	[33]	[33]			
2012									
2013								[35]	
2014		[24]		[24]	[24]				
2015									
2016	[48,68]	[16]	[16,36,48]	[16,48,68]	[16,48,68]		[68]		
2017	[38]		[38]	[20]					
2018	[15,54,55,61]	[15,54,55]		[15,54,55]	[15,54,55]		[15,54,55]		[54]
2019	[18]		[30]	[11,17,30]				[30]	
2020	[12,67]	[12,67]		[12,67]	[12]		[67]		[12,67]
2021	[31]		[31]	[31]					
2022	[28]		[28]	[28]					
2023	[52]	[52]	[52]	[4,52]			[47]		[44]

it offers benefits in re-engineering existing systems [61]. Agent-based simulations further allow for the exploration of emergent behaviors in complex environments.

Table 2. Summary of conceptual IoT and ABC complementation

Characteristic	IoT need	ABC solution
Autonomy	IoT devices or systems should autonomously perform tasks, make decisions, and adapt to changes, without a constant human intervention	Agents can act independently and take decisions based on local observations, strategies and goals, by autonomously responding to stimuli
Decentralization	Centralized systems obstacle scalability, resilience, efficiency, and privacy in key tasks of decision-making, data processing, and resource management across the network	MAS exhibit varying degrees of decentralization, enabling collaboration, coordination, computing and decision-making to achieve individual or shared goals
Cyberphysicality	To seamlessly merge the digital and physical worlds, enabling real or simulated monitoring, control and optimization with sophisticated human-machine interfaces	Exploitation of sensors and actuators networks to interact with the physical world or simulation of realistic agentified scenarios
Intelligence	To autonomously process data, make decisions, and optimize processes through artificial intelligence (AI), machine learning (ML), and analytics, transcending mere execution of commands to achieve real-time understanding and learning	Integrating Context-Awareness, Proactivity, and Adaptability introduces a new dimension of intelligence that was less accessible with traditional IoT methodologies
Interoperability	To unlock their full potential and foster innovation, heterogeneous IoT devices, systems, and services need to seamlessly work together and efficiently exchange data, despite their diversity	To provide common (agent) frameworks, protocols and standards (e.g. FIPA, SOAP, REST) for exchanging data and representing/sharing information in consistent format

On these basis, complex, dynamic, situated and autonomous systems are naturally suited to the agent-oriented perspective. Given the strong conceptual alignment between Agents/MAS and SOs/IoT systems, ABC has been used to speed-up the development of SOs and IoT systems [60]. A summary of the matching characteristics between IoT and ABC can be found in Table 2 and they drive the following analysis.

ABC can facilitate the cooperation between SOs and humans [18] but, with the proliferation of SOs, the traditional paradigm of simplistic human interaction proves inadequate for effectively assisting IoT Systems. Consequently, the topic of **autonomy** becomes a crucial area for discussion, especially when it comes to defining its boundaries [28]. Zooming out, IoT devices must be also cooperative entities in order to orchestrate collective actions towards a high-level goal. Such a **decentralization** [15] aims to boost scalability, resilience and efficiency within the MAS, where local and global goals are successfully achieved by resorting on *(i)* advanced decision-making capabilities and autononomic properties [60], supported by AI and ML techniques, and *(ii)* **cyberphysicality** and context-awareness, enabled by the exploitation of sensor and actuator devices to fill the gap between digital and physical worlds [32,33]. Through these skill, IoT devices can transcend mere execution of commands to achieve real-time

Table 3. Relevant agent-based works with their features; H - Heterogeneity, I - Interoperability; Cy - Cyberphysicality, A - Autonomy; Co - Cooperation.

Surveyed Work <*subject, ref* >	ABC Modelling		ABC Programming					ABC Simulation	
	Fine	*Coarse*	*H*	*I*	*Cy*	*A*	*Co*	*Pure*	*Hybrid*
Digital Factories, [11]	✓		✓	✓	✓		✓	✓	
Health-aware Guides, [12]			✓	✓	✓		✓		
tuProlog, [16]			✓	✓					
OASIS, [17]		✓							
Cognitive Human-Robot Interaction, [18]		✓	✓	✓	✓	✓	✓		✓
SMARTSAN, [20]	✓					✓		✓	
Social-Aware Smart Parking, [24]	✓		✓	✓	✓	✓	✓		✓
Territorial Emergency Management, [25]	✓		✓	✓	✓	✓	✓		✓
Cloud-of-Things, [30]	✓		✓		✓		✓	✓	
Smart Workshops, [31]	✓		✓		✓		✓		✓
MAPS, [33]	✓		✓	✓	✓		✓	✓	
WSNs, [32]		✓	✓	✓	✓	✓	✓		
ACOSO, [37]	✓		✓	✓	✓	✓	✓		✓
Opportunistic IoT, [38]	✓		✓	✓	✓	✓	✓		✓
ACOSO, Omnet++, [36]		✓	✓	✓	✓	✓	✓	✓	
High-Level Architecture Cloud, [35]		✓	✓	✓	✓	✓	✓		✓
Service-Oriented, [44]		✓	✓	✓	✓		✓		
Patient Tracking, [52]	✓						✓		✓
Smart Factory, [54]	✓		✓	✓	✓	✓	✓		✓
HBA, [55]	✓		✓		✓		✓	✓	
ACOSO-Meth, [61]	✓		✓	✓	✓	✓	✓		
ISN, [67]	✓				✓		✓	✓	

understanding and learning, thus achieving an **intelligence** level that elevates them to truly Smart Object. However, due to the marked and distinctive heterogeneity of the IoT domain, autonomy, decentralization, cyberphysicality, and intelligence cannot prescind also from **interoperability** [37,61], and semantic technologies are key enablers by providing a common framework for representing and sharing information in a machine-understandable format. By using ontologies (e.g., OASIS that maps agent behaviors, configurations, requests, and task executions [17]) and semantic annotations, different systems can interpret and exchange data accurately and thereby enhancing communication. This type of shared understandings creates trust among systems and enables seamless interoperability, by having a standardized way for each system to interpret the data [55].

Having established the conceptual alignment between ABC principles and IoT needs in the light of key autonomy, cyberphysicality, decentralization, intelligence and interoperability characteristics, we now move the discussion towards a development-oriented perspective. Indeed, we explore how the ABC marked a significant advancement in IoT systems engineering by enhancing their modeling, programming, and simulation. Table 3 summarizes main highlights of this analysis.

2.1   Agent Based Modelling for IoT

Agent-Based Modeling effectively encapsulates the essential characteristics of both SOs and IoT systems. This modeling approach inherently integrates the autonomy, proactivity and context-awareness that are specific to an SO system. Furthermore, additional features that are not captured intrinsically can easily be articulated through the use of agent-related concepts. For example [38] proposes a novel approach to modeling by *(i)* providing a metamodel in which high-level representations are provided to outline a service overview and *(ii)* providing an operational model, in which the services are formalized. Going beyond service-related modeling aspects, in [60] Authors give emphasis to the agents' roles and behaviours. Predefined roles are context-dependent and specify agent behaviors and goals, while custom models react to environmental stimuli and are not constrained by preset templates. Despite differences in approach, all methods aim to abstract SO features for early development phases. However, the need for further research on modeling agent interactions in physical environments is highlighted, alongside the potential socio-cultural impacts of a cooperative SO-based IoT. Finally, some concepts such as negotiation, competition, cooperation and delegation between agents and other entities [66] have been deeply covered in conventional computer systems and can still be applied for an effective IoT representation [31,53,67]. Concluding, agent-based modeling provides an an articulated body of knowledge to provide a solid foundation for subsequent stages of agent-based programming and simulations in the IoT domain.

2.2   Agent-Based Programming for IoT

The significant heterogeneity in resources and communication protocols within IoT ecosystems as well as the need of programming complex behaviours have prompted the adoption of an agent-oriented approach for creating consistent interfaces and transparently interacting diverse SOs and resources.

A first research line pertained the programming of communication and coordination interfaces either by using already existing communication standards like IEEE FIPA (Foundation for Intelligent Physical Agents)[2] or indirectly by supporting SOs Virtualization [65], for the sake of a major accessibility and integration of the agentified SOs. In both cases, to achieve the semantic interoperability, shared ontologies and knowledge representation [60] are necessary to facilitate the deployment of both existing and forthcoming application.

A second research line, instead, focuses on mechanisms for adaptive and efficient utilization of system resources. Indeed, agent-based programming promotes the availability of proper interface to either interact and integrate devices such as sensors and actuators. The work presented in [32] introduces an agent-based approach for high-level programming of Wireless Body Area Network (WBAN) applications. It demonstrates that the agent approach offers advantages not only during the design phase of a WBAN application but also throughout the implementation phase, enabling faster prototyping of sensor node code compared to

---

[2] http://www.fipa.org/ accessed on March 9, 2026.

using low-level APIs. Provided with contextual data and interoperable interfaces, agents can instill smartness and autonomy into SOs and implement autonomic and cognitive capabilities [59]. Consequently, systems that are appropriately developed and trained, these systems are capable of autonomously addressing more complex challenges. Being Context-Aware, Proactive and Adaptive introduces a novel dimension of intelligence previously less accessible through conventional IoT methodologies [37, 60, 68].

2.3   Agent-Based Simulation for IoT

Deploying IoT ecosystems is a challenging task, influenced by various factors including density, network layout, unpredictable traffic, and the expense of hardware and its installation. These challenges become even more pronounced in large-scale environments like smart cities, smart parking, smart buildings, and smart agriculture. Here, the deployment process becomes more expensive, prone to errors, and time-consuming. Undertaking a deployment that later encounters unforeseen issues, necessitating changes, can be extremely costly. As a result, simulating IoT systems before actual deployment plays a crucial role in estimating, validating, and verifying their performance, models, and protocols [60].

Simulations for agent-oriented IoT systems of various scales (small, medium and large) have been conducted [36] by using the Omnet++ simulation platform. Regardless of the scale—small, medium, or large—simulation results show that an increase in the number of SOs contributes to network traffic, thereby diminishing performance, especially when reliable protocols are used. This underscores the importance of conducting simulations prior to actual system deployment to optimize the performance objectives of all system components. Other studies have focused on proposing a novel and full-fledged approach to IoT service modeling, aiming to fully support IoT service development according to opportunistic properties [38]. They are applied to a case study focused on crowd safety at a large mass event. This approach can be effectively used to analyze, simulate, and validate any IoT service prior to its actual deployment.

Although pure agent-based simulators can successfully validate SOs interactions and operations of SOs, they typically outline quasi aseptic simulation environments, distant from the real cyberphysical IoT ecosystem. This detachment arises because they tend to either overlook or simplistically address issues related to low-level communication and mobility. Consequently, a new direction in research is emerging that advocates for a hybrid method. This method combines agent-oriented modeling with network-based simulation to offer a more comprehensive and realistic representation [60].

3   Agentified IoT Applications and Platforms

3.1   Applications

Building upon the synergies between IoT and ABC, numerous smart applications have been developed across diverse fields which can be fundamentally traced back to three domains: *(i)* smart city [20,24,42,55], *(ii)* smart industry [4,31,54,67] and (iii) smart healthcare [12,25,33,48,52].

With respect to the smart cities domain [24,42], highlight the interconnection of devices and intelligent agents to create more efficient, sustainable, and livable urban environments. Agent-Based IoT systems harness the power of real-time data collection and autonomous decision making as innovative solutions to some pressing challenges in modern urban areas. They can optimize traffic flow, energy consumption, reduce congestion or swiftly analyze emergency situations. Building on the importance of agents, [20] proposes SMARTSAN, a recommendation system tailored for smart cities. This system utilizes a peer-to-peer (P2P) social agent network to form groups of agents associated with geographically close users and objects. These groups provide personalized service recommendations while dynamically adapting to user changing needs. Local groups connect to a global social network, allowing users to discover services managed by agents outside their immediate vicinity. Through their social capabilities, agents form networks that capture and encode valuable information about actors and relationships within the smart city. By enabling personalized recommendations, facilitating social interactions, and integrating diverse services, agents significantly enhance smart city functionality and user experience. Together, these advancements demonstrate the pivotal role of agents in the evolution of smart cities. In [55], the authors propose a semantic-based MAS framework designed to augment automation and adaptivity within the domains of Home and Building Automation (HBA). This framework employs semantic annotations in OWL2[3] to enrich agent profiles, service descriptions, and requests, thus facilitating interactions that are both machine-understandable and human-readable. Within this system, agents are configured to establish social relationships autonomously, engage in independent interactions, exchange information, and coordinate ambient resources, thus fostering enhanced collaboration and resource optimization. Agents assume a pivotal role in decision-making processes, collaborative service, resource discovery, and semantic matchmaking. This approach enables the effective retrieval and prioritization of pertinent resources in response to specific requests.

With respect to the second application domain, the IoT and ABC duo can optimize many of the tasks of traditional factories by exploiting agent characteristics [11]. Digitalization of factories must take into account the simplicity of agents in order to manage complex manufacturing tasks, human interaction for when real factories are managed through digital abstractions and real-time constraints in a MAS system as the digital factory requires real-time data exchange among the virtual and the real IoT based factory. For example, in [30] a Trust-Based algorithm for forming groups of agentified mobile vehicles within an industrial scenario is discussed. The algorithm considers trust relationships, local reputation, and voting mechanisms to match devices and groups based on trust measures, aiming to improve IoT device activities. Furthermore, the seamless integration and coordination of diverse robotic systems within industrial

---

[3] https://www.w3.org/TR/owl2-quick-reference/ accessed on March 9, 2026.

environments such as Smart Workshops are critical to addressing the intricate challenges posed by various manufacturing and logistical activities. In [31] the focus is just on the deployment of Automated Guided Vehicles (AGVs) within collaborative frameworks designed to enhance the efficiency of storage, picking, and transportation tasks across multiple workshop areas. This research introduces an innovative agent-based framework capable of facilitating the automatic formation of virtual, ephemeral teams comprising mobile, intelligent devices with superior performance metrics. These "agentified" AGVs, each equipped with distinct capabilities, are identified as prime candidates for executing both standard operational tasks and extraordinary assignments. This is achieved by not only enhancing the productivity within a given workshop area but also by assigning an agent to support each AGV, thereby fostering a synergistic work environment among robotic coworkers. The proposed MAS efficiently distributes the informational burden across the entire network of AGVs, eliminating the dependency on a singular, centralized data repository. Furthermore, the presence of a Manufacturing-Manager (MM) agent is crucial for overseeing production lines. This agent is specifically tasked with monitoring the performance metrics of workshop agents and forming the optimal team(s) of AGV collaborators based on established trust measures. Through this approach, the paper gives a method for maximizing the potential of AGVs in industrial settings, highlighting the importance of agent-based systems in evolving the dynamics of modern manufacturing and logistics. Similarly, [54] proposes the use of a MAS as a means for intelligent cooperation between smart manufacturing components in smart factories. MAS is seen as a well-elaborated approach to overcome the lack of appropriate cooperation in smart factories. It is also relevant to highlight the importance of using existing standards such as OPC-UA (OPC Unified Architecture)[4] for service-oriented industrial communication infrastructure and AutomationML for semantic data exchange to achieve the required connectivity and interoperability for intelligent cooperation in smart factories. The proposed solution includes a service-based online model of the system represented in AutomationML, which meets the requirements for system information acquisition by MAS. A prototypical implementation is presented to validate the solution in a lab size production system, where MAS enables intelligent cooperation between smart manufacturing components, addresses the need for self-organization, self-optimization, and self-learning capabilities, and supports the acquisition of system information and knowledge management in production systems, thus eventually enabling efficient decision-making and optimization. Finally, [67] presents a formal MAS framework for coordinating Industrial Symbiotic Networks (ISNs - collaborative industrial practices that involve sharing resources and reducing costs at the collective level) as cooperative games. The paper focuses on the implementation problem of ISNs, which involves distributing the collectively obtainable benefits among the involved firms in a fair and stable manner, proposing the use of Marginal Contribution Nets (MC-Nets) as rule-based cooperative game representations to combine regulations and ISN games without affecting expressiveness. The paper

---

[4] https://reference.opcfoundation.org accessed on March 9, 2026.

utilizes a normatively-coordinated MAS to guarantee stability and fairness in ISNs, coordinating the behavior of industrial agents to balance benefits allocation among agent groups.

Finally, in the smart healthcare domain, software agents and ML [1,41] enables the personalization of patient care and the efficient management of resources, ensuring timely interventions and monitoring. The development of a new organizational model leveraging ABC and ML is discussed in [52], where data collection is facilitated through an IoT architecture to perform indoor localization of patients within the operating compartment. Furthermore, the architectural framework is designed to incorporate a distribution of several agents (used for collection of data, processing, location tracking, communication and notification) thereby ensuring the optimal utilization of resources and enhancing the overall performance of the system. This approach introduces resilience and adaptability, significantly improving the healthcare delivery process. Authors of [33] has presented MAPS, a mobile agent framework for Sun SPOT sensor platform that can actually support the development of applications integrating wireless body sensor networks (BSNs) and building sensor and actuators networks (SANs). The agent paradigm, its methodology and technology are indeed ideal candidates for engineering those integrated scenarios where context-awareness, mobility support and versatility are inherent requirements.

Wrapping up, it can be concluded that the exploitation of ABC is increasingly pervasive. Regardless of the specific application domain, anyway, particular emphasis should be reserved to semantic technology, in order to enable transparent communication among devices and thus creating integrated systems. In this direction, the OASIS ontology, introduced in [17], provides a framework for integrating services and behaviors across interconnected devices. It exploits behavior templates to manage generalized models of behaviors and tasks. Within this ontology, agent behaviors are defined as sets of objectives, where each objective comprises multiple tasks. Agents initiate actions by sending requests either to a request dispatcher or directly to the target agent. These agents are key to executing actions and achieving objectives, enabling coordination and collaboration among devices. By facilitating seamless integration, OASIS ensures effective communication and synchronization across networks.

3.2   Platforms

By leveraging the principles of MAS, IoT systems can efficiently manage and analyze the vast amounts of data generated, making decisions in real-time and adapting to changes without human intervention. Platforms provide the tools and environments needed to translate theoretical ideas into operational systems. Agent-based IoT platforms harness these capabilities to address complex challenges inherent in dynamic and distributed environments.

Transitioning to the foundation of IoT system development, in [37] the agent-oriented ACOSO methodology is introduced and applied for engineering SO-based IoT systems of different complexities and scales. ACOSO stands as a domain-neutral, comprehensive agent-based approach supporting the principal engineering phases of IoT systems and applications. This paper outlines and examines the primary development requirements of IoT systems, previously discussed, highlighting how ASCO effectively meets these essential requirements. During the analysis phase, ACOSO exploits a high-level SO metamodel used to describe basic SO features that shares main features with other IoT architectural standards such as IEEE P2430[5], AIOTI[6], and IoT-A[7] domain models. As the methodology progresses, this model is specialized and detailed through the design and implementation phases. More specifically, in the design phase, an ACOSO-based SO metamodel specializes the metamodel in order to shape the system's functional components, along with their relationships and interactions. The implementation phase introduces a JADE-based ACOSO metamodel that refines the design model for a specific implementation using JADE [9] (software framework for developing MAS in compliance with the FIPA, simplifying the implementation of agent-based applications). ACOSO goals is to facilitate SO development by means of metamodels that are present at different levels of abstractions, completely detached from any application-specific context. This approach significantly broadens the methodology's applicability, offering a standard within the heterogeneous landscape of IoT. The need for a comprehensive development methodology in the case of IoT systems is crucial, as to enable the dynamic cooperation among cyberphysical SOs in any IoTIoT application that requires distributed computation, proactivity, intelligence.

In [33] a domain-specific framework for intelligence management of WSAN (Wireless Sensor and Actuator Networks), named BMF, is discussed. It enables proactive monitoring of spaces and control of devices. The main functionalities of it are: *(i)* adaptive coordination of an extensive array of sensors and actuators; *(ii)* organization and categorization of the various components or elements of buildings in a structured manner, using both logical and physical groupings; *(iii)* intelligent sensing and actuation techniques; *(iv)* integration of heterogeneous WSNs; *(v)* flexible programming. In particular, BMF comprises two processing layers: a Low-Level Processing (LLP) layer that handles data acquisition from sensors, actuator control, in-node processing, scheduling of sensing and actuation requests, data and request routing, dynamic node addressing, and group management; and a High-Level Processing (HLP) layer that facilitates device discovery and management, group-based programming of sensors and actuators, adaptation of heterogeneous devices, and support for higher-level application-specific components. Another development in the design of the BMF has introduced an agent-oriented approach, termed A-BMF. This innovative design utilizes agents and their supporting infrastructure to enhance the management capabilities of BMF. It consists of coordinator agents (CAs) that operate in the base stations and sensor agents (SAs) that run on the sensor nodes, thereby facilitating management in large buildings with multiple floors and diverse environments.

---

[5] https://standards.ieee.org/ieee/2430/7045/ accessed on March 9, 2026.
[6] https://aioti.eu/ accessed on March 9, 2026.
[7] https://www.iot-a.eu/ accessed on March 9, 2026.

Finally, SPINE [8] is an open-source domain-specific framework for developing WBSN applications, providing high-level abstractions and rapid prototyping capabilities. It consists of two main components: one on the coordinating node and one on the sensor nodes, allowing for the distribution of signal processing and classification functions. The framework includes an application-level communication protocol for managing communication between nodes and the coordinator, supporting customization of messages to fit application needs. SPINE offers lightweight Java APIs for managing sensor nodes and issuing service requests, promoting interoperability and portability across different devices. In [33] SPINE plays a crucial role in the WBSN application for real-time human activity monitoring by offering vital signal processing and data management capabilities. It allows for the efficient implementation of application-specific logic, including the synchronization of sensor data and the processing of this data for activity recognition. The integration of SPINE with the JADE agent-based system underscores the framework's versatility and utility in supporting complex WBSN applications.

4   Agents in the Continuum: Edge Intelligence and Future Directions

The Computing Continuum [26] is defined by the strategic deployment of a device-edge-cloud architecture, designed to optimally run service-oriented applications across various network segments—cloud, edge, or devices—tailored to immediate system requirements and operational demands. This dynamic adaptability highlights the flexibility and robustness of IoT systems. Moreover, the emergence of the device-edge-cloud paradigm accelerates the transition towards a cohesive computing ecosystem, significantly enhancing the development and efficiency of complex IoT ecosystems. This represents a pivotal shift towards a more integrated, IoT-centric future. The ABC framework is well-positioned for effective integration with key computing paradigms and technologies that are crucial in the IoT ecosystem, and therefore, within this computing continuum. ABC can be applied at any level individually, from agentified smart devices, through the edge, and into the cloud, traversing each layer of the entire continuum. It seamlessly collaborates with these complementary paradigms and technologies, fostering a synergistic relationship that significantly enhances and propels the ongoing evolution and development of the computing continuum [6].

This integration not only underscores ABC's potential beyond being an isolated framework but also highlights its role as a foundational element in the dynamic advancements of the continuum and as a strong candidate to standardize a framework to control this continuum. In the following, the aforementioned computing paradigms are defined, the agent's role in each one is highlighted, and relevant use cases are presented.

4.1 Device

The first agentified smart devices were WSNs, which served as the cornerstone technology for IoT. These devices enabled the collection, processing, and transmission of data through wireless sensor nodes that are often limited in resources and dispersed throughout the monitored area. In the early 2000s, WSNs began to proliferate, finding their use in a wide array of applications such as ambient assisted living, structural health monitoring, and e-health. These applications have since gained prominence within the IoT sphere [2, 7]. Thus, WSNs not only preceded the IoT revolution by setting a foundational framework for interconnected devices, but also remain an integral component of the IoT infrastructure. This relationship underscores the critical role of WSNs in the evolution and expansion of IoT systems, highlighting their importance in facilitating a seamless, interconnected digital environment that can adapt to a variety of scenarios and demands.

Given the limited resources of wireless network infrastructures—such as constrained bandwidth and the computational, storage, and energy limitations of some of this devices integrating smart, mobile, and autonomous agents offers significant benefits. These agents enhance WSNs by managing critical functions including sensing, filtering, preprocessing, storage, and communication, along with essential services like timer management and resource access. Furthermore, they facilitate a distributed, intelligent decision-making process by enabling the selective activation of sensor nodes. This optimizes energy consumption and minimizes bandwidth usage. By processing and reducing the volume of sensory data directly on the nodes and employing context-aware filtering and clustering, these agents significantly decrease data redundancy. This leads to more efficient and sustainable operations of WSNs.

Building upon the foundational role of WSNs in the IoT, recent advancements have focused on enhancing the intelligence and autonomy of agent-based systems in other IoT devices. Microcontrollers and development boards such as Arduino, ESP32, and Raspberry Pi have been instrumental in this evolution, enabling the development of multi-agent system (MAS) applications on these platforms. This progression has facilitated the creation of more intelligent and autonomous IoT devices, capable of complex decision-making and improved interconnectivity [43, 47, 51].

For example, in [33], the authors delve into how agent technology profoundly enhances the adaptability, coordination, and overall efficiency of WSNs and IoT systems. They underscore the inherent adaptiveness of agents within their operational environments, demonstrating how this feature is crucial for imbuing WSNs and IoT systems with flexible, responsive properties. Highlighting the importance of coordination among agents, the paper elucidates how such dynamic entities are vital for ensuring synchronized actions within WSNs, thereby facilitating the achievement of system-wide goals. The research further investigates the synergy between agents and sensors, advocating for the use of agent technology in the design of efficient agent-based WSN architectures. This approach fosters the development of methodologies and tools tailored to support the complete lifecycle of WSN applications. Moreover, the authors discuss the deployment of mobile agents in the architectural design of WSN systems, as well as in the creation of services and applications, to enhance data processing capabilities, task autonomy, and the system's flexibility in responding to various sensed events, thereby providing a comprehensive framework for leveraging agent technology in enhancing WSN and IoT infrastructures.

4.2 Edge Computing

Edge Computing [19,62] brings computational and storage resources closer to the sources of data generation. This approach significantly enriches IoT applications with improved context-awareness, swift responsiveness, enhanced privacy, increased robustness, superior operational efficiency, and integrated edge intelligence [63,64]. By reducing bandwidth usage and energy consumption, edge computing with edge intelligence [5] infuses IoT systems with the capability for real-time analytics and expedited decision-making at the data source. Applications such as video analytics, personal healthcare monitoring, and autonomous vehicle operations benefit considerably. Furthermore, edge intelligence ensures local data processing, addressing privacy and security concerns by minimizing sensitive information transmission over potentially insecure networks. This method not only conserves bandwidth but also reduces energy costs, contributing to more sustainable and cost-effective IoT solutions. Ultimately, edge computing, augmented with edge intelligence, marks a crucial technological evolution, advancing the capabilities and effectiveness of IoT applications across various sectors [23].

Within the decentralized context of edge computing, there's a critical demand for SOs to exhibit autonomy, interoperability, and intelligence—despite inherent software and hardware limitations. This requirement underscores the significance of the ABC framework. The ABC framework empowers SOs with the capability for autonomous, context-aware, and intelligent behavior, crucial for the collaborative success of IoT applications based on edge computing. This includes enhancing edge intelligence by enabling these objects to process data and make decisions locally, without relying on centralized control. It grants agentified SOs the autonomy to sense and react to their environments, thereby enabling decentralized control over both SOs and network resources through cognitive algorithms and specialized data aggregation methods. Such capabilities ensure smart decision-making, dynamic task scheduling for enhanced flexibility, and efficient resource utilization, all integral to boosting edge intelligence. Furthermore, the ABC framework integrates privacy measures tailored for SOs, highlighting the paramount importance of protecting user privacy in a connected ecosystem. With these integrations, the ABC framework markedly boosts the operational efficiency and security of edge computing environments. It stands as a pivotal enabler for harnessing the full potential of edge computing within the IoT ecosystem, thereby fostering the creation of more agile, efficient, and secure applications. This makes the ABC framework a key contributor to the advancement of edge intelligence, optimizing the performance and security of IoT applications in various sectors.

For example in [47], authors explore the deployment of agents in IoT with edge computing as a mechanism to enable distributed artificial intelligence, facilitating intelligent collaboration among autonomous entities across a network towards shared goals. The integration of MAS within edge computing is examined through different lenses, including system architecture, resource management, task allocation, and optimization techniques. Specifically, agent platforms like DEMOCLE are highlighted for their innovation in offering agent capabilities to embedded devices within edge computing environments. DEMOCLE distinguishes itself by allowing logic/declarative agent programming in C++, leveraging object orientation, macros, and modern language features such as lambdas, thereby addressing a significant challenge in the domain. Furthermore, these platforms are equipped with sensor libraries that enable seamless interaction with common microcontroller peripherals, enhancing the agents' ability to communicate with external sensors like timers, digital input pins, and ADC channels. Such capabilities are particularly impacting in applications requiring intricate sensor interaction, as demonstrated in healthcare patient monitoring scenarios, where embedded devices equipped with sensors and wireless connectivity benefit from the advanced programming features offered by platforms like DEMOCLE.

4.3 Cloud Computing

Cloud Computing significantly enhances the capabilities of systems by facilitating computation at an extreme scale and enabling the integration, storage, and analysis of large, dynamic, and diverse datasets. Within the IoT landscape, it provides robust support even for devices with limited resources, emerging as a foundational technology that propels the functionality and development of IoT [49]. By leveraging cloud platforms, IoT systems can offload heavy processing and data management tasks to the cloud, thus overcoming the inherent computational and storage limitations of many IoT devices. This strategy not only streamlines the processing of vast amounts of data generated by these devices but also supports advanced analytics and intelligent decision-making processes. Consequently, cloud computing not only broadens the scope of potential applications for IoT but also significantly contributes to the sophistication, efficiency, and scalability of IoT solutions, making it an indispensable component in the development and deployment of smart, connected ecosystems. Building on the critical role of cloud computing in enhancing system capabilities and overcoming device limitations within the IoT, it becomes a pivotal facilitator for the development and operation of agent-based smart objects, even those with constrained resources. Cloud computing enables these "agentified" SOs to perform complex functionalities locally—facilitated through the virtual aggregation of SOs and the composition of SOs services—while offloading computation and data management to powerful remote servers. This dual approach effectively and transparently mitigates any hardware or software limitations that the SOs might have. Furthermore, the virtualization of agentified SOs, alongside the strategic offloading of their data and computation, not only maximizes the efficiency and potential of each SO but also simplifies the remote management of their resources. Through cloud computing, the IoT ecosystem evolves into a more dynamic, flexible, and scalable network, where smart objects can achieve a higher level of intelligence and functionality, paving the way for more advanced IoT applications and services.

For example, in [35], the authors highlight the crucial role of agents within the IoT ecosystem in conjunction with cloud computing. These software entities, designed to operate autonomously and make decisions based on their environment, seamlessly interact with other agents, humans, and the broader IoT infrastructure. The paper highlights the significant boost that the cloud computing paradigm provides to IoT objects by supplying them with enhanced computing and memory resources. This support enables the objects to perform more complex tasks and adhere to system-wide policies effectively. Within this framework, agents are able to leverage the extensive resources of the cloud platform, such as storage, processing power, and communication capabilities, which facilitates the creation of new virtual smart object agents through the process of meta-aggregations. The authors argue that the integration of agent-oriented middleware with cloud platforms is essential for the effective management of large-scale IoT systems. This integration enables the development of agent-based IoT systems that utilize cloud resources to significantly improve application functionality and scalability, thus increasing the autonomy, decision-making capacity, and collaborative potential of agents within IoT systems.

4.4 Computing Continuum

As seen in the previous paragraphs, ABC has been applied at various levels individually. Now, it can also be applied across the entire continuum. ABC significantly amplifies the capabilities of the computing continuum and IoT applications through dynamic and flexible management of complex distributed environments. By leveraging autonomy and cooperation, agents can process local data independently and collaborate to address challenges, reflecting the distributed nature of the computing continuum. This approach not only guarantees scalability as IoT ecosystems grow but also enhances resource efficiency across cloud, edge, and device layers. The context-aware decision-making of agents facilitates adaptive workflows and application migrations, ensuring operations remain optimal under varying conditions. Furthermore, the inherent fault tolerance and decentralized control within these agents enhance the resilience and robustness of IoT systems, which are essential for continuous operation despite potential failures or attacks. Through edge-based processing, agents promote real-time data responsiveness, minimizing latency. Moreover, the agents' ability to perform intelligent data management—via local filtering and aggregation—improves data quality while reducing bandwidth requirements. Overall, ABC offers a robust framework for addressing the complexities of the computing continuum, propelling advancements in the efficiency, scalability, and resilience of IoT ecosystems.

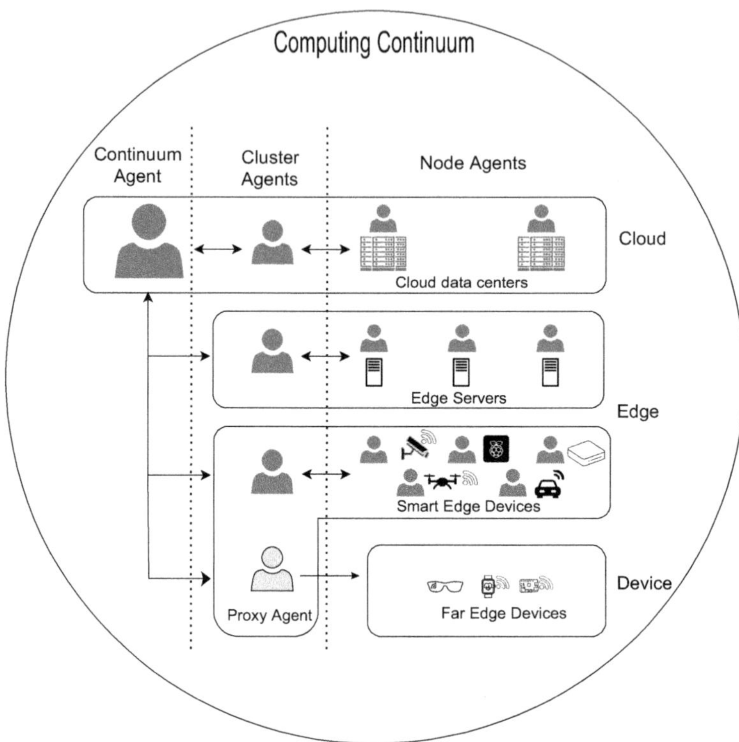

Fig. 3. Agentified MLSysOps Infrastructure to address the computing continuum.

In their exploration, the authors of [44] emphasize the potential of the MLSysOps framework[8], a groundbreaking fusion of intelligent agents, microservices, and ML techniques, designed to revolutionize automation within the dynamic Computing Continuum. This framework marks a significant leap beyond traditional paradigms, offering a sophisticated approach to embedding intelligence across the continuum spectrum, thus enhancing operational efficiency and adaptability composed by different type of agents as shown in Fig. 3. Each node in the continuum is monitored by a node agent that tracks the resources and services running on it. At a higher organizational level, cluster agents collect information from groups of node agents or applications and make decisions based on this data. Similarly, at the highest level, a continuum agent gathers information from groups of cluster agents and makes decisions accordingly.

All agents employ a ML approach that includes the MAPE loop (Monitor, Analyze, Plan, Execute) [56] to determine the best orchestration positions for services. This approach also takes into account IoT devices that can be resource constrained. Since nodes cannot directly run a node agent, a proxy agent is used

---

[8] https://mlsysops.eu/ accessed on March 9, 2026.

to fulfill this role. While acknowledging the roles of Service-Oriented Architecture and microservices architectures, the paper places a stronger focus on how MLSysOps transcends these technologies' limitations. By integrating intelligent agents with ML and microservices, MLSysOps promises to usher in a new era of agile, distributed services that can seamlessly operate across diverse organizational and operational contexts, signaling a paradigm shift towards more intelligent, autonomous digital service ecosystems.

Summarizing, the integration of distributed computing with the IoT marks a significant evolution in enhancing the performance, efficiency, and scalability of applications across IoT ecosystems. As we explore the integration of agents with WSNs, cloud computing, edge computing, and continuum computing, the synergy between these elements and the ABC framework stands out as a vital driver for the evolution of IoT. This convergence aims to redefine efficiency, autonomy, and scalability across the entire computing landscape. Implementing the ABC framework to complement edge intelligence initiatives empowers smart objects to conduct data processing and analysis at the network's edge, bringing about a revolution in resource management and decision-making efficiency. Such integration not only promises enhanced responsiveness and contextual awareness in IoT applications but also paves the way for the development of complex, distributed, and intelligent systems. These future systems, designed for autonomous operation and equipped with predictive analytics, will address the emerging needs for privacy, security, and personalized services in a hyper-connected environment. As we advance, the blend of agents with these computing paradigms will undoubtedly lead to groundbreaking applications and challenges, steering the IoT ecosystem toward an era of unprecedented interconnectivity and intelligence.

5   Conclusion

As its name suggests, the WOA workshop was established 25 years ago to investigate the transformation of Objects into Software Agents, focusing on the added autonomy, reactivity, and proactivity they bring to computational systems. In the last 15 years, as Smart Objects have been "agentified", they significantly returned to WOA, embodying a fusion of intelligence and physicality within networked environments. This large body of knowledge, along with other relevant related work, has been summarized in this chapter in order to explore the core requirements and characteristics of IoT landscape, and the pivotal role of ABC in addressing these needs.

Through a comprehensive analysis, we have demonstrated how ABC aligns with the demands of IoT, substantiated by various studies and papers that have effectively utilized agents within this domain. Our discussion extended into the realm of ABC modeling, programming, and simulation processes, highlighting their critical contributions to the development and optimization of IoT applications. By showcasing agentified IoT applications and the platforms supporting them, we have illustrated the practical implementation and advantages of integrating agents into the IoT ecosystem. Furthermore, our exploration into the synergy between agents and emerging computing paradigms - such as WSN, cloud computing, edge intelligence, and the computing continuum - has underscored the transformative potential of this integration. Citing specific examples, we have revealed how this fusion not only enhances system efficiency and responsiveness but also opens up new avenues for innovation and research in IoT ecosystem.

Acknowledgment. This work was co-funded by the European Union – Next Generation Eu - under the National Recovery and Resilience Plan (NRRP), Mission 4 Component 1 Investment 4.1 - Decree No. 118 (2nd March 2023) of Italian Ministry of University and Research - Concession Decree No. 2333 (22nd December 2023) of the Italian Ministry of University and Research, Project code D93C23000450005, within the Italian National Program PhD Programme in Autonomous Systems (DAuSy). We also acknowledge financial support under the National Recovery and Resilience Plan (NRRP), Mission 4, Component 2, Investment 1.1, Call for tender No. 1409 published on 14.9.2022 by the Italian Ministry of University and Research (MUR), funded by the European Union–NextGenerationEU–Project "Entrust: usEr ceNtric plaTform foR continoUS healThcare"–CUP H53D23008110001 - Grant Assignment Decree No. 1382 adopted on 01-09-2023 by the Italian MUR.

This work was also co-funded under the Italian MIUR, PRIN 2017 Project "Fluidware" (CUP H24I17000070001), and under the "MLSysOps" Project (Grant Agreement 101092912) funded by the European Community's Horizon Europe Programme. For the purpose of open access, the authors have applied a CC BY public copyright license to any Author Accepted Manuscript version arising from this submission.

References

1. Alpaydin, E.: Machine Learning. MIT Press (2021). https://mitpress.mit.edu/9780262529518/machine-learning/
2. Bajaj, K., Sharma, B., Singh, R.: Integration of WSN with IoT applications: a vision, architecture, and future challenges. In: Integration of WSN and IoT for Smart Cities, pp. 79–102. Springer, Cham (2020). https://doi.org/10.1007/978-3-030-38516-3_5
3. Baldoni, M., Baroglio, C., Bergenti, F., Garro, A. (eds.): WOA 2013 – 14th Workshop "From Objects to Agents", CEUR Workshop Proceedings, vol. 1099. Turin, Italy (2013). http://ceur-ws.org/Vol-1099/
4. Baldoni, M., Baroglio, C., Ditano, V., Micalizio, R., Tedeschi, S.: Agents for industry 4.0: the case study of a production cell. In: Falcone et al. [27], pp. 167–180. http://ceur-ws.org/Vol-3579/paper12.pdf
5. Barbuto, V., Savaglio, C., Chen, M., Fortino, G.: Disclosing edge intelligence: a systematic meta-survey. Big Data Cogn. Comput. **7**(1), 44 (2023). https://doi.org/10.3390/bdcc7010044
6. Beckman, P., et al.: Harnessing the computing continuum for programming our world. In: Abbas, A., Khan, S.U., Zomaya, A.Y. (eds.) Fog Computing: Theory and Practice, chap. 7, pp. 215–230. Wiley (2020). https://doi.org/10.1002/9781119551713.ch7
7. Begum, K., Dixit, S.: Industrial WSN using IoT: a survey. In: 2016 International Conference on Electrical, Electronics, and Optimization Techniques (ICEEOT), pp. 499–504. IEEE (2016). https://doi.org/10.1109/ICEEOT.2016.7755660

8. Bellifemine, F., Fortino, G., Giannantonio, R., Gravina, R., Guerrieri, A., Sgroi, M.: SPINE: a domain-specific framework for rapid prototyping of WBSN applications. Softw.: Pract. Exp. **41**(3), 237–265 (2011). https://doi.org/10.1002/spe.998

9. Bellifemine, F., Caire, G., Dominic, G.: JADE: A Software Framework for Developing Multi-Agent Applications. https://jade.tilab.com/. Accessed 25 Nov 2024

10. Bergenti, F., Monica, S. (eds.): WOA 2019 – 20th Workshop "From Objects to Agents", CEUR Workshop Proceedings, vol. 2404. Parma, Italy (2019). http://ceur-ws.org/Vol-2404/

11. Bicocchi, N., Cabri, G., Leonardi, L., Salierno, G.: Intelligent agents supporting digital factories. In: Bergenti and Monica [10], pp. 29–34. http://ceur-ws.org/Vol-2404/paper05.pdf

12. Bordini, R.H., Mascardi, V., Costantini, S., El Fallah Seghrouchni, A., Lespérance, Y., Ricci, A.: Transcultural health-aware guides for the elderly. In: Calegari et al. [13], pp. 135–146. http://ceur-ws.org/Vol-2706/paper8.pdf

13. Calegari, R., Ciatto, G., Denti, E., Omicini, A., Sartor, G. (eds.): WOA 2020 – 21st Workshop "From Objects to Agents", CEUR Workshop Proceedings, vol. 2706. Bologna, Italy (2020). http://ceur-ws.org/Vol-2706/

14. Calegari, R., Ciatto, G., Denti, E., Omicini, A., Sartor, G. (eds.): WOA 2021 – 22nd Workshop "From Objects to Agents", CEUR Workshop Proceedings, vol. 2963. Bologna, Italy (2021). http://ceur-ws.org/Vol-2963/

15. Calegari, R., Ciatto, G., Mariani, S., Denti, E., Omicini, A.: Logic programming in space-time: the case of situatedness in LPaaS. In: Cossentino et al. [21], pp. 63–68. http://ceur-ws.org/Vol-2215/paper_11.pdf

16. Calegari, R., Denti, E., Mariani, S., Omicini, A.: Towards logic programming as a service: experiments in tu Prolog. In: Santoro et al. [58], pp. 79–84. http://ceur-ws.org/Vol-1664/w14.pdf

17. Cantone, D., Longo, C.F., Nicolosi Asmundo, M., Santamaria, D.F., Santoro, C.: Towards an ontology-based framework for a behavior-oriented integration of the IoT. In: Bergenti and Monica [10], pp. 119–126. http://ceur-ws.org/Vol-2404/paper18.pdf

18. Cantucci, F., Falcone, R.: A computational model for cognitive human-robot interaction: an approach based on theory of delegation. In: Bergenti and Monica [10], pp. 127–133. http://ceur-ws.org/Vol-2404/paper19.pdf

19. Cao, K., Liu, Y., Meng, G., Sun, Q.: An overview on edge computing research. IEEE Access **8**, 85714–85728 (2020). https://doi.org/10.1109/ACCESS.2020.2991734

20. Comi, A., Rosaci, D.: SMARTSAN: a P2P social agent network for generating recommendations in a smart city environment. In: De Meo et al. [22], pp. 108–112. http://ceur-ws.org/Vol-1867/w19.pdf

21. Cossentino, M., Sabatucci, L., Seidita, V. (eds.): WOA 2018 – 19th Workshop "From Objects to Agents", CEUR Workshop Proceedings, vol. 2215. Palermo, Italy (2018). http://ceur-ws.org/Vol-2215/

22. De Meo, P., Postorino, M.N., Rosaci, D., Sarnè, G.M.L. (eds.): WOA 2017 – 18th Workshop "From Objects to Agents", CEUR Workshop Proceedings, vol. 1867. Scilla, RC, Italy (2017). http://ceur-ws.org/Vol-1867/

23. Deng, S., Zhao, H., Fang, W., Yin, J., Dustdar, S., Zomaya, A.Y.: Edge intelligence: the confluence of edge computing and artificial intelligence. IEEE Internet Things J. **7**(8), 7457–7469 (2020). https://doi.org/10.1109/JIOT.2020.2984887

24. Di Nocera, D., Di Napoli, C., Rossi, S.: A social-aware smart parking application. In: Santoro and Bergenti [57], pp. 24–29. http://ceur-ws.org/Vol-1260/paper4.pdf

25. Domnori, E., Cabri, G., Leonardi, L.: A multi-agent approach for territorial emergency management. In: Fortino et al. [34], pp. 74–80. http://ceur-ws.org/Vol-741/ID4_DomnoriCabriLeonardi.pdf
26. Dustdar, S., Pujol, V.C., Donta, P.K.: On distributed computing continuum systems. IEEE Trans. Knowl. Data Eng. **35**(4), 4092–4105 (2022). https://doi.org/10.1109/TKDE.2022.3142856
27. Falcone, R., Castelfranchi, C., Sapienza, A., Cantucci, F. (eds.): WOA 2023 – 24th Workshop "From Objects to Agents", CEUR Workshop Proceedings, vol. 3579. Roma, Italy (2023). http://ceur-ws.org/Vol-3579/
28. Falcone, R., Sapienza, A.: The role of decisional autonomy in user-IoT systems interaction. In: Ferrando and Mascardi [29], pp. 77–87. http://ceur-ws.org/Vol-3261/paper6.pdf
29. Ferrando, A., Mascardi, V. (eds.): WOA 2022 – 23rd Workshop "From Objects to Agents", CEUR Workshop Proceedings, vol. 3261. Genova, Italy (2022). http://ceur-ws.org/Vol-3261/
30. Fortino, G., Fotia, L., Messina, F., Rosaci, D., Sarné, G.M.L.: Supporting agent CoT groups formation by trust. In: Bergenti and Monica [10], pp. 71–76. http://ceur-ws.org/Vol-2404/paper11.pdf
31. Fortino, G., Fotia, L., Messina, F., Rosaci, D., Sarné, G.M.L., Savaglio, C.: A trust model to form teams of agentified AGVs in workshop areas. In: Calegari et al. [14], pp. 61–71. http://ceur-ws.org/Vol-2963/paper2.pdf
32. Fortino, G., Galzarano, S.: Programming wireless body sensor network applications through agents. In: Omicini and Viroli [50], pp. 137–144. http://ceur-ws.org/Vol-621/paper20.pdf
33. Fortino, G., Galzarano, S., Gravina, R., Guerrieri, A.: Agent-based development of wireless sensor network applications. In: Fortino et al. [34], pp. 123–132. http://ceur-ws.org/Vol-741/ID19_FortinoGalzaranoGravinaGuerrieri.pdf
34. Fortino, G., Garro, A., Palopoli, L., Russo, W., Spezzano, G. (eds.): WOA 2011 – 12th Workshop "From Objects to Agents", CEUR Workshop Proceedings, vol. 741. Rende, Italy (2011). http://ceur-ws.org/Vol-741/
35. Fortino, G., Russo, W.: Towards a cloud-assisted and agent-oriented architecture for the Internet of Things. In: Baldoni et al. [3], pp. 60–65. http://ceur-ws.org/Vol-1099/paper15.pdf
36. Fortino, G., Russo, W., Savaglio, C.: Simulation of agent-oriented Internet of Things systems. In: Santoro et al. [58], pp. 8–13. http://ceur-ws.org/Vol-1664/w2.pdf
37. Fortino, G., Russo, W., Savaglio, C., Shen, W., Zhou, M.: Agent-oriented cooperative smart objects: from IoT system design to implementation. IEEE Trans. Syst. Man Cybern. Syst. **48**(11), 1939–1956 (2017). https://doi.org/10.1109/TSMC.2017.2780618
38. Fortino, G., Russo, W., Savaglio, C., Viroli, M., Zhou, M.: Modeling opportunistic IoT services in open IoT ecosystems. In: De Meo et al. [22]. http://ceur-ws.org/Vol-1867/w16.pdf
39. Garro, A.: Agent-based computing for science and engineering: back to the future and beyond.... In: Mascardi and Omicini [46]
40. Gokhale, P., Bhat, O., Bhat, S.: Introduction to IOT. Int. Adv. Res. J. Sci. Eng. Technol. **5**(1), 41–44 (2018). https://doi.org/10.17148/IARJSET.2018.517
41. Jordan, M.I., Mitchell, T.M.: Machine learning: trends, perspectives, and prospects. Science **349**(6245), 255–260 (2015). https://doi.org/10.1126/science.aaa84

42. Lagana, F., De Carlo, D., Calcagno, S.: An agent-based system to monitor an energy biomass process. In: De Meo et al. [22], pp. 31–36. http://ceur-ws.org/Vol-1867/w6.pdf
43. Lefemmine, O.L., Meck, T.C., Logan, K.T., Pelz, P.F.: Agent-based control of fluid systems using microcontrollers: development and integration. In: Fluid Power Systems Technology: BATH/ASME 2024 Symposium on Fluid Power and Motion Control, p. V001T01A035. American Society of Mechanical Engineers (2024). https://doi.org/10.1115/FPMC2024-141218
44. Loaiza, M., Savaglio, C., Arijo, N.H., Aloi, G., Fortino, G., Gravina, R.: Agents in software development architectures. In: Falcone et al. [27], pp. 66–77. http://ceur-ws.org/Vol-3579/paper5.pdf
45. Madakam, S., Ramaswamy, R., Tripathi, S.: Internet of things (IoT): a literature review. J. Comput. Commun. **3**(5), 164–173 (2015). https://doi.org/10.4236/jcc.2015.35021
46. Mascardi, V., Omicini, A. (eds.): The Agents Journey: Twenty-five Years of Multi-agent Systems at WOA. Lecture Notes in Computer Science – State-of-the-Art Surveys. Springer, Cham (2026)
47. Messina, F., Santoro, C., Santoro, F.F.: A declarative C++ agent platform for agent-based edge computing. In: Falcone et al. [27], pp. 206–215. http://ceur-ws.org/Vol-3579/paper16.pdf
48. Montagna, S., Omicini, A., Angeli, F.D., Donati, M.: Towards the adoption of agent-based modelling and simulation in mobile health systems for the self-management of chronic diseases. In: Santoro et al. [58], pp. 100–105. http://ceur-ws.org/Vol-1664/w17.pdf
49. Nazari Jahantigh, M., Masoud Rahmani, A., Jafari Navimirour, N., Rezaee, A.: Integration of Internet of Things and cloud computing: a systematic survey. IET Commun. **14**(2), 165–176 (2020). https://doi.org/10.1049/iet-com.2019.0537
50. Omicini, A., Viroli, M. (eds.): WOA 2010 – 11th Workshop "From Objects to Agents", CEUR Workshop Proceedings, vol. 621. Rimini, Italy (2010). http://ceur-ws.org/Vol-621/
51. Palanca, J., Rincon, J.A., Julian, V., Carrascosa, C., Terrasa, A.: IoT artifacts: incorporating artifacts into the SPADE platform. In: Novais, P., Carneiro, J., Chamoso, P. (eds.) Ambient Intelligence – Software and Applications – 12th International Symposium on Ambient Intelligence, Lecture Notes in Networks and Systems, vol. 483, pp. 69–79. Springer, Cham (2021). https://doi.org/10.1007/978-3-031-06894-2_7
52. Pellegrino, M., et ak,: A system for tracking patients in the operating room – a pilot study. In: Falcone et al. [27], pp. 181–190. http://ceur-ws.org/Vol-3579/paper14.pdf
53. Rosaci, D., Sarnè, G.M.L.: Looking for the best partners. In: Mascardi and Omicini [46]
54. Rosendahl, R., Cala, A., Kirchheim, K., Lueder, A., D'Agostino, N.: Towards smart factory: multi-agent integration on industrial standards for service-oriented communication and semantic data exchange. In: Cossentino et al. [21], pp. 124–132. http://ceur-ws.org/Vol-2215/paper_20.pdf
55. Ruta, M., Scioscia, F., Loseto, G., Gramegna, F., Pinto, A., Sciascio, E.D.: Semantic-based social intelligence through multi-agent systems. In: Cossentino et al. [21], pp. 96–102. http://ceur-ws.org/Vol-2215/paper_16.pdf
56. Rutten, E., Marchand, N., Simon, D.: Feedback control as MAPE-K loop in autonomic computing. In: Software Engineering for Self-Adaptive Systems III. Assurances: International Seminar, Dagstuhl Castle, Germany, 15–19 December 2013,

Revised Selected and Invited Papers, pp. 349–373. Springer, Cham (2017). https:// doi.org/10.1007/978-3-319-74183-3_12

57. Santoro, C., Bergenti, F. (eds.): WOA 2014 – 15th Workshop "From Objects to Agents", CEUR Workshop Proceedings, vol. 1260. Catania, Italy (2014). http:// ceur-ws.org/Vol-1260/

58. Santoro, C., Messina, F., De Benedetti, M. (eds.): WOA 2016 – 17th Workshop "From Objects to Agents", CEUR Workshop Proceedings, vol. 1664. Catania, Italy (2016). http://ceur-ws.org/Vol-1664/

59. Savaglio, C., Fortino, G., Zhou, M.: Towards interoperable, cognitive and autonomic IoT systems: an agent-based approach. In: 2016 IEEE 3rd World Forum on Internet of Things (WF-IoT), pp. 58–63. IEEE (2016). https://doi.org/10.1109/ WF-IoT.2016.7845459

60. Savaglio, C., Ganzha, M., Paprzycki, M., Bădică, C., Ivanović, M., Fortino, G.: Agent-based Internet of Things: state-of-the-art and research challenges. Futur. Gener. Comput. Syst. **102**, 1038–1053 (2020). https://doi.org/10.1016/j.future. 2019.09.016

61. Savaglio, C., Leppänen, T., Russo, W., Riekki, J., Fortino, G.: Re-engineering IoT systems through ACOSO-Meth: the IETF CoRE based agent framework case study. In: Cossentino et al. [21], pp. 81–89. http://ceur-ws.org/Vol-2215/paper_ 14.pdf

62. Shi, W., Cao, J., Zhang, Q., Li, Y., Xu, L.: Edge computing: vision and challenges. IEEE Internet Things J. **3**(5), 637–646 (2016). https://doi.org/10.1109/JIOT.2016. 2579198

63. Shi, Y., Yang, K., Jiang, T., Zhang, J., Letaief, K.B.: Communication-efficient edge AI: algorithms and systems. IEEE Commun. Surv. Tutor. **22**(4), 2167–2191 (2020). https://doi.org/10.1109/COMST.2020.3007787

64. Singh, R., Gill, S.S.: Edge AI: a survey. Internet Things Cyber-Phys. Syst. **3**, 71–92 (2023). https://doi.org/10.1016/j.iotcps.2023.02.004

65. Vlacheas, P., et al.: Enabling smart cities through a cognitive management framework for the Internet of Things. IEEE Commun. Mag. **51**(6), 102–111 (2013). https://doi.org/10.1109/MCOM.2013.6525602

66. Wooldridge, M.: Agent-based computing. Interoperable Commun. Netw. **1**, 71–98 (1998)

67. Yazdanpanah, V., Yazan, D.M., Zijm, W.H.M.: A multiagent framework for coordinating industrial symbiotic networks. In: Calegari et al. [13], pp. 38–53. http:// ceur-ws.org/Vol-2706/paper9.pdf

68. Zambonelli, F.: Towards a discipline of IoT-oriented software engineering. In: Santoro et al. [58], pp. 1–7. http://ceur-ws.org/Vol-1664/w1.pdf

AI Infrastructure: From Gigastructure to Edge Intelligence with Multi-Agent Systems

Andrea Omicini[1(✉)], Alessandro Ricci[1], and Viviana Mascardi[2]

[1] Department of Computer Science and Engineering (DISI), Alma Mater Studiorum–Università di Bologna, Cesena, Italy
{andrea.omicini,a.ricci}@unibo.it

[2] Department of Computer Science, Bioengineering, Robotics and Systems Engineering (DIBRIS), Università degli Studi di Genova, Genova, Italy
viviana.mascardi@unige.it

Abstract. The rise of generative AI and LLMs is reshaping the global landscape of computational infrastructures. Massive investments in hardware and software are required, raising pressing questions about technological monopolies, digital divides, and the role of public institutions. Recalling the historical evolution of ICT infrastructures, we argue in this paper for a different long-term perspective on AI development—one where agents and MASs serve as the conceptual and technical foundation of scalable, sustainable, and open AI frameworks. Such an approach can help address the challenges of sustaining AI research within public contexts and promote democratic control over AI technologies and applications in the public interest.

Keywords: AI Infrastructure · Multi-Agent Systems · Open Science · Neurosymbolic AI · Internet of Intelligent Things · Digital Divide · Public Interest · AI & Democracy

1 AI Infrastructure Today: Towards Gigastructure

The popularisation of artificial intelligence (AI) is still quite a recent phenomenon, which has basically taken everyone's life by storm. Every contemporary human capable of using a personal device has nowadays access to an unprecedented amount of knowledge typically delivered by LLM-based applications; and generative AI apps have extended the impact of AI technologies even further—to music, images, videos, animation, ...

However, the world-wide accessibility of generative AI applications does not come cheap, and has instead pushed the demand for computational and network resources beyond any previously-imaginable limit. In fact, the training, testing, and deployment of large language models (LLMs) not only require massive datasets, but also ask for the availability of a specialised technological infrastructure developed on an enormous scale. The unprecedented level of the currently-available computational and networking infrastructure – which we refer to as

V. Mascardi and A. Omicini (Eds.): *The Agents Journey*, LNCS 16395, pp. 366–384, 2026.
https://doi.org/10.1007/978-3-032-22940-3_14

AI *gigastructure*, here and henceforth – requires a corresponding and equally-unprecedented level of financial investments. However, few are the organisations that can actually afford that level of investments. Mostly, they are private technology giants, which are rapidly overcoming public organisations—governments and academia: while in 2019 the public sector was controlling more than 60% of the AI supercomputers, in 2025 companies in the private sector own almost 80% of the AI supercomputers—see Fig. 1.

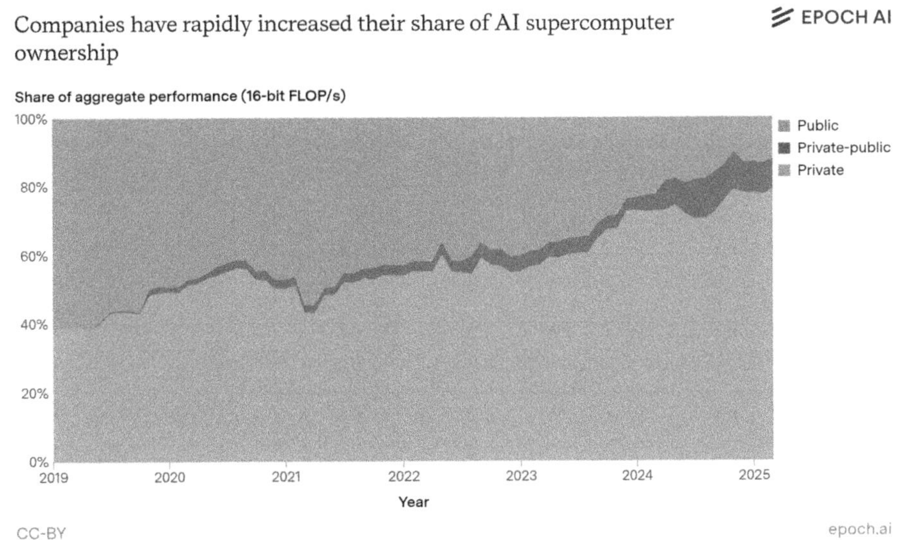

Fig. 1. In the last years, private companies have steadily increased their share of AI supercomputer ownership over public sector [89].

As we are quite accustomed to hear and read bold claims about research from the private sector, whereas the academia keeps on producing most of the actual scientific results, the imbalance in the availability of supercomputing resources for public organisations threatens public research on AI wherever in the world universities are mostly public. In the words of AI scientists Fei-Fei Li, "Public-sector investment in AI is so abysmal. Not a single university today can train a ChatGPT model... academia cannot fully develop its own versions so that it can be used for more open scientific research. That is a problem." [63]

So, the first critical questions becomes: Can public universities keep the pace with private organisation research on AI? Or, instead, should academic researchers just give up, or, leave academia for the big giants in the private sector to pursue their research goals in the field of intelligent systems? Should scientific and technological departments within public universities just leave AI research to rich private organisations, and focus instead on less money-intensive research themes? Should, in the end, the public sector lose control of the AI landscape completely, and leave it all to technological monopolies?

Meanwhile, the centralisation of the AI infrastructure in the hands of a few (private) bodies capable of affording the required financial investments also has a detrimental impact on the geopolitical side. Fact is, private organisations owning the AI gigastructure are primarily based in the United States (75%) and China (15%), with Europe significantly lagging behind (less than 5%), other countries like Japan owning small amounts, and even continents like South America and Africa practically out of the global picture—see Fig. 2.

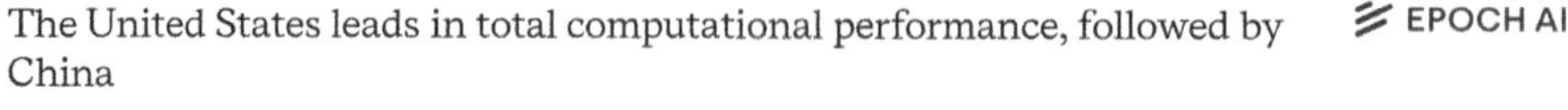

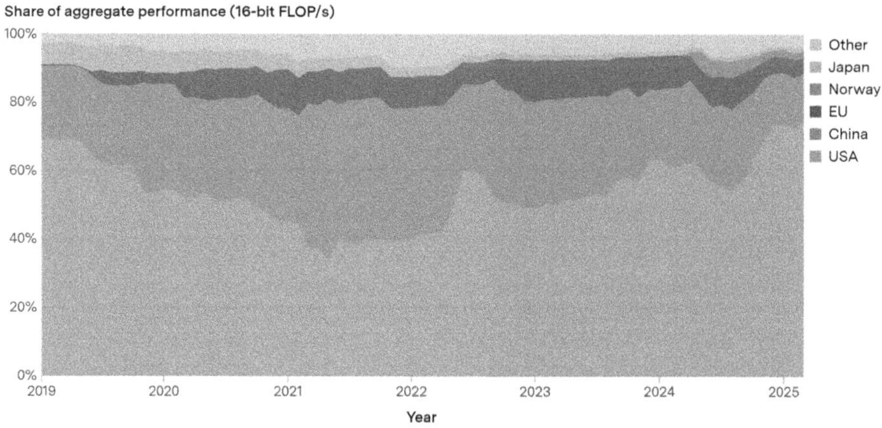

Our dataset covers an estimated 10–20% of global aggregate AI supercomputer performance as of March 2025. While coverage varies across companies, sectors, and hardware types due to uneven public reporting, we believe the overall distribution remains broadly representative. Future country shares may change dramatically as exponential growth continues in both AI chip performance and production volume. We are visualizing all countries that held at least a 3% share at some point in time.

                                                    epoch.ai

Fig. 2. Geopolitical share of AI supercomputer ownership [89].

Even though European countries are among the richest on the planet, only by considering it as a whole Europe possesses the economic capacity to compete— and then, what about, say, African or South American countries? The whole development of the AI gigastructure is apparently exacerbating the geopolitical imbalance in AI capabilities, which seriously threatens to negatively impact on the potential of development of most countries in the world.

So, the next questions becomes: are we witnessing the emergence of a new kind of digital divide – a huge, geopolitical one –, based no longer on essential information and communication technology (ICT) features, such as Internet access, but rather on access to AI tools and infrastructure? A digital divide where only few superpowers on Earth are able to secure their control over a significant portion of the overall AI gigastructure, quickly gaining industrial and military predominance over the rest of the world?

So, in the remainder of this chapter we try and answer those two fundamental questions about our future as it is going to be predictably shaped by the development of the AI infrastructure: *(i)* Should universities abandon AI research and leave it to the technology monopolists? *(ii)* Is the AI gigastructure going to drive an unbridgeable technology wedge between few superpowers and the rest of the planet?

In spite of the magnitude of the above questions, and – perhaps more critically –, of their economic, social, and geopolitical nature, in this chapter we mostly adopt a scientific and technical viewpoint, showing how agents and multi-agent system (MAS), working as the fundamental reference paradigm for the engineering of intelligent systems [101], can provide us with a less catastrophist perspective on the foreseeable future of AI technology and infrastructure—and of the world to come for all of us.

2 AI Infrastructure Tomorrow: A Perspective

Actually, both critical questions make (more) sense when their common premise is acknowledged: which is, that the future of the AI relies on an overwhelmingly-costly computational & networked infrastructure—which is basically the stage where we found ourselves now, at the end of the first quarter of the 21st century. To put it simply, this means that the future we envision is one where increasingly large datasets are fed to ever-larger models to build massive centralised AI architectures running over a vast distributed computational infrastructure—the AI gigastructure.

However, before we simply accept such a premise, some further considerations need to be made. First of all, we need to address the fundamental issue of technical obsolescence, whose pace in AI is seemingly accelerating: new model architectures, new hardware accelerators, new training techniques emerge frequently, rendering existing infrastructure outdated within a few years. Unlike traditional infrastructure investments – like transportation and urban commodities – AI infrastructure is going to require continual reinvestment, rather than mostly maintenance expenses. On the one hand, this apparently suggests that even fewer governments and private monopolies will be actually able to sustain the costs of an always up-to-date AI infrastructure. On the other hand, early investors may miss dynamics such as a steep reduction in hardware costs accompanied by increasing software efficiency. Conversely, investors who enter at the "right time" could in principle benefit from lower costs, possibly without suffering the drawbacks of a late market entry.

Yet, a deeper question still needs to be asked: Will the need for such an intensive infrastructure persist indefinitely? Or, instead, is it possible that future innovations would make AI development more efficient, more distributable, more sustainable, obliterating the need for a gigastructure for AI applications? Is there the chance that breakthroughs in algorithmic efficiency or new paradigms could significantly alter the forthcoming AI infrastructure landscape?

In order to get the chance to have a glimpse about the future of the AI infrastructure, it may be instructive to take a quick look back at the historical evolution of ICT. First of all, the initial phase of ICT was characterised by centralised mainframes accessible only to a few people and organisations, and with the widespread idea that a handful of exceptionally powerful computers would have provided enough computational power to the whole planet. Even thought Thomas Watson is typically misquoted for technology myth-busting ("I think there's a world market for maybe five computers"), he was still actually referring to a new IBM supercomputer in terms of numbers that would nowadays make us smile.

Instead, as we now know, that stage was followed by the miniaturisation and democratisation of computing through microcomputers, first, and personal devices, then—with industry leaders often unable to see what was coming—such as "There is no reason for any individual to have a computer in his home" (Ken Olsen, CEO of Digital Equipment Corporation, 1977), or Microsoft's Steve Ballmer "There's no chance that the iPhone is going to get any significant market share".

The advent of the Internet, first, and cloud computing, then, continued the trend, decentralising access and functionality across distributed systems. More recently, the rise of edge and fog computing has further pushed intelligence to the periphery, allowing small, cheap, networked devices to perform sophisticated computations.

Overall, the historical pattern is clear: initial centralisation, with a few super-costly, super-powerful computational units doing all the work, is followed by a progressive decentralisation process, with huge numbers of distributed low-power and low-cost computational units. The question now is whether AI infrastructure will follow the very same trend, or, instead, it will keep on growing towards gigastructure stimulated by exponentially growing AI application requests. Could the future of AI be marked by distributed intelligence across edge devices [28], rather than centralised supercomputing hubs? And, in case, which computational paradigms would drive us in that direction, harnessing the complexity of AI applications, and preventing the need for the AI gigastructure?

3 Agents and MAS as the AI Paradigm

3.1 Agentic AI

The very idea of agentic AI exploded in the AI landscape in the last few years [64], based on the fundamental idea that *intelligent systems should be built around "intelligent, autonomous AI agents that can reason, plan, and adapt"* [27]. Two essential things about the concept of agentic AI should be made crystal clear from the very start, before we proceed: *(i)* that idea is not new at all, heading back to the original notions of agents and MAS in the scientific literature [73], *(ii)* what is new there is the predominant notion of agent as an LLM/generative AI container.

So, the novelty of the agentic AI approach is mostly coming from the widespread diffusion and spectacular power of generative AI technologies and frameworks, such as OpenAI's Operator[1] or Stanford's Self-Taught Reasoner (STaR) [102]. On the other hand, the notion that agents and MAS provide intelligent systems engineers with the most expressive and coherent foundation for the design, development, and deployment of AI systems is a long-standing one, in academia, and can be dated back at least to the last decade of the 20th century. At the time, the three original and most important agent conferences – AGENTS (International Conference on Autonomous Agents), ICMAS (International Conference on Multi-Agent Systems), and ATAL (International Workshop on Agent Theories, Architectures, and Languages) – were born, which later merged into the annual International Conference on Autonomous Agents and Multiagent Systems (AAMAS) [59]. More or less at the same time, Workshop on Objects and Agents (WOA) was initiated [41], where ideas like "the deliberative capability of an agent is the natural place for whichever sort of intelligence is needed, in whichever form." [78] were immediately shared by the community.

3.2 MASs for Intelligent Systems

So, multi-agent systems (MASs) have long been a staple in classical AI research, in particular since the emergence of the DAI (distributed artificial intelligence) research area [77]. There, an agent is typically understood as an autonomous software entity capable of perceiving its environment, reasoning, taking actions to achieve goals—yet, a social entity [82], capable of non-trivial interaction within a multi-agent system. In turn, a MAS consists of multiple interacting agents, coordinating their behaviour in some way [31], possibly exhibiting some form of collective intelligence—e.g., [37].

MASs offer a robust and flexible framework for the engineering of intelligent systems [101], since they provide a uniform and coherent way to encapsulate all the many different AI techniques available, from rule-based reasoning to machine learning, within modular and interacting components [87]. Agent-oriented software engineering (AOSE) [39] further extends these ideas by offering methodologies and tools for building large-scale [85], adaptive systems out of agent-based abstractions [46]. Safety requirements of critical applications are a fundamental research topic inside the AOSE community, where formal and semi-formal approaches for testing and verification of agents and MASs have been and are still being developed [8, 11, 13, 14, 38, 56, 60, 68, 96, 100].

What are the basic ideas here, in short? *(i)* The software engineering principle of *encapsulation* applies to intelligence, too, and agents are the fittest containers for intelligence—so, for any AI technique and method. *(ii)* Agents of whatever specific sort can be assigned specific *goals* or tasks that require a specific sort of intelligence in order to be achieved or completed. *(i)* Complex intelligent systems can be built around the *divide et impera* principle, based on multiple intelligent agents each one pursuing its own goal/task with its limited intelligence, knowledge, and capabilities, *coordinating* [31] with other autonomous agents within a MAS so as to achieve the global (intelligent) system goal.

---

[1] Previously at https://operator.chatgpt.com/, since 17/7/2025 part of ChatGPT as a ChatGPT agent—see https://openai.com/index/introducing-operator/.

So, bottom line, agentic AI is basically just the standard MAS view over intelligent systems engineering, but enhanced with the almighty tools and whistles of contemporary generative AI—which spells distributed artificial intelligence (DAI), in the end [77]: as nowadays any non-trivial computational system is mostly nothing but a distributed one, almost any intelligent system is a distributed intelligent system since its design, and not just for the distributed infrastructural support. Which is why, in the end, AOSE [46] has been synonymous with intelligent systems engineering since its very inception.

What are the potential consequences of that, in terms of the AI infrastructure? Some clues could come from exploring the issues of *edge intelligence* [28]—in the remainder of this section.

3.3   MASs for the Internet of Intelligent Things (IoIT)

The same trajectory of physical distribution and miniaturisation of computational devices that lead us from centralised mainframes to pervasive computing is nowadays observable in the area of AI —where the notion of *pervasive intelligence* [51] is going to play a central role in the next decades. There, in particular, the growing computational power in embedded systems and the expansion of IoT devices are laying the foundation for the Intelligent Things (IoIT). Beyond traditional Internet of Things (IoT), which focuses first and foremost on connectivity and data acquisition, IoIT emphasises autonomous decision-making, exploitation of local knowledge, and situated intelligence.

As discussed elsewhere in this book [28], MASs are ideally suited to work as the sources of abstractions, technologies, and methodologies for the IoIT. Individual agents can be exploited as to handle situated interaction [34,70,98]; to handle local knowledge [47,53,86]; to rationally reason and suitably (re)act in physical and augmented environments [6]. MASs can work as distributed aggregators of knowledge [29] and intelligence, providing for agent coordination [31,71] even on the large scale [85].

Notions such as *micro-intelligence* [34] can then flourish at the device level, reducing the need for constant communication with centralised servers, in the same way as techniques for *localised learning* [36] align well with the DAI interpretation of intelligent systems intrinsically driven by the MAS paradigm. In fact, MAS provide intelligent systems engineers with a structured approach for coordinating device-level intelligence across networks, as "the incorporation of intelligent agents has become widespread to provide smartness within distributed system as well as to design and manage complex scenarios, such as the device- edge- cloud continuum and IoT ecosystem" [65].

So, rather than the AI gigastructure, a likely projection for the future of the AI infrastructure is the one of a *pulverised infrastructure* [54] where smart agents of any sort, suitably coordinated within large-scale MAS, will provide the conceptual, technical, and methodological foundations for the design, development, and deployment of intelligent systems.

Yet: which kind of agents are going to work as the basic components for the forthcoming AI systems?

3.4 MASs for Neurosymbolic Systems

As witnessed by the first years of WOA, in their first decades agent models and technologies mostly developed along two parallel lines: *(i)* rational agents based on a logically-sound architecture [7] – *á la* belief-desire-intention (BDI) [6,44,72,75,76,91] –, mostly focussing on classic AI issues, such as automated reasoning and planning, using symbolic approaches [99], and *(ii)* middleware agents – *á la* JADE [15,16,19,22,23,26,88] –, mostly focussing on the language paradigm shift (from objects to agents), as well as on computational autonomy for harnessing the many issues of distributed systems [25]. The subsequent, overwhelming success of deep learning (DL) led to an intense yet heterogeneous flow of research activities, where DL techniques are integrated with agent-oriented models and technologies in many different ways – e.g., [62,67,96] –, obviously including agent-based modelling & simulation (ABMS)—e.g., [4,66,97].

In the last years, however, the impact of agentic AI techniques has pushed many researchers and practitioners in the area of intelligent system to focus on the almost trivial notion of agents as software containers for DL and generative AI technologies. There, the integration of subsymbolic techniques within the agent frameworks mostly occurs at the syntactic level [1]—so that the expressive power of the agent and MAS abstractions is mostly wasted. Yet, the widespread adoption of subsymbolic techniques has brought into the MAS scenario the same AI issues – transparency, interpretability, trustability [95], accountability, ... – that have led to the recent emergence of explainable artificial intelligence (XAI) as one of the hottest research areas [61]. There, one of the most promising research lines involves the integration of symbolic and subsymbolic techniques into neurosymbolic ones [35], a hybrid approach to intelligent systems that combines the raw power and effective capabilities of subsymbolic approaches with the interpretability and reasoning ability of symbolic systems.

Agents and MAS serve as the ideal architectural layer for this integration. Within an agent, subsymbolic components – e.g., neural networks (NNs) – can handle perception and pattern matching, while symbolic components can manage logic, reasoning, and explanations [2,20,69,90]. Neurosymbolic agents become then the containers where heterogeneous AI paradigms coexist and cooperate fruitfully, making the overall MAS more powerful and effective, and at the same time more understandable, explainable, and trustworthy.

However, if neurosymbolic agents – and MAS whose components are neurosymbolic agents – are the conceptual, technical, and methodological foundation of forthcoming AI systems, one might argue that each of them would require the same huge amounts of computational & networking resources as current generative AI applications do. Yet, first of all, neurosymbolic agents can be designed and implemented so as to exploit subsymbolic techniques – such as generative AI ones – only when actually required by the task at hand, while relying on symbolic techniques – which are typically less computationally intensive – for their general operation.

Also, at the core of AOSE is the notion of agent *society* [78,81], enabling (de)composition techniques like *zooming* [74], which promote fine-grained goal and task (dis)aggregation and stepwise refinement—so that the computational load of every agent can in principle be adjusted to *its* computational power. For instance, one already quite visible trend in knowledge-intensive intelligent systems is partitioning application knowledge into very specific application subdomains, train some individual agents over each subdomain – which typically do not require huge computational resources, e.g. [40] – and make them cooperate within a MAS covering altogether all the application knowledge. Also, real application domains often do not require the full power of general-purpose AI approaches, so that simplification and reduction techniques can be used to exploit AI techniques on constrained devices–even hyper-constrained devices, as in the case of [3].

In the end, it seems safe to conclude that neurosymbolic agents, too, can be expected to suitably fit the "device-edge-cloud continuum and IoT ecosystem" [65], providing for edge intelligence, specifically, and for the general needs of intelligent systems, as well, without necessarily require the support of the AI gigastructure.

4   The Future of AI Infrastructure: Some Answers

In Sect. 1 we summarise the two fundamental questions to be faced when reasoning about the future of the AI infrastructure:

(i) should universities abandon AI research and leave it to the technology monopolists?, and *(ii)* is the AI gigastructure going to drive an unbridgeable technology wedge between few superpowers and the rest of the planet?

which we can finally try and answer—the latter in Sect. 4.1, the former in Sect. 4.2.

4.1   The Future of AI Infrastructure is Agent-Based

Definitely, the future of AI does not belong exclusively to massive, superpowerful, centralised infrastructures. The most likely trajectory for intelligent systems will presumably include all the possible spectrum of (networked) computational devices, from a number of large supercomputers down to a myriad hyper-constrained embedded devices—balancing the drive in opposite directions, centralisation vs. decentralisation.

Far beyond the current wave of agentic AI, agents and MASs are going to provide the conceptual and technical means to build intelligent systems of any sort. AOSE methods and processes will shape the forthcoming tide of well-designed intelligent systems, allowing engineers to adapt them to the available computational infrastructure—up to a point, as obvious. In particular, MASs can bridge the gap between large-scale infrastructures and decentralised networks, since they can be either deployed on high-performance servers or embedded within edge devices. Neurosymbolic agents, such as *self-explaining agents* [79], demonstrate how a MAS can exploit effective AI subsymbolic techniques while maintaining interpretability, transparency, and trustability—without necessarily depending on a large and costly infrastructure.

Since agents and MASs date far back than the notion of agentic AI, a large, interconnected, worldwide scientific community (which obviously includes the Italian one, grown around twenty-five years of WOA) is already in place, mostly from public institutions, sharing common values such as open science, and prone to listen to the needs of the global citizens of the world—so that the benefits of AI can be shared by everyone on the planet, and the dangers of AI can be limited for everyone at the best of human knowledge. So, for instance, the MAS community has already developed a suitable set of open standards through the FIPA[2] standardisation body [43], which are also actively sustained by the research work—e.g., [30,80]. Also, agent-based notions like *electronic institutions* [12] and *social norms* [92] seemingly provide MAS engineers with a straightforward path towards intelligent systems that are not only powerful and promoting sustainable infrastructure principles, but also more easily aligned with democratic values and ethical norms.

4.2   AI and Public Interest: The Issue of Research

The current dominance of private corporations in AI technology has sparked intense debate, with someone (mostly from private organisations themselves) claiming that universities and public institutions should step back from AI research due to the high costs involved, arguing that the resource requirements has already placed meaningful AI research beyond the reach of academia. That would be a grave mistake. AI technologies already impact every facet of human life, from healthcare to education, from governance to employment: leaving their development solely in the hands of private entities would threaten transparency, accountability, and ethical oversight. Moreover, public norms and regulations, while essential, typically lag behind technological change, and are often insufficient on their own to safeguard public interests—and private ownerships are not historically the best remedy for that problem.

Luckily, public institutions have already reacted constructively and proactively to the risk of losing control of a relevant asset such as AI research and technology: from US[3] to China[4] and Singapore,[5] from EU[6] to UK[7] and Canada,[8] from India[9] to Japan,[10] all the richest countries in the world have implemented

---

[2] http://www.fipa.org.

[3] https://www.nsf.gov/news/nsf-announces-100-million-investment-national-artificial.

[4] https://www.chinadaily.com.cn/a/202504/18/WS6802358ea3104d9fd38204b5.html.

[5] https://nsstc.niar.org.tw/en/highlights/analysis/2024-07-29.

[6] https://digital-strategy.ec.europa.eu/en/policies/european-approach-artificial-intelligence.

[7] https://www.ukri.org/opportunity/responsible-ai-uk-keystone-projects.

[8] https://ised-isde.canada.ca/site/ai-strategy/.

[9] https://www.pib.gov.in/PressReleasePage.aspx?PRID=2108810.

[10] https://www.meti.go.jp/english/policy/0704_001.pdf.

big public AI funding programs; and many other countries all over the world have done/are doing the same – e.g., in Africa[11] –, at the best of their economic power and sociopolitical context.

However, significantly increasing public funding dedicated to AI is just the first step towards the main goal of preserving democratic oversight and ensuring socially beneficial outcomes. Also, efforts to foster competitive AI research within (public) universities and public research institutions and to promote connections with private sector will be essential, in particular where small and medium-sized enterprises (SME)[12] – whose size typically makes access to AI research problematic – are numerous and relevant. Along this line, Open Science presents a promising path forward, since it emphasises transparency, reproducibility, and collaboration. Yet, it is already evident – even in the academic environment – that any effort toward openness of science should in some way navigate the complexities of intellectual property, data privacy, and (perhaps mostly, today) security. Academic freedom is vital to this effort, offering a foundation for independent exploration and innovation—and maybe for that very reason often under attack.[13]

Nonetheless, academic freedom alone may not suffice in the medium to long term. Alternative paradigms should be pursued, looking for approaches that could reduce reliance on massive computational infrastructure – what we called the AI gigastructure –, and lead us instead towards more flexible, scalable, and inclusive AI architectures. As we discussed in Sect. 3, that is precisely the role that agents and MASs are expected to play in the next decades, working as the main paradigm for the design, development, and deployment of the intelligent systems to come.

5   Conclusion

In conclusion, the dominance of the AI gigastructure in the hands of few private technology giants is not an inevitable future. Drawing from historical trends in ICT as well as from the expressive power of agents and MAS – as well as from more than three decades of academic research –, we argue first of all that the future of AI infrastructure will likely include every size of computational devices, from large supercomputers down to constrained embedded devices.

AOSE offers a paradigm enabling intelligent systems engineers to scale across infrastructural levels—from centralised data centres to distributed edge networks. In the long term, agents and MAS are likely to become the cornerstone of AI infrastructure, offering a balanced response to the challenges of digital divide, public oversight, and technological monopolisation. In that, they represent not only a technical solution but a socio-technical framework for responsible AI.

---

[11] https://blog.startuplist.africa/articles/ai-revolution-in-africa-2025.

[12] https://eur-lex.europa.eu/eli/reco/2003/361/oj/.

[13] https://www.nytimes.com/2025/08/19/us/politics/trump-universities-financial-penalties.html.

That path, however, strongly depends on the support from public institutions: goals, fundings, and proper regulations from governments; research, open science and technology from public research bodies, such as universities. Whereas many governments worldwide are already pushing in that direction, twenty-five years of research results at WOA – most of which from Italian public universities – suggest that the academic community, too, is ready to accept the challenge.

Acknowledgments. This chapter was partially supported by *(i)* "ENGINES – ENGineering INtElligent Systems around intelligent agent technologies" project, funded by the European Union – Next Generation EU within the framework of the National Recovery and Resilience Plan NRRP – Mission 4 "Education and Research" – Component 2 – Investment 1.1 "National Research Program and Projects of Significant National Interest Fund (PRIN)" – Call PRIN 2022 – D.D. n. 104 of 02/02/2022, under grant number 20229ZXBZM, *(ii)* the "AEQUITAS" project funded by European Union's Horizon Europe research and innovation programme under grant number 101070363, *(iii)* PNRR âĂŞ M4C2 âĂŞ Investimento 1.3, Partenariato Esteso PE00000013 âĂŞ "FAIR—Future Artificial Intelligence Research" âĂŞ Spoke 8 "Pervasive AI", funded by the European Commission under the NextGenerationEU programme.

Disclosure of Interests. The authors have no competing interests to declare that are relevant to the content of this article.

References

1. Agiollo, A., Calegari, R., Ciatto, G., Magnini, M., Omicini, A., Sabbatini, F.: Intelligent agents from symbolic to neurosymbolic systems: The quest for integration. In: Mascardi and Omicini [73]
2. Agiollo, A., Ciatto, G., Omicini, A.: Graph neural networks as the copula mundi between logic and machine learning: a roadmap. In: Calegari et al. [33], pp. 98–115. http://ceur-ws.org/Vol-2963/paper18.pdf
3. Agiollo, A., Omicini, A.: Load classification: a case study for applying neural networks in hyper-constrained embedded devices. Appl. Sci. **11**(24) (2021). https://doi.org/10.3390/app112411957. special issue "Artificial Intelligence and Data Engineering in Engineering Applications"
4. Albericci, T., Cecconello, T., Gibertini, A., Vizzari, G.: A curriculum-based reinforcement learning approach to pedestrian simulation. In: Calegari et al. [33], pp. 224–240. http://ceur-ws.org/Vol-2963/paper11.pdf
5. Alderighi, M., Baldoni, M., Baroglio, C., Micalizio, R., Tedeschi, S.: WOA 2024 – 25th Workshop "From Objects to Agents", CEUR Workshop Proceedings, vol. 3735. Bard, AO, Italy (2024). http://ceur-ws.org/Vol-3735/
6. Amato, A., Di Martino, B., Venticinque, S.: BDI intelligent agents for augmented exploitation of pervasive environments. In: Fortino et al. [58], pp. 81–88. http://ceur-ws.org/Vol-741/ID16_AmatoDiMartinoVenticinque.pdf
7. Ancona, D., Briola, D., Ferrando, A., Martelli, M., Mascardi, V.: 25 years of declarative agent technologies in Italy. In: Mascardi and Omicini [73]
8. Ancona, D., Briola, D., Ferrando, A., Mascardi, V.: MAS-DRiVe: a practical approach to decentralized runtime verification of agent interaction protocols. In: Santoro et al. [94], pp. 35–43. http://ceur-ws.org/Vol-1664/w7.pdf

9. Armano, G., Paoli, F.D., Omicini, A., Vargiu, E.: WOA 2003 – 4th Workshop "From Objects to Agents". Pitagora Editrice Bologna, Villasimius, CA, Italy (2003). http://giuseppevizzari.github.io/WOA-proceedings-archive/woa-2003.html

10. Baldoni, M., Baroglio, C., Bergenti, F., Garro, A.: WOA 2013 – 14th Workshop "From Objects to Agents", CEUR Workshop Proceedings, vol. 1099. Turin, Italy (2013). http://ceur-ws.org/Vol-1099/

11. Baldoni, M., Baroglio, C., Berio, G., Marengo, E.: Declarative representation of curricula models: an LTL-and UML-based approach. In: Baldoni, M., Boccalatte, A., De Paoli, F., Martelli, M., Mascardi, V. (eds.) WOA 2007 – 8th Workshop "From Objects to Agents", pp. 34–41. Seneca Edizioni Torino, Genova, Italy (2007). http://woa07.dibris.unige.it/papers/BaldoniDeclarative.pdf

12. Baldoni, M., Baroglio, C., Capuzzimati, F., Micalizio, R.: Endowing business artifacts with a normative coordination layer. In: De Meo et al. [48], pp. 71–77. http://ceur-ws.org/Vol-1867/w13.pdf

13. Baldoni, M., Baroglio, C., Martelli, A., Patti, V.: Conformance and interoperability in open enviroments. In: De Paoli et al. [49], pp. 151–157. http://ceur-ws.org/Vol-204/P11.pdf

14. Baldoni, M., et al.: Personalization, verification and conformance for logic-based communicating agents. In: Corradini et al. [42], pp. 177–183. http://lia.deis.unibo.it/books/woa2005/papers/25.pdf

15. Baldoni, M., Boella, G., Dorni, M., Mugnaini, A., Grenna, R.: powerJADE: Organizations and roles as primitives in the JADE framework. In: Baldoni et al. [17], pp. 84–92. http://www.pa.icar.cnr.it/woa08/materiali/paper/paper_1.pdf

16. Baldoni, M., Boella, G., Grenna, R.: Modeling organizations and roles using a middleware Jade-based. In: Bergenti [21], pp. 100–107. http://www.ailab.unipr.it/woa09/papers/Baldoni.pdf

17. Baldoni, M., Cossentino, M., De Paoli, F., Seidita, V.: WOA 2008 – 9th Workshop "From Objects to Agents". Seneca Edizioni Torino, Palermo, Italy (2008). http://www.pa.icar.cnr.it/woa08/materiali/Proceedings.pdf

18. Baldoni, M., De Paoli, F., Martelli, A., Omicini, A.: WOA 2004 – 5th Workshop "From Objects to Agents". Pitagora Editrice Bologna, Torino, Italy (2004). http://lia.deis.unibo.it/books/woa2004/atti.pdf

19. Bellifemine, F., Poggi, A., Rimassa, G., Turci, P.: An object-oriented framework to realize agent systems. In: Corradi et al. [41], pp. 52–57. http://giuseppevizzari.github.io/WOA-proceedings-archive/pdfs/woa2000/WOA11.pdf

20. Beretta, D., Monica, S., Bergenti, F.: Capturing a recursive pattern in neural-symbolic reinforcement learning. In: Falcone et al. [55], pp. 17–31. http://ceur-ws.org/Vol-3579/paper2.pdf

21. Bergenti, F.: WOA 2009 – 10th Workshop "From Objects to Agents". Seneca Edizioni Torino, Parma, Italy (2009). http://www.ailab.unipr.it/woa09/papers/

22. Bergenti, F., Caire, G., Gotta, D.: Agents on the move: JADE for android devices. In: Santoro and Bergenti [93], pp. 44–47. http://ceur-ws.org/Vol-1260/paper9.pdf

23. Bergenti, F., Iotti, E., Poggi, A.: Outline of a formalization of JADE multiagent systems. In: Di Napoli et al. [52], pp. 123–128. http://ceur-ws.org/Vol-1382/paper19.pdf

24. Bergenti, F., Monica, S.: WOA 2019 – 20th Workshop "From Objects to Agents", CEUR Workshop Proceedings, vol. 2404. Parma, Italy (2019). http://ceur-ws.org/Vol-2404/

25. Bergenti, F., Monica, S.: Rethinking software agents as building blocks of software systems. In: Mascardi and Omicini [73]

26. Bergenti, F., Petrosino, G.: Overview of a scripting language for JADE-based multi-agent systems. In: Cossentino et al. [45], pp. 57–62. http://ceur-ws.org/Vol-2215/paper_10.pdf
27. Biswas, A., Talukdar, W.: Building Agentic AI Systems: Create intelligent, autonomous AI agents that can reason, plan, and adapt. Packt Publishing Ltd (2025). https://www.packtpub.com/en-it/product/building-agentic-ai-systems-9781801079273
28. Bouleanu, D.C., Loaiza Carrillo, M.A., Savaglio, C., Bădică, C., Gravina, R., Fortino, G.: From objects to agents, and back to smart objects: software agents for intelligent Internet of Things (IoT) systems. In: Mascardi and Omicini [73]
29. Bouquet, P., Serafini, L., Zanobini, S.: Semantic coordination in systems of autonomous agents: The approach and an implementation. In: Armano et al. [9], pp. 179–186. http://giuseppevizzari.github.io/WOA-proceedings-archive/pdfs/woa2003/17.pdf
30. Briola, D., Locoro, A., Mascardi, V.: Ontology agents in FIPA-compliant platforms: a survey and a new proposal. In: Baldoni et al. [17], pp. 68–75. http://www.pa.icar.cnr.it/woa08/materiali/paper/paper_7.pdf
31. Cabri, G., Leonardi, L., Mariani, S., Zambonelli, F.: Coordination of software agents: models and languages. In: Mascardi and Omicini [73]
32. Calegari, R., Ciatto, G., Denti, E., Omicini, A., Sartor, G.: WOA 2020 – 21st Workshop "From Objects to Agents", CEUR Workshop Proceedings, vol. 2706. Bologna, Italy (2020). http://ceur-ws.org/Vol-2706/
33. Calegari, R., Ciatto, G., Denti, E., Omicini, A., Sartor, G.: WOA 2021 – 22nd Workshop "From Objects to Agents", CEUR Workshop Proceedings, vol. 2963. Bologna, Italy (2021). http://ceur-ws.org/Vol-2963/
34. Calegari, R., Ciatto, G., Mariani, S., Denti, E., Omicini, A.: Logic programming in space-time: The case of situatedness in LPaaS. In: Cossentino et al. [45], pp. 63–68. http://ceur-ws.org/Vol-2215/paper_11.pdf
35. Calegari, R., Ciatto, G., Omicini, A.: On the integration of symbolic and sub-symbolic techniques for XAI: a survey. Intelligenza Artificiale 14(1), 7–32 (2020). https://doi.org/10.3233/IA-190036. special issue for the Twentieth Edition of the Workshop 'From Objects to Agents'
36. Calegari, R., Denti, E., Mariani, S., Omicini, A.: Towards logic programming as a service: Experiments in tuProlog. In: Santoro et al. [94], pp. 79–84. http://ceur-ws.org/Vol-1664/w14.pdf
37. Casadei, M., Gardelli, L., Viroli, M.: Collective sorting tuple spaces. In: De Paoli et al. [49], pp. 173–180. http://ceur-ws.org/Vol-204/P01.pdf
38. Casadei, M., Viroli, M.: A framework to specify and verify computational fields for pervasive computing systems. In: De Paoli, F., Vizzari, G. (eds.) WOA 2012 – 13th Workshop "From Objects to Agents". CEUR Workshop Proceedings, vol. 892, pp. 72–81. Milano, Italy (2012). http://ceur-ws.org/Vol-892/paper2.pdf
39. Ciancarini, P., Wooldridge, M.J.: Agent-Oriented Software Engineering, Lecture Notes in Computer Science, vol. 1957. Springer, Cham (2001). https://doi.org/10.1007/3-540-44564-1. 1st International Workshop (AOSE 2000), Limerick, Ireland, 10 Jun. 2000. Revised Papers
40. Ciatto, G., Agiollo, A., Magnini, M., Omicini, A.: Large language models as oracles for instantiating ontologies with domain-specific knowledge. Knowl. Based Syst. 310, 112940:1–22 (2025). https://doi.org/10.1016/j.knosys.2024.112940
41. Corradi, A., Omicini, A., Poggi, A.: WOA 2000 – 1st Workshop "From Objects to Agents", Atti di Congressi, vol. 1195. Pitagora Editrice Bologna, Parma,

Italy (2000). http://giuseppevizzari.github.io/WOA-proceedings-archive/woa-2000.html

42. Corradini, F., De Paoli, F., Merelli, E., Omicini, A.: WOA 2005 – 6th Workshop "From Objects to Agents". Pitagora Editrice Bologna, Camerino, MC, Italy (2005). http://lia.deis.unibo.it/books/woa2005/atti.pdf

43. Cossentino, M., Hopmans, G., Odell, J.: FIPA standardization activities in the software engineering area. In: Armano et al. [9], pp. 71–77. http://giuseppevizzari.github.io/WOA-proceedings-archive/pdfs/woa2003/23.pdf

44. Cossentino, M., et al.: GIMT: a tool for ontology and goal modeling in BDI multi-agent design. In: Santoro and Bergenti [93], pp. 81–88. http://ceur-ws.org/Vol-1260/paper10.pdf

45. Cossentino, M., Sabatucci, L., Seidita, V.: WOA 2018 – 19th Workshop "From Objects to Agents", CEUR Workshop Proceedings, vol. 2215. Palermo, Italy (2018). http://ceur-ws.org/Vol-2215/

46. Cossentino, M., Sabatucci, L., Seidita, V.: Designing agent-oriented systems. In: Mascardi and Omicini [73]

47. Costantini, S., Tocchio, A.: Learning by knowledge exchange in logical agents. In: Corradini et al. [42], pp. 1–8. http://lia.deis.unibo.it/books/woa2005/papers/1.pdf

48. De Meo, P., Postorino, M.N., Rosaci, D., Sarnè, G.M.L.: WOA 2017 – 18th Workshop "From Objects to Agents", CEUR Workshop Proceedings, vol. 1867. Scilla, RC, Italy (2017). http://ceur-ws.org/Vol-1867/

49. De Paoli, F., Di Stefano, A., Omicini, A., Santoro, C.: WOA 2006 – 7th Workshop "From Objects to Agents", CEUR Workshop Proceedings, vol. 204. Catania, Italy (2006). http://ceur-ws.org/Vol-204/

50. De Paoli, F., Manzoni, S., Poggi, A.: WOA 2002 – 3rd Workshop "From Objects to Agents". Pitagora Editrice Bologna, Milano, Italy (2002). http://giuseppevizzari.github.io/WOA-proceedings-archive/woa-2002.html

51. Delicato, F.C., Al-Anbuky, A., Wang, K.I.K.: Editorial: smart cyber-physical systems: toward pervasive intelligence systems. Futur. Gener. Comput. Syst. **107**, 1134–1139 (2020). https://doi.org/10.1016/j.future.2019.06.031

52. Di Napoli, C., Rossi, S., Staffa, M.: WOA 2015 – 16th Workshop "From Objects to Agents", CEUR Workshop Proceedings, vol. 1382. Naples, Italy (2015). http://ceur-ws.org/Vol-1382/

53. Di Nitto, E., Pianciamore, M., Selvini, P.: The role of agents in knowledge management. In: De Paoli et al. [50], pp. 29–34. http://giuseppevizzari.github.io/WOA-proceedings-archive/pdfs/woa2002/22.pdf

54. Domini, D., Farabegoli, N., Aguzzi, G., Viroli, M.: Towards intelligent pulverized systems: a modern approach for edge-cloud services. In: Alderighi et al. [5], pp. 252–270. http://ceur-ws.org/Vol-3735/paper_19.pdf

55. Falcone, R., Castelfranchi, C., Sapienza, A., Cantucci, F.: WOA 2023 – 24th Workshop "From Objects to Agents", CEUR Workshop Proceedings, vol. 3579. Roma, Italy (2023). http://ceur-ws.org/Vol-3579/

56. Ferrando, A., Malvone, V.: Hands-on VITAMIN: a compositional tool for model checking of multi-agent systems. In: Alderighi et al. [5], pp. 157–169. http://ceur-ws.org/Vol-3735/paper_12.pdf

57. Ferrando, A., Mascardi, V.: WOA 2022 – 23rd Workshop "From Objects to Agents", CEUR Workshop Proceedings, vol. 3261. Genova, Italy (2022). http://ceur-ws.org/Vol-3261/

58. Fortino, G., Garro, A., Palopoli, L., Russo, W., Spezzano, G.: WOA 2011 – 12th Workshop "From Objects to Agents", CEUR Workshop Proceedings, vol. 741. Rende, Italy (2011). http://ceur-ws.org/Vol-741/

59. Gini, M., Ishida, T., Castelfranchi, C., Johnson, W.L.: AAMAS 2002: Proceedings of the 1st International Joint Conference on Autonomous Agents and Multiagent Systems: Part 1. Association for Computing Machinery, New York, NY, USA (2002). https://doi.org/10.1145/544862

60. Giordano, L., Martelli, A., Terenziani, P., Bottrighi, A., Montani, S.: A temporal approach to the specification and verification of interaction protocols. In: Corradini et al. [42], pp. 171–176. http://lia.deis.unibo.it/books/woa2005/papers/24.pdf

61. Gunning, D.: Explainable artificial intelligence (XAI). Funding Program DARPA-BAA-16-53, DARPA (2016)

62. Habbash, N., Bottoni, F., Vizzari, G.: Reinforcement learning for autonomous agents exploring environments: an experimental framework and preliminary results. In: Calegari et al. [32], pp. 84–100. http://ceur-ws.org/Vol-2706/paper5.pdf

63. Hammond, G.: AI scientist Fei-Fei Li: "Maths is pretty clean. Humans are messy". Financial Times (2025). https://www.ft.com/content/d5f91c27-3be8-454a-bea5-bb8ff2a85488

64. Huang, K.: Agentic AI: Theories and Practices. Springer, Cham (2025). https://doi.org/10.1007/978-3-031-90026-6

65. Loaiza, M., Savaglio, C., Arijo, N.H., Aloi, G., Fortino, G., Gravina, R.: Agents in software development architectures. In: Falcone et al. [55], pp. 66–77. http://ceur-ws.org/Vol-3579/paper5.pdf

66. Lombardo, G., Pellegrino, M., Poggi, A.: Unsupervised continual learning from synthetic data generated with agent-based modeling and simulation: A preliminary experimentation. In: Ferrando and Mascardi [57], pp. 116–126. http://ceur-ws.org/Vol-3261/paper9.pdf

67. Losapio, G., Minutoli, F., Mascardi, V., Ferrando, A.: Smart balancing of e-scooter sharing systems via deep reinforcement learning. In: Calegari et al. [33], pp. 83–97. http://ceur-ws.org/Vol-2963/paper16.pdf

68. Maggi, P., Sisto, R.: Experiments on formal verification of mobile agent data integrity properties. In: De Paoli et al. [50], pp. 131–136. http://giuseppevizzari.github.io/WOA-proceedings-archive/pdfs/woa2002/15.pdf

69. Magnini, M., Ciatto, G., Omicini, A.: A view to a KILL: knowledge injection via lambda layer. In: Ferrando and Mascardi [57], pp. 61–76. http://ceur-ws.org/Vol-3261/paper5.pdf

70. Mariani, S., Omicini, A.: TuCSoN coordination for MAS situatedness: towards a methodology. In: Santoro and Bergenti [93], pp. 48–57. http://ceur-ws.org/Vol-1260/paper11.pdf

71. Mariani, S., Omicini, A.: Multi-paradigm coordination for MAS: integrating heterogeneous coordination approaches in MAS technologies. In: Santoro et al. [94], pp. 91–99. http://ceur-ws.org/Vol-1664/w16.pdf

72. Mascardi, V., Demergasso, D., Ancona, D.: Languages for programming BDI-style agents: an overview. In: Corradini et al. [42], pp. 9–15. http://lia.deis.unibo.it/books/woa2005/papers/2.pdf

73. Mascardi, V., Omicini, A.: The Agents Journey: Twenty-five Years of Multi-agent Systems at WOA. Lecture Notes in Computer Science – State-of-the-Art Surveys, Springer (2026)

74. Molesini, A., Omicini, A., Ricci, A., Denti, E.: Zooming multi-agent systems. In: Müller, J.P., Zambonelli, F. (eds.) Agent-Oriented Software Engineering VI, Lecture Notes in Computer Science, vol. 3950, pp. 81–93. Springer, Heidelberg (2006). https://doi.org/10.1007/11752660_7. 6th International Workshop (AOSE 2005), Utrecht, The Netherlands, 25–26 Jul. 2005. Revised and Invited Papers
75. Morreale, V., Bonura, S., Francaviglia, G., Centineo, F., Cossentino, M., Gaglio, S.: Reasoning about goals in BDI agents: The PRACTIONIST framework. In: De Paoli et al. [49], pp. 187–194. http://ceur-ws.org/Vol-204/P20.pdf
76. Morreale, V., et al.: PRACTIONIST: a framework for developing BDI agent systems. In: De Paoli et al. [49], pp. 4–5. http://ceur-ws.org/Vol-204/D02.pdf
77. O'Hare, G.M., Jennings, N.R.: Foundations of Distributed Artificial Intelligence. Sixth-Generation Computer Technology, Wiley, Hoboken. hardcover edn. (1996). https://www.wiley.com/en-gb/Foundations+of+Distributed+Artificial+Intelligence-p-9780471006756
78. Omicini, A.: From objects to agent societies: abstractions and methodologies for the engineering of open distributed systems. In: Corradi et al. [41], pp. 29–34. http://giuseppevizzari.github.io/WOA-proceedings-archive/pdfs/woa2000/WOA07.pdf
79. Omicini, A.: Not just for humans: explanation for agent-to-agent communication. In: Vizzari, G., Palmonari, M., Orlandini, A. (eds.) AIxIA 2020 DP — AIxIA 2020 Discussion Papers Workshop. AI*IA Series, vol. 2776, pp. 1–11. Sun SITE Central Europe, RWTH Aachen University, Aachen, Germany (2020). http://ceur-ws.org/Vol-2776/paper-1.pdf
80. Omicini, A., Ricci, A., Rimassa, G., Viroli, M.: Integrating objective & subjective coordination in FIPA: A roadmap to TuCSoN. In: Armano et al. [9], pp. 85–91. http://giuseppevizzari.github.io/WOA-proceedings-archive/pdfs/woa2003/07.pdf
81. Omicini, A., Ricci, A., Viroli, M.: Artifacts in the A&A meta-model for multi-agent systems. Auton. Agents Multi-Agent Syst. **17**(3), 432–456 (2008). https://doi.org/10.1007/s10458-008-9053-x. special issue on Foundations, Advanced Topics and Industrial Perspectives of Multi-Agent Systems
82. Omicini, A., Tolksdorf, R., Zambonelli, F.: Engineering Societies in the Agents World, Lecture Notes in Artificial Intelligence, vol. 1972. Springer Berlin Heidelberg (2000). https://doi.org/10.1007/3-540-44539-0. 1st International Workshop (ESAW'00), Berlin, Germany, 21 Aug. 2000. Revised Papers
83. Omicini, A., Viroli, M.: WOA 2001 – 2nd Workshop "From Objects to Agents". Pitagora Editrice Bologna, Modena, Italy (2001). http://giuseppevizzari.github.io/WOA-proceedings-archive/woa-2001.html
84. Omicini, A., Viroli, M.: WOA 2010 – 11th Workshop "From Objects to Agents", CEUR Workshop Proceedings, vol. 621. Rimini, Italy (2010). http://ceur-ws.org/Vol-621/
85. Omicini, A., Zambonelli, F.: Coordination of large-scale socio-technical systems: challenges and research directions. In: Di Napoli et al. [52], pp. 76–79. http://ceur-ws.org/Vol-1382/paper11.pdf
86. Passadore, A., Grosso, A., Boccalatte, A.: Indexing enterprise knowledge bases with AgentSeeker. In: Bergenti [21], pp. 69–75. http://www.ailab.unipr.it/woa09/papers/Passadore.pdf
87. Perini, A., Bresciani, P., Giorgini, P., Giunchiglia, F., Mylopoulos, J.: Towards an agent oriented approach to software engineering. In: Omicini and Viroli [83], pp. 72–77. http://giuseppevizzari.github.io/WOA-proceedings-archive/pdfs/woa2001/pdf/19.pdf

88. Petrosino, G., Iotti, E., Monica, S., Bergenti, F.: Prototypes of productivity tools for the Jadescript programming language. In: Calegari et al. [33], pp. 14–28. http://ceur-ws.org/Vol-2963/paper4.pdf

89. Pilz, K., Rahman, R., Sanders, J., Heim, L.: Trends in AI supercomputers (2025). https://epoch.ai/blog/trends-in-ai-supercomputers

90. Pisano, G., Ciatto, G., Calegari, R., Omicini, A.: Neuro-symbolic computation for XAI: towards a unified model. In: Calegari et al. [32], pp. 101–117. http://ceur-ws.org/Vol-2706/paper18.pdf

91. Ribino, P., Cossentino, M., Lodato, C., Lopes, S., Sabatucci, L., Seidita, V.: Ontology and goal model in designing BDI multi-agent systems. In: Baldoni et al. [32], pp. 66–72. http://ceur-ws.org/Vol-1099/paper12.pdf

92. Robol, M., Giorgini, P., Busetta, P.: Applying social norms to implicit negotiation among non-player characters in serious games. In: Santoro et al. [10], pp. 23–28. http://ceur-ws.org/Vol-1664/w5.pdf

93. Santoro, C., Bergenti, F.: WOA 2014 – 15th Workshop "From Objects to Agents", CEUR Workshop Proceedings, vol. 1260. Catania, Italy (2014). http://ceur-ws.org/Vol-1260/

94. Santoro, C., Messina, F., De Benedetti, M.: WOA 2016 – 17th Workshop "From Objects to Agents", CEUR Workshop Proceedings, vol. 1664. Catania, Italy (2016). http://ceur-ws.org/Vol-1664/

95. Sapienza, A., Cantucci, F., Castelfranchi, C., Falcone, R.: Trust evolution in agent and multi-agent systems: a computational modeling perspective. In: Mascardi and Omicini [73]

96. Unniyankal, H., Belardinelli, F., Ferrando, A., Malvone, V.: RMLGym: a formal reward machine framework for reinforcement learning. In: Falcone et al. [55], pp. 1–16. http://ceur-ws.org/Vol-3579/paper1.pdf

97. Vidali, A., Crociani, L., Vizzari, G., Bandini, S.: A deep reinforcement learning approach to adaptive traffic lights management. In: Bergenti and Monica [24], pp. 42–50. http://ceur-ws.org/Vol-2404/paper07.pdf

98. Vizzari, G., Bandini, S.: Coordinated change of state for situated agents. In: Baldoni et al. [18], pp. 69–76. http://giuseppevizzari.github.io/WOA-proceedings-archive/pdfs/woa2004/11.pdf

99. Vozna, A., et al.: Evolution of programming languages in agent systems and the role of computational logic. In: Mascardi and Omicini [73]

100. Yan, E., Burattini, S., Hübner, J.F., Ricci, A.: Towards a multi-level explainability framework for engineering and understanding BDI agent systems. In: Falcone et al. [55], pp. 216–231. http://ceur-ws.org/Vol-3579/paper17.pdf

101. Zambonelli, F., Omicini, A.: Challenges and research directions in agent-oriented software engineering. Auton. Agents Multi-Agent Syst. **9**(3), 253–283 (2004). https://doi.org/10.1023/B:AGNT.0000038028.66672.1e. special Issue: Challenges for Agent-Based Computing

102. Zelikman, E., Wu, Y., Mu, J., Goodman, N.D.: STaR: self-taught reasoner bootstrapping reasoning with reasoning. In: Proceedings of the 36th International Conference on Neural Information Processing Systems (NIPS 2022). Curran Associates Inc., Red Hook, NY, USA (2022). https://dl.acm.org/doi/10.5555/3600270.3601396

Author Index

V. Mascardi and A. Omicini (Eds.): *The Agents Journey*, LNCS 16395, p. 385, 2026.
https://doi.org/10.1007/978-3-032-22940-3